The Complete **BUILDER'S GUIDE** to

Hot Rod
CHASSIS AND SUSPENSION

Jeff Tann

CarTech®

CarTech®
CarTech®, Inc.
39966 Grand Avenue
North Branch, MN 55056
Phone: 651-277-1200 or 800-551-4754
Fax: 651-277-1203
www.cartechbooks.com

© 2010 by Jeff Tann

All rights reserved. No part of this publication may be reproduced or utilized in any form or by any means, electronic or mechanical, including photocopying, recording, or by any information storage and retrieval system, without prior permission from the Publisher. All text, photographs, and artwork are the property of the Author unless otherwise noted or credited.

The information in this work is true and complete to the best of our knowledge. However, all information is presented without any guarantee on the part of the Author or Publisher, who also disclaim any liability incurred in connection with the use of the information and any implied warranties of merchantability or fitness for a particular purpose. Readers are responsible for taking suitable and appropriate safety measures when performing any of the operations or activities described in this work.

All trademarks, trade names, model names and numbers, and other product designations referred to herein are the property of their respective owners and are used solely for identification purposes. This work is a publication of CarTech, Inc., and has not been licensed, approved, sponsored, or endorsed by any other person or entity. The Publisher is not associated with any product, service, or vendor mentioned in this book, and does not endorse the products or services of any vendor mentioned in this book.

Edit by Scott Parkhurst
Layout by Elly Gosso

ISBN 978-1-61325-140-9
Item No. SA185P

Library of Congress Cataloging-in-Publication Data

Tann, Jeff.
  The complete builder's guide to hot rod chassis and suspension / by Jeff Tann.
    p. cm.
  Includes bibliographical references and index.
  ISBN 978-1-934709-18-4
  1. Hot rods. 2. Automobiles—Chassis. 3. Automobiles—Springs and suspension. I. Title.
  TL236.3.T36 2010
  629.2'4—dc22

2010013716

Title Page:
This solid front axle suspension works great, provides a comfortable ride, and stops quickly when necessary. It also has a nice traditional appearance, which is perfect for this 1935 Ford.

Back Cover Photos

Top Left:
The differential is supported by tubular traction bars that connect to a mounting point under the transmission mount. The differential also features tubular shock absorbers that connect to tabs on the axle housing and strong mounts that are connected to the Model A crossmember. The exhaust also connects to the rear crossmember.

Top Right:
Looking at the differential from the front, you can see the double-kicked-up chassis that provides a low ride height for the rear of the Model A. This chassis also has a crossmember for the rear control arms that keeps the differential from twisting forward or backward. Also visible are the Wilwood parking-brake calipers.

Middle Left:
The upper portion of the shock absorber is connected to the frame mount. The upper portion of the shock is attached with the bolt and locknut that came in the kit.

Middle Right:
The original center portion of the crossmember is removed, and a new split-wishbone crossmember is installed in its place. Here, the top section of the crossmember is cut out to make access to some connections easier.

Bottom Left:
While I was attending a car show, I saw this Model A for sale; it was equipped with a Jaguar front suspension. Apparently, there were several kits available for installing the suspension in street rods. The upper A-arm brackets are angled to allow the installation of front fenders.

Bottom Right:
When the crossmember is located properly and secured at both ends, it is tack welded to the frame.

CONTENTS

Preface 4
Introduction 6

Chapter 1: Hot-Rod Chassis Modifications 12
   Early Hot-Rod Transmission Selections 14
   Build or Buy a Hot-Rod Chassis? 15
   Crossmember Installation 16
   Installing a Universal Power-Brake Assembly 20
   1935-and-Later Chassis 22
   Total Cost Involved Engineering Chassis Selections 25
   Detailing a 1940 Ford Chassis 26
   Detailing a 1931 Ford Chassis 28
   Tools 32

Chapter 2: Solid Front Axle Suspensions 36
   Installing a Posies Dropped-Front-Axle Kit and Wilwood Disc Brakes 37
   Installing a Unisteer System on a Model A Chassis 48

Chapter 3: Independent Front Suspensions 53
   Corvair System 53
   Jaguar System 54
   Opel System 55
   Mustang II System 56
   Installing a Heidts Economy Mustang II IFS System 58
   Installing a Total Cost Involved Engineering 1933–1934 Ford IFS 67

Chapter 4: Solid Rear Axle Suspensions 81
   Installing a Posies Rear Spring Kit in a 1933–1934 Ford Chassis 84
   Installing a Heidts Triangulated Four-Link Suspension System 96

Chapter 5: Independent Rear Suspensions 104
   Jaguar System 104
   Corvette System 124
   Kugel System 126
   Heidts System 126
   Picture Gallery of Independent Rear Suspensions 139

Source Guide 142

PREFACE

The author's $105 1930 Model A coupe, circa 1960. It represents the start of his lifelong career in hot rodding, most of which would be spent owning at least one Model A Ford in one form or another. This is the car that started it all, and it's evil ride characteristics prompted a decades-long quest to find a truly comfortable, effective suspension/chassis setup for hot rods like it.

I moved from Van Nuys, California, to Northridge, California, in 1959 and, being a car enthusiast, the first thing I noticed was that all of the older kids in the neighborhood had Model A Ford hot rods. I thought the cars were really cool, so I worked odd jobs in the area until I had enough money to buy a Model A Ford. I purchased a nice 1930 coupe in 1960 for $105, and that was the start of my hot-rod hobby, and as it turned out, my occupation. During the 1960s, I built a number of Model A street rods, but the one thing they all had in common was an uncomfortable ride.

After owning a variety of early Fords, in 1967 I purchased a 1928 Model A Ford coupe that I planned to turn into a show car. When I was finished with the car, it featured a chrome-plated, dropped-tube front axle, and the rear end was a chrome-plated Olds differential that came out of K.S. Pittman's 1940 Willys gasser race car. The differential had all of the race-car mounts, so I set it up exactly the way it was in the Willys, hoping the ride quality would be softer than that of a stock Model A. It was an improvement, but it remained stiff. Obviously, the car hooked up well with the race car setup and rear slicks. When the coupe was finished, it was a really nice-looking car, and it did win its class at the World of Wheels car show two years in a row.

When the coupe was in the building stages, several of my hot-rod friends and I formed a San Fernando Valley hot-rod club called the Hard Times. In 1970, the club had a barbecue at a member's house, and

The author's 1928 5-window Ford Model A coupe, circa 1971. It was one of the first rods to sport a full Jaguar independent rear suspension setup. This uncaged, fully chromed Hamilton Automotive setup has worked wonderfully for four decades and is still under the car today. This same car is still in the author's posession, and probably will remain so for a long time to come.

one of the new members in attendance had a Model A sedan that had just been equipped with a Jaguar independent rear suspension. He was touting the virtues of the Jaguar suspension, so I asked him if I could go for a ride in the car. He said, "Sure," so I jumped into the sedan and went for a spin around the neighborhood. The owner wasn't kidding; the sedan had a very smooth ride and absorbed even the worst bumps. I was sold, so the following Monday I was on the phone looking for a wrecking yard that had a Jaguar independent rear suspension for sale.

By the end of the day, I found a nice XKE IRS that was selling for $250. The installation looked complicated, so I contacted Hamilton Automotive in Van Nuys, California, because I knew that shop was installing Jaguar differentials in T-buckets. The sedan that introduced me to the Jaguar rear still had the differential in the original cage, but, since my coupe was a show car, I wanted the unit out of the cage so that all of the parts could be chrome-plated. Hamilton Automotive's T-buckets had exposed Jaguar suspensions then (1971), and the shop was located a block away from where I was working. Curt Hamilton and the crew did the installation, and when it was being installed, Curt showed me the engineering that went into one of his installations. His slogan was "Bullet Proof," and the unit certainly was when he was finished. When I took the coupe for the first drive with the new Jaguar differential, I was extremely pleased with the ride and handling of the coupe, not to mention how nice it looked. I still own that coupe, and it was upgraded a few years ago. In the process, I updated it with a Heidts independent front suspension. I am sold on independent-suspension systems in early-model street rods. I am also aware that if you are building a car to fit into a certain period style, the I-beam and tube-suspension systems are the only way to go. In this book, I show a variety of suspension/component installations on the front and rear of a chassis. At the end of the book, a comprehensive buyer's guide lists the places where you can find the parts to build your own chassis or buy a new one.

INTRODUCTION

Hot rodding is a hobby that started in the late 1930s, but this book covers hot-rod chassis from the later era—the mid 1950s forward. Over the years, there have been a number of improvements in chassis construction. In the early days, you had to use Ford parts; later, aftermarket hot-rod parts companies appeared, and today, new products are being created by these manufacturers. This book covers both I-beam-style suspension systems and street-rod independent-suspension systems for the front of a street rod. I also cover rear-differential installations and independent-rear-suspension systems. This book starts by looking at an original late-1950s-style chassis, and also shows you some professional chassis that are currently being built.

This book contains everything you need to know about hot-rod suspension systems. In it is information for you to build rear-suspension systems the correct way and to install a suspension system into your chassis properly. The I-beam and dropped-tube suspensions are the standards used today for traditional street rods (such as '32 highboy roadsters and most highboy-style early street rods), because nostalgic styling has returned to the hobby. The independent-front-suspension (IFS) system is the standard for 1935-and-later cars, because you can't see one under the fat fenders, so I show you how to install an IFS unit into a street-rod chassis.

A Brief Hot-Rod History

A question that is asked often is: "When did the hot-rod hobby get started?" The term "hot rod" dates back to the late 1940s, when Pete Petersen named his automotive publication *Hot Rod*. Before that, the modified roadsters and coupes had a variety of names, one of which was "Gow Jobs."

The origin of hot rodding can go back to the late 1800s, when Henry Ford started building horseless carriages. Ford built his first quadricycle in 1896, because he thought a motor-powered carriage would be better and easier to use than a smelly horse-driven carriage. The unique vehicle was amazing, but he received almost no publicity, so only a small number of people knew of its existence. Over the next few years, Henry Ford built several horseless carriages, each vehicle being more advanced than the previous ones. Finally, in 1899, Ford was receiving some desperately needed publicity, and a variety of wealthy investors noticed his new invention and wanted to get involved.

In an effort to get more publicity and the required financial backing that he needed to start a car company, Henry Ford raced a stripped-down horseless carriage that he built in 1901, and that modified race car certainly could be considered one of the earliest hot rods. After winning that race, Ford received the notoriety he needed to get the financial backing to launch his own car company. Ford was quick to realize that the emerging interest in auto racing helped to sell cars, so he constructed another racing car that was basically a chassis with an engine, and Barney Oldfield drove it. The early race car set an unbelievable and breathtaking top-speed record of 64.5 mph in 1903, and that set a precedent for the dry-lakes top-speed racing events

INTRODUCTION

that followed years later. During this same period, Louis Chevrolet was also building race cars, and I have to say that some of the stripped-down cars he built could also be considered early hot rods.

Most of the early automobile manufacturers built and raced race cars for publicity, but there were a number of other people—early car enthusiasts—modifying cars for their own use on the street and in emerging racing endeavors. Some of the enthusiasts wanted faster cars, while others just wanted their cars to look nicer than the factory models. A milestone in hot rodding occurred in 1932, when Ford released its first flathead V-8 engine, but it wasn't until several years later, when dry-lakes racing started to become popular in California, that the sport took hold. The lag between Ford's first flathead V-8 engine and the dry-lakes racing was the time it took for the cars to become affordable for teenagers and younger enthusiasts.

It is interesting to note that the flathead V-8 engine was being tested in 1930 and 1931 and was originally scheduled for release in 1933. Model A Ford passenger-car sales were dropping in 1930 and 1931, due to the Great Depression, so Henry Ford thought that if the V-8 engine could be introduced earlier, it would stimulate more sales and make the company more money. The Model A was supposed to run with only small changes through 1932, so Henry installed the V-8 into a Model A to see how it worked, and the result was a car whose chassis flexed and twisted a little from the additional power. The stock Model A engine was developing 40 hp, and the new V-8 engine was developing 65 hp, but that was enough to create noticeable chassis flex. Henry told his son, Edsel, to make the necessary changes to the Model A chassis to handle the additional horsepower. Edsel could have easily done that with some additional chassis gussets, but, being a designer and stylist, he took advantage of the assignment and created an all-new car with a sturdier frame. The frame rails were exposed, and that eliminated the need for splash aprons; the bodies were similar to the Model A's, but they had refined lines and no sun visor. When Edsel made the changes, every body style available had to be changed, and that was a huge undertaking, considering the number of bodies being manufactured and offered for sale. The '32 Fords were great-looking cars, and the V-8 engine did catch everyone's attention, but the big change was very expensive, wasn't really necessary. And since many people were out of work and couldn't afford to buy a new Ford anyway, the end result was that the Ford Motor Company lost $75 million. Thanks, Edsel!

Sales of the '32 Ford were low, but enthusiasts did like the new V-8 engine, even though it had a lot of problems in the first year, they saw plenty of potential for creating additional horsepower. Ford engineers continued to improve the flathead V-8 engine, and it didn't take long before the engine became reliable. Performance enthusiasts and automotive engineers at the time began to develop performance parts to improve the horsepower of the flathead V-8 engine, and that activity became the start of the speed-parts industry. Enthusiasts found out that increasing the engine's compression ratio and changing the cam profile improved the engine's horsepower. When those changes were done, the engines could handle more gasoline, so multi-carburetion was needed.

The young enthusiasts modified their engines and tested them on California's dry lakes to set top-speed records. The dry lakes were popular, because they were perfectly flat and long, making them the perfect places to test the cars' top-speed potential. The Ford flathead was one of the racers' favorites, but enthusiasts brought out a variety of different cars with four-cylinder and six-cylinder engines. Soon, the Southern California Timing Association (SCTA) was formed to sanction this new style of racing, and dry-lakes and salt-flats racing is still going strong today. The SCTA came up with different classes for the cars that were racing and started keeping the top-speed records. Dry-lakes racing was growing in popularity in the late 1930s, but World War II interrupted it.

Many Southern California dry-lakes racers joined the armed forces and were getting correspondence from the SCTA and other friends about the dry-lakes racing that was still going on, and those soldiers were telling friends about the fun they were having before the war started. Before long, other soldiers became interested in the hobby. Many of the mechanically astute fellows who'd joined the Army, Navy, and Army Air Force became mechanics and fabricators, and in their positions they learned many new tricks that they used on their cars when they returned from the war. Many of the young men learned how to weld, work machine tools, and fabricate parts out of blocks of steel and aluminum. Some of the fellows who joined the Air Force or Navy were trained to work on airplane engines,

INTRODUCTION

and the engines were far advanced over their automotive counterparts, so many of these men learned how the airplane engineers were building horsepower. The fabrication and mechanical skills that the young servicemen learned in the service were used later when they came home and started working on their cars.

After the war ended, many soldiers returned to California, and dry-lakes racing became even more popular than it was before the war. It was at this time that many of the stripped-down, dry-lakes race cars were also being driven on the street. Some of the cars were beaters that were only meant to go fast, while others were nice-looking cars as well as fast. The racers started lowering the cars to get less air flowing under the body, which helped the cars' stability at speed. The old, skinny tires and large-diameter wheels were replaced with 15- and 16-inch steel wheels and wider tires that improved the handling of the cars.

It was evident that many of the emerging young car enthusiasts were fascinated by the appearance of the racing roadsters, but dry-lakes racing didn't interest them because the California desert was dusty, extremely hot in the summer, and very cold in the winter. Pictures of the custom-built roadsters started appearing in publications, and before long, enthusiasts all across the country wanted to build a car that looked like a dry-lakes race car, even though the closest dry lakes were thousands of miles away. Many of the enthusiasts built street-driven cars that resembled the race cars, and they also spent money getting the engines running strong and the cars looking nice. Hot rods may have started in California, but it didn't take long for the hobby to grow throughout the United States and, eventually, beyond.

The original dry-lakes race enthusiasts liked '32 Ford roadsters because they were low priced, lightweight, and, most importantly, already set up to run flathead engines and 3-speed manual transmissions; so it was easy to swap in the stronger-running later-model engines and transmissions. Roadsters were low priced, because most car owners preferred cars with windows. Starting in the days of the Model T, most people wanted enclosed bodies, and the overwhelming sales leader year after year was the two-door sedan. The interest in closed cars didn't change in the 1940s and 1950s, so enthusiasts started modifying coupes and sedans, using the styling features of the dry-lakes race cars.

Modifications included lowering the front and the use of modern wheels and tires. Some of the dry-lakes racers also started to race coupes, and they found out that chopping the top made them go faster. As I mentioned earlier, the number of '32 cars produced was low, so many of the car enthusiasts started building Model A Fords, Model T Fords, and 1933 and 1934 Fords. The enthusiasts also liked the 1940 Fords, but the cars were still fairly expensive after the war, so they weren't turned into hot rods until the early 1950s. Many really nasty-looking early coupes and sedans were being built, and that increased the interest in the hobby. The more hot rods that were being built, the more other car guys saw them and wanted to build one of their own.

The 1940 Ford coupes and two-door sedans also became popular with enthusiasts after the cars became affordable because the stock engine could be beefed up, and the later-model 59AB flathead engines were an easy drop-in. The 1939 and 1940 Fords were also very aerodynamic for the time, and that gave them a racing advantage over many of the other cars. The 1939 and 1940 Fords also looked really nice with only a minor amount of styling changes, so the enthusiasts could spend more money on the engines.

Chevy passenger cars were also being modified but, up until 1937, Chevy's bodies used a wood framework, and that made the bodies heavier than comparable Ford bodies. Similar to those enthusiasts who were building parts for the Ford flathead engine, some enthusiasts were also building parts for the Chevy straight six-cylinder engine. The Chevy engine used an overhead-valve design, and it actually had more potential than the Ford V-8 engine.

In the late 1940s, Pete Petersen, a public-relations man and car enthusiast, recognized the renewed and growing interest in dry-lakes racing and the emergence of street versions of the cars, so he thought it would be interesting to have a car show featuring the modified roadsters, coupes, and sedans. The car show became a reality and, soon after, he decided to release a publication dedicated to the specialty cars. He wanted a generic name, in order to show all types of specialty cars in the publication, so he called it *Hot Rod*, after the connecting rods used in the engines (after the engines were at running temperature, they had hot rods, and it wasn't unusual to see them flying through the block when the racing engines blew up). The name was also generic enough to let the magazine feature dry-lakes race cars, street modified roadsters, coupes and

INTRODUCTION

sedans, track roadsters, and other custom cars as well. The magazine was first published in 1948, and it introduced the California hot-rod and custom-car culture to the rest of the United States.

After the magazine's debut, it didn't take long before people called any modified roadster or coupe a hot rod (some people incorrectly called and still call the street rods roadsters, even though they were and are actually coupes and sedans). The newer cars that were being modified were called customs. *Hot Rod* magazine also featured a variety of modified cars of all vintages, such as coupes and sedans from any early vintage. And before long, all of the older cars were being modified, or hot rodded. As the magazine grew nationally, young car enthusiasts from all over the country started building cars similar to the ones that they were seeing in the magazine.

Many of the hot roadster and coupe owners unintentionally created a new type of racing that was basically an acceleration test to see which of two cars could accelerate faster; prior to that, racers tested only the top speed of their car. This new style of racing, being done on public streets, became extremely popular. It outraged the older people in their neighborhoods and communities, because it could be very dangerous. This type of racing required high horsepower and chassis modifications to maximize the power output for quick bursts of speed. It didn't take long before the street racer, hot coupe, and roadster owners became looked upon as juvenile delinquents, or criminals in general. This certainly was not good publicity for the growing hot-rod hobby.

Wally Parks saw a need for sanctioned acceleration racing events, so he established the National Hot Rod Association (NHRA) in an effort to get the racers off of the streets. Acceleration racing was called drag racing, and it was determined that 1/4 mile would be the length of the race. After the war, there were many abandoned Air Force landing strips, and they were perfect for safe and sane 1/4-mile drag-racing events.

Parks determined that many race classes were needed, so that the racing could be fair for everyone who participated. The early racers knew that the lighter the car was, the faster it could go, so stripped-down cars were being built. That was the start of the dragster, or rail job. A dragster was basically a chassis with a powerful engine. There were also classes for roadsters, coupes, and newer cars. The classes were divided by power and weight. The drag-racing events became very popular, and they brought many racers off the streets. Over the years, the sport grew nationwide. This form of racing was also responsible for the creation of many new speed-parts manufacturers.

Finally, there were two sanctioned forms of racing for hot rods (drag and dry-lakes), and both grew in scope, but there were also young fellows who just wanted cool-looking cars. They were more interested in displaying their custom-crafted cars than racing them. Car shows also became popular, and some of the cars being built were innovative and extremely nice-looking. Car shows were also popular for the custom fans, and before long, there were rod-and-custom shows being held all over the country; one of the best is the Grand National Roadster Show, which was started in 1948 and is still going strong today. Hot-rod building was very popular throughout the 1950s and early 1960s, but it slowed down when factory hot rods, called muscle cars, were introduced. Many would-be hot rodders decided to go down to their local car dealership and purchase a car that could turn 14-second, 1/4-mile times right off the showroom floor. Many of these cars were "grocery getters" by day and fast race cars on the weekends. Another advantage of these cars to enthusiasts was that they could get a car loan to buy one.

We can thank Norm Grabowski's *Kookie* car and the Tommy Ivo T-bucket for keeping the hot-rod hobby alive during the muscle-car years. Hot-rod enthusiasts loved the T-bucket featured in the TV show *77 Sunset Strip,* so several companies were formed to offer T-bucket kits with fiberglass bodies and custom-made chassis. The best part was that the T-buckets were very affordable and easy to build, so they kept the hot-rod hobby alive from 1964 to 1970.

In 1969, a new term, street rod, was coined by Tex Smith in order to change the hoodlum image of hot rods. That name took hold, and it actually did change the image of the hobby. Street rodding took off in the 1970s when the factory muscle cars went away, due to low-octane-gas regulations and swelling insurance rates. Rodding also received a big boost in popularity from professional T-bucket manufacturers, because they also built components for many other cars being built at the time. It was easy to see that some people had the interest in cars, but they had no tools or talent to build them, so professional hot-rod shops that would build turnkey street rods started opening up.

INTRODUCTION

T-bucket manufacturers were the first companies to see that enthusiasts were willing to buy a hot rod that had a fiberglass body and custom-made chassis, so when certain rare cars—such as the '32 Ford roadster—became very difficult to find, they reasoned that a fiberglass replica might be a marketable replacement. Before then, fiberglass companies were making Model T–based bodies and sheetmetal replacement parts (such as fiberglass fenders and grille shells). As it turned out, the fiberglass manufacturers were right; the aftermarket bodies became extremely popular with street-rod enthusiasts.

Other enthusiasts with engineering backgrounds thought custom-made chassis would also become a necessity, and several companies across the nation were formed to make custom chassis. Thanks to the hot-rod aftermarket, the street-rod hobby started to grow, and it is still going strong today.

Hot-Rod Suspension Systems in the 1950s and 1960s

Hot-rod suspension systems in the 1950s were very basic and generally consisted of mildly modified original suspension components and some newer Ford parts, such as hydraulic brakes. The early hot rodders preferred the '32 Ford chassis, because they were relatively strong and originally equipped with flathead V-8 engines and 3-speed manual transmissions. It was easy to upgrade a chassis with a later, more refined, and powerful flathead engine and newer 3-speed transmission. Ford didn't change the mounting points of the engine and transmissions from year to year, so they could be bolted in place without the need for fabrication work. Welding equipment was not as common as it is today, because it was expensive and generally was only found in specialized shops, and they were stick-style arc welders. Because many of the early hot rods were being built by young guys with limited funds, these specialized shops were cost prohibitive. The more desirable welding machines, such as TIG welders, were very expensive and were generally only found in heavy industrial businesses, such as aircraft manufacturers. Over the years, that changed, and most car enthusiasts can afford basic welding equipment that is relatively easy to use. The old gas welders are still available for certain jobs, but MIG welders that were introduced in the late 1970s have replaced the old stick-style arc welders and are available in 110-volt configurations for light-duty work and 220-volt setups for more heavy-duty applications. Some enthusiasts have both a 110-volt welder (perfect for light-duty body repairs) and a 220-volt welder (for heavy-duty chassis welding). Most hot-rod shops also have TIG welding machines, because they provide welds that are visually attractive and are stronger than other welding methods.

The Ford flathead engine was popular with hot rodders in the early 1950s, but several really powerful overhead-valve V-8 engines were being released by Cadillac, Oldsmobile, and Chrysler, and they caught the attention of hot rodders. Many of these engines were developing a lot more horsepower in stock form than most horsepower-modified flathead engines could produce. When they were originally released, the engines were very expensive, but it was only a matter of time before the later-model, overhead-valve V-8 engines could be adapted into a Model T, Model A, or '32 chassis. These powerful engines opened up new problems for the early hot rodders, because even the '32 chassis wasn't strong enough to handle the additional horsepower.

When I was in high school, I was looking for a hot rod to buy, and I remember driving a Model A coupe, with a stock chassis, powered by a 1957 Olds engine. It was a scary ride, to say the least! When you stabbed the throttle, it was always a surprise, because the coupe went everywhere but straight, and the body twisted in several directions. Henry Ford learned that there were chassis problems when he installed a flathead V-8 in a Model A chassis meant to have a 40-hp, four-cylinder engine; the Oldsmobile engine was developing 200 hp more than the original flathead, so you can imagine how much that chassis was flexing. When early hot rodders started making engine improvements, they found out that they also had to make chassis upgrades. I considered buying that Olds-powered rod, but I knew that it needed to be disassembled in order to strengthen the chassis. I decided to pass.

Henry Ford wasn't interested in changes if he didn't have to make them, so the single buggy-spring-style suspension system that was used on the earliest Model T Ford remained in use (although vastly improved) up until 1948. Many engineering improvements were made in the basic design, such as spring rates and the location of the springs. Starting in 1932, the differential was moved in front of the spring position, and that allowed the rear spring to have more travel. The spring travel softened the ride quality in the rear of the car, and with some tricks (such as tapering the ends of the individual spring leaves), the suspension travel could be vastly improved. The front suspension had the spring mounted on top of the axle, and that design remained until 1935, when Ford mounted the spring in front of the axle. The changes to the front and rear mounting points of the springs allowed more travel to improve the ride quality of these early Fords and, in 1935, it became very acceptable. The chassis were also stronger than the ones used during the early Model T days.

There are six different Ford chassis designs from before 1949. They start with the simple, rectangular-shaped Model T chassis, which is followed by the Model A chassis that tapers from the front to the rear. Both the Model T and Model A chassis are constructed of what appears to be C-channel, but they are actually stamped from flat steel plate. After those is the '32 chassis, which is larger than the Model A's and features a curved taper design. The '32 chassis is a one-year design that was made for the new flathead V-8 engine, and it is also stamped steel, but it is larger than the original Model A-style chassis. The '32 chassis features a strong center crossmember that is used as a mount for the transmission. The fourth chassis is the one that was developed for the 1933 and 1934 Ford passenger cars, which had the bodies channeled over the frame. Ford added additional crossmember bracing in this chassis, because the flathead horsepower was slightly increased. In 1935, another very strong frame was designed for the new, larger Ford, and it is more than strong enough to handle the flathead engine. When hot rodders install a later-model overhead-valve V-8 engine of moderate horsepower, the chassis is still acceptable, although additional bracing makes it even better. The 1935 Ford was the beginning of what hot rodders call the fat-fender cars. The frame released in 1935 was used until 1940, with only minor changes to the body mounts. In 1941, Ford introduced a new, stronger frame with a two-inch longer wheelbase, and it was used until car production stopped during World War II. When the war was over, the new 1946 Ford continued to use the same basic 1941 chassis design, and it remained until 1948. The newer chassis is strong, offers a very comfortable ride, and can handle a stronger V-8 engine with only minor structural improvements.

Early on, Chevrolets weren't as popular as Fords for performance applications, because they were equipped with six-cylinder engines. Additionally, the sheetmetal-tacked-to-a-wooden-frame body design (used through 1936) was heavy, and cars that sat abandoned for any length of time didn't last long, because of termite infestation and dry rot.

Although performance-minded enthusiasts didn't like the Chevy as much as the Ford, the general public did like Chevrolet, and it sold more cars than Ford. The reason for this can be attributed to Chevrolet's superior mechanical engineering. The engineers at Chevrolet were influenced by the other General Motors divisions that were producing more expensive cars, so the company spent more time on chassis construction and suspension design. As a result, the engineers designed a more-comfortable, softer-riding, dual-parallel-leaf-spring design. This suspension system worked well and didn't have the roll characteristics of Ford's transverse-spring design.

In 1937, Chevrolet improved the ride quality of its cars with knee-action suspension, which was a precursor to later independent front suspensions. That year, too, Chevrolet started making an all-steel body, and it eventually became a favorite with hot rodders and drag racers. Chevrolet also offered safer, more reliable hydraulic brakes before Ford did, which was another reason buyers selected a Chevy over a Ford. From a design standpoint, Fords were more attractive than the early Chevys, but they didn't have the comfortable ride, agile handling ability, and superior stopping power.

Ford may have been the car preferred by most performance enthusiasts, but that isn't to say that there weren't Chevrolet performance enthusiasts. Many Chevrolet enthusiasts found that the overhead-valve Chevy engine had plenty of performance potential, and that was proven in drag racing during the 1950s and early 1960s. Chevrolet had beautiful body designs in the early years, so even though the cars had wooden body frames, street enthusiasts still turned them into hot rods. The 1937-and-newer Chevys also became very popular, and that popularity continues today.

CHAPTER 1

HOT-ROD CHASSIS MODIFICATIONS

The early hot rodders learned that the air flowing under a car's body at high speeds added unwanted lift, and that deteriorated the car's stability, which slowed the car. The hot rodders started lowering the front of the cars, and some even lowered the cars all the way around, with more lowering done in the front. Early rodders found that the best way to lower the front suspension without changing the basic ride characteristics was to heat up and re-bend (drop) the ends of the axle. This wasn't an easy task, because special forging equipment was needed, but before long, there were companies (such as Mor-Drop) that were dropping axles in various heights from 2 to 4 inches. The 3-inch drop was the most common, because it allowed a substantial drop and didn't decrease the car's safety by weakening the ends of the axle.

The hot rodders also noticed that, by reversing the main front-spring mounting eyes, the cars could be lowered another inch. There were many spring manufacturers that could take a normal spring main leaf, turn the spring eyes around, and re-arch the spring. Eventually, an aftermarket company, Posies, started offering reversed-eye springs; the company is still making them.

The rodders also lowered the front end by using smaller-diameter tires in the front and larger-diameter tires at the rear to provide more traction. This big-and-little tire combination is called a rubber rake. The lowered front suspension and the use of small tires in the front and big tires in the rear quickly became the hot rod look, and soon many different types of cars were using the stance to sport a racy appearance.

All of the early Fords use a wishbone-shaped support system to keep the front axle straight in the frame. The wide end of the wishbone

This beautiful '32 Ford chassis represents the traditional solid axle suspension (both front and rear) at its highest level of detail and nostalgia. The stock Ford transverse springs are still in place, but the entire car has been artfully lowered to acheive perfect stance. While the ride quality cannot be truly outstanding with this style of suspension in place, it was built to represent a past era, which it does beautifully.

connects to the outer ends of the axle, and the narrow end connects to the transmission crossmember. The rear of the support uses a ball-type connection at the end, allowing it to move up and down freely as the spring flexes. This system works fine, and it was used from the Model T days on up with changes in size and strength.

When rodders install more modern V-8 engines in pre-1949 Ford chassis, the stock crossmember has to be removed, and a custom one must be fabricated for the transmission being used. Even when an early transmission is used with a later-model V-8, the wishbone support won't clear most V-8 oil pans, so it has to be split for clearance. This is moderately easy to accomplish. The cast-iron end of the wishbone can be cut off, and the tubular part of the wishbone can be fabricated to use a Ford tie-rod ball joint that will also allow up-and-down movement. Some of the rat-rod and traditional-car builders use this system for the hot rods they create.

The wishbone-radius-rod system was used for many years. But in the 1970s, a new Pete & Jake's four-bar system was designed that actually worked better than the wishbone style, and before long, most of the new street rods were using it. The four-bar setup is still one of the most popular ways to support an I-beam or tubular-style front suspension. Rodders choosing to build nostalgic or traditional-style street rods are reverting to the hairpin radius rods to get the old-fashioned appearance, because they just plain look cool.

When the early, lowered cars were driven at higher speeds, they were noticeably more stable, but one of the problems encountered was that of slowing them back down. The factory mechanical brakes used on 1932-and-older Fords were poor at best, so the hot rodders started upgrading their roadsters and coupes with 1939–1948 Ford hydraulic brakes. It didn't take long before many of the 1928–1938 Fords were upgraded, even cars that were just used for basic transportation. The upgrade was a simple bolt-on affair and could be done over a weekend.

When the hot rodders started to install stronger overhead-valve V-8 engines in Model A or '32 Fords, they quickly found that the chassis were not adequate to handle the horsepower, as the frames would twist. To correct this, the C-channel frames, which were riveted together originally, were welded solid. The welded frames didn't flex as much, but they were still very weak. Some rodders started to box the frame in critical areas, and that process really made a big difference. Rodders boxed the frame by adding 3/16- or 1/4-inch steel plate to the inside of the frame to turn it into something that resembled rectangular steel tubing.

In many cases, hot rodders also added crossmembers to gain additional support and keep chassis flex to a minimum. This was especially important in cars that were used for drag racing. As I said earlier, in the early days, only metal-fabrication shops had welding machines, so welding the corners of the frame and boxing the chassis was an expensive process for a teenager on a very limited budget. Back then, there were no shops specializing in hot-rod fabrication, but that changed in the 1960s.

The wishbone radius rods may not be the best-looking system, but the design works fine. When the wishbone-style radius rods are made out of chrome-moly tubing, they are plenty strong. Some early rodders wanted a nicer-looking system, so they borrowed a design from the race cars of the time and used hairpin-style radius rods; radius rods really look nice when they, along with the front axle, are chrome-plated.

CHAPTER 1

Early Hot-Rod Transmission Selections

Most of the early hot rods used upgraded Ford parts, such as later-model (1936 through 1948) differentials and dropped-I-beam axles. The early Ford differentials used a torque tube to connect the differential to the transmission, and that was fine if a flathead engine was powering the car. The torque tubes from the later-model cars had to be shortened when they were used in early-model hot rods. The early differentials weren't strong, but hot rodders quickly found out that the transmission was the weak link in these early machines. Even a strong-running flathead could strip the gears in an early transmission. The most commonly used transmission was a 1939 Ford unit, because it was stronger than the previous transmissions, and the stick shifter is built into the transmission.

In 1940, Ford changed to a column-shifted transmission, but it wasn't stronger than the 1939 tranny. The 1939 Ford transmission was widely used and seemed to work with a mildly-built flathead engine for street use and dry-lakes racing, but it didn't stand up to drag racing when a car was running sticky tires. By the mid 1950s, the powerful new Buick, Olds, Cadillac, and Chrysler V-8 engines were being installed in the hot rods, and the early Ford transmissions simply weren't built to handle the increased torque and horsepower.

One good stab of the throttle, and the early transmissions would strip the gears right off the input shaft and cluster gear. The Ford transmissions had straight-cut gears that weren't very strong, so some rodders modified the transmissions with stronger Lincoln-Zephyr diagonally cut gears. When the Zephyr-geared transmissions were used, the power could be transferred through the transmission more effectively, but then the early Ford differential gears could be stripped under hard acceleration.

If you were racing your early Ford and blew the 1939 transmission, fixing it was no easy task. In order to remove the transmission, the differential had to be disconnected and moved back to allow enough room to unhook the driveline and move the transmission rearward. Rodders who faced this problem a few times wanted a stronger driveline that could handle

This '32 chassis was originally modified in the early 1960s, and it is the foundation for a 1929 Ford highboy roadster. The chassis features boxed frame rails and a very strong tubular crossmember to keep the frame from flexing.

You can see the '32 Ford truck, 4-inch-dropped, I-beam axle that was chrome plated and detail painted yellow. A truck axle was used, because it is stronger than a passenger-car axle; the drop was done by Mor-Drop in the San Francisco area. The suspension features a reversed eye spring, and the axle is supported with chrome-plated hairpin radius rods. A close look also reveals the 1940 Ford front brakes with chrome-plated backing plates, which are also detail painted yellow. Another interesting feature is the Model A front crossmember that was installed; it effectively lowers the car more than 1 inch. It was also laid back a little to increase the caster of the front axle. Notice that the front frame horns were also boxed and that the spreader bar was welded to the boxing plates.

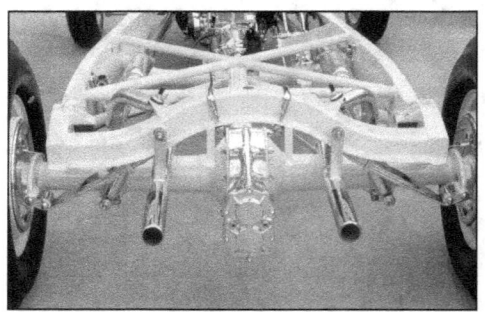

This roadster features a 1940-Ford-style differential outfitted with a Halibrand quick-change center section. The early Ford housing "bells" were narrowed, and 9-inch Ford ends were installed so that stronger later-model, pull-out axles could be used. The rear brakes were upgraded to 1956 Ford pickup brakes, because they are larger and stronger. The roadster features a '32 rear spring, but to lower the rear of the roadster, the original spring mount was changed over to a Model A mount. The rear frame horns originally used for gas-tank mounting were cut and finished. Notice that the rear springs also feature reversed eyes, and the shackles are connected to custom spring mounts.

HOT-ROD CHASSIS MODIFICATIONS

The differential is supported by tubular traction bars that connect to a mounting point under the transmission mount. The differential also features tubular shock absorbers that connect to tabs on the axle housing and strong mounts that are connected to the Model A crossmember.

The large tubular crossmember supports the transmission, but is also used to mount the master cylinder and the brake and clutch pedals. In keeping with the early roadster design, the steering consists of an early Ford steering shaft that connects to a 1956 Ford pickup steering box. The early steering box is very popular in 1960s-style street rods. This frame features all of the early tricks, but the detailing is much nicer than what was found in the early days, unless the car was built for show.

Complementing the car's early style, the engine features finned-aluminum valve covers, a variety of chrome-plated parts (such as the water pump and pulleys) and a polished tri-power intake manifold topped by three Rochester carburetors. Other nostalgic features include the early Corvette exhaust manifolds and the Joe Hunt magneto ignition.

the horsepower. The answer came in the form of open drivelines and modern transmissions, and that certainly included automatics.

Before going any further, check out the accompanying photos of a '32 Ford chassis that uses many nostalgic chassis-building techniques, along with some of the improvements the early rodders were using.

Build or Buy a Hot-Rod Chassis?

When an enthusiast purchased an old car in the 1950s and 1960s, he had to work with the original chassis to turn it into a hot rod. Rodders who were building Model T Fords modified the original chassis or purchased stronger Model A frames as the foundation for their hot rods, and they made the modifications that were required, with an emphasis on strength. The fellows who purchased Model A Fords had to strengthen the stock frame, and in order to do a good job and get the frame looking show ready, they had to fill all of the holes that were used to secure the mechanical-brake brackets.

If you are not familiar with a stock Model A frame, there are plenty of unnecessary holes after the mechanical brakes are removed. In fact, all of the frames from 1928–1938 that use mechanical brakes have an array of bracket holes that need to be filled. If you want to install any high-horsepower engine in a 1928–1934 Ford, the riveted frame connections have to be welded solid, and the frame rails need boxing. The '32 frame is stronger and was built to handle a whopping 65 hp, so when a highly modified, later-model flathead that produces 150 hp is installed, some strengthening is required.

Today, the basic Chevy 350-ci engine that street rodders like to use is developing around 350 hp, and the guys and gals who prefer modern engines are using LS1 and LS2 engines that develop more than 400 hp. That means that the chassis that is being used, whether it is one from a Model A, a '32, a 1933, or a 1934, will require a lot of strengthening to handle the horsepower. If you are using a stock chassis, that means it will require boxing from front to rear, and it will need strong crossmembers. If it is going to be a show car, then all of the modifications will have to be done well so that the frame looks nice. If you are interested in modifying your street-rod chassis with a crossmember that looks nice and works terrific, the following shows you how to do it.

Crossmember Installation

1 The original chassis had good frame rails, but it was missing the factory crossmember. The street-rod shop started improving the frame by boxing the front frame rails and installing a Heidts IFS system. The shop also boxed the rear frame rails when the Ford 9-inch differential and Heidts triangulated four-bar system was installed.

2 This close view of the frame rail shows where the original crossmember was cut out. The new crossmember uses this same mounting area.

3 The street-rod shop fabricated most of the parts that were used in this installation, but it did start with a Total Cost Involved Engineering transmission mount that the company uses in its Model A chassis. Here, the width of the mount is being measured so that a custom crossmember can be made.

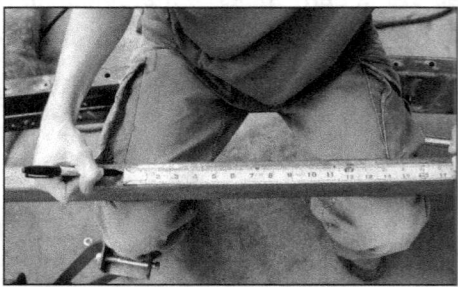

4 Rectangular steel tubing is used to form the center crossmember section. Accurate measurements are crucial.

5 The rectangular tubing is cut to length by using a large chop saw.

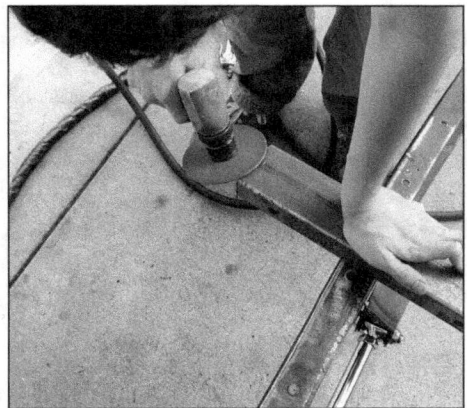

6 A 5-inch angle sander dresses and smoothes both ends of the rectangular tubing.

7 The center crossmember section is centered in the Total Cost Involved Engineering transmission mount, and then two holes are drilled for through bolts.

8 Using two sections of strap steel to hold the crossmember section in place, the unit is positioned parallel to the side of the frame, allowing sufficient clearance for the transmission's shifter arms.

9 After properly locating the center section of the crossmember, the rear section is positioned to see how it fits.

10 The rear section is marked for cutting, and the angle is noted. The crossmember ties into the rear frame boxing for additional strength.

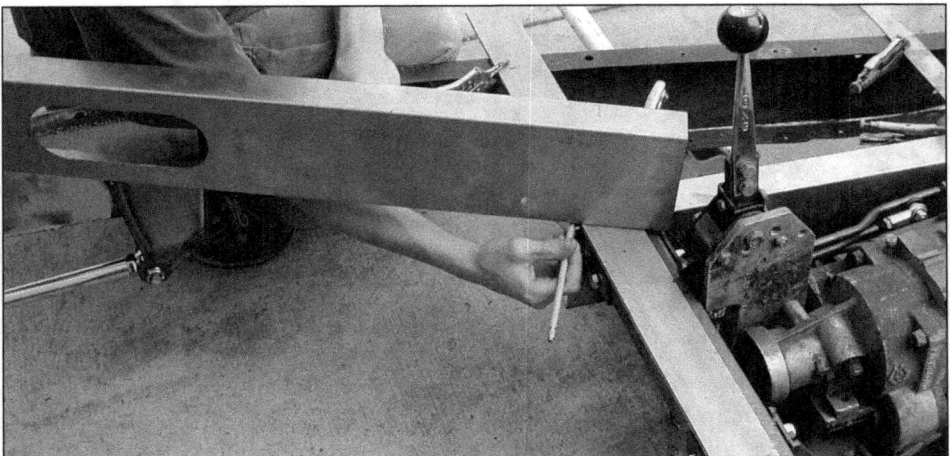

11 The front part of the rear boxing section also is marked for cutting; again, the angle is indicated.

CHAPTER 1

12 A large chop saw cuts the rear crossmember section. After that, the angles on the side are cut with a small cut-off tool according to the marks made.

13 The two boxing sections are tack welded together, and this process includes tacking the center boxed-tubing section. When it is finished, all three sections are welded together.

14 The rear boxing section is also welded to the rear portion of the frame. A close look reveals a hole in the boxing section that can be used for exhaust routing.

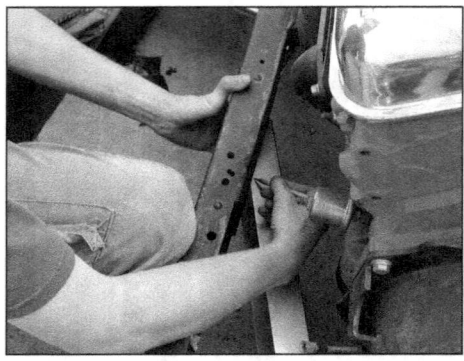

15 Now, the front boxing section can be installed. Here, the joining angle is being drawn onto the crossmember section.

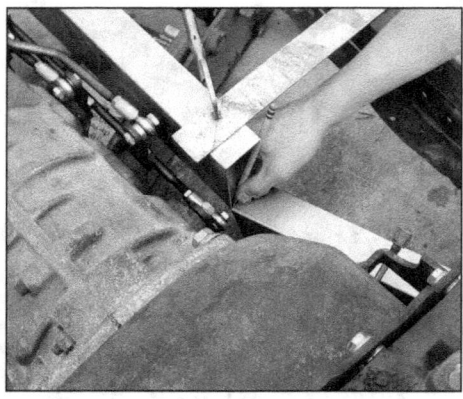

16 The front crossmember section is also marked for length, and the required angle is indicated.

17 The front section, including the required angles, is cut with a plasma cutter. After it is cut, the ends are smoothed with a 5-inch sander.

18 The crossmember section is installed and tack welded to the frame rail. The other side is tack welded to the center cross-member section. Note that this crossmember section is being welded to the area where the original section was located.

19 Here is the front section after being connected to the frame and the center section. There is plenty of clearance around the engine and transmission.

HOT-ROD CHASSIS MODIFICATIONS

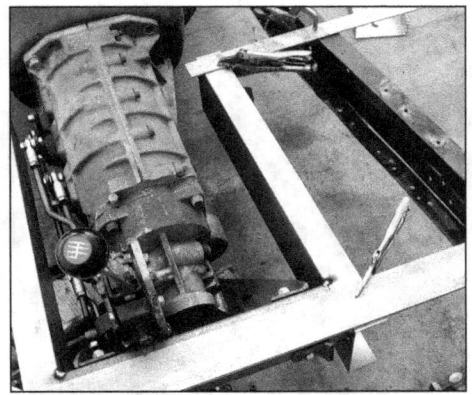

20 Using the same procedures, the other crossmember side is finished.

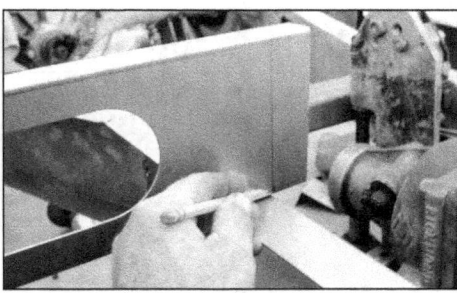

21 After both sides are finished, two braces are made to strengthen the crossmember. The small brace is stretched from the side of the frame to the new crossmember, and the length required is marked.

22 The frame side also must be marked for cutting. Both sides are cut, because the hole for the exhaust has to be centrally located.

23 The brace is welded to the frame and to the new crossmember. This brace strengthens the center portion of the frame where the transmission mount is located.

24 The shop installs the body to determine the position for the pedals. When the pedals are in the correct location, the mounting bracket is tack welded to the frame.

25 Here are the brake pedals and the master-cylinder mount after the bracket was welded to the frame. You can also see the brace for the crossmember.

26 After the crossmember sections are tack welded together, and everything works well, the sections are finish welded.

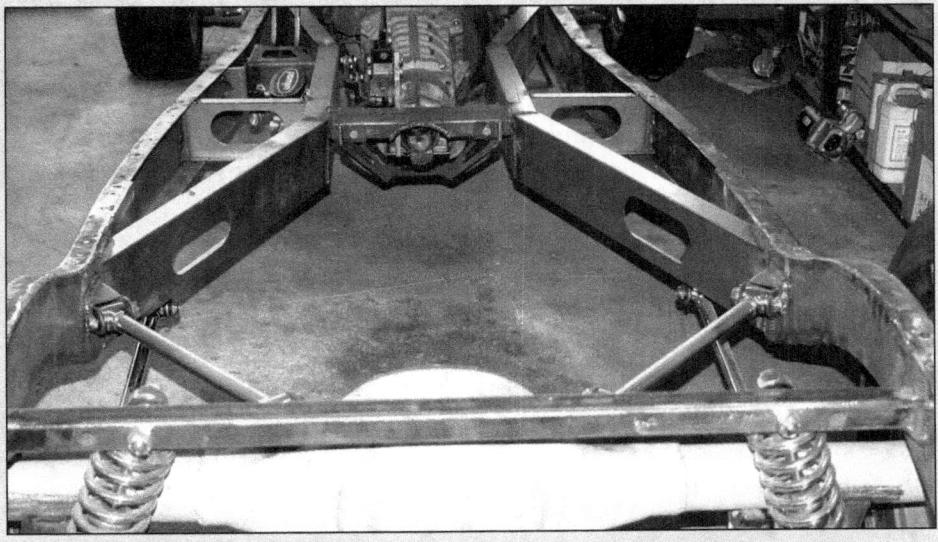

The frame after the crossmember installation. It works great, and it also looks good, because the shop made sure that one side was a mirror image of the other side.

Installing a Universal Power-Brake Assembly

Another problem you will run into is how to hook up a brake pedal (if you are running an automatic transmission) or brake and clutch pedals (if you plan to install a manual transmission). In the early days, some rodders used swinging pedals that mounted to the firewall; that way, the master cylinder also mounted to the firewall. This was a logical way to mount both the brake pedal and master cylinder, and some hot rodders are still using that system. However, most rodders prefer a clean firewall, so they build a street rod with the pedals coming up through the lower firewall and toe board.

A problem with the firewall mount is that the engine compartment can appear very busy when a power booster is used. When pedals that come through the lower firewall and toe board are installed, the master cylinder can be mounted under the car where you can't see it. By mounting the components underneath, the firewall and engine compartment can be kept clean. If you are building a street rod and are trying to come up with a way to install your pedals, I show an example of how a pedal-and-master-cylinder assembly was installed in a 1947 Chevy pickup truck chassis. The installation is very similar in all of the other street-rod applications.

Classic Performance Products offers brake kits for a variety of street rods and classic trucks. The company offers kits for 1928–1940 Ford frames, as well as many other booster kits for GM and Chrysler products. Many kits are available for later-model cars of every vintage. If you have a car that Classic Performance Products doesn't offer a kit for, the company sells a universal booster kit that can be installed in many vehicles. The kits come complete with bracket assemblies and power boosters with master cylinders. Today, there are many small-diameter booster and master-cylinder assemblies that can easily be installed under a car without the worry of a clearance problem.

Pedal Assembly Installation

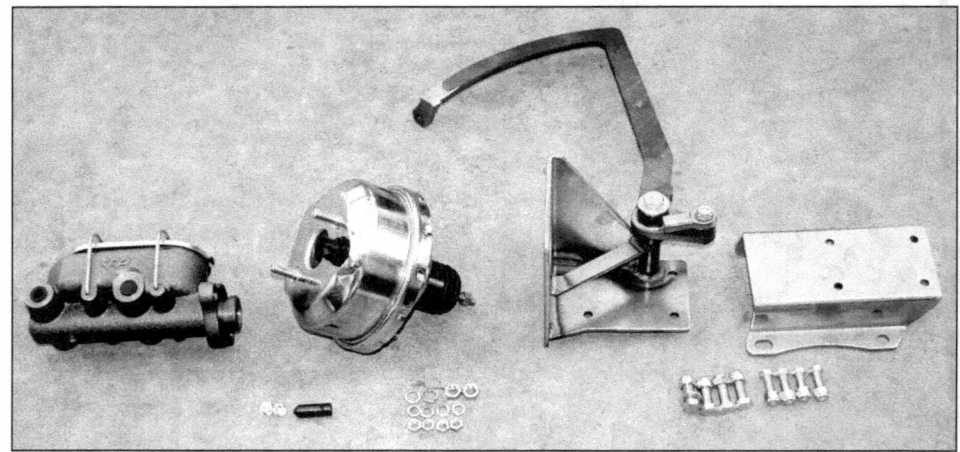

1 The 1947 through early 1955 Chevy brake kit comes with everything needed to complete the installation. This kit includes the brake-pedal assembly, the frame bracket, the power booster, the master cylinder, and all of the required hardware.

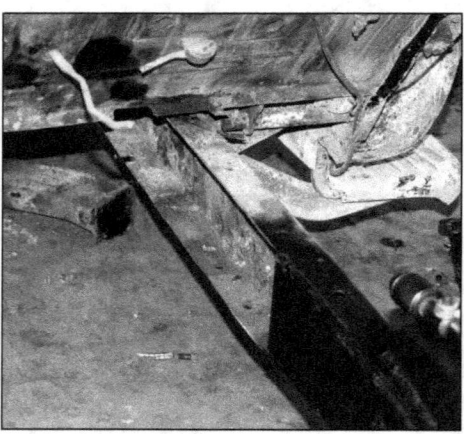

2 The original pedal assembly is removed from the frame. All of the mounting holes remain and are used by the kit.

3 The mounting bracket is installed into the frame, and then it is lined up with the original holes. Here, a lower mounting bolt and locknut are being installed.

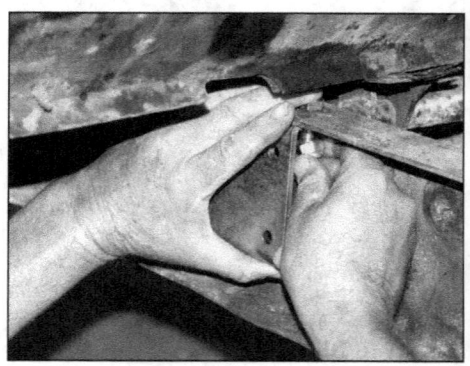

4 The bracket also makes use of the upper mounting holes. Here, a bolt and locknut are being connected finger tight.

5 After all of the bolts and locknuts are installed, they are tightened with a box-end wrench and a power ratchet wrench.

6 The brake pedal is removed from the unit so that it can be installed in the firewall. The hole is small, so the brake pedal must be inserted when the pedal mount is 90 degrees to the firewall.

7 Here is the pedal after it was inserted through the original hole. The kit was designed so well that it makes use of the original pedal hole.

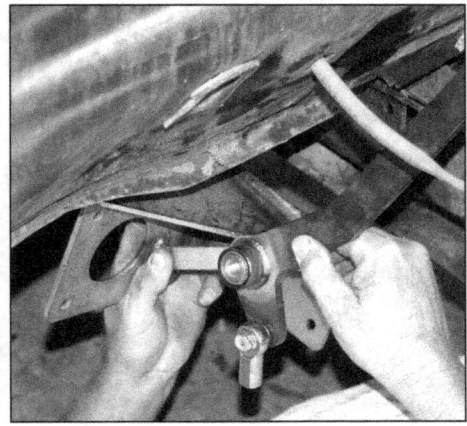

8 The pedal is reinstalled on the power brake bracket. It's a good idea to lubricate the shaft on which the pedal rides.

9 The pedal assembly is connected to the frame bracket with the bolt supplied in the kit.

10 After the bolts are installed finger tight, they are secured with a power ratchet wrench and an open-end wrench.

11 The nylon ball end-fitting is installed on the end of the power booster assembly. This fitting screws on and can be adjusted to the correct length.

12 This plunger also must be installed in the master cylinder before it is bolted to the power booster.

CHAPTER 1

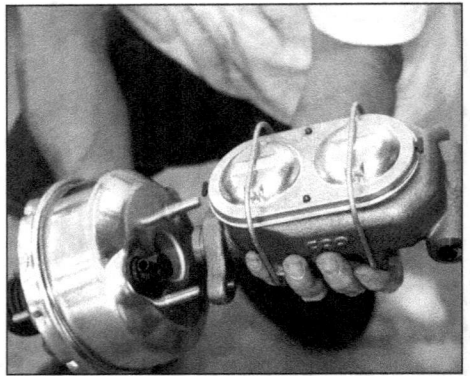

13 The master cylinder is lined up with the two studs on the power booster assembly. Notice that the cap and the booster are coated with rainbow cad plating.

14 The two nuts and washers are installed and tightened.

15 The four studs on the power booster are inserted in the bracket holes.

16 The four nuts are installed, and then they are tightened with a long box-end wrench.

17 The power booster plunger rod connects to the brake-pedal assembly with the bolt and locknut supplied in the kit.

18 In a few hours, the old truck was outfitted with a new power-brake assembly. The next step is installing the brake lines.

1935-and-Later Chassis

In 1935, Ford came out with a new chassis that was larger and much stronger than previous versions. This chassis features larger side rails and a center crossmember that connects to the frame and becomes a double wall for the outside rails in the front and rear of the frame. This is an excellent design, and because of the double wall, the chassis is much stronger than a single-wall chassis. The 1935–1940 frames were built to handle a more powerful flathead engine. When they were being designed, the engineering team knew that the engines would increase in power over the years, and that is why the frames were built with increased strength.

From personal experience, I know that the frames can handle around 250 hp in stock form without any major problems. If a 350-plus-hp engine is going to be installed, the frame requires strengthening in the corners and boxing in the front and rear. The frame can be boxed in the middle for additional strength. When a large engine and transmission are installed, the stock center crossmember connection must be altered; so when new parts are installed, they should be as strong as the parts that were removed.

The nice thing about the 1935–1940 chassis is that there are several companies that make kits to improve the suspension. Posies and other companies make a dropped-front-axle assembly that provides a split-wishbone kit. There are several kits that replace the original center crossmember connection with new parts that are strong and allow the installation of a Turbo 350 transmission when it is hooked to a small-block Chevy engine. There are also kits that allow the builder to install dual parallel leaf springs and a late-model differential. Many of the kits available can be bolted on, but additional strength can be added if the parts are welded on.

Rodders who are building a 1935–1940 Ford or a 1941 pickup truck can go from a stock frame to a nice street-rod chassis in a couple days and, if you use the bolt-on kits, it only requires normal hand tools for most of the changes. The front-suspension kit is the only one that requires heating and bending (using a gas welder) and the installation of weld-on fittings for the Ford tie-rod ends. There are some kits for the earlier frames but many rodders purchase a new chassis, because it is cost effective.

If you are building a Model A Ford, the stock chassis can be boxed, new crossmembers can be installed, and the rear of the chassis can be enhanced for a coil-over-shock

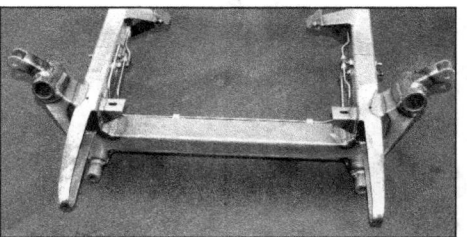

When Total Cost Involved Engineering designed a Model A chassis, it wasn't done with a one-size-fits-all mentality. The engineers at the company know that every street rodder wants his or her street-rod style, so many options are available for every chassis it builds, from the little Model A frame shown here to the larger 1935 through 1940 Ford chassis. This group has a chassis with an IFS and a standard four-link system at the rear. The chassis in the middle is designed for a Pro Street application, and it has a few custom modifications that were requested by the owner. The other chassis features a stock front crossmember that will be used with a dropped-tube axle and a special rear suspension that Total Cost Involved Engineering engineered for closed-cab pickups and roadster pickups. All of these styles are available for all of the other chassis the company builds.

Total Cost Involved Engineering also offers a Model A chassis that works with the stock dropped-front-axle arrangement seen here. The brackets on the side are shock-absorber mounts.

Total Cost Involved Engineering offers a variety of Model A chassis for many different applications and personal preferences. Enthusiasts who want a state-of-the-art Model A can order independent front suspension. This A chassis has the IFS crossmember.

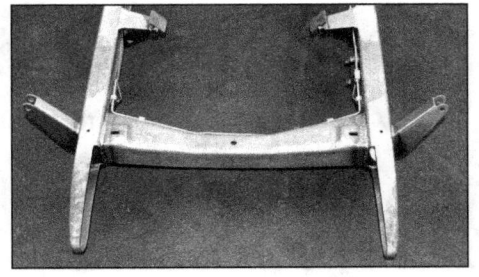

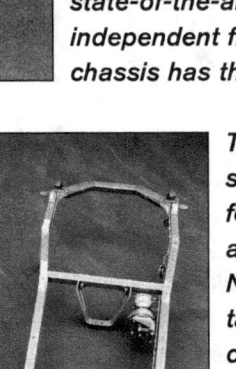

The most common rear-suspension arrangement features coil-over shocks and a four-link setup. Notice how the frame rails taper at the rear for better clearance. The round pads on both sides of the rear cross-member are designed for the body's rear body-to-chassis mounts.

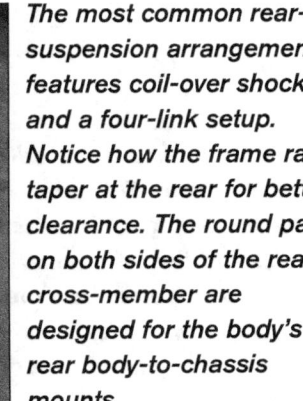

If you are building a Model A closed-cab pickup or roadster pickup, choose this chassis. The cross-member is modified to offer more clearance for the pickup bed. Even the stock Ford chassis required a hole and a box in the wood bed for frame clearance. This frame doesn't.

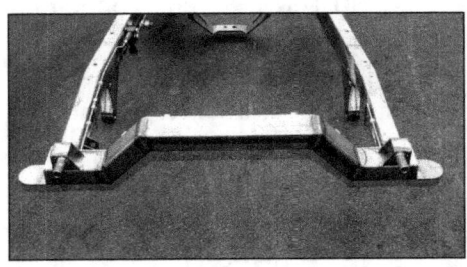

Performance enthusiasts may want a Pro Street chassis, and Total Cost Involved Engineering offers one. This chassis is narrower at the rear and is built to work with a narrowed rear end that is equipped with a four-link setup. The chassis also features a driveshaft loop.

suspension or an independent rear suspension. If you don't have the ability to do the fabrication upgrades yourself, the time it takes to have a hot-rod shop do it for you can become cost prohibitive. Even professional rod shops have problems because, to do the boxing and frame modifications correctly, the frame needs to be held in a jig to keep it from bending or twisting when the work is being done. Besides the normal fabrication work, there are holes all over the frame that have to be filled and ground flat, and that process can get expensive. Most rod shops tell you that you can save money by purchasing a new chassis, and there are several companies that offer them.

When fiberglass bodies became available, there was a need for new chassis, because it wasn't easy to find a good original one. Some fabrication companies saw the demand for new chassis, so they started building them. The most difficult chassis was that of the '32, because the frame rails had to be stamped to get the shape correct. Other chassis were more straightforward, and most companies started making chassis for Model A and 1935–1940 Fords. Several companies started making chassis for Chevys, although some of the Chevy chassis were stronger and easier to modify. Chassis companies are very busy, and they offer a variety of frames using different suspension methods.

When designing a street rod, you have to select the parts that go with the style of the street rod. If you want an early-1960s-style car, you probably want something similar to the '32 shown at the beginning of this book. If you are not building a nostalgic car and want a common style that works well, you can equip

Total Cost Involved Engineering Chassis Selections

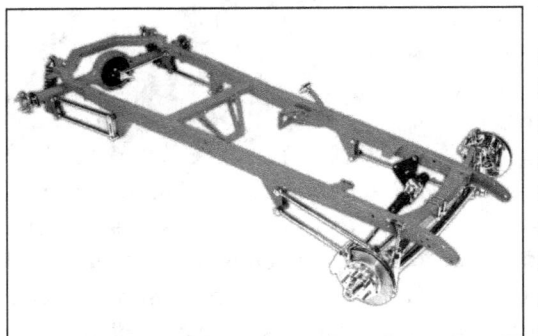

This Model A chassis has a premium dropped axle with a stainless package, and it features an optional Unisteer rack-and-pinion system. In the rear, the coil-over-shock system is hooked to a 9-inch Ford differential, and a four-link system and a Panhard bar are used. The boxed chassis features a sturdy crossmember for the transmission mount, side-mount engine mounts for a small-block Chevy engine, and a pedal that will hook to a small power booster.

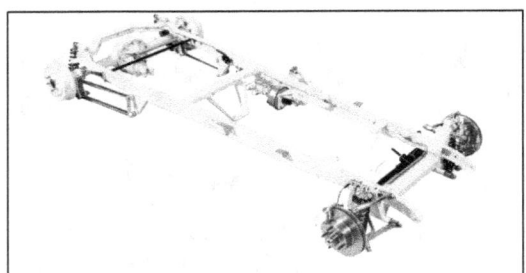

Independent front suspension is available on a Model A chassis, and this one is equipped with custom IFS and the stainless package. In the rear are a coil-over-shock system hooked to a 9-inch Ford differential and a four-link system with a Panhard bar. This particular chassis also features an optional anti-roll bar. The pedal assembly connects to the small power booster and dual master cylinder. Steering is handled by a rack-and-pinion system.

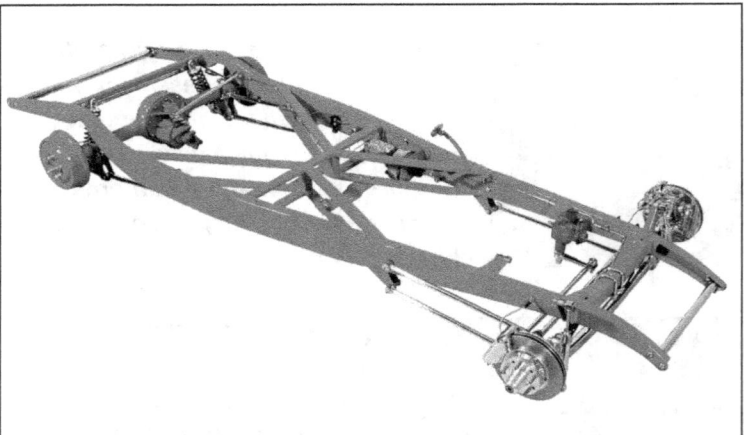

Total Cost Involved Engineering manufactures really nice '32 chassis that have a lower reveal that is exactly like the one on the original chassis. This particular chassis features a dropped-tube front suspension that is held in place with a four-bar system. This chassis also sports a premium dropped axle and the stainless package. The rear includes a Ford 9-inch differential with coil-over shocks, and the differential is held in place by a four-link system with a Panhard bar. Notice how the extra-strong, rectangular-tube crossmember is designed for use with a variety of transmission selections. This chassis has polished-aluminum Wilwood disc brakes and a standard steering box. This is the perfect chassis for a traditional highboy roadster.

HOT-ROD CHASSIS MODIFICATIONS

If you are building a full-fendered '32 hot rod, and want a comfortable-riding street rod that is fun to drive, this is the chassis for you. It features an independent front suspension with rack-and-pinion steering, and the rear has a Ford 9-inch with coil-over shocks and a four-link system with a Panhard bar. If you want front and rear independent suspension, you can add an optional Jaguar, Heidts, or Kugel IRS; those are available for all chassis, from the Model A to the 1935 through 1940 chassis. This chassis also has a bracket for the pedal and master-cylinder assembly, and it uses the super-strong, rectangular-tube crossmember.

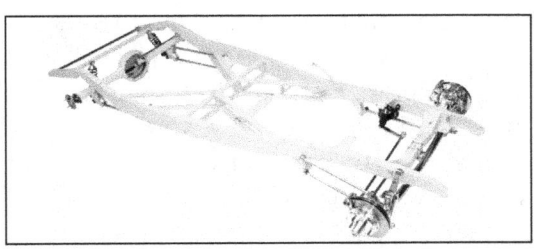

The stock 1933 through 1934 Ford chassis was strong in stock form, but the Total Cost Involved Engineering chassis is extremely strong with the sturdy boxed frame rails and the rectangular-tube crossmember. The chassis features a custom tube front suspension with a four-bar system. Additionally, this chassis has the standard cross-steer system. The chassis includes a Ford 9-inch differential suspended on coil-over shocks, and it is held in place with a four-link system with a Panhard bar. This chassis also features Wilwood polished-aluminum front disc brakes.

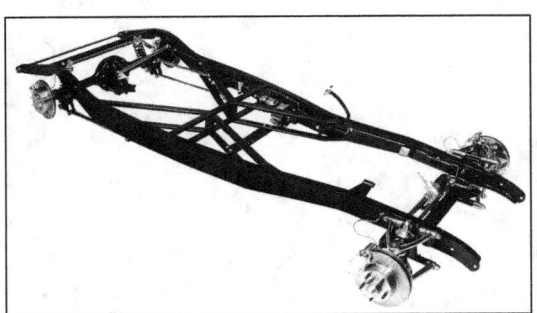

If you want a 1934 Ford coupe that looks great and has a soft, stable ride, order a 1933 through 1934 Ford chassis with an independent front suspension. This coupe features optional Wilwood disc brakes and rack-and-pinion steering. The chassis also includes a pedal assembly and bracket for the power booster and dual master cylinder. Additionally, there is a Ford 9-inch differential riding on coil-over shocks, and they are held in place with a four-link system with a Panhard bar. A close look also reveals that this chassis sports the optional rear-disc-brake package.

Street rodders building a fat-fendered car can make one that rides smooth and handles fantastic by purchasing a Total Cost Involved Engineering chassis with an independent front suspension and a parallel-leaf spring rear suspension. This 1935 through 1940 chassis features a Mustang II front suspension outfitted with GM-style brakes. Also shown is the pedal assembly and bracket for the power booster and dual master cylinder.

your car with a dropped-tube front suspension with a coil-over-shock/four-link rear suspension. This is a very common style used on highboy roadsters, coupes, and sedans, because the front suspension adds to the traditional appearance of the car. If you prefer an early car with fenders, you might opt for an independent front suspension with a coil-over-shock/four-link rear suspension, or you might choose a Jaguar, Kugel, or Heidts independent rear suspension.

Pre-1934 cars use a variety of chassis and suspension systems, because you can see the suspension parts, but the 1935–1940 chassis are primarily equipped with independent-front-suspension systems, with the owner's choice of parallel leaf springs or coil-over-shock/four-link suspension systems. Independent front suspensions are preferred on the later street rods, because you really can't see the front suspension, and when installed, the 1935–1940 street rods have a better ride quality, a positive steering, and an improved turning radius.

Total Cost Involved Engineering Chassis Selections

Total Cost Involved Engineering is one of the first companies to build custom chassis. The company was founded in 1974 and quickly became the leading chassis manufacturer.

Today, the company offers chassis for 1928–1940 Ford cars and 1941 Ford pickup trucks. The custom chassis are very strong and are designed for use with original bodies as well as custom fiberglass bodies.

Detailing a 1940 Ford Chassis

Total Cost Involved Engineering offers a range of chassis in a variety of suspension levels. Although the chassis that are featured at car shows and in the catalog are painted to look nice, they are delivered as bare steel. When you get the chassis, you have to determine how you would like it to look, and then it is painted and plated to look nice. With the previous chassis, all of the parts on the front and rear suspension were polished or chrome-plated to look great, because they're visible. The project chassis illustrated here will be used under a 1940 Ford sedan, so expensive chrome plating is pointless. However, the owner still wanted a nice-looking chassis, so it was painted.

Rodders have choices regarding chassis detail. Some prefer powder coating the chassis, while others prefer painting it. With today's high-impact urethane paints, it is difficult to tell the difference until it is color sanded and rubbed out.

The 1940 chassis was detail painted using single stage urethane, and the price of doing it was reasonable, compared to powder coating. We call this detailing process economy detailing, because it can be done for less than $250.

Building a street rod can be extremely expensive, so the following is an example of a chassis that looks great but doesn't break the bank. At first, chrome plating many of the suspension parts was considered, but that would have cost a fortune. This is a 1940 Ford sedan, and most of the undercarriage will never be seen when the body is on the chassis. The Total Cost Involved Engineering chassis was in bare metal, the frame was finished with paint detailing.

This sedan will be driven to outdoor shows and other events; it is definitely not going to be an ISCA "show-only" sedan. Many people powder coat their chassis, but that is another process that is very expensive. For this frame, the painters used a quart of Spectramaster Red DuPont single-stage paint, and for some contrast, a quart of DuPont Silver single-stage paint. The frame and differential were painted red, and the gas tank and suspension parts were painted silver.

If you are handy with a spray gun, single-stage urethane paint can be applied to look better than powder coating, and it is very durable. Another advantage is that the frame can be smoothed in areas with body filler, so the end result can look better than a powder-coated chassis. The early Hemi engine used in the chassis was already detailed with polished aluminum and chrome plating, so it wasn't included in the expense of the chassis detailing. The total cost for detailing this chassis was less than $400, and that included the primer. The results turned out very nice; it proves how you can detail your fat-fender car's chassis without spending a fortune.

Economy Detailing

Joe Reath built this early Hemi engine years ago, and it features Hot Heads aluminum heads, a Hot Heads dual-quad intake manifold, a set of Hot Heads valve covers, a pair of Carter carburetors, and an O'Brien Truckers air cleaner. When this engine was built, all of the aluminum parts were polished, and the steel parts were chrome plated.

1 The chassis is outfitted with a Carter fuel pump and a Fram fuel filter. The fuel pump is painted red to match the chassis, and the parts of the Fram filter that aren't chrome plated are also painted red. Both of the parts are located close to the Rock Valley gas tank.

2 The Rock Valley stainless-steel gas tank is silver, and it's secured to the frame with polished stainless-steel bolts. You can also see the gasoline sending unit for the Classic Instruments gas gauge.

3 The early Hemi engine has to power a Chevy Turbo 350 transmission, so an adapter kit from Performance Automotive Warehouse is used. This kit comes complete with the aluminum adapter plate, a flex-plate, a starter motor, a tap kit, and all necessary hardware. A Chrysler transmission could be used, but it is larger and more difficult to hook up. The transmission is coated with silver paint.

4 The front suspension features silver A-arms, spindles, and shock absorbers, and they contrast nicely with the bright red paint. The airbags were inspected and cleaned before they were reinstalled.

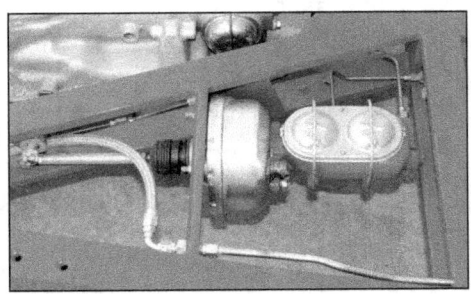

5 The chassis has a dual master cylinder with a power booster. The master cylinder is painted red, and the gold-cad-plated parts remain as delivered. The polished stainless-steel brake lines are a nice touch.

6 A close look at the front suspension reveals the silver-painted upper and lower A-arms, the silver spindle, and a hint of the red Stainless Steel Brakes calipers.

7 The Ford 9-inch differential was smoothed and painted red, and the driveshaft and four bars were painted silver. The Panhard bar was also painted silver. A Wilwood proportioning valve is mounted to the frame.

CHAPTER 1

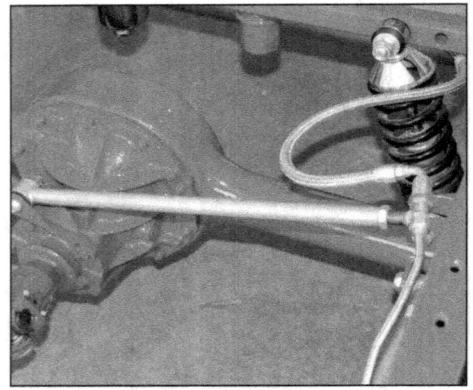

8 *The differential is red, the Panhard bar is silver, and the coil-over shocks are billet aluminum with black springs. The braided, stainless-steel hose connects to the polished-stainless-steel hard line.*

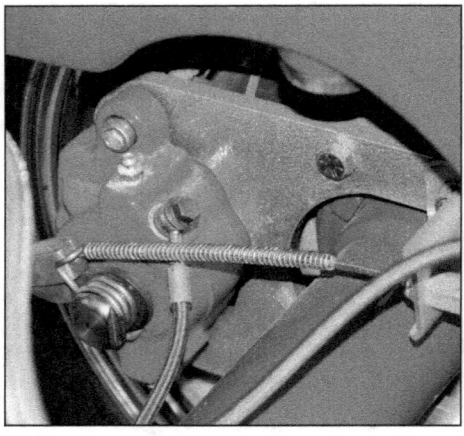

9 *A close look at the rear brakes reveals the silver caliper bracket and the red Stainless Steel Brakes caliper. This brake has a manual-parking-brake system.*

10 *The rear of this car is suspended by Total Cost Involved Engineering coil-over shock absorbers. The rear shock bracket has three settings so you can raise or lower the rear of the car.*

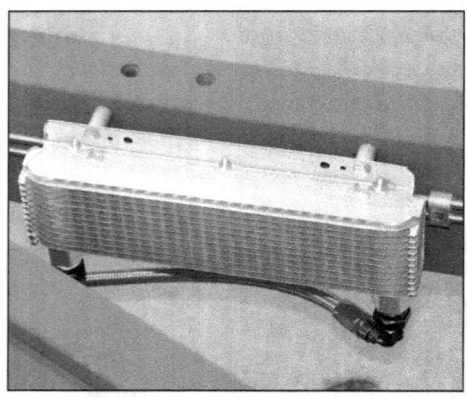

11 *A B&M transmission cooler is used, and it hooks to the transmission with braided-steel lines.*

12 *The front suspension comes from Total Cost Involved Engineering. The A-arms, spindles, and power rack-and-pinion steering unit are painted silver. The chassis is bright red DuPont single-stage paint, and it certainly provides a smooth, shiny finish.*

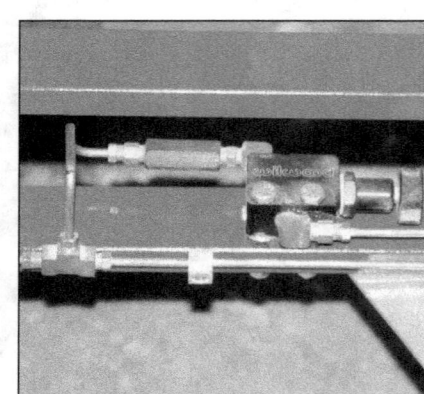

13 *The brake system features polished-stainless-steel brake lines, a Wilwood proportioning valve, and residual valves for the front and rear disc brakes.*

14 *The silver power-rack-and-pinion steering system connects to polished-stainless-steel U-joints and a steering rod. The bracket is mounted low on the frame to clear the huge Hemi engine.*

Detailing a 1931 Ford Chassis

The fellow who is building this Model A wants to have a nice-handling and smooth-riding street rod, so it is equipped with a Jaguar rear suspension and a Total Cost Involved Engineering independent front suspension. He wanted the undercarriage to be show worthy, so in the process of building the car, the chassis was built to work well and look nice, too. This car is a little different, because the chassis features all of the state-of-the-art chassis components, but the car was built in a very traditional style. One of the traditional aspects of this car is the power combination, which consists of a 425-ci Buick nailhead engine connected to a Turbo 400 transmission. The polished American Racing wheels also add to the Model A's traditional appearance.

Model A Detailing

1 This 1931 Model A chassis features a Jaguar rear suspension riding, Aldan adjustable coil-over shocks, and a Total Cost Involved Engineering independent front suspension. Before the chassis was assembled, the frame and components were painted with red urethane paint.

2 A close look at the front suspension reveals the polished-stainless-steel upper and lower A-arms, stainless-steel spindles, chrome-plated sway bar, and chrome-plated coil-over shock absorbers. This suspension provides a nice comfortable ride, and it looks fantastic.

3 The rear suspension features a bright red center section that is outfitted with a Posi-Traction unit with 3.42:1 gears. The upper dog-bone shafts are Jaguar sedan units, and the lower control arms were shortened to provide a 56-inch-wide differential. The aluminum hubs were cut back slightly to show the U-joint, and the sides were drilled for a nice appearance. Four Aldan shocks are used to provide a smooth ride and adjustable ride height. All of the aluminum parts are polished to a high shine, and many other parts are chrome-plated.

CHAPTER 1

4 *Looking at the differential from the front, you can see the double-kicked-up chassis that provides a low ride height for the rear of the Model A. This chassis also has a crossmember for the rear control arms that keeps the differential from twisting forward or backward. Also visible are the Wilwood parking-brake calipers.*

5 *This chassis is outfitted with a large Turbo 400 transmission, so the brake booster and the battery area aren't very big. In order to make this area work, the Model A features a small, but powerful, battery that connects to the starter motor on the driver side.*

6 *The rack-and-pinion steering unit is painted red to match the frame. The U-joint connection travels rearward to connect to the steering column. All of the brake lines are fabricated from stainless steel, and they are polished to a high shine.*

7 *This Model A is different, because it's equipped with a 425-ci Buick nailhead engine that was rebuilt with quality performance parts. The engine is red to match the frame and body and the aluminum parts, including the timing-chain cover, are polished to a high shine.*

8 The frame is outfitted with a Carter electric fuel pump and a Fram fuel filter, and both are detailed with red paint. All lines on the car are outfitted with aircraft fittings and braided-steel line.

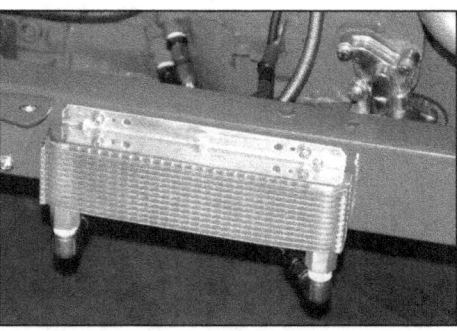

9 A B&M polished-aluminum transmission cooler is used, and it is connected to the outside of the frame where it gets cool airflow. The lines travel under the frame to the transmission fittings.

10 A single stainless-steel brake line travels to a T-fitting that provides brake fluid to the two inboard calipers. Visible is the emergency-brake caliper that is installed after the body is installed on the frame.

11 The Jaguar center section is equipped with a later-model Jaguar finned-aluminum cover that is polished to a high shine. The covers are rare, so the owner was lucky to find one. The dual brake lines running to the two polished Wilwood calipers are also visible.

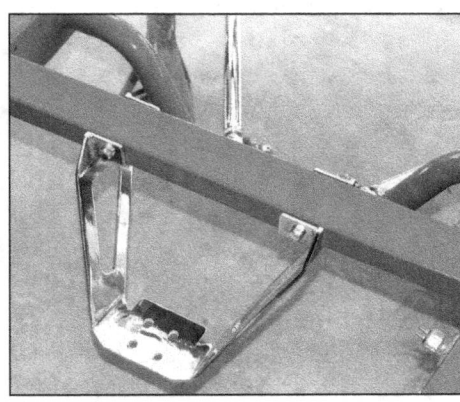

12 The transmission mount is modified to accept the Buick engine; it is chrome plated for a nice appearance.

13 In order to save space, this Model A is equipped with a small power booster connected to a dual master cylinder. The power booster features gold cad plating, and the master cylinder is red to match the chassis.

14 The nicely engineered independent front suspension and Wilwood brakes with vented rotors. The rotors are detail painted red for a nice appearance.

15 The brake pedal is modified slightly to clear the transmission bell housing and driver-side-mounted starter motor. The pedal assembly is red to match the chassis, plus it looks nice inside of the car. All of the lines are connected to the frame and engine with small nylon clips.

16 This chassis features polished American Torque Thrust wheels wrapped with BF Goodrich tires. The polished-aluminum Wilwood caliper peeks through the windows in the wheels.

Tools

Our 1940 Ford project chassis was modified by the owner to accept a Chrysler engine and Turbo 350 transmission. Using the simple detailing tips mentioned, the chassis looks terrific and didn't cost a ton to complete. The engine will be seen when the hood is up, so it received all of the polished and plated detail parts. Many street-rod enthusiasts prefer to purchase a frame that is ready to go, because most enthusiasts do not have the tools, time, or ability to turn a stock frame into a street-rod masterpiece. In the 1960s, I built a variety of street-rod frames, but even though I have the ability to modify a frame, I prefer to buy one that's ready to go, because it is cost and time efficient.

Some rodders take pride in working on their own chassis, and that is a credit to them. If you think you would like to modify your own chassis, there are a number of tools you need to do the job correctly. The first item you need is a large air compressor with at least a 60-gallon tank; compressors are available from many sources. A large one is expensive, but it will be the workhorse of your shop, so you want a quality unit. The compressor powers air tools, and it is necessary if you plan to paint the chassis and car. The compressor should be plumbed with a good water-trap system, so that the air tools and spray equipment stay in good condition. It is essential to have a good water trap, especially when you are using paint-spraying equipment. It is also a good idea to drain the compressor and the water trap before any spray painting.

Frame building also requires welding equipment, such as a 220-volt MIG welder, a quality TIG welder, or both. Most frame modifications can be done with a MIG welder, and from a cost standpoint, it is less expensive than a TIG welder. Many shops prefer the TIG welder because the welds look nicer, and it is more flexible. You can weld very thin or thick metal, but learning how to use it is more difficult than learning how to use a MIG welder.

Another important tool is a plasma cutter. The plasma cutter can cut pencil-thin lines through sheetmetal. It is great for making chassis modifications, cutting sheetmetal to use as frame-boxing material, and situations where metal has to be cut and shaped.

When chassis work is being done, such as boxing the frame and attaching brackets, the chassis will look better when the welds are ground and smoothed. The heavy-duty welding work requires an aggressive grinder, so use a heavy-duty electric unit. A large grinder has a lot of torque, so care has to be used when handling one. When welding smaller areas, use a small grinder.

One of the most important tools is an air compressor. Many shop tools are air powered, and a strong compressor is required to power air-gobbling tools, such as 3-inch cut-off wheels and small air sanders. The air compressor is also used to operate paint-spraying equipment and finish sanders. I recommend buying a large compressor with at least a 60-gallon tank.

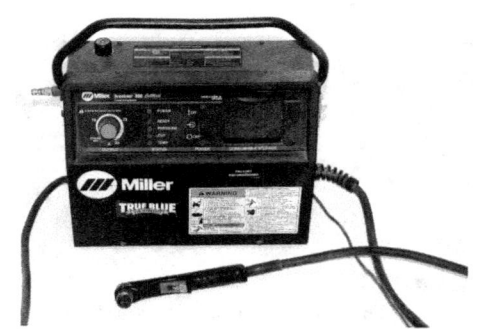

A chassis fabricator needs a plasma cutter. The plasma cutter can slice through metal with a pencil-thin line. After you get used to it, you can make frame-boxing plates, intricate brackets, notches in the frame, and many other items that require metal cutting.

Plumb the compressor with a water trap in the line. Water condenses in the compressor, and it enters the lines, ends up in your air tools, or introduces water drops in your paint. It's always a good idea to drain the compressor tank once a week, and drain your water trap at the same time.

When building a hot-rod chassis, you need welding equipment. There are many different welders available, from small 12-volt machines to mega-dollar TIG welders. Most professional shops have a 220-volt MIG welder (that is perfect for just about any chassis operations) and a TIG welder (which delivers some of the strongest welds you can make). If you have a home shop, you can probably get by with a good MIG welder for most chassis applications.

When you box a frame, the welds need grinding to get the frame looking nice. This is not an easy job, and it can't be done with a little grinder. In order to grind large, long welds, use a heavy-duty grinder. This grinder cuts through the welds quicker than any other type of machine, but only use it to a point, because after the welds are manageable, they should be finished off with a smaller grinder.

Use a 5-inch grinder to flatten small welds on your chassis parts; it's the grinder that can finish the metal after using the large grinder. Air grinders are very handy and can be purchased from many retail tool establishments.

Related to the grinders is a 5-inch angle sander to clean up bracket installations, and it can also be used to follow up the work done by the large grinder.

Every hot-rod and chassis builder needs a variety of 3-inch cut-off wheels, because they are used for fabrication, from making small gussets to making complex brackets. All shops also need a 2- and 3-inch angle sander or grinder, because they are perfect for grinding small areas and preparing areas for welding. The 3-inch grinder can also follow the 5-inch sander to get the metal smoother and formed correctly. Small hand grinders are important to have when building a frame, and there are several kinds that do the job. Another electric grinder that works well for heavy welding slag is a small hand grinder with a stone instead of paper-backed grinding discs.

It is impossible to build a chassis without power drills. Both air-powered and heavy-duty electric drill motors are recommended, but air units work well because they are smaller and easier to use in tight areas. Additionally, an angle drill motor is nice to have, because it can fit into extremely tight areas.

CHAPTER 1

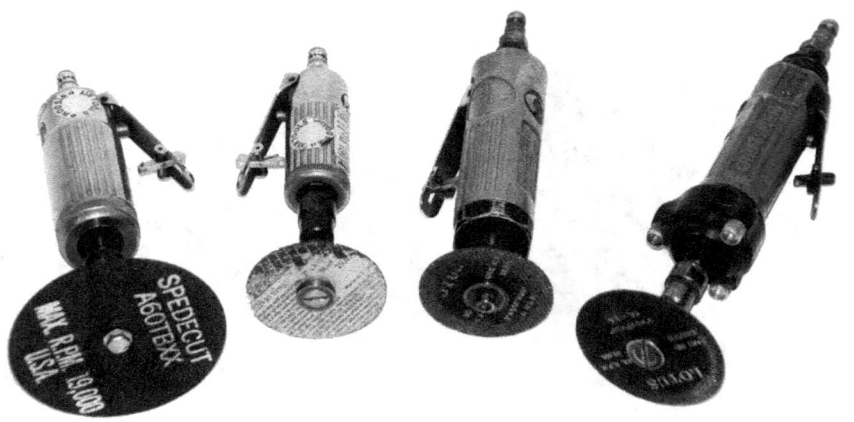

Buy 3-inch cut-off wheels. The super-thin stone blade cuts through sheetmetal or thick steel with ease. The cut-off tool has so many uses that most rod shops use them every day. This group of cut-off wheels includes one that is outfitted with a 4-inch blade.

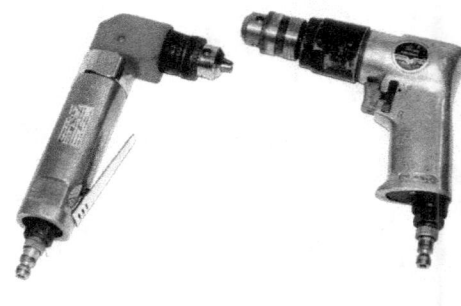

Buy an assortment of hand drills. Shown are an air-powered standard drill (right) and an air-powered angle drill (left), which is used in tight areas. You also need a heavy-duty electric drill with a 1/2-inch chuck.

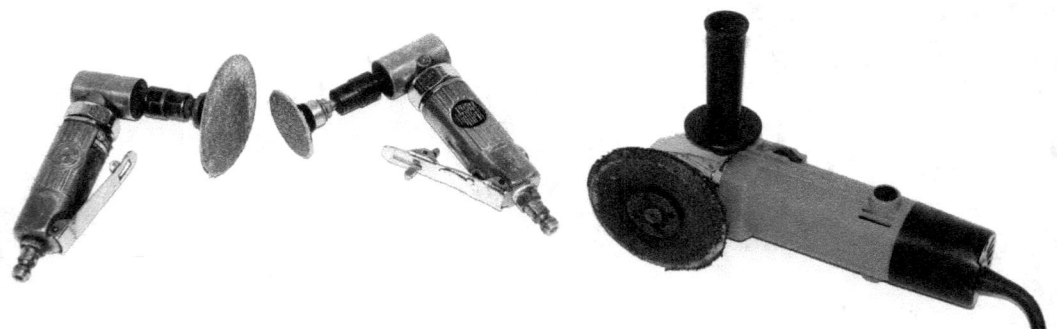

These two small angle sanders are outfitted with 3- and 1¾-inch sandpaper. These small tools are finish grinders, and they are used to clean up cuts made by the plasma cutter, finish brackets, clean metal prior to welding, and more. The small sander is perfect for getting into areas that the 3-inch unit can't.

This smaller grinder is useful for cleaning up welds on certain areas of the frame. It uses a stone rather than sandpaper, and it is very effective.

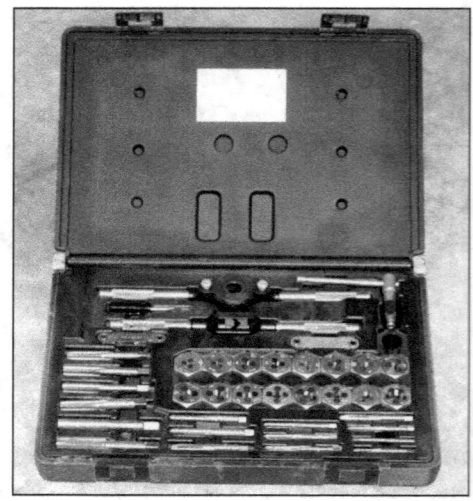

There are many areas on a frame, including brackets and mounting points for brake-line clips, that have to be drilled and tapped. If possible, get a full line of taps and dies. The taps come in handy after the frame is painted, to clean out small holes that have paint inside.

When building a chassis, many holes have to be tapped to secure brake-line clamps and small brackets. The taps can also be used to clean out nuts after they've been welded to the frame, although many builders prefer using nut inserts. It is also a good practice to tap the nuts in the frame after it has been painted or powder coated.

The most important part of building a chassis is making the correct measurements, so it is necessary to have a couple measuring tapes and an angle finder. If you have to cut thin sheet steel and want a clean cut, you can do a great job with a small air saw. If you plan to paint your frame instead of powder coating it, you should have paint-spraying equipment, such as a low-cost HVLP spray gun for applying primer and another quality HVLP spray gun for applying the finish paint. If you do paint the frame and street rod, you also need special sanders for polishing the paint and a quality buffer to get the paint shiny.

You can have all the tools you want in your garage, but if you don't know how to use them, you will never get a chassis built. Building a chassis can be very complex, because starting from scratch isn't easy.

If you have a friend who is a good metal worker, or one who has built a few street rod chassis, you have the advantage of that knowledge to help you.

In the old days, everything had to be hand fabricated, but today there are companies that can sell you parts that have been engineered and fabricated by experts. If you want instant gratification, you can order a chassis from a variety of street-rod chassis manufacturers. If you prefer to build your own chassis, you have to know how to weld; although there are some bolt-on parts you can use, the majority of the parts required to finish your chassis will have to be welded on.

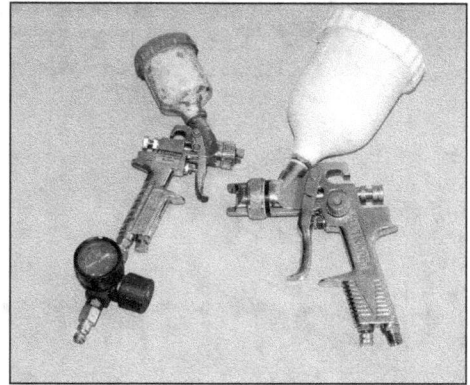

Frames can be powder coated or painted, depending on how nice you want the frame. If the frame is painted, more work can be done to smooth the frame before it is painted, and then it can be color sanded and rubbed out, just like the body paint. If you paint the chassis, use a spray gun or two to coat the frame. Notice the small gun that can be used to get into small, tight spaces in the frame.

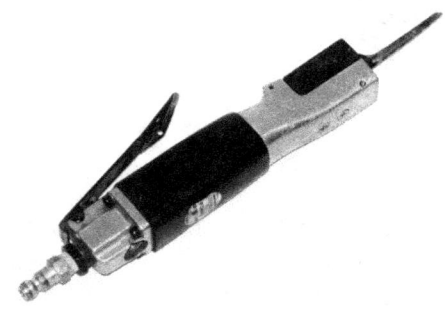

There are times, generally on thin metal, when an air-powered saw is perfect for making brackets and trimming thin metal parts. It is good to have one, but you can build a chassis without one.

If you plan to polish the frame, color sand it with fine-grit sandpaper first. On long, flat areas of the frame, the job can be speeded up with a small air-powered sander, like this one that is designed for use with 1,000-grit-and-finer sandpaper.

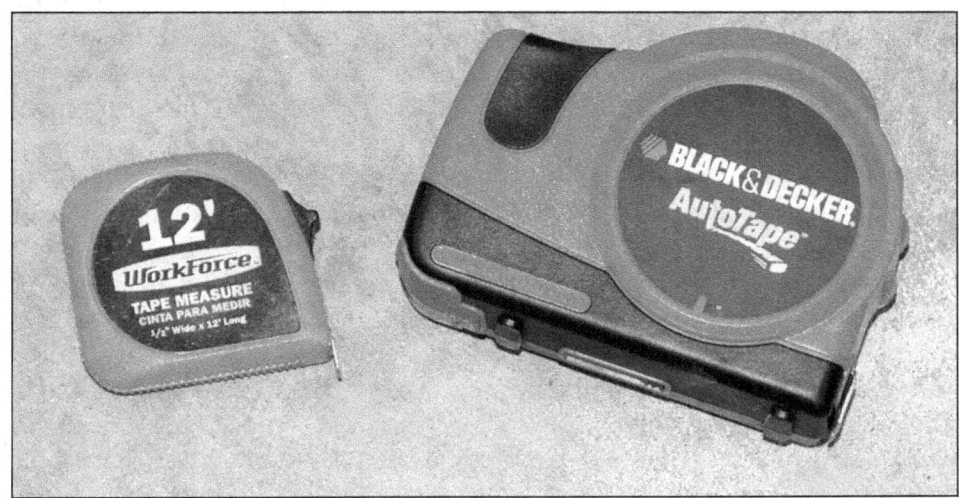

There is an old saying, "Measure twice, and weld once." That simply means that measuring is the most important part of building a chassis. You want to make sure that the brackets are in the correct location, the front-suspension crossmember isn't crooked, and the frame is square when the transmission crossmember is being installed. It is important to have tape measures and an angle finder.

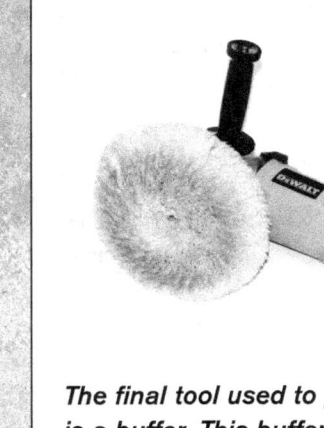

The final tool used to polish a frame is a buffer. This buffer turns at a lower speed than a grinder, and it is lightweight, so it is easy to handle. This buffer is actually a two-speed unit, and it is currently equipped with a buffing pad. After the wool pad is used, the buffing process is finished with a foam pad.

CHAPTER 2

SOLID FRONT AXLE SUSPENSIONS

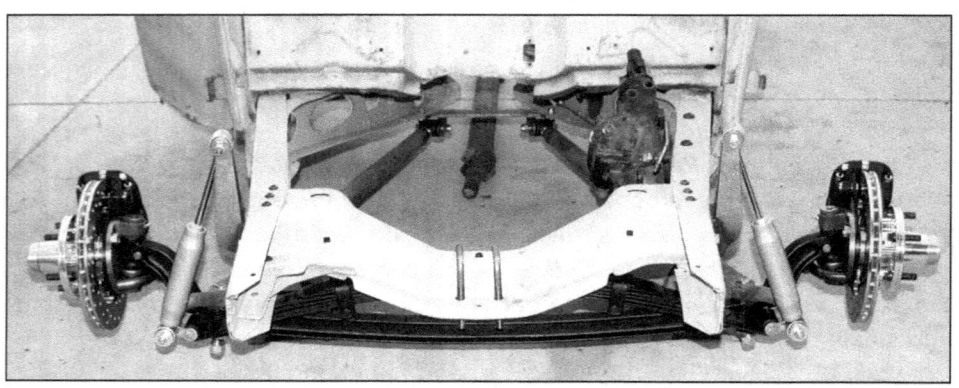

The front suspension is finished and ready to roll. This suspension works great, provides a comfortable ride, and stops quickly when necessary. It also has a nice traditional appearance, which is perfect for this 1935 Ford.

The chassis featured in this chapter is the foundation for a 1932 Ford pickup originally modified in the early 1960s. The car was used as basic transportation over the years and recently underwent a total restoration. The chassis was restored to the way it was originally modified, but many improvements were made to make it even stronger to handle the 350-ci Chevy engine and Turbo 350 automatic transmission.

Early hot rodders were limited to using I-beam axles and early Ford parts. Ford actually used tubular axles in 1937 on some cars, but they are very rare and are better suited for T-bucket-style cars that use suicide-style suspension, because they can't be effectively dropped. The I-beam-suspension systems are still being used on many street rods, and some aftermarket companies offer brand-new dropped axles, so you don't have to have your axle dropped anymore.

The dropped-I-beam axles work fine, can be made to have a fairly soft ride, and handle well with some of the newer parts that are available. A front spring can be made to handle the weight of the front of your car so that ride quality can be improved. Previous-generation hot rodders had to deal with springs that were designed for the weight of a four-cylinder engine or an early flathead V-8. If you are trying to build a budget street rod without chrome-plated and polished parts, an I-beam suspension system is an economical way to lower your street rod. Of course, if you are looking for a cool-appearing front suspension, a chrome-plated I-beam can be quite outstanding.

The installation of a dropped-axle I-beam suspension system in a car from the late 1920s to the late 1940s is relatively straightforward and can be done with normal hand tools, a gas welder (for heating and bending), and a MIG welding machine. The following pages show you how to install a dropped axle into a 1935–1940 Ford street-rod chassis. These are all new parts, but the installation process is the same as was done in the early days. If you are trying to keep your car purely traditional, you may want to install 1939–1948 Ford hydraulic brakes, but our project car will have modern, superior stopping power.

SOLID FRONT AXLE SUSPENSIONS

Installing a Posies Dropped-Front-Axle Kit and Wilwood Disc Brakes

If you are building a street rod, there are many front-suspension systems to choose from. Some of the suspension systems are expensive, and others are more reasonable, but all of them work well when they are installed properly. If you are building a traditional or nostalgic-styled street rod, you may want to use a dropped-I-beam- or tube-axle arrangement. When this particular street rod, a 1935 Ford, was in the planning stages, a nostalgic appearance and economical suspension system were both important factors.

The owner of this street rod wanted to build a chassis that would ride and handle well, be safe, and have the look of a late-1950s or early-1960s street rod. When the owner was looking for an economical suspension, the best deal he found was a kit being offered by Posies, Inc. The company calls it the In Da Dirt kit, and it comes with all of the parts required to install a dropped-front axle into a 1935–1940 Ford frame. It's also important for a street rod to be able to stop as quickly as the new car in front of it, so adequate brakes are a necessity. The owner selected Wilwood disc brakes, because they work great and are in the price range he could afford.

The Posies kit comes complete with all the parts required, providing the car you are building has a stock front suspension, because some of the original parts are reused. There are some small differences between an early frame and a later one, so it is a good idea to talk to Posies and let the company know exactly what you have.

The installation required a MIG welder, a gas welder with a rosebud tip, a drill motor with a good selection of drills, a chop saw, and a variety of normal hand tools. It takes the average builder about two days to install this suspension from start to finish, or a little bit longer if you are a first timer. If you are interested in building a nice, nostalgic 1935–1940 Ford, this economical kit is exactly what you are looking for.

The Wilwood disc brakes used on this installation make the car capable of stopping as quickly as a new car, and that is important if you plan to drive on city streets and highways. New cars have two- and four-wheel disc brakes so they can stop quickly, and you want to make sure your car does the same. In the early 1960s, just about all of the cars were equipped with four-wheel drum brakes, so equipping a street rod with them was perfectly safe, because most of the lightweight hot rods could stop quicker than the heavy sedans of the time. The 1939–1948 drum brakes are still used on some street rods, but you have to keep a longer stopping distance between your car and the one in front of you.

Posies Economy Suspension Installation

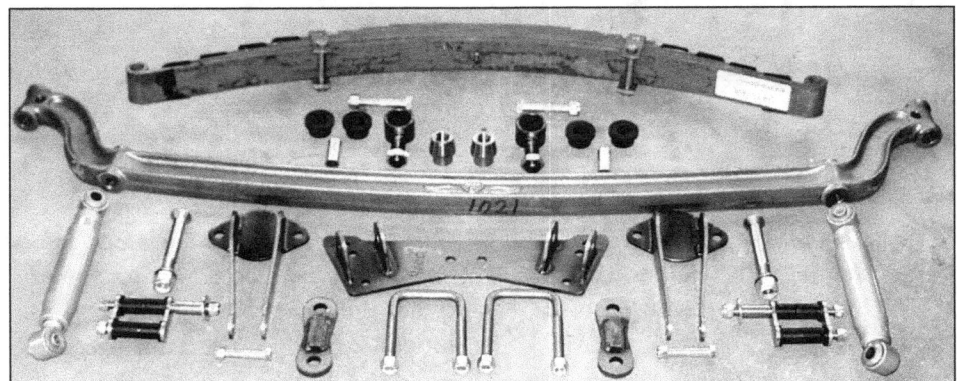

1 *The Posies front-suspension kit comes with a dropped axle, a new front Super Slide spring with reversed eyes, a split-wishbone kit, shock absorbers and brackets, and all of the hardware you need to complete the installation.*

2 *Using the measurements in the instructions, the original wishbone axle-support system is measured in preparation for splitting.*

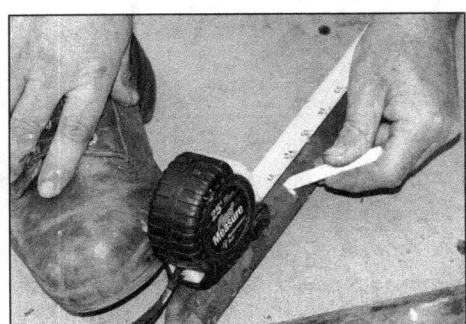

3 *The wishbone is marked for cutting at 36½ inches back from the center of the perch hole. This is done on both sides of the wishbone.*

CHAPTER 2

4 A large chop saw cuts both sides of the wishbone. This can be done with a 3-inch cut-off wheel, but it would take much longer and wouldn't be cut as straight.

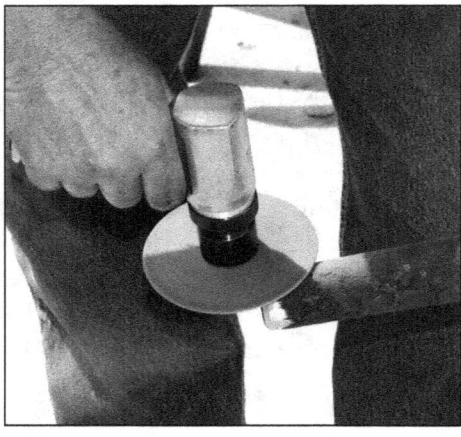

5 After the wishbone is cut, the end is dressed with a 5-inch air sander. De-burr the inside of the tube.

6 The Posies kit comes with a machined-and-threaded end that has to be installed in the tube. It is a tight fit, so some persuasion may be necessary. Notice that the end of the wishbone is angle sanded back for a stronger weld.

7 Using a MIG welder, the end bung is securely welded to the tube.

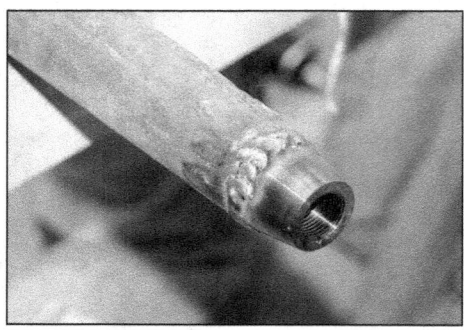

8 The end after it is welded to the tube. The end is designed so that the weld can be sanded smooth for a nice, clean appearance.

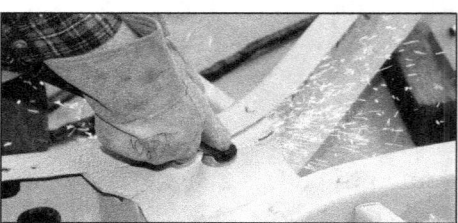

9 The original center portion of the crossmember is removed, and a new split-wishbone crossmember is installed in its place. Here, the top section of the crossmember is cut out to make access to some connections easier.

10 After the center portion of the crossmember is removed, the rivets are cut, and the side sections are removed. The side sections require some persuasion with a large hammer. If you don't have a gas welder, or just prefer a cleaner method, the rivets can be sanded flat, the heads can be center punched, and the rivets can be drilled out.

11 After the crossmember is removed, the frame rail is sanded smooth with a 5-inch angle sander.

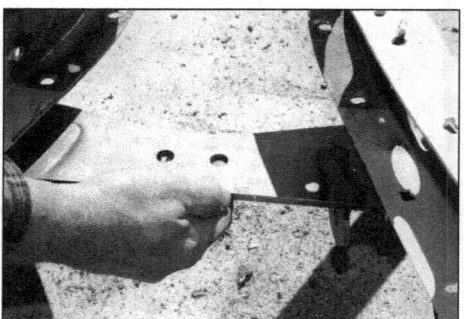

12 The crossmember is designed to bolt to the frame rails so it can be removed if the transmission needs servicing. Notice that this mount is a support for the split wishbones as well as a mount for the transmission, providing you are installing a Chevy engine with a Turbo 350 transmission.

SOLID FRONT AXLE SUSPENSIONS

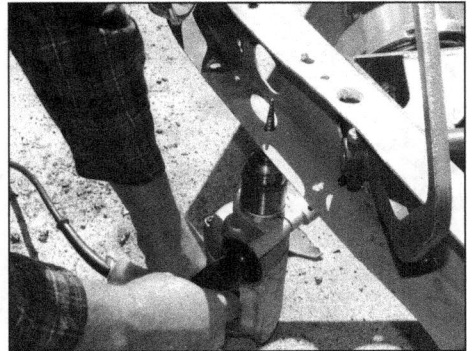

13 The mount uses two of the existing holes, one per side, so they are opened up with a step drill. The other two holes have to be drilled using the mount as a guide.

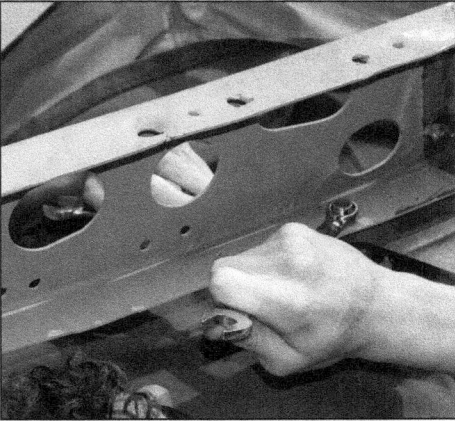

14 The transmission/split-wishbone bracket is attached by using the bolts and locknuts in the kit.

15 The wishbone ends are designed to use large rubber dual-sided bushings. The bushings are installed first.

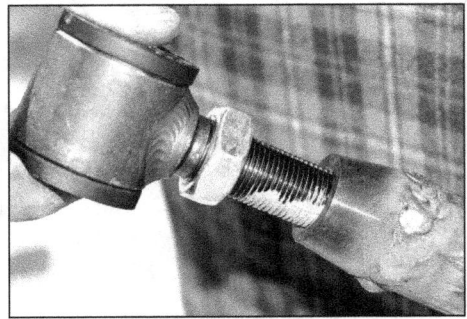

16 After the bushings are installed, the split-wishbone end is screwed into the fitting that is welded to the wishbone. Coat the threads with anti-seize lubricant so adjustments can be made later.

17 The split wishbones are connected to the wishbone bracket with the large bolts that come in the kit. Both wishbones are installed at this time.

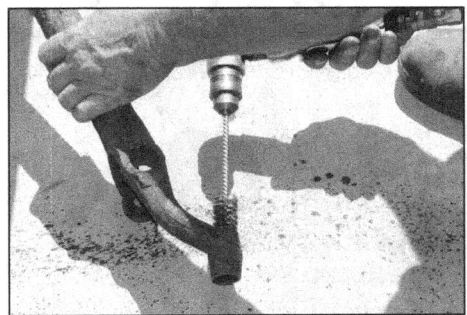

18 The original wishbones are a little rusty, so the spring perch is honed to make sure it is clean. Later, the suspension will be disconnected, and it will be painted shiny black.

19 Using the hone, the perch holes are cleaned so that the bolt slides through easily.

20 The bare axle is covered with black paint to keep it from rusting. Later, all of the parts will be removed and professionally painted.

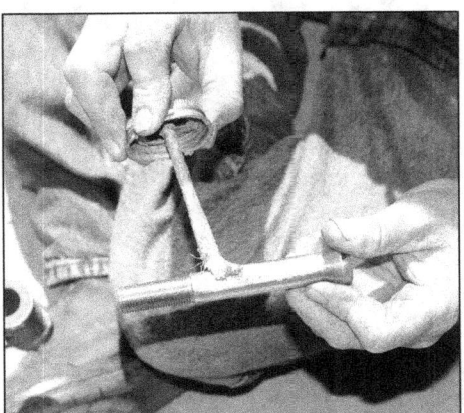

21 The special perch bolts are coated with anti-seize compound to make sure they are lubricated.

CHAPTER 2

22 The axle is connected to the wishbone using the special perch bolts.

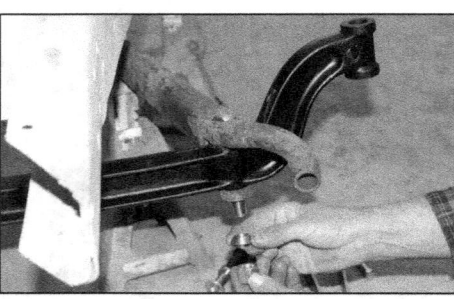

23 The perch bolt is connected with this specially tapered spacer and locknut.

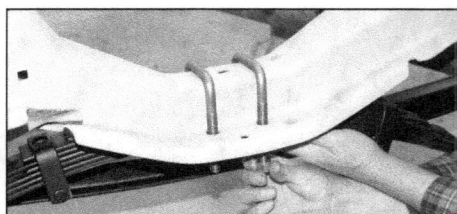

24 The spring is installed and centered in the frame, and then the U-bolts and lower spring plate are installed. Initially, the bolts are connected finger tight.

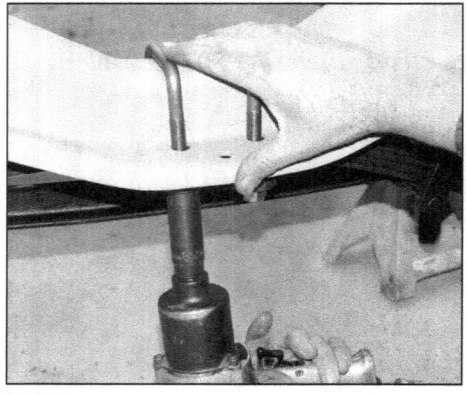

25 After the nuts are installed finger tight on the U-bolts, they are tightened fully with an impact gun.

26 When the wishbone is split, the ends are mounted farther apart than they were in the stock location. That changes the alignment of the spring-shackle mounts, as seen here. In this position, there is some spring bind.

27 The Posies kit comes with instructions that show how the shackle mount must be modified to align with the spring.

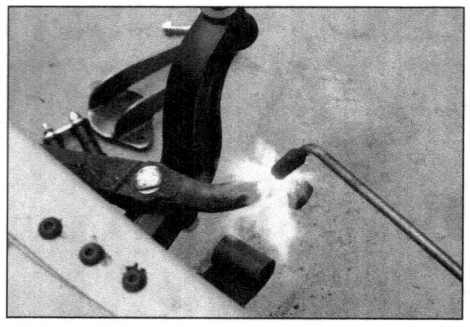

28 Following the instructions, the spring-shackle mount is heated with a gas torch and a rosebud tip. After the mount is red hot, a long rod is installed, and the shackle mount is bent to line up with the spring.

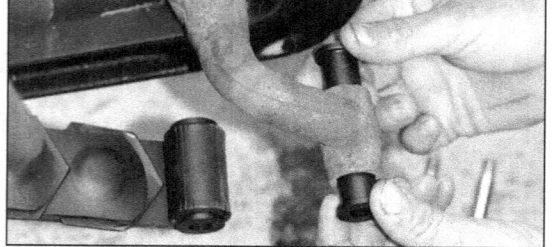

30 The kit comes with rubber bushings for the spring mount, so they are installed before the spring is attached.

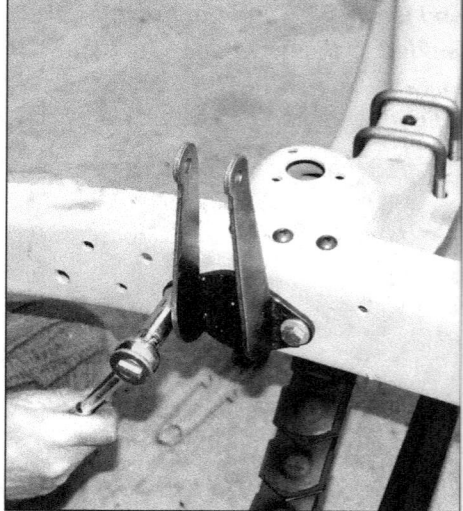

29 As the spring mount cools, the shock brackets are bolted to the frame. The mount actually uses the bolt holes that were used to mount the stock lever-action shock absorber.

SOLID FRONT AXLE SUSPENSIONS

31 The spring is installed with the perches in the kit. The upper bolt is extra long, because it is used to mount the shock absorber.

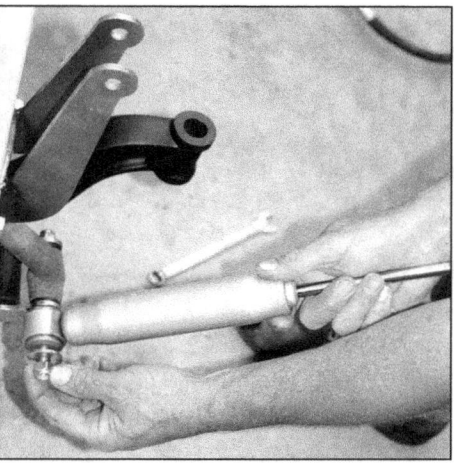

32 The shock is installed on the lower mount, and a washer and a locknut are fastened finger tight.

33 The upper portion of the shock absorber is connected to the frame mount. The upper portion of the shock is attached with the bolt and locknut that came in the kit.

34 After the upper shock bolt is tightened, the lower locknut is secured.

35 The front suspension is installed and ready for the brake system. This axle arrangement lowers the car approximately 5 inches.

Installing the Brakes

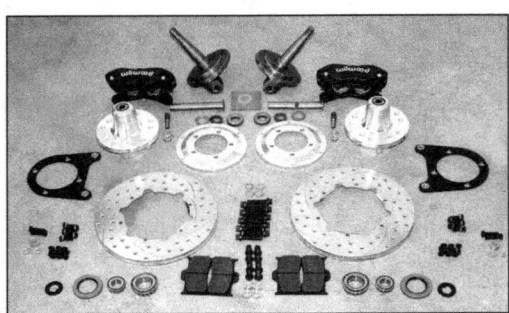

1 Excellent stopping power is very important to keep a driver out of trouble, so the chassis is equipped with Wilwood disc brakes. The kit comes complete with the rotors, calipers, caliper brackets, bearings, and all hardware required to mount the brakes. The spindles are aftermarket units and are copies of original 1940 Ford units. Kingpin kits are available from a variety of restoration suppliers.

2 The new bushings are coated with grease and installed in the spindles.

3 The spindles are installed on the axle using new kingpins.

THE COMPLETE BUILDER'S GUIDE TO HOT ROD CHASSIS AND SUSPENSION

CHAPTER 2

4 The kingpin kit comes with a bearing that slides under the axle. Some shims are supplied in the kit, and this particular installation requires one per side.

5 The spindle moves on the kingpin, but it remains stationary. A pin is installed to keep the kingpin in place. When the kingpin is installed, it is important to line up the notch with the hole in the axle.

6 The pin acts as a wedge, so it must be pounded in with a lead hammer to get it seated.

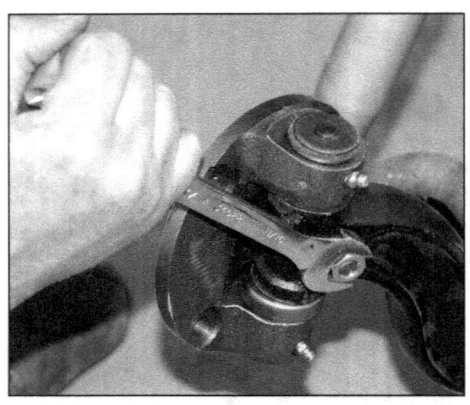

7 The pin is secured with the nut and lock washer supplied in the kit.

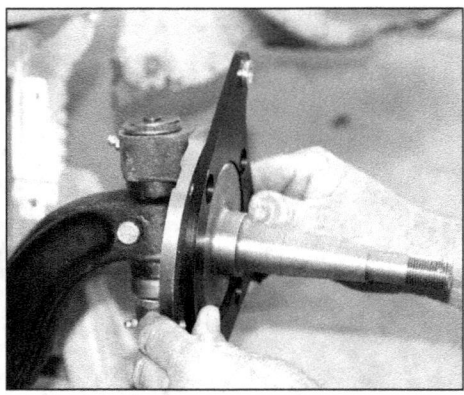

8 The caliper brackets are installed on the spindles; the holes must line up.

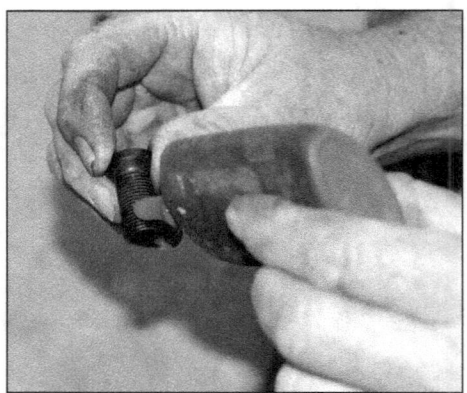

9 The caliper-bracket bolts are coated with Loctite to keep them from backing out.

10 The upper-caliper brackets are connected to the spindle with the washers and nuts supplied in the kit.

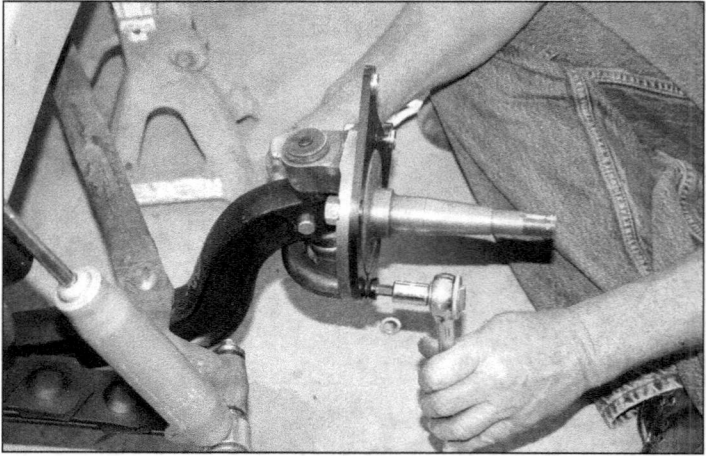

11 The lower Allen bolts are secured through the spindle to the steering arms with an Allen socket and socket wrench.

SOLID FRONT AXLE SUSPENSIONS

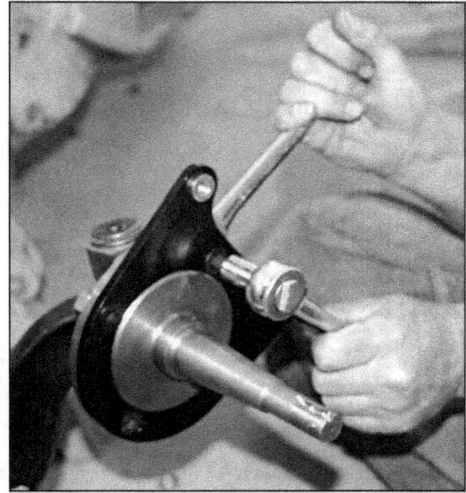

12 The upper bolts are also tightened with an Allen socket and socket wrench on one side and an open-end wrench on the other side.

13 The lug bolts are coated with anti-seize compound. This is done to keep the steel bolts from reacting with the aluminum hub assembly.

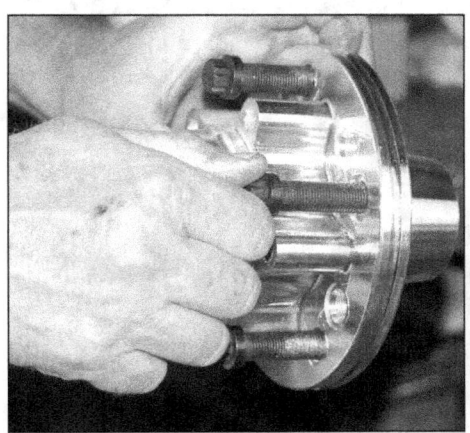

14 The Wilwood kit comes with screw-in lug nuts, because the hubs have two different bolt patterns. In this case, the car is running a GM rear axle, so the bolts are screwed into the 5-on-4¾ pattern.

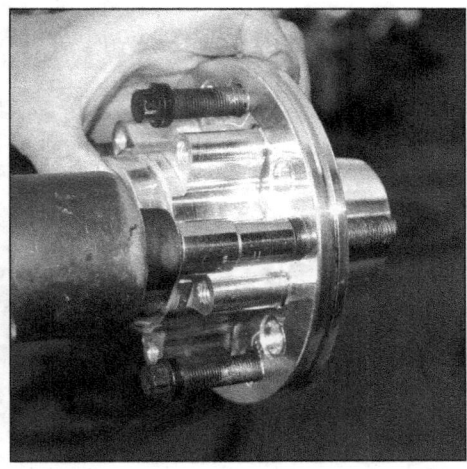

15 The bolts are tightened with an impact gun to get them super tight. If they are not tight enough, they can back out when you try to remove the lug nuts.

16 After the lug nuts are installed, the rotor adapter is connected to the hub. There is a dish to the adapter, so make sure it is facing in the correct direction.

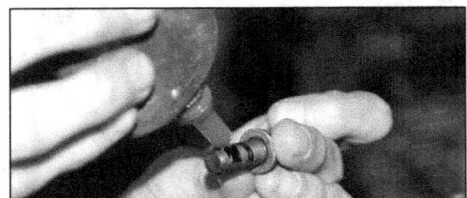

17 The rotor-adapter bolts are coated with Loctite to make sure they don't back out. This washer also has to be installed.

18 The rotor adapter is installed with the button-head Allen bolts. The bolts are tightened to 180 in-lbs.

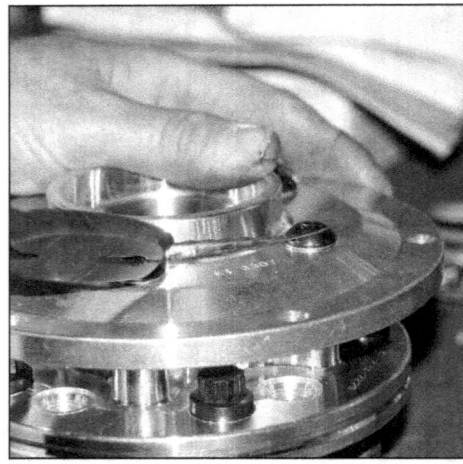

19 The button-head Allen bolts are drilled for safety wire. The wire is installed with safety-wire pliers.

20 The rotor-adapter plate is installed after the safety wire. This ensures that the bolts stay in place.

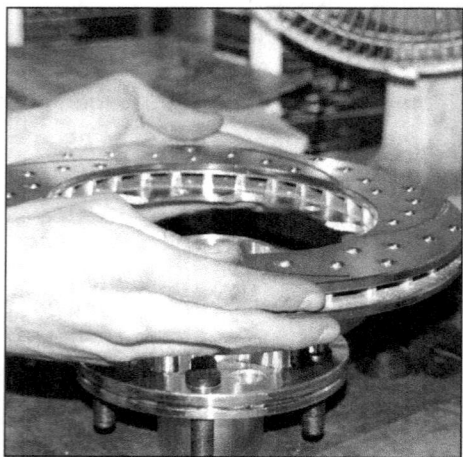

21 The hex-head rotor bolts are coated with Loctite to secure them to the adapter plate.

22 The hex-head rotor bolts are coated with Loctite to secure them to the adapter plate.

23 The hex-head bolts are installed, tightened, and then torqued to 180 in-lbs.

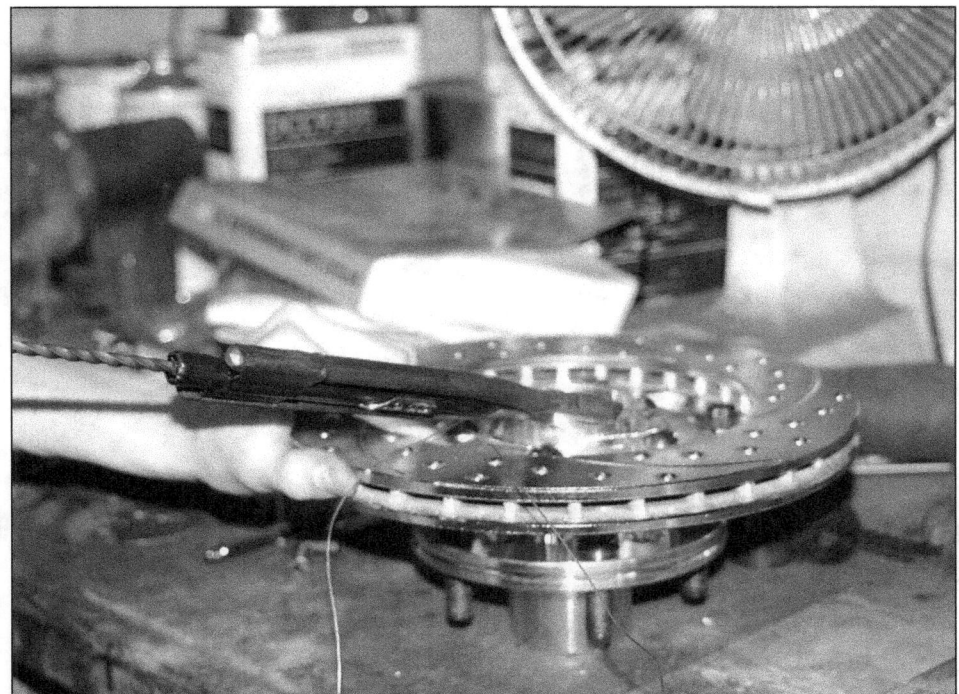

24 The hex-head bolts are also drilled for safety wire. The wire is installed and twisted with safety-wire pliers.

26 After the bearing is seated, the grease seal is installed. A light layer of grease is spread on the seal prior to installation.

27 Using a bearing-packing tool, the large inner bearing is loaded with high-temperature disc-brake bearing grease. The races come installed in the hub assembly. The bearing is carefully installed in the rotor with the taper facing outward.

25 The rotor assembly with the safety wire installed. The safety wire is important, because it keeps the bolts from backing out.

28 The grease seal is installed with a seal-installation tool. It has to be tapped down until the seal is flush with the surface of the hub.

CHAPTER 2

29 The rotor is slipped over the spindle, and then the rear bearing is seated on the spindle.

30 The front bearing is installed, along with the large flat washer. That is followed by the large castle nut.

31 The nut is tightened, but only to the point of being snug. When the rotor is spun, it should make one revolution. When the nut is secured properly, it is lined up with the nearest hole, and a cotter pin is then installed.

32 After the rotors are installed, the aluminum hub cover can be twisted on.

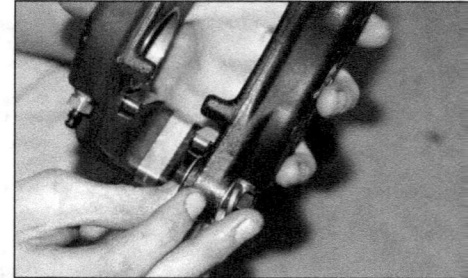

33 Install the caliper. Look closely because there is the bolt, a large washer, a small washer, and a thin shim on the inside where it connects to the bracket.

SOLID FRONT AXLE SUSPENSIONS

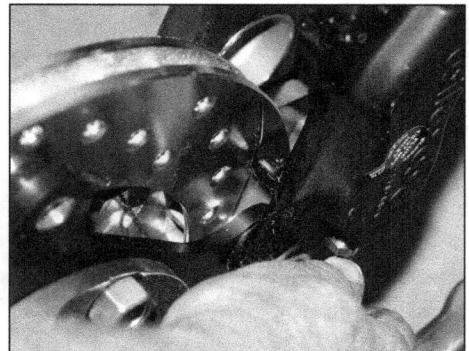

34 The caliper is mounted to the spindle on the backside first. The bolt should only be finger tight at this point.

35 The caliper is moved downward until the hole in the caliper lines up with the bracket. Now, both bolts can be tightened.

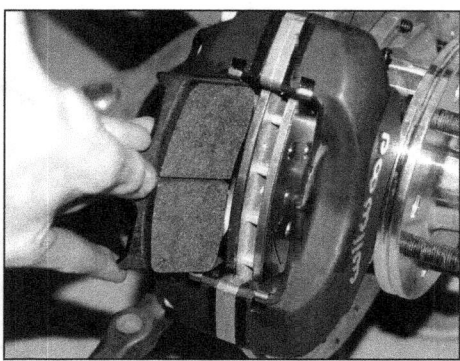

36 The brake pads load from the top, and that makes brake-pad changes easy. Make sure that the caliper is centered over the rotor.

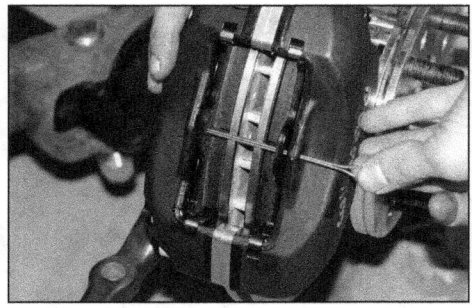

37 The brake pads are secured with a large cotter pin. The pin is positioned through the holes in the caliper and the holes in the brake pads.

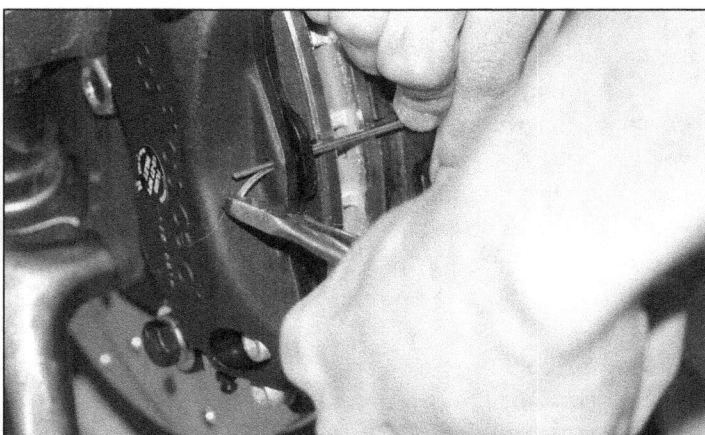

38 The end of the cotter pin is bent so it stays in place, but it's not bent not too much, because it needs to be removed when the pads are changed.

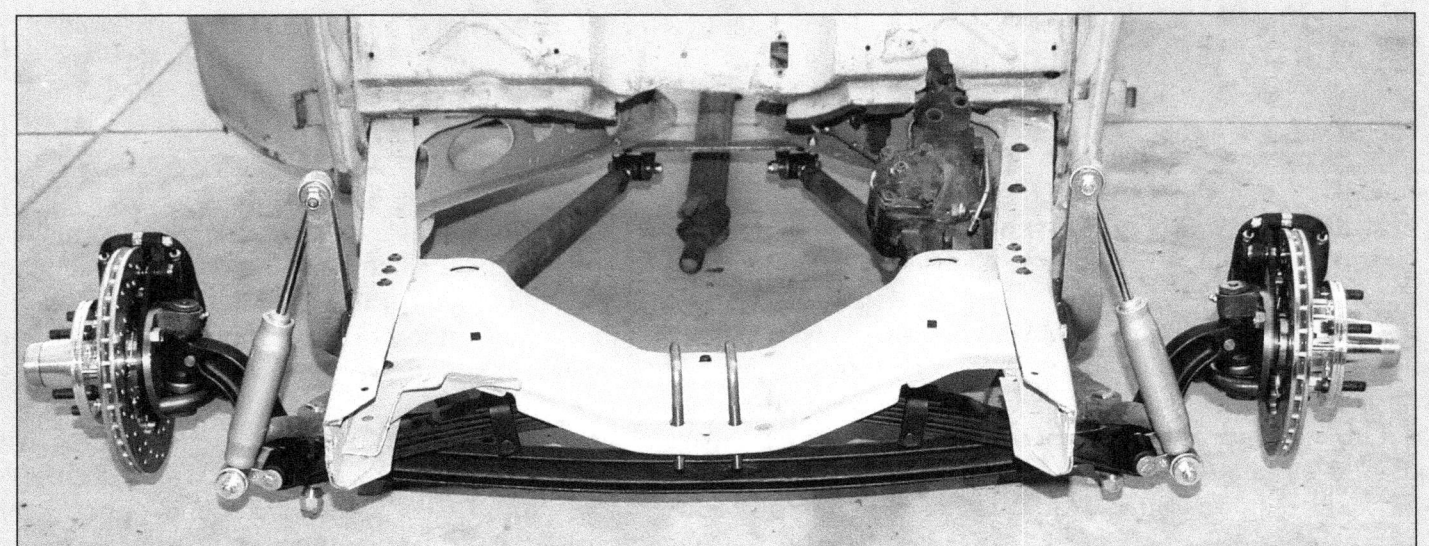

The front suspension is finished and ready to roll. This suspension works great, provides a comfortable ride, and stops quickly when necessary. It also has a nice traditional appearance, which is perfect for this 1935 Ford.

THE COMPLETE BUILDER'S GUIDE TO HOT ROD CHASSIS AND SUSPENSION

CHAPTER 2

Unisteer

The I-beam axle is still the traditional front axle used on street rods of every style, but in the late 1960s, several companies, primarily T-bucket manufacturers, started fabricating tube axles from heavy-wall chrome-moly tubing. Initially, this type of axle was used on T-buckets, but several manufacturers started making dropped-tube axles for Model A, 1932, 1933, and 1934 Ford street rods. The tube axles worked well and looked nice, especially when they were chrome plated, and most of the axles were built to work with chrome-moly hairpin radius rods. The later-model, fat-fender 1935–1948 Fords continued to be equipped with the dropped-I-beam axles, basically because they were hidden from sight (unless you stuck your head under a fender) and worked fine. Many rodders also felt that the solid I-beam was stronger and a better choice for a heavier street rod. The dropped-tube axles were designed for cars with a spring that sat on top of the axle. The dropped-tube axles for T-buckets were done in a suicide style, where the axle sat in front of the spring.

Many of the cars being built are using the early-style suspension systems, because they want the cars to have that 1950s and 1960s styling. The biggest problem with the early suspension systems is the steering quality of the cars. If you had an early car, the steering was marginal, so hot rodders looked at other steering systems from newer cars. In the early days, many rodders used 1940 Ford steering boxes, and later, 1956 Ford pickup steering systems became popular. Both worked better than the earlier steering, but both generally had a degree of slop in the steering.

In the 1960s, rodders started using Mustang steering units, and they worked well, but they had to be hooked up on the frame with a drag link that traveled to a bracket on the driver-side spindle. However, there was always some bump steer. Corvair steering was also used with a similar-style installation, and it had the same problem; it had some slop in the steering. The best system that rodders used was the Vega cross-steering method, where the steering drag link traveled under the engine to the passenger-side spindle. The cross-steer system eliminated the bump-steer problem associated with the Mustang and Corvair steering boxes, and Vega-style steering is still used on street rods with I-beam and tube axles.

When independent-front-suspension systems started to become popular, they relied on rack-and-pinion steering, and hot rodders loved the positive steering units. Even the best early hot-rod steering systems had a degree of play in the steering, so it was obvious that rack-and-pinion was the way to go. There is a new system for I-beam and tube axles that features a single rack-and-pinion-style steering system called the Unisteer system. This unit is easy to install and works great; it can improve your steering system.

Installing a Unisteer System on a Model A Chassis

One of the biggest problems with early-style, I-beam, front suspension systems is the steering can be a little sloppy. The slop generally comes from junkyard steering boxes that may require rebuilding. However, even with a rebuilt steering box, the front-steer Mustang or cross-steer Vega steering is not as positive as a rack-and-pinion steering system. That was the problem with our project Model A, plus the Vega steering box was not located properly. Since the fellow just purchased the car, he wasn't sure if the steering box was an old used unit or a rebuilt unit.

The Model A roadster pickup was delivered to a street-rod shop for some improvements, and that included the steering system. After inspecting the front suspension, the I-beam setup was found to be fine, but the steering wasn't, because the Vega steering box was located too far forward. The shop informed the owner that he could change the position of the steering box, but a better improvement would be the installation of a Unisteer steering setup because it would provide the positive steering he was looking for. The Unisteer system is a rack-and-pinion-style steering unit that features a single arm that connects to the cross-steer hole on the passenger-side spindle. It is designed be a direct replacement

SOLID FRONT AXLE SUSPENSIONS

Unisteer Installation

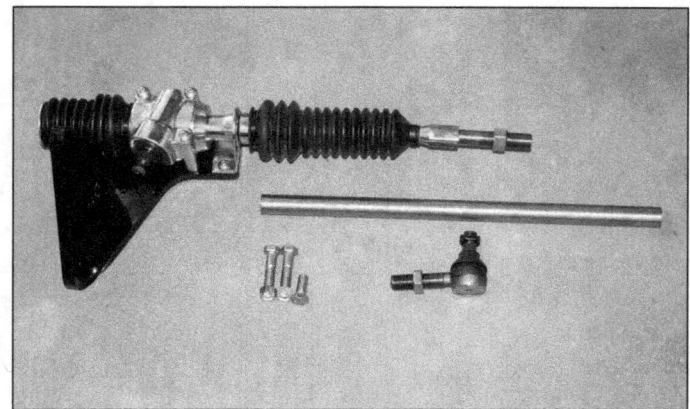

1 The Unisteer system comes with the steering unit, a steering arm, a ball joint, and a steering mount that is designed to bolt to the Vega steering-box mount.

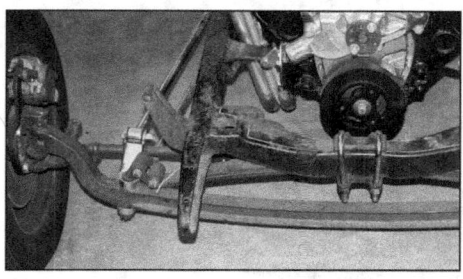

2 It's obvious that this front suspension has been sitting for a while before the car was purchased. A close inspection reveals that the dropped axle is in good condition, and it is riding on a reversed-eye spring. The front suspension is fine, except for the steering system that wasn't installed properly.

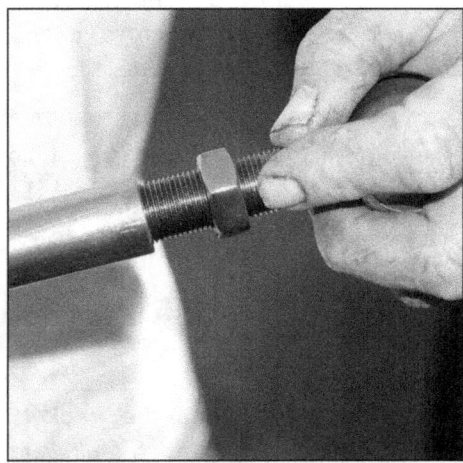

3 The steering arm in this kit is adjustable, because the same system can be used on everything from a 1928 Model A to a 1934 Ford. Installing a jam nut on the steering arm is the first step of this installation.

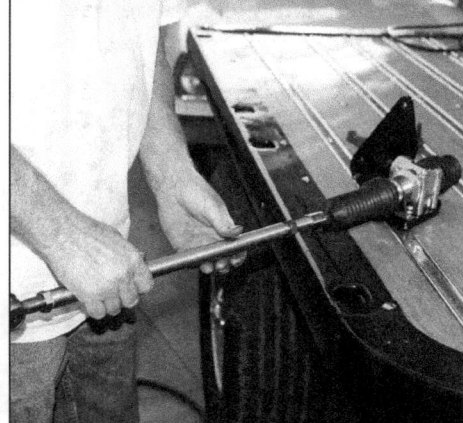

4 After the jam nut is installed, the steering rod is connected to the arm of the steering unit. Notice that the ball joint is also connected to the steering rod.

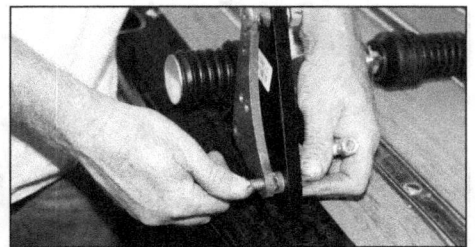

5 The Vega steering-box mount is removed from the frame first, and then it is bolted to the bracket that comes with the Unisteer assembly.

of the Vega steering box. The owner agreed that it was what he wanted, so the system was installed on his Model A.

The first thing that had to be done was the removal of the mounting bracket for the Vega steering, because it had to be relocated. Because some changes had to be made, the tools required to perform this installation included a MIG welder and an assortment of normal hand tools.

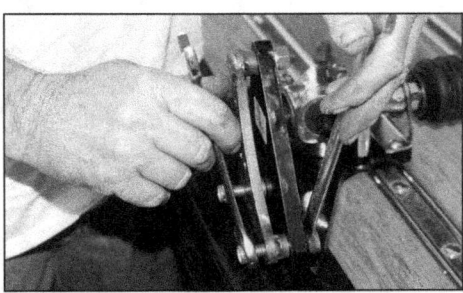

6 The bolts are tightened with a pair of open-end wrenches. They should be snug at this point, but not too tight, because they will be removed before the installation is complete.

7 The ball joint is connected to the spindle. Some steering-arm adjustments may have to be made before the steering unit can be lifted into place.

THE COMPLETE BUILDER'S GUIDE TO HOT ROD CHASSIS AND SUSPENSION

8 The ball joint is tightened at this point to make sure the measurements were done correctly.

9 The steering unit is raised up in the frame, and when it is in the correct location, the bracket is clamped against the frame. The steering arm should be adjusted so that the bracket is resting against the frame. Fortunately, the frame was boxed prior to this installation.

10 The steering is in the correct location when the cross-steer arm is parallel to the tie rod.

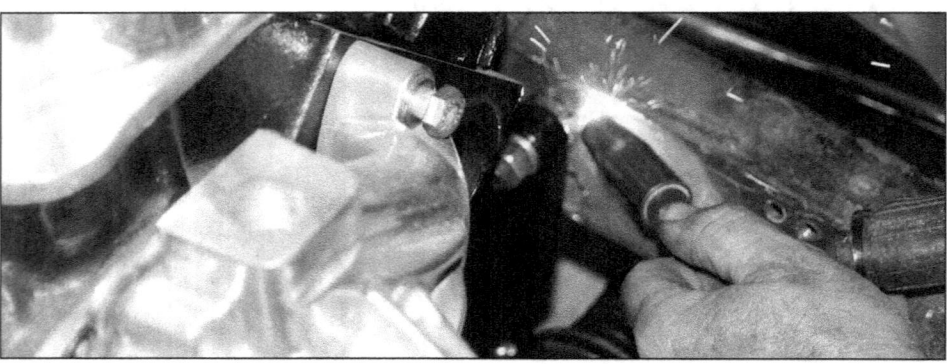

11 After the bracket is located properly, the Vega steering bracket is tack welded to the frame.

12 To make sure that the bracket is securely located, a tack weld is also done on the frame side of the bracket.

13 The front suspension is elevated so that the steering system can be tested.

14 A U-joint is installed on the steering rack, then the steering unit is turned from one side to the other to see the steering travel. The steering has full travel, and the steering unit is easy to turn.

SOLID FRONT AXLE SUSPENSIONS

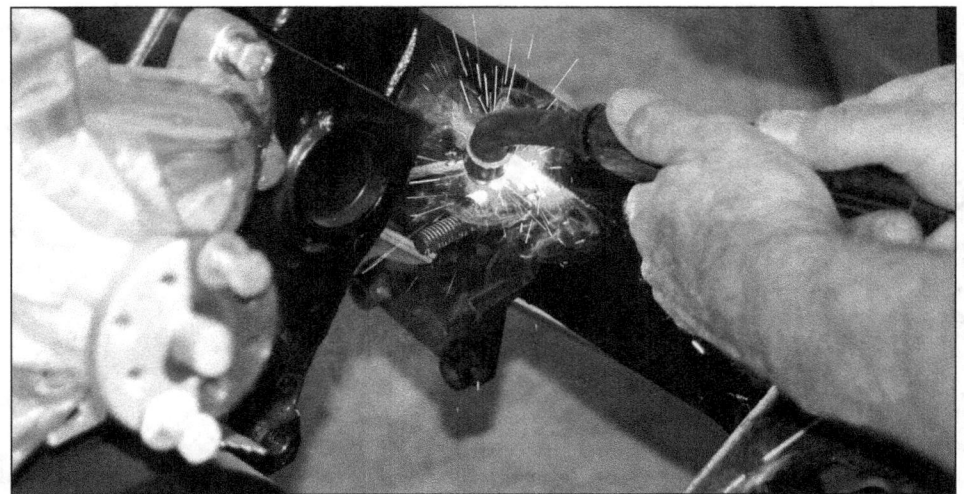

15 The Unisteer system is disconnected from the Vega bracket in preparation for welding. After the Unisteer unit is removed, the bracket is welded to the frame.

16 The Vega bracket after being welded to the frame. The connection to the boxed frame is very strong.

17 The welded Vega bracket is allowed to cool, and then the Unisteer bracket is connected to the Vega bracket.

18 Flat washers and lock washers are used on both sides of the brackets to make sure the steering system remains tight.

19 One of the two lower bolts is tightened with an open-end wrench (left). The upper bolt is also secured with a large open-end wrench (right).

20 The steering arm can be reconnected at this point. Some adjustment may be required to get the steering centered perfectly.

21 After the castle nut is installed and tightened, it is secured with a small cotter pin.

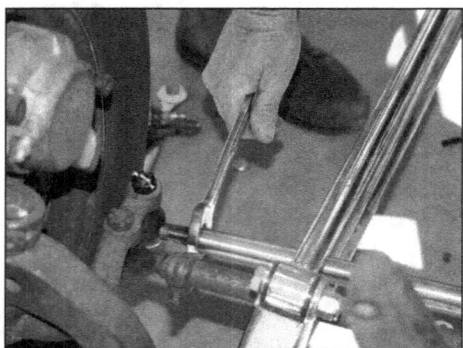

22 After the steering is installed and the ball joint is connected, any adjustments are made and the jam nut is secured.

23 Looking at the center of the car, the steering-arm jam nut and steering-arm nut require tightening to keep the arm secure and at the correct length.

The finished steering box is secured to the frame. This system clears the engine without a problem, and it gives this Model A roadster pickup positive steering. The best part is that the system didn't cost a fortune.

CHAPTER 3

INDEPENDENT FRONT SUSPENSIONS

The finished front suspension looks great, and it provides excellent ride comfort and easy steering.

Street-rod builders are always looking for an improved suspension system, so when the little Corvair was released, some builders thought its components were a perfect solution. This Corvair suspension was installed in a Model A chassis with a front-mounted, rack-and-pinion steering system.

In the 1950s, most Ford street rods used dropped-I-beam axles riding on stock transverse leaf springs. The ride quality was marginal, but the engine weight did allow the spring to work properly. Today, there are several companies that manufacture dropped-I-beam and tube axles, and the springs and shock absorbers are improved, so it's possible to get the stock-style suspensions working well. If a hot-rod builder wants to create a traditional fenderless hot rod, a dropped-front axle is the only way to go to follow the theme, and the appearance is exceptional when the parts are chrome plated.

It really doesn't matter how good the solid I-beam axle works, an independent front suspension always works better. That's why every new car manufactured today uses an independent-front-suspension (IFS) system. In the early days, many hot-rod owners and builders were looking for a way to improve the front suspensions of their rides by adapting something from a newer car. Most of the front suspensions being used were large and clunky, and they certainly were not attractive on the front of a street rod.

Corvair System

When the Corvair was released, it was smaller than most cars, and the front suspension could be removed in one piece, so street rodders thought it was a good candidate for use in later-model 1930s and 1940s cars where the front suspension couldn't be easily seen.

The Corvair IFS was adapted to many cars, but they didn't perform to expectations. The problem was finding a good steering mechanism that worked correctly, because they used front steering in the original car. Builders were trying to turn the steering arms around, and they didn't work properly when they were backwards. In the 1960s, rack-and-pinion steering was rare, so that steering method wasn't considered. Eventually, people adapted front-mounted rack-and-pinion systems to the Corvair, and they worked better, but by that time, most rodders had given up on the idea.

Jaguar System

When street-rod builders started adapting Jaguar rear-suspension systems to street-rod chassis and found how well they worked, some decided to do the same thing with the front. The Jaguar front suspension was small, delicate-appearing, and looked attractive because it didn't use large coil springs. Jaguar actually used torsion bars that were similar to those on Chrysler cars.

The front suspension actually provided a smooth, comfortable ride quality, so many early cars were equipped with them, and many are still being used today. In the 1970s, several companies started making installation kits, and each was a little bit different. Kugel Komponents was one of the major installation shops

This show-quality Model T features a fully chrome-plated Jaguar front suspension. Features include small, delicate upper and lower A-arms; a centrally located tube shock; a chrome-plated spindle with disc-brake caliper; and a rear-mounted rack-and-pinion steering system.

Jaguar rear suspensions are perfect for street-rod chassis. The street rod's ride quality is as good as a Jaguar's, and if you have ever driven an early Jag, it is very comfortable. This Model T has a Jaguar suspension in front and a Jaguar suspension in the rear.

Snow White in Fresno, California, installed a Jaguar suspension on a really nice Model A. The suspension works great, and it looks really nice under a 1929 Model A front fender.

INDEPENDENT FRONT SUSPENSIONS

early on, and it continued to do the installations until it created its own suspension systems. When installed properly, the front-suspension systems were the perfect width for a variety of early Ford and Chevy models. Since the suspension systems were introduced when early-model cars were popular, most of the Jaguar front-suspension systems can be seen in Model T, Model A, and Model B Fords, as well as early Chevys.

The Jaguar suspension system looks nice under cars with fenders, especially when the parts are chrome plated. If you have access to a Jaguar front-suspension system and want to adapt it to your street rod project, you can contact Snow White in Fresno, California, which can help you.

Opel System

In the late 1960s and early 1970s, the Opel GT was introduced, and it looked like a miniature Corvette. Since Opel was a subsidiary of General Motors, the similarity was not by chance. The suspension was also similar, and it featured independent A-arms that were suspended with a transverse leaf spring. Since the car was a miniature version of the

The Opel suspension features a rear-mounted rack-and-pinion system that is perfect in many early cars.

While I was attending a car show, I saw this Model A for sale; it was equipped with a Jaguar front suspension. Apparently, there were several kits available for installing the suspension in street rods. The upper A-arm brackets are angled to allow the installation of front fenders.

When the Opel GT was introduced, it had upper and lower A-arms and a transverse leaf spring for suspension. The suspension was small, nice appearing, and was a good width for most street rods. Mark Laeger, a rod builder, saw the potential of the unit and released a front crossmember to mount the suspension parts. This Opel front suspension is under a Model A Ford, and in chrome-plated form, it looks nice, and it also works well.

The transverse leaf spring is mounted to the lower A-arm. Note the tube shock absorber, the steering arm, and Opel disc brakes.

Looking at this installation from the rear, you can see the torsion bar that attaches to the lower A-arm. The nice thing about this front suspension is that the car it was removed from weighed about the same amount as a Model A or Model T with a Chevy small-block engine.

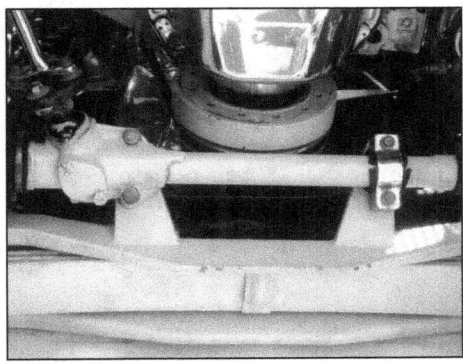

A close look at the rack-and-pinion steering system and the transverse leaf spring mounted to the custom crossmember.

CHAPTER 3

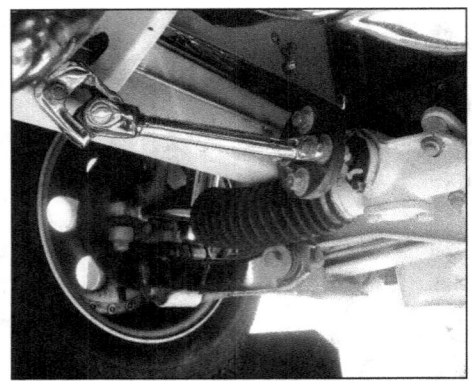

The rack-and-pinion system hooks to a steering shaft in much the same way most modern IFS systems do. This system was very advanced when it was installed. Today, you would be hard pressed to find an Opel GT suspension system.

Corvette, the suspension was also small and delicate, and it turned out to be a good system to install under a Model T, Model A, or even a '32 Ford, or under early Chevrolets or Plymouths.

The front suspension wasn't well suited for larger late-1930s and early-1940s cars, because it really wasn't strong enough. The Opel system never became popular. The suspensions were introduced when rodders started building the later-model fat-fender Fords from 1935 on up. The other problem was the transverse spring was designed for a lightweight car and engine, and it had to be strengthened for a car that was running a heavy V-8. When the front suspension was set up properly, it worked well and provided a smooth, comfortable ride and positive steering.

Mustang II System

Many of the front-suspension systems available today are based on the Mustang II, which was introduced in 1974. The Shay replica Model A was directly responsible for the use of Mustang II suspension parts. The Shay Model A was a fiberglass replica that featured all Ford parts so that the car could be fixed by a Ford dealership. The car was built on a custom chassis that featured a Mustang II front suspension, a Ford rear differential, and a Pinto four-cylinder engine. When the replica Model A was released, it looked like a Model A from a distance, but up close, it was easy to tell that it was a reproduction. Shay sold a number of the cars, but they didn't catch on as hoped. The company eventually went out of business, and many of the parts were liquidated for extremely low prices. One of the first companies to take advantage of the suspension parts that were available was Progressive Automotive. It released a crossmember that adapted Mustang II parts into street-rod frames.

Kugel Komponents in Southern California is well known for installing Jaguar rear and front suspensions into hot-rod chassis. The company was doing a large number of the installations, but Jerry Kugel was having a difficult time finding the Jaguar parts in wrecking yards. After the parts started getting hard to find, he began designing his own front- and rear-suspension systems based on what he learned from the Jaguar components.

He designed and manufactured his own spindles, machined his own A-arms out of stainless steel, and carefully engineered his own front crossmember, making sure it worked well and had an attractive appearance. He also designed a rear suspension based on the Jaguar, but he wanted it to match the front. In the process of building his rear suspension, he eliminated the parts that he

When John Buttera's sedan made its debut at the Early Times Car Club's hot-rod run at Knott's Berry Farm in 1974, it became the hit of the show. This sedan had power steering, power windows, power brakes, air conditioning, and many other nice features. This sedan also had front and rear suspension upgrades that were years ahead of their time.

INDEPENDENT FRONT SUSPENSIONS

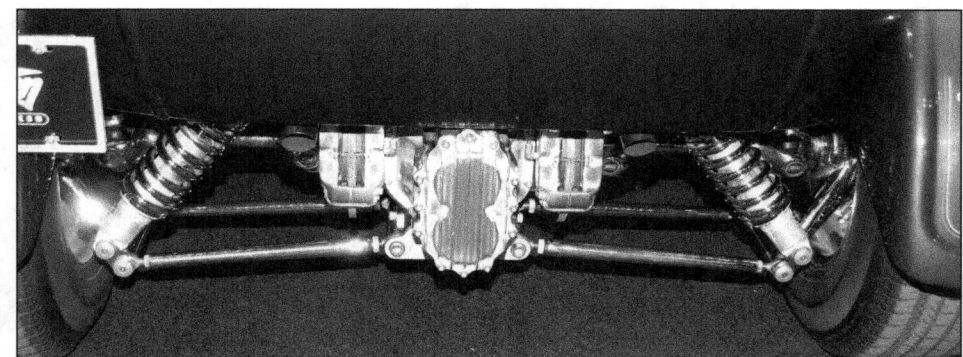

The rear featured a highly modified Jaguar suspension that eliminated the stock lower control arms and replaced them with a lightweight tubular control arm that is very similar to that used on Heidts and Kugel suspension systems. Buttera's design also used a pair of coil-over shocks instead of the four used on a stock Jaguar.

Buttera also used his race-car knowledge and designed a front suspension system that featured tubular upper and lower A-arms and a very short coil-over shock absorber for suspension. A power rack-and-pinion unit handled the car's steering. This car was featured in many magazines, and it influenced many future suspension designs.

When Jerry Kugel designed his suspension, all of the parts were machined out of stainless steel. Notice the relief design in the A-arms that matches the same design found on the IRS support arms. Kugel also designed and manufactured his own spindles long before the Mustang II suspensions were released and used. When he designed the suspension, coil-over shocks were introduced, and he thought that they were easier to use than torsion bars.

thought were unattractive and replaced them with his own delicate-appearing—but very strong—parts. As it turned out, he was the first to offer aftermarket independent front- and rear-suspension systems, and his products certainly influenced suspension systems being crafted by others when the Mustang II suspensions became popular.

Street rod enthusiast and engineer Gary Heidt was interested in the Mustang II suspension systems when a friend told him that if someone could tailor crossmembers for specific frames, he could make a fortune. Heidt thought about what his friend said and decided to design custom crossmembers for the Model A and '32 chassis, initially, and later

When Jaguar suspension systems started to get difficult to find, Jerry Kugel, the owner of Kugel Street Rod Komponents, used his engineering expertise and Jag suspension experience to create his own independent front and rear suspensions. This is the top-of-the-line unit that features high-strength, cast-stainless-steel A-arms and specially designed spindles.

designed units for the 1933–1940 Ford chassis.

He didn't like the strut rod and the clunky appearance of the factory upper and lower A-arms, so he designed a tubular A-arm suspension using the Mustang II spindle and rack-and-pinion steering system. Instead of using the stock Mustang II spring, the Heidt's suspension featured adjustable coil-over shocks. Heidt also designed other lower-cost

CHAPTER 3

suspension systems that used normal coil springs and shock absorbers, and that kit became very popular.

Installing a Heidts Economy Mustang II IFS System

After persuasion from his street rod enthusiast friend, Gary Heidt decided to work on a front-suspension system based on Mustang II suspension components. The original Mustang II suspension used clunky-appearing upper and lower A-arms, plus the lower arm required a strut rod, so Heidt eliminated those parts and designed tubular upper and lower A-arms that effectively eliminate the need for strut rods. Heidt did retain the front spindles, springs, and rack-and-pinion steering system. He also designed several new crossmembers for Model A, 1932, and 1933–1934 Fords that not only worked great, but installed easily.

Our project 1934 Ford chassis was equipped with a standard I-beam-style front crossmember when it was purchased, but it was only tacked in place, because the owner was going to install a Heidts economical independent-front-suspension system. The owner knew from experience that the Heidts suspension systems work well, offer excellent ride control, and provide superior steering. The best part was the basic system is reasonably priced, and the owner felt that it was a bargain. Combine that with the GM-style disc brakes, and you can see that it's a very nice suspension system for a very low price. The kit that the owner ordered included the crossmember, tubular upper and lower control arms, GM brakes, and a standard rack-and-pinion steering system.

The installation is very straight forward, so the only important and necessary procedure is making sure that all of the measurements are correct. This is an easy installation if you have the necessary tools, which consist of a MIG welder, a 3-inch cut-off wheel, a small 3-inch angle sander, a degree indicator, and normal hand tools. Since this frame was already boxed for strength, the installation was accomplished in a day without a problem. Here is a close look at how it was done.

Heidts System Installation

1 *The Heidts economy IFS kit comes complete with the cross-member, upper and lower A-arms, springs, GM disc brakes, rack-and-pinion-steering system, and all brackets and hardware needed to finish the installation.*

 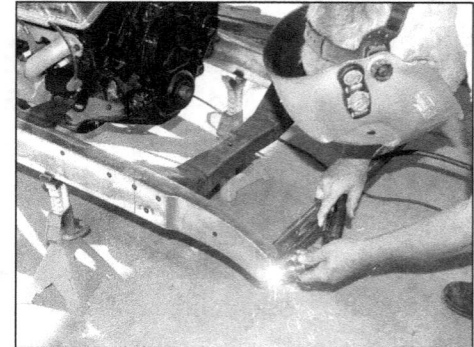

2 *The installed crossmember must be removed, but before that can be done, a temporary front brace must be installed to keep the chassis in place. Here, a thick-wall tube is connected to the front of the chassis. It is welded to one side in two areas, and then welded to the other side.*

INDEPENDENT FRONT SUSPENSIONS

3 The crossmember was only tack welded to this chassis. After the crossmember is installed, the tack welds are cut with a 3-inch cut-off wheel.

4 It appears that the crossmember is only tack welded on the top, but there are actually two welds on the bottom side. They have to be cut to release the crossmember.

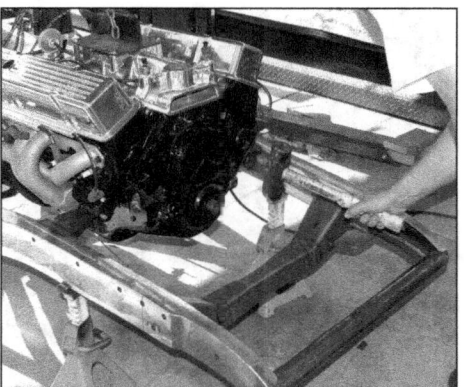

5 After all of the tack welds are cut apart, the crossmember is removed with a little persuasion. A few whacks with a large hammer, and the cross-member falls out.

6 The remaining tack welds on the side of the frame are sanded smooth with a 3-inch angle sander.

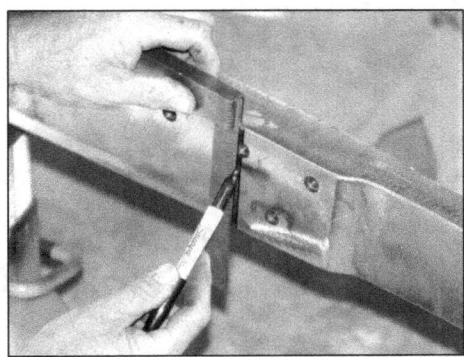

7 On a custom frame, the center point of the crossmember lines up with the rear-fender brace hole. The center is marked with a felt pen.

8 The center of the crossmember is marked, too. This is used to position the unit during installation.

9 The crossmember is installed on the floor jack, and then it is raised into place. The jack keeps the crossmember where it belongs and tight to the frame while the welding is being done.

THE COMPLETE BUILDER'S GUIDE TO HOT ROD CHASSIS AND SUSPENSION

CHAPTER 3

10 The center line on the frame is lined up with the center line on the crossmember. This crossmember is designed well, because it fits perfectly without any trimming.

11 Following the directions, the frame angle and crossmember angle are checked to make sure both measurements are correct.

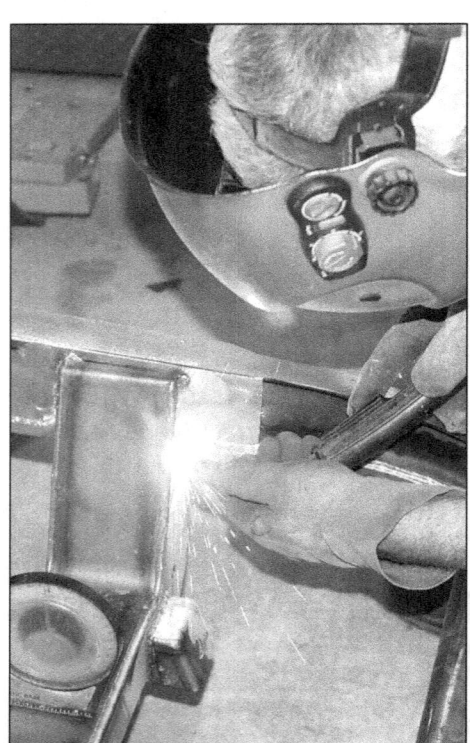

12 When the crossmember is lined up in the frame, the center-line-to-center-line dimensions are checked from one side of the frame to the other. After confirming it is in the correct location and square, the crossmember is tack welded to the frame. Several tacks are used to keep it firmly in place.

13 Using the measurement supplied, the upper spring hats are positioned for welding. Make sure they are on the correct side by checking the marks on the bottom side.

14 After the upper spring hats are in the correct location, they are tack welded in place.

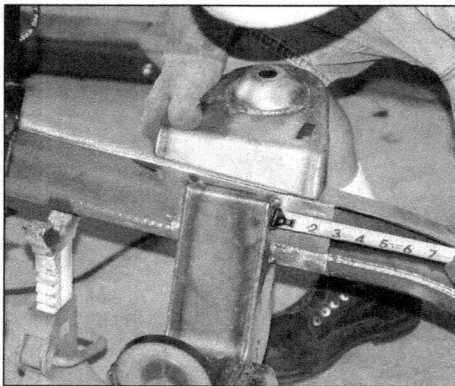

15 The hat on the other side is also carefully measured to make sure it is in the correct location.

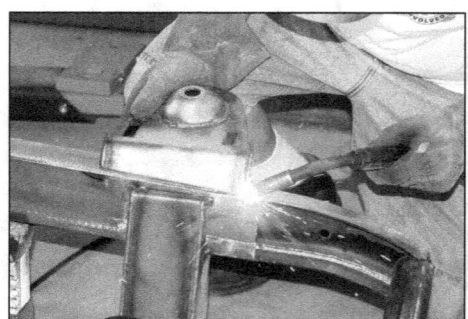

16 After the upper spring hat is located properly, it is tack welded to the frame. Several tack welds are used to secure the upper hat to the frame.

60   THE COMPLETE BUILDER'S GUIDE TO HOT ROD CHASSIS AND SUSPENSION

INDEPENDENT FRONT SUSPENSIONS

17 The hole in the crossmember is drilled out to work with the stock Mustang II A-arm that uses a smaller bolt. Since this kit has tubular A-arms, drill the hole to size with a 5/8-inch drill bit.

18 Since the stock A-arm is not used, a tubular spacer must be installed inside of the crossmember, and another must be welded to the outside. The long, lower A-arm bolt is used to keep the spacers straight while the tubes are being welded.

19 The other spacer tube must be welded to the crossmember. The long bolt is holding both of the spacers in place and in alignment while the welding is being done.

20 The inner tube is tack welded in place first on both sides. Two long tacks are used to keep the tube securely in place.

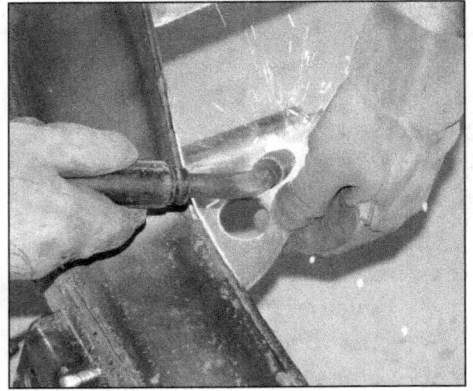

21 The kit contains a brace for the lower A-arm tube. It is tack welded to the frame and to the tube.

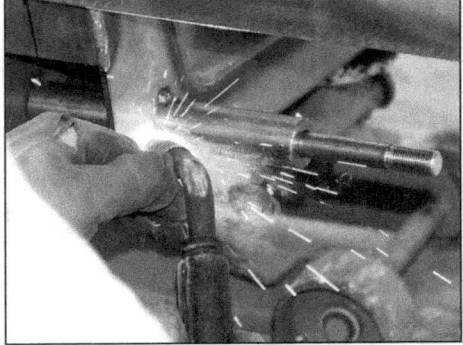

22 The outer tube is tack welded to the crossmember. This tube is used to secure the lower A-arm, so it needs to be strong.

23 When the measurements are finished and the parts are installed correctly, they are welded to the frame.

24 Here is the frame after all of the welding is completed. This connection is very strong and should provide years of service.

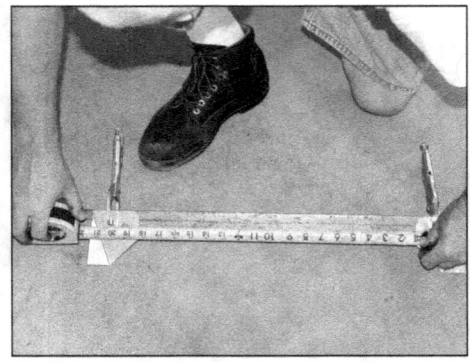

25 The radiator braces are installed next. They are positioned properly by lining them up, measuring, and connecting to a piece of bar stock with locking pliers.

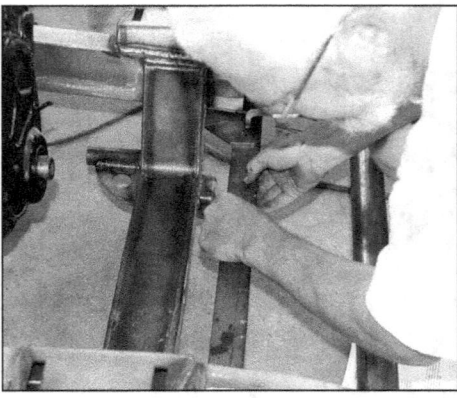

26 The bar stock is lined up next to the frame, but the corner of the radiator mount rubs against the weld in the crossmember.

27 In order for the radiator mount to align with the frame, the corner must be cut slightly for clearance. A band saw can be used for this.

28 After the corners are cut, the radiator mounts are able to fit tightly against the frame.

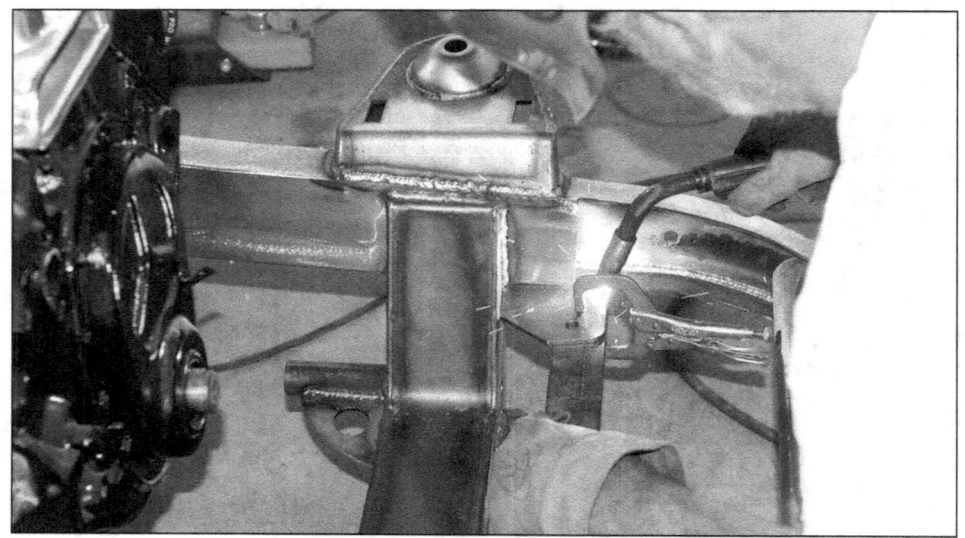

29 After they are in place, the radiator mounts are tack welded to the frame. The bar stock is removed, and the mounts are welded to the frame.

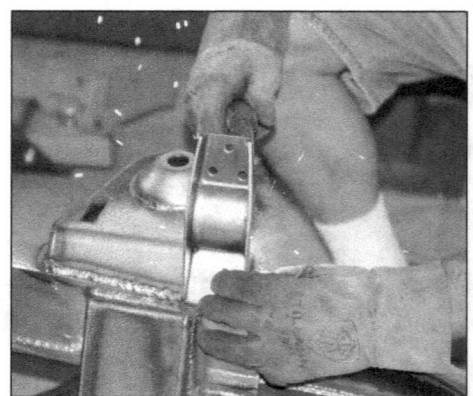

30 This Heidts kit comes with a new mounting location for the fender braces. The new mounting brackets must be welded to the frame, and then the fender brace must be shortened accordingly.

INDEPENDENT FRONT SUSPENSIONS

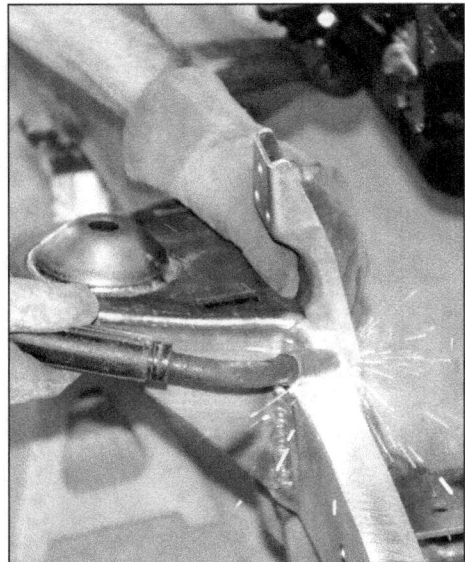

31 Following the directions in the kit, the fender braces are welded to the upper spring hats.

32 After the lower tubes are welded to the chassis, the heat expansion and shrinkage changes the fit of the lower A-arm bolts. In order to remedy the situation, the tubes are drilled to provide the clearance necessary.

33 The drill is not long enough to pass through the tubes, so they must be drilled from both sides.

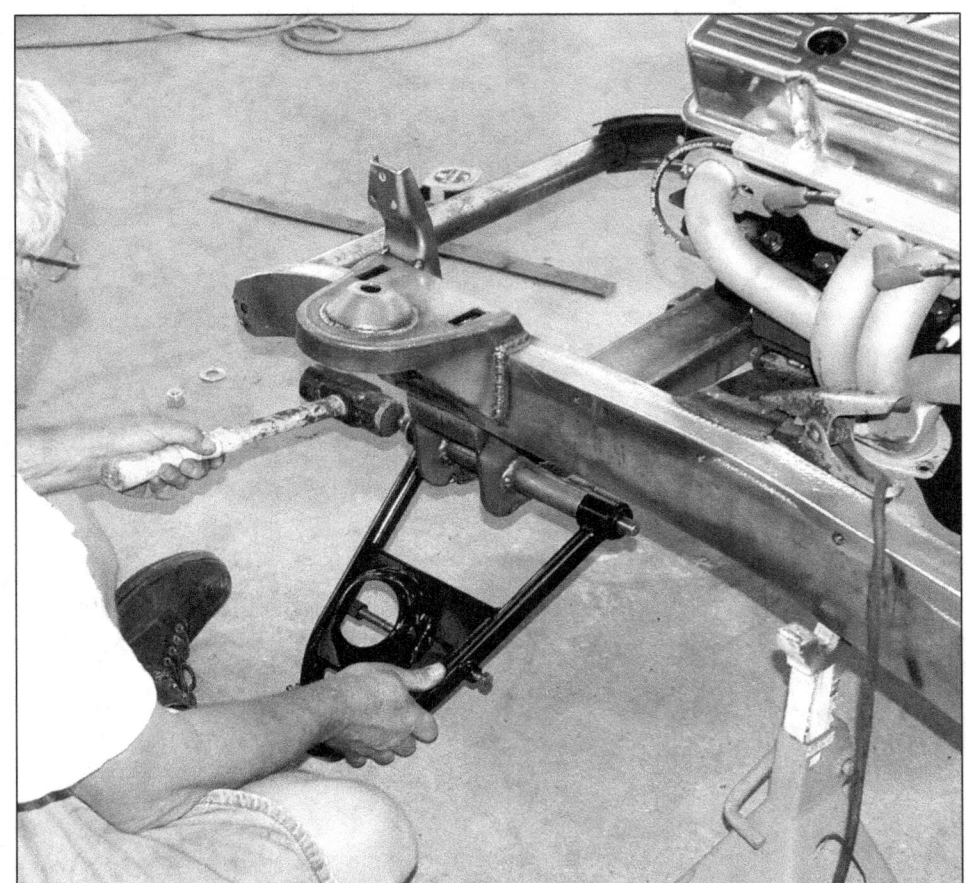

34 The lower A-arm is aligned with the tubes, and then the long bolt is installed. Even after the drilling, the bolts may be snug, so they must be installed with a little persuasion.

35 The spring is installed in the spring pocket, and then it is installed on the lower A-arm. The jack is used to elevate the lower A-arm.

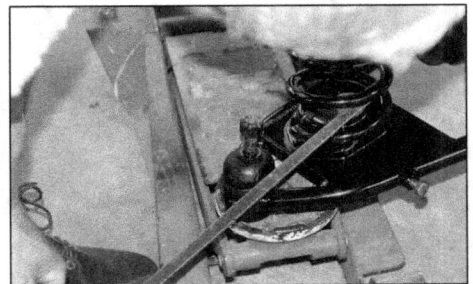

36 The spring may not seat properly on the lower A-arm, so it is pried over, using a long bar, until it pops over the lower mount.

THE COMPLETE BUILDER'S GUIDE TO HOT ROD CHASSIS AND SUSPENSION

CHAPTER 3

37 The spring after being mounted correctly at the top and bottom. The jack remains until the upper A-arm and spindle are connected.

38 The spindles are installed on the lower A-arms with castle nuts supplied in the kit. The castle nuts should be snugged and secured with cotter pins.

39 The upper A-arm is connected to the spring hat with slider bolts supplied in the kit. The bolts are designed to move forward and backward when the front suspension is being set up.

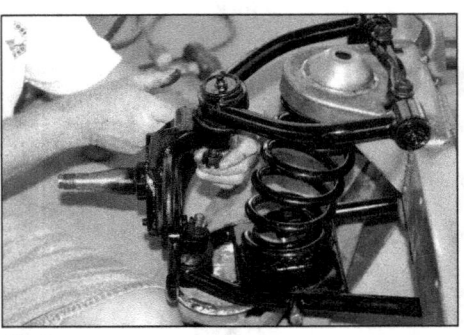

40 The upper A-arm is connected to the spindle with the castle nut supplied in the kit. After it is tight, it is secured with a cotter pin.

41 The upper-ball-joint connection is tightened, and then the castle nut is secured with a cotter pin.

42 The upper A-arm is set midway in the travel. This is a good place to start, but the camber, caster, and alignment have to be set properly at an alignment shop.

43 The shock is inserted through the hole in the lower A-arm and is aligned with the hole in the top of the spring hat. After the shock is installed with a rubber bushing on both sides of the hole, a washer and nut are installed to keep it in place.

INDEPENDENT FRONT SUSPENSIONS

44 The shock bolt is torqued, and a jam nut is installed to keep it in place.

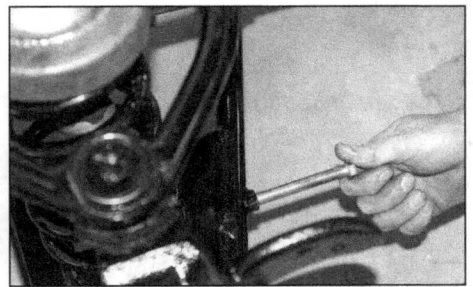

45 The shock connects on the lower side with this long bolt, which passes through the tube in the lower A-arm. It is secured to the other side of the A-arm with a built-in nut plate.

46 The inner bearing and seal is installed in the rotor, and then the rotor is installed on the spindle. After the rotor is in place, the small front bearing is installed. Make sure the bearings are coated with high-temperature disc-brake bearing grease.

47 The large washer and spindle nut are installed, and a large pliers is used to tighten them. The spindles should be tight, but loose enough to allow a half spin when you turn the rotor.

48 After the spindle bolt is tight, a castle-nut cover and a cotter pin are installed to keep it in place, so it doesn't back off.

THE COMPLETE BUILDER'S GUIDE TO HOT ROD CHASSIS AND SUSPENSION

CHAPTER 3

49 The GM brake calipers are installed. The units connect to the spindles with two special Allen bolts.

50 The suspension system after the brakes are installed. This system works great, offers a soft ride, and provides ample stopping power.

51 The Heidts front suspension kit comes with a Mustang II rack-and-pinion steering unit.

52 The rack is aligned with the bracket holes, and then the large bolts are connected. This unit mounts to the front of the crossmember.

53 The rack is secured to the crossmember by using two large box-end wrenches, one on each side of the bracket.

INDEPENDENT FRONT SUSPENSIONS

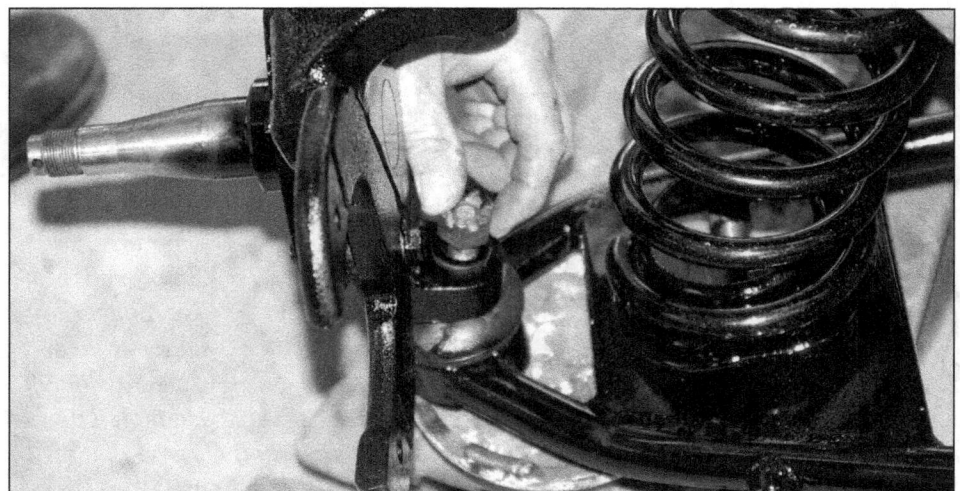

54 *The rack ball joints are connected to the spindle with 3/4-inch castle nuts. When they are tight, they are secured with cotter pins.*

55 *The front-end brace is removed. This is done by cutting the spot welds with a 3-inch cut-off wheel.*

The Heidts economy front suspension after installation. It looks great, and it provides a soft ride and positive steering.

Installing a Total Cost Involved Engineering 1933–1934 Ford IFS

Our project 1934 Ford cabriolet was built in the late 1970s and was a state-of-the-art car at the time. The resto-styled hot rod features dual parallel leaf springs in the rear and a dropped-I-beam front end that was updated with disc brakes. After driving the cabriolet to rod runs all over southern California for quite a while, the owner, Don Wilson, decided that he wanted power steering so that his "better half" could drive the cabriolet with ease.

Following all of the advancements in street-rod technology that he saw at rod runs, Wilson started thinking about installing an independent front suspension that could be outfitted with a power rack-and-pinion steering system. In the end, he has a car that is easy to steer, and he also has steering that is completely positive. In addition, the car has an improved ride, superior stopping power, and with the Total Cost Involved Engineering show-quality suspension, an attractive appearance.

A basic Total Cost Involved Engineering suspension-system kit comes with a standard rack-and-pinion steering system but, for a few dollars more, an optional power rack is available. This installation kit came with a new front crossmember, tubular upper and lower A-arms, Aldan coil-over shocks, a sway bar, Mustang dropped spindles (complete with rotors and Wilwood brakes), and the power rack-and-pinion steering unit. An attractive front suspension was desired, so the chrome package was specified. The installer also thought that the car would look better if the chassis was painted after the welding work was completed.

The installation required several tools, which included a MIG welding machine, a plasma cutter, a few small grinders, normal hand tools, and in this case, a spray gun to primer and paint the chassis. The total installation took about three days to perform, and the cabriolet looks great, sits low, and is fun to drive.

1934 Cabriolet IFS Installation

1 This 1934 Ford is receiving important updating. First, the front sheetmetal parts must be removed.

2 The owner of the car wants power steering and an improved suspension appearance. It is very difficult to install power steering to the existing suspension, and chrome plating costs a fortune; it's more cost effective to install a completely new front suspension.

3 The shop is installing a Total Cost Involved Engineering front-suspension system. This kit comes with the special front crossmember, tubular upper and lower A-arms, Aldan coil-over shocks, a sway bar, and Mustang II spindles, complete with rotors and Wilwood calipers. The kit also comes with all of the hardware and brake lines required to complete the installation.

4 The shop starts the installation by disconn-ecting the four-bar radius rods. The existing suspension must be removed before the new one can be installed.

5 The steering U-joint bolts are disconnected so the steering unit can be removed.

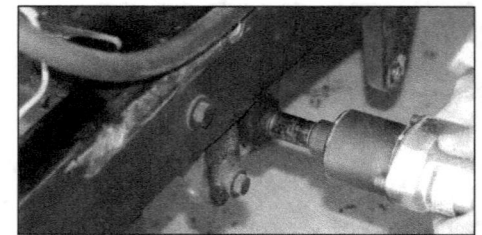

6 The steering box is held in place with three large bolts. Using an impact gun, the bolts are removed.

INDEPENDENT FRONT SUSPENSIONS

7 After the bolts are removed, the steering box is lowered and disconnected from the steering wheel at the U-joint connection.

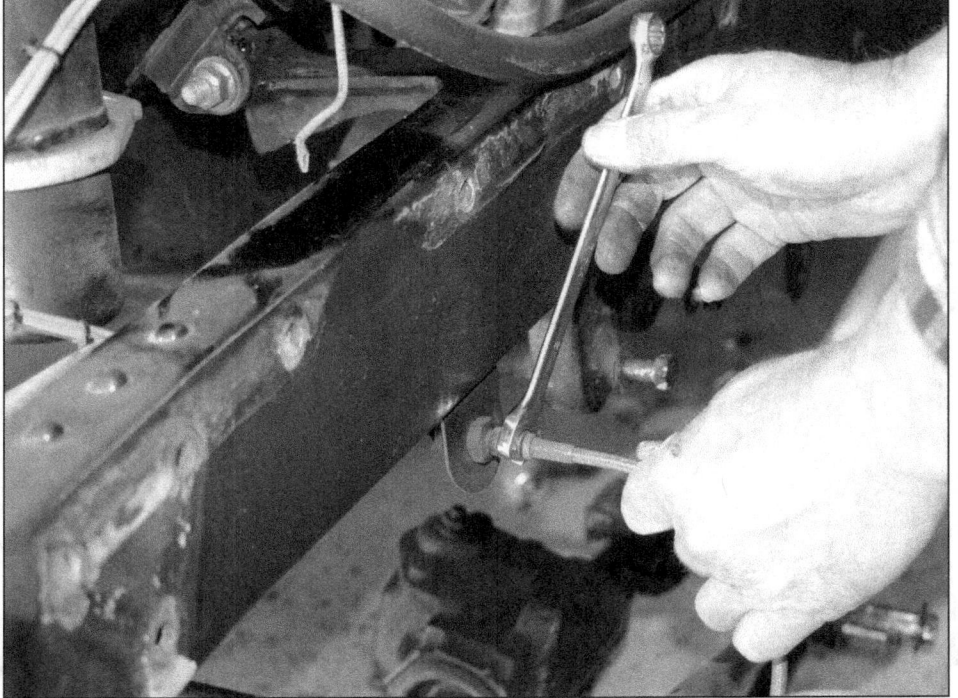

8 The brake lines must be removed from the small tabs on the frame. The kit comes with new brake lines.

9 The final step in removing the front suspension is disconnecting the front U-bolts that secure the spring in the front crossmember. After they are disconnected, the front suspension is removed.

10 The old crossmember must be removed. However, before that is done, a temporary crossmember must be tack welded in place to keep the frame rails from moving.

11 After the temporary crossmember is secured, the stock crossmember is removed. The stock crossmember is secured to the frame with rivets, so if one wants to save the unit, the rivets must be drilled out. In this project, the crossmember was scrapped, so it was cut out of the frame with a plasma cutter.

THE COMPLETE BUILDER'S GUIDE TO HOT ROD CHASSIS AND SUSPENSION

12 The old four-bar mounts are removed. It may be more difficult than it looks, because the mounts are made out of 3/4-inch-thick bar stock. Several passes are made with the plasma cutter before the mount is disconnected.

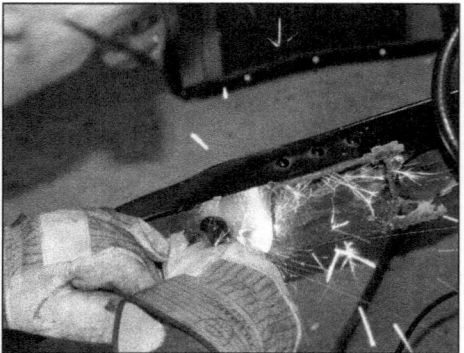

14 The rest of the front crossmember is removed. A plasma cutter is used to cut out the sides of the crossmember.

15 Sometimes, a little friendly persuasion must be used to remove the existing crossmember. This section is removed so that this area can be boxed before the new crossmember is installed. The boxing plate sits inside of the frame rails to match up with the boxing that is already there.

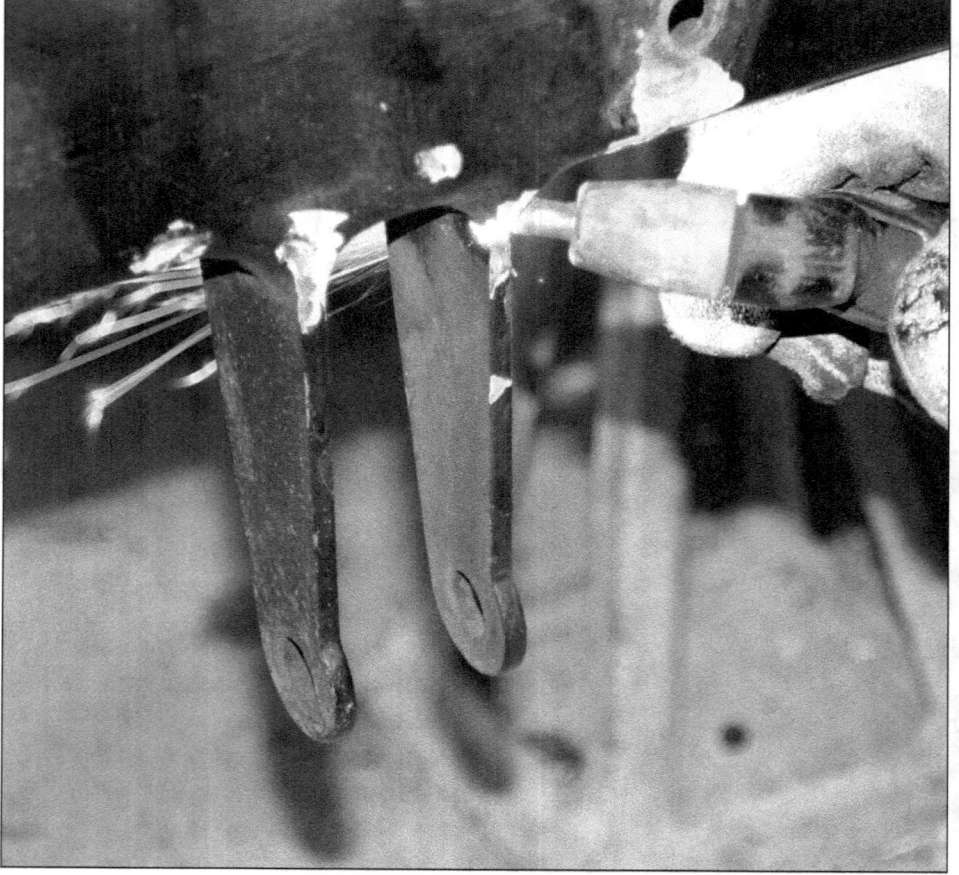

13 Although this front suspension isn't using a Panhard bar, there are mounts on the frame for one, so they must be removed with a plasma cutter.

16 The frame is dressed with a small hand grinder to get it looking good.

17 The crossmember center line is found, and by using the measurements in the kit, the frame rails are also marked in the correct location. The crossmember is lifted into place with a floor jack. It is measured, the angle is checked, and when everything is perfect, the crossmember is tack welded to the frame.

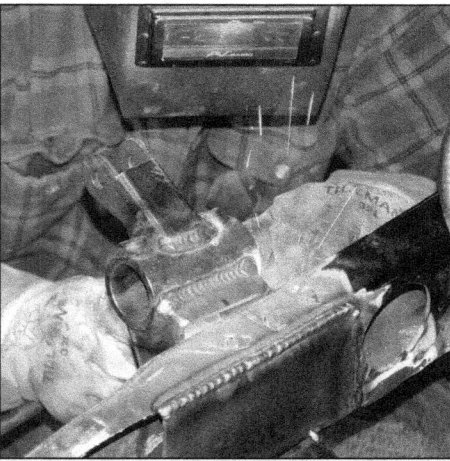

18 After the measurements are checked again to make sure the crossmember is installed correctly, it is finish welded in place. Notice that the frame is boxed in this area.

19 A die grinder is used to cut the tack welds, and the temporary crossmember is removed.

20 The crossmember is held in place with the floor jack when it is tack welded. Notice that the frame is boxed on both sides prior to the installation of the new crossmember.

21 The entire frame is sanded and cleaned before it is primered to keep the bare-metal areas from rusting. At this point, the fender braces must be installed.

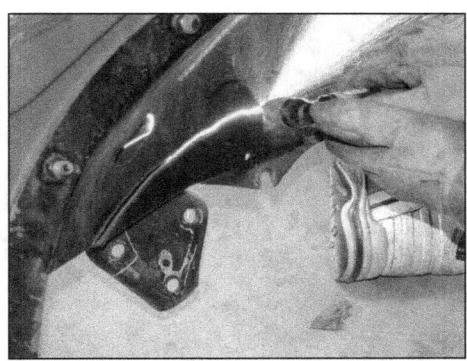

22 The inner fender must be trimmed slightly to get the fenders to fit. The fenders are held in place, and then the fender braces are marked where they must be cut to fit.

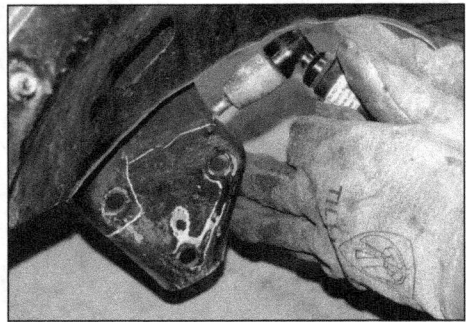

23 Using the measurements made on the fender brace, a cut is made accordingly with a plasma cutter.

24 After the fender brace is cut, it is smoothed with a small hand grinder. The paint is removed from the brace prior to welding it to the frame.

CHAPTER 3

25 The inner fender pan is also cleaned with a small hand sander to get it smooth. The fender is installed, and the brace is tack welded to the frame. When that is finished, the brace is disconnected from the fender, and the fender is removed.

26 The frame is sanded and painted. The paint on the frame matches the paint on the body.

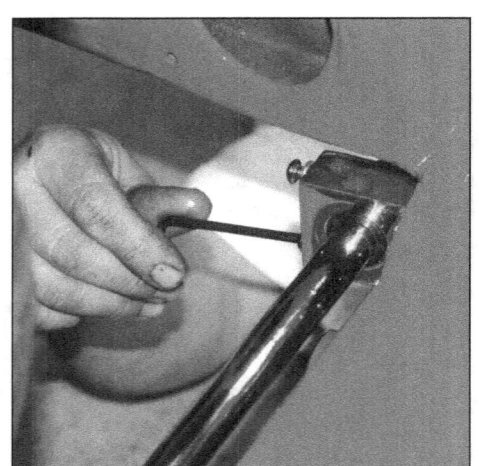

27 The front-suspension installation begins by installing the sway bar. It is secured with two small Allen-head screws. The sway bar is held in place by a Teflon bushing that sits inside of an aluminum block.

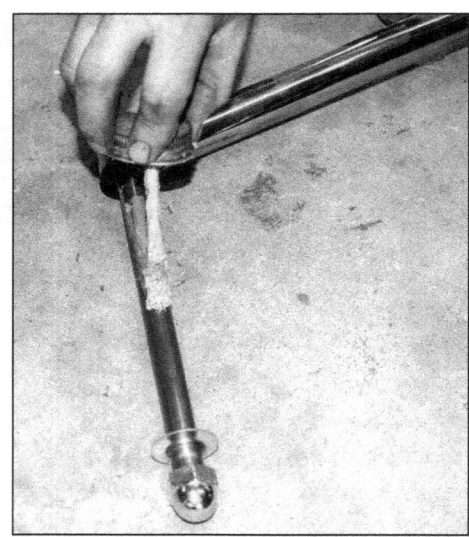

28 The lower A-arm is held in place with a long bolt. It is coated with anti-seize compound before it is installed.

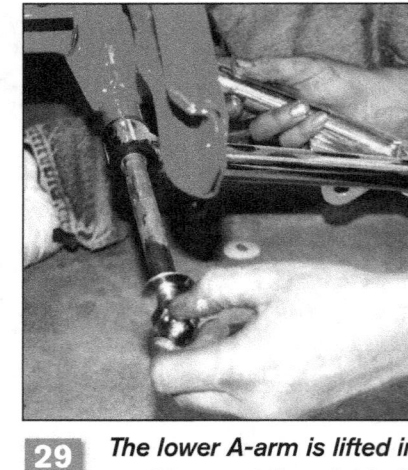

29 The lower A-arm is lifted into position, and then the bolt is installed. Notice that the kit comes with polished stainless-steel washers to cover and secure the Teflon bushings.

30 The coil-over shock is installed. It is secured at the top with an Allen-head button screw and at the bottom with a long screw that is also used to secure the sway-bar connection.

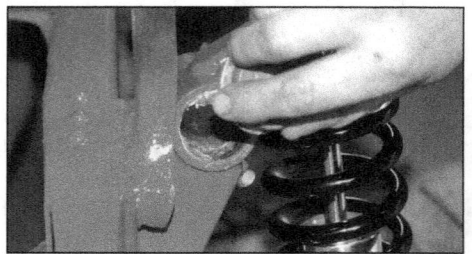

31 The hole for the eccentric bushing is also coated with anti-seize compound prior to the installation of the upper A-arm.

72   THE COMPLETE BUILDER'S GUIDE TO HOT ROD CHASSIS AND SUSPENSION

32 The eccentric bushing is installed. This eccentric bushing is used to adjust the camber and caster of the vehicle. When the adjustments are correct, jam nuts hold the eccentric bushing in place.

33 The upper A-arm is lifted into position, and then the long rod is installed. It is secured with a Nylock nut.

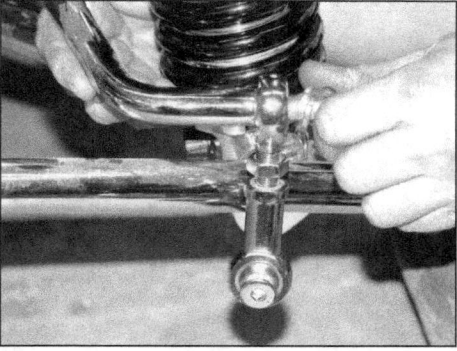

34 The sway bar is attached with a special connector that uses small Heim joints. The sway bar is threaded and is connected with a fine-thread Allen-head button screw.

35 The spindles, rotors, and brakes are set up by Total Cost Involved Engineering to make sure they are done correctly. The entire system is connected to the upper and lower A-arms.

36 This kit features Wilwood polished-aluminum calipers and vented rotors. These brakes slow down the lightweight cabriolet without a problem.

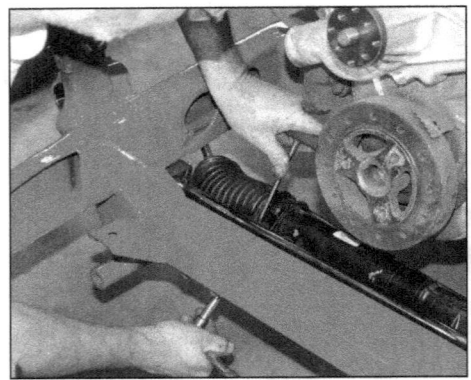

37 The power rack-and-pinion steering system connects to the backside of the crossmember. It is held in place with four bolts.

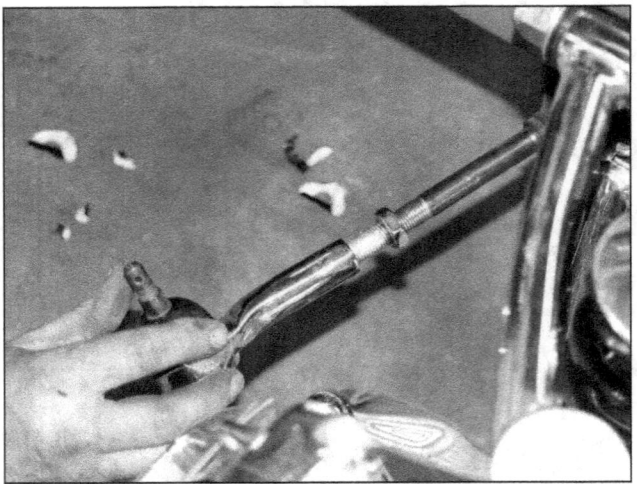

38 The chrome-plated tie-rod ends are connected to the rack-and-pinion unit, and then the ends are connected to the spindles. After all of the parts are in place, the bolts are tightened; the cotter pins are installed where necessary; and the camber, caster, and alignment are set as close as possible. After the car is finished, it goes to the alignment shop to set it up perfectly.

39 The finished front suspension looks great, and it provides excellent ride comfort and easy steering.

40 The 1934 Ford sits super low but the stance can be adjusted, if desired. A few turns on the spanner ring of the coil-over shocks, and the hot rod can be raised a little.

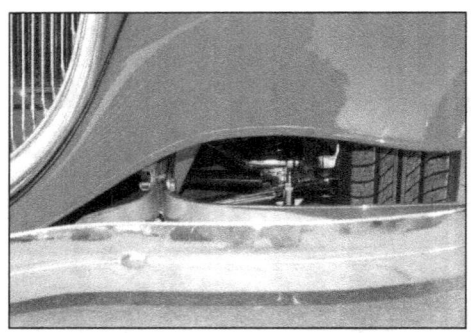

41 The year 1934 marks the last in which a Ford's front suspension is easily seen. When one looks under the fender, that person sees the intricate chrome-plated independent front suspension.

From the side, the car sits just right with the independent front suspension.

Model A IFS Installation

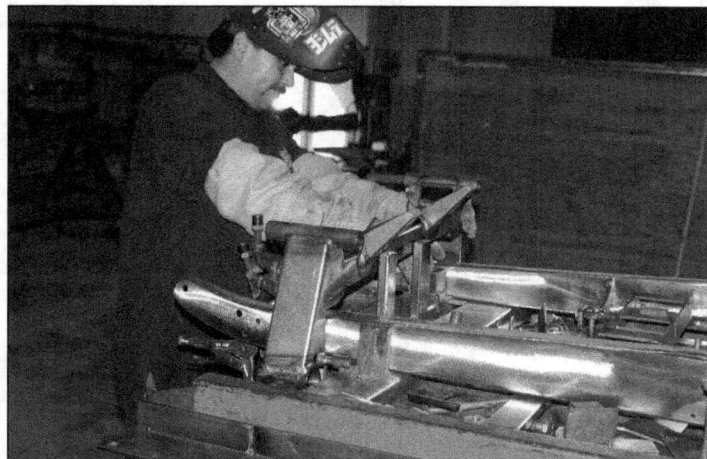

1 The fellows at Total Cost Involved Engineering are installing the front crossmember using a jig that makes the installation easier and more accurate. Here the one-piece crossmember is being installed on the chassis. The crossmember is a well-designed unit so it can be installed without a jig for homebuilders. Careful measuring is the key to success.

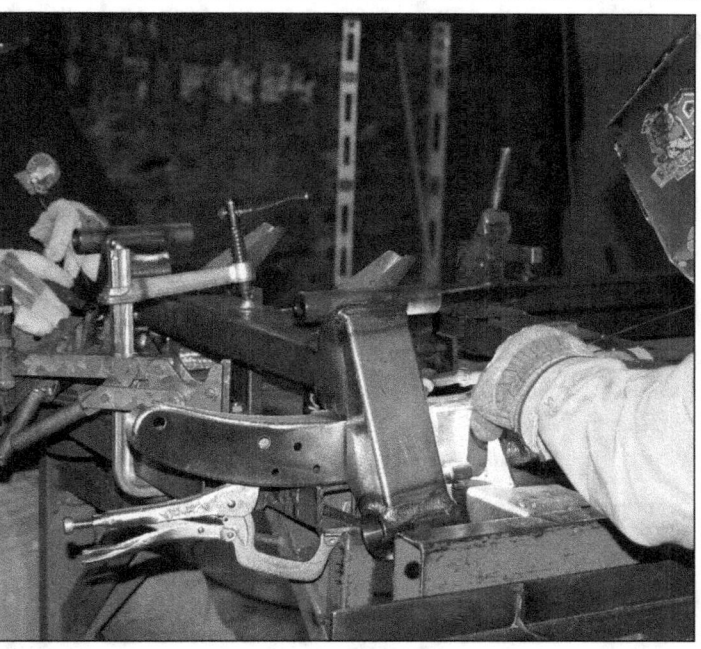

2 After the crossmember is lined up and measured, it is tack welded to the chassis.

3 The chassis is turned over, and then the angle of the crossmember is determined and more measuring is done to make sure the crossmember was sitting square in the chassis. When the measurements are correct, the crossmember is TIG welded to the frame rails.

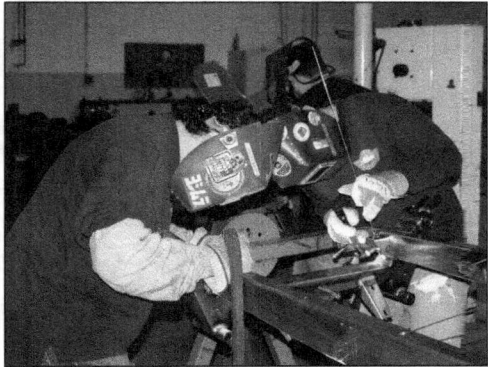

4 Here the fellows at TCI are TIG welding the crossmember into the chassis. In this case they also have to install the radiator support tabs.

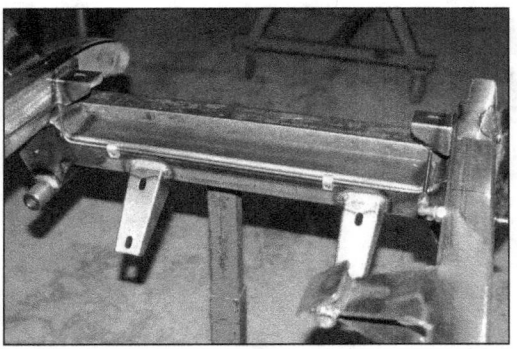

5 Here is the finished crossmember connected to the frame along with the radiator support tabs. If you look closely you can also see the stainless-steel brake lines that run from side to side and to the master cylinder, which is not shown.

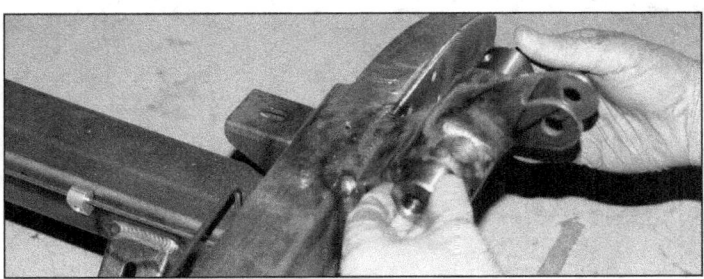

6 The eccentric is installed in the upper crossmember boss. Since this is an eccentric, turning it pushes the upper A-arm outward or moves it inward. Moving it backward for forward also changes the front suspension angle.

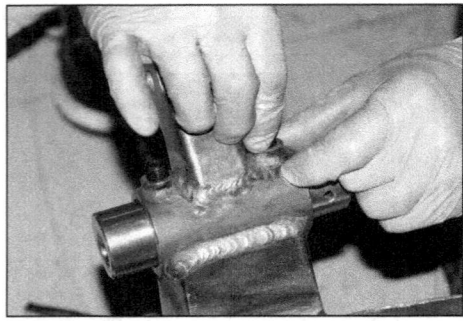

7 In the process of setting the camber and caster measurements the eccentric adjustments are made. When the measurements are correct the eccentric is held in place with these two Allen-head set screws.

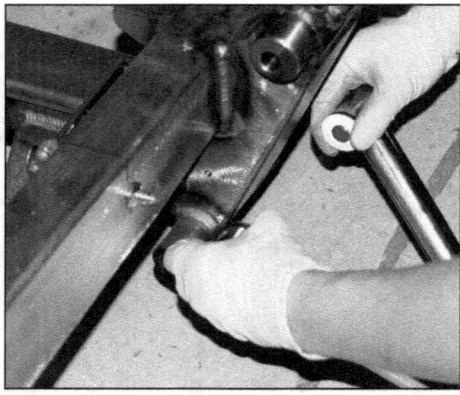

8 The lower A-arms are installed first with the long bolt. It is a good idea to coat the bolt with anti-seize to keep everything lubricated.

9 Sometimes the lower control arm bolt needs some persuasion to get the bolt to seat correctly. After it is in place, the nut can be installed and secured.

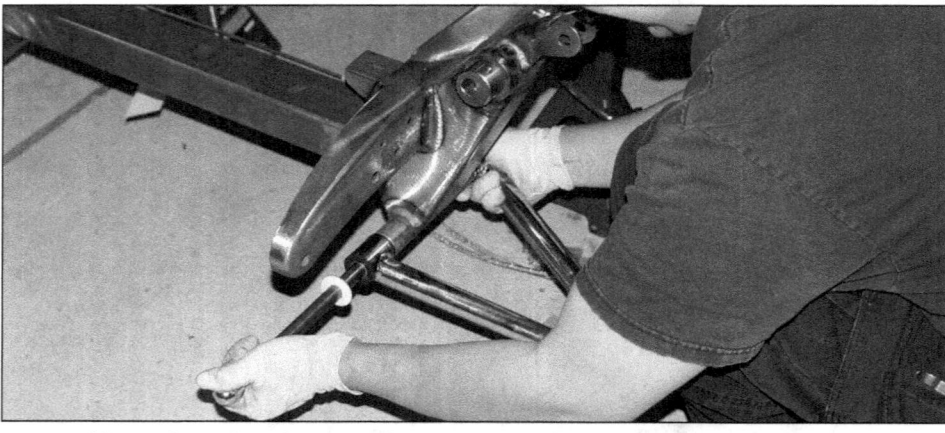

10 Here, the other A-arm is being installed with the large bolt. Remember to lubricate the bolt before it is installed.

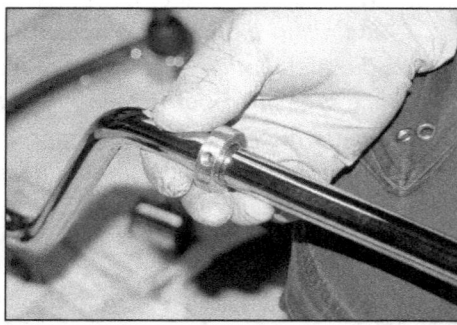

11 The Model A front suspension installation features a sway bar. The installation was started by installing the two set-screw retainers that are used to center the sway bar.

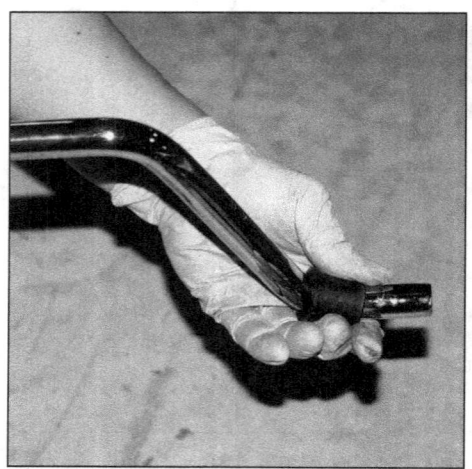

12 The sway bar is secured to the frame with two brakets and nylon insulators Here the insulator is being installed on the sway bar.

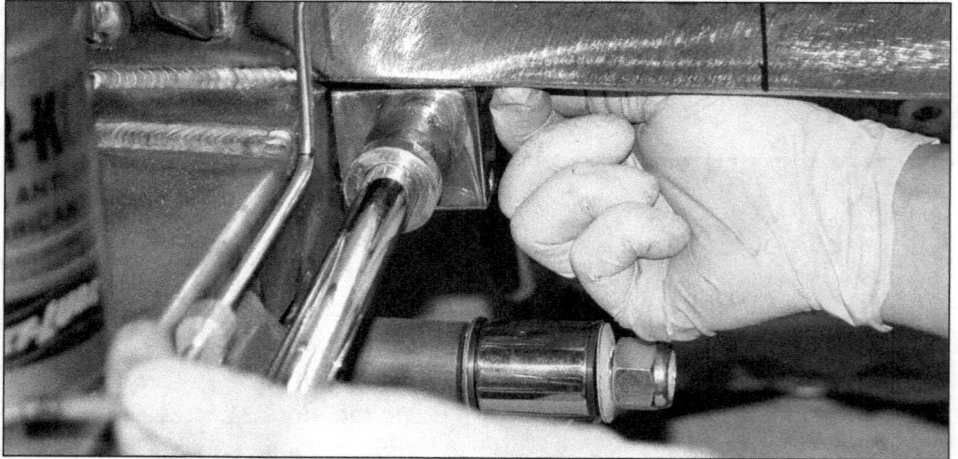

13 The sway bar is being held to the frame by two square aluminum brackets. The bracket fits over the sway bar, the insulator is pushed into the bracket, and then the sway bar is centered and is held in place by the set-screw retainers.

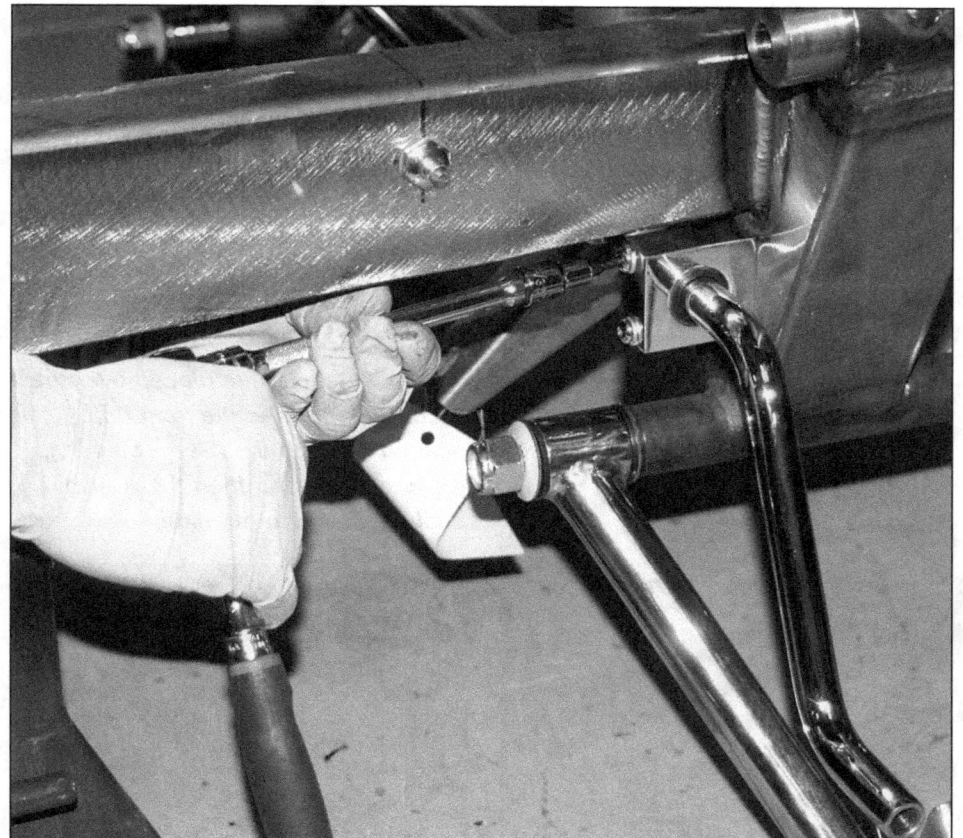

14 Here the bracket is being secured to the frame with a socket wrench and two button-head Allen fasteners.

15 The special TCI All-American coil-over shock is being secured to the upper mount.

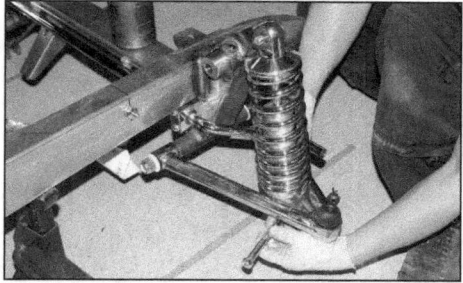

16 After the shock is connected to the top bracket it can be connected to the lower A-arm with a long bolt. The bolt is longer than necessary because it is also used to mount the sway bar.

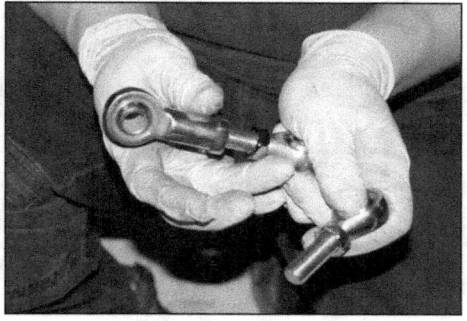

17 The sway bar link is made out of male and female Heim joints screwed together. The length of the link can be determined and set with the lock nut.

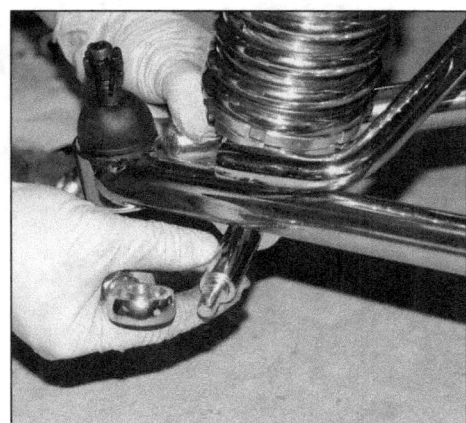

18 The fastener that secures the coil-over shock is also used as a connection point for the sway bar link. Notice how the shank has been turned down at the front to accept the washer and lock bolt.

CHAPTER 3

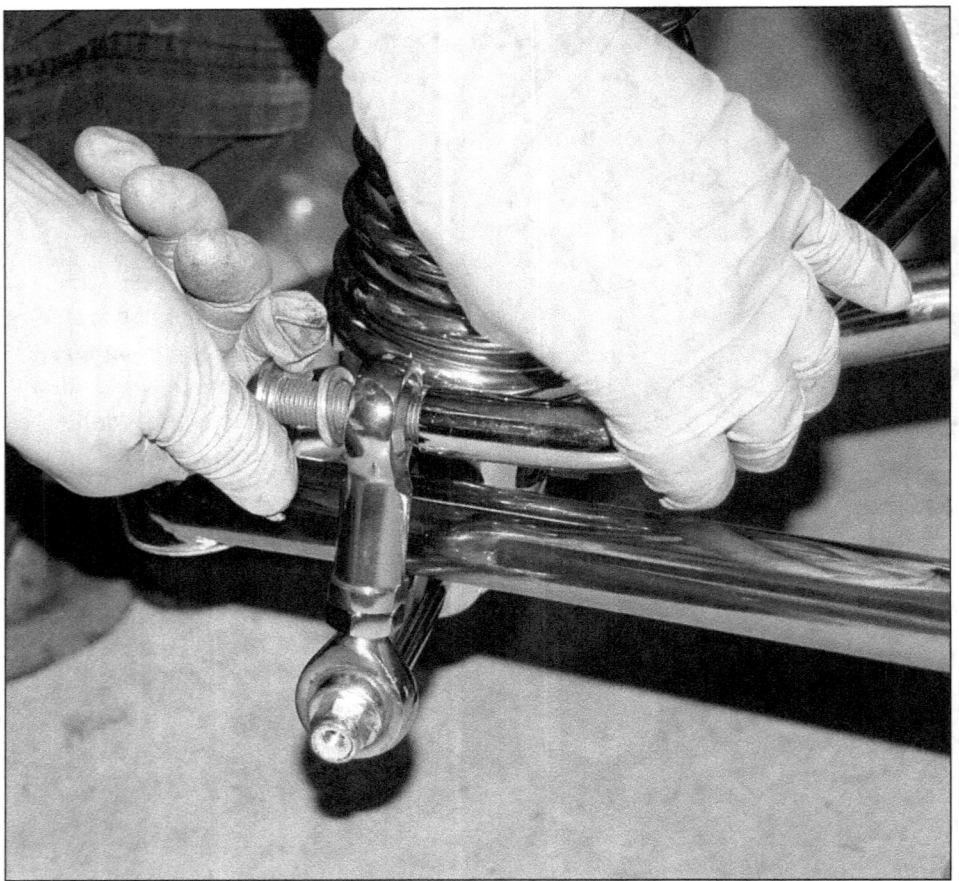

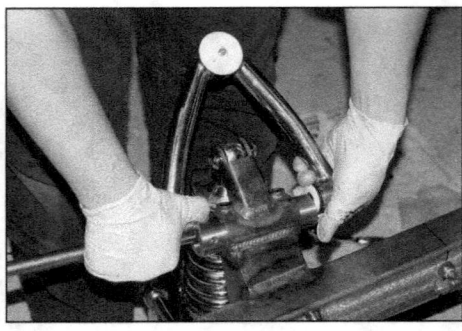

19 The link is connected to the lower bolt and then the button-head Allen bolt is secured to the sway bar. Here it is being screwed into the end of the sway bar. The bolt should be coated with anti-seize.

20 Now the upper A-arm can be installed. It is placed over the eccentric and then the long bolt passed through the A-arm bushing, the eccentric, and then the A-arm bushing on the other side.

21 This is a tight fit but it goes through just fine with a little friendly persuasion. After one side is connected the other side is installed.

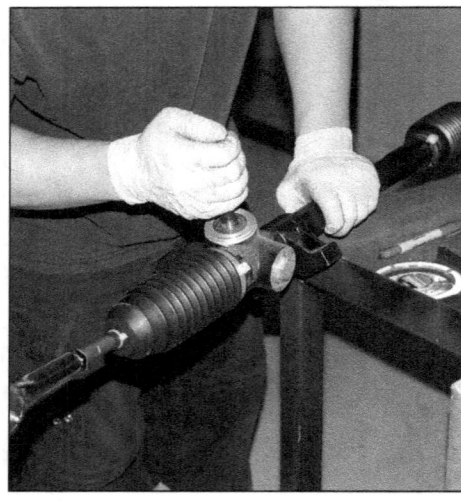

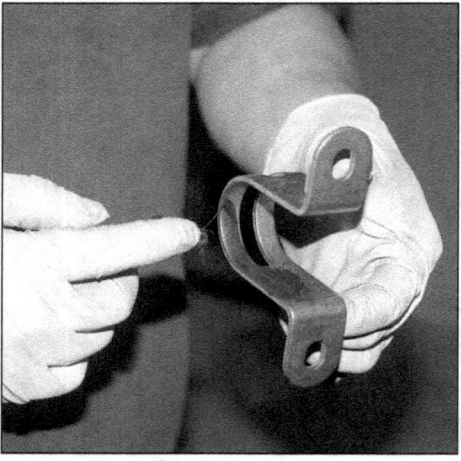

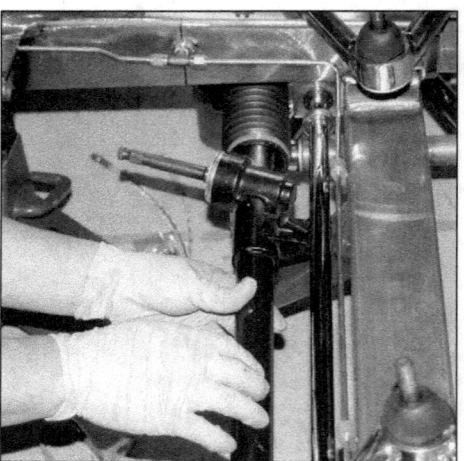

22 The rack-and-pinion shaft is turned to one side and then to the other to find the center position. The rack should be in the center position when it is installed.

23 The rack is held in place on one side with a built-in boss, but on the other side, this bracket is used. Here the inside of the bracket is being covered with a light coat of grease.

24 Here the rack is being set onto the brackets to make sure it fits correctly. After it is in place, the two button-head Allen bolts are installed to secure the driver side of the rack.

INDEPENDENT FRONT SUSPENSIONS

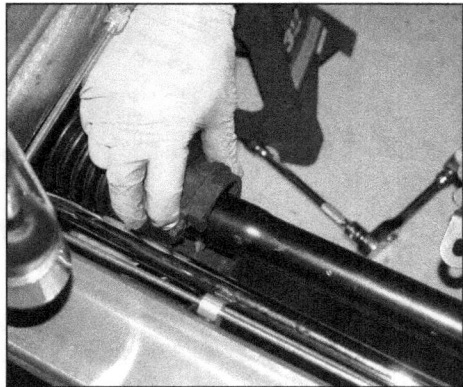

25 The rubber insulator is installed on the rack shaft at the point of connection. The rubber should be centered over the two bolts that will be used to secure the connection.

26 The bracket is installed over the rubber insulator and then it is bolted to the chassis.

27 The bracket secured the rack to the chassis on one side. On the other side the rack has a built-in bracket that is bolted to the chassis. Both connections are made with button-head Allen bolts.

28 When the TCI kit arrives at your door, the spindle and the brake assembly will be assembled. In this case it is a polished-aluminum Wilwood brake assembly. Here the assembly is being installed on the lower A-arm ball joint.

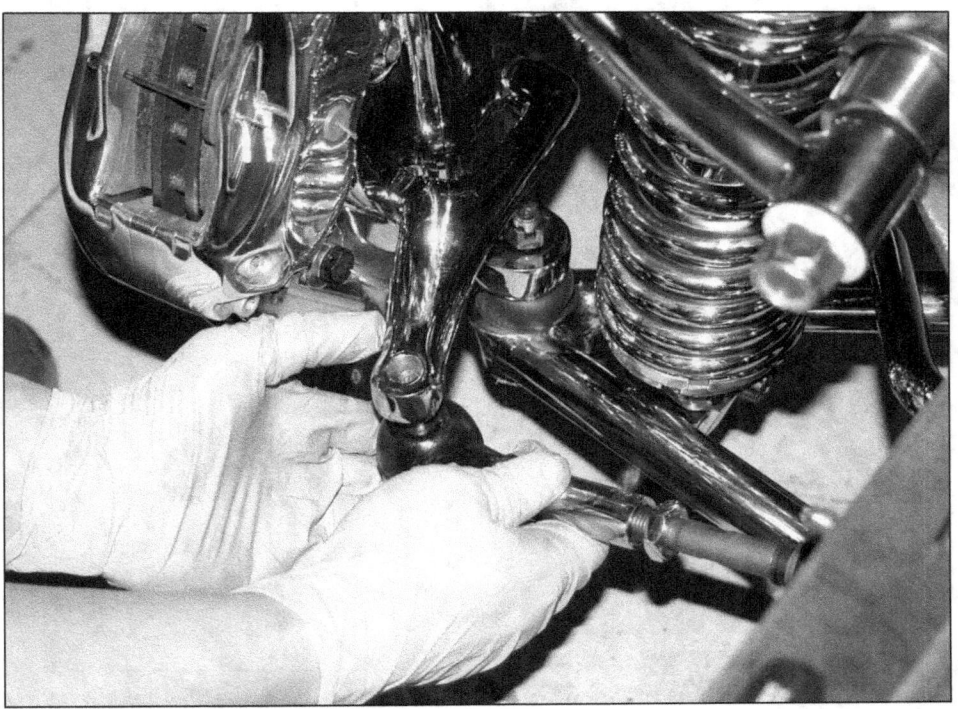

29 The upper A-arm is moved downward and the ball-joint tapered shaft is installed in the spindle.

THE COMPLETE BUILDER'S GUIDE TO HOT ROD CHASSIS AND SUSPENSION

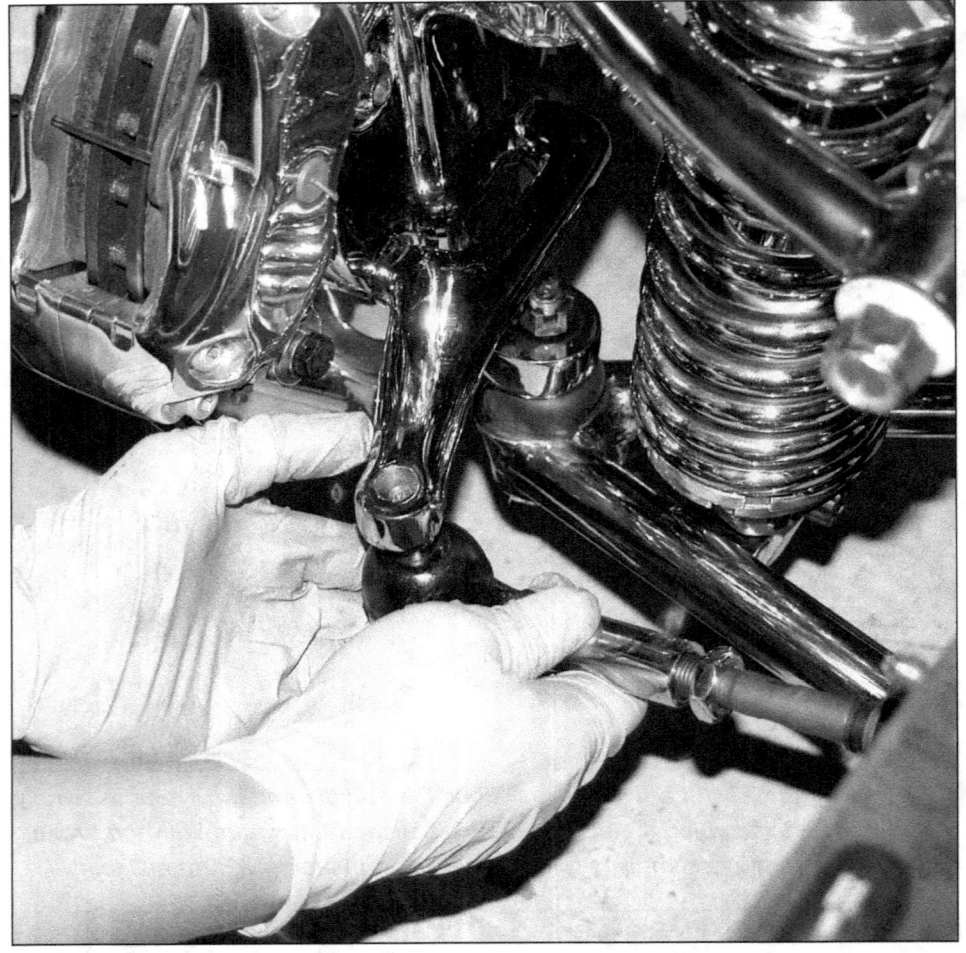

30 The two rack ends are installed in the spindles. All of the ball joints have tapered shafts so they can only be installed one way. If only a small number of threads are showing, the ball joint shaft is probably upside down.

31 After connections are made, and they are done correctly, the castle nuts can be secured, and each will require a cotter key to keep them in place.

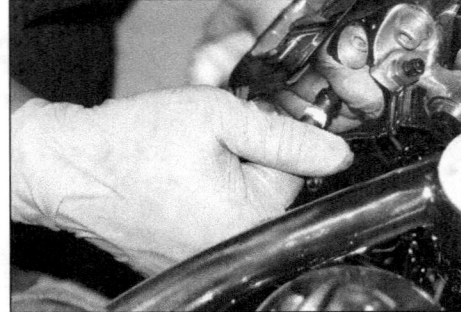

32 Both of the calipers have to be equipped with a brake fitting or the aircraft line. Here, the blue-anodized aluminum fitting has been covered with Teflon tape and is being secured to the Wilwood caliper.

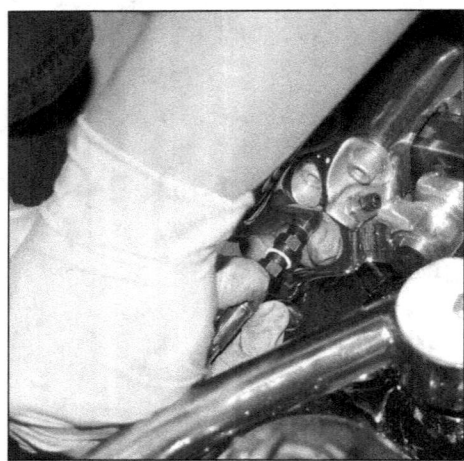

33 The braided steel line is being connected to the fitting. The line must be very tight to maintain a good seal.

The finished assembly looks terrific and works even better. This assembly appears to be very complex, but if you take if one step at a time, it is very easy to install.

CHAPTER 4

SOLID REAR AXLE SUSPENSIONS

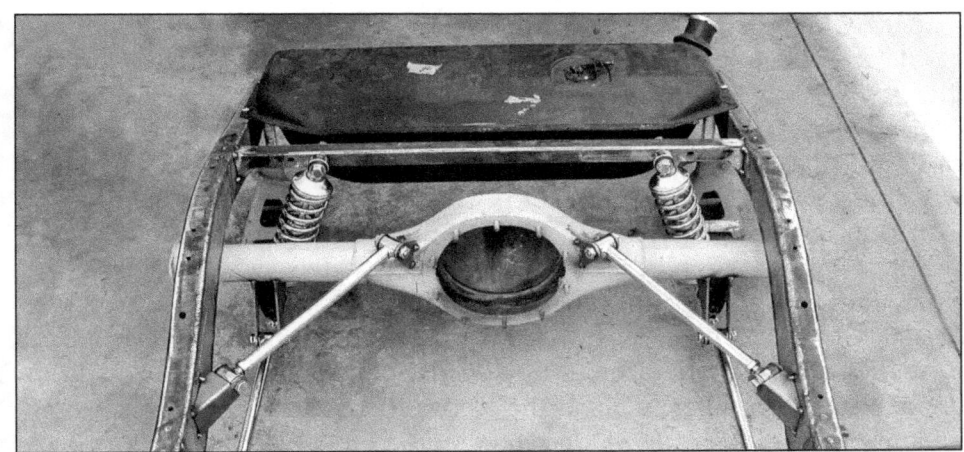

While solid-axle-suspension designs lack the flash and ultra comfort of independently-sprung systems, they also lack the high pricetag and inevitable custom fabrication IRS setups command. They can still look great and offer a fine ride, as this four-link setup clearly shows.

It should come as no surprise that the early Model A and '32 rear-axle assemblies were designed to handle the respective horsepower/torque of the car's engine, the tire size, and the weight of the car. The Model A Ford's stock engine developed 40 hp, and the car was offered with 21-inch wheels (in 1928 and 1929) and 18-inch wheels (in 1930 and 1931); cars from all four years ran on skinny tires. The Model A, depending on body style, weighed about 2,500 pounds, so the rear differential was designed to handle a little more weight than that, and it was built to handle the engine's power. The '32 Ford offered both a four-cylinder engine and a V-8 engine, had wider tires, and weighed a little more than the Model A, so the rear differential was improved to handle the additional power. Because of cost considerations, the four-cylinder model received the same differential as the V-8 model. Many of the early dry-lakes roadsters used the '32 differentials, but they didn't last long when hot rodders installed modern flathead engines with double the power of the original engines.

The Model A and '32 differentials were also different in suspension design, because the Model A axle had the spring mounted on top of it, and the '32 Ford axle had the spring mounted behind it. Edsel Ford didn't like the rough ride provided by the Model A spring-position design, so the '32 spring was mounted behind the axle, to allow more spring travel, and that provided a more comfortable ride. The differentials offered from 1932–1948 used the behind-the-axle spring design, and they all shared the same width, so they were interchangeable with a few modifications in torque-tube length. Many of the early hot rodders upgraded their cars with rear-axle assemblies from later-model Fords. Many of the dry-lakes race cars were upgraded with later-model differentials after the stock ones didn't make the grade.

In the late 1930s and early 1940s, Ford offered an overdrive rear-axle assembly that was vacuum operated.

THE COMPLETE BUILDER'S GUIDE TO HOT ROD CHASSIS AND SUSPENSION

The Columbia rear differential had a low gear as the standard axle ratio and a high gear as the overdrive axle ratio. This Columbia differential was actually a little stronger than the standard Ford axle, so it became popular with hot rodders. The overdrive ratio was perfect for top-speed racing, and the standard gears were better for drag-racing applications. From my personal experience, I drag-raced a 1940 Ford powered by a 322-ci Buick engine and never had a problem with the two-speed differential. Additionally, the overdrive gear was so high that, with the original engine, the overdrive only worked when the car was not climbing a grade, even a small one. The stock engine did not have enough torque to make the car climb a small grade; however, when the Buick engine was installed, the engine made the car climb any grade, any time, when the overdrive was being used.

In an effort to improve the strength of the early Ford rear-axle assemblies, an aftermarket company, Halibrand Engineering, designed a quick-change center section. It was stronger than a stock differential, and it also allowed the axle gear ratios to be changed quickly by removing the rear cover and swapping gear sets. This differential was primarily designed for sprint-car-style race cars so that the gears could be changed according to the track size; similar units are still being used in stock-car race cars today.

When these differentials were released, hot rodders really liked the quick-change feature. The gears could be changed for high-speed activities (such as dry-lakes racing on one day) and acceleration activities (such as drag racing the next day). The aluminum quick-change center sections also looked nice, and because they provided a performance appearance, many street-driven roadsters and coupes were also upgraded with the differentials. The down side of the quick-change differentials was that the rear-axle center sections were very expensive, noisy, and could be easily heard inside of the car. Some hot rodders thought the noise was cool; for others, the noise drove them crazy. Many of the hot rods being built today that are going for a traditional style are being equipped with quick-change differentials; they look great, and many of the large models can handle extremely high horsepower.

Before the mid 1950s, rodders didn't have a lot of differential choices, because there were only a few cars with open drivelines, and most were wider than what was needed to install in a street rod. Many GM cars were still using torque-tube drivelines into the mid 1950s. In 1955, several GM cars changed to open drivelines, and soon after, Ford introduced the 9-inch differential, so the options opened up for hot-rod installations. However, it took a few years before they were available for a reasonable price.

The 1955–1957 Chevy differential was a good choice for street rods, because it wasn't too wide and it was strong enough to handle a 300-hp engine, if it was going to be used in a racing application. On the street, the Chevy differential could handle even more power if the car was driven easy. Pontiac and Oldsmobile also introduced an open-driveline differential, and it was much larger and stronger than the Chevy unit, because the cars were being built with larger engines with more power than Chevrolet's cars. This large, extremely strong, over-engineered differential quickly became the choice of drag racers, because they were almost impossible to break. The tires—even slicks—would spin before the differential would break, so they were regularly used in gasser-style race cars.

When the street enthusiasts started to notice what the drag racers were using, they copied them. The Pontiac and Oldsmobile differentials were not only strong, but they looked husky, and in street rods where the rear end could easily be seen, such as a Model A Ford, they were very desirable. The only problem was that the Pontiac and Oldsmobile differentials quickly grew in width, and a lot of work had to be done to them to work in race cars and street rods. Some racers modified the differentials, but many started to change to a narrower Ford differential that was also very strong. The Ford 9-inch started to be used after it became difficult to find the early, narrow, Pontiac and Oldsmobile differentials.

If you look through early car magazines, you see many street rods with their rear tires sticking out past the rear fenders. Back then, that look was very acceptable, but things changed when the Ford Mustangs were released, and rodders started to equip their street rods with narrower differentials. In the early days, it was difficult to find a shop that could narrow a differential to fit under a street rod. In the 1960s, there were only a few shops that had the machinery to narrow a differential, and if you did find one, the cost of doing it was extremely expensive.

Fortunately, Ford started building a variety of small cars, such as the Fairlane, Falcon, Mustang, and (later) the Maverick with differentials that were the perfect width for most hot rods. The six-cylinder differentials weren't used, because they weren't strong enough and only offered four lugs for the wheels. The V-8 differentials were stronger and offered five lugs for the wheels. Some of the high-performance big-block-powered Fairlanes and Mustangs were actually equipped with 9-inch differentials instead of the smaller 8-inch ones used in regular cars, and they became very popular with street-rod enthusiasts. The problem was, only a small number of the 9-inch differentials were used in the Mustangs and Fairlanes, so you had to be lucky to find one. Wrecking-yard owners quickly found out that street rodders wanted them, so that prompted the wrecking-yard owners to increase the price.

In the mid to late 1960s, most of the street rods being built were for the highway and car shows. There were still enthusiasts racing cars at the dry lakes and drag strips, but now those cars were specialized for the racing endeavors and were never driven on the street. Rodders who could find them were equipping their cars with the stronger 9-inch Ford differential, but many hot rodders were using the 8-inch Ford unit, because it could handle the power delivered by a small-block Chevy or Ford engine. By the mid 1960s, the majority of the rods were running 283 and 327-ci Chevy engines and 289-ci Ford engines. The 8-inch differential was easy to find, priced right, and came in a wide array of gear applications; the most common ratios were 3.00:1 and 3.25:1, and both were perfect for highway use. The 8-inch Ford differential was also used with leaf springs, so only minor modifications were necessary to adapt them for use in a 1935–1948 Ford street rod.

Changing to a new differential became popular in the 1960s, but the problem many rodders ran into was how to adapt the differential to street-rod chassis. Some rodders were looking at what the factories were doing, and they started designing leaf-and-coil-spring systems that improved the ride on many early cars. The fellows who had Model A Fords really benefited from a new suspension design; a coil-spring system done correctly with lightweight springs, which offered a reasonable ride quality.

I remember attending many early rod runs, and after street-rod enthusiasts looked at the exterior and interior of a car, they walked around to the rear of the car and looked underneath. They were looking at some of the suspension designs others were using to see if the designs were better than what they were using. Hot rodders in the 1970s started driving their street rods longer distances, and they wanted a car that had a comfortable ride quality. In the mid 1960s, suspension-quality coil-over springs became readily available.

On many '32 Fords, enthusiasts installed a late-model differential in the same way they installed a stock one, but in many cases, there was a center-housing clearance problem. There were several ways to work around that problem; one method involved cutting away part of the rear crossmember and using a Model A spring and rear crossmember. Some '32 Ford chassis were equipped with rear coil springs, and others used quarter-elliptic springs. Some rodders equipped the '32 chassis with dual parallel leaf springs, but the springs were too short to work correctly. Most rodders chose to keep the original rear spring, because it could be made to offer an acceptable ride, and in doing so they would have to modify the differential accordingly.

The dual-parallel leaf spring had merit on 1933-and-newer chassis, and since Ford differentials became a staple in most hot rods, the differentials could be equipped with parallel leaf springs. Rodders found out that it was easy to adapt the differentials to the early Ford chassis by using parts found in wrecking yards. The only change necessary was moving the spring pads on the axle to the correct width for the car, and that depended on where the mounts would be positioned.

Wrecking-yard springs were used in many cases, but rodders who wanted a superior ride quality visited their local spring shop and had

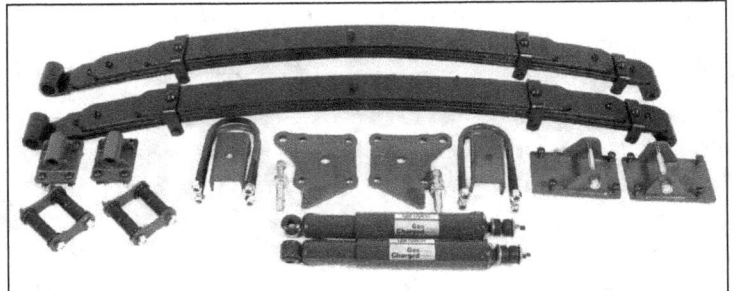

Total Cost Involved Engineering offers a parallel-leaf-spring kit for Chevrolet and Ford street rods. The kit features 2-inch-lower leaf springs, a shock kit, mounting brackets, weld-on axle brackets, hardware, and instructions. This particular kit fits a 1937–1939 Chevy.

springs made for the weight of the rear of the car. In the process, they also had the centering pin located in the correct position. The dual-parallel leaf spring doesn't require traction bars, unless the car is going to be used for drag racing, so the installation was very easy to accomplish. In the old days, the rodders had to use wrecking-yard or custom-made parts to make the swaps, but today there is a variety of companies that sell everything you need in kit form.

Installing a Posies Rear Spring Kit in a 1933–1934 Ford Chassis

In 1933, Ford made some big strides forward in automotive styling and engineering. It was Ford's first body that was factory channeled over the frame, giving the 1933 model a long, low profile. In order to accomplish this, the frame design was changed drastically from the Model A and '32 designs. It was built with a strong center crossmember and an arch in the rear to clear the rear-axle housing. In stock form, the rear end was suspended by a single transverse leaf spring, which worked well for the time, but it also promoted some sway when the car was going around corners.

Our 1933 project roadster frame required some updating. The old suspension was removed, and a new one was required to give the roadster a smoother and more stable ride. There were several ways to accomplish that, but the rod shop building the frame decided to install a Posies dual-parallel-leaf-spring kit. The shop has installed several of the kits in other cars and found that they offer a smooth ride combined and good handling. The best part is that the kit is reasonably priced.

The kit comes with all of the parts required to accomplish the installation, but the rod shop decided to make a few improvements to the frame before installing it. The shop boxed the rear frame section to improve the strength of the chassis. Then, it created a C-notch in the frame for more axle clearance. Both of the improvements make this frame better and allow the axle to sit at the lowest level of the adjustable spring brackets.

This installation can be done by a seasoned street rodder, but if you are a novice, it might be more than you can handle. The tools required to perform this installation include a plasma cutter, a MIG welder, a large hand grinder, a small angle sander, and normal hand tools. In this project, the tubing used to make the C-notch was cut with a large power metal saw.

Posies Leaf Spring Kit Installation

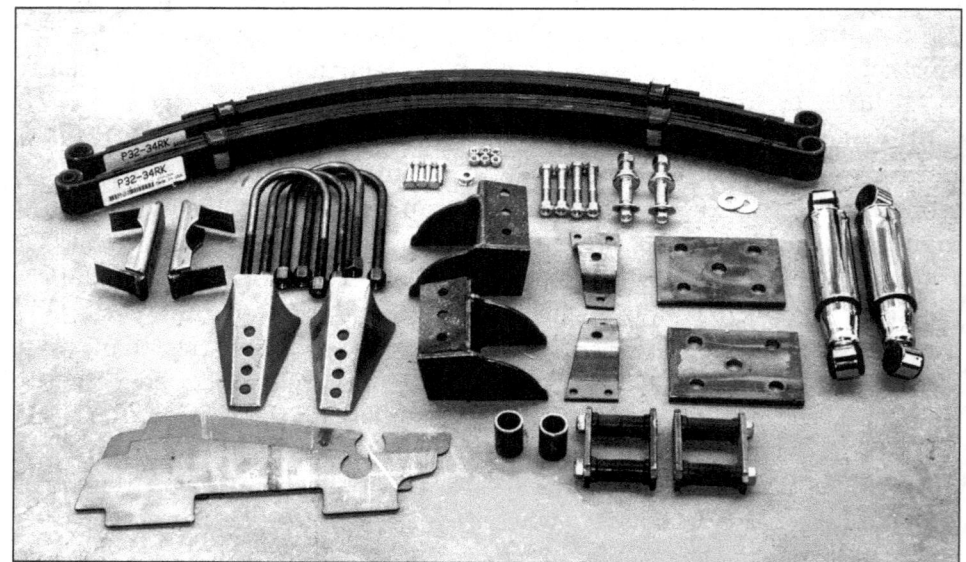

1 *The Posies dual-parallel-leaf-spring installation kit comes with two springs calibrated for the weight of a 1933–1934 Ford roadster. It also comes with two front frame brackets, two rear frame brackets with bungs, two shackles, four U-bolts, two spring plates, two axle brackets, two shock brackets, and a pair of shock absorbers. All of the hardware needed to finish the installation is also included.*

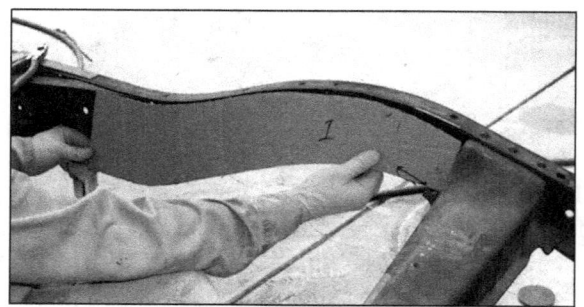

2 *Using the frame as a guide, a cardboard template is cut to fit the rear rails. There may be a slight difference from side to side, so if there is a problem, you can make two templates.*

SOLID REAR AXLE SUSPENSIONS

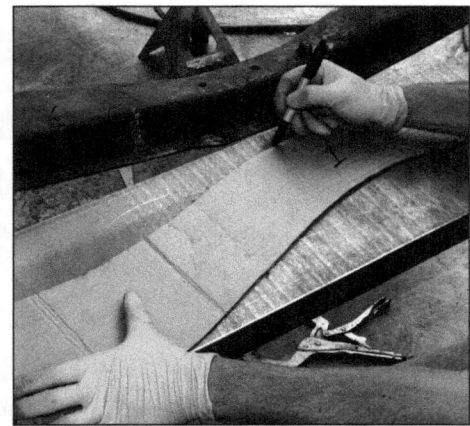

3 Following the template, the outline is drawn on a piece of 3/16-inch sheet steel.

4 Following the outline that was just made, the frame boxing plate is cut out of the sheet steel with a plasma cutter.

5 The boxing plate is placed in the vise, and the edge is sanded smooth with a large body grinder.

6 The frame section in front of the rear crossmember is sanded to bare metal with a large body grinder. This is necessary to promote the welding step.

7 Using a body grinder, the coating on the sheet steel is sanded to bare metal. This makes the welding easier.

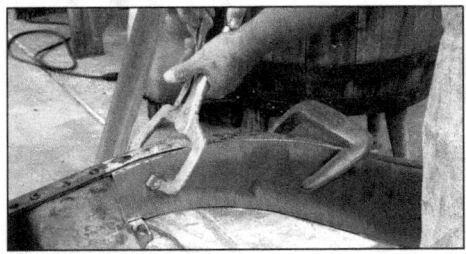

8 The boxing plate is carefully positioned on the frame, and it is held there with two clamps. If some trimming is necessary, this is the time to do it. In this example, the boxing plate is perfect.

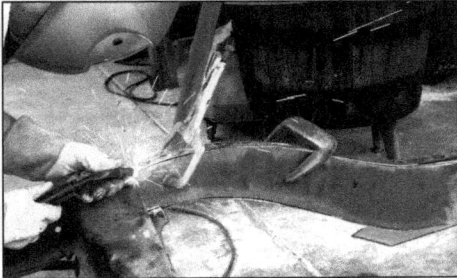

9 The boxing plate that is held tightly to the frame with clamps is tack welded to the frame. Several tacks are made to hold it securely in place.

10 The boxing plate after it is tack welded to the frame. At this point, the spring brackets can be welded on.

CHAPTER 4

11 Using the axle center line as a guide, marks are made 15½ inches forward on both sides of the frame. The spring holes in the bracket must line up with that measurement. After the bracket is aligned, it is tack welded in place.

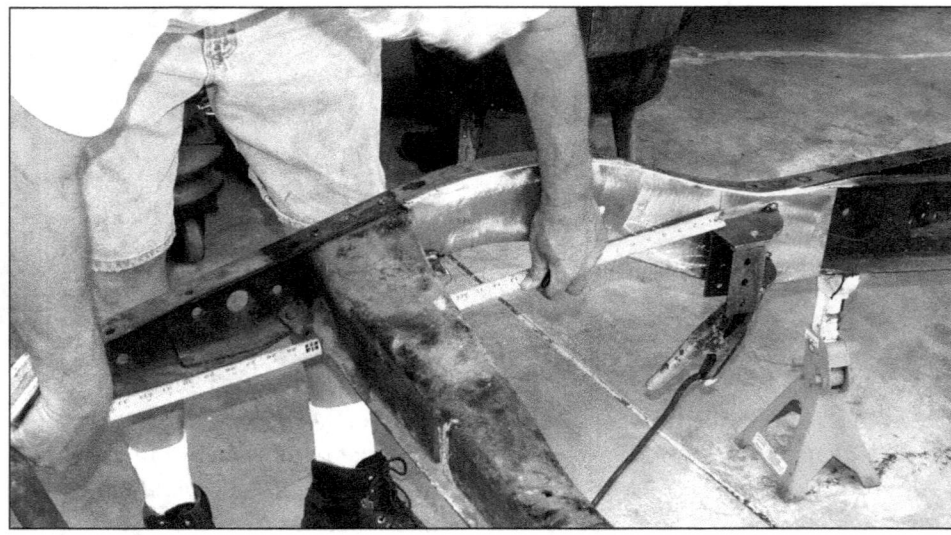

12 The rear-spring hanger must be located 34½ inches back from the front-spring bracket holes.

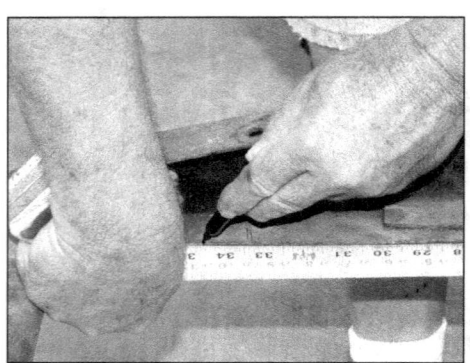

13 The frame is marked at 34½ inches. The bung is centered with this mark.

14 The bung is held in place while the circumference is marked for drilling. This bung must be welded in place at a slight angle to match the angle of the spring.

15 The hole is drilled slightly larger than the bung size with a hole saw. This is done to allow flexibility while lining up the bung at the correct angle before it is welded in place.

16 A rear boxing plate must be welded in place before the bung is welded to the frame. Here, the plate is placed in the frame to see how it fits.

SOLID REAR AXLE SUSPENSIONS

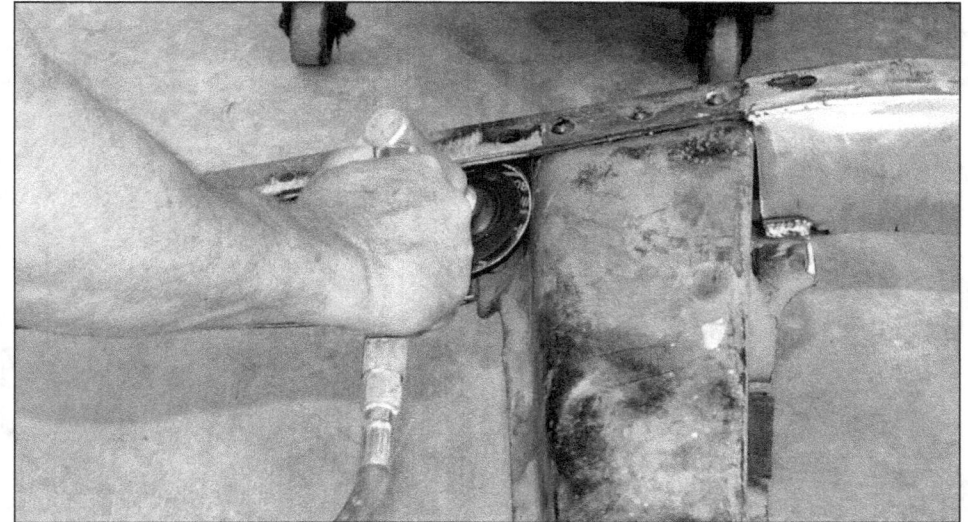

17 The perimeter of the frame is sanded to bare metal to promote welding. Some sanding is also required where the bracket meets the rear crossmember.

18 The bracket is placed back in the frame, lined up, and tack welded to the frame.

19 The bung is also tack welded to the frame to keep it secure while the spring angle is checked.

20 The bung is also tack welded to the outside of the frame.

21 The spring is connected to the frame bracket to check the fit of the spring and bracket. Notice that at this point the bracket is only tack welded to the frame so that changes can be made, if necessary.

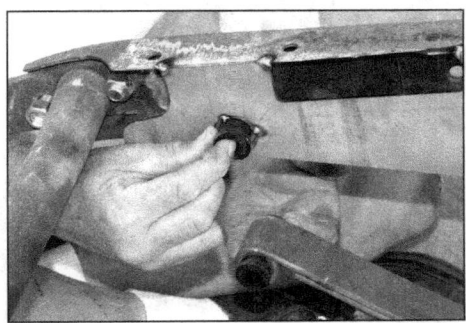

22 The urethane bushings are installed in the frame bung and spring prior to the installation of the spring perch.

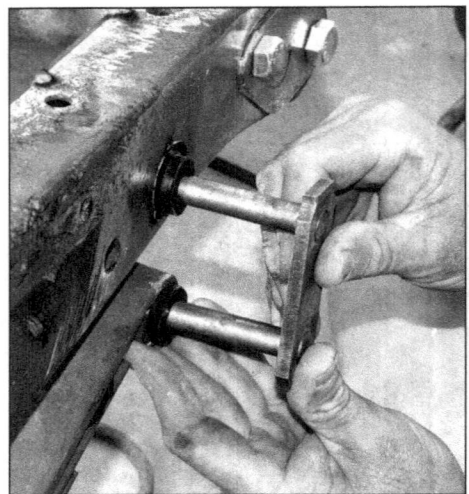

23 The spring perch bolts are coated with lubricant before it is installed in the spring and frame bracket.

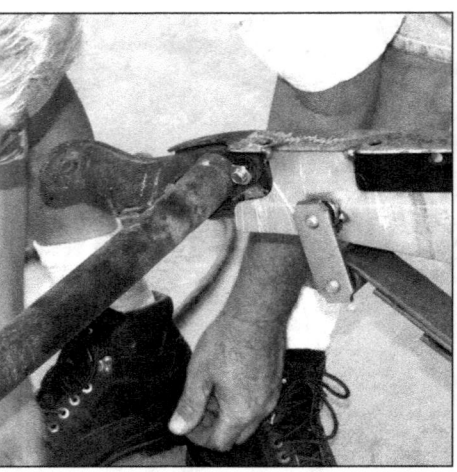

24 The angle of the bung is correct, and the other side of the shackle fits right on. It is easy to see that the springs will work perfectly without any binding.

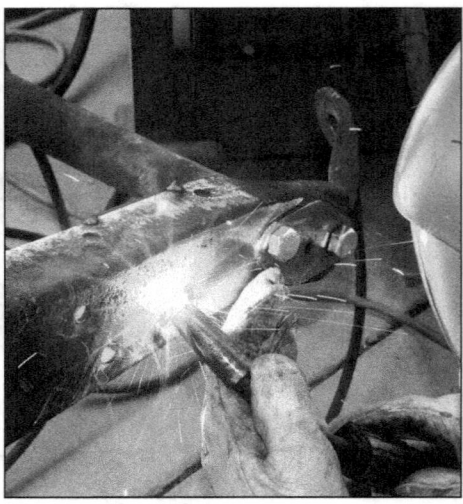

25 The spring is disconnected, and the urethane bushings are removed, then the bung is finish welded to the frame.

26 The boxing plate is also finish welded to the frame. If the lower section doesn't line up as well as at the top, it must be hammered at the bottom to butt against the frame rail.

27 After the welding is complete, the frame-to-boxing-plate connections are sanded smooth. The bung welds are also sanded smooth for a nice appearance and proper bushing fit.

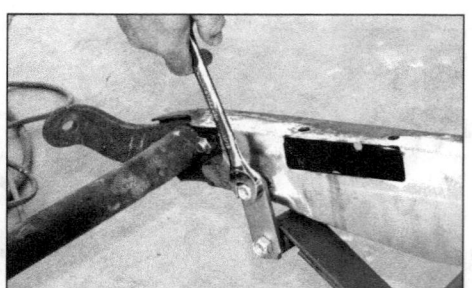

28 The springs are attached again to make sure they line up properly. If they work fine, remove them again so that the front brackets can be finish welded to the frame.

SOLID REAR AXLE SUSPENSIONS

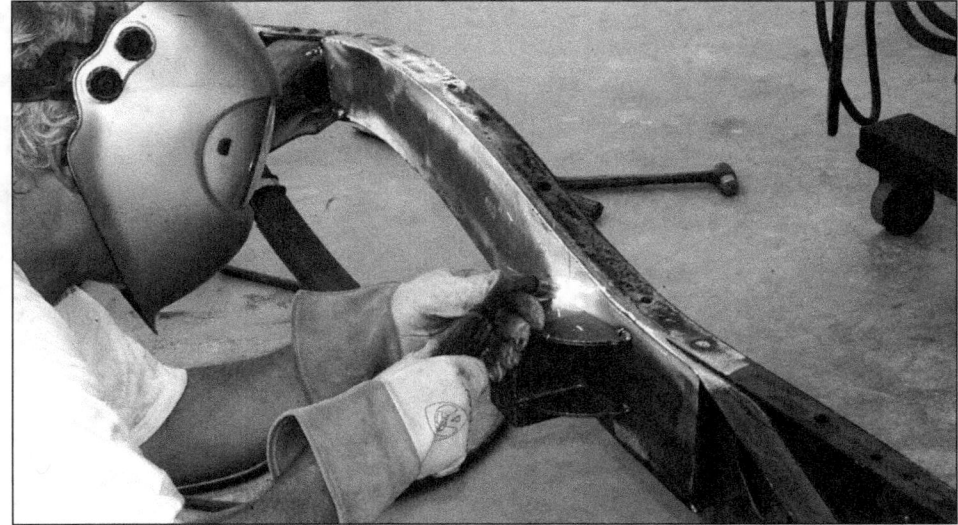

29 The front brackets are finish welded to the frame on the sides and on the inside.

30 The bracket after it is welded to the frame. It will work great, and it looks nice.

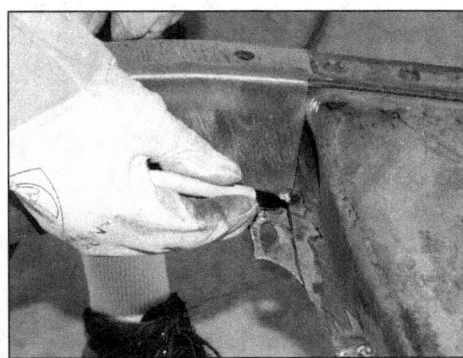

31 This small section of the rear crossmember must be removed. The section is marked for cutting.

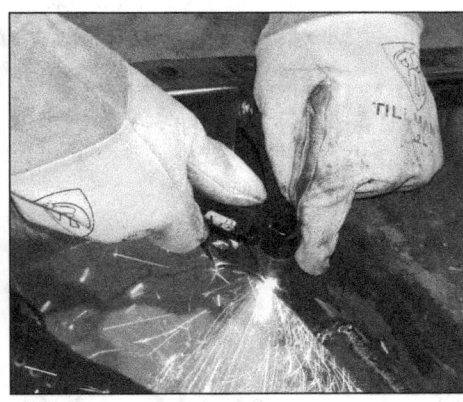

32 Using a plasma cutter, cut the small section of the crossmember.

33 A 4½-inch piece of tube steel is cut with a power cutter to 2 inches wide. This is used to form the C-notch in the frame.

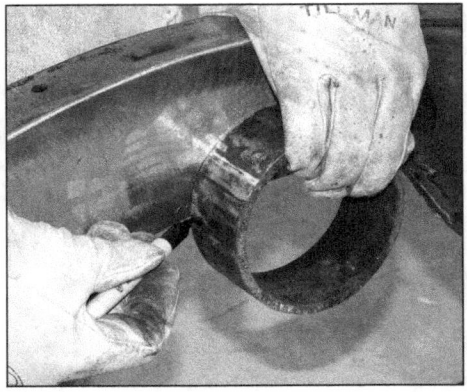

34 The tube is placed against the frame using the rear-axle center line as a guide. It is marked accordingly for cutting.

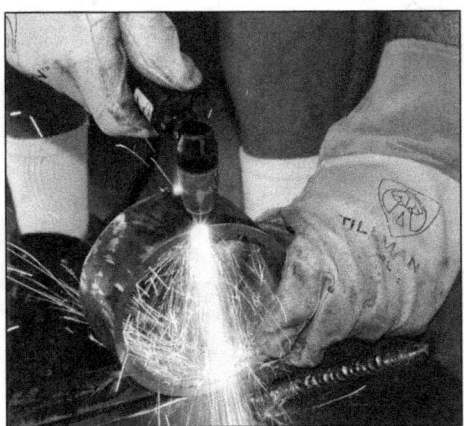

35 The tube is cut in half, and the two halves are used as the C-notches on each side of the frame.

36 Using a T-square, the position of the C-notch on the inside of the frame is marked on the outside.

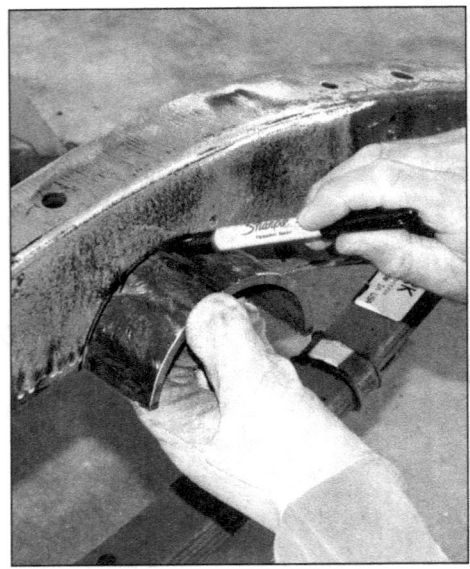

37 Using the marks as a guide, the diameter of the tube half is drawn on the frame for cutting.

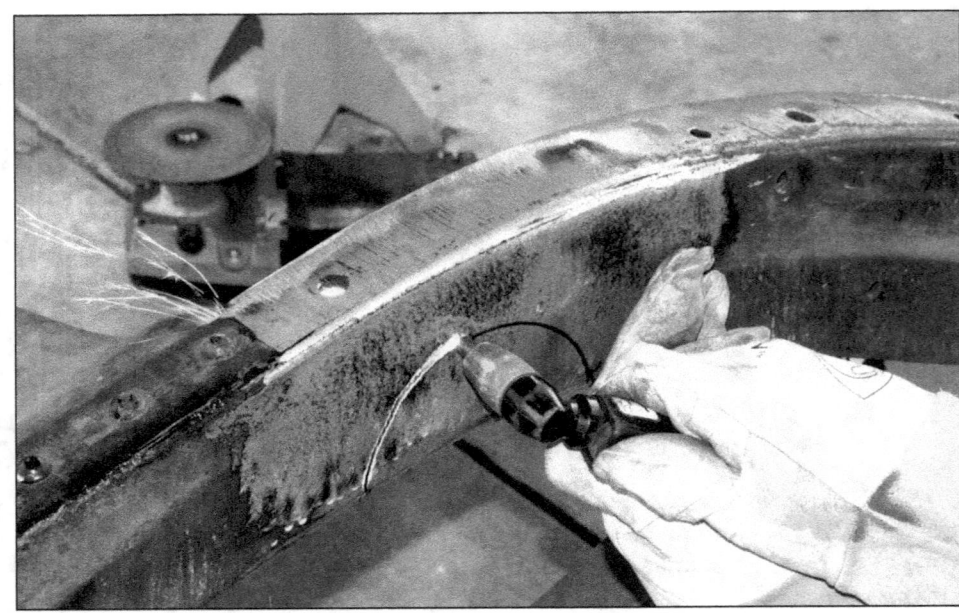

38 Following the lines just drawn, the frame is cut with the plasma cutter. It is also cut along the bottom, so the section of the frame can be removed.

39 This section of the frame is double walled; after the first section is removed, the inside remains.

40 Remove the inside frame section. Using the cut line as a guide, the frame is cut.

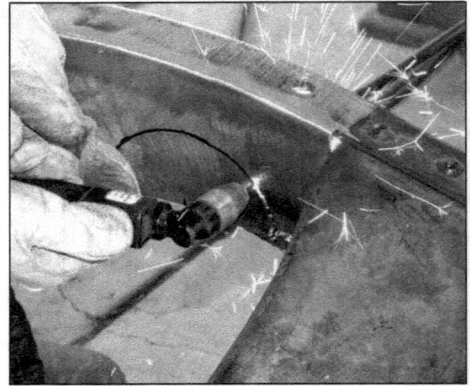

41 The inside section of the frame is cut by following the drawn line. It is also cut along the bottom to remove the frame section.

SOLID REAR AXLE SUSPENSIONS

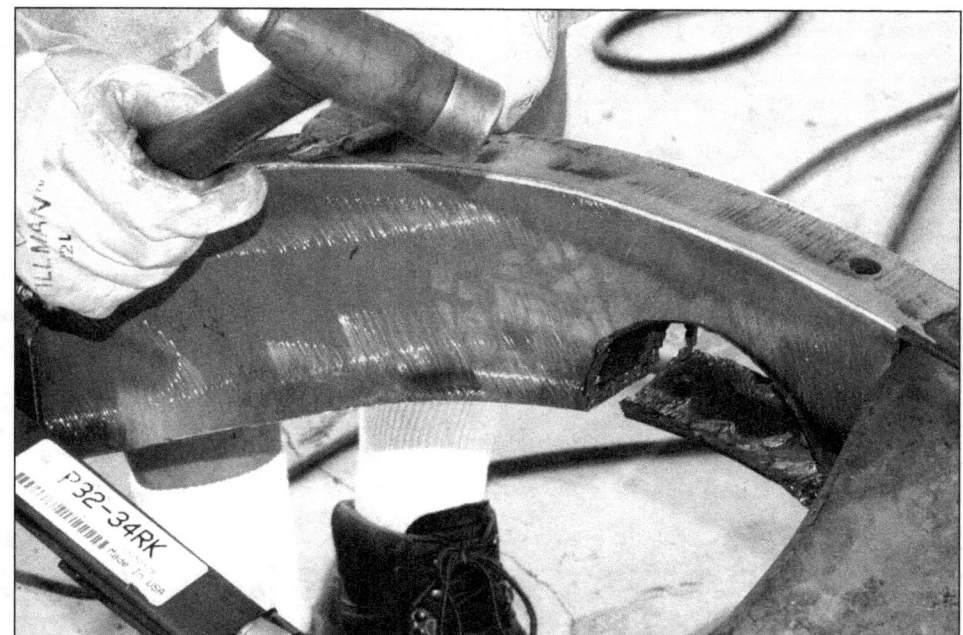

42 *A small chunk of the double frame remains at the bottom of the frame. Both sides are cut with the plasma cutter, and then it is removed with the hammer.*

43 *After the section is cut, the perimeter is sanded smooth with a small 3-inch angle sander.*

44 *The plasma-cut edges of the C-notch tube are also cleaned with a 3-inch angle sander.*

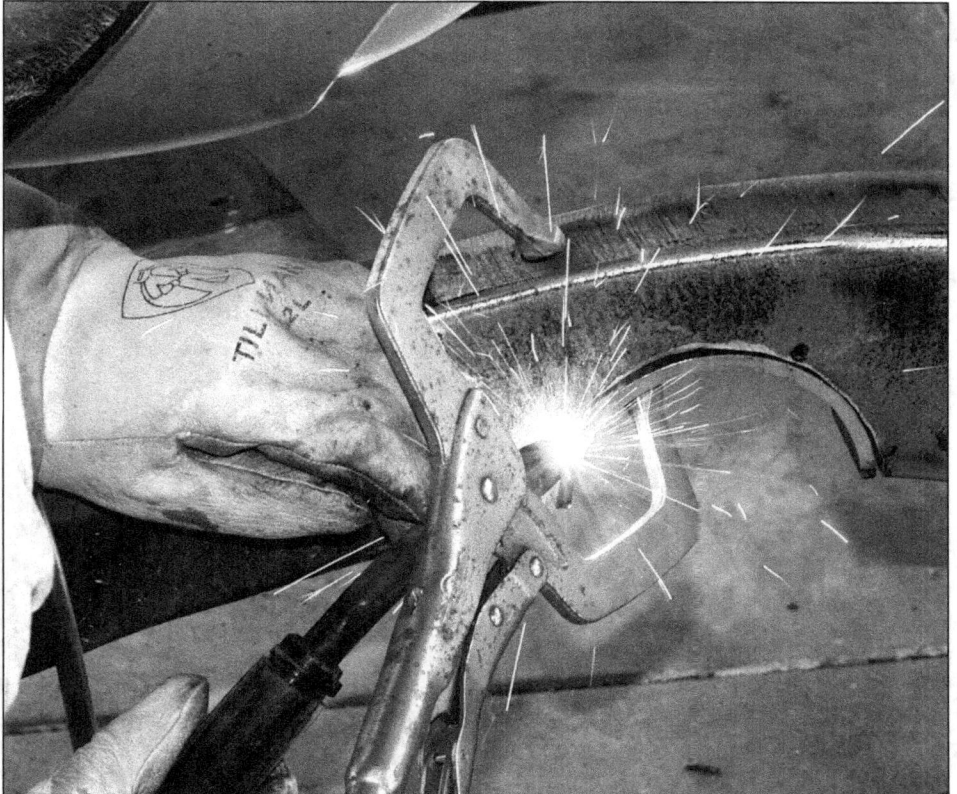

45 *The tube section is trial fit into the C-notch holes. Since both sides of the frame are cut separately, some trimming may be necessary to get the tube to fit perfectly.*

46 *The tube section is connected to the frame to keep it secure, and then it is finish welded to the frame. The thick metal tube is used to make sure the structural integrity of the frame is maintained at the point of C-notching.*

THE COMPLETE BUILDER'S GUIDE TO HOT ROD CHASSIS AND SUSPENSION

47 Both sides are welded securely to the frame, and then the section is sanded smooth.

48 After the sanding is completed, the C-notch looks like the frame was made that way.

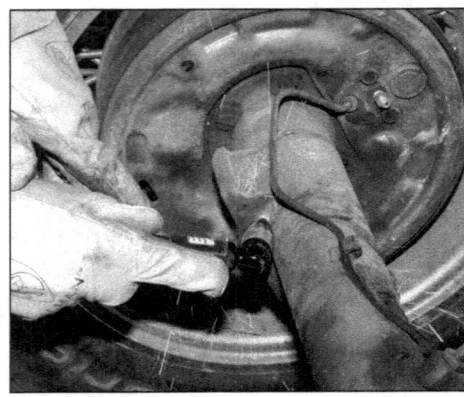

49 The stock frame pads on the 8-inch Ford rear end are in the wrong place, so they must be removed. This is done with a plasma cutter.

50 After the spring pads are removed, the residue is sanded off with a large hand grinder.

51 Since the new spring pads are located inboard of the old ones, the axle must be sanded in preparation of installing the new spring pads.

52 The springs are connected to the brackets at the front, and then the axle is rolled under the car and positioned in the approximate position where it is to be mounted.

SOLID REAR AXLE SUSPENSIONS

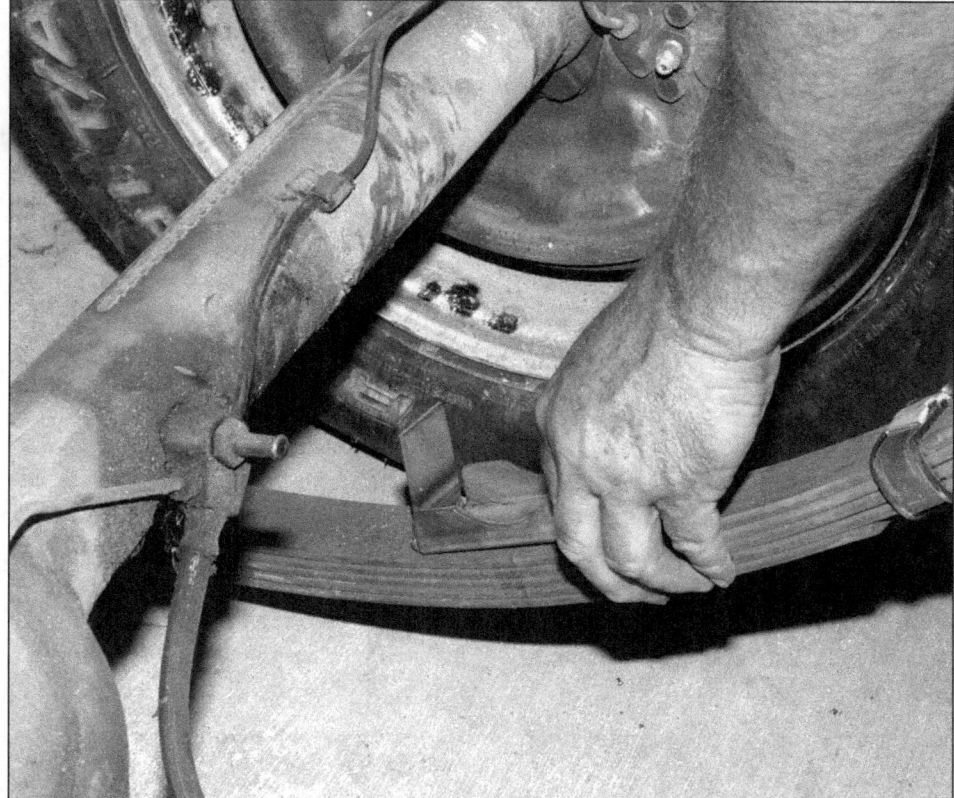

53 The new spring pads are located over the centering bolt in the spring.

54 The shackles are installed so that the springs are at the correct ride height.

55 The axle is placed on the spring pad that is located with the centering bolt. Notice that the area where the new spring pad is to be mounted is sanded to bare metal.

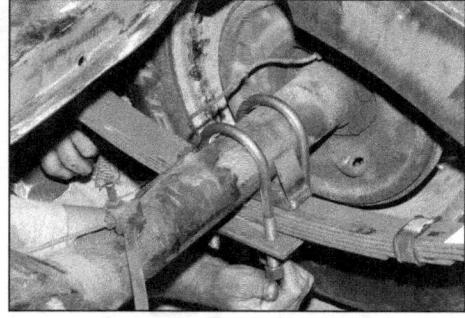

56 The U-bolts and spring plate are connected to the axle. The bolts must be finger tight so that the axle can be moved from side to side and up and down to make the proper adjustments.

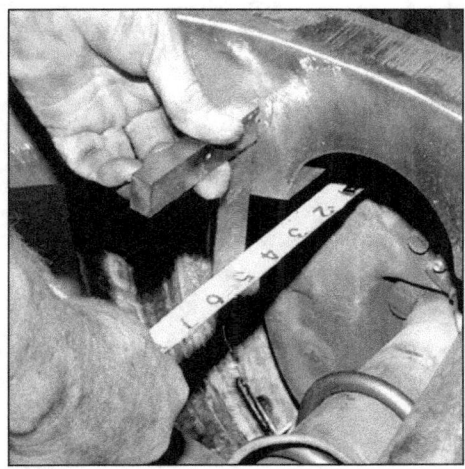

57 The axle housing must be moved from side to side until it is centered in the frame. Measurements must be taken accordingly.

CHAPTER 4

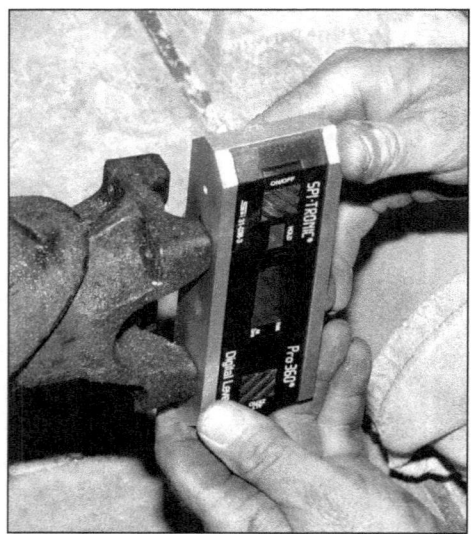

58 The axle pinion angle is set with a digital angle finder. After the axle is centered and the pinion is set, the U-bolts are tightened to keep the axle in place.

59 After the axle is tight in the frame, the axle pad is welded to the axle housing. This pad is tack welded first, and then it is removed and finish welded later.

60 This kit comes with adjustable spring brackets, so the kit is designed with adjustable shock brackets. The bracket is held up to the frame to check the fit. The axle is sanded to bare metal in the area where the bracket is to be connected.

61 The bracket is held in place, and then it is tack welded to the axle housing.

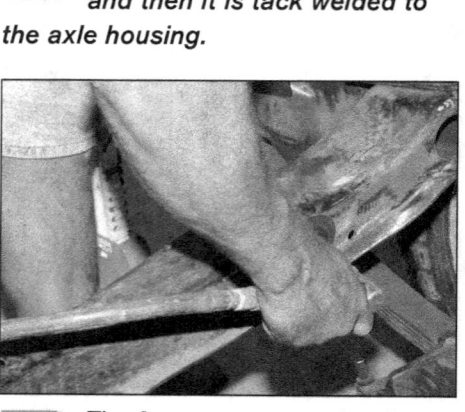

62 The frame crossmember is sanded to prepare it for the installation of the upper spring brackets.

63 The upper spring bracket can be bolted or welded on. In this example, it is welded to the frame. According to the instructions, it can be mounted 9 to 10 inches from the side of the frame. This installer split the difference at 9½ inches from the frame.

SOLID REAR AXLE SUSPENSIONS

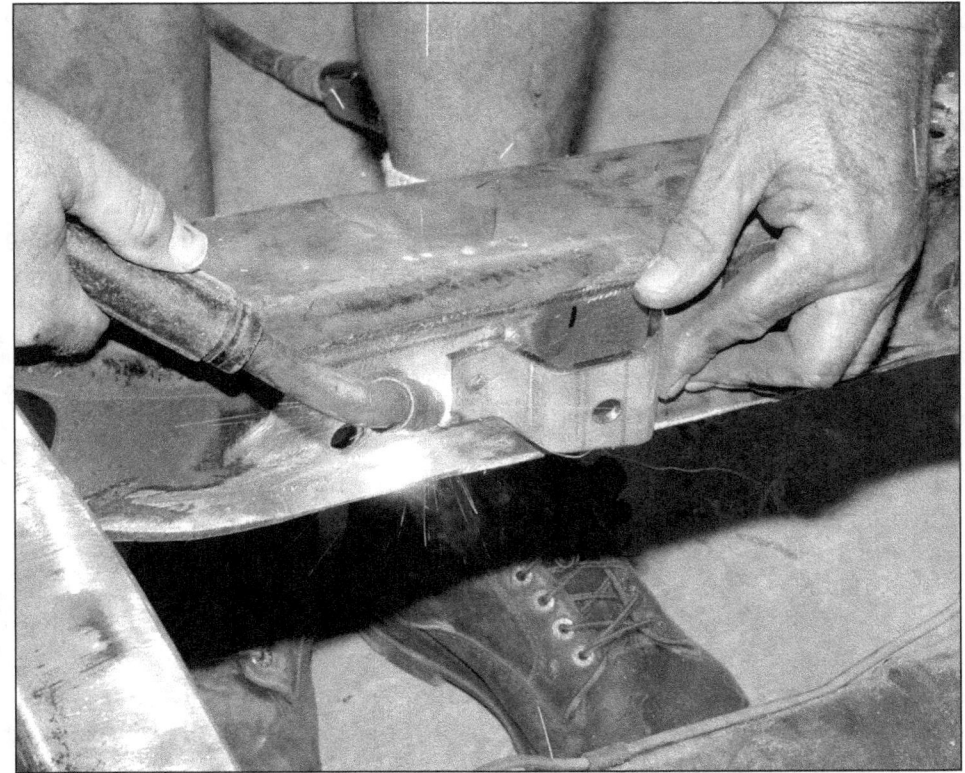

64 *The bolt hole is aligned with the mark, and then the bracket is tack welded to the frame.*

65 *The shock absorber is mounted to the axle housing and to the crossmember. This is done to check the clearance and make sure there is no interference.*

66 *The shock is tightened at the top and bottom. The brackets are finish welded to the chassis and axle housing.*

67 *The springs are installed and ready for detailing. This system works great and provides a nice ride and excellent handling. The installation takes about two days.*

CHAPTER 4

The high-tech chassis isn't a cheap date, with its fully chrome-plated Jaguar rear suspension and the polished stainless-steel Total Cost Involved Engineering front suspension. This system works great, but it may well be out of reach for some street rodders.

Going back to the 1960s, the Jaguar rear suspensions gave hot rod builder Kurt Hamilton an idea. He was installing Jag rear ends into T-buckets and Model A Fords and was outfitting the differentials with the factory coil-over shocks. He also knew that Koni was making an improved adjustable shock for the racing Jaguars, so he wondered how the shock would work when it was adapted to a Ford 8- or 9-inch differential. He contacted Koni and had them make a coil-over shock to his specifications, and then he designed a Ford 9-inch system that used the shocks for suspension, a four-link arrangement to keep the differential in place, and a Panhard bar that kept the differential from moving from side to side. After the street rod was finished, he found out that the system worked well. The system didn't give as smooth of a ride as a Jaguar rear suspension, but it was quite acceptable; importantly, though, it was more affordable for the average hot rodder. After doing the first installation, he did more coil-over installations into street rods, and he was selling the coil-over shocks to a variety of other hot-rod builders.

It didn't take long for other builders to use his basic idea, and before long, several companies began offering kits for coil-over shock installations. The kits are straightforward, but they require a skilled chassis builder with the correct equipment to accurately complete the installation.

The system is the most common rear-suspension system found on street rods, because it offers a comfortable ride, and it looks nice.

The four-link suspension systems can be done in two basic ways. Most kits use the system that features four bars connected between the axle housing and a specific area of the frame so that no forward motion or axle twisting can happen. The side-to-side movement is controlled by a bar that connects to a bracket on the center section and to an area on the side of the frame. This is called a Panhard bar, and it keeps the movement in check and centers the differential. All of the bars are made out of heavy-duty chrome-moly tubing for strength.

There is another four-bar design—a triangulated four-link—that is based on a GM chassis design, and it is also used on race-car applications. Because the four links are triangulated, the system doesn't require a Panhard bar. Two heavy-duty bars run from the bottom of the axle housing to a point on the frame, and two other bars run at an angle from the axle housing to the frame; those bars not only keep the axle from twisting, they also center the axle in the frame and keep it in place. This system works great, and the difficulty of installation is about the same as the regular four-link system.

Installing a Heidts Triangulated Four-Link Suspension System

In the process of planning and designing a street rod, the components have to work together as a cohesive package. If you are using a 283-ci Chevy engine for power, the chassis components don't necessarily have to be as strong as the ones required for a 454-ci engine. You can use the same parts, but that might be overkill, and a more expensive way to build the car.

In the process of building our 1934 Ford project roadster, strength was important, because the engine is a 502-hp 502-ci Chevy engine backed by a 6-speed manual transmission. The immense torque and power produced by the engine meant the stock 1934 Ford frame had to be fortified to handle the power of the big-block. It was also important to have a strong rear-suspension system to transfer the power to the pavement, so a Ford 9-inch differential is used, and it has been upgraded with strong Strange axles. The builder wanted a rear-end setup that could handle the torque, so a Heidts triangulated four-link system with coil-over shocks was used. This is a similar design to what many drag cars use, and it works great in this application.

The differential is equipped with a Strange limited-slip unit, so with the triangulated four-link system, the hot rod should be able to go straight when the pedal hits the metal. A nice feature about the Heidts system is the quality of construction and the ease of installation. The most difficult part of the installation was narrowing the differential, and that required a good deal of knowledge and a special fixture to keep the differential straight when it was welded back together.

This particular installation required several special tools, so it may be something that should be done by a full-service rod shop. In this case, the shop needed a chop saw, a metal lathe, a large hand grinder, a MIG welder, a plasma cutter, and normal hand tools.

SOLID REAR AXLE SUSPENSIONS

Heidts Triangulated Four-Link

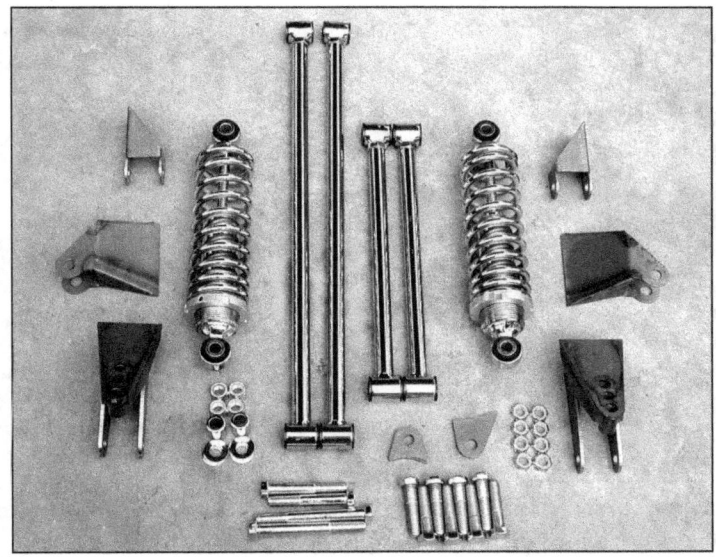

1 This 1934 Ford chassis is going to be upgraded with a Heidts triangulated four-link suspension system. The parts in the kit include the four bars, brackets, coil-over shocks, and all of the hardware required to complete the installation.

2 The stock 1934 chassis before installation. In stock form, with an 855-hp flathead engine, this chassis is strong enough, but with 502 hp, some strengthening is required.

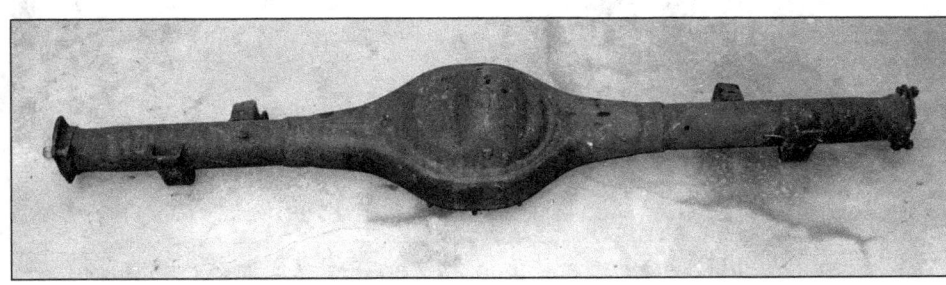

3 Before the four-link setup is installed, the Ford 9-inch differential must be narrowed to fit under the stock 1934 Ford fenders.

4 The Goodyear tires and American Racing rims are placed under the fenders, allowing about 1 inch of clearance on each side. After the tires are mounted correctly, the mounting flange-to-flange distance is measured.

THE COMPLETE BUILDER'S GUIDE TO HOT ROD CHASSIS AND SUSPENSION 97

CHAPTER 4

5 The Wilwood disc-brake offset also is measured, so that the rear end can be narrowed and work with the rear-disc-brake system.

6 After all of the measurements are made, the axle tubes are cut with a chop saw at the area where they were originally joined.

7 The axle tube is cut, and then the end of the tube is turned down, so it slides into the housing. The housing is cleaned of metal shavings and debris.

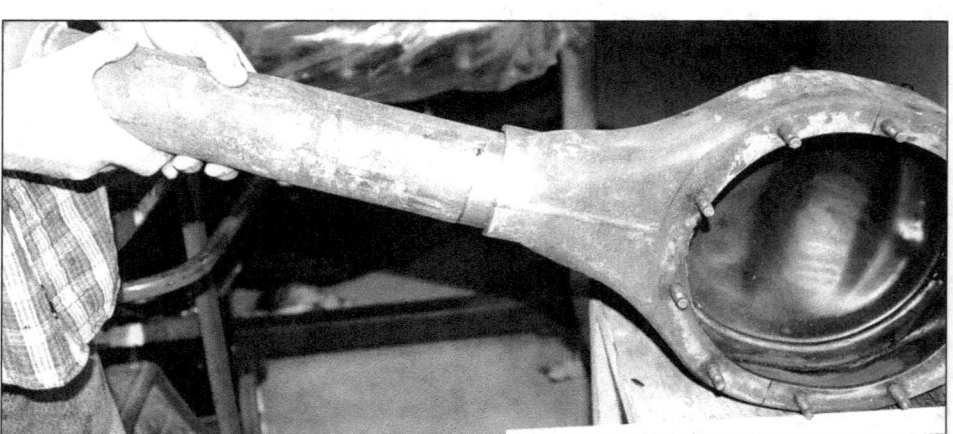

8 Both axle tubes are cut, and then they are installed into the housing. The tubes must be installed so that the flange on each end is parallel and sitting in the correct location.

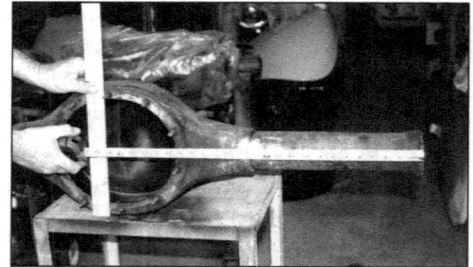

9 Using the housing center bolt as a guide, the axles are measured accordingly. Since Ford uses an offset pinion, one axle tube is shorter than the other one.

10 The tube on the other side is measured to make sure it is spaced correctly. After both tubes are measured, the entire rear axle is measured from side to side.

98 THE COMPLETE BUILDER'S GUIDE TO HOT ROD CHASSIS AND SUSPENSION

SOLID REAR AXLE SUSPENSIONS

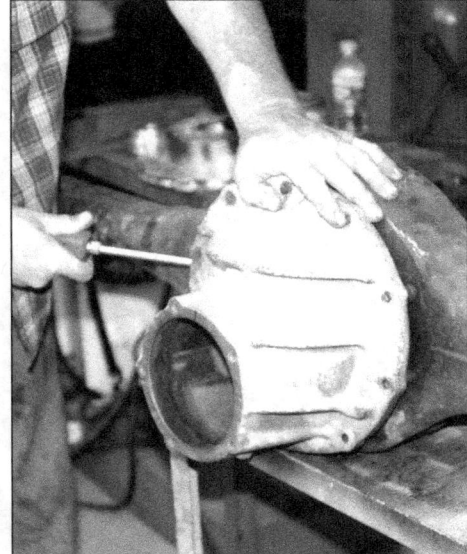

11 The center section is connected to the housing in preparation for the installation of a fixture that holds the axle straight when the welding is done.

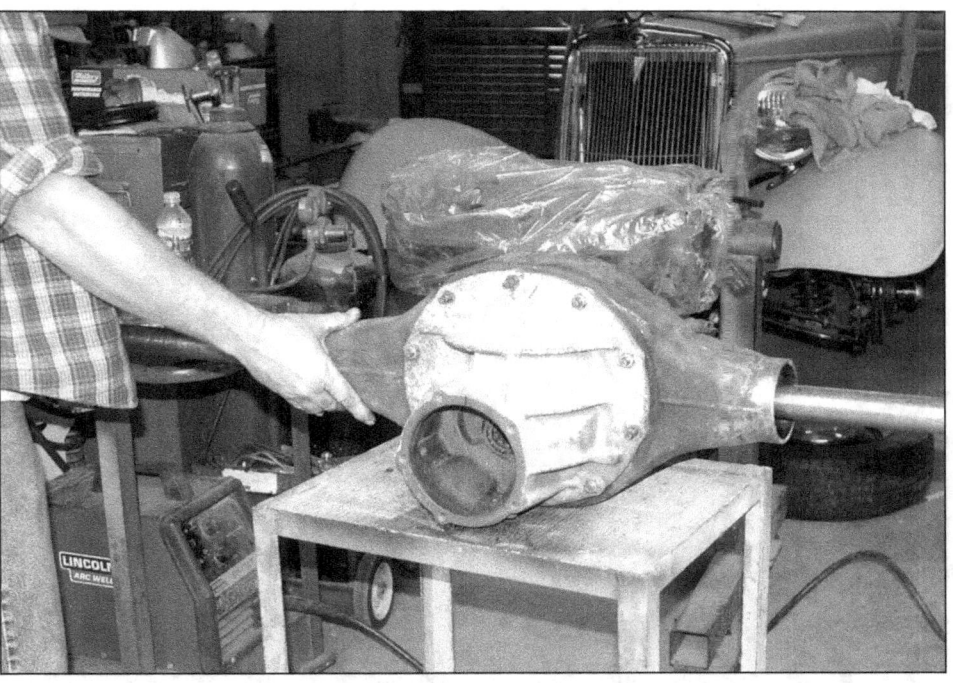

12 The fixture is a long straight piece of round stock with machined aluminum parts that take the place of the bearings.

13 This fixture has aluminum fittings that fit into the bearing holes to hold the axle perfectly in line. One of the aluminum fittings is being installed into the bearing flange of the tube.

14 After the fixture is installed in the housing, the tubes are welded to the housing. There is a great deal of heat produced during the welding process, so without the fixture, the housing and tubes can warp from the heat.

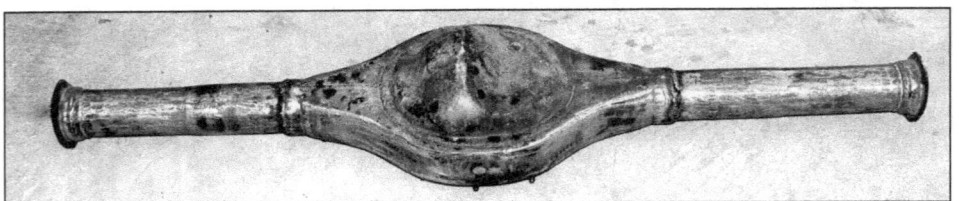

15 The axle housing after the welding is completed. After the housing was finished, the strong Strange Engineering axles and limited-slip unit were ordered from Art Morrison Enterprises.

16 After the axle housing is finished, the four-link installation begins. The rear of the frame is sanded to bare metal in preparation for boxing the chassis.

17 First, a cardboard template for the chassis boxing plate is made.

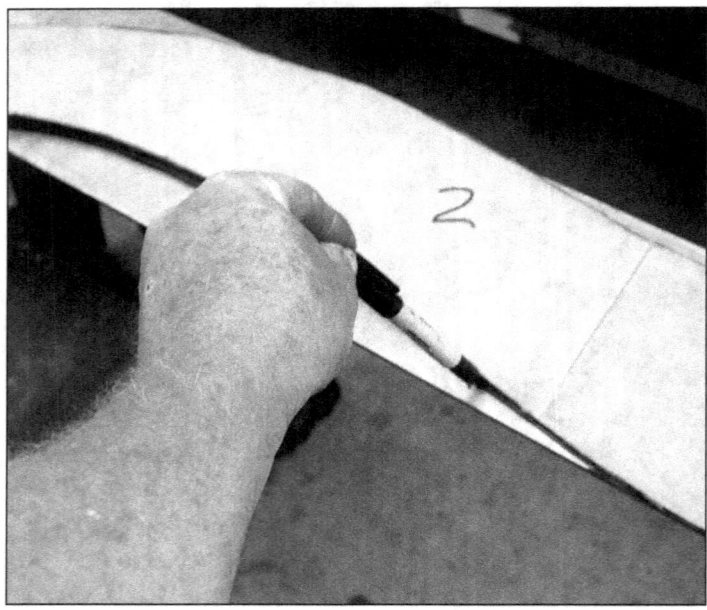

18 After the template is made, the pattern is transferred onto a section of 3/16-inch plate steel. The same pattern is used for both sides of the frame.

19 After the pattern is marked on the plate steel, it is cut to size using a plasma cutter. After the cuts are made, the section is sanded smooth with a 5-inch air sander.

SOLID REAR AXLE SUSPENSIONS

20 A new crossmember is used in this installation, so the existing one is cut off at the point where it is marked. This allows the boxing plate to be longer than it would have been had the crossmember remained installed.

21 The crossmember is cut by using an oxy-acetylene cutting torch. Cutting it can also be done with a plasma cutter or a 3-inch cut-off wheel.

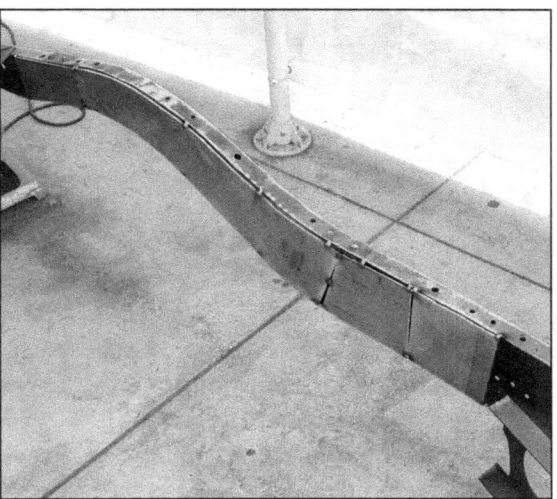

22 The frame after the boxing sections are tack welded. This long boxed section adds plenty of strength to the rear of the frame.

23 The axle housing is sandblasted and painted with primer to keep it from rusting. The combination shock mount and four-bar bracket is located on the axle housing.

24 The paint is removed from the axle housing at the position where the brackets will be installed. The side-to-side position of the brackets must be measured.

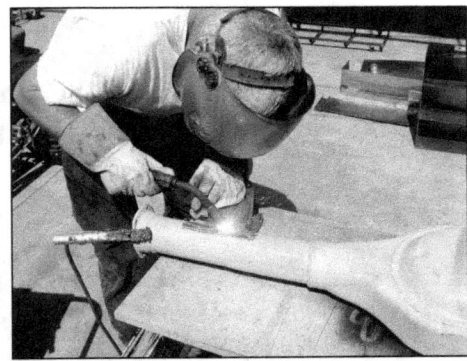

25 The bracket is tack welded to the axle housing. This is done on both sides, and it's important that both brackets are parallel.

THE COMPLETE BUILDER'S GUIDE TO HOT ROD CHASSIS AND SUSPENSION

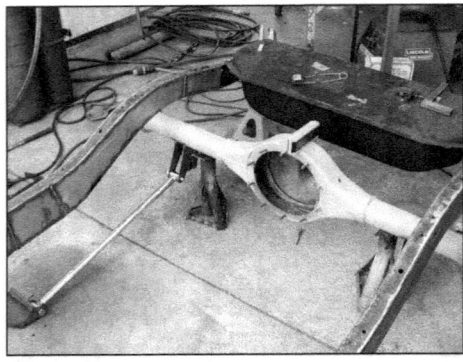

26 The axle housing is placed on jack stands under the frame so that it can be rotated slightly. Here, the pinion angle of the housing is being set.

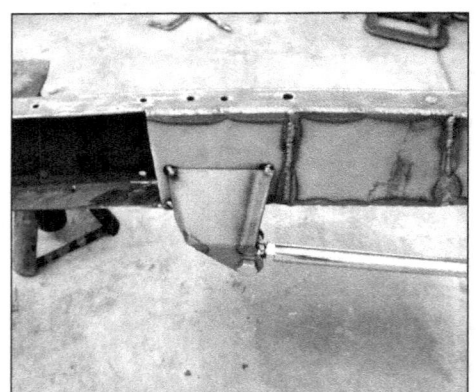

27 After the pinion angle is set, the side brackets are tack welded to the frame.

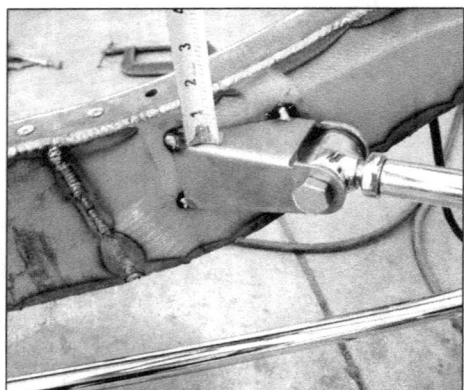

28 Using the measurements in the kit, the triangulation bar brackets are tack welded to the frame. These bars allow the up-and-down differential movement, but they don't allow any side-to-side movement.

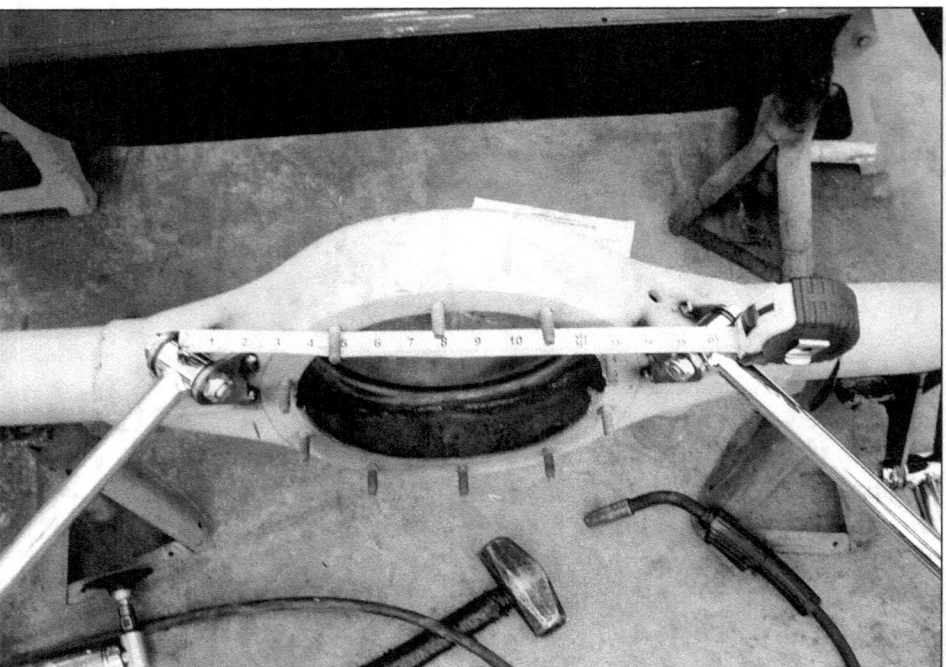

29 After the triangulation bar brackets are tack welded to the frame, the brackets on the other end are aligned with the differential. The brackets are measured to make sure that they are positioned correctly, and then they are tack welded to the housing.

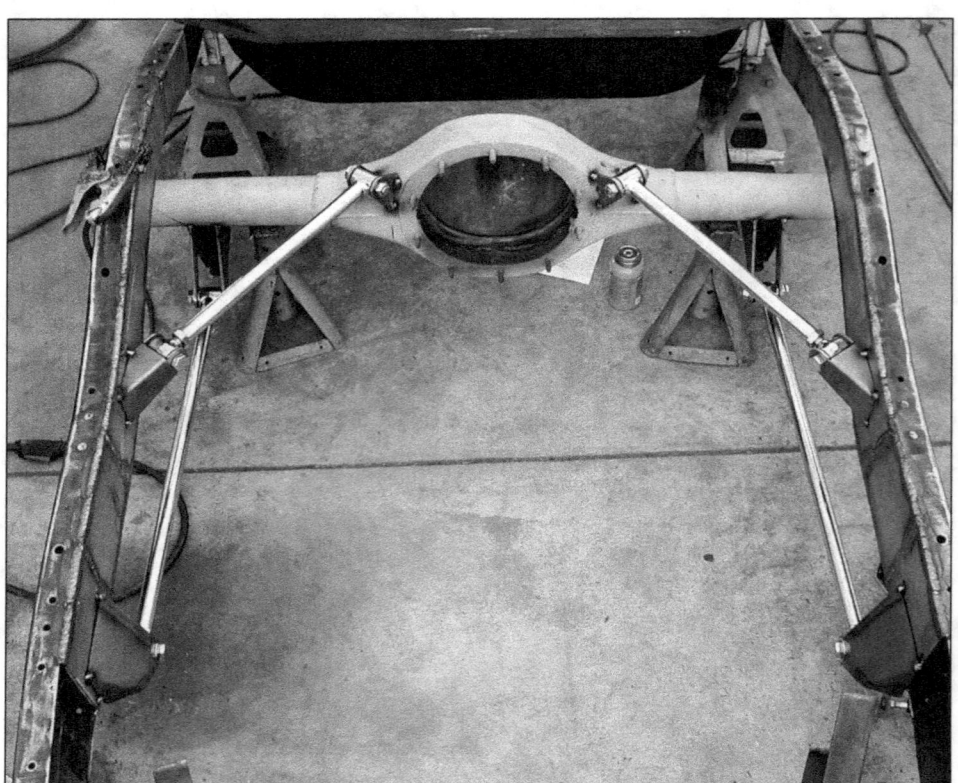

30 The housing with the four-link system installed. This setup works great and looks nice as well.

SOLID REAR AXLE SUSPENSIONS

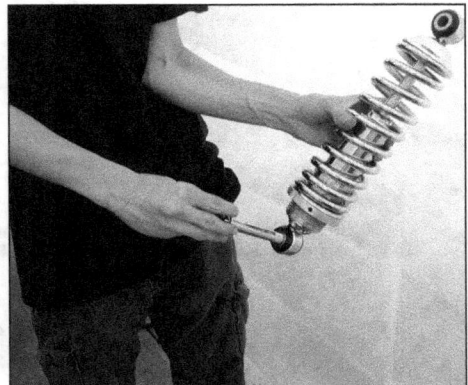

31 This 1934 Ford will be equipped with Heidts chrome-plated adjustable coil-over shocks. Here, the bottom mount bolt is being installed.

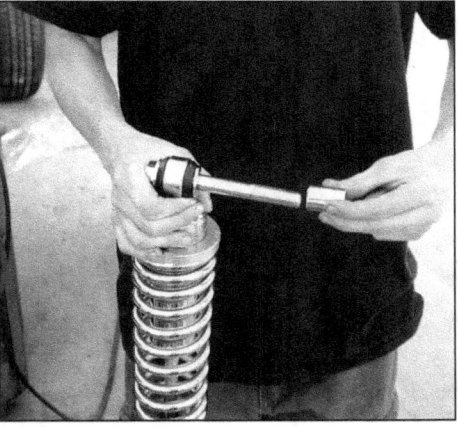

32 The bottom bolt requires a spacer that allows room between the shock and axle housing.

33 The shock is connected to the combination bar and shock bracket.

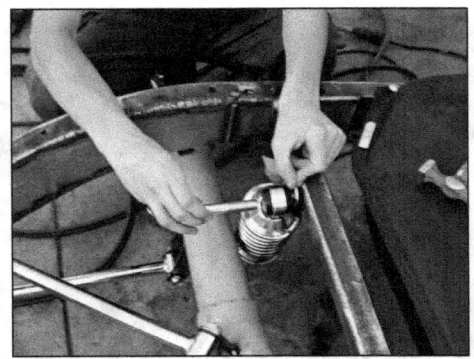

34 The other end of the coil-over shock is connected to the square-tube upper mounting bracket. This bar is not part of the kit, so it must be fabricated.

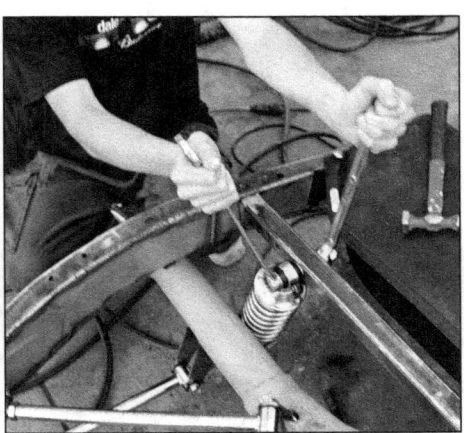

35 This bolt is tightened to secure the shock to the bracket prior to welding the bar to the frame.

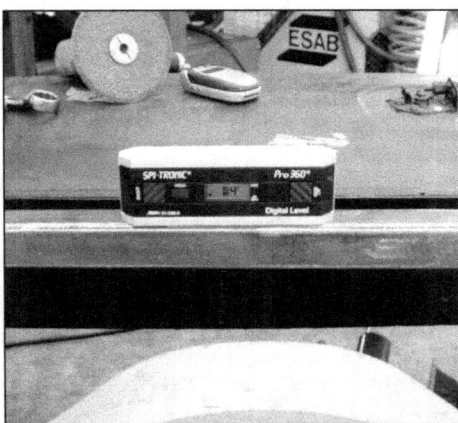

36 The bar must be level in the frame, so check it with an angle finder.

37 After the upper shock bracket is in place and is level in the frame, it is tack-welded in place. After it is in the frame, check the measurements, and then finish weld it in the frame.

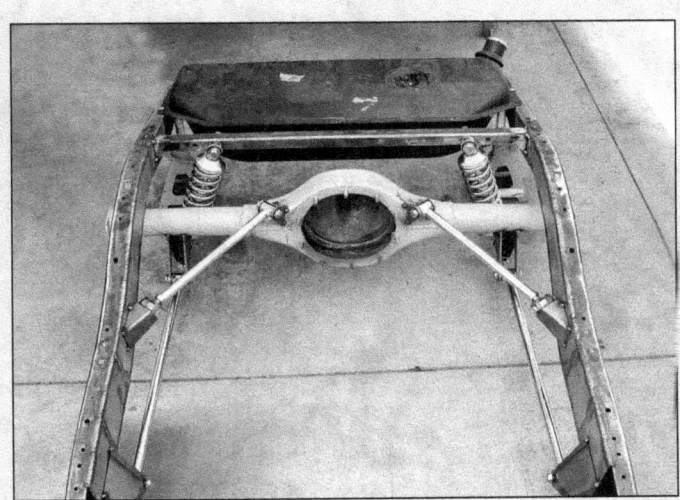

The frame after the four-link-system installation. This is a strong installation that is fully adjustable to keep the roadster going in a straight line under hard acceleration. The Heidts coil-over shocks provide a comfortable ride.

CHAPTER 5

INDEPENDENT REAR SUSPENSIONS

Ford's transversely-sprung solid axles were rather primitive, but effective in stock shape. They typified the era, as all American cars of the time had similar designs, engineered for unimproved roads and to simply survive, more than to offer any kind of comfort. The emergence of paved roads encouraged the evolution of automotive suspension systems, and eventually the independent design was refined and mass produced. The first independent rear suspension truly capable of life under a hot rod was the Jaguar system in 1961. The second was the Corvette system in 1963. Both formed the basis for hot-rod IRS setups, which continue to this day.

Jaguar System

In the 1950s and 1960s, rodders spent plenty of time scrounging through wrecking yards looking for parts for their rod projects. It would

Using many Jaguar design features, Heidt's Hot Rod Parts developed its own independent-rear-suspension system. The custom center section features a Ford 9-inch carrier and gears, custom-made lower control arms, Wilwood inboard disc brakes, and Heidt's coil-over shocks.

be impossible to tell you who discovered the benefits of a Jaguar independent rear suspension in a street rod. The new XKE was introduced in 1961, and it was available as a coupe or roadster. The Jag's monocoque body was very aerodynamic, and the chassis design featured a tubular-front-frame structure that was based on the race cars of the time. The company's engineering for the new sports car was state-of-the-art, so four-wheel-independent suspension was used along with four-wheel disc brakes. The rear suspension featured a caged assembly that could be assembled separately and bolted into the body-and-chassis structure. The front suspension could also be removed easily, and it featured torsion bars instead of leaf or coil springs for a smooth, stable ride.

When the new XKE was released, it became an instant success in England and the United States. The Jaguar independent suspensions were first installed in the 1961 Jags, so finding a number of them in automobile wrecking establishments wasn't likely until years later. Since the rear suspensions came complete in a cage, it could be removed from the Jaguar as a unit, and it was only natural to graft the entire caged suspension into the rear of an early frame. This method worked well, because it used all of the Jaguar's engineered geometry, so the suspension provided a smooth and comfortable ride. The suspension was so nice that the back of the car felt like it was riding on a cloud.

The only problem with the caged suspension system was its appearance. It was easy for rodders to look at the suspension and see the possibilities if it could be removed from the cage and detailed appropriately. The Jaguar suspensions were relatively unknown until Joe Cardoza and Les Urban, two San Francisco Bay area hot rodders, installed one into their 1929 Ford roadster pickups.

The Cardoza story appeared in a 1966 issue of *Rod & Custom* magazine. Cardoza and Urban thought of the idea when they visited a friend in Santa Clara who was working on a Model T. He pulled a Jag differential out of a junkyard to use in his car, and it looked like it would be an easy installation. Right after Cardoza and Urban saw the differential, they felt it'd be a natural fit in their roadster pickups, so they started looking in local junkyards until they found a pair of XKE units.

It was their plan to pull the unit out of the cage, so they came up with an idea of how to do it. Cardoza said the only mistake they made was the way they installed the lower control arm's traction bars. They attached them to the side of the frame, and after driving the car, they soon realized that the arms should be moved inward. The change was made, and the swap was a success. In chrome-plated form, this was the most beautiful suspension that could be installed under any street rod, especially in a Model A Ford, where the entire suspension could be viewed.

After the Jag installation story was featured in the magazine, Cardoza and Urban formed a company (Components Limited of San Jose) that sold Jaguar IRS installation kits, and they also performed a number of installations for other local rodders. The two also looked at the Jaguar front suspension, and both of them installed the torsion-bar units into their own cars and were pleased with the ride and handling. The company was selling installation kits until 1976, when the two men decided to suspend the business.

It is interesting to note that both of their rods are still running fine. While Cardoza's received a minor paint update a few years ago, mechanically, it remains unchanged. This early installation inspired many professional builders to investigate the Jaguar suspension systems. Before long, several new cars were being constructed with Jaguar-based IRS systems.

Professional Shops Un-Cage the Jaguar Rear Suspension

Jaguar rear-suspension systems became very popular with street rodders, but they were hard to find and expensive when a person did locate one. The standard price for a Jag rear suspension ranged from $150 to $250 in the 1960s, and that was what a rodder could buy an entire old car for at the time. Then, after one purchased the rear suspension, it had to be detailed. The most popular way was to chrome plate some or all of the parts, and that process doubled or tripled the price. The differential also had to be installed in the car, which added to the price of the conversion, but it was worth the cost and effort when it was finished.

In the early days, there were a few professional shops that handled installations. Hamilton Automotive was one of the top shops in the San Fernando valley that was capable of installing a Jaguar rear suspension. The company is still in business, and Jaguar suspension installations are still one of its specialties. In Los Angeles, a rodder could contact Kugel Komponents. It was instrumental in installing Jag rear suspensions, and the company also

Snow White, Ltd was established in 1975, and it is one of the leading street-rod shops in central California. The company specializes in Jaguar suspensions and is currently doing several IFS units and chassis.

CHAPTER 5

Ron White stands next to one of the Jaguar rear-suspension systems he has just finished. This one features chrome-plated lower control arms, chrome-plated half shafts, polished hubs, and Wilwood disc brakes.

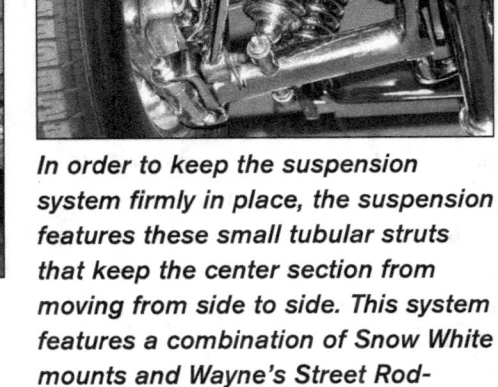

In order to keep the suspension system firmly in place, the suspension features these small tubular struts that keep the center section from moving from side to side. This system features a combination of Snow White mounts and Wayne's Street Rod-fabricated side braces.

This Model A rear crossmember is outfitted with the Jaguar rear-suspension mount for the center section and the two shock mounts. Snow White also makes brackets for Wilwood disc brakes and emergency-brake units.

Long traction bars keep the axle from twisting. The traction bars connect to the factory lower-control-arm mounts and to the frame. The mounting location must be in a parallel line with the control-arm mounting bolts.

The Jaguar suspension in this '32 Ford roadster was installed with parts from Snow White. Since every chassis is a little different, the side mounts and traction bars are custom fabricated. In chrome-plated form like this, Jaguar suspensions have an awesome appearance.

INDEPENDENT REAR SUSPENSIONS

This Jaguar XKE differential was removed from the car and is still in the cage. This IRS is set up for wire wheels so it has a splined hub. When a Jaguar XKE IFS is used in a street rod, a bolt flange drilled for Chevy or Ford wheels has to be welded to the splined area.

Looking at the differential from the front, you can see that the unit is held firmly in place with the cage and the bottom plate. The lower control arms can't move because of the traction bar system.

installed the Jaguar torsion-bar front suspensions. Today, Kugel Komponents offers its own design of independent-suspension systems, due in part to the difficulty in finding the Jaguar units.

In California's central valley, Snow White, Ltd. worked with Jag rear and front suspensions, and it continues to offer an installation kit. Formerly in Huntington Beach, California, and now located in Castle Rock, Washington, is Concours West, another specialist that has installed a large number of Jaguar-based suspension systems. Before long, there were a number of shops that performed installations, but most of them followed the engineering ideas developed by these pioneers.

Identifying a Jaguar Suspension

The Jaguar independent rear suspension was designed initially for the XKE, and it worked so well that the company also installed it in its sedans. The XKE was made from 1961–1971; the XKE3 (the 12-cylinder version) was built from 1971–1974. Jaguar also installed the independent suspension in the 3.8S sedan made between 1963 and 1967 and the later-model XJ6 and XJ12 sedans made from 1969–1987.

Here is a close look at the aluminum hub and spline assembly. When a lug pattern flange is welded to the splined area the width of the rear assembly can be moved inward or outward to get the desired with.

The XKE rear ends are the narrowest, but they were designed for use with knock-off wheels, so they have splined hubs. In order to use an XKE rear end, a flange with a Ford or Chevy bolt pattern needs to be welded on to the hubs. The 3.8S sedan rear suspension is around 55½ inches wide and has a normal hub with the lugs in a standard GM bolt pattern (5 on 4¾ inches). The XJ6 and XJ12 sedan rear ends are 61½ inches wide and have to be narrowed for most street-rod applications. They also feature a standard GM lug pattern. The XKE

Today most of the differentials that can be found are the sedan differentials with the 61½-inch width and Snow White has several of them in their stock pile. These differentials can be narrowed to fit in most street rods or street machines.

V-12 Jaguar rear ends are also 55½ inches wide and are available with both splined and flanged hubs. The XKE V-12 Jaguars were very rare when new, so the chance of finding a rear end out of one of these is unlikely, but not impossible.

If you are looking for a Jaguar rear suspension, you can still find them in auto-wrecking establishments, at swap meets, on the internet, in Recycler-style classified ads, and by word of mouth. My hot-rod friends know that I like Jaguar suspensions, so they are always finding them for me, and I generally buy them when the price is right.

Engineering Aspects: The Jaguar rear-suspension system uses a Dana 44 center section, similar to what is used in a stock 1956 Ford pickup. Jaguar rear ends were designed to be used behind powerful overhead-cam six-cylinder engines that produced close to 300 hp, so they should stand up to most Chevy 350-ci V-8 engines without a problem, if the car is driven normally.

The difference between the standard Dana rear-end assembly and the Jaguar version is the larger size of the ring-gear bolts that strengthen the unit. Even though the rear end is strengthened, a Jag rear end should not be used as a drag-race rear suspension, so sticky tires and an overabundance of torque can create problems for the ring-and-pinion gears, half shafts, and universal joints. The Jaguar Dana rear ends were available with a limited-slip differential, so that is another great feature. XKE rear ends came standard with the limited-slip-differential, but that feature was optional on sedans. There are two different carriers to watch for: one for lower gears, and another for higher gears. The difference is in the gear spacing on the unit itself. Since this is a Dana rear end, there are still plenty of companies that make gears for this unit. Hamilton Automotive told me that it has a variety of gear ratios to choose from, along with all of the other rebuilding parts required. Snow White and Concours West also have a variety of parts available.

Mechanical Aspects: When you look at a Jaguar rear suspension, it looks very intricate and complicated, and in many ways it is. The center section is very similar to a standard Dana, with the only difference being the axle length. The major differences are that the case was designed with a connection for the lower-control-arm mounts, and the short axles connect to half shafts with Chevy-style universal joints. The outside ends up in an aluminum hub assembly, and that is where the difficulty arises. It has to be adjusted just right for the differential to work properly.

Installing a Jaguar Independent Rear Suspension

Some of the first Jaguar installations on a hot rod were done by installing the entire cage assembly into an early Ford or Chevy chassis. That worked fine, but it didn't look nice, so some rodders, such as Joe Cardoza and Les Urban, took the Jaguar rear end out of the cage. The two men studied the cage so that the correct suspension geometry could be used when they reinstalled it into Joe Cardoza's Model A chassis. That installation was featured in *Rod & Custom* magazine, and many other rodders followed. According to Cardoza, the first traction bars that were installed on the side of the frame didn't work properly. The men were the first to realize that the bars need to be connected to a bracket, where the ends of the bars can be spaced to meet at a point parallel to the control-arm mounting bolts.

The Jaguar rear suspension shown here was assembled by Hamilton Automotive in Van Nuys, California, and the chassis was fabricated by Total Cost Involved Engineering. The company builds a variety of chassis, and it has done many Jaguar installations, so the main rear crossmember is something it has in stock. The rest of the assembly was custom made to work with this chassis and Jaguar assembly. This project installation was done in a Model A chassis, but the design features are essentially the same in other Ford and Chevy chassis.

Jaguar Independent Rear Suspension Installation

1 *Total Cost Involved Engineering makes a universal rear Jaguar mount that can be adapted to several chassis. Here, the mount is narrowed to fit into the narrow Model A frame. Oswaldo Guardado cuts it on a large power band saw.*

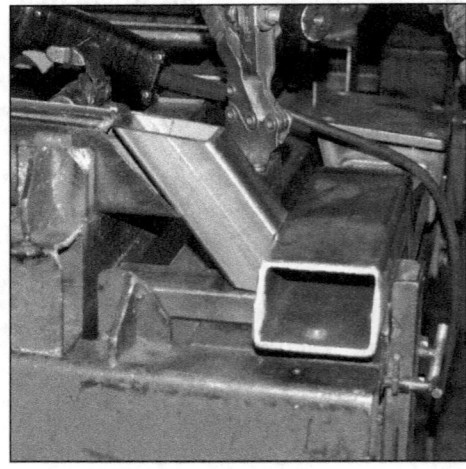

2 *When a Model A chassis is built, it features a kick-up at the rear to lower the car's stance. The tube section is installed and connected to the Jaguar rear mount.*

INDEPENDENT REAR SUSPENSIONS

3 The rear mount is carefully TIG welded to the chassis for maximum strength. The opening in the rectangular tubing and Jag crossmember is stepped for a nicer appearance and additional strength.

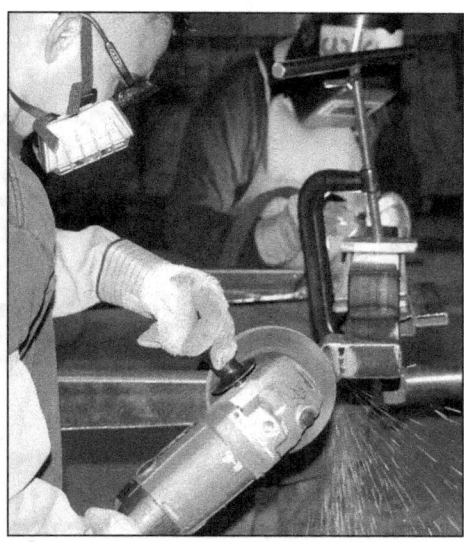

4 After the welding is finished, the chassis is sanded smooth for a nice appearance.

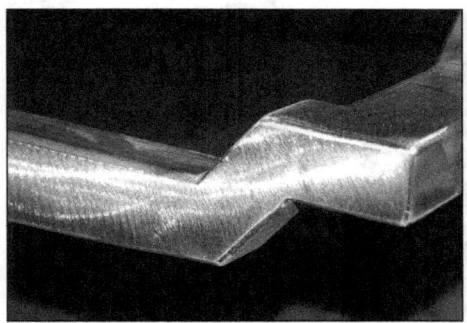

5 The sanded chassis looks great, and it looks as if it was stamped this way. It's difficult to tell that it is constructed from several pieces of metal.

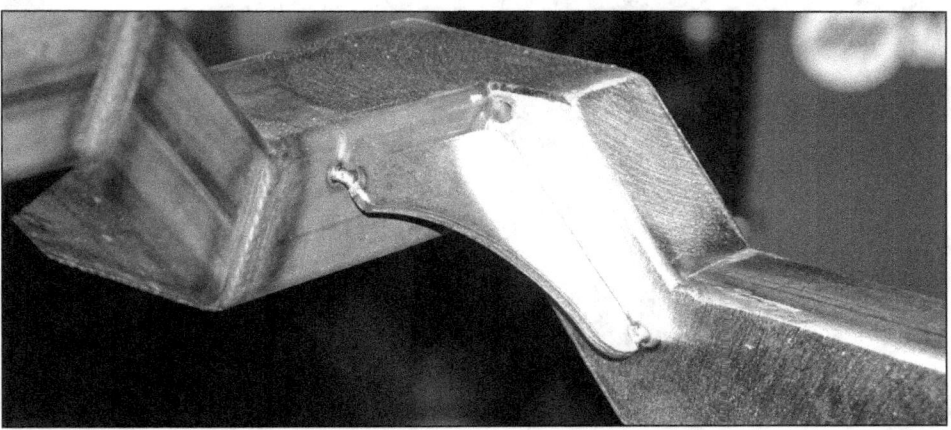

6 Strength is very important, so a small gusset is added to the rear to eliminate any chassis flex. Here is the gusset tack welded in place.

7 The gusset is TIG welded to the chassis on the top and bottom for maximum strength. The gusset has a pleasing shape, so it is also an attractive addition.

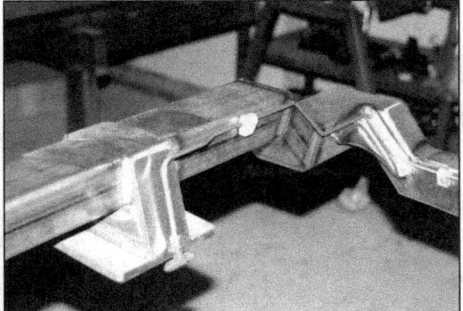

8 After the chassis is finished, the brake lines are added to it. Since the center section doesn't move, the lines to the disc-brake calipers are done after the rear is installed.

9 Jaguar rear suspensions are heavy and awkward to carry, so it should be loaded onto a pallet that can be easily moved with a forklift. Geoffrey Oka attaches the differential center section to the chassis mount using the four large top bolts.

THE COMPLETE BUILDER'S GUIDE TO HOT ROD CHASSIS AND SUSPENSION

CHAPTER 5

10 The suspension should be elevated to the actual ride height, so connect the half shafts to these special brackets. Notice that the Jaguar hubs are cut back slightly and that the struts are drilled with lightening holes.

11 The chassis is elevated to the ride height, and the half shafts are also elevated to where they would sit if the tires were installed. The detailed Jag rear end looks nice in the chassis. Wilwood disc brakes ride on the special Hamilton Automotive brackets.

12 The frame-to-rear-end measurements are made to make sure the chassis is elevated to the correct ride height.

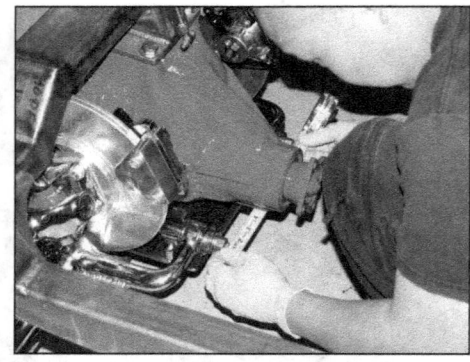

13 The pivot points for the A-arms are measured across, because a bracket will be made and installed between the two lower mounting studs. This bracket is used to control pinion movement.

14 Total Cost Involved Engineering has installed many Jaguar rear suspensions, so the basic mount is in stock. Using the measurement just made, the mounting holes are drilled in the bracket.

15 After the holes are drilled, they are beveled to clean up the connection point.

16 The mount is trial fit to the A-arm studs to make sure it fits properly. After the fit is checked, the ends are bent to make the support-rod connection an easy fit. The original control-arm studs are long enough to be used with the bracket, because originally they were bolted through the cage assembly.

17 The Jag's lower control arms require support rods to keep them in place. The support rods provide the support to keep the lower control arms from moving forward or backward. This is the basic crossmember used as the mounting location. Note that the crossmember is long so it can be used in a variety of chassis applications.

18 The parts required to fabricate the support-rod mounts. The brackets are elongated so that they can be mounted at a slight angle on the crossmember. Tapered threaded ends are used with the appropriate tubing threaded to accept them.

19 Because the tie-rod ends are tapered, in order to mount them properly to the brackets, special bungs must be made and attached to the brackets. Here, the bung is machined on a lathe. The end is flattened and the sides are tapered for a nice appearance.

20 The bung is machined on both sides and then cut in half. This way, there is one bung per bracket.

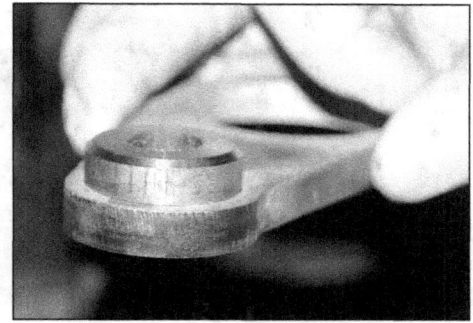

21 Here is the bung placed over the hole in the bracket. This provides the added depth required to secure the tapered tie-rod end.

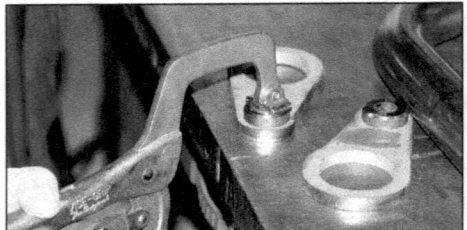

22 It is important that the bung is perfectly aligned over the hole in the bracket before it is welded. The bung is aligned, and then it is clamped to the bracket to keep it from moving.

23 The bung is TIG welded to the bracket. The extra width is needed to work properly with the tapered tie-rod end.

24 The bracket is placed in a bench vise, and then the end is tapered to the size required for the tie-rod end.

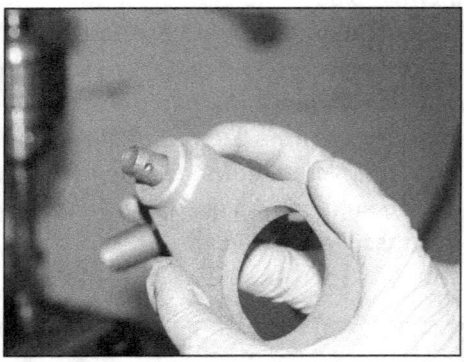

25 After the taper is installed, the shaft of the tie-rod end is trial fit into the bracket. With a good fit, it works fine with the castle nut and cotter pin.

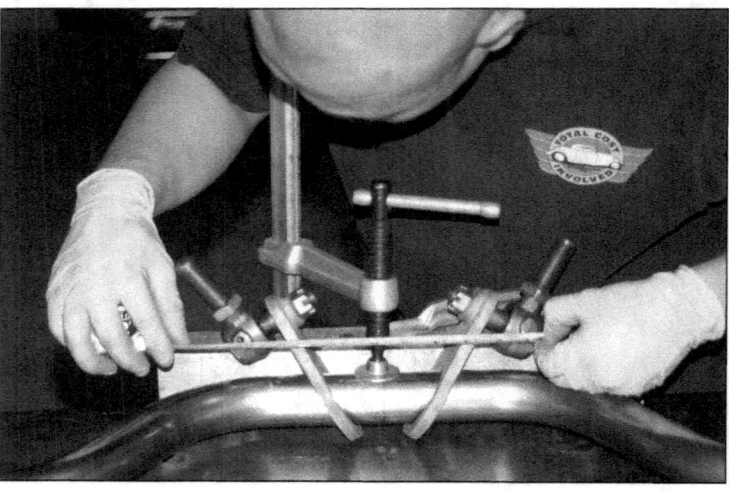

26 The center of the crossmember is marked, and then the brackets are installed. Because the holes are elongated, the brackets can be laid at an angle, which provides good alignment with the original Jag control-arm support rods and brackets. The brackets are measured to make sure the support rods are connected properly. The rod ends should be spaced the same distance apart at the inside width of the two lower-control-arm mounting bolts.

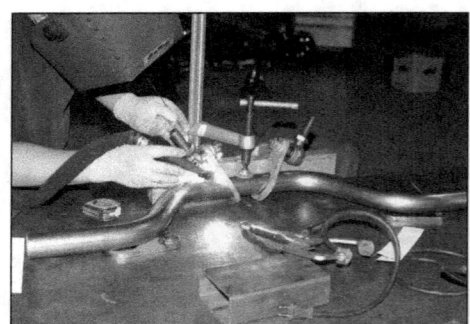

27 The measurements are made and determined to be accurate, so the brackets are tack welded to the crossmember. After the tacks are made, the brackets are measured again, and that is followed by finish welding them to the crossmember. At this point, the crossmember is finished and used later.

INDEPENDENT REAR SUSPENSIONS

28 The pinion-support rods connect to this rectangular-tube crossmember. Here, the tube is cut, and the fit is checked inside of the frame. This is also done to see where the crossmember should be located.

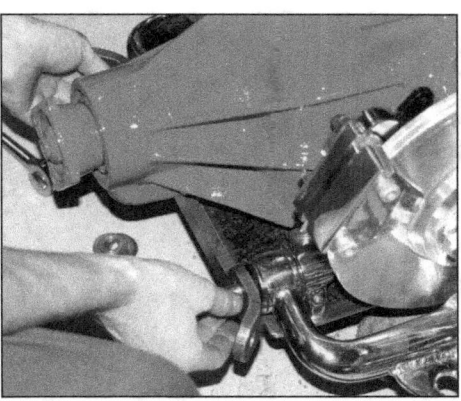

29 The bracket previously shown is bent on each end so that the support rods can be easily connected. The pinion is supported by two strong rods that keep the pinion from trying to move up or down. In the original application, this movement was kept in check by the cage.

30 The frame is marked on each side to show where the pinion brace crossmember should be mounted.

31 In order to mount the crossmember flush with the top of the frame, an aluminum bar is secured to the frame. This keeps the crossmember from being higher than the frame.

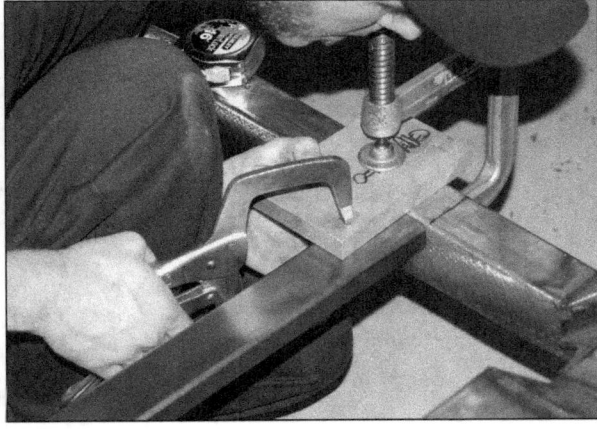

32 The crossmember is clamped to the aluminum bar to keep it flush with the top of the frame. The clamping also keeps it from twisting while it is being welded.

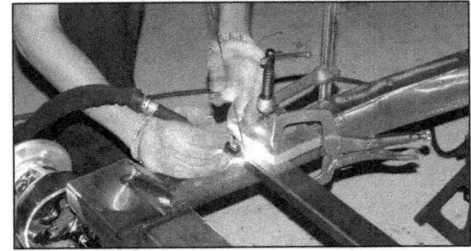

33 When the crossmember is located properly and secured at both ends, it is tack welded to the frame.

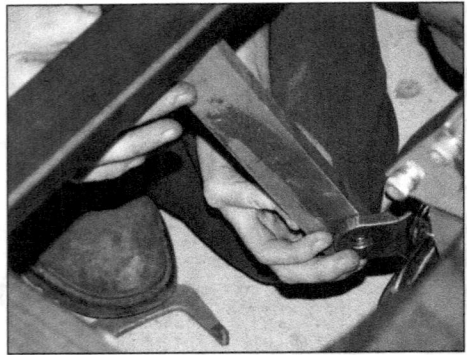

34 Another aluminum bar is used to check the angle between the lower pinion brace and the crossmember. The aluminum bar is clamped to the lower brace to keep it in place.

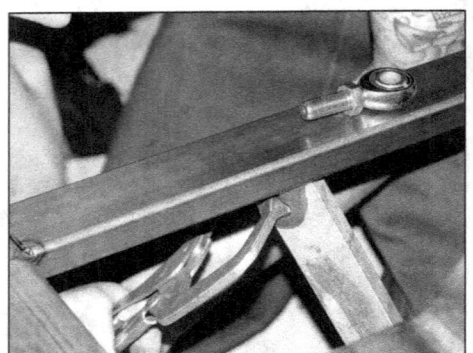

35 Using the bar as a guide, the upper tab connection is clamped to the bar before welding it to the crossmember. It is tack welded to the crossmember after it is in place.

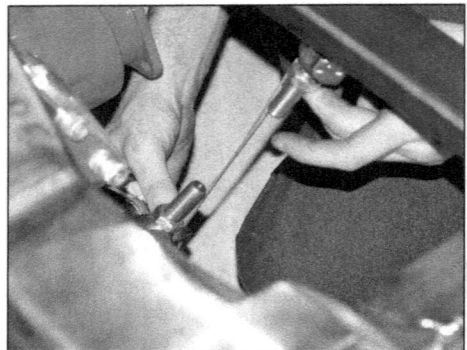

36 The bracket is tack welded to the crossmember, and then the Heim joints are connected to the upper and lower brackets. Holding them in position, a measurement is made for the tube that connects them.

37 Following the measurement just made, two thick chrome-moly tubes are cut accordingly.

38 The tube is installed in the lathe, and then the ends are drilled to size for tapping. The tubes are tapped so that the rods can be lengthened or shortened for a perfect fit.

INDEPENDENT REAR SUSPENSIONS

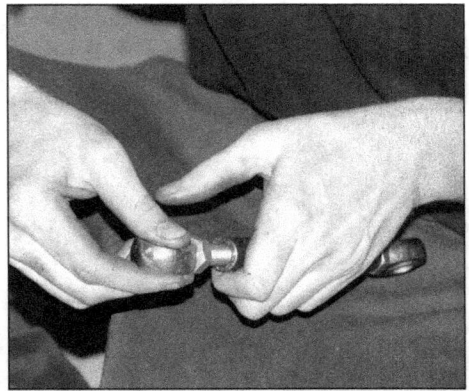

39 The two rod ends are installed in the tube. Notice the jam nuts that keep the heim joints secure.

40 The rods are adjusted to the correct length, and they are secured to the crossmember.

41 The completed cross-member and the support rods. This system keeps the pinion and lower control arms positioned correctly. There is no chance of the unit rocking forward or backward.

42 A 13-inch shock body is used to mark the correct location of the upper shock mount. The angle of the shock changes the ride characteristics of the car. An angle finder is used to get the correct angle of the shocks, to provide the best ride possible.

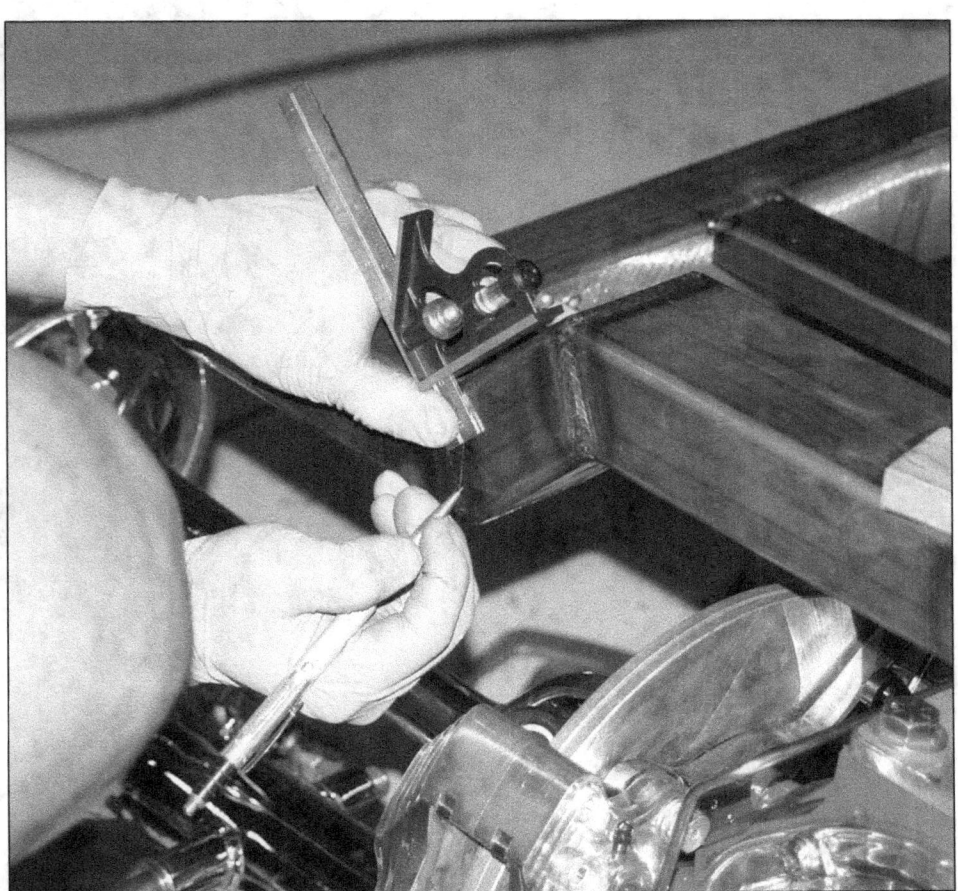

43 After the location is found, the area of the frame is covered with red Dykem, and the mark is scribed.

THE COMPLETE BUILDER'S GUIDE TO HOT ROD CHASSIS AND SUSPENSION

CHAPTER 5

44 The shock-mounting mark is center punched to make the drilling location precise. Using the center-punched mark as a guide, the frame is drilled with a 1/4-inch drill bit. Since this hole must go through both sides of the frame, it is important to keep the drill straight.

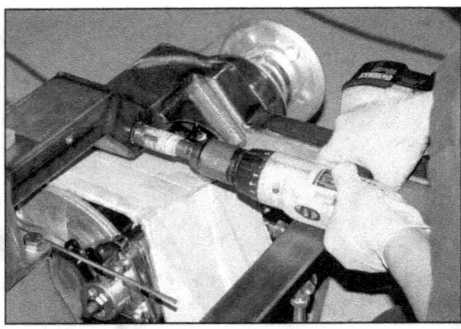

45 The 1/4-inch hole is used as a pilot for the drill with a 1½-inch hole saw. A large piece of tubing connects through the holes from one side to the other, connecting the shocks.

46 The frame is measured to determine the length of the tube to be used. After the measurements are determined, two lengths of tube are cut to size.

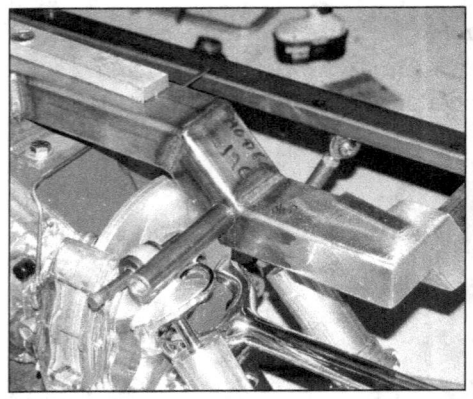

47 The tubes are cut to length, and the inside of the tube is drilled and tapped for a 5/8-inch bolt. After the tube is finished, it is installed through the frame.

48 The tube is a tight fit, so some persuasion is needed to position it properly in the frame.

49 The shock bodies are installed to check the fit. At this point, the tube can be adjusted fore or aft to get the shocks positioned correctly for clearance.

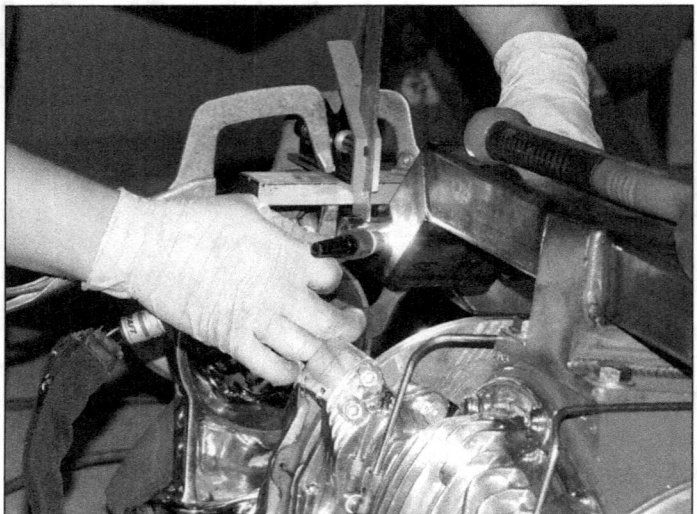

50 The tubes are installed and positioned correctly, and they are TIG welded in place. This application uses four 13-inch Aldan coil-over shocks with 250-pound spring rates.

116   THE COMPLETE BUILDER'S GUIDE TO HOT ROD CHASSIS AND SUSPENSION

INDEPENDENT REAR SUSPENSIONS

51 The control arms are fabricated. The crossmember is installed on the frame in the approximate position of its final location.

52 Measurements are made from side to side and forward and backward to get it in the correct location.

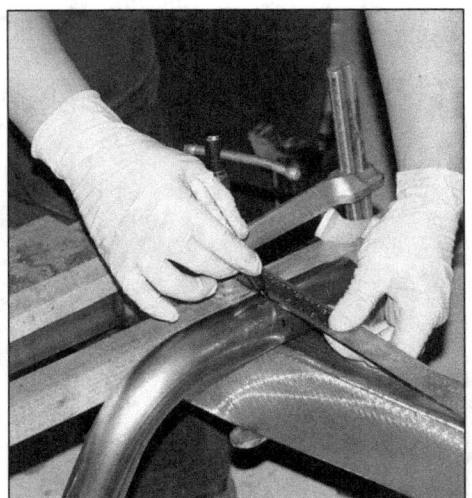

53 Since the frame is tapered just a little, the tube must be cut at a slight angle. Using a straightedge, the line is marked.

54 Josh Huffer cuts the tube along the line. Both ends are cut at a slight angle.

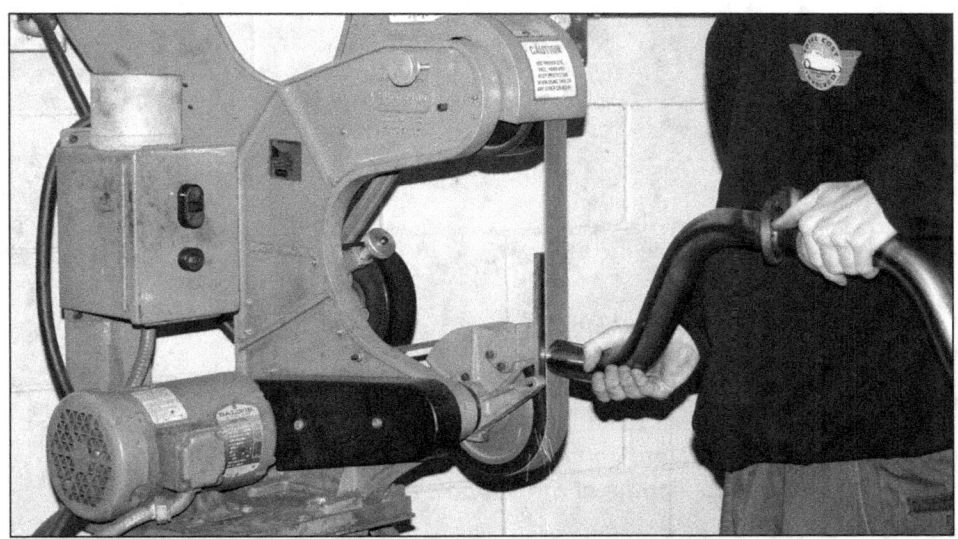

55 The tube is installed in the frame, and some adjustments are necessary. Some sanding is done to get the tube to fit perfectly between the frame rails.

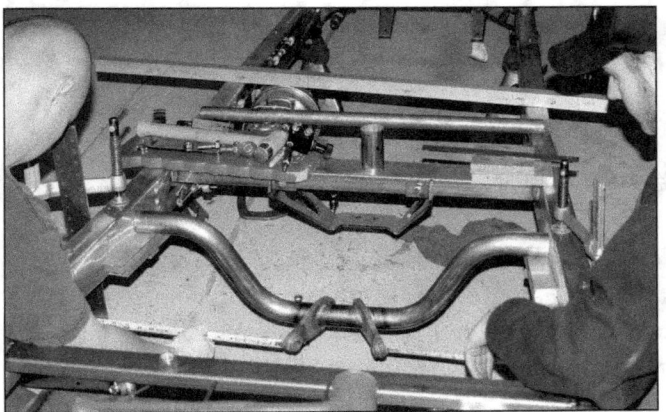

56 A pair of aluminum bars, one on each side, is clamped to the frame to help position the crossmember in the correct location. In this project, the tube sits 1-inch below the top of the frame.

THE COMPLETE BUILDER'S GUIDE TO HOT ROD CHASSIS AND SUSPENSION

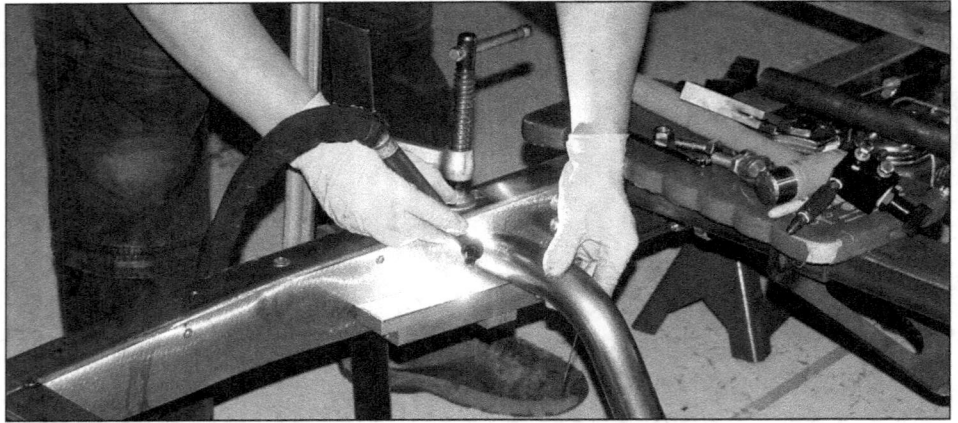

57 The crossmember is TIG welded to the frame on both sides to secure it in the frame. Now that the crossmember is in place, the control arms can be fabricated.

58 The crossmember after it is secured in the frame. Notice how the brackets are facing outward to face the mounting location on the lower control arms.

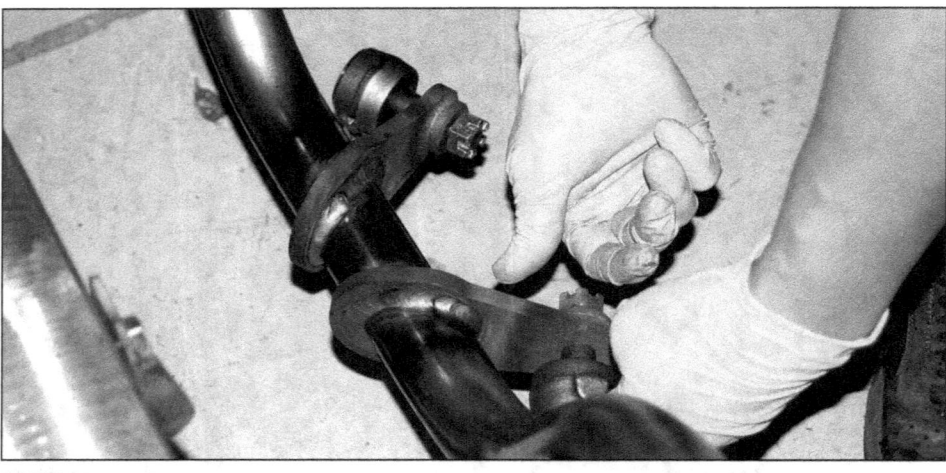

59 The tie-rod ends are connected to the brackets in preparation for measuring the lengths of the support rods.

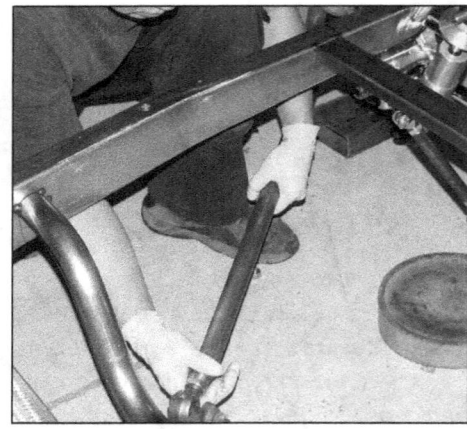

60 The support-rod tubing is positioned, and the final measurements are made.

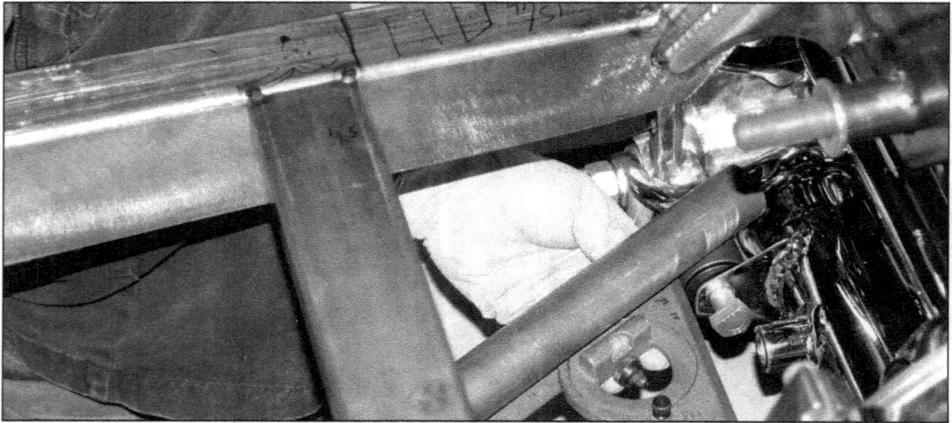

61 The support-rod tubing is cut about 2 inches longer than necessary, because it must be angle cut to work properly with the connection point. Using an angle finder, the angle of the tube to the bushing connection is measured accordingly.

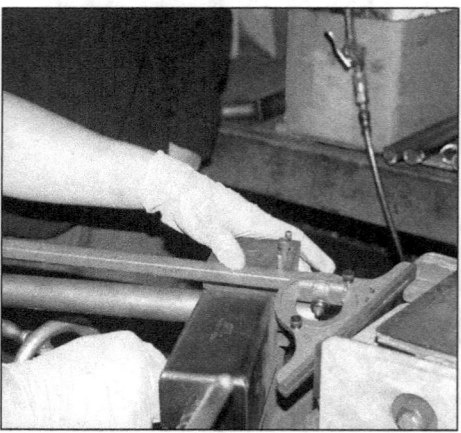

62 After the angle is measured with the adjustable angle finder, the tube is installed in a tubing cutter at the correct angle.

INDEPENDENT REAR SUSPENSIONS

63 Using this special tubing cutter, the tube section is cut to the correct angle.

64 After the cut is made, the tubing ends are sanded for a clean, smooth finish. The ends must be notched to fit the circumference of the bushings that are used.

65 The bushings require removable urethane inserts so that they can be welded to the support-rod tube without heat damage. The bushings are fabricated and are similar to the four-link bushings that the company offers.

66 The bushings are cut to size to fit the inserts. This tube, which is a little too long, is machined to length. The machining ensures that the bushing ends are straight. Both are beveled just a little for a nice appearance.

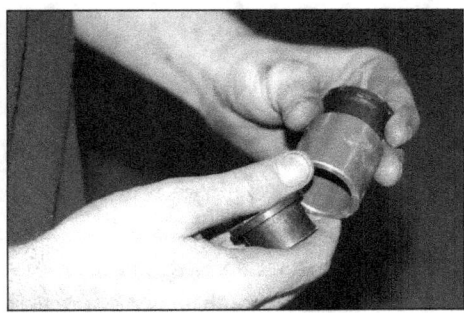

67 The urethane insert is trial fit in the bushing.

68 The bushings are installed into the lower-control-arm bracket with the special factory bolts.

69 The tubing is notched to have a perfect fit against the bushing. The notching is done on a special machine. Because of the angle of the support rod, one side must be notched more than the other.

70 The tube-to-bushing connection is tack welded after the tube is cut to the correct angle. The minimal amount of heat required to do the tack weld doesn't hurt the insert.

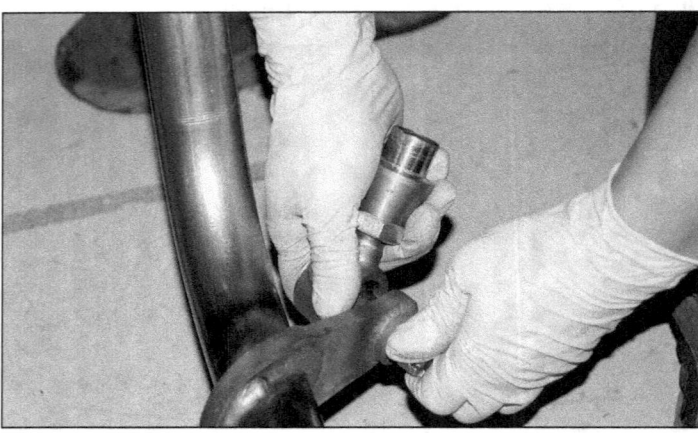

71 The tie-rod end and tapered metal insert are connected to the center crossmember. Now, the support tube can be measured for cutting.

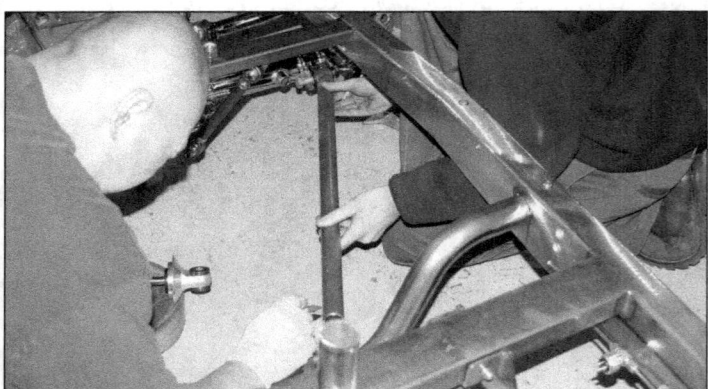

72 After the bushing end is finished, the tube must be cut slightly to work properly with the tapered ends installed in the tube. Here, the support rod is marked for cutting.

73 The support-rod tubes are removed and cut to size on a large band saw.

74 The tube is cut to size, and the tapered threaded ends are installed in the tube. They must line up properly.

INDEPENDENT REAR SUSPENSIONS

75 The tube is tack welded to the tapered threaded end while it is positioned in the crossmember bracket. The small amount of heat required for the tack weld does not hurt the tie-rod end.

76 The threaded ends are finish welded to the tubes and are sanded to look as if they are one piece. Nice-appearing parts are important to pro builders.

77 After everything is fitting properly, the brackets and crossmembers are finish welded. Start by removing the rear end so that the chassis can be moved and flipped over when necessary. Here, Oka is finish welding the crossmember.

78 The frame is turned upside down, and the crossmembers are welded on the bottom side as well. The control-arm support rods and pinion support rods are also finish welded.

THE COMPLETE BUILDER'S GUIDE TO HOT ROD CHASSIS AND SUSPENSION

CHAPTER 5

79 The finishing touch is the installation of the brake lines from the calipers to the line leading up to the master cylinder.

80 The brake lines after they are connected to the Wilwood calipers. Since the rear-end center section doesn't move, hard lines can be installed. If it were a conventional rear end, flex lines would be necessary.

81 Here is the complete assembly done correctly. The pinion support is clean and simple, and the control-arm support rods are spaced correctly. The two tie-rod ends should swivel in a parallel plane with the two inner-control-arm bolts. When they are located properly, there will be no bind and forward or backward movement.

82 A close inspection of the shocks and shock mounts. This angle is correct and provides a nice, soft ride. In this application, the rear end is equipped with Wilwood brakes and a late-model Jaguar finned rear cover for a nice appearance. Hamilton Automotive narrowed the lower control arms, and you can see the gussets that were added for additional strength. The shocks were installed at the same angle they were when they were in the cage.

The Jag rear end finished and ready to go. When installed in a street rod, the appearance of the Jag rear end is stunning. The system looks delicate, but it is actually very strong and durable.

Narrowing a Jaguar Rear Suspension

Jaguar rear-suspension systems come in three different widths, the narrowest being the rare and difficult-to-find early XKE unit. The 3.8S sedan IRS units are probably the most desirable, because they are 55½ inches wide, and that is perfect for Model T through 1948 Ford vehicles, as well as for most of the early Chevys. The XKE Series III cars also used 55½-inch IFS units, but they are very rare. The most common differentials found today are the XJ6 and XJ12 sedan versions, and they are 61½ inches wide. The wide Jaguar IRS might fit into bigger cars and trucks (such as a 1955 Chevy pickup or a 1955–1957 Chevy) without narrowing, but to fit one into an early Ford, it must be narrowed.

The 1961–1971 XKE units have splined ends for knock-off wheels, so a mounting plate must be welded on to adapt standard wheels having a Chevy or Ford bolt pattern. Depending on where this plate is welded, the width of the rear end can be set, and since this is the narrowest unit in the first place, it can be set in a very narrow position. Welding on a bolt-pattern plate is not easy, so it should be done in a machine shop that has the proper equipment—and perhaps even a fixture that will make sure the plate is true after the welding is done. If you have parts from other differentials, it is possible to add a factory bolt flange to the IRS from another unit.

The XJ6 and XJ12 units are the easiest units to find, so they present a unique problem to the builder. Since they are 61½ inches wide, and because 56 inches is optimum for most street rods, they have to be narrowed. The lower control arm can be cut down to size and welded back together. Snow White has come up with a way to narrow, machine, weld, and heat-treat the original dog-bone-style shafts with good results, but some of the other Jaguar specialists prefer to make small driveshaft-style half shafts. The trick here is to make completely new half shafts out of thick-wall tube steel with universal-joint ends. In simple terms, they are constructed like small driveshafts, but the tubing used is a thicker wall. Using this method, you can tailor them to fit in your particular car, and they are very strong.

Jaguar Parts and Installation Kits

Jaguar parts are available from many sources, including Jaguar dealerships, but there are only a few companies that specialize in the parts for street rods and classic Cobras. The companies I have worked with over the years include Hamilton Automotive in Van Nuys, California; Snow White in Fresno, California; and Concours West in Castle Rock, Washington. Total Cost Involved Engineering also makes chassis for Jaguar rear suspensions, and it does follow an approved engineering design.

Snow White started working with Jaguar rear suspensions in 1975 and introduced a rear-end mounting kit that can be welded to a frame to mount the center section and the shock mounts. This center-section mounting plate insulates the differential from the frame for an extremely smooth ride. Since not all chassis are exactly the same, the mounts to stabilize the unit have to be custom fabricated by the chassis builder or car owner.

Hamilton Automotive, established in 1967, specializes in Jaguar rear-suspension systems, so it can do everything from assembly to performing complete installations. When I visited the company recently, I was impressed with the parts it has in stock. If you don't want to scrounge the auto-wrecking establishments to find a unit, Hamilton can build you a rebuilt unit out of the stock on hand. The company just released an installation system to install a Jag suspension into 1953–1956 Ford pickups, as well as early Chevy pickups. Another nice component Hamilton offers is a Wilwood disc-brake conversion kit for later-model Jag suspensions; it also offers disc-brake conversions for the early Jag units. If you want a custom aluminum hub for your street rod, Hamilton can modify yours to reveal a better look at the outer U-joint. Also spotted was an aluminum Jaguar case that was custom made for Cobra kit cars. Hamilton said that the aluminum-center cases are expensive, but I am sure you could talk the company into installing one into a street rod. In polished form, it is awesome.

Hamilton just designed this Jaguar rear mounting bracket assembly for 1953–1956 Ford pickups. This mount should also work in other pickups with a Ford-style ladder frame.

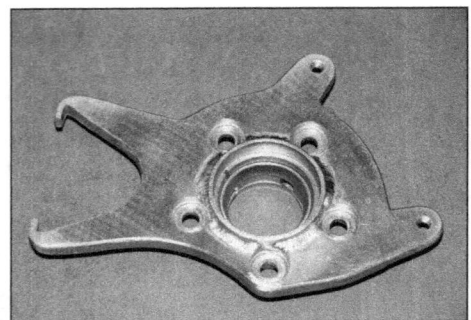
In the past it was very difficult to adapt Wilwood disc brakes to a late-model Jaguar center section. That is no longer a problem because Hamilton has recently released this heavy-duty brake adapter plate that mounts Wilwood calipers and a Wilwood emergency brake.

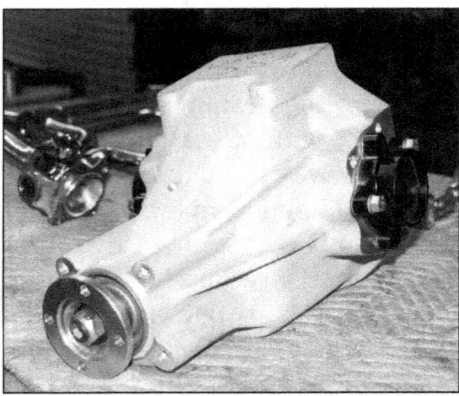
Hamilton told us this aluminum center section was custom made for Jaguar kit cars. He also said this center section is very costly but it sure would look great if it was polished and used under a nice street rod.

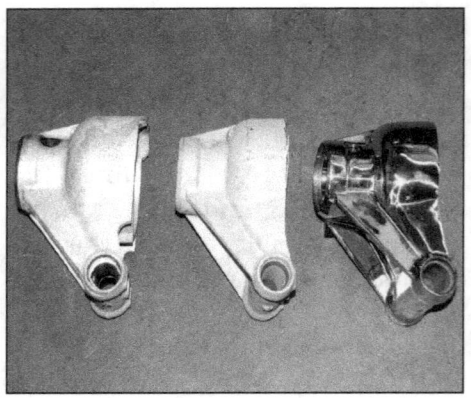
Here is a good look at the difference between a stock aluminum hub, one that is cut down just a little and the last one that is a polished unit. If you want yours modified, Hamilton can do it for you.

Hamilton's warehouse is filled with Jaguar parts and here are some of the control arms in the short length and the long length.

Hamilton also stocks a wide variety of standard and Positraction carriers. He also stocks gear sets for the Jaguar rearends.

Corvette System

The Corvette was introduced in 1953, and only small changes were made to the car's suspension during the model's early years. Later, the engineering and design teams went to work and introduced a state-of-the-art Stingray in 1963 that featured independent front suspension, independent rear suspension, and an entirely new and very sleek body style. In 1963, the front suspension was equipped with disc brakes; however, the rear suspension featured drum brakes. In 1964, GM used disc brakes in the rear, and that was a big improvement.

It took several years for Corvettes to start appearing in wrecking establishments, but when they did, enthusiasts purchased the high-performance engines and rear suspensions to use in a variety of cars. Corvette's early independent rear suspension was very strong and featured large half shafts and a single transverse leaf spring that suspended both sides of the IRS. The center section was based on the Chevy 12-bolt differential, so there were many gear-ratio selections available. The early units were about 56 inches wide, so they could be easily adapted

INDEPENDENT REAR SUSPENSIONS

to street rods. However, every time the Corvette changed, the rear-suspension system grew wider, so some of the later-model IRS systems need narrowing.

The Corvette suspension became a natural resource for hot rodders, but the ride quality was somewhat harsh, like that of the stock Corvette. Some hot-rod builders (including Boyd Coddington) made modifications to the suspension system by changing from a transverse leaf spring to coil-over shocks to improve the ride quality. The suspension system could be tailored to the car it was under by changing the spring rates. The Corvette's system was also a good choice because of its availability; a lot of them were produced, and they were relatively easy to find in wrecking establishments.

Later-model Corvette suspension systems feature a variety of aluminum parts, and with some detailing, the suspension pieces look really nice. The later-model suspension systems are too wide for most street rods, but there are a few companies that build chassis for early Corvettes and 1955–1957 Chevys that feature Corvette suspension.

Corvette independent rear suspensions started appearing in auto-wrecking establishments in the mid 1960s, and rodders started adapting them to street rods and street machines to improve ride and handling. In the early form, they were narrow, so they were a good fit in many hot rods. However, like the ride in an early Corvette, the hot-rod's ride was a little harsh.

Some rod builders liked the Corvette independent rear suspension for its strength and durability, so they improved their cars by fitting them with a coil-over setup. Here's a good example in a Model A sedan. The car has a smooth, quiet ride, and handles well, too.

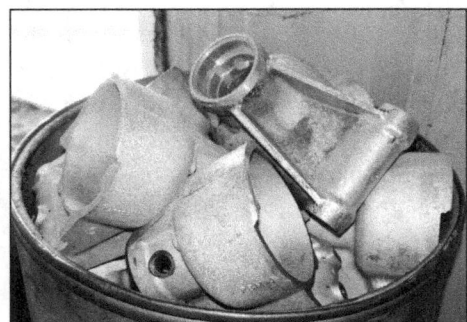

Hamilton has several barrels filled with aluminum hubs like the ones seen here. If you find a differential with a broken hub assembly, or any other part, Hamilton has all of the parts you require.

If you don't have a Jaguar differential, Hamilton can put one together for you from the large volume of parts the company stocks. These center sections are ready to be used as the centerpiece of a show-quality Jaguar rear suspension.

CHAPTER 5

When Jaguar rear suspensions were difficult to find, Jerry Kugel designed his own independent rear suspension using a Ford 9-inch center section in a center case designed by Kugel. The lower control arms are stainless steel and are designed to match the differential's center link, adding to its attractive appearance.

Heidts independent rear suspension systems look nice and you can see the similarity between this suspension and the Jaguar. The special-cast center section is designed for use with a Ford 9-inch carrier. The brakes are inboard and the control arms are connected to Aldan coil-over shocks.

Kugel System

Kugel Kompenents started working on street rods in the early 1960s and was one of the companies that specialized in Jaguar front- and rear-suspension installations. Jerry Kugel, the owner of the company, is very innovative and knew that Jaguar rear suspensions were going to run out sooner or later, so he decided to design his own independent suspension system.

After working on all of the Jaguar suspension systems, Kugel knew that they worked well, so he borrowed some of the engineering features. The Kugel suspension features a Ford 9-inch carrier and ring-and-pinion setup, but everything else is pure Kugel. Similar to the Jaguar unit, the suspension features inboard brakes, coil-over shocks, stainless-steel lower control arms, and hand-fabricated half shafts. Kugel designed his own hub assemblies and bearing-sealing system. Kugel based the engineering on the Jaguar suspension, but the appearance is very different. Kugel also offers the suspension in different widths for various cars.

The nice thing about the Kugel suspension system is that it comes to you fully assembled and connected to the crossmember. The installation is very easy to accomplish; simply follow the detailed instructions that come with the suspension system. All you have to do is find the rear-suspension centerline and the centerline of the crossmember. After the marks are lined up, and the angle of the crossmember is determined, the two parts can be tack-welded together. The suspension can be covered or removed, and then the finish welding is done.

Heidts System

Heidts Hot Rod & Muscle Car Parts is one of the independent-front-suspension leaders, and a few years ago, owner Gary Heidt wanted to design an independent rear suspension that worked well and was reasonably priced. Heidt was quite familiar with the Jaguar suspension, so he based his suspension on that design.

The differential features a Ford 9-inch center section that sits in a cast-aluminum-alloy center housing. The design features inboard brakes, lower control arms, fabricated half shafts, and aluminum hub assemblies. The rear suspension is available in widths from 55 to 62 inches, so it can be used in a variety of cars. The lower control arms are available in steel or polished stainless steel. The suspension features the owner's choice of single or dual Aldan coil-over shocks. The installation kit also comes with forward struts and pinion support links.

Installing a Heidts Independent Rear Suspension

In the 1960s, hot rodders discovered the Jaguar and Corvette IRS systems, and many hot rods were built using them. The Jaguar seemed to be the best one, because it looked terrific and offered a smooth, comfortable ride.

The problem with both was that the rear suspensions were used in limited-production, very-expensive automobiles, so finding them in auto-wrecking establishments was somewhat limited. Most of the Jaguar suspension systems were found in large cities, such as Los Angeles, San Francisco, Dallas, New York, Miami, and Chicago. Stock Jaguars were not readily found in many less-populated areas of the United States, so many local rodders had a difficult time finding them.

Today, original suspension systems are rare, so that's why Heidts Hot Rod & Muscle Car Parts decided to manufacture an independent suspension system that looks as nice as a Jaguar's and offers the same ride quality. It's easy to see that the Heidts suspension was influenced by the Jaguar system, although the lower control arms are very different. The benefit of the Heidts design is that it is offered in several widths, so the company should have one that fits into your car.

The Heidts rear-suspension system is also delivered with a center crossmember and all of the other parts needed to secure the unit into the chassis. If you are wondering about the price, it is about the same as that of a finished Jaguar suspension, and in some cases, it is even less. The Heidts kit is very universal, so it can be installed in a variety of hot rods of every style and vintage.

The Heidts IRS installation covered here pertains to a 1927 Chrysler touring car. Even though this is a rather unique street rod, the basic installation is similar to that for a variety of other cars. In some cases, the procedure will be much easier for other cars. This installation requires metal-working tools, including a MIG or TIG welding machine. If you want a hot rod that looks really cool and rides like a Cadillac, install a Heidts IRS under your street rod.

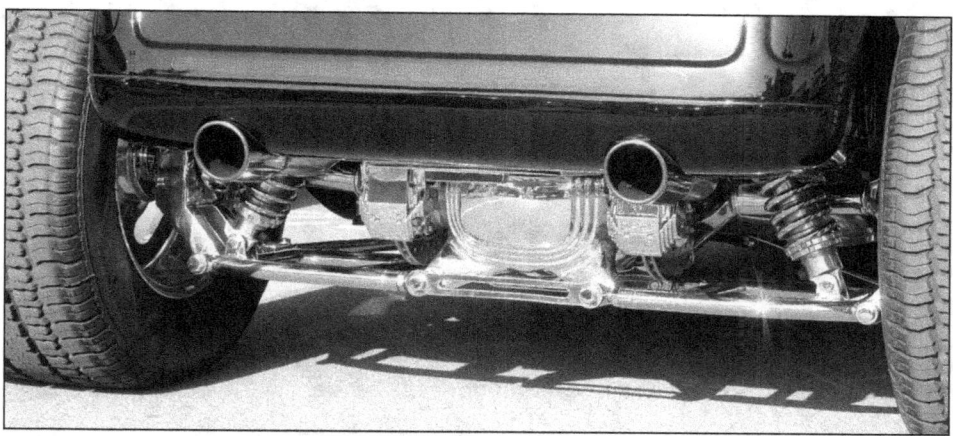

Here is a look at a roadster running a Heidts independent rear suspension. The suspension system looks similar to a Jag but it has a custom-designed differential cover, Wilwood inboard disc brakes, and very delicate appearing lower control arms. Aldan coil-over shocks offer a very pleasant ride quality. The differential can also be ordered with four shock absorbers for a more intricate appearance.

Heidts Independent Rear Suspension Installation

1 The parts that come in a Heidts installation kit. The kit comes with all of the parts necessary to complete the installation, and this particular kit includes top-of-the-line chrome-plated and polished parts.

CHAPTER 5

2 Before a Heidts suspension can even be ordered, the original differential must be removed, and the tires and wheels to be used installed under the fenders.

3 The tires and wheels are placed under the fender in the position that they will be in when the rear suspension is installed. The wheel flange-to-flange distance is measured, and that provides the width of the Heidts rear suspension needed.

4 The axle center line is found, and then it is marked. It is located between the axle bumper-bracket-mounting holes shown by the arrows.

5 In order to do this job correctly, the body is removed from the chassis. This is done by using an engine hoist with two chains attached to the four corners of the body.

6 In this project, after the body was removed, there was a stock crossmember connected to the frame where it would interfere with the Heidts IRS installation.

7 The stock crossmember was in the way, so it had to be removed. The crossmember is removed by using a plasma cutter.

INDEPENDENT REAR SUSPENSIONS

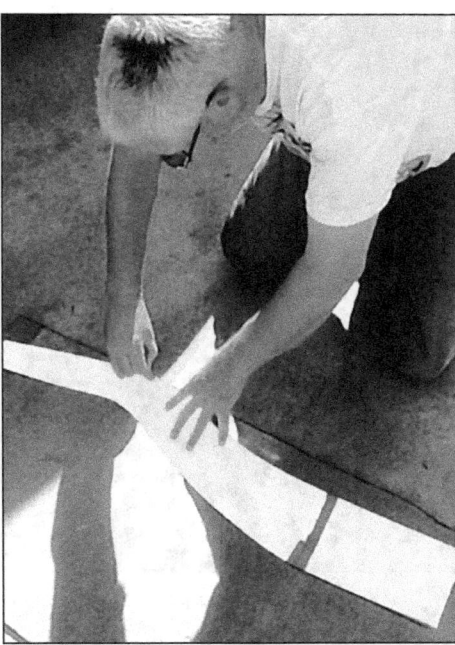
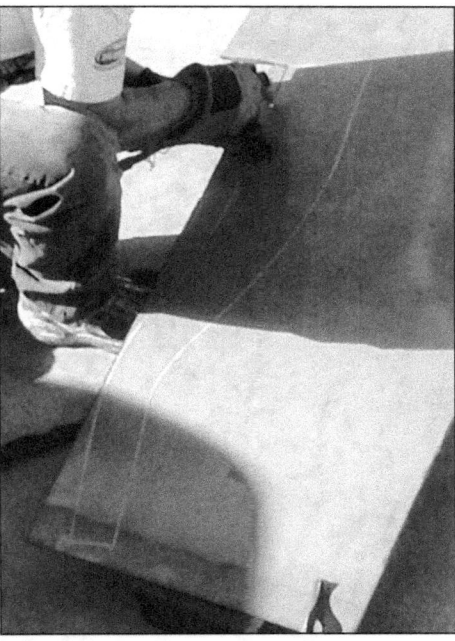

8 The Chrysler frame is a strong unit, but it still needs boxing at the rear for additional strength. A piece of cardboard is marked so that it can be used as a template.

9 After the template is made and cut, the pattern is transferred to a sheet of 3/16-inch steel plate.

10 After the pattern is laid out on the metal using a black felt pen, it is carefully cut with a plasma cutter.

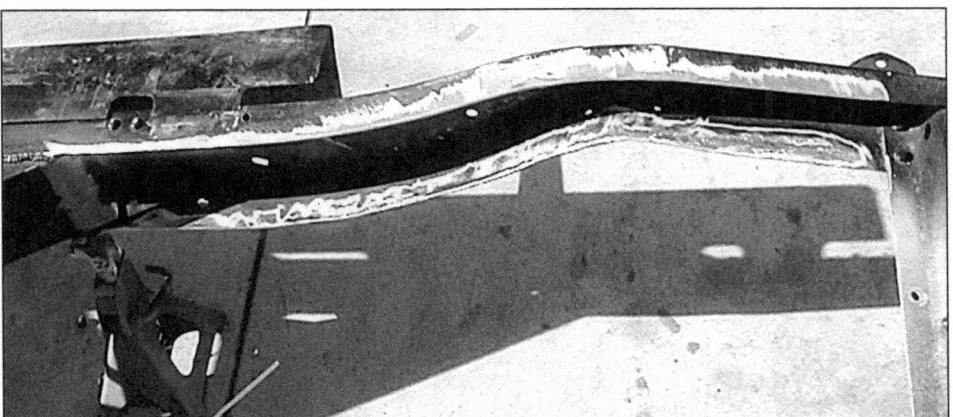

11 In order to get a better and stronger weld seam, the frame is sanded and the edges are beveled by using a large hand grinder.

12 The frame after the grinding is complete. A large section of the frame is now ready for the installation of the boxing plate.

13 The boxing plate is attached to the side of the frame with large clamps. Using a MIG welder, the boxing plate is attached to the frame. It is beneficial to move from side to side and front to rear when the welding is done to spread the heat and avoid warping the frame rail. None of the welds are longer than 1½ inches at a time.

CHAPTER 5

14 After the welding is complete, the frame is sanded with a large electric hand grinder. When the grinding is complete, this area looks like box tubing.

15 After the frame is finished, it is time to assemble the Heidts suspension. The first thing that must be done is to assemble the cast-aluminum center section. Here, the two stub-axle seals are lubricated before being installed.

16 The process begins with the installation of the two stub-axle seals in the housing ends. With the lips pointing inward, the seals are tapped down until the seals bottom out on the shoulder in the bore.

18 The studs are installed by hand first until they hit bottom. Heidts cast this special housing for use with its IRS system, which has an upper mount and an area where the lower control arms are attached. Instead of using a Dana differential, this housing accepts a Ford 9-inch unit for additional strength.

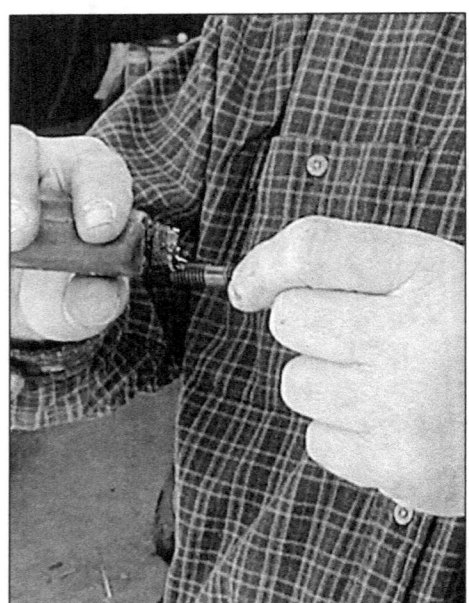

17 The kit comes with several 2- by 3/8-inch studs to attach the third member to the face of the aluminum-alloy rear-end housing. It is important to use thread-locking compound when they are installed to lock them in place.

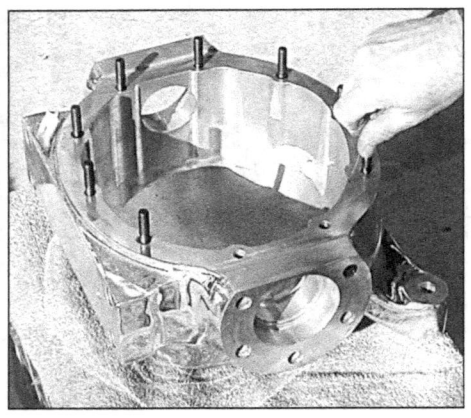

19 A liberal amount of gasket sealer is used on both sides of the third-member gasket.

INDEPENDENT REAR SUSPENSIONS

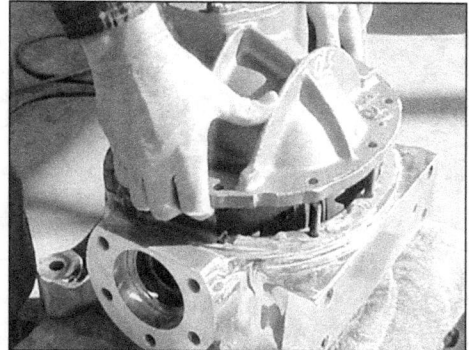

20 Using care, the third member is placed over the studs in the center section. There are copper washers that are used between the aluminum housing and the nuts.

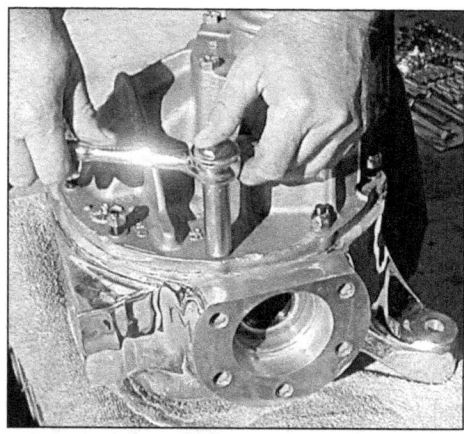

21 The nuts are carefully tightened with a ratchet wrench and a long 9/16-inch socket.

22 A small amount of grease is applied to the splines and seal area of the stub axles prior to installation.

23 The stub axles are installed into the housing. The longer stub axle goes on the passenger side of the housing.

24 Studs must be installed into the side of the housing. The studs are coated with a thread-locking compound and are screwed in until they hit bottom.

25 The caliper-mounting brackets are installed next. The outward side has threaded inserts in it for the calipers to mount to.

26 The optional parking-brake bracket is also attached to the center section. There is a relief in the caliper and parking-brake brackets for the stub seals, and they face inward.

27 There are 10 locknuts and A/N washers provided in the kit. They can now be installed.

CHAPTER 5

28 The front pinion support plate must be installed next. In order to do this, the bolts are removed and longer ones are installed to replace them.

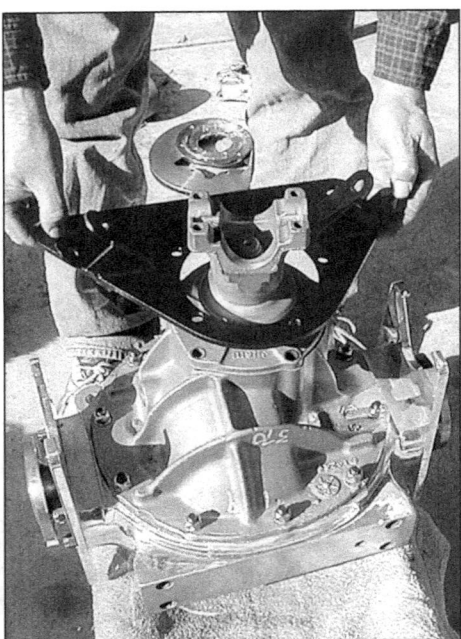

29 The pinion plate is installed around the pinion yoke using the holes available. The ears on the plate are toward the bottom, facing forward.

30 The plate is aligned with the holes, the longer bolts are installed, and then they are tightened with a ratchet wrench. This plate is used to support the front of the center section. If the owner desires, all of the bare-metal parts can be chrome plated or detail painted to match the frame.

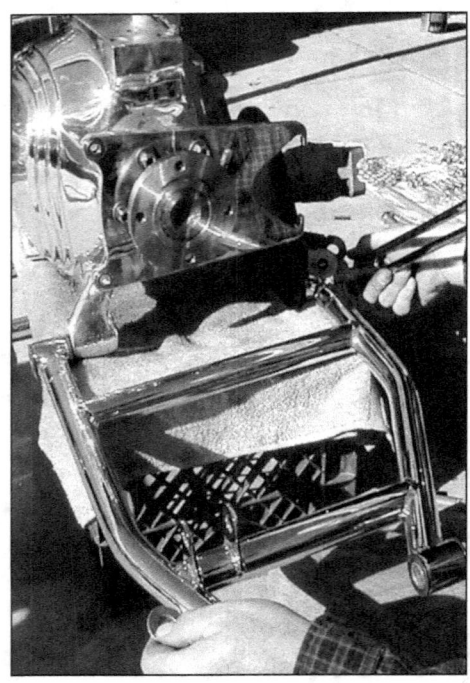

31 After the pinion plate is installed, connect the lower control arms. They attach to the rear-end housing and pinion plate with 5/8-inch bolts, washers, and nuts.

32 There are two tie bars supplied, one for the front and one for the rear, and they are used to take the bolts out of sheer. The shock ears go to the rear.

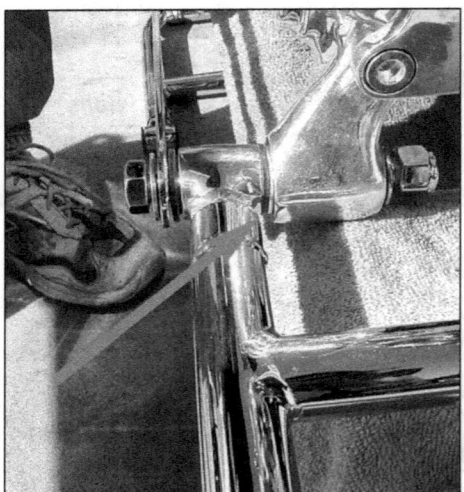

33 There are washers that go between the adjusters and the housing, both front and rear, as shown by the arrow. If they are needed, there are additional shim washers to space the pinion plate and front adjuster. At this point, the nuts and bolts shouldn't be tightened, because the camber is adjusted here by turning the adjusters in or out.

INDEPENDENT REAR SUSPENSIONS

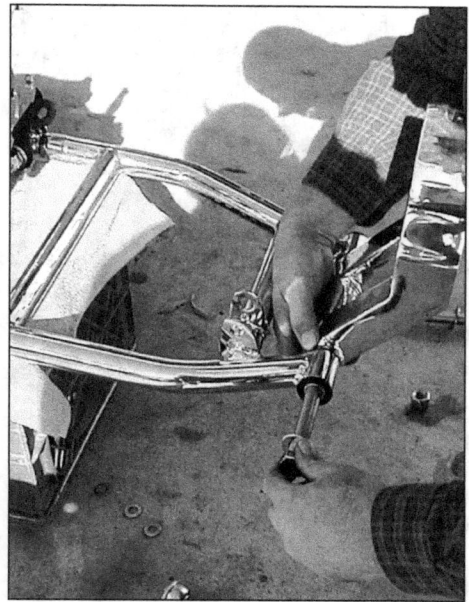

34 The upright assemblies (hubs) are inserted into the outer ends of the control arms, with the supplied washers between the uprights and the control-arm bushings.

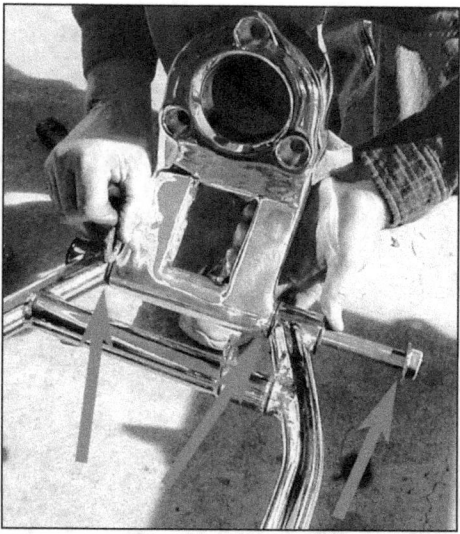

35 There are 10½-inch-long through bolts that fasten the two assemblies together. It is important to install a flat washer between the bolt head and the outer-control-arm bushing. The bolt comes in from the rear.

36 At the other end of the bolt is a "U" bracket that the radius rods attach to later in the assembly. The bracket is held in place by a locknut.

37 The outer bearings are installed into the outer uprights and are secured with the 12-mm socket-head bolts and washers supplied in the kit. A small amount of locking compound is used on the bolt threads.

38 The rotors are attached to the rotor adapters (with the shoulder side of the adapter to the flat side of the rotor) using the 5/16-inch button-head bolts and lock washers. Thread-locking compound is applied on the bolt.

39 Using a torque wrench, the bolts are tightened to 180 in-lbs.

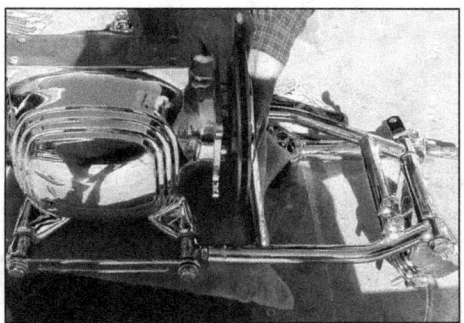

40 With the recessed side of the rotor facing inward, the rotor assemblies are connected to the axle stubs.

CHAPTER 5

41 A liberal amount of grease is applied to the splines of the half shafts.

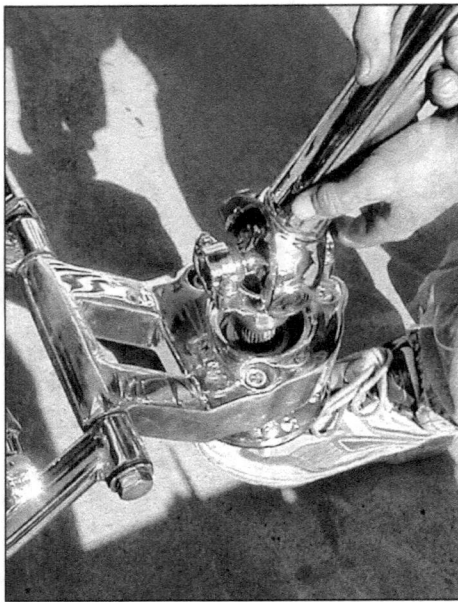

42 The axle shaft is installed in the outer uprights (hub assemblies).

43 The axle shaft is installed in the outer uprights (hub assemblies).

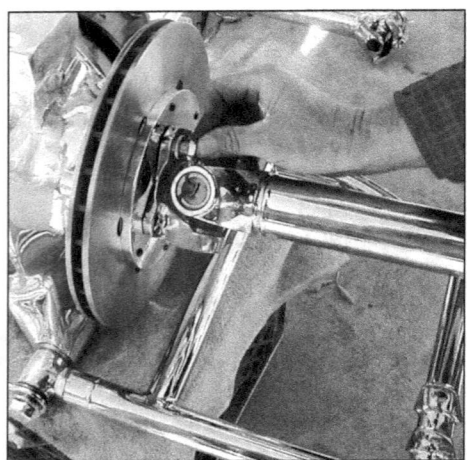

44 Attach the half shafts to the stub axles.

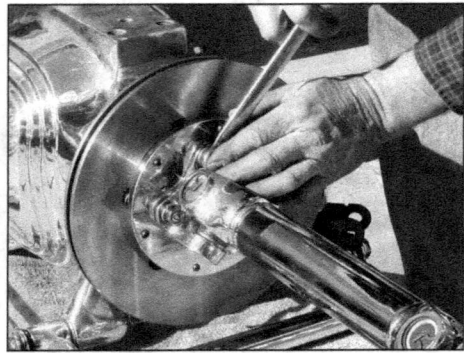

45 Four 7/16-inch bolts are lined up between the half shaft, rotor assembly, and axle stubs, and they are tightened with an open-end wrench.

46 After the bolts are secure, they are tightened to 75 ft-lbs. Before the bolts are installed, thread-locking compound is applied to the threads.

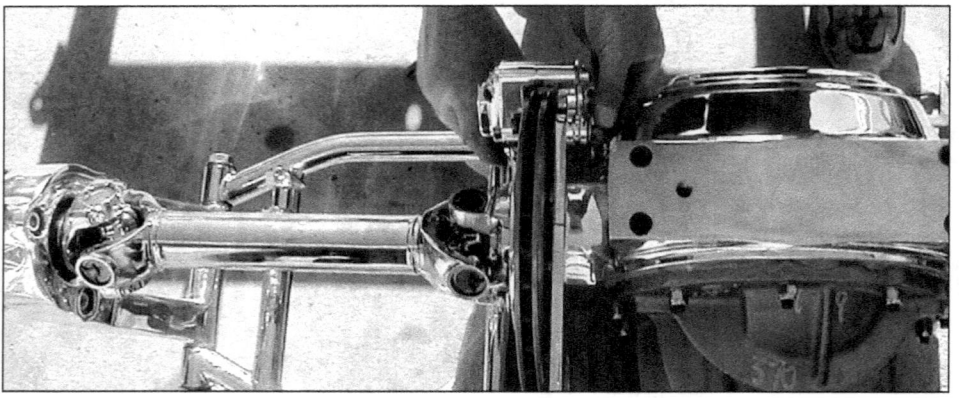

47 The brake calipers come in from the rear. They mount to the plates that were previously installed. The caliper should be centered to the rotor. If needed, there are shims in the kit to adjust them. After they are in place, the 3/8-inch bolts are tightened to 20 ft-lbs.

INDEPENDENT REAR SUSPENSIONS

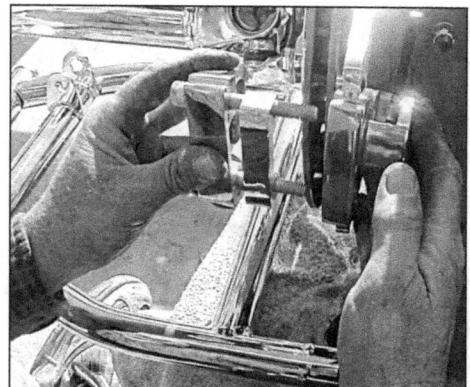

48 The parking-brake calipers are installed next. They fit onto the bracket that faces the front of the car. Before they can be installed, they have to be split in half.

49 After the parking-brake caliper is split, it is installed in the bracket, and then it is connected back together.

50 The rear-end breather is installed next. It is located on top of the rear end housing, next to the crossmember mounting holes on the right side. It is hidden once the crossmember is bolted to the differential housing, so make sure it gets installed before installing the crossmember. Ensure the plug threads are clean and apply sealant prior to installation.

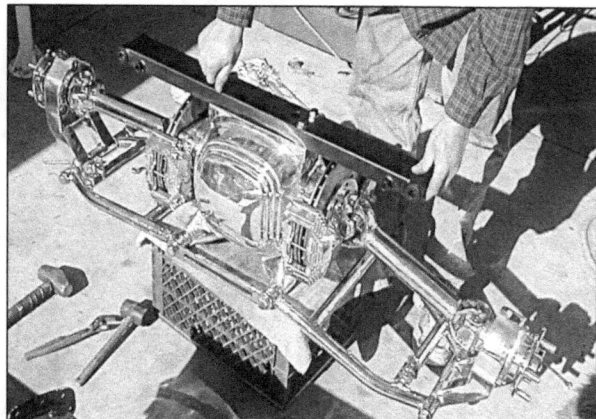

51 The installation of the crossmember is very easy. The crossmember is connected to the aluminum-alloy center section by lining up five holes, three on one side and two on the other. The coil-over-shock mounting holes should be toward the bottom.

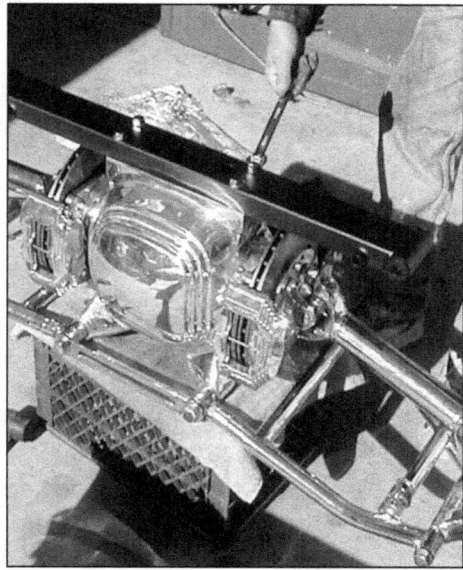

52 The four 1/2-inch mounting bolts are tightened to 75 ft-lbs.

53 Now the Heidts IRS assembly is very complete, and it can be placed in the frame. The third-member is placed on a floor jack, the tires are installed, and the assembly is rolled into place.

54 A close look at the two axle bumper-bracket mounting holes that are left in the frame. Eventually, they become filled with weld and ground down. For now, they provide the axle center line, because a vertical line was drawn between them in the inside of the frame rail.

55 The line is transferred to the top of the frame, and that helps to line up the Heidts crossmember.

56 The center-member-housing crossmember is held in place by two outer brackets. The center line is marked on them as well.

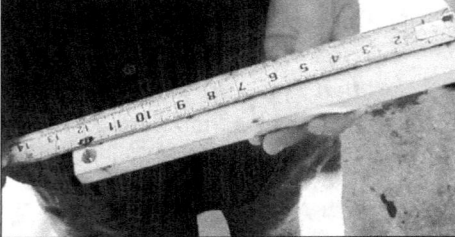

57 The line is transferred to the top of the frame, and that helps to line up the Heidts crossmember.

58 The coil-over shock bolts are used to temporarily secure the straps.

59 The two outer crossmember brackets are bolted to the crossmember. In your case, some minor trimming might be necessary, if you have a frame that tapers from front to back.

60 The rear end is positioned in the chassis, matching the pinion-yoke angle to the transmission angle.

61 Using the angle finder, the crossmember is checked to make sure it is level from side to side and that it is at the correct ride height in the frame.

62 When the Heidts IRS assembly is in the correct location, and all of the angles are correct, tack weld all four corners of the brackets. Notice that the axle center lines line up between the frame and outer brackets.

INDEPENDENT REAR SUSPENSIONS

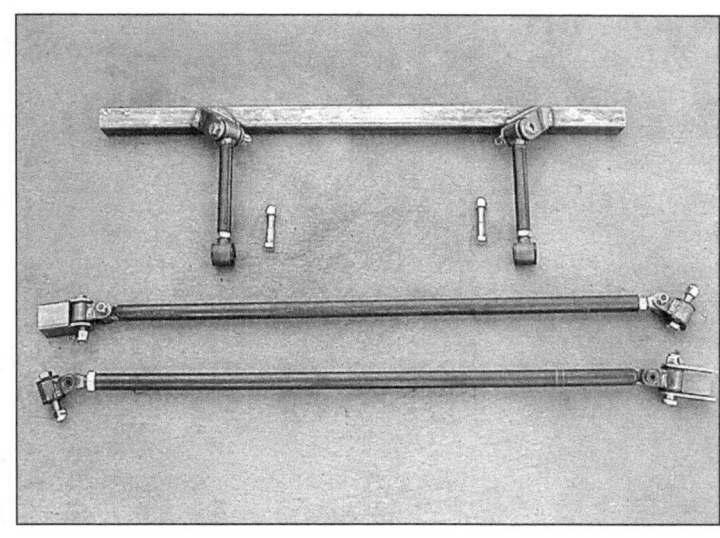

63 The pinion crossmember, links, and radius rods to be installed next.

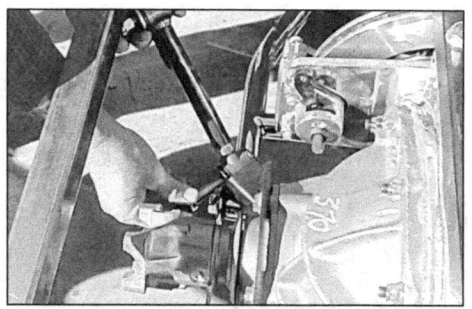

64 The links are installed to the crossmember and also to the pinion plate. These are designed to keep the front of the center section in place to keep it from moving up and down and side to side.

65 The crossmember is lined up; it should be 45-degrees forward and upward.

66 The area where the crossmember meets the frame is marked with chalk, and the areas are measured from side to side to make sure they are the same.

67 When both sides are positioned in the same place, the crossmember is tack welded into the frame.

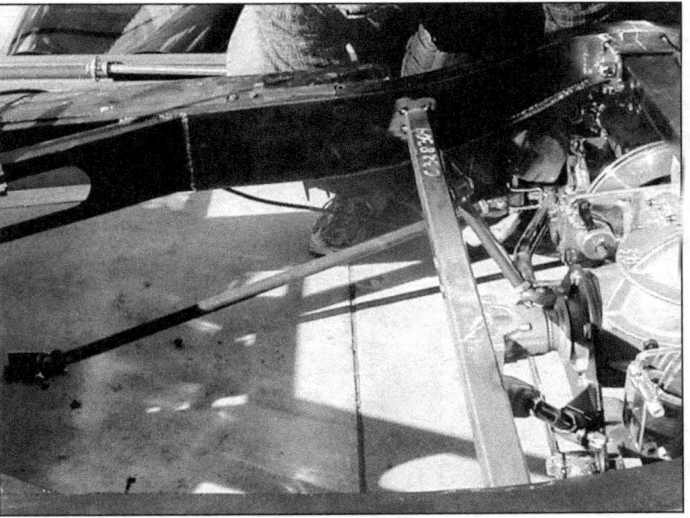

68 The radius rods are installed next. The non-adjustable ends of the radius rods install into the U-bracket on the outer uprights using the 1/2-inch nuts and bolts provided in the kit.

THE COMPLETE BUILDER'S GUIDE TO HOT ROD CHASSIS AND SUSPENSION

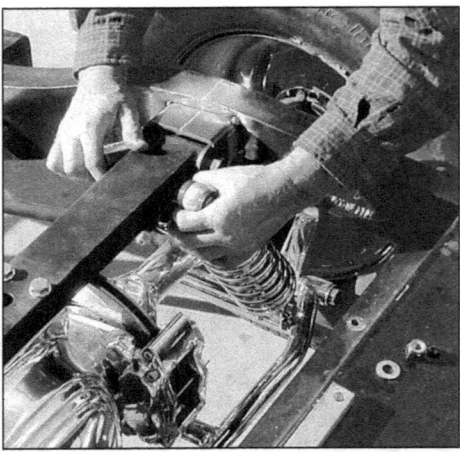

69 The area where the crossmember meets the frame is marked with chalk, and the areas are measured from side to side to make sure they are the same.

70 When both sides are positioned in the same place, the crossmember is tack welded into the frame.

71 The finished rear end. It's very impressive, and the car will handle well and have a smooth, comfortable ride. In order to finish the project, all of the final welding must be done.

72 After all of the welding is completed and the parts are painted and reinstalled, the body is placed back on the frame.

The finished Heidts IRS. Toe-in is 0 degrees, and camber is 0 degrees at ride height.

Picture Gallery of Independent Rear Suspensions

An independent rear suspension will improve your car's ride quality and handling, but there is another basic reason to install one. When you look under the rear of a Model A, Deuce, or 1933–1934 Ford and see an intricate and fully chrome-plated Jaguar or Corvette system, it's an absolutely beautiful thing to see. Rodders hear a variety of comments about the Jaguar suspensions, and one friend of mine said that he was hypnotized by the movement of the half shafts, U-joints, and lower control arms as he was following a car.

Concours West built this Jaguar rear differential and it features the company's billet aluminum hubs, the company's disc brake kit that features Wilwood brakes, and it rides on Aldan coil-over shocks. The center section was also outfitted with a quick-change cover that is available from Speedway motors. Concours West started with a XJ6 differential and narrowed it to 54-inches wide.

This 1911 Model T Ford is awesome and it features a highly modified Jaguar rear differential. It is running a quick-change center section along with custom machined lower control arms.

Many rodders preferred to equip their car with a stronger Corvette rearend especially when they were running high-horsepower engines. This Corvette unit looks great and the suspension was improved with coil-over shocks.

Hamilton Automotive built this beautiful Jaguar rear suspension. It features the company's modified hubs, Aldan coil-over shocks, a Hamilton disc brake kit that features Wilwood brakes, and a late-model Jaguar finned rear-center-section cover.

This nice '32 Ford was an AMBR contestant a few years ago and was detailed to perfection. The roadster features a nicely detailed Jaguar XKE differential that features a Snow White crossmember along with struts and control arm support rods by Wayne's Street Rods. The original XKE coil over shocks were used and they were chrome plated to look terrific.

This XKE Jaguar suspension was installed in this Model A in 1971 and it is still going strong. Several improvements were made in the 1980s and they include the Magoos Wilwood disc-brake kit and the Aldan coil-over shocks. Hamilton Automotive originally built the IRS.

INDEPENDENT REAR SUSPENSIONS

Using many Jaguar design features Heidt's Hot Rod Parts developed their own independent rear suspension system. The custom center section features a Ford 9-inch carrier and gears, custom-made lower control arms, Wilwood inboard disc brakes, and Heidt's coil-over shocks.

Kugel Komponents was one of the first companies to design an independent rear suspension. It features a specially made center section that uses a Ford 9-inch carrier and gears. The Kugel suspension also uses some Corvette components, including the brakes, and it can be equipped with two coil-over shocks or optionally with four coil-over shocks.

Source Guide

If you are building a street rod, there are excellent foundations for your creation; there are many suspension suppliers, all of which build excellent chassis and suspension systems. This list features the manufacturers that build complete chassis, front- and rear-suspension systems, brakes, and various other suspension components. Everything needed can be purchased from these companies by mail or on the Internet.

Art Morrison Enterprises, Inc.
5301 8th Street East
Fife, WA 98424
866-558-1653
www.artmorrison.com
Suspension components and complete frames

Borgeson Universal
91 Technology Park Drive
Torrington, CT 06790
860-482-8283
www.borgeson.com
Steering boxes, universal joints, and steering columns

Chassis Engineering Incorporated
Box 70, 119 N 2nd Street
West Branch, IA 52358
319-643-2645
www.chassisengineeringinc.com
Chassis component kits, suspensions, and complete frames

Classic Performance Products
175 E. Freedom Avenue
Anaheim, CA 92801
800-823-0937
www.classicperform.com
A complete line of brake components

Cornhusker Rod & Custom
402-749-1932
www.cornhuskerrodandcustom.net
Complete chassis

Dutchman Motorsports
P.O. Box 20517
Portland, OR 97294
503-257-6604
www.dutchmanaxles.com
Differential components and complete independent rear suspensions

Eddie's Rod Shop
300 Island Road
Kingsport, TN 37664
423-323-2081
www.eddiesrodshop.com
Complete chassis and bodies

Engineered Components, Inc.
P.O. Box 841
Vernon, CT 06066
860-872-7046
www.ecihotrodbrakes.com
Street-rod brake systems

Fat Man Fabrications
Highway 218
8621-C Fairview Road, Highway 218
Charlotte, NC 28227
704-545-0369
www.fatmanfab.com
Street-rod components, independent front suspensions, and complete chassis

SOURCE GUIDE

Flat Out Engineering
633 W. Katella Avenue, Unit K
Orange, CA 92867
714-639-2256
www.flatout-engineering.com
Independent front suspensions

Gayle Bridges Co.
212 Davis Drive
Hot Springs, AR 71901
501-321-1130
www.gaylebridgesco.com
Independent front suspensions

Heidts Hot Rod & Muscle Car Parts
111 Kerry Lane
Wauconda, IL 60084
847-487-0150
www.heidts.com
Independent front and rear suspensions and chassis parts

Helix Suspension Steering Brakes
201 S.E. Oak Street
Portland, OR 97214
866-470-7542
www.helixsuspension.com
Independent front suspensions and chassis parts

Jim Meyer Racing Products
2795 S.E. 23rd
Lincoln City, OR 97367
800-824-1752
www.jimmeyerracing.com
Independent suspension parts and complete chassis

JW Rod Garage
948 West Silver Beach Road
Belgium, WI 53004
888-414-8787
www.jwrodgarage.com
Independent front suspensions, complete chassis, and chassis parts

Kimbridge Enterprises
7617 160th Street S.E.
Snohomish, WA 98296
425-487-0763
www.kimbridgeent.com
Independent-front-suspension kits and rear-suspension kits

Kugel Street Rod Komponents
451 Park Industrial Drive
La Habra, CA 90631
562-691-7006
www.kugelkomponents.com
Independent-front- and rear-suspension systems

Lobeck's V8 Shop
560 Golden Oak Parkway
Cleveland, OH 44146
440-232-0210
www.lobeckshotrod.com
Chassis components and complete chassis

Magnum Axle Company
P.O. Box 2342
Oakhurst, CA 93644
559-877-4630
www.magnumaxle.net
Front axles and chassis components

Martz Chassis, Inc.
646 Imlertown Road
Bedford, PA 15522
814-623-9501
www.martzchassis.net
Independent-front-suspension systems

Newman Car Creations
3430 El Pomar Drive
Templeton, CA 93465
805-266-9201
www.newmancarcreations.com
Corvette-based chassis

Performance Online, Inc.
2572 E. Fender Avenue, Unit A
Fullerton, CA 92831
800-638-1703
www.performanceonline.com
Independent front suspensions, brakes, and suspension kits

Posies Rods and Customs
219 North Duke Street
Hummelstown, PA 17036-1017
717-566-3340
www.posiesrodsandcustoms.com
Street-rod springs and chassis-improvement kits

Pro Shocks
1715 Lakes Parkway
Lawrenceville, GA 30043
770-995-6300
www.proshocks.com
High-quality coil-over shocks

Roadster Shop
28775 N. Route 83
Mundelein, IL 60060
847-949-7637
www.roadstershop.com
Complete chassis for 1928–1948 Fords and 1930–1935 Chevys

Rod End Supply
P.O. Box 2080
Olathe, KS 66051
913-768-1017
800-284-2902
www.rodendsupply.com
A variety of rod ends and steel and aluminum swedge tubes

SAC Hot Rod Products
625-35 West Katella Avenue
Orange, CA 92867-4619
714-997-3433
www.sachotrod.com
1928–1948 hot-rod chassis

SOURCE GUIDE

Sacramento Vintage Ford
2484 Mercantile Drive
Rancho Cordova, CA 95742
916-853-2244
www.vintageford.com
Dropped axles and chassis components

Shadow Rods
5400 North Michigan Road
Saginaw, MI 48604
989-754-1927
www.shadowrods.com
Complete frames and bodies

So-Cal Speed Shop
1357 E. Grand Avenue
Pomona, CA 91766
909-469-6171
www.so-calspeedshop.com
Complete chassis and chassis components

Speedway Engineering
13040 Bradley Avenue
Sylmar, CA 91342
818-362-5865
www.1speedway.com
Quick-change differentials

Speedway Motors
340 Victory Lane
Lincoln, NE 68528
800-979-0122
www.speedwaymotors.com
Chassis components

Super Bell Axle Co.
(Pete and Jake's Hot Rod Parts)
401 Legend Lane
Peculiar, MO 64078
800-334-7240
www.peteandjakes.com
Complete chassis, chassis components and axle assemblies

Total Control Products
A Chris Alston's Chassisworks, Inc. Brand
8661 Younger Creek Drive
Sacramento, CA 95828
888-388-0298
www.totalcontrolproducts.com
Independent-suspension systems and chassis components

Total Cost Involved Engineering
1416 West Brooks Street
Ontario, CA 91762
800-984-6259
www.totalcostinvolved.com
Independent-suspension systems, complete chassis, and chassis-improvement kits

Unisteer Performance Products
1555 Enterprise Parkway
Twinsburg, OH 44087
800-338-9080
www.unisteer.com
Rack-and-pinion steering systems

Wilwood Engineering
4700 Calle Bolero
Camarillo, CA 93012
805-388-1188
www.wilwood.com
Front and rear disc brake kits and components

www.ingramcontent.com/pod-product-compliance
Lightning Source LLC
Chambersburg PA
CBHW051414070526
44584CB00023B/3423

HIGH-PERFORMANCE
BRAKE SYSTEMS
DESIGN, SELECTION AND INSTALLATION

JAMES WALKER, JR.

CarTech®

Copyright © 2007 James Walker, Jr.

All rights reserved. All text and photographs in this publication are the property of the author, unless otherwise noted or credited. It is unlawful to reproduce – or copy in any way – resell, or redistribute this information without the express written permission of the publisher.

All text, photographs, drawings, and other artwork (hereafter referred to as information) contained in this publication is sold without any warranty as to its usability or performance. In all cases, original manufacturer's recommendations, procedures, and instructions supersede and take precedence over descriptions herein. Specific component design and mechanical procedures – and the qualifications of individual readers – are beyond the control of the publisher, therefore the publisher disclaims all liability, either expressed or implied, for use of the information in this publication. All risk for its use is entirely assumed by the purchaser/user. In no event will CarTech®, Inc., or the author, be liable for any indirect, special, or consequential damages, including but not limited to personal injury or any other damages, arising out of the use or misuse of any information in this publication.

This book is an independent publication, and the author(s) and/or publisher thereof are not in any way associated with, and are not authorized to act on behalf of, any of the manufacturers included in this book. All registered trademarks are the property of their owners. The publisher reserves the right to revise this publication or change its content from time to time without obligation to notify any persons of such revisions or changes.

Edited By: Travis Thompson

ISBN-13 978-1-61325-054-9

CarTech®
39966 Grand Avenue
North Branch, MN 55056
Telephone (651) 277-1200 • (800) 551-4754 • Fax: (651) 277-1203
www.cartechbooks.com

OVERSEAS DISTRIBUTION BY:

Brooklands Books Ltd.
P.O. Box 146, Cobham, Surrey, KT11 1LG, England
Telephone 01932 865051 • Fax 01932 868803
www.brooklands-books.com

Brooklands Books Aus.
3/37-39 Green Street, Banksmeadow, NSW 2019, Australia
Telephone 2 9695 7055 • Fax 2 9695 7355

Front Cover:
There is more to upgrading your brake system than just shopping for the best looking parts. While aesthetics certainly are important, consideration must also be given to system-level performance. Picking the right parts is usually more complicated than physically bolting them on—they have to work together. (Randall Shafer)

Title Page:
During track use, rotors are squeezed with thousands of pounds of clamp force, twisted by thousands of foot-pounds of torque, and heated to over 1,200 degrees F. Heavy cars with large engines such as these only make the demands that much more intense. (Wayne Flynn/pdxsports.com)

Back Cover, Top:
Designing a hot rod brake system from scratch may seem intimidating at first, but the fundamental concepts of gain and balance still apply. What really differentiates these brake systems are unique design and operating requirements that may require different compromises than would be appropriate for an all-out racecar. (Randall Shafer)

Middle:
Because experience is the best teacher, the final four chapters of this book are dedicated to sharing our years of upgrade know-how with you. Whether you are upsizing your front rotors for track use or converting your muscle car from rear drum brakes to rear disc brakes, grab your wrenches and head out to the garage with us. Just be sure to wear your safety glasses! (Randall Shafer)

Bottom:
Motorsports can place extreme demands on your brake system, and if your hardware is not up to the task, performance can suffer dramatically. A solid understanding of brake system fundamentals greatly increases your likelihood of ending up in the winner's circle on race day. (Wayne Flynn/pdxsports.com)

TABLE OF CONTENTS

Biography	5
Acknowledgments	5
Dedication	6
Foreword	6
Introduction	7

Chapter 1: Energy Conversion 9
- The Conservation of Energy 9
- Where Energy Comes From 10
- Friction 10
- Kinetic Energy 11
- Potential Energy 13
- Energy Transformation 14
- Energy and the Brake System 14
- Calculating Brake System Temperature .15
- Importance of Brake Sizing 15

Chapter 2: Tires Stop the Car 18
- The First Law of Motion 18
- Brake Forces 18
- Tire Slip 19
- How Brake Forces are Generated 20
- The Mu-Slip Curve 22
- Choosing the Best Tires 24
- Calculating Maximum Deceleration 25

Chapter 3: Brake System Design 27
- Driver Applied Force 27
- Brake System Overview 28
- Brake Corner Gain 33
- Summing Forces 34
- Overall Brake System Gain 34
- Calculating Deceleration 34
- Calculating Stopping Distance 34
- Brake System Modifications 35

Chapter 4: Brake Balance 37
- Brake Force and Corner Weight 37
- Perfect Balance 38
- Static Weight Distribution 39
- The Second Law of Motion 39
- Dynamic Weight Distribution 40
- The Benefits of Perfect Balance 41
- Front Brake Bias 43
- Rear Brake Bias 43
- Measuring Brake Balance 44
- Changing Brake Balance 44

Chapter 5: Pedals, Boosters and Master Cylinders 46
- Brake Pedal Components 46
- OEM Brake Pedals 47
- Racing Brake Pedals 48
- Brake Boosters 48
- Vacuum Boosters 48
- Hydraulic Boosters 50
- Master Cylinders 50
- Master Cylinder Selection 52
- Rear Brake Pressure Reduction 54
- Balance Bars 54
- Proportioning Valves 55

Chapter 6: Brake Fluid 58
- Brake Fluid 101 58
- FMVSS116 58
- Dry Boiling Point 60
- Wet Boiling Point 61
- Water Adsorption 61
- DOT Ratings 61
- Brake Fluid Compatibility 64
- Brake Fluid Maintenance 64
- Brake Bleeding 65

Chapter 7: Brake Lines and Hoses 69
- Hydraulic Circuit Design 69
- Brake Lines 70
- Flare Fittings 70
- Brake Hoses 71
- Banjo Fittings 72
- Stainless Steel Brake Hoses 73

TABLE OF CONTENTS

Chapter 8: **Brake Calipers** 76
- Hydraulic Gain 76
- Caliper Components 76
- Taper Wear 79
- Piston Count 81
- Caliper Mounting 82
- One-Piece (Monoblock) Calipers 84
- Two-Piece Calipers 84
- Knockback 84

Chapter 9: **Brake Pads** 88
- Brake Pad Terminology 88
- Coefficient of Friction 90
- Coefficient of Friction Stability 91
- Brake Pad Fade 91
- Friction Material Categories 92
- Friction Material Chemistries 93
- Friction Mechanisms 96
- Brake System Break-In 97

Chapter 10: **Brake Rotors** 100
- A Rotor Refresher 100
- Rotor Terminology 101
- Effective Radius 103
- Rotor Sizing 103
- Static Weight and Rotational Inertia ..103
- Rotor Cooling 104
- One-Piece (Fixed) Rotors 107
- Two-Piece (Floating) Rotors 107
- Solid Rotors 109
- Vented Rotors 110
- Cross-Drilled Rotors 111
- Slotted Rotors 112
- Rotor Inspection 113
- Thickness Variation 115

Chapter 11: **Sports Car Brake Upgrade** 118
- The Vehicle 119
- The Objective 119
- Picking the Right Parts 119
- Bolting Them On 121
- The Results 124

Chapter 12: **Racecar Brake Upgrade** 126
- The Vehicle 127
- The Objective 127
- Front Brake Upgrade 127
- Rear Brake Upgrade 129
- Apply System Upgrade 131
- Hoses, Fluids, and Pads 132
- The Results 132

Chapter 13: **Muscle Car Brake Upgrade** 133
- The Vehicle 133
- The Objective 134
- Drum Brakes 101 134
- Picking The Right Parts 134
- Bolting Them On 135
- Buttoning it Up 138
- The Results 138

Chapter 14: **Hot Rod Brake Upgrade** 139
- The Vehicle 139
- The Objective 139
- Front Brake Upgrade 139
- Brake Pedal Considerations 140
- Master Cylinder Upgrade 142
- Brake Line and Proportioning
  Valve Installation 142
- Brake Hoses 143
- Brake Fluid Selection 143
- Parking Brake Installation 144
- The Results 144

Biography

James Walker, Jr. is currently the Supervisor of Vehicle Performance Development at Delphi Corporation. His professional brake system résumé includes employment at Kelsey-Hayes, Saturn, General Motors, Bosch, and Ford.

(Photo courtesy Randall Shafer)

Walker created scR motorsports in 1997, successfully competing in SCCA Club Racing until 2004. Through team scR, he continues to serve as a brake system consultant for StopTech and as a seminar instructor for the Society of Automotive Engineers (SAE).

While this is his first book, Walker contributes to several automotive magazines focusing on high-performance brake system analysis, design, and modification. Originally from upstate New York, he and his family currently reside in southeast Michigan.

Acknowledgments

It was approximately 11:30 PM and I was flying 25,000 feet above Michigan's lower peninsula on a Northwest Airlines commuter shuttle. I was working my way through Chapter 7, finding it difficult to be creative at such a late hour (there's only so much to say about brake hoses), but there's no such thing as spare time when you're on a deadline.

For most of the flight I spent more time keeping my Diet Pepsi from spilling on the keyboard than actually typing. During a particularly long stretch of inactivity, the gentleman sitting next to me leaned over and asked just what exactly I was writing about. When I replied that I was writing a book about high-performance brake systems his eyes got wide in amazement and he asked, "Are you writing it by yourself?"

This was my epiphany. Although my name would be on the cover, at that moment I realized there was no way I could have even contemplated a project of this scope without an enormous cast of characters (and believe me, some of them *are* characters) behind the scenes making me look good. To say thank you to them is not enough; I owe them my gratitude beyond mention.

I first got roped into the field of high-performance brake systems through an unexpected phone call from Bob Lee, then President of StopTech. From day one Bob pressured me to write this book, and with invaluable support from the StopTech technical staff, here we are. A special tip of the hat must also be made to Dan Barnes for parts procurement, Sandor Bota for generating CAD images, and to Matt Weiss for loaning me his couch when passing through town.

Well after getting in over my head, I solicited the services of co-worker Randall Shafer to assist with a photograph or two. What I ended up with was an assistant art director, an image retouch specialist, and a deadline drill sergeant all rolled into one. He is personally responsible for approximately two-thirds of the images in this book—his contribution cannot be overstated. The folks at Delphi Corporation must also receive their own special acknowledgment for allowing us the time and flexibility to work this project into our day jobs.

In addition to Randall's work, prepare to be captivated by the action photography of Wayne Flynn of pdxsports.com. My original request to use 5 to 10 of his shots ballooned over the course of six months to nearly 40 images. There is only so much drama that classic tabletop photography can convey, and Wayne's photos strike the perfect balance between education and entertainment.

Tires receive more than their fair share of coverage in the pages that follow, and Bruce Foss and Steve Boits at Hoosier Racing Tire get their moment in the spotlight for providing images of products made from rubber and string. In addition, much of Chapter 2 was inspired by Paul Haney and his book *The Racing & High-Performance Tire*. If after reading this book you want to know more about tires and tire technology, I highly recommend Paul's book.

Speaking of tires, I also need to thank John Rastetter at The Tire Rack. With the assistance of John and his team, the project BMW in Chapter 11 stops in the shortest possible distance and looks good doing it. Their behind-the-scenes engineering allowed us to take the guesswork out of selecting the best wheel and tire package to fit around our enhanced brake system hardware.

David S. Wallers and the rest of the crew at *Grassroots Motorsports* get two nods. First, I owe them all the thanks in the world for breaking me into the world of freelance automotive journalism back in 1998. The success of that first piece (and the eight-year tsunami of brake system technical articles that followed) led to the book you're holding in your hands. You'll also find a photo or two throughout the book to their credit, but this contribution pales in comparison to the confidence they gave me to put pen to paper in the first place.

Much of the content in Chapter 13 comes courtesy of Nic Cheek and the team at Baer, with additional images to their credit sprinkled throughout the remainder of the book. While I have attempted to reciprocate the favor by answering Nic's endless stream of Corvette brake questions, I'm sure that I have not yet made it up to him in full. I'll keep trying.

I also must give my sincere thanks to Carl Harbert at Hawk Performance for looking over my shoulder through much of Chapter 9. Friction materials are in large part witchcraft and alchemy, but with his help I hope to cut through the marketing propaganda and get to the issues that matter most to the automotive enthusiast.

Finally, Travis Thompson at CarTech receives full credit (perhaps blame is a better word?) for convincing me that writing a book would be a simple ordeal. Only later did I realize that Travis should sell used cars in his spare time. While there's nothing simple about writing a book, his support, encouragement, and guidance kept the fire burning. If this book gets to press on time, it will be purely because of his constant enthusiasm and support of this project.

Dedication

No pain, no gain. While this may be an overused expression, it pretty accurately describes the process of writing a book. The twist here though, is that while the author alone receives the *gain* once the book goes to press, the *pain* during its creation is borne by many others— specifically, those around the author who wonder where he has disappeared to this time to type up a few more paragraphs. Helpful hint to first-time authors: Do *not* start your first book with two children under four years old and a pregnant wife at home. This is not a recipe for family harmony.

For this reason alone I could dedicate this book to my wonderful wife Dana and our three children, Zack, Ethan, and Shelby. The freedom from diaper changes I have received over the past nine months has allowed me the time and energy required to finish on time (okay, more or less on time). However, the support and encouragement I receive from them daily transcends that provided for this book. I am truly blessed to have such an accommodating family and I could not have done this without them supporting me every step of the way. In many ways, their sacrifice was much greater than mine.

I am also deeply indebted to the countless individuals who have helped me to shape and create scR motorsports over the past 10 years. In another classic example of no pain, no gain, I have been graciously afforded the ability to race (and occasionally win) only because of their tireless, selfless, and seemingly endless support. I'm sure that the free beer at Outback Steakhouse helped to lure them in, but they stayed around because of their dedication to my selfish hobby. For this reason, I simply must include the entire scR extended family in my dedication. This is truly *our* book.

FOREWORD

"No, the brakes don't stop the car, the *tires* do!" —James Walker, Jr.

I can't remember the first time I heard Walker utter those words. It was probably in response to an off-handed remark from me. See, even though I'm a writer at *Car and Driver* magazine, I don't always speak in the precise language that we strive to publish each month. Walker, however, loves that kind of precision—and believe me, he knows everything about brakes.

The precise date and time of our first encounter has faded away from my memory. I can, however, remember him coming to my rescue at an SCCA race and helping me sort the brakes on my Honda CRX. Back then I had just finished building the CRX to ITA specifications. I had a lot to learn. I was burning through expensive brake pads at a horrific pace and the pedal feel was horrendously inconsistent and spongy.

You can get all sorts of free advice at every racetrack in the county—and it's usually worth every penny. I had my own ideas, but since I'd spent far more than I could afford on my car, I was desperate to cure my brake problems. I tried everything, hoping I would learn as I went and eventually figure it out.

What struck me first about Walker was that he never tried to push his ideas. He simply explained what he thought I should do and why his techniques would work. He has a knack for cutting through the theory and getting to the practical stuff.

Some say I'm not that bright, but I was smart enough to listen to him about brake-pad management. My Honda has small rotors with flimsy calipers. No matter what you do, the brakes will never feel as good as those on a Porsche 911. But there are certain things you can do that will help— and those tips are just a small part of the information found in this book.

I've always thought that Walker should write a book. In addition to an encyclopedic knowledge of braking systems and vehicle dynamics, he's also quite a good teacher. One time a group of us racers got together and Walker gave us a three-hour class on brake theory. Even though many in the room were automotive engineers, we all learned a great deal. And his lecture was nothing like the painfully boring classes I sat through at engineering school.

Handling is an esoteric, hard-to-define vehicle trait. In a nutshell, it's how a car feels to drive. Almost everything on a car contributes—the driver's seat, the suspension, steering, tires, and yes, the brakes. Brakes that feel and perform the same at every pedal application increase driver confidence, and believe me, confidence makes you go fast. Remember also, that you only have three inputs to control the car: the steering, the throttle, and the brakes.

A good braking system can't turn an evil-handling car into a sweetheart, but bad brakes can seriously erode a good setup. Professional drivers use the brakes as much as the steering to get the car to do what they want. Let's say you're negotiating a fast third-gear corner and the front wheels are sliding and the car is drifting off the optimum line. A lift of the throttle might be all it takes to shift some weight to the front wheels and give them more grip, but if the understeer is severe enough, a light dab on the brakes might be required. I'm simplifying things, but in that scenario, you need a brake system that's easy to modulate because too much braking force will make the understeer worse.

I don't want to get ahead myself, because after reading this book, you'll know practically everything there is to know about brakes. You may be thinking that I've left out the most important part of a car's brakes— stopping the car. Of course Walker has explained that in detail too. But as he would say—it's the tires that stop the car anyway!

Larry Webster
Technical Director
Car and Driver Magazine

INTRODUCTION

Brakes are one of the most important, yet least understood, vehicle systems. Whether you are a commuter, a casual enthusiast, a weekend warrior, or a professional racer, chances are you rely on your brakes day in and day out without giving a second thought to their health and well-being, let alone their function or design. In fact, brakes are typically only given attention after something goes horribly wrong, and in most cases, that's too late.

Fortunately, most factory brake systems are quite robust and reliable under daily driving conditions. However, when used aggressively, brakes can become a problem in a hurry. Be it fluid fade, cracked rotors, tapered pads, or b-b-brake v-v-vibration, a number of maladies are possible and will most likely come to your attention when you can least afford it.

The intent of this book is to help you avoid all of these conditions, and more—but my strategy is to do much more than tell you which calipers, rotors, and brake fluid to install. In other words, the goal is not to give you a shopping list, but to introduce you to the fundamental principles behind each and every component of a modern, high-performance brake system so that you can determine the right parts for *your* application. One size does not fit all, and picking the right parts in most cases is usually much more difficult than actually bolting them on.

Systems, Components, and Installations

This book has been divided into three distinct sections, broken down by the simple questions of why, what, and how. These three sections aim to expand your knowledge, guide your checkbook, and save your knuckles.

Why: Chapters 1 through 4 are dedicated to *brake system fundamentals*. Here you will learn that contrary to popular belief—the brakes don't stop the car! To support this outrageous claim, Chapter 2 goes into the details of what actually occurs to create vehicle deceleration. The answer may surprise you. A complete brake system overview and an explanation of brake balance conclude everything the enthusiast needs to know about the physics of braking.

What: Chapters 5 through 10 join forces to explore *brake component selection*. This is where you'll learn the intimate details of each individual component in a typical high-performance brake system. Calipers, rotors, brake pads, brake hoses, and master cylinders are just a sampling of parts under discussion. Is a floating rotor better than a fixed rotor? What makes DOT 4 brake fluid different from DOT 3? How do I pick the right brake pad? Do red calipers really make the car stop any faster than black calipers? All of these questions and more are answered clearly and concisely to assist in your buying decisions.

When selecting the best brake system components, there's never just one right answer. Whether you're installing new brake pads on your daily driver or upgrading to a full carbon/carbon race system as shown here, the purpose of this book is to introduce you to the tradeoffs and compromises that must be made when modifying your brakes. (Randall Shafer)

The first chapters of this book are dedicated to the overall function and design of high-performance brake systems. Specifically, the information found in Chapters 1 through 4 provides you with the knowledge you need to optimize your brake system for better pedal feel, increased heat capacity, and the ability to out-brake your opponent heading into Turn 1, regardless of what you drive. (Wayne Flynn/pdxsports.com)

INTRODUCTION

How: For those of you who simply want to grab wrenches and head to the garage, leaf back to Chapters 11 through 14, which each showcase a different high-performance *brake system upgrade*. It doesn't matter if you own a slammed sport compact, an exotic performance machine, a big-block muscle car, or a home-built hot rod—these four step-by-step chapters walk you through what it takes to select, install, modify, and maintain your high-performance brake system components. We even get our hands dirty with you along the way.

In summary, whether your objective is shorter stopping distance, reduced brake fade, or you just want the racecar look, there's something in here for you.

Caution: Engineer at Work

Before going any further, one disclaimer must be stated. Although I'm wearing my author hat today, I am an engineer by training and as such, I look at the world a particular way. Consequently, if you thumb through these pages you may find several occasions where I use formulas and equations to reinforce particular points and concepts. Don't panic.

You don't need a calculator while you read these sections, but feel free to play with the numbers if you're into that sort of

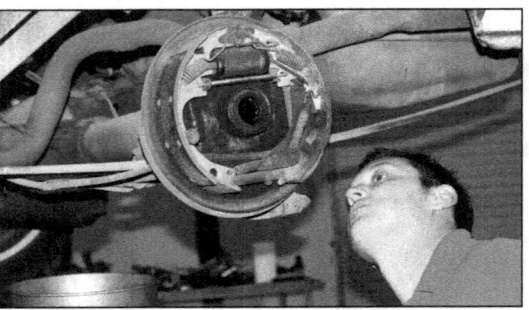

thing. If not, that's just fine too, as the equations only reinforce what's in the text.

Tips, Tricks, and Rumor Control

At scR motorsports, we have personally worn brake pads down through their backing plates and welded them to the caliper pistons. We've spilled gallons of brake fluid underhood. We've used rotors until they cracked in half. Yes, we've even drawn our own blood while bleeding the brakes, as ironic as that may seem. To help you avoid doing the same, the text is periodically interrupted by sidebars to share tips and tricks that we have accumulated over the years so that you can learn from our mistakes. From a stand-alone procedure for brake bleeding in Chapter 6 through the multi-page installation notes found in Chapters 11 through 14, if we've invented a better mousetrap, it's in here.

Finally, I've spent several pages dispelling myths, quelling rumors, and helping you differentiate between hard facts and marketing hype. Advertisements for

If getting your hands dirty is your idea of fun, then Chapters 11 through 14 are just for you. The design, selection, and installation considerations of four unique brake system upgrades, including a drum-to-disc conversion performed on this 1972 Nova, will be explained in detail. There are hints, tricks, and tips here for everybody. (Baer)

calipers with *200 percent better stopping power*, rotors that run *400 degrees cooler*, and brake pads with *incredible bite* abound. While there may be bits of truth in all of it, armed with the information you acquire from reading this book, you'll be able to better separate reality from fanciful claims. Braking knowledge is braking power.

Brake system design combines elements of geometry, trigonometry, fluid dynamics, kinematics, and heat transfer, but don't panic! The primary objective of this book is to explain these sometimes confusing relationships in practical and useful ways so that you can apply these concepts to your own vehicle. (Randall Shafer)

Semi-metallic, non-asbestos organic, ceramic... just to name a few. With so many brake pads on the market, how can you choose? Well, there's more to it than just shape. Armed with the knowledge in Chapter 9, the choice will be that much easier. (Randall Shafer)

Eight years of SCCA club racing tends to destroy a lot of brake system components, and at scR motorsports we sure learned the hard way. Hopefully our lessons learned on the track will prevent you from making the same mistakes. (Dan Gabriel Photography)

CHAPTER 1

ENERGY CONVERSION

If there's just one piece of information you should retain after reading this book, it's that the brakes don't stop the car. Contrary to popular belief, bright red calipers, cross-drilled rotors, and stainless steel brake hoses are not responsible for vehicle deceleration.

That's a pretty hard statement to accept, isn't it? This fundamental concept directly contradicts your own everyday driving experiences. You push on the brake pedal hundreds of thousands of times per year, each time expecting your vehicle to slow down. This is repeated more than one million times over the life of a typical vehicle. You're probably asking yourself right now, "How can those countless observations be wrong?"

Thankfully, the true purpose of brake systems is not based on particle string theory or quantum mechanics. All you need is solid understanding of the First Law of Thermodynamics and the rest will fall into place.

The Conservation of Energy

The First Law of Thermodynamics says that energy (the ability to do work) can neither be created nor destroyed. In other words, the amount of energy found in the universe is constant, and regardless of what you choose to do with it, you can't change the total amount.

(Note here that Albert Einstein later proved that isn't necessarily the case, but exceptions only occur when traveling at the speed of light. Since the vehicles you drive are most certainly *not* traveling at the speed of light, you can ignore Einstein's accurate but irrelevant observations without worry.)

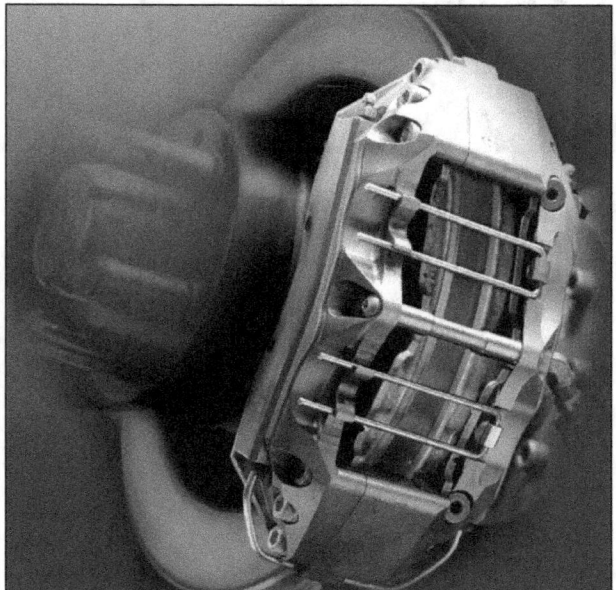

Regardless of their color, size, number of pistons, slots, holes, or sex appeal, the brakes don't stop the car. As you'll learn, they exist solely to convert energy from one form into another. A glowing rotor is a sure sign that the energy conversion process is in high gear. (Hawk Performance)

These vehicles are sitting on the grid, ready to head out on the track. Even if they all were to attain the same top speed on the main straight, they would all have different amounts of kinetic energy because of their differences in weight. (Wayne Flynn/pdxsports.com)

CHAPTER 1

While complex in design and operation, the internal combustion engine only exists to convert the stored chemical energy of gasoline into vehicle kinetic energy. The higher the rate of energy conversion, the more power (and acceleration) the vehicle is capable of producing. Turbochargers certainly add to the excitement. (Randall Shafer)

While the law as stated refers to the universe as a whole, the focus of automotive enthusiasts is quite a bit narrower. From this perspective, *the universe* can be replaced with *the vehicle* and the law still holds true.

In summary, the amount of energy in and around your vehicle is constant, and while you can't change the total amount, you *can* influence which forms that energy takes.

Where Energy Comes From

The primary source of energy in most vehicles comes from the *chemical energy* stored in the bonds holding together molecules of gasoline in the gas tank. The internal combustion engine is a device which takes this stored chemical energy and converts it into a variety of other energy forms with the intended effect of accelerating the vehicle to a given speed and maintaining that speed as long as the driver intends—or until the gas tank is empty.

In this regard, the most useful form of energy coming from the internal combustion engine is *kinetic energy*—the energy of the vehicle in motion. Unfortunately, this only accounts for about 25 to 35 percent of the total energy stored in the fuel. The remaining 65 to 75 percent is converted into relatively useless *thermal energy* (such as heat) lost to the cooling system and stored in the exhaust gasses.

Friction

Since friction is discussed at great length in this book, it makes sense to define it now. In simple terms, friction is the resistance to movement that occurs between any two objects that are in contact with one another. More specifically, any time you attempt to generate relative motion between two objects, there will be a force generated which resists the motion you are trying to achieve. This force is called the *frictional force*.

The simplest example is a block of wood sitting on a table. In order to move the block along the surface of the table, you need to push it with a certain amount of force. The force required to get the block to move is equal to the weight of the block multiplied by the amount of

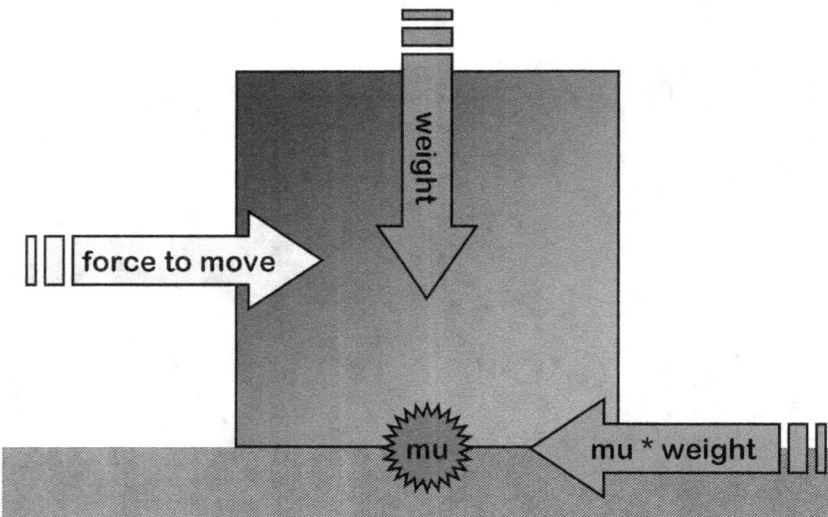

The force due to friction (green arrow) is equal to the coefficient of friction, or mu (blue star), multiplied by the object's weight (red arrow). This is equal to the force required to move the object along the surface (yellow arrow). As a result, the lower the coefficient of friction, the easier the object will be to move.

ENERGY CONVERSION

Aerodynamic drag is just one mechanism that can convert a vehicle's kinetic energy into heat. Although the contribution from aerodynamic drag is small while driving around town, it's the only mechanism available for an airborne vehicle – hit the brakes if you want, but they won't help you slow down! (Wayne Flynn/pdxsports.com)

friction, or resistance, found between the block and the table. This level of resistance is called the *coefficient of friction*. In equation form:

Force required to move the object (lb) = coefficient of friction (unitless) x weight of the object (lb)

From this relationship you can see that lower coefficients of friction result in lower forces required to move the block. For example, the block would be easier to push along a polished granite tabletop than along a piece of 60-grit sandpaper because the coefficient of friction is lower on the tabletop.

In addition, once these two objects are moving relative to each other there is an energy transformation at the interface. This is the frictional force at work. The most common form of energy transformation is converting kinetic energy into thermal energy. As a result, when the block slides along the table, both the block and the tabletop will increase in temperature because they absorb the heat generated due to friction.

Subsequent chapters explore some of the different ways friction is developed, but for now let it suffice to say that friction always makes the conversion to kinetic energy more difficult than it needs to be. Unfortunately though, like death and taxes, you just can't escape from frictional forces.

Kinetic Energy

The kinetic energy of a vehicle in motion is proportional to its weight and its speed through the following relationship:

Kinetic energy (ft-lb) = vehicle weight (lb) x vehicle speed^2 (MPH^2) ÷ 29.9 (a conversion factor)

(Continued on page 13)

Vehicle Kinetic Energy Comparison

The following table compares the total kinetic energy of six unique vehicles at four different speeds. Due to the nature of energy calculations, the units are given in foot-pounds. Since torque also is expressed in units of foot-pounds this can be a little confusing at first, but regardless of the units used, note the extreme differences in kinetic energy between the various conditions.

Kinetic Energy (in ft-lb)

	35 mph	75 mph	150 mph	225 mph
200-lb soap box derby car	8,194	37,625	150,502	338,629
400-lb race kart	16,388	75,251	301,003	677,258
600-lb sport bike	24,582	112,876	451,505	1,015,886
1,900-lb formula car	77,843	357,441	1,429,766	3,216,973
3,000-lb passenger car	122,910	564,381	2,257,525	5,079,431
80,000-lb tractor-trailer	3,277,592	15,050,167	60,200,669	135,451,505

Kinetic energy is a function of a vehicle's speed and weight. Consequently, a 1,900-pound formula car traveling at 50 mph possesses approximately the same amount of kinetic energy as a 400-pound race kart traveling at nearly 110 mph. (Wayne Flynn/pdxsports.com)

While not all of these vehicles are capable of reaching the speeds listed, the data allows for some interesting comparisons. For example, a 600-pound sport bike at 150 mph has less kinetic energy than a 1,900-pound formula car traveling at half that speed, while an 80,000-pound tractor-trailer traveling at just 35 mph has the same amount of kinetic energy as a 1,900-pound formula car traveling at over 225 mph!

CHAPTER 1

Converting Potential Energy into Kinetic Energy

Meet Jack. In the following sequence of images, he'll be demonstrating how potential energy is converted into kinetic energy. Note: this is a trained professional on a closed course. Do not attempt this at home. (Randall Shafer)

Sitting at the top of the ramp, Jack's car isn't moving. Therefore, it doesn't possess any kinetic energy. However, because of its elevation relative to its surroundings, it does possess potential energy. The amount of potential energy is equal to the weight of the car multiplied by its height above the base of the ramp. Assuming a weight of 0.10 pounds and a height of 0.5 feet, the total potential energy stored in the car would be 0.05 ft-lbs. (Randall Shafer)

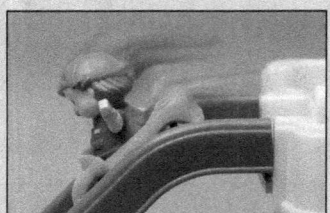

The instant that the car begins to move, the transformation from potential energy to kinetic energy begins. As the car continues to travel down the ramp, the amount of kinetic energy grows rapidly while the amount of potential energy decreases at an equal but opposite rate. (Randall Shafer)

Once Jack's car reaches the bottom of the ramp, all of its potential energy has been converted into kinetic energy. For this reason, his car will attain its highest speed at the bottom of the ramp. Assuming no losses to friction, his car would achieve a top speed of 3.9 mph. (Randall Shafer)

Because tires are forced to flatten out as they contact the road, they naturally resist rolling. This is called rolling resistance. Because of this phenomenon, the tires will rise in temperature as they are driven down the road. Drag racers use skinny front tires like the one shown here because they have less rolling resistance. (Hoosier Racing Tire)

Regardless of the mechanism of energy conversion, a vehicle must get rid of all of its kinetic energy to stop. Unfortunately for the owner of this racecar, its right front corner was used to absorb a great deal of its kinetic energy. (Wayne Flynn/pdxsports.com)

ENERGY CONVERSION

(Note that technically it's vehicle mass and not vehicle weight that contributes to kinetic energy, but this is a subtle point that only engineers will find important. The conversion factor of 29.9 found in the equation takes care of that detail.)

From this equation, you can see that doubling vehicle weight will double the kinetic energy, but doubling the vehicle speed will increase kinetic energy by a factor of *four*. This occurs because kinetic energy is a function of the speed term squared. The table provided in the Vehicle Kinetic Energy Comparison sidebar compares the kinetic energy found between several different types of vehicles traveling at various speeds.

Whether your vehicle is powered by natural gas, methanol, electricity, or uranium, the concept is the same. Some form of chemical energy stored onboard the vehicle is converted into kinetic energy as the vehicle accelerates. Different engine and energy source combinations may change the efficiency of the energy conversion, but for the automotive enthusiast, the more kinetic energy the better!

Potential Energy

While internal combustion engines are typically used to provide kinetic energy for passenger vehicles, a second form of energy comes from Mother Earth directly. Potential energy is the name given to the energy stored in a body (a vehicle in this case) that is elevated relative to its topographical surroundings. The energy is simply there because gravity is pulling it back toward planet earth.

The potential energy of a vehicle is proportional to its weight, its elevation, and the pull of gravity by the following formula:

Potential energy (ft-lb) = vehicle weight (lb) x vehicle height (ft)

For example, a vehicle parked on a steep hill has zero kinetic energy (because the speed is zero), but it does have potential energy due to its elevation on the hill. If the parking brake were released, the vehicle would accelerate down the hill, converting potential

Potential Energy and Speed

The following table illustrates how much speed a vehicle could theoretically generate if it were allowed to coast from the top of a given hill all the way to the bottom, as in a soapbox derby competition. The elevation change of five feet approximates a mild driveway slope; 48 feet is the official elevation change during the All-American Soap Box Derby Championship held annually in Akron, Ohio, and 14,100 feet represents the descent from Pikes Peak in Colorado to sea level.

	Maximum Speed (in MPH)		
	5 feet	48 feet	14,110 feet
200-lb soap box derby car	12	38	650
400-lb race kart	12	38	650
600-lb sport bike	12	38	650
1,900-lb formula car	12	38	650
3,000-lb passenger car	12	38	650
80,000-lb tractor-trailer	12	38	650

The first interesting point is that the numbers suggest the maximum theoretical speed is independent of the vehicle weight. While this is true from an analytical perspective, in the real world there are factors such as energy loss due to tire resistance to rolling (the frictional heating of the tires), aerodynamic drag (heating of the air), and driveline frictional losses (heating of the bearings and lubricants), which could influence the actual speed attained. The real-world result is that the vehicle with the lowest frictional losses (the highest efficiency) would have the highest speed at the bottom of the hill. In most cases, a larger, heavier vehicle will be less efficient than a smaller, lighter vehicle because of additional rolling resistance (more weight on the tires) and extra wind resistance (more frontal area).

The second point of interest is that in theory all six vehicles would attain a speed of nearly 650 mph by simply coasting down from Pikes Peak! Practical experience tells you that this is not possible for the same reasons just listed. Tire rolling resistance, aerodynamic drag, and frictional losses in various driveline components all convert potential energy in their own way. As a result, instead of converting 100 percent of the potential energy to kinetic energy, many parts of the vehicle would just get hot.

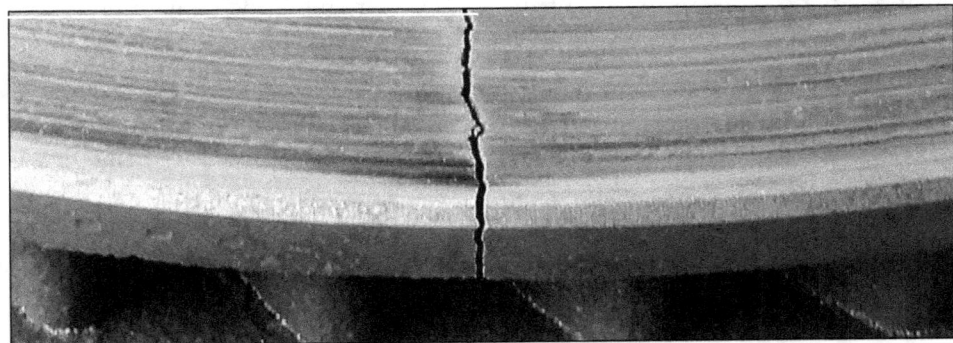

Extreme brake temperatures can cause all sorts of brake system problems. In the case of this stock Corvette Z06 rear rotor, high temperatures contributed to this crack in the outboard friction disc. The inboard friction disc remained intact, suggesting that it was running at a lower temperature.

CHAPTER 1

Heavy vehicles have some of the largest brake system components. In these applications, size is not dictated by high speeds, but rather by extreme vehicle weight. A typical passenger vehicle front brake assembly is shown on the left, while the one on the right is from a Ford F-350 work truck. (Randall Shafer/Delphi Corporation)

Brake temperatures can rise very quickly during high-performance driving. The orange wire shown coming out of the caliper above is actually a thermocouple lead to monitor brake pad temperatures on the track. The yellow connector on the strut allows for quick pad replacement without losing measurement capability. (Randall Shafer)

energy into kinetic energy. At the bottom of the hill the vehicle would have no more potential energy (at the bottom of the hill there is no more elevation difference) but because the vehicle is speeding along, it would have a great deal of kinetic energy.

Energy Transformation

In order for a vehicle in motion to slow down, it must get rid of some or all of the kinetic energy it possesses. Remembering that energy can neither be created nor destroyed, the only alternative is to transform it into some other type of energy to decelerate the vehicle. Before discussing the brakes, however, it's important to understand that the kinetic energy of a vehicle in motion can be converted into several other forms of energy *without* using the brakes. For example:

1. Energy is required simply to roll a tire along the road surface (also called rolling resistance). Consequently, the tires absorb some of the vehicle's kinetic energy by heating the surface temperature of the tread material.

2. Axles, differentials, bearings, and the engine itself require a certain amount of energy to overcome their own internal friction. As a result, these parts absorb some of the vehicle's kinetic energy by increasing their temperature and the temperature of the lubricants found inside them.

3. Shoving a vehicle through the air requires energy as well—stick your arm out the window of a fast-moving vehicle to feel this effect firsthand. This aerodynamic drag effect is responsible for the absorption of some of the vehicle's kinetic energy by increasing both the temperature of the displaced air and of the temperature of the vehicle body panels.

4. While not highly desirable, running the vehicle into a fixed object will certainly decrease its kinetic energy, usually with dramatic results. Whether it is a tree, another vehicle, or the turn-3 wall at Martinsville, the vehicle's kinetic energy will be used to deform body panels, frame rails, and who knows what else.

These four factors are certainly enough to convert all of your vehicle's kinetic energy into other forms all by themselves. However, with the exception of striking an immovable object, the *rate* of energy conversion is not sufficient enough to produce an acceptable level of deceleration. Just imagine how far you'd have to plan ahead if you had to rely on aerodynamic drag alone to stop at every stop sign!

Energy and the Brake System

And now, the moment you have all been waiting for: *The primary function of the brake system is to convert the kinetic energy of a vehicle in motion into thermal energy, or heat.* Naturally, the practical effect is to cause the vehicle to slow down, but an energy transformation must be made in order for the vehicle to change its speed at all. Remember, no kinetic energy change equals no change in speed.

So there you have it. The brakes do not stop the car—they simply convert energy from one form into another.

ENERGY CONVERSION

Calculating Brake System Temperature

In addition to performing its primary function of energy conversion, the brake system is also responsible for absorbing the heat it generates. After all, during the process of transforming kinetic energy into thermal energy, the heat needs to go somewhere. As a result, the brake system components can get quite warm during use.

If you know the amount of kinetic energy, the weight of the brake system components that are absorbing the energy, and the material they are made from, you can determine the rise in temperature of those brake system components as follows:

Rise in temperature (degrees F) = kinetic energy (ft-lb) ÷ weight of the brakes (lb) ÷ 77.8 (assuming cast iron)

(Note that this equation assumes all of the brake system components that absorb energy are made from cast iron. While that may be a reasonable generality, in practice it would be necessary to identify all of the different component materials and evaluate them individually.)

From this relationship it's apparent that the rise in temperature of the brakes is directly proportional to the kinetic energy in the brake system and the weight of the brake system components. What does this mean in plain English? Glad you asked…

Importance of Brake Sizing

Heat is the primary enemy of the brake system. Relatively speaking, cool brakes are happy brakes. Hot brakes are not happy brakes. The warmer the brakes, the higher the likelihood of excessive brake pad wear, rotor cracking, wheel bearing lubricant failure, brake fluid chemistry changes, caliper seal degradation, and so forth. The details of these maladies are discussed in later chapters, but in general cooler brake system components reduce the chances of undesirable brake system behaviors.

To this end, the equation for brake system temperature rise indicates that the relative increase in temperature is

ABS and Energy Conversion

Since anti-lock braking systems (ABS) are practically standard equipment on most modern vehicles, it's appropriate to discuss how they figure into the energy conversion equation. In short, they really don't.

At the very highest level, ABS relies on speed information from sensors located at each of the four wheels. Based on this information, it can calculate if any tires are rotating more slowly than the vehicle speed would suggest. This phenomenon is called tire slip (more to come in Chapter 2), and if the tire slip exceeds a preset threshold, ABS reacts by temporarily reducing brake fluid pressure to those individual wheels that display unacceptable levels of slip.

ABS can assist the driver in maintaining vehicle control when stopping on slippery surfaces, but it cannot change the total amount of kinetic energy that must be converted into heat. In other words, ABS does not let your vehicle drive around the laws of physics (or snow banks, as shown here). (Randall Shafer)

Naturally there are more details, but fundamentally ABS cannot change the total amount of vehicle kinetic energy. Through the cycling of brakes it can redistribute the energy to different components in the brake system, but a fixed amount of energy based on the vehicle's speed and weight still needs to be dissipated for the vehicle to stop.

directly proportional to the kinetic energy being dissipated. In other words, if kinetic energy goes up, temperature goes up. If kinetic energy goes down, temperature goes down.

However, the equation also indicates that brake temperatures are *inversely* proportional to the weight of the brake system components. In simple terms, if the overall weight of the brakes goes up, temperature goes down. If the weight of the brakes goes down, temperature goes up. Because of this important relationship between temperature and weight, engineers often refer to the weight of the brake system components as the *thermal mass*. It's a term you will see often throughout the course of this book, so file it away in your cerebral card catalog for future reference!

This is exactly the reason that big, heavy vehicles have large brake system components. It isn't necessarily to provide any more braking effort—it's to give the kinetic energy (heat) somewhere to go. From the kinetic energy comparison sidebar, we know that at any given speed the 80,000-pound tractor-trailer has to dissipate 26 *times* more kinetic energy than the 3,000-pound passenger car. If they used the exact same brake systems, the tractor-trailer brakes would experience 26 *times* the temperature increase of the passenger car. Consequently, tractor-trailer brakes are much larger than passenger car brakes because they need more thermal mass.

Conversely, the 400-pound race kart only has to deal with about 13 percent of the kinetic energy of the 3,000-pound passenger car, so its brake system components can be scaled down accordingly. This is why race kart rotors are only about six inches in diameter and less than 1/4 inch thick. They need less thermal mass because they need to store less thermal energy.

Summary

So what can you do to increase the thermal performance of your own brake system? Make it heavier. Everything else being equal, more thermal mass results in lower brake temperatures, and lower brake temperatures result in happier brake sys-

50 mph is not just 50 mph

"So," you think to yourself, "during a stop from 50 mph, the brake system must convert 50 mph worth of kinetic energy into thermal energy. Since a stop from 75 to 25 mph also dissipates 50 mph worth of speed, I bet the amount of kinetic energy is the same too, right?" In order to find out, the table below was generated for three different 50-mph stopping events.

Kinetic Energy Dissipated (in ft-lbs)

	50 to 0 mph	75 to 25 mph	100 to 50 mph
200-lb soap box derby car	16,722	33,445	50,167
400-lb race kart	33,445	66,890	100,334
600-lb sport bike	50,167	100,334	150,502
1,900-lb formula car	158,863	317,726	476,589
3,000-lb passenger car	250,836	501,672	752,508
80,000-lb tractor-trailer	6,688,963	13,377,926	20,066,890

Even though the speed difference in all three scenarios is the same 50 mph, the kinetic energy of the stops from 75 to 25 mph is double that of the stops from 50 mph and the stops from 100 to 50 mph triple the energy of the stops from 50 mph. From this data, it becomes quite apparent that 50 mph is not just 50 mph!

Race karts can achieve extremely high speeds, but because of their low weight, they don't need very much thermal mass capability at all. The single rear rotor on this Rotax Max kart absorbs nearly all of its kinetic energy, yet it measures only 8.00 inches in diameter and 0.56 inches in width.

ENERGY CONVERSION

tem components. Bigger is generally better.

How much bigger is too big then? Based on the physical size restrictions in and around the wheels, it's kind of difficult to put too large of a brake on a passenger car from a practical perspective. Usually if it fits inside the wheels that came on the vehicle you're in good shape. However, every application is different, and Chapters 11 through 14 go into more specifics.

Although not mentioned yet, brake cooling also plays a significant role in brake temperatures, but that topic is reserved for upcoming chapters. After all, if we covered everything in Chapter 1, there would be no need for a Chapter 2. And, as you are probably hoping, that's where you are going to learn what actually *does* stop the car.

The upgraded front rotor on this 2004 Corvette Z06 measures 14.0 inches in diameter and 1.3 inches in width. Because the stock 17-inch front wheels will not fit over a rotor this large without interference, they need to be replaced with 18-inch wheels.

Brake Temperature Sample Calculations

Typically, brake systems are happiest working in the 100-to 500-degree Fahrenheit range. Once brake temperatures begin to reach 700 to 900 degrees F, performance typically begins to suffer. In severe racing environments it is not uncommon to reach temperatures of 1,200 to 1,400 degrees F, but the materials and components used in these special applications are designed to survive under these demanding conditions (for the length of one race, anyway).

The following table was developed to show how large an impact thermal mass can have on brake temperatures. For all examples, a single stop from 75 mph was used to determine the vehicle's kinetic energy. The temperature rise was then calculated based on total vehicle brake system weights of 5, 50, and 500 pounds (assumed to be made of cast iron).

Brake System Temperature Rise (in degrees F)

	5 lbs	50 lbs	500 lbs
200-lb soap box derby car	97	10	1
400-lb race kart	193	19	2
600-lb sport bike	290	29	3
1,900-lb formula car	919	92	9
3,000-lb passenger car	1,451	145	15
80,000-lb tractor-trailer	38,689	3,869	387

(Note that the temperatures listed are averages of all of the components that absorb energy. In reality the parts will not all rise in temperature at the same rate, nor will they even display uniform temperature themselves; however, doing an analysis by averaging makes the math easy enough that you don't need a PhD in the room to help you.)

The data above shows that it is possible to have brakes that are too big and/or too small for the job! For example, using 50 pounds worth of brake system components on an 80,000-pound tractor-trailer would generate enough heat to melt the cast iron brake components right off of the vehicle (the melting point of cast iron is approximately 2,800 degrees F). And, while a 600-pound sport bike with 50-pound brake system components would have extremely low brake temperatures (a rise of only 29 degrees F from 75 mph), the brake system components would probably weigh more than the entire wheel and tire assembly, making the bike difficult to accelerate and/or steer.

Author's disclaimer: The table above assumes that 100 percent of the vehicle's kinetic energy will be absorbed by the brake system, when in fact the number is closer to 50 to 75 percent for relatively aggressive stops. For this reason, the numbers listed above are higher than those you would actually measure on a vehicle, but the trends and orders of magnitude are representative of the real world.

CHAPTER 2

TIRES STOP THE CAR

As you just learned in Chapter 1, brakes do not stop the car—they simply convert energy from one form into another. The responsibility of stopping the car falls solely on the tires, or more specifically the tire-to-road interface. Only these four palm-sized patches of rubber that are in contact with the road below (the contact patches) govern how quickly a car will stop.

Of course, a poorly designed or malfunctioning brake system can certainly *prevent* a vehicle from achieving its maximum deceleration rate, but the best stopping performance each and every time is dictated by the tire-to-road interface. A few simple equations are used later in this chapter to illustrate this point, but for the next few pages sit back and hang tight. It's now time to talk about another law.

The First Law of Motion

You may recognize Sir Isaac Newton as the guy who allegedly defined the concept of gravity when an apple fell on his head one afternoon. However, for a few paragraphs you should look past that rather major accomplishment and focus on the first of his three stated Laws of Motion.

(Note that Newton's First Law of Motion is not to be confused with the First Law of Thermodynamics from Chapter 1. Apparently, every physicist wants to be known for discovering the first law of something or other.)

Paraphrasing Newton with a reasonable degree of accuracy, the First Law of Motion states that an object at rest will stay at rest unless it is acted upon by an external force. Conversely, it also states that an object in motion will stay in motion unless it too is acted upon by an external force. In other words, things sitting still will just sit still until you push them and things that are moving continue to move until you do something to stop them.

Brake Forces

Applying Newton's First Law of Motion to vehicle brake systems is relatively straightforward. It goes something like this: Once in motion, a vehicle essentially will not slow down or stop unless it is acted upon by an external force, or what can now be called a *brake force*.

So where do these brake forces come from? Essentially, they result from any mechanism that absorbs a vehicle's kinetic energy (they are one and the same). Consequently, this merits a brief revisit of

The brakes don't stop the car—that's the tires' job! For this reason, tires come in a wide variety of shapes, sizes, and designs to optimize the available brake force. The lack of a tread pattern on this tire makes it a poor choice for wet-weather performance, but a great choice for racing when the track is dry. (Hoosier Racing Tire)

Brake forces can come from a variety of sources other than the brake system. For example, if a mischievous co-driver were to force a car traveling at highway speeds into first gear, the resulting driveline friction forces would be transmitted immediately back to the driven wheels. Not that we speak from experience here...

energy transformation factors from Chapter 1, now adding in the resulting brake force contributions for each mechanism:

1. *Rolling resistance brake forces* result from the body and tread of the tire resisting deformation at the contact patch. As the tire flattens out against the road, a force is generated that resists the motion of the vehicle.

2. *Axle, differential, bearing, and engine brake forces* result from rotating and reciprocating friction. As these components mesh and rub together, they resist any motion between themselves, which is then mechanically transferred to the tire-to-road interface.

3. *Aerodynamic brake forces* result from the vehicle simply traveling through the air. As the vehicle attempts to push the air out of its path, the air molecules react by resisting the motion. In other words, the air is not happy with the situation and it pushes back (the sensation you get from holding your hand out of the car window).

4. *Mechanical deformation brake forces* result from running the vehicle into a fixed object. Again, this is a highly undesirable, yet highly effective, way of stopping a vehicle. Turn 3 at Martinsville pushes back pretty hard, as do trees and telephone poles.

So, while it is nice to be aware of these secondary brake force mechanisms, the whole point of this book is to understand the contribution of the brake system components. Consequently, the rest of this chapter leaves these factors behind and focuses on brake forces occurring at the tire-to-road interface as a result of brake system operation.

Tire Slip

Tire slip, or simply slip, is the single most important concept in understanding any aspect of vehicle performance (at least in my humble opinion). Without slip, vehicles could neither accelerate, nor decelerate, nor turn, as a tire can only generate force when it is slipping. As you'll learn in a few moments, a tire that is not slipping is free rolling, or coasting, and a free-rolling tire does not generate any force at all (except for the small amount of brake force due to its internal rolling resistance).

Before going any further, let's clarify one important point: A tire does not need to be spinning wildly or skidding out of control to be slipping. Although these conditions are a result of a significant amount of slip, there are many other times where a slipping tire does not actually *look* like it's slipping at all. Yet for all practical purposes, any time your vehicle is in motion, its tires are slipping, even though you can't see it with the naked eye.

Applying this concept to brake system performance is relatively straightforward. In order for a tire to generate a brake force, it must be slipping relative to the road surface in the direction of travel (normally to a very small level, but it is slipping nonetheless). If a tire is not slipping, it is not generating any brake force (again, ignoring the brake force due to its internal rolling resistance).

Although that may sound odd, it makes more sense by taking a moment to formally define slip. Tire slip can be quantified mathematically by the following equation:

Tire Slip Calculations

The data in the table below illustrates how much tire slip would be present for given combinations of tire speed and vehicle speed.

	Tire speed	Vehicle speed	Tire slip
Condition 1	50 mph	50 mph	0%
Condition 2	45 mph	50 mph	10%
Condition 3	0 mph	50 mph	100%

So, what do these numbers mean? Well, a few observations can quickly be made:

1. Condition 1 indicates that when the tire speed (50 mph) is the same as the vehicle speed (50 mph), there is zero slip present. Because this is a free-rolling condition, there is no brake force present between the tire and the road. The vehicle will be coasting.

2. Condition 2 indicates that when the tire slows down (45 mph) relative to the vehicle (50 mph), the slip level increases (10 percent in this case). This is the slip range where most normal braking occurs.

3. Condition 3 represents a tire that has stopped spinning (0 mph) although the vehicle continues to speed along (50 mph), resulting in 100-percent slip. This is the classic "brakes locked up" situation, which is usually accompanied by screeching sounds and billowing tire smoke. Note that this condition is also commonly referred to as sliding or skidding and is generally an undesirable way to slow down a vehicle.

100 percent tire slip, also known as wheel lock, occurs if a vehicle is still moving yet the tire is no longer rotating. This may be amusing for the spectators, but it's not the most effective way to achieve the best possible stopping distance. (Wayne Flynn/pdxsports.com)

CHAPTER 2

Different surface textures, environmental conditions, and slip levels can influence the brake force contribution from the adhesive, deformation, and the mechanical wear modes of friction. For example, water on the road surface partially separates the tire from the road, greatly reducing the available adhesive friction. This results in extended stopping distances. (Wayne Flynn/pdxsports.com)

Although ABS is designed to prevent such theatrics, pulling the fuse and stomping on the brake pedal is an effective way to force the tires to achieve 100-percent slip. While this technique won't generate the shortest possible stopping distances, the resulting skid marks provide evidence that rubber is physically removed from the tire under these conditions. (The Tire Rack)

$$\text{Tire slip (\%)} = (1 - \{\text{speed of the tire (mph)} \div \text{speed of the vehicle (mph)}\}) \times 100$$

What this implies is that in order for a tire to generate brake force, it must be spinning more slowly than the speed of the vehicle would suggest. However, looking at this relationship in tabular format is somewhat easier on the eyes. For this reason, make your way over the tire slip sidebar for a different look at this slightly perplexing situation.

How Brake Forces are Generated

So now that you know that slip is required to generate force, how exactly does the slipping tire generate brake force? As the tire rolls along without slip, there is constant interaction between the tire and the road, yet with the exception of a small amount of rolling resistance, there are no brake forces generated. However, as soon as a torque is applied to the tire by the brake system (more to come in Chapter 3), it wants to slow down.

Unfortunately for the tire, the car does not want to slow down, and consequently the tire is forced to stretch and distort. This is because there is resistance, or friction, at the tire-to-road interface that prevents the tire from decelerating as rapidly as it would like. Few things are more fun than getting a group of contact physicists together in a room and asking them why and how tires generate these forces, but for now it makes more sense to break it down into simple, bite-sized pieces.

Tires used for racing in the rain are optimized to take maximum advantage of the deformation effect, since water on the track greatly reduces the adhesive effect. The rain tire shown here uses extremely soft rubber compounds to enhance deformation, while large, open channels molded into the tread face purge water from the contact patch in an attempt to increase adhesion. (Hoosier Racing Tire)

Adhesive Effects

Any time two objects in nature come in contact with one another, there are momentary electrostatic bonds formed between them. In other words, to some extent they want to stick together. One of the best practical examples is that of garden-variety duct tape. The adhesive characteristics of the tape allow it to effectively stick temporarily wherever it is placed.

This same mechanism is in effect as the tire rolls along the road. During braking, the contact patch is continuously forming adhesive bonds with the road surface below, which resist the tire's desire to decelerate—after all, if the tire were hanging in mid-air, it would slow down much more quickly when the brakes were applied. While in this case the adhesive effect may not be as pronounced as it is with duct tape, the rubber tire will

TIRES STOP THE CAR

A tire operating at 100-percent slip is generating a significant amount of brake force through the mechanical wear mechanism. Unfortunately, this wear will be concentrated at one location on the tire tread. The resulting flat spot causes significant vibration and less-than-optimal performance if it isn't replaced immediately. (The Tire Rack)

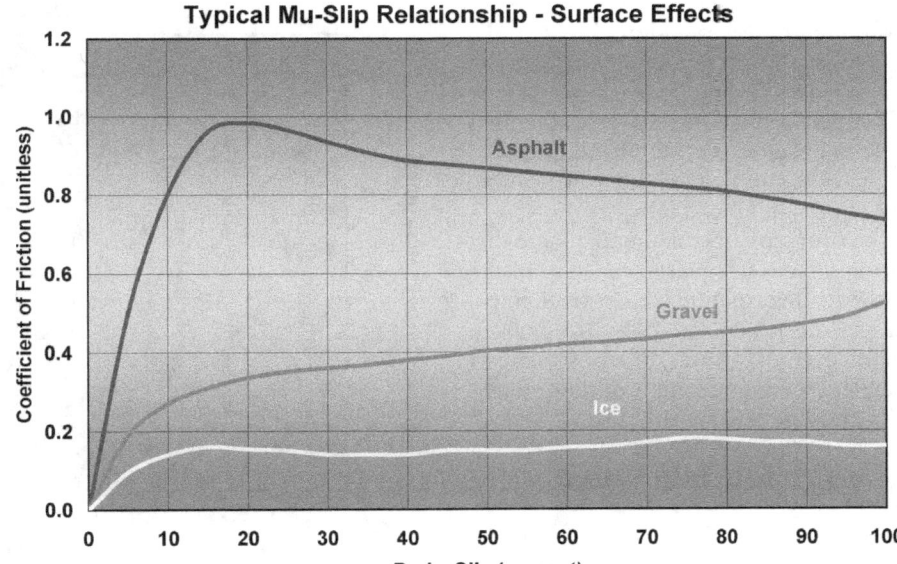

A mu-slip curve relates a tire's brake force potential to its level of slip, with every tire and surface combining to generate a unique mu-slip relationship. The blue curve shown here is typical of a street car tire on a dry, paved road, with a maximum coefficient of friction of approximately 0.95. This particular tire reaches this level when operating at 18-percent slip. However, notice that when driving on ice and gravel, the maximum coefficients of friction (as well as the shapes of the curves themselves) can change dramatically!

elastically deform, and consequently slip, when brake torque is applied. The force of the electrostatic bonds formed between the tire and the road is the first component of the total brake force.

Deformation or Keying Effects

Although all objects found in nature are deformable to a certain extent, rubber has a relatively high amount of built-in elasticity. Because of this characteristic, when weight is placed on a tire, it deforms into any irregularities in the road surface. Different varieties of rubber deform to different extents, but fundamentally as more weight is applied, more rubber is forced down into the road surface. As a result, the tire becomes mechanically interlocked with the textured road surface.

During braking, the contact patch is continuously keying with the passing road surface, which resists the tire's desire to decelerate. The rubber molecules pressed into the road surface resist being dragged along (they would much rather stay stuck in the crevices in the road surface than be pulled along it), which results in the tire body elastically deforming when brake torque is applied. The force required to stretch the tire body is the second component of the total brake force.

Mechanical Tearing or Wear Effects

Although similar to the deformation effect, mechanical tearing is sort of like mechanical interlocking gone bad. As load and texture combine to squish more and more rubber molecules into the road surface, it's possible to create a situation where enough brake torque is present to physically rip away bits of rubber in the tread area and leave them stuck in the road

ABS and Tire Selection

Because the ABS algorithm relies on tire slip calculations to determine if ABS control is required, much of its calibration is based on assumed tire mu-slip characteristics. In nearly all cases, these assumptions are based on the mu-slip characteristics for the vehicle's original brand and size of tire.

What this means to the enthusiast is that if you're upgrading your tires for any reason, the existing ABS calibrations might not be optimized for the new tire's mu-slip characteristics. Unfortunately there are no user-programmable changes that can be made to remedy this situation. Unlike some engine computers, which allow for flash reprogramming, ABS controllers are off-limits.

The reality is that in most cases ABS is tolerant of small changes made in tire mu-slip characteristics, but instrumented testing would most likely demonstrate that the system could benefit from calibration optimization. Every application is different, but in general the overall benefits of the new tire may very well outweigh the small loss in ABS performance.

behind the moving vehicle. In other words, the tire leaves skid marks.

During this extreme braking, the tire tread is violently worn away by the passing road surface, which further resists the tire's desire to decelerate. The force required to rip apart the tire tread is the third component of the total brake force.

In summary, the total brake force that a tire produces is equal to the sum of the adhesive, deformation, and mechanical tearing forces generated during a given braking event. However, one of the largest variables in the generation of these forces is the absolute level of tire slip.

The Mu-Slip Curve

Up to this point, tire slip and brake force have been discussed as two relatively discrete phenomena. It's now time to permanently link them together, because when it comes to vehicle braking, tire slip and brake force are inseparable.

Unfortunately, the fundamental equation that defines the relationship between slip and force is not easy to derive—there are many complex interactions at play. In fact, the most common way to relate slip and force is not to calculate anything at all, but rather to make measurements and plot the results. And, as an added twist, in order to simplify the plots it's typical to measure a tire's effective coefficient of friction, or mu (pronounced mew), as determined by the following relationship:

*Mu (unitless) =
measured brake force (lb) ÷
weight acting on the tire (lb)*

This relationship can then be plotted graphically to illustrate a tire's mu-versus-

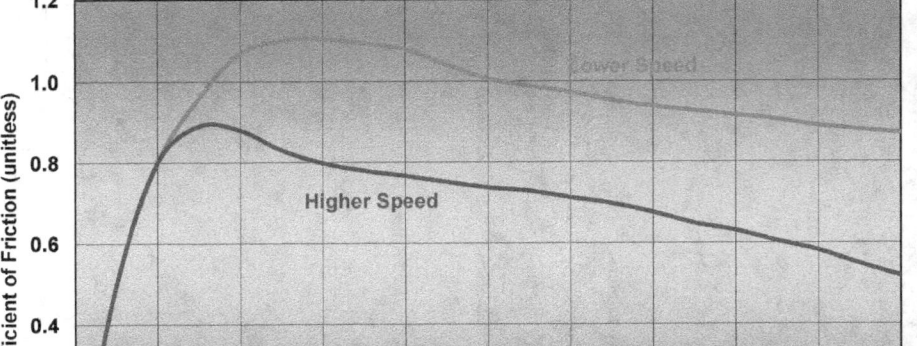

Vehicle speed can also influence the mu-slip relationship. In general, as speed increases the maximum coefficient of friction decreases, while at lower speeds tires are able to generate higher coefficients of friction. Lower speeds can also decrease a tire's sensitivity to slip, as demonstrated by the wide plateau between 20- and 40-percent slip.

slip relationship. In the auto industry these are most commonly referred to as *mu-slip curves* and define, in an indirect way, how much brake force a tire will generate at a given level of slip.

So why is this important? Because the mu-slip relationship can tell us how much deceleration (how short of a stopping distance) a given tire can provide.

Mu-Slip Considerations

While the concept of the mu-slip curve may sound elegant, there is never just a single mu-slip relationship. The mu-slip curve is a moving target and countless factors can influence its shape and size.

A typical dry asphalt road surface contains irregularly shaped protrusions that temporarily bond to the tire as it passes by. However, contaminants found on the road surface such as water, ice, snow, or sand can limit the effectiveness of the bonding. In some cases, this can drastically reduce the maximum brake force possible. (The Tire Rack)

Just a few are discussed here to get you thinking.

Effect of Surface: Every surface that the vehicle encounters will cause the tire to display a different mu-slip relationship. You know this from firsthand experience, as driving on glare ice certainly is a different experience than driving on a typical paved road. The seat of your pants tells you that glare ice does not allow the tire to generate as much force as it would on dry pavement, but why?

Looking back a few paragraphs, you can now explain this real-world observation. When driving on a slippery surface, or even just a wet one, the ability of a tire to generate adhesive, deformation, and mechanical wear forces can change dramatically. For example, a thin layer of water on an otherwise typical paved road can prevent the tire from generating adhesive forces, much like a layer of water prevents duct tape from sticking effectively. The water may also interfere with the tire's ability to generate deformation and/or mechanical wear forces, but in any case the end result is that the overall level of available brake force will go down.

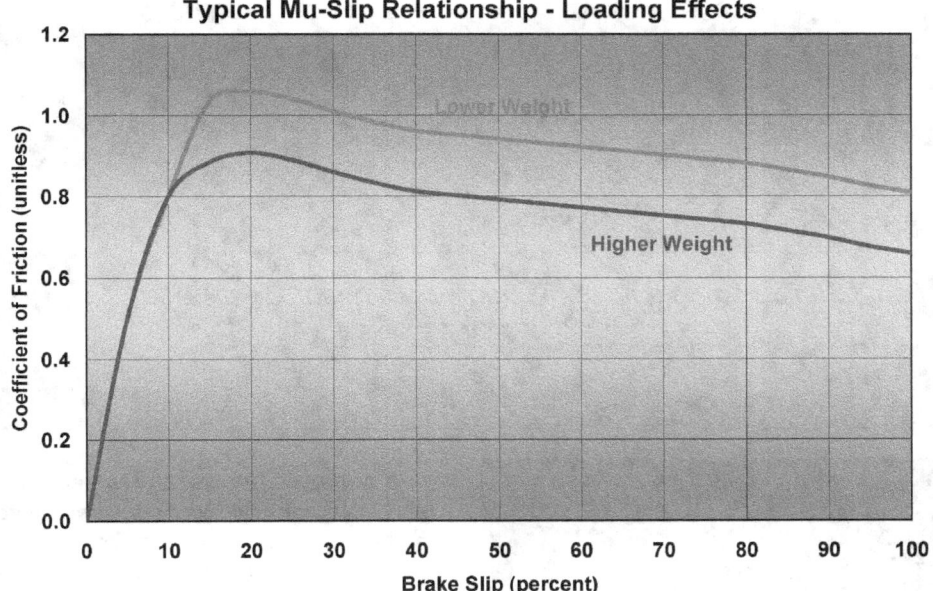

Because tires are sensitive to load, increasing the weight on the tire decreases its effective coefficient of friction. Conversely, removing weight from a tire increases its efficiency, thereby allowing it to generate higher coefficients of friction. This is one of the primary reasons that competition vehicles are made as light as possible.

Effect of Speed: As a vehicle is driven, it experiences a broad range of speeds. No surprise there. However, without any warning whatsoever, the tire's ability to generate brake force changes with these variations in vehicle speed. In general, tires are capable of generating their highest brake forces at low speeds and gradually lose brake force capability as speeds rise. Why? Because at lower speeds the tire has more time to establish its electrostatic bonds and mechanical interlocking (keying) with the road surface, enhancing the total brake force available.

Hand-in-hand with changes in brake force are changes in the maximum sustainable slip. Typically, a tire continues to provide increasing brake force at elevated slip levels as speed drops because the tire again has more time to establish interactions with the road surface.

When you combine these two effects, the result is slower speeds yielding stronger bonds at higher levels of sustainable slip. The practical application here is that during a given braking event, a vehicle will decelerate from high speed to low speed, whatever those speeds may be. Therefore, most vehicles achieve their highest rate of deceleration right before they stop moving. In other words, the mu-slip curve changes throughout the duration of the stopping event, gradually increasing the total available brake force until the braking event ends.

The caveat is that for cars with wings (real aerodynamic pieces, properly adjusted; not peel-and-stick spoilers), the added downforce created by these devices is highest during the initial brake application and decreases for the duration of the stop. For this reason, a vehicle utilizing aerodynamic aids might actually achieve its highest rate of deceleration at the beginning of the braking event.

Effect of Loading: Tires are adaptable, yet naturally lazy objects. They gladly generate braking forces regardless of how much weight they are asked to support, but as the load upon them increases, their efficiency drops. Said differently, as weight is added to a vehicle the tire's brake force capability goes up but at a decreasing rate. They do more work, but really are not too happy about it.

Because of this phenomenon, adding weight to a vehicle increases its stopping distance (decreased deceleration) and removing weight from a vehicle decreases its stopping distance (increased deceleration). The amount of change will be a function of how much weight is at play

If you are driving around on tires from days gone by, simply upgrading to modern radial performance rubber can make a significant improvement in stopping distance. Although this 1969 Chevelle SS is still equipped with four-wheel drum brakes, its modern tires allow it to decelerate with enhanced confidence (until the drum brakes overheat, anyway). (Randall Shafer)

CHAPTER 2

A tire's treadwear rating can sometimes be used as an indicator of a tire's performance capability, with lower values suggesting softer, stickier compounds. While most passenger car tires have tread wear ratings of 300 to 500, the tire shown has a rating of only 20, indicating that although it may be great for track use, it probably wouldn't last many miles on the street. (Randall Shafer)

Warmer tire temperatures generally lead to better braking performance—to a point, that is. Most racing tires tend to generate maximum output at temperatures between 180 and 220 degrees F. Go much above these levels, however, and performance can fall off dramatically. Heavier cars like this BMW typically generate higher tire temperatures than smaller, lighter cars. (Wayne Flynn/pdxsports.com)

and how sensitive the tire is to the change, but fundamentally to achieve the shortest possible stopping distance, the vehicle should be made as light as possible.

Choosing the Best Tires

Because of the wide variety of surfaces, speeds, loads, and road conditions, experienced in daily driving, selecting a "one size fits all" tire is an exercise in futility. Yes, it's true that most people select a single tire, usually of the all-season variety, but a tire that works well on the racetrack is probably not suitable on icy roads. There's a reason that Formula 1 cars don't race on snow tires!

In order to optimize high-performance braking under typical conditions (clean, dry pavement), tires typically adhere to the following recipe. This is a blatant oversimplification, but in general, high-performance tires use low durometer (soft) rubber compounds and shallow tread depths. In extreme cases (such as racing applications), there may not be any tread pattern at all.

However, for the best stopping performance on snowy roads, the recipe looks a

Snow tire design usually incorporates very soft tread compounds with complex tread patterns. The snow tire above also has multiple thin grooves, or sipes, cut into each individual tread block that increase the number of biting edges to enhance traction in snow and on ice. (The Tire Rack)

little bit different. Although low durometer rubber compounds are still employed, the real difference is that snow tires have deep tread depths with aggressive tread patterns.

Rubber Durometer

Earlier in this chapter you learned that rubber's highly elastic nature allows it to generate brake force due to adherent bonding, mechanical deformation, and mechanical wear. The absolute level of brake force is ultimately limited by how much rubber is able to come into contact with the road below, and higher levels of elasticity generally allow for more deformation into the peaks and valleys at the road surface interface.

A tire's treadwear rating (found molded into the tire's sidewall) is the only published indicator of the rubber's relative elasticity. Roughly speaking, lower numbers indicate softer, and usually better performing, tires (most performance street tires have ratings between 120 and 220, with competition tires even lower). Higher numbers (600+) reflect tires that act more like bricks than rubber, lending themselves to improved fuel economy at the expense of braking performance.

When designing a tire for the best possible stopping performance, it is desirable to manufacture it from the softest rubber possible, regardless of the surface condition. Hence, both high-performance tires and snow tires use soft rubber compounds. However, the downside is that softer materials tend to generate higher operating temperatures due to all of the deformation, or squirming, occurring at the contact patch.

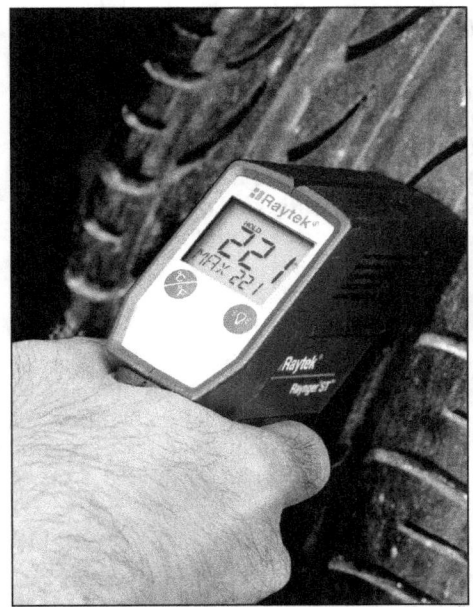

Tire temperatures indicate how hard a tire is working. For this reason, a pyrometer is typically used to measure tire temperatures at the end of every track session. The pyrometer shown here uses infrared technology to measure the tread surface temperature, while probe-type pyrometers more accurately measure the tread core temperature. (Randall Shafer)

The seat of your pants tells you that vehicles take longer to stop on ice than they do on asphalt. This is because the coefficient of friction of most tires on ice is much lower than it would be on dry pavement. Consequently, the maximum rate of deceleration is lower as well. (Randall Shafer)

Now on one hand, elevated tire temperatures are a good thing. As the tire heats up it becomes even *more* elastic, which allows it to form better bonds with the road surface. This is exactly why race tires need a few laps to "warm up" before they operate at their peak levels. Typically, a happy race tire operates in the neighborhood of 180 to 220 degrees F and is designed to withstand these conditions for the duration of its intended lifespan.

The flip side is that additional heat leads to better performance *until* the point at which the tire begins to overheat. Once a tire exceeds its optimum operating temperature it actually begins to break down and starts to lose its ability to generate brake force. This in turn results in even higher temperatures and more deformation, which perpetuates the condition until the tire quite literally self-destructs and fails. This is generally viewed as a bad thing and explains the preponderance of tire engineers walking around the paddock holding tire pyrometers and clipboards. So in summary, soft is good, but *too* soft is bad.

Tread Pattern and Tread Depth

A tire's tread pattern is essentially an escape path for any contaminants between the tire and the road that could prevent optimized traction. Be it water, mud, snow, or sand, a tread pattern offers the offending material a route to exit from the contact patch, thereby allowing for enhanced tire-to-road contact. Tire engineers would argue that it isn't quite that cut and dry, but it's sufficient for now.

Based on the type of surface expected, tread patterns can vary greatly. A tire designed for use in deep, off-road sand differs greatly from a tire designed for use on a formula car in the rain. Snow tires with thousands of tiny grooves, or *sipes*, cut into the tread blocks look altogether different from tires designed for mud with their massive, blocky tread lugs. In any case though, these unique tread patterns are designed to optimize the tire-to-road interface.

Tread patterns can be a good thing, but the downside of a tread pattern is that as tires slip and generate forces, the individual tread blocks squirm around a good bit. This results in—you guessed it—heat. Just like tires that are made from rubber that is too soft, a tire with a deep tread pattern will overheat and fall off in performance quicker than a tire with shallow tread pattern.

Now, if contaminants are not expected during the operating life of the tire, it is common to construct them without any tread pattern whatsoever. In the racing world, these tires are typically referred to as *slicks* due to their lack of features cut into the tread surface. While slicks generally offer other benefits as well (very high force potential due to very soft tread compounds), their reduced rate of internal heat generation makes them standard equipment in any racing series where they're allowed.

Calculating Maximum Deceleration

Since this is a book about brakes, you could argue that enough time has already been spent studying the details of tires and tire design. However, if Chapter 2 ended now you'd be missing the cherry on top. Pay close attention, as what you're about to learn may completely change your perspective on high-performance brake system upgrades.

For two chapters now you've heard that the brakes don't stop the car, yet when people decide to modify their brake systems, be it for the street or for the track, it usually stems from a desire to have their vehicles stop in a shorter distance. Yes, heat management and energy conversion are great, but shorter stopping distances are typically first and foremost on the want list, right? What these people really need is a different tire, not a better braking system. Here's the physics to prove it.

When Newton's First Law of Motion was discussed earlier, the text neglected to state another very important relationship between objects and forces. Cutting straight to the chase, if a force is applied to an object, it will change speed as a result of the force being applied. In other words, if you apply a brake force to your vehicle it will decelerate.

Applying this back to a vehicle in motion, you end up with the following relationship:

*Brake force (lb) =
vehicle weight (lb) x vehicle deceleration (g)*

However, you also learned that brake force is also defined as the relationship between the weight acting on the tire and the effective coefficient of friction. Rearranging the equation from a few pages back and substituting vehicle weight for tire corner weight (because there are four tires on the vehicle) yields:

*Brake force (lb) =
vehicle weight (lb) x mu (unitless)*

So, now you have been exposed to two different equations for brake force. One of the nice things about equations is that if you have two equations that equal the same thing, you can set them equal to one another to see what falls out of the mess. In this particular case you end up with:

*Vehicle weight (lb) x
vehicle deceleration (g) =
vehicle weight (lb) x mu (unitless)*

Almost there. Now, dividing by vehicle weight (therefore taking it out of the equation) leaves you with:

Vehicle deceleration (g) = mu (unitless)

If you managed to stay alert for all of that you now see that vehicle deceleration (in units of g's) is always equal to the effective coefficient of friction between the tire and the road. This proves, in no uncertain terms, that the tires stop the car.

Summary

So what can you do to increase the deceleration performance of your own brake system? The answer here is simple: forget the brake system and invest in the right set of tires. From road racing to rock crawling, from drag racing to snow rallying, there are optimized tires for every application. Choose wisely, as the tire sets the ultimate limit of deceleration each and every time.

With that said, there are plenty of ways in which substandard brake system design can *prevent* the tire from achieving its maximum deceleration. In addition,

If the road is dry and clean, no tread pattern at all is the way to go. Many street tires approximate this level of design, but only true racing slicks eliminate patterns in the tire tread completely. The tire shown here displays two shallow circumferential tread grooves, which only exist to make the tire legal by DOT standards. This permits the use of this tire in racing classes that require street-legal tires. (Hoosier Racing Tire)

at deceleration levels *below* the maximum, the brake system can certainly impact the effort required by a driver to bring a vehicle to rest. It should come as no surprise then that this is exactly where Chapters 3 and 4 are headed.

Before getting too far ahead of ourselves, though, it is necessary to take a 30,000-foot look at the brake system, starting with the driver pressing on the brake pedal and ending where the tire makes contact with the road below. Volumes of brake knowledge are headed your way, but through it all don't forget that the brake system is simply trying to enable the tire do all of the work it is capable of performing.

Surface Effects on Maximum Deceleration

A vehicle's maximum deceleration is always limited by the maximum coefficient of friction available at the contact patch. While the values shown below are approximate, they are quite representative of what you can expect to encounter in the real world with typical performance tires.

	Mu peak (unitless)	Maximum deceleration (g)
Glare ice	0.1–0.2	0.1–0.2
Wet grass	0.2–0.4	0.2–0.4
Packed snow	0.3–0.6	0.3–0.6
Loose gravel	0.4–0.7	0.4–0.7
Wet pavement	0.6–0.8	0.6–0.8
Dry pavement	0.8–1.0	0.8–1.0
Dry pavement with race tires	1.3–1.6	1.3–1.6

While tire selection is critical to brake system performance, tire care can be just as important. In most cases, this is as simple as maintaining the appropriate inflation pressure at all times. Tires that are either under inflated or over inflated may compromise braking performance. (Randall Shafer)

CHAPTER 3

BRAKE SYSTEM DESIGN

If you skipped over the first two chapters, you missed the big news: brakes don't stop your car. If you didn't skip them, well, now you have heard it again. In case you have not caught on by now, this is a point that needs to be driven home.

Yet you know that when you press on the brake pedal the vehicle will, in most cases, slow down. Usually, the more you push on the pedal, the more deceleration you feel. Heck, the vehicle might even stop. Eventually, anyway.

Chapter 1 taught you that between the effects of tire rolling resistance, driveline frictional losses, and aerodynamic drag, the kinetic energy of the vehicle in motion can be absorbed without the need for a separate vehicle brake system. However, there are often times when the *rate* of energy conversion is not sufficient enough to produce an acceptable rate of deceleration (such as driving around town, let alone on a race track). This is where the brake system steps in, and certain modifications may prove useful to the casual driver, high-performance enthusiast, and pro racer alike.

Now, before analyzing the benefits (and tradeoffs!) of adjustable proportioning valves, 6-piston calipers, floating rotors, DOT 5.1 brake fluid, and stainless steel braided brake lines, it's necessary to take a high-level look at a typical brake system. Knowing the roles of the individual components will better prepare you for the detailed discussions to come.

Driver Applied Force

Brake systems are fitted to vehicles in order to increase their deceleration capability. They accomplish this task by converting energy at a higher rate than the aforementioned passive mechanisms. In fact, the rate of energy conversion is limited only by the tractive capability of the tires and the thermal capacity of the brake system components.

None of this matters one bit, however, if the driver does not press on the pedal in the first place. If you neglect the effects of tire rolling resistance, driveline frictional losses, and aerodynamic drag for the rest of this chapter, it's only the force exerted by the driver on the brake pedal that creates slip (and hopefully force) at the contact patch. It's not quite like Fred Flintstone, but all of the force the brake system generates ultimately comes from the driver's leg.

Of course, most people are not strong enough to decelerate a 3,000-pound vehicle at a reasonable rate from even 20 mph using only their leg muscles. The brake system is therefore designed to amplify the leg force generated by the driver (while of course still converting kinetic energy into heat). This brings forward the concept of brake system *gain*.

Gain

Gain is really nothing more than a fancy way of saying multiplication. The brake system gain relates the amount of brake system force input to brake system force output. In equation form:

$$\text{Brake system gain (unitless)} = \text{total brake force (lb)} \div \text{driver's leg force (lb)}$$

For example, if a leg force of 50 pounds on the brake pedal nets a total brake force of 2,000 pounds at the four contact patches, the brake system gain is 40. You could also say that the system increased force at a 40-to-1 ratio, or that the gain was 40:1.

So where does the brake system gain come from? In brief, each of the brake system components is designed to provide its own gain through some type of mechanical advantage. The overall brake system gain is therefore equal to the individual brake system component gains all multiplied together.

If a brake system is designed properly, even the very weakest driver should be capable of generating enough leg force to decelerate the vehicle at the limit defined by the tire-to-road interface. This dictates that every vehicle has a unique gain requirement. As a result, much of the art of brake system design revolves simply around developing the appropriate amount of gain.

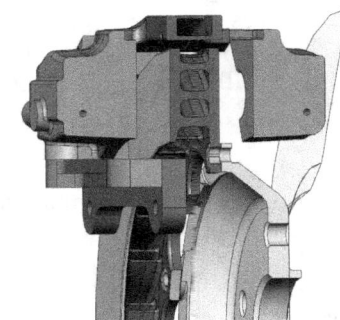

Although the tire ultimately stops the car, it's the combined contributions of the brake system components that multiply the driver's leg force to stop the car. For this reason, methodical brake system design is required to ensure that all performance expectations are met. (StopTech)

CHAPTER 3

The gain of a brake system component is simply the relationship between the force coming in and the force going out. In the case of a brake booster, the ratio of these two forces is called the boost gain. (Randall Shafer)

amount of amplification, or gain, is a function of the brake pedal *leverage*.

You probably learned the concept of leverage on a teeter-totter—the farther you sit from the middle (the pivot point, or fulcrum), the more weight you can lift on the other end. In the case of the brake pedal assembly, the fulcrum is at the top of the brake pedal arm, the brake pedal pad is on the opposite end, and the output rod is somewhere in between. Based on the distance between these features, the pedal ratio can be defined as:

Pedal ratio (unitless) = distance, pad to fulcrum (in) ÷ distance, output rod to fulcrum (in)

Because the distance from the pad to the fulcrum is longer than the distance

Force Distribution

In addition to amplifying the driver's leg force, the brake system must also distribute all of this amplified force to the four corners of the car, ultimately directing it to the four tire contact patches. It may also need to modify the brake force distribution as a function of deceleration, speed, or vehicle loading.

While brake force distribution is a critical responsibility of the brake system, you'll need to wait until Chapter 4 to learn more. For the remainder of this chapter, the focus is on brake system gain.

Brake System Overview

It's now time to analyze the mechanical attributes, the functional responsibilities, and gain characteristics of each individual brake system component. Note that this is required reading before jumping to Chapters 5 through 10 which go into much deeper detail!

The Brake Pedal

Most people are already familiar with the brake pedal *pad*—it's where you press to make the your vehicle stop. But while most of you are aware of the part of the pedal that makes contact with your foot, two equally important components of the pedal assembly, the *output rod* and *fulcrum*, are generally out of sight. Together, these three separate parts define the brake pedal assembly.

The primary function of the brake pedal assembly is to harness and multiply the force exerted by the driver's leg. The

---

How Much Gain is Enough?

To illustrate the variability in gain from vehicle to vehicle, the following table demonstrates how brake system gain can be influenced by just vehicle weight alone. Note that this analysis assumes a maximum driver leg force of 50 pounds and a deceleration limit of 0.9g for each vehicle.

	Gain Required
400-lb race kart	7.2:1
1,900-lb formula car	34.2:1
3,000-lb passenger car	54:1
80,000-lb tractor-trailer	1,440:1

Even though the assumptions listed might not be perfectly accurate for each vehicle, it becomes quite clear that there is not one optimum value for brake system gain. A brake system designed to generate 0.9g on a 1,900-pound formula car would only generate 0.02g if installed on an 80,000-pound tractor-trailer.

The overall brake system gain is a function of how much absolute force is required to stop the vehicle. Due to its weight, this 60,000-pound airport snowplow requires much more brake system gain than a typical passenger car. (Randall Shafer)

Conversely, if the 3,000-pound passenger car brake system were installed on the 400-pound race kart, only 6.7 pounds of driver leg effort would be required to achieve maximum deceleration. This would make the brake system response less progressive than desirable. In fact, with a gain this high, the brake pedal would be so sensitive that it could probably be replaced with an on-off switch to achieve the same result.

In summary, if the gain is too low the vehicle will be difficult to stop with reasonable leg efforts. If the gain is too high, the brake system response may be touchy or grabby. Determining the proper gain comes down to driver preference, and the careful selection of components will allow you to tailor it to meet your needs.

from the output rod to the fulcrum, the pedal ratio is a value greater than one. For example, if the distance from the pad to fulcrum was 12.00 inches and the distance from the output rod to the fulcrum was 3.75 inches, the pedal ratio would be 3.2:1.

In order to calculate the brake pedal output force, one simply needs to multiply the driver leg force and the pedal ratio as follows:

Brake pedal output force (lb) = driver leg force (lb) x pedal ratio (unitless)

To put some real-world numbers into the equation, if a driver leg force of 41 pounds were multiplied by the previously defined 3.2:1 pedal ratio, the output rod force would equal approximately 131 pounds. At first glance this would appear to be a good thing, and in one regard, it is.

Unfortunately, gain isn't a free lunch. More gain brings more force multiplication, but at the cost of increased pedal stroke, or travel, which is generally viewed as undesirable. For example, doubling the pedal ratio to 6.4:1 would double the output (approximately 262 pounds of output rod force), but would require the pedal to travel twice as long of a distance to achieve this result.

The primary design compromise for the brake pedal therefore becomes juggling pedal ratio and pedal travel. You can't have your cake and eat it too.

The Brake Booster

The brake pedal output rod force is fed through the firewall and into the back of the brake booster. Brake boosters, or simply boosters, come in many colors, shapes,

The brake pedal is really just a big lever under the dash. As driver applies leg force to the brake pedal, the output force is amplified based on the pedal's geometry. (Randall Shafer)

Vehicles that advertise "power brakes" (like this 1969 Chevelle SS) use a brake booster to increase the brake pedal output force. Because the booster uses engine intake manifold vacuum to perform this task, making changes to a vehicle's camshaft timing, runner design, air cleaner geometry, and a host of other horsepower modifiers can degrade the booster's performance. (Randall Shafer)

and sizes, yet they are all designed to do the same thing—they amplify brake pedal output rod force. The booster's inner workings can be quite complex, but fundamentally they rely on a pressure differential working across an internal diaphragm or piston to create a booster output force that is proportional to the brake pedal output rod force. In equation form:

Booster output force (lb) = brake pedal output force (lb) x boost gain (unitless)

Continuing the example, given a boost gain of 5.9:1 (typical for a conventional passenger vehicle brake booster), you can calculate that a 131-pound brake pedal output rod force would be translated into 774 pounds of booster output force.

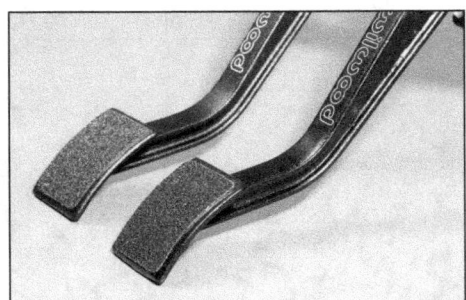

Because the driver can apply a significant amount of leg force to the brake pedal arm, it must be made strong enough to avoid excessive bending or deflection. The photo above compares an I-beam-shaped brake pedal arm on the right to a thinner clutch pedal arm on the left. (Randall Shafer)

Before continuing on to the next component in the analysis, it should be noted that the brake booster is not necessarily a required component. In fact, many racing vehicles are specifically designed *without* a brake booster in mind. Like any other mechanical device there are compromises in its design, and sometimes the benefit of increased gain does not justify the offsetting penalties of weight, cost, and complexity.

The Master Cylinder

The next step is to convert the amplified force from the booster into hydraulic fluid pressure. The master cylinder, consisting of a piston in a sealed bore filled with brake fluid, performs this task.

As the booster output force pushes on the back side of the master cylinder piston, the piston pushes against the fluid, creating hydraulic pressure. It's really that simple; however, in order to determine how much pressure is generated by the master cylinder, it's necessary to rely on yet another equation:

Master cylinder pressure (psi) = booster output force (lb) ÷ master cylinder piston area (square inches)

Assuming a typical master cylinder piston diameter of 1.00 inches (with an area of about 0.79 square inches), 774 pounds of booster output force will generate 986 psi. (While that may seem like a ridiculous amount of pressure, it is actually quite common for brake systems to operate at pressures between 1,000 and 2,000 psi.)

Because the equation for pressure is force *divided* by area, the equation predicts that decreasing the master cylinder piston diameter increases the pressure at a given force. In the example above, if the master cylinder piston diameter were to be reduced from 1.00 inches to 0.875 inches, the calculated system pressure would increase from 986 psi to nearly 1,288 psi!

Given this level of understanding, it may seem desirable to use the smallest diameter master cylinder possible. However, since there is always some compliance in the brake system (see the compliance sidebar for more on this topic), the master cylinder has to contain enough brake fluid to fill the hydraulic volume created by the flexing and distortion of the brake components during pressurization. Unfortunately, the best way to provide hydraulic volume is to increase the diameter of the master cylinder, which, as you just learned, reduces the pressure at a given force!

The primary design compromise for the master cylinder therefore becomes balancing pressure output and volumetric needs. There's never an easy answer, is there?

The Brake Fluid, Brake Lines, and Brake Hoses

On the surface, the brake lines and brake hoses have one of the easiest jobs in the brake system. They only need to transport pressurized brake fluid away from the master cylinder to the four corners of the car. How hard can that be?

Because of compliance (you will read the compliance sidebar, right?), it would be ideal to use the most rigid material possible for transporting the fluid. However, since the brake components at the wheel ends (the calipers, pads, and rotors) are usually free to move relative to the vehicle body, a flexible (and therefore compliant) portion of brake hose is required somewhere in the system.

At the same time, the fluid itself should be as incompressible as possible and *oh-by-the-way* should be resistant to extreme heat (to prevent boiling), extreme cold (to prevent freezing), and should not corrode the brake lines from the inside (to prevent leakage). This is hardly a simple task after all!

In nearly every application, rigid steel tubing is used for the majority of the plumbing (the brake lines) while a short length of rubber-coated polymer tubing is used to make the connection to the moving parts (the brake hoses). Brake fluid is the medium that is used to transmit the pressure, and merits its own discussion in Chapter 6.

In any case, regardless of the compliance of the components or the chemistry of the brake fluid, the relationship between the pressure in and the pressure out is as follows:

Caliper input pressure (psi) = Master cylinder pressure (psi)

This is an example of a system where the gain is 1:1—the pressure in equals the pressure out. Certainly the components may swell and expand as they transmit pressure through the system, but the pressure will be the same at all locations within the system.

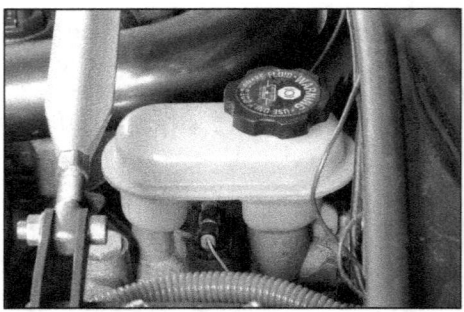

The master cylinder's role is to convert the force from the brake booster into hydraulic fluid pressure. While it may seem counterintuitive, smaller pistons generate higher pressures while larger pistons generate lower pressures. (Randall Shafer)

In most applications, the master cylinder is attached directly to the brake booster as shown above. In the early days of the automobile, however, it was not uncommon to find them mounted on opposite sides of the engine compartment. (Delphi Corporation)

As stated in Chapter 4, it may be desirable to modify the hydraulic fluid pressure going to the rear brakes. The most common way to accomplish this task is to install an inline proportioning valve. Although they all look similar from the outside, the inner components are custom-fit to each application. (Randall Shafer/Delphi Corporation)

Although brake boosters are common on passenger cars, they typically aren't found in dedicated racing applications. Why? Because race engines generally don't produce enough vacuum to support the booster's operation. Racers don't like the additional weight either! (Wayne Flynn/pdxsports.com)

Brake System Compliance

In case you haven't noticed, whenever an object is pressurized internally it expands in volume. In other words, it swells or grows in size. Balloons, beach balls, and brake systems all fall into this category, although the amount of expansion varies greatly based upon each object's *compliance*.

Compliance simply relates the amount of expansion to the amount of pressure. In the brake world, this is called the *Pressure-to-Volume*, or the P-V, relationship.

There are usually two sources of compliance in a brake system. The first is due to mechanical clearances. As the driver attempts to build pressure in the brake system, the components must first move around and take up any gaps that may have opened up since the brakes were last applied. The running clearance between the stationary brake pad and the spinning rotor face is a good example of a mechanical clearance that must be eliminated before pressure can be generated. Because fluid volume, or displacement, is required to push the brake pads against the rotor, the driver must move this fluid from the master cylinder to the calipers. As a result, the brake pedal needs to travel some small amount.

The second form of compliance is due to the natural compressibility of the brake pads, the flexibility of the brake hoses, and mechanical deformation of the caliper seals. All of these components (and more!) stretch and distort, effectively increasing the hydraulic volume in the brake system. As a result, the brake pedal needs to move even more once pressure is present.

Ultimately, it's possible to graph the relationship between brake system pressure and brake system compliance. The resulting P-V curve illustrates clearly how non-linear this relationship can be.

Because compliance results in brake pedal travel, it's generally viewed as undesirable. Therefore, when designing a brake system it's critical to minimize the clearances and gaps between components while simultaneously increasing the stiffness of the pressurized parts. When it comes to compliance, less is certainly more!

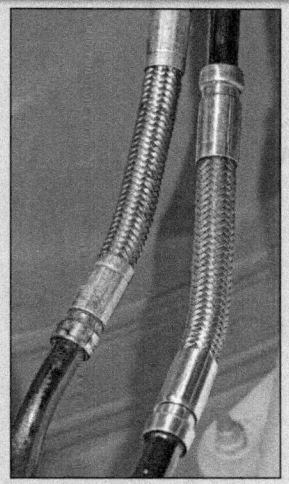

Flexible rubber brake hoses expand whenever you use the brakes. As a result, the master cylinder needs to fill them with additional brake fluid as pressurization occurs. Covering the hoses with stainless steel braiding as shown can help to reduce this effect. (Randall Shafer)

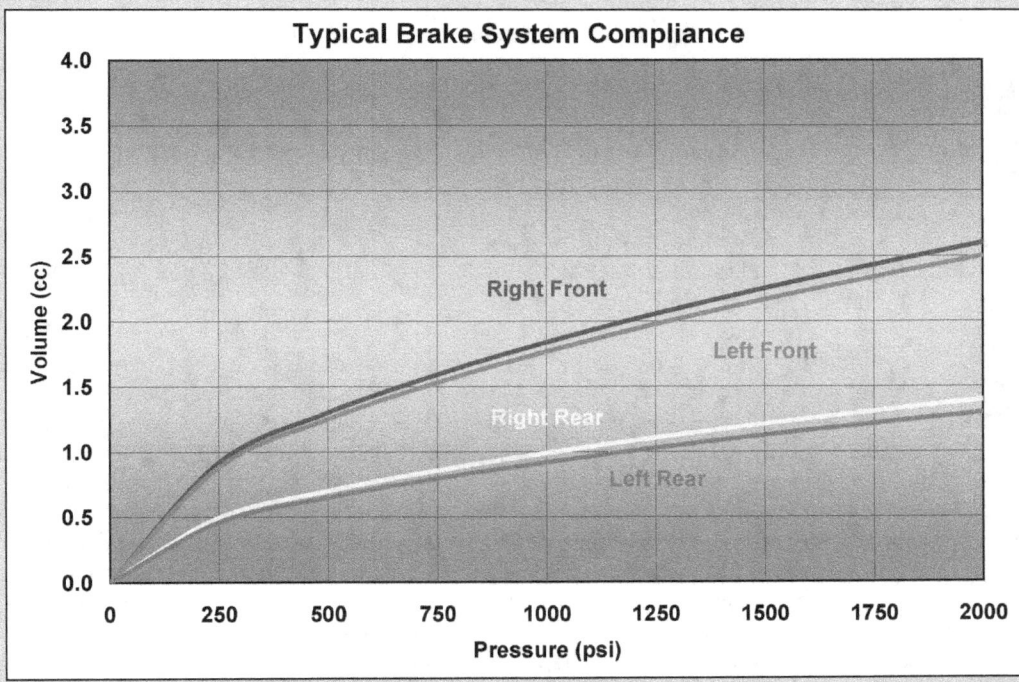

The P-V relationship graphically illustrates how much brake fluid volume must be added to the brake system hydraulic circuit to attain pressurization. The four lines above represent four separate brake assemblies on the same vehicle. In this example, the total system displays a compliance of approximately 7.8 cc at 2,000 psi.

The Calipers

Calipers are one of the most visible components of the brake system, yet sometimes are the most misunderstood. Like the master cylinder, the simplest calipers are not much more than a piston in a sealed bore with brake fluid on one side of the piston. However, while the master cylinder uses mechanical force to generate hydraulic pressure, calipers do exactly the opposite by using hydraulic pressure to generate mechanical force.

In order to calculate the amount of clamp force generated by a single caliper, you simply need to know the incoming pressure and the area of the caliper piston or pistons on the inboard side of the caliper. This is essentially the equation for the master cylinder turned around backwards:

*Caliper clamp force (lb) =
master cylinder pressure (psi) x
inboard caliper piston area (in^2) x 2*

Continuing the example, assume that the 986 psi generated at the master cylinder has traveled through the brake lines and brake hoses and is pushing against one piston in a floating caliper (more in Chapter 8)

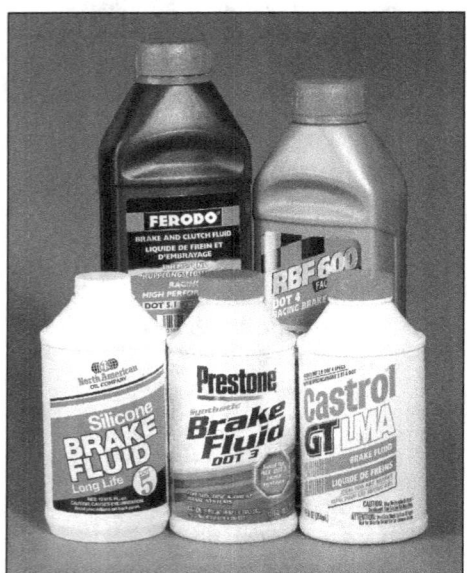

Brake fluid is the medium through which pressure is transmitted from the master cylinder to the calipers. In order to maintain the ability to perform this task, it must not freeze, boil, foam, froth, or otherwise change from its liquid state. (Randall Shafer)

Nothing screams high-performance louder than huge slotted rotors showing through the wheels. While yellow and red calipers add to the visual excitement, their bright colors don't provide any additional braking performance over basic black.

with a diameter of 2.125 inches. With an effective caliper piston area of approximately 7.09 square inches, this caliper will generate just about 6,991 pounds of clamp force under these conditions. If you recall that the input force to the master cylinder was 774 pounds, you can calculate the *hydraulic gain* of brake system to be approximately 9:1.

Where did this gain come from? Not by coincidence, the ratio of the master cylinder piston area (0.79 square inches) to the inboard caliper piston area doubled (7.09 square inches) is also 9:1. This concept of hydraulic gain is also employed by devices such as the common hydraulic floor jack. By changing the ratio of piston sizes on either end of a hydraulic circuit, the gain can be tailored to whatever level is required.

As you have probably already guessed, increasing the caliper piston diameter increases the clamp force for a given input pressure. Unfortunately, this (again) is not a free lunch. Selecting larger caliper piston diameters to generate more hydraulic gain may seem like a good idea at first, but the tradeoffs mirror those found when selecting a master cylinder.

In general, increasing the caliper piston diameter increases compliance, which in turn increases the pedal travel of the system. This means that increasing the caliper piston diameter also increases the displacement of the system, which can ultimately limit master cylinder selection (larger calipers generally require larger master cylinders, but more in Chapter 5).

More gain, more compliance, more pedal travel. Round and round it goes.

The Brake Pads

A brake pad's primary role is to be pushed against a spinning rotor friction disc with thousands of pounds of caliper clamp force. What a thankless job! There is a lot of black magic surrounding the chemistry, composition, and formulation of the brake pad friction material, but what matters here in Chapter 3 is the coefficient of friction between the brake pad and the surface of the rotor.

The friction force between the brake pad and rotor decelerates the rotor/wheel/tire assembly. It's also responsible for converting kinetic energy into thermal energy, but by focusing on just the forces for a minute, one can define the friction force by the following relationship:

*Brake pad friction force (lb) =
caliper clamp force (lb) x
coefficient of friction (unitless)*

In this particular example, let's assume the brake pads have a coefficient of friction of 0.32. Based on the caliper clamp force of 6,991 pounds, the brake pad friction force calculates out to only 2,237 pounds—a decrease of 68 percent. In other words, a gain of *less* than 1:1.

Some simple analysis indicates that the gain of the brake pads is equal to their coefficient of friction. In the case above, a coefficient of 0.32 leads to a gain of 0.32:1. A coefficient of friction of 0.54 would lead

BRAKE SYSTEM DESIGN

The master cylinder and caliper generate mechanical advantage in exactly the same way as a hydraulic floor jack. Large motions and low forces are converted into small motions and high forces much like a mechanical lever. (Randall Shafer)

Brake pads are the primary sacrificial interface in the brake system. In order to prevent premature wear and tear of the rotor, their coefficient of friction is typically lower than 0.35 but can be as high at 0.60 in racing applications. The pads shown here are for use with a carbon/carbon racing brake system. (Randall Shafer)

to a gain of 0.54:1 and would result in a higher brake pad friction force, but is still much less than 1:1.

So why not use the highest coefficient of friction possible in order to maximize the gain? If you were told the answer now there would be no need for Chapter 9, but the tradeoffs and compromises that must be made in brake pad selection encompass not only gain due to the coefficient of friction but also thermal sensitivity, output variation, and wear characteristics. One size does not fit all.

The Rotors

Drilled or slotted, floating or fixed, solid or vented—regardless of their design, rotors exist to convert the brake pad friction force into wheel torque. Like all forms of torque, wheel torque is just a function of a force being applied at a distance from the center of a rotating system:

*Wheel torque (ft-lb) =
brake pad friction force (lb) x
[rotor effective radius (in) ÷
12 (a conversion factor)]*

Rotor effective radius is described in more detail in Chapter 10, but in most applications it can be approximated with a reasonable degree of accuracy by the following equation:

*Approximate rotor effective radius (in)
= [rotor diameter (in) ÷ 2] −
[caliper piston diameter (in) ÷ 2]*

If you now assume that the example vehicle has a rotor diameter of 14.0 inches, the effective radius will be approximately 5.94 inches. (Note that this is based on the caliper piston diameter of 2.125 inches mentioned a few paragraphs back.)

Now, using your calculated effective radius of 5.94 inches and a brake pad friction force of 2,237 pounds, the equation tells you that approximately 1,107 foot-pounds of torque will be generated in the rotating rotor/wheel/tire assembly. Yes, you read that correctly—over *one thousand* foot-pounds of torque will be generated at this corner of the vehicle.

Don't forget that while all this torque is being generated, the rotor must also absorb the thermal energy generated by the brake pad rubbing against the rotor friction disc. Talk about multi-tasking!

The Wheels and Tires

Because the wheel and tire are rigidly attached to the rotor and hub, the wheel torque will attempt to decelerate the whole enchilada. However, because the contact patch does not *want* to be decelerated by the torque, a force will be generated between the tire and the road at the contact patch that opposes the motion of the vehicle.

The equation to calculate contact patch force looks just like the equation to calculate wheel torque, but in reverse:

*Contact patch force (lb) =
wheel torque (ft-lb) ÷ [tire rolling radius (in)
÷ 12 (a conversion factor)]*

Assuming a tire with a rolling radius of 12.65 inches (approximately half of a typical tire's outer diameter), the equation reveals that a force of approximately 1,050 pounds is being requested between the tire and road, opposing the motion of the vehicle. As you learned in Chapter 2, the force only materializes if the mu-slip relationship allows for a force of this magnitude, but for the moment assume that the tire is not limiting the contact patch force.

Brake Corner Gain

Recalling that calculating gain is just a matter of dividing an output force by an input force, you can quickly develop an equation for the gain of one individual brake corner:

*Brake corner gain (unitless) =
contact patch force (lb) ÷ driver's leg force (lb)*

If the vehicle actually generated 1,050 pounds of contact patch force as described above, you can calculate the brake system gain for this one corner of the vehicle to be 25.6:1. In other words, the brake system increased the driver's original input of 41 pounds 25.6 times.

Now, in order to stop the car, all that is necessary is to add up all four contact patch forces (remember, there is a contact patch force acting on every wheel with a brake) and run through a little more math. In case you haven't noticed, brake engineers just love math…

The rotors acts as the primary brake system heat sink. For this reason, the rotors are made as large as possible to increase their thermal mass, yielding lower operating temperatures. In high-performance applications, lower operating temperatures are almost always a good thing. (Randall Shafer/Baer)

Summing Forces

Before you can sum up all the forces, however, there is one last fact to consider—the contact patch forces are not equal at all four corners of the car. All of Chapter 4 is spent explaining this phenomenon, but for the sake of this exercise, estimate that the rear contact patch forces are only 20 percent as large as the front contact patch forces. Therefore, if each front tire generates 1,050 pounds of contact patch force then you can estimate that each rear contact patch generates 20 percent of that, or 210 pounds.

Regardless of the actual forces, the equation for total brake system force simply boils down to adding up the forces at the four corners of the car:

Total brake force (lb) = [Front contact patch force (lb) x 2] + [Rear contact patch force (lb) x 2]

Adding up the four corners now reveals a total of 2,520 pounds of total brake force acting on the vehicle between the four tires and the road. Take a deep breath—you're almost done being pummeled with brake system math.

Overall Brake System Gain

Retracing your footsteps back to the very first equation rolled out in this chapter, you can finally calculate the *overall brake system gain*. All that's required is to divide the total contact patch force of 2,520 pounds by the driver's original leg force of 41 pounds. In this case, running the final numbers through the calculator returns an overall brake system gain of 61.5:1. Said differently, the entire brake system, from the brake pedal to the contact patch, amplified the driver's leg force 61.5 times.

Calculating Deceleration

Since you have now determined the total brake force, you can calculate vehicle deceleration in the same way you learned in Chapter 2 with only a small amount of additional formula manipulation:

Vehicle deceleration (g) = total brake force (lb) ÷ vehicle weight (lb)

Assuming a vehicle weight with driver of 3,410 pounds, you can plug-and-chug to discover that a total brake force of 2,520 pounds yields a vehicle deceleration of approximately 0.74g.

Calculating Stopping Distance

If, at the end of all this data crunching, you have established vehicle deceleration, you can perform one last calculation to determine vehicle stopping distance from any given speed. The equation takes the following form:

Stopping distance (ft) = vehicle speed^2 (mph) ÷ vehicle deceleration (g) ÷ 29.9 (a conversion factor)

For example, from 60 mph, a vehicle decelerating at 0.74g would require approximately 163 feet to come to a complete stop. Double the speed to 120 mph though, and the stopping distance extends out to a lengthy 651 feet, or four times the distance required from 60 mph.

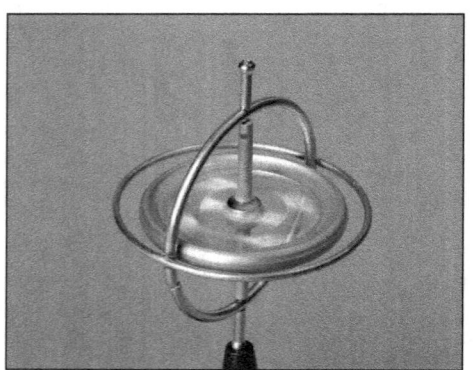

While massive rotors may sound like a good idea, going too big can be just as bad as too small. Rotors that are oversized act like large gyroscopes, making the rotating assembly difficult to turn. At high speeds, this can have a profound negative impact on a vehicle's handling characteristics. (Randall Shafer)

ABS and Overall Brake System Gain

In general, ABS does not contribute to overall brake system gain. In fact, when not performing active control of brake fluid pressure, the ABS functions as just another brake line, albeit a very complex and expensive one.

However, new algorithms exist that can cycle the ABS in such a fashion that the overall brake system gain can be greatly increased on demand. Called Panic Brake Assist (PBA), this technology uses a sensor (typically on the brake pedal arm or in the brake booster) to detect if the driver is using the brakes in an emergency fashion. If the driver then applies too little leg force, PBA cranks up the gain to bring the vehicle to maximum deceleration even though the driver has not responded adequately.

Does it sound like the vehicle is thinking too much on the driver's behalf? Perhaps, but testing clearly shows that in many cases an untrained or distracted driver can reduce their emergency stopping distance by nearly 50 percent with these systems active.

BRAKE SYSTEM DESIGN

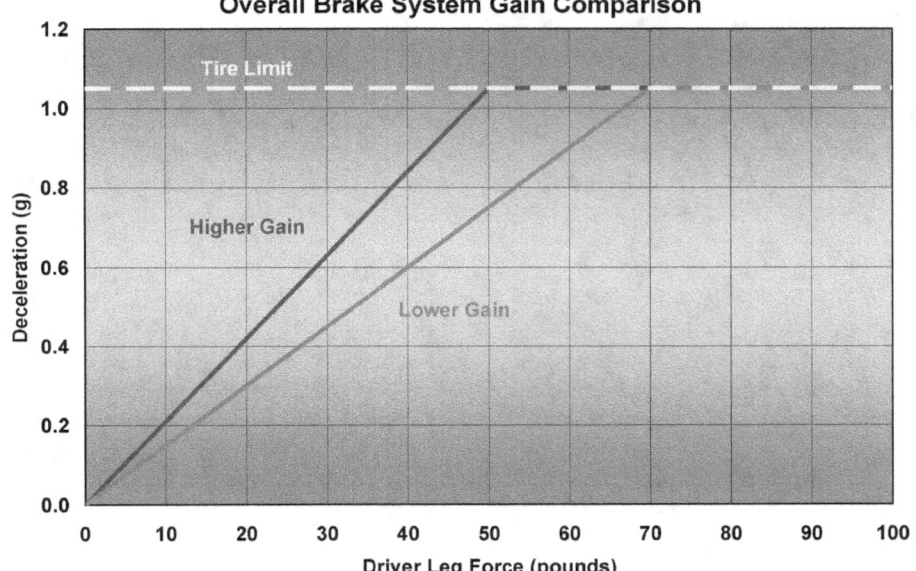

The overall brake system gain relates the driver's leg force to the total brake force. Consequently, the brake system represented by the blue line would require less pedal effort to achieve deceleration than the brake system represented by the red line. The limiting factor for both, however, is the tire-to-road interface, shown here as a dashed yellow line at 1.05g.

Therein lays the fundamental relationship between speed and stopping distance: Doubling the speed quadruples the distance required to come to rest. Why? Because, as the equation above shows us, stopping distance is a function of the speed *squared*. It's that whole kinetic energy concept resurfacing again. But enough of that—in both cases the vehicle is now stopped. No more equations for a while. Honest.

Brake System Modifications

So, if changing brake system components does not necessarily provide shorter stopping distances, then why even consider modifications in the first place? Why not just leave the brakes alone and buy better tires? Quite simply, making changes to your brake system can have a very real, very significant impact on four *other* areas of brake system performance other than stopping distance.

Driver Tuning

Brake system component sizes can be tweaked to adjust the overall brake system gain to suit the driver's tastes. Some drivers prefer a high, hard pedal while others prefer a longer stroke. Some drivers prefer more pedal effort than others. In this regard, tuning your brakes is a lot like tuning your shocks—every driver likes something a little bit different, and there's no right answer within certain functional limits. The proper selection of components can make or break the driver's perception of the brake system.

Operating Temperature

Increasing brake system thermal mass (primarily by increasing rotor size) can be of benefit *if* there is a thermal concern in the brake system. If your brakes work consistently under your driving conditions (street, race, or otherwise), then adding size to the braking system accomplishes nothing more than increasing the weight and/or the overall rotational inertia of your vehicle, even though you may prefer the look!

Aesthetics aside, if high temperatures are having an adverse effect on brake system performance, then you may want to consider upsizing the hardware. Cooler brakes are always happier brakes.

Thermal Robustness

In many cases, your budget, rulebook, or both can prevent you from installing components that can significantly decrease operating temperatures. Under these conditions, it may be possible to modify your existing brake system to operate more consistently at elevated temperatures.

Regardless of your system configuration, selecting brake fluid and brake pads that are robust to high temperatures can greatly extend the operating range of your

If a vehicle's total brake force can be calculated, then so can its deceleration. Dividing the total brake force (in pounds) by the vehicle weight (also in pounds) yields deceleration in units of g. (Wayne Flynn/pdxsports.com)

Tuning Brake System Gain

By now your head is probably swimming with thoughts of larger caliper pistons, more aggressive brake pads, tiny master cylinder pistons, and so forth. These components can and should be adjusted in small steps to achieve a feel that the driver prefers, but the process of making the proper selections can be quite overwhelming.

So what gain is most appropriate? There is no one right answer, but in general a higher overall brake system gain requires lower driver leg forces to achieve deceleration, but with longer pedal travel. Lower overall brake system gains typically require higher driver leg forces to achieve deceleration, but with shorter pedal travel.

Tuning overall brake system gain involves more than mathematically selecting the proper components. Just as important is tailoring the brake pedal effort and travel to the driver's preference. Some drivers prefer a firm pedal with high effort while others prefer low efforts with a longer stroke. (Wayne Flynn/pdxsports.com)

The following table summarizes what the effects might be of changing any of the brake system components we covered in Chapter 3. This should get you well on your way toward shopping for the right set of components for your application.

Overall Brake System Gain Cheat Sheet

System Parameter	For More Gain	For Less Gain
Brake pedal ratio	increase	decrease
Brake booster gain	increase	decrease
Master cylinder piston diameter	decrease	increase
Caliper piston diameter	increase	decrease
Brake pad coefficient of friction	increase	decrease
Rotor effective radius	increase	decrease
Tire rolling radius	decrease	increase

Sports car, racecar, muscle car, or hot rod, the primary reason for making any brake system upgrade is to reduce operating temperatures. Certainly the benefits of reduced brake pedal travel and enhanced curb appeal should not be trivialized, but bigger brakes have only one purpose: to increase thermal mass. (Randall Shafer)

brake system. The heat will certainly find its way into other components (wheel bearings, for example) and may lead to the premature wear-out of others (increased rotor cracking is quite common), but these characteristics are inherent to any system with undersized thermal mass, quality brake fluid and brake pads, or not.

Compliance

Any changes that you can make to reduce compliance will increase the overall efficiency of the brake system. More efficient components can decrease the total pedal travel, improve system reaction times, and provide more stop-to-stop consistency, just to name a few. Think of it as blueprinting your brake system.

Summary

In summary, brake system modifications can help make your vehicle more consistent, more predictable, and more user friendly during braking. Better pedal feel, higher thermal capabilities, and longer component life are all on the table, and the chapters that follow walk you through how to achieve these results step by step.

As the saying goes, if you want to stop *just once* in the shortest possible distance, buy the right tires. However, if you want to stop *consistently* in the shortest possible distance, it's time to upgrade your brakes.

Extreme brake temperatures are not just detrimental to brake system components. The wear seen on this wheel bearing inner race resulted from the grease in the bearing losing its lubricating properties during intense braking activity. (Randall Shafer)

CHAPTER 4

BRAKE BALANCE

One of the most critical, yet least understood, brake system attributes is brake system balance. This single design parameter can make or break (no pun intended) a vehicle's stopping distance performance. Even with the very best brake system components installed on your vehicle, improper brake system balance can prevent the tires from operating at their maximum decelerations simultaneously, resulting in vehicle deceleration performance that is far from optimized.

Improper brake system balance can also create undesirable vehicle dynamic responses. From a premature loss of vehicle steering during braking to dynamic instability while braking in a turn, the ramifications of improper balance can extend far beyond a few additional feet of stopping distance.

Unfortunately for the automotive enthusiast, screwing up a vehicle's brake balance is pretty darn easy to do. Later in this chapter you'll be presented with a table of those factors that can influence brake balance, but let it suffice to say that just about anything and everything brake related, suspension related, and tire related can have an effect (both positive *and* negative) on brake balance.

A vehicle with a balanced brake system creates brake forces at all four tires simultaneously that are equal to the maximum forces that each tire can sustain independently. You could also say that a balanced brake system is one that brings all four tires to their independent maximum coefficients of friction at the same time. In either case, defining perfect brake balance is quite a bit easier than designing a system that can pull it off.

Brake Force and Corner Weight

In Chapter 2 you learned that the maximum brake force a particular tire can generate is equal to the coefficient of friction of the tire-road interface (mu in the equation below) multiplied by the amount of weight being supported by that corner of the car:

Brake force at one tire (lb) = corner weight (lb) x mu (unitless)

To use real numbers, a single tire supporting 500 pounds of the total vehicle weight with a peak coefficient of friction of 0.9 (a typical value for an all-season tire on a dry asphalt road) could generate, in theory, a maximum of 450 pounds of braking force. Recall that this also would result in

Even with the very best brake system components, improper brake balance can wreak havoc on vehicle braking dynamics. Stopping distance certainly can suffer as well. (Wayne Flynn/pdxsports.com)

Tires generate brake forces through adhesive, deformation, and mechanical wearing modes of operation. Based on the surface, condition, and level of slip, a tire may be operating in one, two, or all three modes simultaneously. Tire smoke usually indicates too much mechanical wearing! (The Tire Rack)

HIGH-PERFORMANCE BRAKE SYSTEMS: DESIGN, SELECTION AND INSTALLATION

CHAPTER 4

In this example, a single tire is supporting 750 pounds of vehicle weight (red arrow) with a peak coefficient of friction, or mu, of 1.1 (blue star). Therefore, this tire could generate, in theory, a maximum of 825 pounds of braking force (yellow arrow). The brake force would oppose the direction of travel (green arrow). (Randall Shafer)

a maximum deceleration contribution of 0.9g at that one wheel.

Now if you were to place an additional 200 pounds on the same tire (700 pounds total), the maximum brake force rises to 630 pounds (this assumes that the peak coefficient of friction remains at 0.9). From this calculation you can see that an increase in maximum brake force does not result in higher deceleration (still 0.9g in this case). Why? Because the tire has more weight on it, and that additional weight requires its own additional force to decelerate.

Based on this relationship, you can also predict that reducing the weight on the tire reduces the maximum brake force sustainable by that corner. In the example above, if the weight were reduced to 300 pounds, a maximum of only 270 pounds of brake force would be available at that corner (again, assuming the same coefficient of friction).

Perfect Balance

From all of these equations, ideal brake balance can be boiled down to one simple relationship. For perfect brake balance under all conditions:

Real-Life Brake Balance Success Story

How big of an impact can brake balance have on vehicle performance? It varies by application, but even with the very best brake system components, super sticky tires, and impeccable installation, skewing your brake balance can lengthen stopping distances dramatically. So much for those fancy red calipers...

To illustrate this point, here is a real-life brake balance success story reproduced with permission from *Grassroots Motorsports* during their Porsche 914-4 restoration.

"Our initial stopping distance measurements were not quite world-class. Even though we had installed Yokohama AVS Intermediate 195/60ZR15s at all four corners, we were recording stopping distances of 150 to 160 feet from 60 mph. There was obviously room for improvement.

"We then began to slowly adjust the proportioning valve until we were just barely on the verge of rear lock-up. We dialed back a tiny bit for a safety factor and again ran our stopping distance tests. Note that if you are doing this at home, you should be prepared just in case you go a bit too far and need to deal with the back end of the car getting all out of shape. A large parking lot or airstrip (as opposed to a crowded four-lane highway) is really the best place for this sort of thing.

"As stated earlier, the adjustable proportioning valve is a must-have item for anyone performing a 914-4 caliper swap. Our new stopping distance from 60 mph was now a scant 121 feet—on par with many of today's premier sports cars. Apparently the brake bias was significantly holding us back from optimizing our new components."

Paying attention to brake balance can pay huge dividends at the track. The 60 mph stopping distance of the Porsche 914-4 shown here went from 160 feet to 121 feet simply by setting the brake proportioning valve to an optimum position. (David S. Wallens/Classic Motorsports)

In this particular application, the stopping distance from 60 mph was reduced by approximately 34 feet—a whopping 22 percent! If you consider that out-braking your opponent by just two feet every lap for a twenty lap sprint race can result in a three to four car-length advantage at the checkered flag, a 22-percent decrease in stopping distance in every braking zone is sure to get everyone's attention.

In order to determine a vehicle's static weight distribution, weigh the front and rear axles of the car. The percent front weight is the front axle weight divided by the total weight. The percent rear weight is the rear axle weight divided by the total weight. A nice set of scales will do the math for you, though. (Randall Shafer)

Either at rest or while coasting, every vehicle has a static weight distribution. Due to its rear-engine layout, this Porsche 911 has approximately 38 percent of its weight on the front axle and 62 percent of its weight on the rear axle prior to braking. (Daniel Mainzer)

$$\text{Front brake force (lb)} \div \text{front vehicle weight (lb)} = \text{rear brake force (lb)} \div \text{rear vehicle weight (lb)}$$

Therefore, one could surmise that in order to design a perfectly balanced brake system you would just:

1. Weigh the front axle and rear axle of the car.
2. Design the front axle and rear axle brake components to deliver brake forces in the same ratio as the front-to-rear weight distribution.
3. Pat yourself on the back for achieving perfect brake balance.

For example, a vehicle with equal (or 50/50) front-to-rear weight distribution would appear to require front and rear brakes that generate the same amount of brake force simultaneously. In other words, the front brakes would provide 50 percent of the total required brake force and the rear brakes would provide the other 50 percent of the total required brake force.

Looking at a different scenario, it would appear that a vehicle with 60/40 front-to-rear weight distribution would require front brakes that provide 60 percent of the total brake force while the rear brakes would contribute the remaining 40 percent of the total required brake force. Why? Because of the extra weight being supported by the nose of the car.

In mini-summary, a perfectly balanced brake system generates brake forces at the front and rear axles in exact proportion to the front and rear axle weights. Like most things in life though, calculating brake balance is not as simple as it may appear and designing a braking system to these static conditions would neglect the most important factor in the brake balance equation—the effect of *weight transfer* during braking.

Static Weight Distribution

Let's assume you have a 2,500-pound vehicle with an unknown static weight distribution. If you are only concerned with the vehicle at rest, it's easy to determine the weight on each wheel. You just need to find some corner weight scales and weigh it.

The sum of the front individual corner weights (left front + right front) is equal to the front axle weight, and the sum of the rear corner weights (left rear + right rear) is equal to the rear axle weight. For example, if the sum of the front individual corner weights is 1,250 pounds and if the sum of the rear individual corner weights is also equal to 1,250 pounds, then you could say that the vehicle has 50/50 weight distribution. That is, half of the vehicle's weight (50 percent) is being supported by the front axle, and the other half of the vehicle's weight (the remaining 50 percent) is being supported by the rear axle.

The total weight of the vehicle is equal to the sum of the two axle weights (our original 2,500 pounds), and this weight can be thought of as acting through (or existing at) the vehicle's center of gravity, or CG. Simple, right?

The Second Law of Motion

Now this is all fine and good while the vehicle is sitting still, but as soon as the vehicle begins to decelerate the effective weight on each corner of the vehicle changes. This is once again because of the relationship between forces, objects, and their accelerations. You have been exposed to this concept a few times now without much fanfare, but fundamentally all things in nature are also bound by Newton's Second Law of Motion which states:

Force (lb) = weight (lb) x acceleration (g)

From Chapter 2 you hopefully remember Newton's First Law of Motion, which states that things won't move unless you apply a force to them. With Newton's Second Law of Motion you now see the interdependency between how hard you push on something (force) and how quickly it will change speed (acceleration). Simply stated, a small force results in a

During braking, weight is transferred from the rear axle to the front axle. Assuming a weight of 3,200 pounds, a CG height of 20 inches, a wheelbase of 104.5 inches, and a deceleration of 1.2g, this vehicle will transfer 735 pounds from its rear axle to its front axle. (Wayne Flynn/pdxsports.com)

small acceleration while a larger force results in a larger acceleration.

(Note that purists would rather write the equation above as *force = mass x acceleration*. However, the equation written above, with the units as stated, is equally valid. Apologies are extended to any engineers or physicists who are offended by this simplification.)

So far you have seen this equation applied to determine maximum decelerations, brake forces, and other related stuff. Now it's time to turn it around to see how a decelerating vehicle is affected by this same relationship.

Dynamic Weight Distribution

Like vehicle weight, all deceleration forces must also act through the vehicle's CG. In other words, all of these various forces acting on the vehicle can be thought of as pushing on the vehicle at its CG. However, unlike the total vehicle weight, which acts *vertically* through the CG, the deceleration force acts *horizontally* through the CG. When coupled with the fact that the CG is located somewhere above the ground, the total amount of weight transferred will be equal to:

Weight transfer (lb) = total vehicle weight (lb) x acceleration (g) x CG height (in) ÷ wheelbase (in)

The net result is effective weight transfer from the rear axle to the front axle during braking in direct proportion to the rate of deceleration. This also explains why you are thrown forward against the seatbelts during rapid deceleration—your body is experiencing its very own inertia reaction to the deceleration force acting upon it.

If this concept is applied to the 2,500-pound vehicle discussed earlier, you can get an understanding of just how much weight is being transferred during a given braking event. Assuming a deceleration of 0.9g (again, this is about the limit for most all-season tires on a dry asphalt road), a CG height of 22 inches, and a wheelbase of 102 inches, the calculated front-to-rear weight transfer is approximately 485 pounds.

Calculating the new front and rear axle weights is now just a matter of adding the transferred weight to the front axle and subtracting it from the rear axle. This results in a new front axle weight of 1,735 pounds (1,250 static + 485 dynamic) and a new rear axle weight of only 765 pounds (1,250 static - 485 dynamic). Naturally, the total vehicle weight remains constant at 2,500 pounds.

Effect of Weight Transfer on Brake Balance

Back to the task at hand: brake balance. Armed with your newfound knowledge of weight transfer, you can calculate that your vehicle, which had 50/50 weight distribution at rest, displays approximately 70/30 weight distribution when decelerating at 0.9g. The practical implication is that if you designed a brake system for perfect brake balance at 50/50 weight distribution, the brake balance will be far from optimal at 70/30 weight distribution.

This would result in a vehicle that would have too little front brake force contribution relative to the weight on the front axle and too much rear brake force contribution relative to the weight on the rear axle. In other words, the rear brakes will be doing more than their fair share of the total braking. From this point forward, this too-much-rear-brake condition will be known as being *rear biased*.

If you were to study this long enough, you might eventually conclude that the

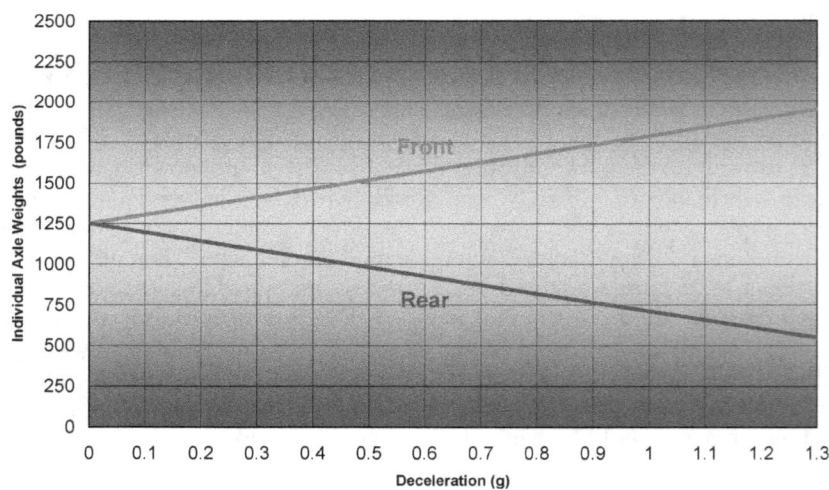

As deceleration increases, so does the amount of weight transferred from the rear axle to the front axle. While the rate of weight transfer (the slope of the red and blue lines) is a function of vehicle wheelbase, CG height, and deceleration, the total vehicle weight never changes.

BRAKE BALANCE

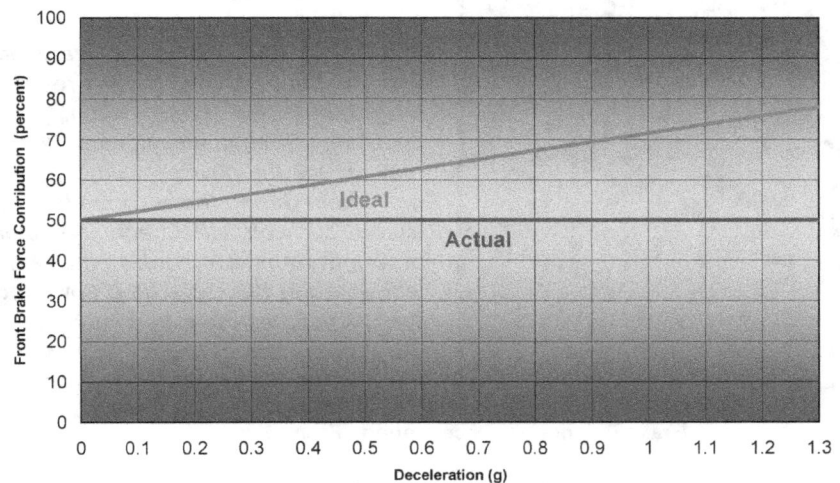

If brake system balance is calculated without taking weight transfer effects into account, the vehicle will always be underutilizing the front brakes. For this reason, the vehicle is said to be rear biased. As a result, the vehicle may be unstable during heavy braking.

only time when this vehicle has perfect balance is when it is not braking at all. Kind of ironic, isn't it? Weight transfer sure throws a wrench in brake system design.

The Benefits of Perfect Balance

Stopping distance is minimized by distributing brake forces so that all four tires are simultaneously generating their maximum deceleration. Why is this important? Well, in a racing application, the vehicle with a perfectly balanced brake system is able to hit the brakes a fraction of a second later going down the back straight. What racer wouldn't want that?

In the real word though, if brake force is continuously increased, one axle of the vehicle will eventually lock up, or skid, before the other. Naturally, if the vehicle is perfectly balanced at the point of maximum deceleration all four tires would skid simultaneously, but rarely does this ever happen in practice. There are simply too many variables at play that prevent this ideal condition from occurring on a regular basis.

Balance in Racing Applications

All of these conflicting considerations can quickly make perfect brake balance seem like an unachievable goal. However, if you're trying to optimize a brake system for *just one particular deceleration level*, say the point of maximum deceleration, it becomes much easier. In fact, this is how balance is addressed in most racing applications. After all, how often does a racecar decelerate at 0.4g? Not very often!

Based on a race vehicle's physical dimensions, weight distribution, and tire performance, maximum deceleration and total weight transfer can be readily calculated. From there, it's a simple matter of calculating the dynamic weight distribution, and presto! You can now calculate the optimum distribution of front and rear brake forces.

Getting back to the 2,500-pound vehicle, you can now calculate the front and rear brake force needs at maximum deceleration. Assuming a maximum deceleration of 1.3g, the same CG height of 22 inches, and the same wheelbase of 102 inches, the calculated front-to-rear weight transfer is approximately 701 pounds.

As before, calculating the new front and rear axle weights is now just a matter of adding the transferred weight to the front axle and subtracting it from the rear axle. This results in a new front axle weight of 1,951 pounds (1,250 static + 701 dynamic) and a new rear axle weight of only 549 pounds (1,250 static - 701 dynamic).

These quick calculations reveal that the vehicle, which had 50/50 weight distribution at rest, displays approximately 78/22 weight distribution at maximum deceleration. Therefore, the next step would be to modify the brake system to distribute brake forces in this same ratio by increasing the gain of the front brake system components and/or decreasing the gain of the rear brake system components.

However, this staggering brake of force output through component gain adjustment is a rough design exercise at best. Consequently, devices such as balance bars and tandem master cylinders are commonly used to fine-tune the system performance, but those details are saved for discussion in Chapter 5.

Balance in Street Applications

Unfortunately, this design philosophy works well for racing vehicles, but it falls apart on the street. If you go back to the race vehicle above, you have already calculated that this same vehicle displays 70/30 weight distribution at 0.9g, but 78/22 weight distribution at 1.3g. In fact, you could plot out weight distribution versus deceleration and the resulting graph

Nearly every car on the road today has rear brakes that are physically smaller than the front brakes. Although this is primarily driven by thermal mass requirements, it's also a function of brake balance. For these two reasons, the rear rotor on this Saturn racecar measures only 9.8 inches in diameter. (Randall Shafer)

Although a vehicle's body may pitch forward dramatically during braking (or may roll to one side during cornering), this isn't the cause of weight transfer. In fact, the body motions are the result of weight transfer. For this reason, installing stiffer suspension springs may reduce the physical body movement during these dynamic events, but won't affect actual amount of weight transferred unless the vehicle is lowered at the same time (lowering the CG reduces the total amount of weight transfer). (Wayne Flynn/pdxsports.com)

would show that this vehicle would only be perfectly balanced at the point of maximum deceleration.

Under all conditions other than the point of maximum deceleration, the vehicle has too much front brake force contribution relative to the weight on the front axle and too little rear brake force contribution relative to the weight on the rear axle. In other words, the front brakes are doing more than their fair share of the total braking. From this point forward, this too-much-front-brake condition will be known as being *front biased*.

While this may be acceptable for racing vehicles, which primarily operate at one deceleration level (maximum deceleration), street vehicles tend to operate under a much wider range of decelerations. Because of this need to achieve perfect balance under a wider range of operating conditions, designing a perfectly balanced brake system for street vehicles is a more involving task.

How do you accomplish this seemingly impossible feat, you ask? Through the use of mechanical devices (proportioning valves) or electronic means (dynamic rear proportioning), street vehicles are capable of operating at near ideal brake

Right: The proportioning valve is a device which, when properly implemented, can provide balanced brake system performance over a broad range of deceleration levels. Unfortunately one size does not fit all, so care must be taken when installing and adjusting these little mechanical wonders. Improperly adjusted, they can do more harm than good.

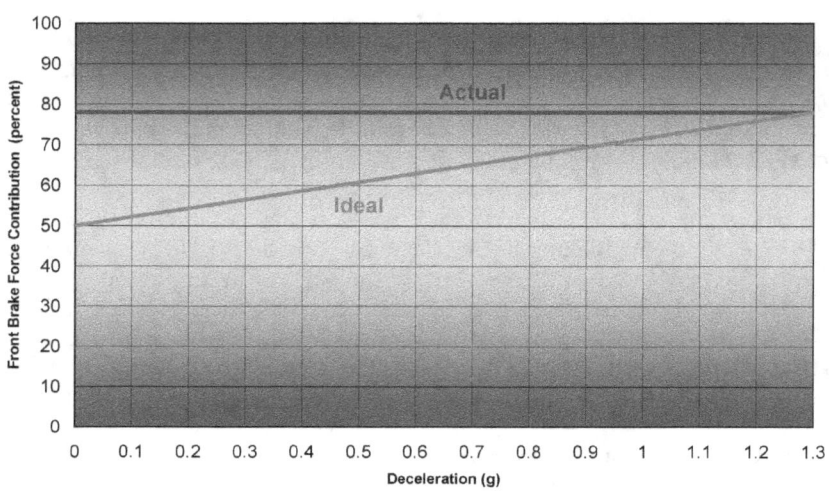

Above: If brake system balance is optimized only at the point of maximum deceleration, the vehicle will be front biased under all non-limit braking conditions. While this may be acceptable for a racing vehicle (and, in fact, is exactly how a balance bar operates), it prematurely wears out the front brake components during everyday use.

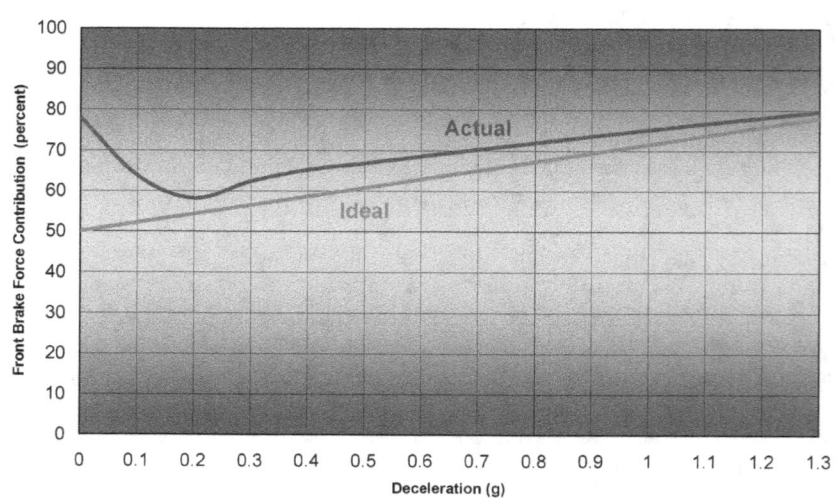

balance over a much wider deceleration range than their racing counterparts. The inner workings of proportioning valves are analyzed in detail in Chapter 5, but for now it is necessary to take a closer look at the benefits of perfect balance and the ramifications of excessive front and rear bias.

Front Brake Bias

As you just learned, if the front tires lock up before the rear tires, the vehicle is considered front biased, as the front tires are the limiting factor for deceleration. From the mu-slip curves in Chapter 2, recall that attempting to increase brake force after the peak coefficient of friction is reached only serves to decrease the available brake force, thereby reducing the overall level of deceleration.

In other words, if a vehicle is severely front biased, the front tires will lock before the rear tires are at their peak coefficient of friction. This prevents all four tires from achieving their maximum deceleration simultaneously, thereby increasing the vehicle's stopping distance. Sure doesn't sound like the hot ticket for better lap times, does it?

The negative effects of front bias extend beyond increased stopping distance, though. A vehicle with excessive front bias is also more prone toward understeer while braking. I could devote a chapter or two to why the vehicle reacts in this fashion, but in summary, if the front tires are being overworked by the brake system, they have less ability to get the vehicle to change direction. Just like the vehicle that

If a vehicle is front biased, its front tires will lock up well before the rear tires. While stopping distance will surely suffer as a result, the driver also loses the ability to steer. The vehicle will not spin, but it may still end up in the weeds. (Wayne Flynn/pdxsports.com)

If a vehicle is rear biased, its rear tires will lock up well before the front tires. There will certainly be a negative impact to stopping distance, but in extreme cases the car will spin out of control and off the road instead of sliding in a straight line. (Wayne Flynn/pdxsports.com)

pushes its way through corners all day long, a vehicle that is heavily front biased will be slow and frustrating at turn-in, but relatively benign and easy to drive.

A third side effect of excessive front bias is extreme front brake pad wear. If the front brakes are generating more than their fair share of heat, then they achieve higher overall temperatures. Higher temperatures result in higher wear rates, and brake pad life may suddenly become an issue.

Rear Brake Bias

Now, if the rear tires lock up before the front tires, the vehicle is considered rear biased, as the rear tires are now the

ABS/DRP and Brake Balance

As you're learning, a vehicle's intrinsic brake balance is purely a function of base brake system design and vehicle weight transfer during braking. In other words, ABS and Dynamic Rear Proportioning (DRP) do not play a part in defining the vehicle's optimum brake balance and sound selection of brake system components is still a requirement for an ABS/DRP-equipped vehicle.

Because ABS and DRP prevent tires from reaching excessive levels of slip, they can be effective at masking some small levels of front and rear bias at high levels of deceleration. However, if brake system modifications have completely distorted the vehicle's fundamental brake system balance, premature cycling of the ABS and/or DRP at low deceleration levels will most likely be the result.

limiting factor for deceleration. As before, the mu-slip curves in Chapter 2 illustrated that attempting to increase brake force after the peak coefficient of friction is reached only serves to decrease the available brake force, thereby reducing the overall level of deceleration. No need to beat this dead horse any further—any brake bias at all, front or rear, increases stopping distances.

Up to this point it would appear that both front bias and rear bias are equally distasteful, but here's the twist: In complete contrast to a vehicle with front bias, a vehicle with excessive rear bias is prone toward oversteer while braking. Again the details are left to another time and place, but in summary if the rear tires are being overworked by the brake system they have less ability to resist any vehicle yaw dynamics.

In other words, a severely rear biased car is a scary, twitchy ride under braking, resulting in a bad case of the white-knuckle syndrome. Envision an imaginary co-pilot yanking up on the park brake handle in the middle of every corner and you begin to get the idea. It might be a rush to drive at speed, but a vehicle with excessive rear bias is horribly slow on the stopwatch.

The third side effect of excessive rear bias is extreme rear brake pad wear. It's the whole heat and energy thing all over again. If the rear brakes are generating more than their fair share of heat, they achieve higher overall temperatures, potentially resulting in, you guessed it, shorter brake pad life.

Measuring Brake Balance

Brake balance can be measured in several ways. Auto manufacturers mount wheels on the vehicle that are equipped with strain gauges to measure brake torque at each wheel. Since brake torque can be used to calculate brake force, all that is left is to combine the vehicle parameters mentioned earlier (wheelbase, CG height, static weight distribution) to calculate brake balance for that particular stopping event. This is the most precise method of measuring brake balance; however, there are simpler and cheaper methods that the enthusiast can employ (such as the stopping distance method that follows) with reasonable accuracy.

Is 100% Rear Bias Really a Bad Idea?

While you can use fancy equations to calculate the percent front or rear bias for a particular combination of brake forces and axle weights, you don't need a calculator to tell you that if a vehicle only has front brakes then the rear brakes are not being fully utilized! Therefore, a vehicle that only has front brakes is 100 percent front biased under all deceleration conditions.

By the same reasoning, a vehicle that only has rear brakes will always be operating at 100 percent rear bias. Now, after all the doom and gloom predicted for even a partially a rear biased vehicle, how can this be at all desirable?

Take the example of a typical racing kart. There are no brakes on the front wheels. Out back, a single disc and caliper combine to provide braking through the rear tires only. Voilà–100 percent rear bias!

Does 100 percent rear bias result in unavoidable disaster? Not necessarily. Race vehicles such as this Rotax Max kart are designed with only a single rear brake assembly. Consequently, they always operate at 100 percent rear bias. In this case, the reduction of complexity and the decrease in rotational inertia more than make up for any brake bias inefficiency.

This may seem like a bad idea at first glance, but like all other considerations in racing, brake system design is driven by compromises. In this case, the additional static weight, system complexity, and rotational inertia (more on this in Chapter 10) of the front brake system components would decrease performance to the point that the benefits of brake balance would not be worth the tradeoffs. As a result, this kart's design only incorporates a rear brake assembly.

Naturally, this design may require the driver to employ a different driving style than if the vehicle were equipped with a four-wheel brake system. Its tendency to oversteer while braking in a turn would definitely deter most drivers from staying on the brakes any longer than necessary after turn-in.

Changing Brake Balance

In order to ensure stable braking for the mass public, nearly all auto manufacturers design their vehicles to be slightly front biased under all conditions. Consequently, if you measure the stopping distance of a vehicle as delivered from the showroom floor, you have a good baseline for a vehicle with 5 to 10 percent front brake bias.

If changes are made to a vehicle that can affect brake balance, re-measuring stopping distance can show you if you took a step in the wrong direction. For example, it's not uncommon to install more aggressive front brake pads (which would increase front bias) and see stopping distances go up 5 percent or more. Due to their even higher coefficients of friction, dedicated race front brake pads can result in even *longer* stopping distances assuming no other changes are made to the vehicle to correct the exaggerated front bias condition.

The most dramatic front bias effects are usually brought about by brake upgrades that are not properly matched to the intended vehicle. Chapter 11 exercises the calculations to perform these enhancements without destroying brake balance, but unfortunately too many swaps do not take brake balance into account.

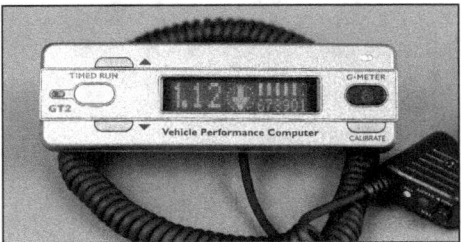

The best way to determine if your brake balance is optimized is to measure your stopping distance both before and after your modifications. Devices such as this Passport GT2 Vehicle Performance Computer can provide repeatable estimates of stopping distance at a reasonable cost. (Randall Shafer)

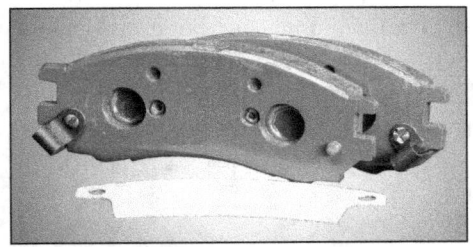

It doesn't matter if you are upgrading calipers, rotors, or brake pads—all of these components have the potential to alter your vehicle's brake balance. However, green paint has been proven to have no significant impact on braking performance. (Randall Shafer)

These poor vehicles end up with both bigger rotors and larger caliper pistons, which serve to drastically increase front brake bias. While the new system is rock-solid stable under braking, stopping distances can go up dramatically.

The flipside can be seen by making changes to increase the amount of rear bias. Because the auto manufacturers leave a little bit of wiggle room in their designs, it's usually possible to make small changes to decrease the front bias and end up with slightly shorter stopping distances than stock. Keep in mind, however, that there is only so much of this wiggle room to play with. After a point, decreased front bias can result in rear bias, which can make the vehicle unstable during hard braking.

Summary

So what can you do to optimize the brake balance of your own brake system? Well, it takes equal measures of educated planning and vehicle testing, but the rewards of optimized brake balance can be yours if you make the effort.

First, as you go about modifying your vehicle for the street or for the track, be aware that changes in the brake system as well as changes in the vehicle's ride height, weight distribution, or physical dimensions can swing brake balance all over the place. Coming chapters allow you to determine the theoretical impact your modifications may have on brake balance.

Second, the only sure-fire way of actually knowing that your brake balance has been optimized is to measure stopping distance both before and after your modifications. Increases in distance from the stock configuration, or from your modified baseline, indicate a change in brake balance for the worse.

Third, if even after careful consideration and design you manage to totally skew your balance into the weeds, you may need to install a balance-correcting device such an adjustable proportioning valve to squeeze out that last three feet of stopping distance. Instead of going into those details here, they'll be shared in Chapter 5.

Once the brake system has achieved perfect balance it's still up to the tires to generate brake forces, but don't forget that poor brake balance can lengthen stopping distances significantly, sticky tires or not.

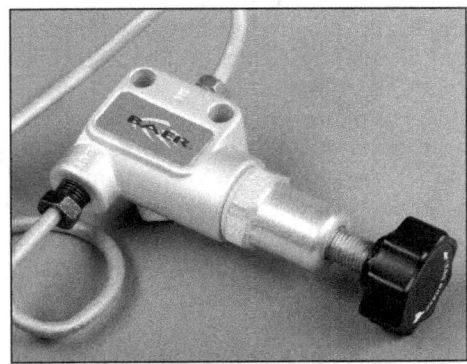

An adjustable proportioning valve can help fine-tune brake system balance. We'll talk about the inner workings of this extremely simple, yet complex, piece of hardware in Chapter 5. (Randall Shafer/Baer)

Factors that can Impact Brake Balance

Because there are so many variables that can influence brake balance, the following table summarizes how several common modifications can change a vehicle's ideal brake balance relationship. Many of these individual factors are covered in the chapters that follow, so feel free to stop back for a refresh after a few more pages.

Factors That Increase Front Bias	Factors That Increase Rear Bias
Increased front rotor diameter	Increased rear rotor diameter
Increased front brake pad coefficient of friction	Increased rear brake pad coefficient of friction
Increased front caliper piston diameter(s)	Increased rear caliper piston diameter(s)
Decreased rear rotor diameter	Decreased front rotor diameter
Decreased rear brake pad coefficient of friction	Decreased front brake pad coefficient of friction
Decreased rear caliper piston diameter(s)	Decreased front caliper piston diameter(s)
Lower center of gravity	Higher center of gravity
More static weight on rear axle	Less static weight on rear axle
Less static weight on front axle	More static weight on front axle
Less sticky tires (lower deceleration limit)	More sticky tires (higher deceleration limit)

CHAPTER 5

PEDALS, BOOSTERS AND MASTER CYLINDERS

The apply system (sometimes called the actuation system) exists in order to amplify the driver's leg force and then convert it into hydraulic fluid pressure. In nearly all cases, the apply system functionality is not assigned to a single device. Instead, most apply systems accomplish this task by dividing the total responsibility among several discrete components.

While there are many different types of apply systems, most conventional vehicles use a combination of brake pedals, brake boosters, and master cylinders to get the job done. Variations on this recipe abound, but the fundamental objective remains the same: increase the applied force and turn it into pressure.

There is, however, one addendum. As you just learned in Chapter 4, brake pressure distribution between the front brakes and rear brakes can be used to optimize a vehicle's brake balance. Consequently, the apply system may also contain additional devices which limit, regulate, or proportion the rear brake line pressure.

The pages that follow walk through these various components in detail, starting with the driver's primary interface to the brake system: the brake pedal.

Brake Pedal Components

The brake pedal's primary role is to mechanically increase the force exerted by the driver's leg on the brake pedal pad. Remember, it's essentially the amplified force from the driver's leg that creates slip at the tire contact patches.

The brake pedal accomplishes this task as a direct result of its lever-based geometry. There are many different designs available, but all rely on the following series of individual components to get the job done.

Brake Pedal Pad

The *brake pedal pad* is simply where the driver provides mechanical force input to the brake system. Most OEM systems use a ribbed rubber pad molded over a steel or composite core, but exotic-looking brake pedal pads made from cast aluminum and/or with weight-saving holes

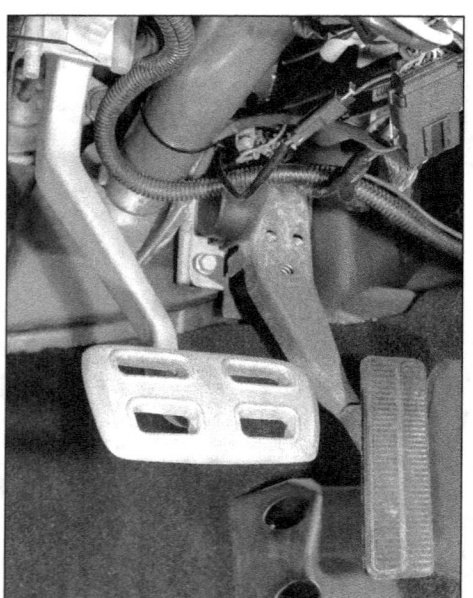

Most brake pedal pads are constructed from steel with textured molded rubber covers. The pedal shown here is actually made from cast aluminum for weight savings. Regardless of the aesthetic impact, the material of the pad itself doesn't impact the brake pedal output. (Randall Shafer)

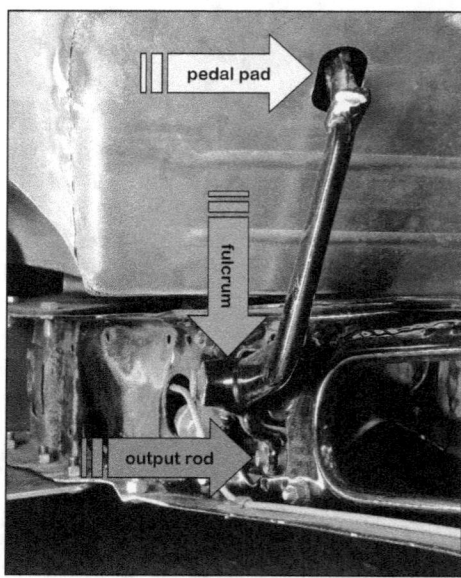

In most modern production vehicles, the brake pedal fulcrum is located at one end of the brake pedal arm. However, in many hot rod applications, the fulcrum (green arrow) is found between the brake pedal pad (yellow arrow, inside vehicle) and output rod (red arrow, under vehicle). In either case, the pedal ratio is calculated using the same equation. (Randall Shafer)

are now becoming more commonplace. Regardless of its construction, the pad should be large enough that the driver will not miss the pedal in a panic, small enough that it won't get hit by accident, and textured enough to prevent the foot from slipping off in the heat of battle.

Fulcrum

The *fulcrum* is found on the opposite end of the brake pedal assembly from the brake pedal pad. This is the pivot point for the moving components of the brake pedal assembly. Usually it's nothing more than a steel pin riding in a self-lubricating bronze bushing.

If your vehicle is equipped with a vacuum booster, the brake pedal output rod is most likely attached to the brake booster with a clevis joint. Shown here sticking out of the back side of the booster, the eyelet fits around a pin on the brake pedal arm, mechanically coupling the two components together. (Delphi Corporation)

Output Rod

The *output rod* transmits the brake pedal output force from the brake pedal assembly to the next device in the brake system (typically a brake booster of some sort). Since it must swing through an arc as it travels, it's usually located with a clevis bracket or, in racing applications, a spherical bearing, to allow for an angular misalignment between the two adjacent components.

Brake Pedal Arm

The *brake pedal arm* is the largest component in the brake pedal assembly. Its function is to locate the brake pedal pad at one end, the fulcrum at the opposite end, and the output rod somewhere

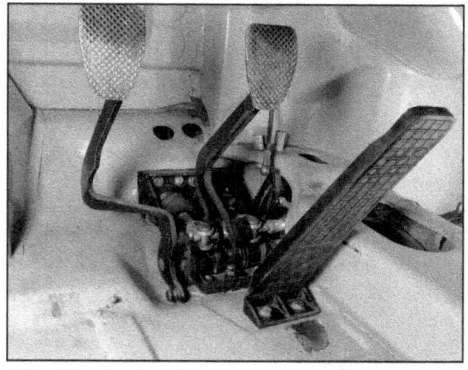

Ideally, the brake pedal arm should not bend or deflect during use. To make the arm as stiff as possible, it can be shaped like an I-beam or can be boxed along its entire length. This pedal simply uses extremely thick steel for its construction—crude, but effective. (Randall Shafer)

in-between. In some racing applications the fulcrum is placed between the pad and the output rod, but the concept is still the same.

Due to the large leg forces a driver may be capable of applying, the brake pedal arm must be structurally sound to prevent deformation or collapse during severe use. For this reason, it's usually designed to resemble an I-beam in cross-section with webbing often added for additional strength.

Brake Switch

The final component of the brake pedal assembly is the *brake switch*. This is the device used to illuminate the tail lamps of the vehicle when the brakes are

Although many brake switches employ a threaded mount for simple adjustment, this doesn't mean that you should tamper with its setting. The adjustment feature is typically used for manufacturing flexibility at the vehicle assembly plant and not for tweaking later. (Randall Shafer)

applied. In most applications, it consists of a mechanical plunger on/off switch actuated by the brake pedal arm, but in some custom applications it's common to have a pressure-actuated switch mounted in one of the master cylinder hydraulic lines.

There are many mechanical switches in use that allow you to adjust the plunger mechanism. In general, they should never be modified once they leave the factory. However, if you are changing other aspects of the apply system, it may be necessary to adjust the threaded mechanism to only illuminate the brake lamps when the driver applies the brakes.

After adjusting the brake switch, it's a good idea to put the vehicle on jack stands and turn each of the road wheels by hand, since an over-adjusted brake switch can result in continuous brake drag. If the wheels are more difficult to rotate than before the adjustment, chances are the switch needs to be returned to its original position.

OEM Brake Pedals

The brake pedal arm geometry (the location of the output rod relative to the brake pedal pad and the fulcrum) defines the pedal ratio. Note that this relationship holds true regardless of the location of the output rod relative to the fulcrum:

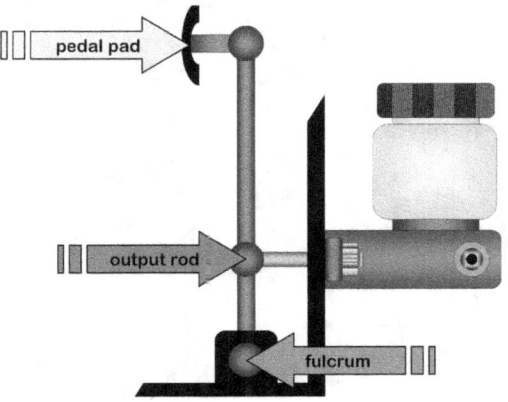

The brake pedal ratio is calculated by dividing the linear distance from the brake pedal pad to the fulcrum by the length from the output rod to the fulcrum. The larger the difference between the two distances, the more gain the brake pedal provides.

*Pedal ratio (unitless) =
distance, pad to fulcrum (in) ÷
distance, output rod to fulcrum (in)*

Typical brake pedal ratios (on conventional vehicles with vacuum boosters) are in the range of 3.5:1 to 4.5:1. Back in the days before booster assist became common, pedal ratios were more often in the range of 6.0:1 to 9.0:1. While these older designs certainly provided more mechanical advantage than most modern brake pedals, the corresponding increase in pedal travel made them undesirable.

As you learned back in Chapter 3, the primary design exercise becomes trading pedal ratio for pedal travel. In most street applications though, this is an academic point at best because modifying the brake pedal arm is a complex task best left to an experienced fabricator. This is not an area for novice experimentation.

Racing Brake Pedals

Despite the warning above, there may be times when modification of the brake pedal becomes necessary to offset a change elsewhere in the brake system. The most common need arises when a vacuum booster is removed from the brake system in a racing application. In this situation, the reduction in gain must be offset through a variety of different means starting with the brake pedal ratio.

Given the space and packaging limitations of a typical passenger vehicle, the maximum brake pedal ratio attainable is approximately 5.5:1 to 6.5:1. A brake pedal with a higher ratio usually won't fit under the dash conveniently, at least if you are trying to modify the stock brake pedal arm to achieve this level of gain (which you probably shouldn't be doing anyway).

Consequently, the best way to achieve a higher brake pedal ratio is to replace the OEM brake pedal with an aftermarket unit. Several makes and models exist, and should be selected based on your mounting needs (floor mount, firewall mount, or overhung), packaging constraints, and, of course, desired pedal ratio.

Brake Boosters

Although the details weren't covered in Chapter 3, you've already learned that the brake booster is designed to further amplify the brake pedal output rod force. The ratio of input force to output force can be expressed as a linear gain as follows:

*Booster output force (lb) =
brake pedal output force (lb)
x boost gain (unitless)*

While there are a number of different designs in use, an overwhelming majority of vehicles use a vacuum-assisted booster. The rest either use a hydraulically assisted device to perform the booster function, or they simply go without.

Vacuum Boosters

From the outside, *vacuum boosters* resemble a large metal can. Typically found sandwiched between the firewall and the master cylinder, their simple outward appearance belies the complexity found inside.

The vacuum booster provides gain by dividing the volume inside the can into two chambers separated by a semi-

The power valve is where the action takes place in a vacuum booster. Functioning as a stand-alone mechanical control system, it meters atmospheric pressure into the rear chamber of the vacuum booster as the driver applies force to the brake pedal. (Randall Shafer/Delphi Corporation)

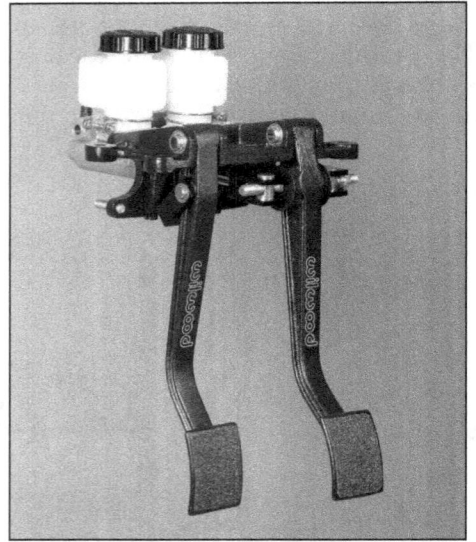

If you need more gain than the OEM brake pedal is capable of providing, invest in a racing brake pedal arrangement. Most, like the assembly shown here, aren't designed to be used with vacuum boosters, so the master cylinders are mounted directly to the bracket. (Randall Shafer)

From the outside, vacuum boosters look deceivingly simple. However, their complex inner workings are finely tuned to provide additional gain for the force delivered by the brake pedal. Resist the temptation to open one up, for there are no user-serviceable parts inside! (Randall Shafer/Delphi Corporation)

flexible, moving *diaphragm* (an elaborate name for a thin piston). While the engine is running, a vacuum line from the engine's intake manifold draws nearly all of the air out of the booster, creating a vacuum on both sides of the diaphragm. Because there is equal pressure (or lack thereof, really) on both sides of the diaphragm, it remains in place without doing anything at all.

When the brakes are applied, the vacuum booster works its magic. The incoming force from the brake pedal output rod cracks open a small labyrinth-like passageway in the booster internal *power*

PEDALS, BOOSTERS AND MASTER CYLINDERS

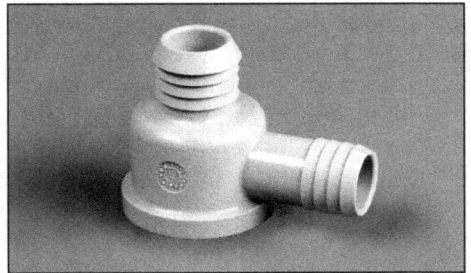

Because the available engine vacuum is subject to fluctuations during typical driving, a check valve is installed between the intake manifold and the vacuum booster. This allows the booster to retain vacuum for operation even after the engine has been shut off. (Randall Shafer/Delphi Corporation)

In autocross competition, some drivers choose to apply the brakes with their left foot while continuing to hold the throttle open with their right foot. This can result in vacuum depletion without an opportunity to recharge. Consequently, you may lose some boost gain midway through the course. (Wayne Flynn/pdxsports.com)

valve. This then allows a small amount of air to enter the rearmost chamber of the booster (the one closest to the brake pedal or firewall), creating a pressure difference between the two chambers separated by the diaphragm.

Because the diaphragm is not locked in place, it moves slightly away from the high-pressure chamber toward the low-pressure chamber, and as it moves it drags the booster output rod along with it. More brake pedal output force allows more air into the rearmost chamber, resulting in more pressure difference and consequently more movement.

The force coming out of the vacuum booster therefore is a function of the pressure difference across the diaphragm and the area of the diaphragm itself:

Booster output force (lb) = pressure difference (psi) x area of diaphragm (in²)

In summary, vacuum booster gain is a function of both power valve design (pressure difference) and diaphragm size (area). For this reason, larger boosters generate higher output forces.

Tandems and Triples

Because booster output is a function of diaphragm size, it would appear that one would want to install the largest booster possible to maximize the booster output force. While this is certainly true, packaging space underhood may not be large enough to fit a large-diameter, single-diaphragm booster.

Equivalent Booster Areas

In order to maximize vacuum booster gain, it's possible to install either one large diaphragm or multiple smaller diaphragms. The following tables illustrate various designs and their effective areas.

Booster Diaphragm Area (in square inches)

	Diaphragm 1	Diaphragm 2	Diaphragm 3	Total
Single 7"	38.5	n/a	n/a	38.5
Single 8"	50.2	n/a	n/a	50.2
Single 9"	63.6	n/a	n/a	63.6
Single 10"	78.5	n/a	n/a	78.5
Single 11"	95.0	n/a	n/a	95.0
	Diaphragm 1	Diaphragm 2	Diaphragm 3	Total
Tandem 6"+7"	28.3	38.5	n/a	66.7
Tandem 7"+7"	38.5	38.5	n/a	76.9
Tandem 7"+8"	38.5	50.2	n/a	88.7
Tandem 8"+8"	50.2	50.2	n/a	100.5
Tandem 8"+9"	50.2	63.6	n/a	113.8
	Diaphragm 1	Diaphragm 2	Diaphragm 3	Total
Triple 6"+6"+6"	28.3	28.3	28.3	84.8
Triple 6"+6"+7"	28.3	28.3	38.5	95.0
Triple 6"+7"+7"	28.3	38.5	38.5	105.2
Triple 6"+7"+8"	28.3	38.5	50.2	117.0
Triple 7"+7"+8"	38.5	38.5	50.2	127.2

From these tables you can see that if an area of 95 square inches is desired, one can select a single 11-inch diaphragm, tandem 8-inch diaphragms, or triple diaphragms measuring 6, 6, and 7 inches in diameter. All provide an equivalent level of boost assist. As always, the right answer depends on what fits your packaging space and, of course, your budget.

Fortunately, it's also possible to increase total booster diaphragm area by packaging multiple, smaller diaphragms in series with one another inside the same housing. The total diaphragm area will be equal to the areas of the smaller, individual diaphragms added together.

The sidebar illustrates some of the more common diaphragm arrangements, but in general, *tandem boosters* (two diaphragms) and *triple boosters* (three diaphragms) trade a reduction in diameter for an increase in overall length. Although the ultimate volume of booster may remain unchanged, a booster shaped like a sausage is sometimes easier to install than one shaped like a life preserver.

High-Performance Considerations

Because vacuum booster gain is also a function of the pressure difference across the diaphragm, any changes to the engine that influence intake manifold vacuum can impact the booster's efficiency. For example, installing a performance camshaft with increased valve overlap may be great for top-end horsepower, but the resulting lumpy idle reduces the maximum level of vacuum available to the booster. Consequently, braking performance may suffer as the maximum boost gain decreases.

Vehicle usage can also influence vacuum booster performance. Since most engines generate maximum vacuum at or near idle, the vacuum booster relies on this operating condition to recharge itself before each application of the brakes. If the engine is not permitted to achieve an idle state between brake applications (for example, the weekend autocrosser who uses their left foot for braking while keeping the throttle open with their right foot), the vacuum stored in the booster will be depleted, resulting in a complete loss of boost gain until vacuum is available once again.

For these reasons and more, vacuum boosters are typically not found on dedicated racing vehicles. Between the lack of vacuum, sustained high-speed operation without returning to idle, and increased packaging space required, the benefits simply do not outweigh the costs.

Hydraulic Boosters

In a few select applications, there simply isn't enough space for a conventional vacuum booster, yet the vehicle needs the additional gain. The late-model SN95 Mustang GT falls into this category, as the cylinder heads on its 4.6-liter V-8 were too wide to accommodate the booster used on the 3.8-liter V-6 Mustangs. Packaging space aside, other vehicles may not able to use vacuum boosters because their engines do not generate sufficient vacuum to provide consistent operation (the turbocharged Buick Grand National, for example).

On the other end of the vehicular spectrum are large trucks with diesel engines. Because these powerplants don't have a throttle plate in the intake system, they don't generate any appreciable vacuum, even at idle, making it rather difficult to justify the installation of a vacuum booster.

In cases such as these, a *hydraulic booster* may be substituted for a conventional vacuum booster. These devices operate much in the same fashion as a vacuum booster, but use pressurized hydraulic fluid from the power steering system to provide assist. The design of internal passages and valves control the gain during use.

Most hydraulic boosters are found in applications where the engine cannot produce enough vacuum on its own for reliable vacuum booster functionality. However, this 2004 Mustang Mach I uses a hydraulic booster because the wide cylinder heads on its 32-valve engine would crash into a vacuum booster. The large hydraulic lines shown entering the booster are carrying pressurized power steering fluid.

While they're smaller in diameter than a vacuum booster, hydraulic boosters weigh significantly more and require plumbing into the power steering system for proper operation. Auto manufacturers only use hydraulic boosters when they're designed into a corner, and you probably should too.

Master Cylinders

Once the driver's leg force has been sufficiently amplified by the brake pedal and brake booster, it's up to the master cylinder to convert it into hydraulic fluid pressure. Compared to the intricate vacuum and hydraulic boosters just mentioned, master cylinders are far less complex.

Body

The *master cylinder body's* primary function is to act as a pressure vessel. In other words, it must rigidly constrain a fixed volume of brake fluid when pressurized. In early vehicles, master cylinder bodies were made from cast iron, but modern bodies are almost exclusively fabricated from cast aluminum. In the aftermarket it's not uncommon to find bodies molded from composite materials for weight savings, but their relatively low burst strength make them unsuitable in most OEM applications.

Piston

The *master cylinder piston* serves to generate pressure in the hydraulic circuit. Usually fabricated from aluminum, the

In nearly all modern production vehicle applications, the master cylinder contains two separate pistons. This is a measure taken for redundancy in case of a hydraulic leak. The complex geometry of the internal components ensures partial system operation even if one hydraulic circuit is completely failed. (Randall Shafer/Delphi Corporation)

PEDALS, BOOSTERS AND MASTER CYLINDERS

piston receives the amplified driver's leg force on one side and transmits it to a fixed volume of brake fluid on the other side.

Seals

The *master cylinder seals* act as one-way valves, capturing pressure downstream of the piston during use, but allowing for rapid return flow to the master cylinder when the brakes are released. Shaped like a cup in most cases, they're susceptible to wear with time and should be considered an item for inspection on a regular basis as a vehicle ages.

More Stomping Power?

Master cylinder swaps are among one of the more common brake system modifications, yet the impacts are often the least understood. For example, this advertisement from a brake component supplier promotes their 19-mm master cylinder upgrade as follows:

"The 914 and very early 911s originally came with a 17-mm master cylinder. The 914-6 and later 911s came with a 19-mm master cylinder that allowed the driver to apply more direct pressure to the brake system. The 19-mm unit is externally almost identical to the 17-mm unit, and is a direct bolt-in replacement. Pedal travel is reduced a little bit, but I never really noticed any discernable change. The more direct result is a bit more stomping power on the pedal."

Since pressure is equal to force *divided* by area, you can calculate that the upgraded 19-mm master cylinder piston (with an area of 283 square millimeters) will actually generate 25 percent *less* pressure overall than the original equipment 17-mm master cylinder piston (with an area of 227 square millimeters). This is the same as reducing the overall system gain by 25 percent. In other words, the driver will need to press on the brake pedal 25 percent harder with the 19-mm master cylinder installed.

On the other hand, increasing the master cylinder piston diameter certainly improves brake pedal travel, or firmness. By how much? Not by coincidence, going from a 17-mm piston to a 19-mm piston decreases pedal travel by the same 25 percent. The effects of pressure and travel are equal but opposite. Less travel always requires higher efforts and vise-versa.

A common misconception is that a larger master cylinder results in a higher overall brake system gain. In reality, just the opposite is true—smaller master cylinders provide increased gain. A larger master cylinder results in reduced pedal travel, though, which some drivers prefer. (Randall Shafer)

Unfortunately for the owner above, the improvement in pedal travel was not significant enough to be discerned in daily use. However, it could be that the improvement in feel was misinterpreted as *more direct pressure* and *increased stomping power*.

The real story here is a 25-percent *decrease* in overall brake system gain without a perceptible improvement in pedal feel. It's up to the end user to decide if that should be considered an upgrade or not.

Return Spring

When the driver releases the brake pedal, it's desirable to relieve the pressure in the hydraulic circuit as rapidly as possible. For this reason, most master cylinders are fitted with a *return spring* to force the piston back to its home position when the brakes are released. Because it requires driver leg force to overcome the spring during brake applications, it unfortunately also has the effect of reducing the overall system gain.

Note that in some applications there may also be a return spring found in the vacuum booster and/or on the brake pedal arm. In a given application, all of these springs are deigned to work together, so removing or altering their design may impact residual brake pressure.

Reservoir

Because the volume of brake fluid in the hydraulic system fluctuates over time due to wear and compliance, it's necessary to carry an onboard supply of additional brake fluid to accommodate this need. Consequently, a *reservoir* of brake fluid is found on or near the master cylinder with enough brake fluid volume to support complete brake pad wear-out.

A reservoir *cab* usually seals the brake fluid from the atmosphere with a rubber bellows device, and in most applications contains printed information related to the chemistry of the brake fluid inside. Any time the cap is removed, it's a good idea to clean the area around it first to prevent contamination from falling into the reservoir during service.

Most reservoir caps are sealed with a flexible rubber bellows. This feature allows brake fluid to be drawn into the hydraulic circuit as needed without exposing it to air. (Randall Shafer/Delphi Corporation)

CHAPTER 5

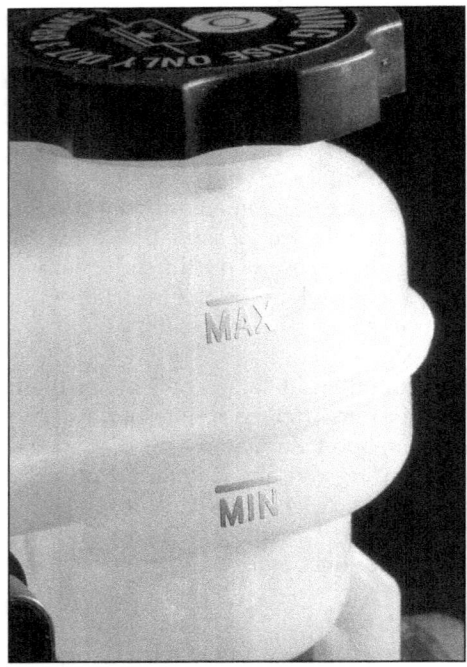

Every reservoir has a marking for the maximum fluid fill level. Note that the fluid should only be at this level when new brake pads and brake rotors are installed at all four corners. It's completely normal for the fluid level to drop over time as the brake components wear out. (Randall Shafer/Delphi Corporation)

While many older reservoirs were constructed from cast iron, modern designs incorporate a semi-transparent polymer such as nylon to permit examination of the brake fluid without removing the cap. This also prevents exposing the brake fluid from moisture in the air any more than necessary during service and inspection.

Master Cylinder Selection

The very simplest master cylinder designs incorporate a single piston acting against a fluid-filled cavity in a machined body. As the booster output force pushes on the back side of the piston, the piston pushes against the fluid, creating hydraulic pressure as defined by the relationship below:

Master cylinder pressure (psi) = booster output force (lb) ÷ master cylinder piston area (in²)

Since force is divided by area to calculate pressure, it becomes apparent that the smaller the master cylinder piston, the greater the pressure. Conversely, increasing master cylinder diameter decreases the pressure generated. Ultimately this means that smaller pistons provide higher system gains and larger pistons provide lower system gains, as counter-intuitive as this may seem.

Master Cylinder Volume

Because of brake system compliance (if you skipped the compliance sidebar in Chapter 3, now would be a good time to go back and read it), the master cylinder can only generate pressure if it's able to transfer additional brake fluid into the hydraulic circuit. More pressure requires more brake fluid. The geometry of the master cylinder stipulates that the maximum volume of brake fluid that can be provided is equal to:

Master cylinder volume (in³) = piston stroke (in) × piston area (in²)

This equation clearly shows that reducing piston stroke, piston area, or

Up until the late 1960s, it was common for vehicles to have a single circuit master cylinder generating pressure for all four brake assemblies, like on this 1966 Chevy II SS. While elegant in design, a single hydraulic leak would lead to a complete loss of braking capability. Modern brake systems incorporate redundant hydraulic circuits (and hence multiple outlet ports) to retain partial braking capability in the event of a leak. (Randall Shafer)

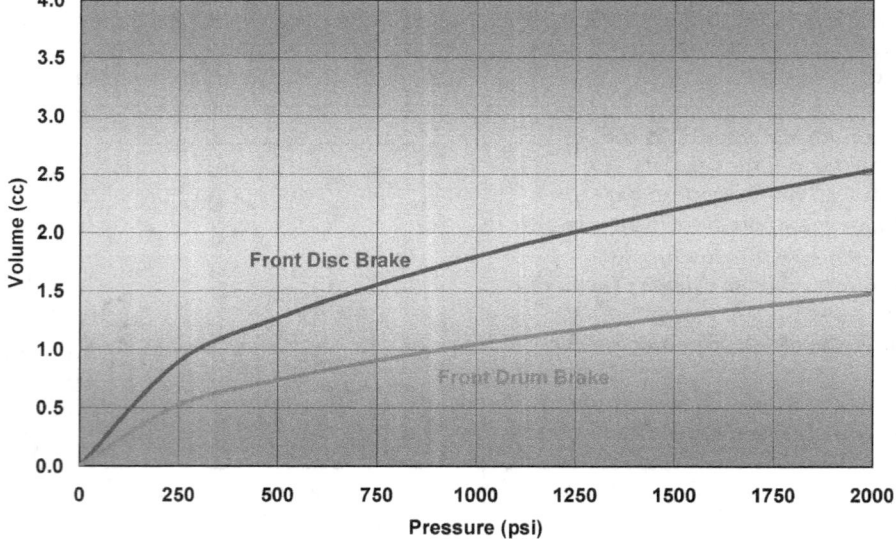

As the P-V curves above demonstrate, different brake systems can have very different amounts of compliance, even in the same application. For this reason alone it may be necessary to consider a master cylinder swap when converting this example vehicle from front drum brakes to front disc brakes.

PEDALS, BOOSTERS AND MASTER CYLINDERS

both reduces the maximum volume of brake fluid that the master cylinder is capable of transferring to the hydraulic circuit. Therefore, if the master cylinder piston size is downsized in the quest for increased gain, you can see that increasing the piston stroke is necessary to regain the lost volume capability.

If the stroke is not increased to offset the loss in volume, the master cylinder may bottom out during use, artificially limiting the maximum pressure that the driver is able to generate. As critical as this attribute may be to proper brake system performance, it's unfortunately not given enough consideration during many brake upgrade projects, especially on older vehicles.

For example, four-wheel drum brakes characteristically require far less brake fluid volume for operation than four-wheel disc brakes. Therefore, when converting a drum brake-equipped vehicle to disc brakes, it's imperative that the disc brake master cylinder is installed at the same time (unless of course they were designed to be the same from the factory). Failure to do so may result in severely limited pressure capability.

Tandem Master Cylinders

In the early days of the automobile, it was not uncommon to have a single master cylinder piston generating pressure for the brakes at all four wheels simultaneously. However, government regulations now dictate that every modern brake system must use a *tandem master cylinder* to build and distribute pressure in parallel between two separate hydraulic circuits (see chapter 7). The reasoning is that if there is a leak in one of the hydraulic circuits, the remaining half of the brake system is still able to generate pressure in some capacity.

In order to allow for pressure generation in a semi-failed condition, there are a few more bits and pieces added to the internal design of a tandem master cylinder. In the end though, the basic functionality remains unchanged from the single master cylinder designs of old.

Dual Master Cylinders

In contrast to the tandem master cylinders found on nearly every production vehicle today, a *dual master cylinder* arrangement is the standard method of building and distributing brake fluid pressure on dedicated racing vehicles. Using one brake master cylinder for the front calipers and a separate brake master cylinder for the rear calipers, hydraulic redundancy is maintained but more flexibility is possible in selecting unique front and rear master cylinder piston sizes.

While triple master cylinders are the hot ticket in circle track racing, they're a bit redundant in road racing applications. In general, unless your vehicle only turns left, a dual-master cylinder arrangement is sufficient. (Wayne Flynn/pdxsports.com)

Because it's extremely difficult, if not impossible, to adapt a dual master cylinder setup to an OEM brake pedal, an aftermarket racing brake pedal is usually required to make the conversion. In addition, dual master cylinders preclude the ability to use either a vacuum brake booster or a hydraulic brake booster, so the reduction in gain must be made up by other brake system components.

When sizing a dual master cylinder system, it's critical to note that optimum brake system balance requires that the rear brake line pressure be lower than the front brake line pressure during most aggressive driving circumstances. Consequently, the rear master cylinder piston is generally larger in diameter than the front master cylinder piston. An adjustable linkage between the two master cylinders can help to fine-tune the pressure ratio, but those details are still a few paragraphs away.

Triple Master Cylinders

Under the premise of more must be better, in many oval track racing vehicles it is common to find a *triple master cylinder* arrangement underhood. The concept is that brake line pressure cannot only be adjusted between the front brakes and rear brakes, but also independently

In dedicated racing vehicles, it's common to use one master cylinder for the front calipers and a second master cylinder for the rear calipers. To keep things balanced, it's typical for the front master cylinder to be of a smaller diameter than the rear master cylinder, but both must be sized for each individual circuit's P-V relationship. (Randall Shafer)

CHAPTER 5

In order to optimize a race vehicle's brake balance, a balance bar is used to control the force applied to the front and rear master cylinder pistons. A remote adjustment (the threaded horizontal rod) allows the driver to fine-tune balance on the fly. (Randall Shafer)

ABS and the Apply System

In general, ABS performance is largely unaffected by modifications made to a vehicle's brake pedal, brake booster, and master cylinder. This is because changes made to these components act no differently than a driver who applies different inputs to the brake pedal. However, as you learned back in Chapter 4, making changes to the vehicle's brake balance can have unintended side effects. Specifically, if the vehicle displays large amounts of front or rear bias after improper balance bar adjustment or poor proportioning valve selection, the ABS may be prone to premature cycling.

Additional disclaimers need to be made for vehicles equipped with traction control and/or electronic stability control. In these applications, brake fluid is drawn from the master cylinder reservoir and is rapidly pressurized at individual corners of the vehicle. Consequently, any modifications made to the apply system fluid flow path can have an impact on the rate of pressure build, and therefore the effectiveness of traction control and/or electronic stability control performance.

between the left front and right front wheels to help the vehicle turn while braking. Because these vehicles only operate in one fashion—go fast, turn left, repeat—their brake system can be optimized more than a conventional vehicle, which must turn both left *and* right while braking.

Rear Brake Pressure Reduction

To this point, it has been suggested several times that methods exist to modify the brake fluid pressure being routed to the rear brakes. While the strategies may vary by design, fundamentally the brake system must deliver less pressure to the rear brakes than the front brakes. Therefore, an additional piece of hardware is necessary to control the brake fluid pressure making its way to the rear brakes.

Balance Bars

On vehicles equipped with dual master cylinders, it is common to use a mechanical reaction linkage that divides the driver's amplified leg force between separate front and rear master cylinders. Known as a *balance bar* or *bias bar*, this device controls the ratio of driver leg force acting on the individual front and rear master cylinder pistons. When adjusted in concert with the previously selected master cylinder piston sizes, the balance bar determines the ratio of brake fluid pressure between the front and rear hydraulic circuits.

Due to the geometry of the balance bar, true brake pressure proportioning between the front and rear hydraulic circuits can be achieved. While this can provide application-specific customization of the front and rear brake line pressures, the primary benefit is that a balance bar can be packaged to allow

Production vehicles typically use a proportioning valve to regulate rear brake pressure. From the factory, their settings are fixed, but several aftermarket models like the one shown here incorporate an adjustment knob or lever to allow the user to customize the brake balance for their individual vehicle. (Randall Shafer/Baer)

adjustment of the front-to-rear proportioning ratio while at speed.

In other words, an adjustable balance bar allows the driver to make on-the-fly balance changes for wet weather, varying track conditions, or decreasing fuel load. The complexity of this device (along with the necessary dual master cylinder setup) makes it highly impractical for street use, but on the track it simply cannot be beat

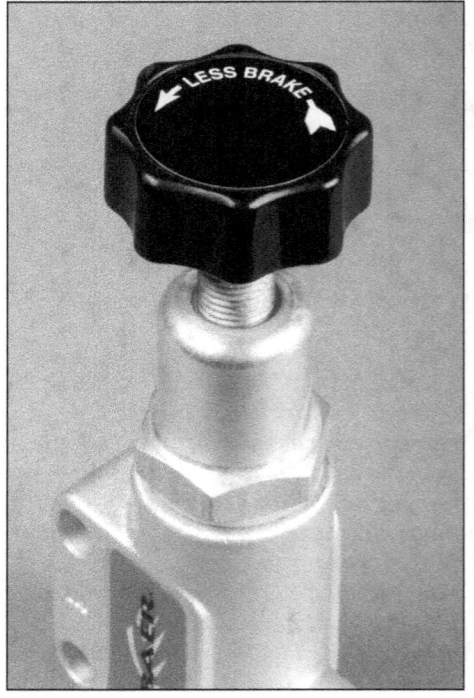

54 HIGH-PERFORMANCE BRAKE SYSTEMS: DESIGN, SELECTION AND INSTALLATION

PEDALS, BOOSTERS AND MASTER CYLINDERS

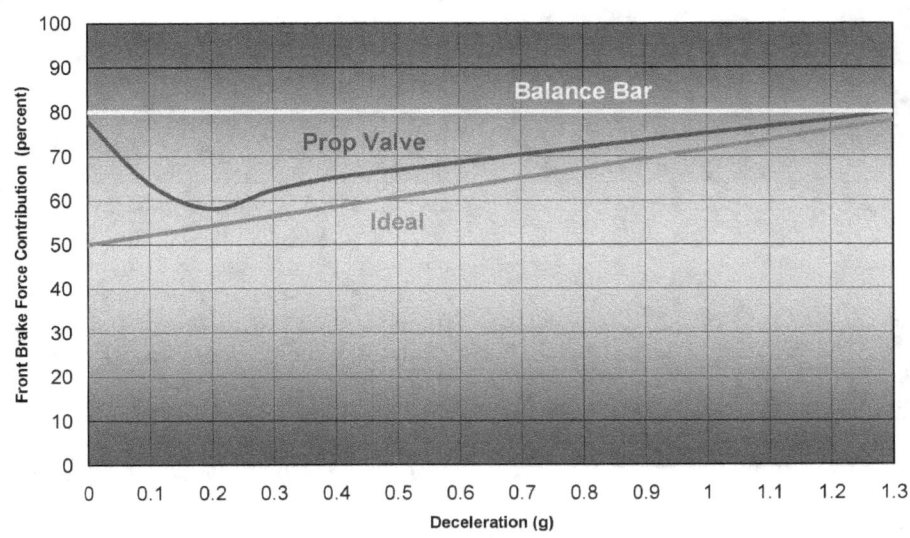

Brake Balance vs. Deceleration

Many strategies exist for controlling the rear brake pressure. The three curves above illustrate the relationship between front and rear brake pressure for the ideal balance condition (red line), the balance bar solution (yellow line), and the proportioning valve (blue line). Although the balance bar can be adjusted to provide ideal balance at maximum deceleration, the proportioning valve provides much better control under typical driving conditions.

for ease of adjustment, hence its nearly universal presence in dedicated racing vehicles.

The only real disadvantage to the balance bar is that it can only be adjusted to provide optimized brake balance at one deceleration level—usually the point of maximum deceleration. At lower deceleration levels the vehicle will display increasing levels of front bias. (Technically you *could* adjust the balance bar to optimize brake balance at any deceleration level, but deceleration beyond that point would lead to an unstable rear-biased condition.)

Proportioning Valves

It can be argued that conventional *proportioning valves*, or *prop valves* for short, should really be referred to as *braking force regulators* or *brake pressure regulating valves*. While their name might imply true proportional control, in reality they impart a more complex level of brake pressure regulation than the balance bar is capable of providing.

Unlike the balance bar, which is installed upstream of the master cylinders, proportioning valves are fitted to the hydraulic lines downstream of the master cylinder pistons. Therefore, they cannot impact the pressure generated, but they can restrict its flow to the rear brake assemblies under certain conditions.

Knee Point and Slope

At low master cylinder pressures, proportioning valves allow equal pressure to both the front and rear brake assemblies. In other words, they won't modify the pressure to the rear brakes at all. This is usually desirable, since at low decelerations there is minimal weight transfer and the rear brakes can do more work.

However, once the proportioning valve *knee point* is reached, the rear brake pressure continues to build, but at a slower rate, or *slope*, than the front brake pressure. Therefore, unlike the balance bar, which provides optimum bake balance at only one deceleration level, systems that use proportioning valves can achieve optimum balance over a wide range of deceleration levels. This benefit is relatively meaningless in racing applications where the vehicles are always operating at maximum deceleration (where the balance bar should be optimized), but it's a great advantage on the street for uniform brake pad wear and vehicle stability when braking in a turn.

OEM Proportioning Valves

Although this conflicts with the enthusiast's innate desire to tinker, you should resist the urge to tamper with *OEM proportioning valves*. In general, they are well matched to the vehicle's

Factory proportioning valves come in all shapes and sizes. Without a thorough understanding of their internal workings, though, they should not be taken apart or modified by the enthusiast. The proportioning valves shown here are actually screwed into the vehicle's master cylinder outlet ports. (Delphi Corporation)

A proportioning valve's operation is governed by the design of its internal spring and armature. The spring preload determines the kneepoint, while the geometry of the armature dictates the rate of pressure rise after the kneepoint has been reached. (Randall Shafer/Delphi Corporation)

CHAPTER 5

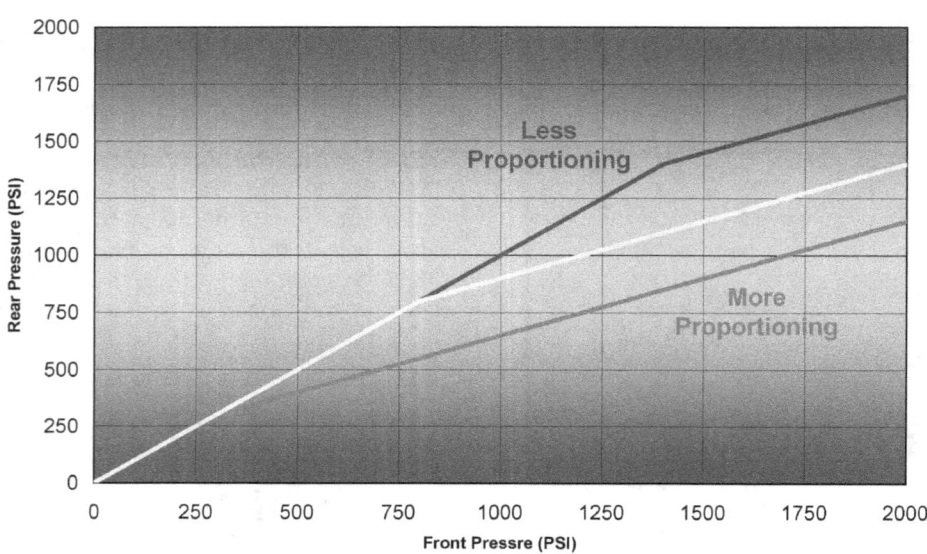

Adjustable proportioning valves vary the spring preload but not the armature geometry. Consequently, only the proportioning valve kneepoint can be adjusted by the driver. In general, increasing preload increases the kneepoint for higher rear brake pressures (blue line) while decreasing preload decreases the kneepoint for lower rear brake pressures (red line).

In most applications, adjustable proportioning valves are mounted in the vehicle to allow the driver full control over brake balance. In this particular application, the valve was mounted underhood by the crew chief in order to prevent adjustment while on the track.

original brake system and there are no parts inside that should be modified by ambitious owners. Unfortunately, some are externally adjustable so the temptation to fiddle with them is right there in front of us!

From a design perspective, the OEM proportioning valve knee point is dictated by the selection of a hold-off spring, and the slope is a function of the internal armature, or piston, geometry. These parts are generally staked in place, but are sometimes serviceable with threaded interfaces. Again, these are not components that should be swapped or modified without extensive knowledge of proportioning valve design.

Height-Sensing Proportioning Valves

The Achilles heel of mechanical proportioning valves is that they must be designed as a best compromise for use under all conditions. High speed, low speed, fully loaded, and empty vehicle scenarios must all be evaluated and figured into proportioning valve selection.

In order to adapt a proportioning valve's output to vehicle loading conditions, many applications use a *height-sensing proportioning valve*. Commonly found on light-duty trucks and several European passenger sedans, these devices connect the proportioning valve to a mechanical linkage between the rear axle assembly and the vehicle body structure. As vehicle loading is increased, the linkage acts on a cam that raises the preload on the proportioning valve spring. This increases the proportioning valve knee point, helping to take advantage of the increased brake force sustainable at the rear tires.

Aftermarket Proportioning Valves

While most enthusiasts should never attempt to modify an OEM proportioning valve, in some circumstances it may be necessary to adjust the rear proportioning to a different level than the factory specification. Consequently, an *aftermarket proportioning valve* might just be the solution, but there are several rules of engagement that must be considered before installation.

First, an aftermarket proportioning valve should *never* be installed if the OEM proportioning valve is still in place.

Proportioning valves plumbed in series with one another can do nasty, unpredictable things.

Second, aftermarket proportioning valves should *never* be installed in the front hydraulic brake circuit. This error would create a significant amount of rear brake bias. Front brake line pressure should always be dictated by the driver's leg force—only the rear brake line pressures should be considered candidates for proportioning.

Third, an aftermarket proportioning valve cannot reconcile or make up for horrible mismatches in brake system sizing. Regardless of the proportioning valve used, the intrinsic brake system balance needs to be close to optimized from the start. This is the only way that a proportioning valve can truly be effective.

Fourth, without the resources of a major automotive manufacturer there's no way of knowing if an aftermarket proportioning valve has been optimized for your particular application. Consequently, this is a classic case of buyer beware. Anecdotal advice and recommendations from other users are the only pieces of information you have to make your decision.

Adjustable Proportioning Valves

Many aftermarket proportioning valves feature a user-adjustable knee point. Through either a multi-position ratcheting lever or an infinitely adjustable threaded knob, spring preload is varied to modify the knee point but the slope remains fixed based on the armature design. While these devices allow quick and easy adjustment of rear brake proportioning, both knee point *and* slope are critical to system performance if optimum brake balance is desired over the entire range of vehicle deceleration.

Consequently, the typical performance of an *adjustable proportioning valve* is somewhere between the performance of a balance bar and an OEM proportioning valve. Brake balance can still be optimized at the point of maximum deceleration and will be close to optimum at lower decelerations, but most likely will not be finely tuned for driving around town.

When dialing in an adjustable proportioning valve for optimum performance, the valve should first be set to the maximum amount of rear brake pressure reduction (the lowest spring preload). Progressively more aggressive brake stops should then be performed at increasing levels of rear brake contribution until the point at which the rear brakes lock before the front brakes, or the point at which the vehicle becomes unstable under braking. Once this point is reached, a slight adjustment back on the valve should be all that is required to enable ideal brake balance at maximum deceleration.

Summary

So what can be done to increase the performance of your apply system? Much depends on your individual needs, but in general you must select the proper combination of components to provide the pressure your vehicle requires.

The brake pedal and booster must work as a team to amplify the force exerted by the driver's leg. Gain is the name of the game, but don't forget that vacuum boosters are sensitive to changes in engine performance. Also, remember that removing a booster always requires a change in the brake pedal (increased ratio) and master cylinder sizing (smaller diameter) to recoup the loss in gain.

Master cylinder selection boils down to trading off pressure build performance (smaller diameters) with decreased brake pedal travel (larger diameters). The happy medium provides an acceptable level of pressure without a spongy feel.

In most applications, you should make every attempt to plan and select your caliper, brake pad, and rotor modifications so that you are able to retain and reap the benefits of the stock proportioning valve. Don't stray too far from the factory balance in the first place, and you will be well ahead of the game.

If more extreme modifications force you to scrap the stock proportioning valve and replace it with an aftermarket unit, be advised that selection and adjustment are not to be taken lightly. While there is more than one way to achieve optimum balance at the point of maximum deceleration, a conservative approach of slowly increasing rear brake contribution will prevent unintended (and undesirable) braking instability.

Although the apply system is not the most glamorous part of the brake system, you do not want to be sitting on the grid second-guessing your decisions. Proper upfront selection of gain and balance provides your vehicle with worry-free braking lap after lap. (Wayne Flynn/pdxsports.com)

CHAPTER 6

BRAKE FLUID

Without a doubt, brake fluid is near the top of most enthusiasts' lists of boring brake subjects. It may even rival the ashtray and cup holder for the all-time most boring vehicle part ever. Yet in spite of its low score on the "cool-o-meter," brake fluid is one of the most vital components to your vehicle's brake system performance, and ultimately to its overall safety.

How then can it be neglected for years and years and years at a time? This may not surprise you, but some people don't change their brake fluid for the entire life of their vehicle and don't even think twice about it.

But don't worry—help has arrived. You're about to learn everything you ever need to know about the very lifeblood of your vehicle's brake system. If you're not itching to run to the garage with a bleeder bottle by the time you're done reading this chapter, you might want to check your pulse.

Time, temperature, and moisture are the three primary enemies of your vehicle's brake fluid. The only visual indication of degraded brake fluid performance is a change in fluid color over time from light yellow (the beaker on the right) to a dark, muddy brown (the beaker on the left). (Randall Shafer)

Brake Fluid 101

Brake fluid's functional responsibility is to transmit the force from the master cylinder piston or pistons to the calipers at the four corners of the vehicle. It does this by allowing itself to be pressurized. Based on the hydraulic gain of the brake system, there may be an increase in the force delivered to the calipers, but the brake fluid and distribution system fundamentally do not provide any gain on their own. This relationship was covered in Chapter 3, but can be summarized by the following equation:

Caliper input pressure (psi) = Master cylinder pressure (psi)

The brake fluid found in the master cylinder reservoir is not pressurized, even during brake application. This fluid is drawn into the hydraulic circuit only as needed due to long-term changes in brake system volumetric consumption, such as when brake pads are worn down to their backing plates. (Randall Shafer/Delphi Corporation)

While that may sound simple, there are several other demands placed on the brake fluid that could prevent it from performing its intended function. For this reason, the National Highway Traffic Safety Administration, or NHTSA, an agency of the Department of Transportation, or DOT, has established a Federal Motor Vehicle Safety Standard, or FMVSS, dedicated to brake fluid performance.

FMVSS116

In FMVSS116, NHTSA has identified no less than 14 properties of brake fluid worthy of government regulation. By law, if the fluid cannot pass one or more of the 14 requirements the product cannot claim compliance to DOT standards.

If all of FMVSS116 were to be duplicated here in this book, over 22 pages of text would be required. The sidebar provides a more detailed list of these items, but for now it makes the most sense to summarize four of the key requirement categories from the perspective of the typical automotive enthusiast.

The Fluid Should Not Solidify

As stated a few paragraphs back, brake fluid is able to transmit force across a distance because it able to be pressurized. While this may be obvious, the pressurization of brake fluid is much easier to accomplish when it's in its natural fluid state than when it is frozen solid in the brake lines and hoses.

Therefore, a critical requirement for brake fluid is that it must maintain its fluid state even in the presence of extremely low ambient temperatures. Because ambient

BRAKE FLUID

One of brake fluid's most important characteristics is its ability to maintain a fluid state even in the presence of extremely cold ambient temperatures. For this reason alone, water would make a very poor brake fluid in climates where temperatures drop below freezing! (Randall Shafer)

temperatures routinely fall well below 32 degrees F, this immediately eliminates water from the list of potential brake fluids.

The Fluid Should Not Vaporize

As stated a few paragraphs back, brake fluid is able to transmit force across a distance because it's able to be pressurized. While this may be just as obvious as it was moments ago, the pressurization of brake fluid is much easier to accomplish when it's in its natural fluid state than after it has boiled into gaseous form in the brake lines and hoses.

Brake fluid fade occurs if the brake fluid vaporizes during use (note that this is quite different from *brake pad fade*, which is covered in Chapter 9) and is characterized by a brake pedal that falls nearly to the floor of the vehicle when pressed by the driver. This increase in pedal travel is accompanied by a partial or complete loss of deceleration capability, which results in extended stopping distances. This condition tends to make drivers a bit uncomfortable, to say the least.

Therefore, a critical requirement for brake fluid is that it must maintain its fluid state even in the presence of extremely high ambient temperatures. However, there is a large amount of heat generated by the brake system itself. In fact, the heat coming from the brake system can greatly overshadow any effects of ambient heat. Remember from Chapter 1 that rotor temperatures of hundreds of degrees Fahrenheit are not all that uncommon, even in everyday driving.

For this reason, the *boiling point* of brake fluid is one of its important physical attributes. In fact, to the racer it may be the single most critical performance criteria.

The Fluid Should Not Attack Seals

Before you get the impression that I'm referring to the protection of an endangered species, this requirement simply implies that brake fluid should not adversely affect the performance or longevity of the hydraulic seals in the master cylinder, proportioning valves, and calipers. This requirement not only applies to chemical compatibility, but also to any lubricating properties that the fluid may need to possess.

(Author's note: no seals were harmed in the writing of this book.)

Of paramount important to the racer, brake fluid must also maintain its fluid state in the presence of extremely high temperatures. For reliable performance on the track, dry boiling points well over 500 degrees F are often required. (Wayne Flynn/pdxsports.com)

Brake fluid fade occurs when the brake fluid changes in state from a liquid to a gas. Unfortunately for the driver, brake fluid in vapor form is much more compressible than it is in liquid form, resulting in little, if any, braking effectiveness. Under these circumstances, the best one can hope for is a gravel trap to stop the car. (Wayne Flynn/pdxsports.com)

Brake fluid's compressibility indicates how much the fluid shrinks in volume when it's pressurized. For the best brake pedal feel, fluid with the lowest compressibility possible is desired. This is just one of the reasons that silicone-based DOT 5 fluid is not recommended in high-performance applications—its chemistry makes it much more compressible than DOT 3 and DOT 4 fluids. (Randall Shafer)

The Fluid Should Not Be Compressible

When Newton (yes, the same Newton from Chapter 2) was not preoccupied defining the laws of motion, he took some time to study fluids and discovered that all of them—without exception—were compressible to some degree. In other words, when they are pressurized they decrease in volume. For this reason, when brake fluid is pressurized it shrinks in reaction.

While this does not pose a performance concern with the fluid, it does result in extra brake pedal travel. For this reason, selecting a brake fluid with low compressibility can result in significant improvements in brake pedal feel.

Dry Boiling Point

During competitive events, mild track use, or even spirited street driving, it's not uncommon to see rotor temperatures well in excess of 800 degrees F. While not all of this heat is seen by the caliper body, the brake fluid behind the piston can easily reach 300 degrees F, with severe applications resulting in even higher temperatures.

Fortunately, brake fluid manufacturers have found a way to formulate brake fluids that can perform in these extreme operating conditions without even breaking a sweat. When new, most common brake fluids have dry boiling points of well over 400 degrees F. Unfortunately though, these very same fluids also have an Achilles heel.

Although the glowing front brakes on this Subaru indicate their temperature is well over 1,200 degrees F, the brake fluid does not experience quite the same level of heat during use. The temperature of the brake fluid in the caliper is probably closer to 300 to 400 degrees F. (Wayne Flynn/pdxsports.com)

Detailed FMVSS116 Requirements

In all, FMVSS116 calls out 14 different performance requirements over 22 pages for brake fluid sold in the United States. Listed here, in their official order of appearance, are those properties under NHTSA's microscope:

1. Dry boiling point
2. Wet boiling point
3. Kinematic viscosity
4. pH value
5. Chemical stability
6. Corrosion
7. Fluidity and appearance at low temperature
8. Evaporation
9. Water tolerance
10. Compatibility
11. Resistance to oxidation
12. Effects on rubber
13. Stroking properties (lubrication capability)
14. Fluid color

While each requirement spells out specific performance criteria in gory detail, all were developed with a single objective in mind: ensuring that brake fluid maintains its ability to transmit force under a wide range of operating conditions.

A brake fluid's wet boiling point is defined by NHTSA as the effective boiling point when the fluid contains 3.7 percent water content by volume. This value is typically found advertised on the side of the bottle along with the fluid's dry boiling point. (Randall Shafer)

Diffusion explains how moisture can find its way through the walls of nylon master cylinder reservoirs. Modern polymers have been formulated to be more resistant to this phenomenon, but nothing beats a good old-fashioned cast iron reservoir for moisture protection. (Randall Shafer)

Even the rubber seals found in the caliper body are subject to moisture migration by diffusion. Unfortunately, the water that passes through these seals contaminates the brake fluid that is most likely to see the highest temperatures, resulting in increased opportunity for brake fluid fade. (Randall Shafer/StopTech)

Wet Boiling Point

If even a small amount of water is adsorbed into brake fluid, the boiling point can plummet to *less than half* of the original value. Because of this sensitivity to water content, FMVSS116 regulates two unique boiling point conditions: the *dry boiling point* and the *wet boiling point*. For uniformity in testing, NHTSA defines the dry boiling point at zero-percent water content by volume and the wet boiling point at 3.7-percent water content by volume.

Ironically then, one of brake fluid's most important characteristics is the ability to adsorb water. Yes, you read that correctly! In spite of brake fluid's boiling point sensitivity to water content, it readily adsorbs water *by design*.

Water Adsorption

Whether you like it or not, water is omnipresent in nature and finds its way into nearly everything. In the case of a brake system, the mechanism of *diffusion* allows moisture (water vapor) in the air to enter the hydraulic system through microscopic pores in the rubber brake hoses, the nylon master cylinder reservoir, and the various rubber seals. As if by magic, even a completely sealed brake system rises in water content over time.

Sadly, there's nothing neither you nor I can do about this situation and if left unchecked, the water will rot away the brake system from the inside out. If you never change your brake fluid, this is exactly what happens.

Consequently, most brake fluid is *hygroscopic* in nature—it adsorbs this unwanted house guest in order to reduce

All cans of brake fluid contain an airtight seal when new. This seal is applied at the factory and should not be removed until immediately before the brake fluid is to be used. Once opened, the can should either be used completely or discarded. (Randall Shafer)

This particular brand of brake fluid takes its name from its low moisture activity (LMA) formulation. Its advertised wet boiling point of 311 degrees F allows it to just barely meet the DOT 4 requirement. (Randall Shafer)

the rate of brake system internal corrosion. As an added benefit, the solution state prevents the individual water molecules from collecting and freezing when exposed to temperatures below 32 degrees F and from boiling when exposed to temperatures above 212 degrees F.

Note that this is also the reason that brake fluid is packaged in sealed containers. Once the seal is broken, the irreversible process of water adsorption begins. For this reason, once you open a new container of brake fluid you should either use the entire contents immediately or discard the remaining portion. An open can of brake fluid left on the shelf for even a few months will degrade rapidly in boiling point performance.

DOT Ratings

FMVSS116 also provides a DOT rating system for brake fluids. Specifically, fluids are classified as being DOT 3, DOT 4, or DOT 5. So, what exactly is contained in the DOT specification? More importantly, what is *not* contained in

DOT 4 fluids are not all created equal; however, they all must adhere to minimum government standards established by FMVSS116. This DOT 4 brake fluid advertises a dry boiling point of 594 degrees F even though the minimum required is only 446 degrees F. (Randall Shafer)

CHAPTER 6

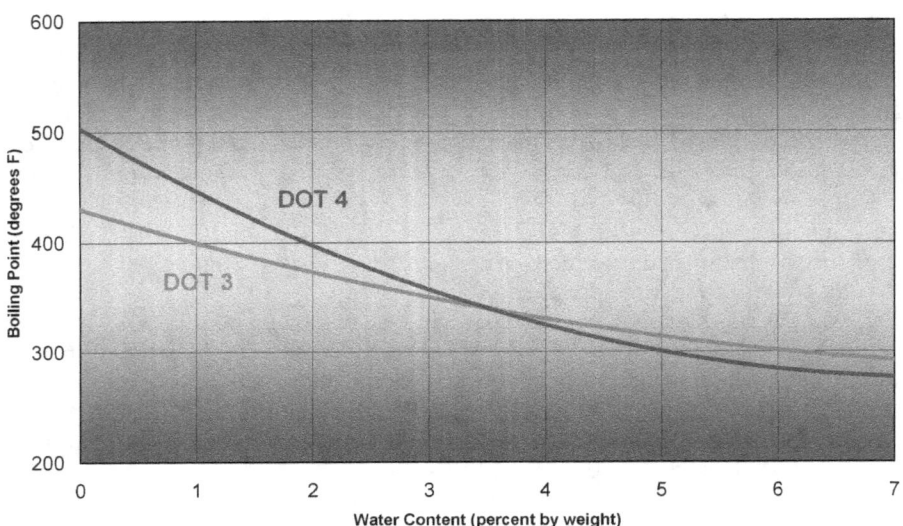

The graph above illustrates the typical boiling point performance of DOT 3 (red line) and DOT 4 (blue line) brake fluids with increasing water content. Although DOT 4 fluids display higher dry boiling points, they tend to degrade more quickly than DOT 3 fluids. This suggests that more frequent fluid replacement is required when using DOT 4 fluids.

DOT 5 brake fluids contain a purple dye to help identify them visually, as shown in the beaker on the left. Non-silicone-based brake fluids generally have a light yellow color, as shown in the beaker on the right. (Randall Shafer)

DOT specification? A quick look through FMVSS116 reveals all you need to know.

DOT 3 Fluids

DOT 3 fluids are usually glycol ether based, but that isn't because they're required to be. In fact, FMVSS116 makes no mention whatsoever about the chemical compounding of brake fluids—it simply dictates the fluid physical properties. However, the brake fluid industry has by consensus decreed that glycol ether fluids are the most economical way to meet DOT 3 requirements.

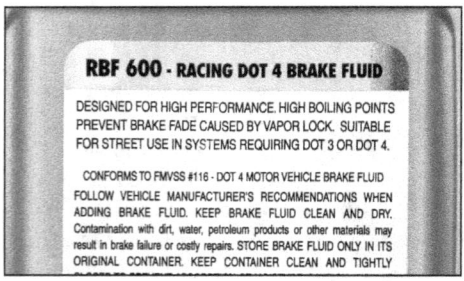

In general, all DOT 3, DOT 4, and DOT 5.1 brake fluids can be mixed without concern. DOT 5 fluids on the other hand cannot be added to any of these other fluids, as their physical composition makes them chemically incompatible. (Randall Shafer)

By FMVSS116 definition, DOT 3 fluids must have a minimum dry boiling point of 401 degrees F and a minimum wet boiling point of 284 degrees F. That's really about all the specification says as far as the average user is concerned.

DOT 4 Fluids

DOT 4 fluids are also glycol ether based, but have a measure of borate esters thrown in for increased immunity to water adsorption. Because of their enhanced chemistry, DOT 4 fluids have a more stable boiling point during the early portion of their lives. However, once the fluid does actually begin to adsorb water, its boiling point typically falls off more rapidly than the average DOT 3 fluid.

By FMVSS116 standards, DOT 4 fluids must have a minimum dry boiling point of 446 degrees F and a minimum wet boiling point of 311 degrees F. Do these more stringent requirements make DOT 4 fluids better than DOT 3 fluids? Well, it's not quite that simple.

Remember, the boiling points listed in FMVSS116 are minimums, and as such there are some DOT 3 fluids available with higher boiling points than some DOT 4 fluids. The real impact of using DOT 4 fluids is that you should change the fluid more often than if you select a DOT 3 fluid, if for no other reason than the rapid fall off in boiling point with time.

DOT 5 Fluids

DOT 5 fluids are typically entirely different animals than DOT 3 and DOT 4 fluids. Why? Because their extremely high boiling point requirements—509 degrees F dry and 356 degrees F wet—usually dictate a silicone-based chemistry to achieve the desired results. Their high boiling points, however, make them appear at first glance like just the ticket for severe-duty applications. In addition, they also tend to have much, much lower viscosities, which improve cold weather performance dramatically.

So why not just pour it in and go? Well, the first strike against DOT 5 fluids is that there is more space for air to fit between the individual molecules than in DOT 3 or DOT 4 fluids. I'm not talking about large bubbles of air that are visible to the naked eye, but rather microscopic

DOT 5.1 brake fluids are required to meet stringent DOT 5 requirements, but are formulated from glycol ether base stocks. This allows them to be mixed with DOT 3 and DOT 4 fluids without negative side effects. They may also be referred to as DOT 4 Plus or Super DOT 4 fluid. (Randall Shafer)

DOT Brake Fluid Ratings

The following table summarizes key minimum performance requirements and typical chemical compositions for DOT 3, DOT 4, DOT 5, and DOT 5.1 brake fluids. While fluid color and labeling requirements may be important to NHTSA, rarely do racers select brake fluid based on these criteria...

Property	DOT 3	DOT 4	DOT 5	DOT 5.1
Dry boiling point (degrees F)	401	446	509	509
Wet boiling point (degrees F)	284	311	356	356
Chemical composition	Glycol Ether	Glycol Ether/ Borate Ester	Silicone	Glycol Ether/ Borate Ester

amounts of air that are finely dispersed, or entrained, in the brake fluid molecular matrix.

Since molecules of air are *much* more compressible than any fluid, the sensation at the brake pedal is like stepping on a big squishy spring. For this reason, silicone-based DOT 5 fluids are typically not favored in applications where high brake line pressures are present or when firm brake pedal feel is a critical attribute.

The second strike against DOT 5 fluids is that they cannot be mixed with or added to DOT 3 or DOT 4 fluids. The two chemistries are simply not miscible with one another, much like the proverbial combination of oil and water. Even with the best of intentions, it's relatively impossible to completely purge an existing system of old brake fluid when doing a fluid change, resulting in pockets of the silicone-based fluid being isolated from the glycol ether-based fluid.

The third strike against DOT 5 fluids is that they do not chemically adsorb water like the glycol ether-based fluids. While this may lead to favorable boiling point performance numbers, it can result in localized areas of boiling, freezing, and internal corrosion. Remember, brake fluid is *supposed* to adsorb water...

DOT 5.1 Fluids

Historically, DOT 5-level performance (specifically boiling points and viscosity) could only be achieved with silicone-based fluids. However, modern compounding has created glycol ether-based fluids, which now meet DOT 5 performance levels in these critical areas. Consequently, the DOT 5.1 name was created to differentiate between these two very different chemistries that *both* meet DOT 5 performance requirements.

In brief, DOT 5.1 fluids are simply DOT 4-type fluids that meet DOT 5 performance requirements. Because DOT 5.1 fluids are glycol ether based, they can usually be mixed with or added to DOT 3 or DOT 4 fluids without concern. In some circles they are even referred to as *DOT 4 Plus* or *Super DOT 4* fluids because they are more similar to a conventional DOT 4 fluid by chemistry than they are to a conventional DOT 5 fluid.

While it may not be obvious, the big advantage of DOT 5.1 fluids is that they possess the compressibility characteristics of DOT 3 and DOT 4 fluids while simultaneously providing DOT 5-level boiling points and viscosities over a wide range of temperatures. In one sense, it's the best of both worlds.

The beaker on the left contains visual proof that DOT 3 and DOT 5 brake fluids are not chemically compatible with one another. Just minutes after mixing a small amount of DOT 3 (light yellow) with DOT 5 (purple), complete separation of the two fluids is observed. A beaker containing only DOT 3 fluid is shown on the right for comparison. (Randall Shafer)

Upgrading your brake fluid requires more effort than simply pouring in the new stuff. While selecting the proper boiling point range and DOT rating are certainly critical to your success, a funnel also helps if your hands are not too steady. (Randall Shafer)

CHAPTER 6

When considering a brake fluid upgrade, it's best to first determine the type of fluid that came in your vehicle from the factory. Typically the brake fluid specification can be found printed on the brake fluid reservoir cap. (Randall Shafer)

In general, if your vehicle was designed for a particular type of brake fluid, you should make every attempt to stick with that fluid. For example, if your vehicle was designed with DOT 3 fluid in mind, the internal components of the system (seals, brake hoses, and fittings for example) were specifically designed and tested for compatibility with DOT 3. Replace it with DOT 4, and the system may not necessarily react in a positive fashion to the new borate esters floating around.

Another incompatibility scenario is common to clutch master cylinders that share a fluid reservoir with the brake mas-

While many sport bikes come from the factory filled with DOT 4 brake fluids for high-performance operation, several cruiser bikes are equipped with DOT 5. Why? Because glycol ether-based DOT 4 fluids eat through their paint if it is spilled during assembly or service. (Randall Shafer)

ter cylinder. In this case, just changing the brake fluid viscosity and/or lubricating properties may cause the clutch system hydraulic seals to wear at an increased rate. What starts as an annoying squeak might eventually become a prematurely worn hydraulic seal.

So does this mean that a brake fluid upgrade is out of the question? Absolutely not! It simply means that when upgrading your DOT 3 fluid to an ultra-high boiling point DOT 5.1, extra care and attention must be placed on hydraulic system maintenance and inspection.

And what about changing to DOT 5? Because most vehicles come from the factory with glycol ether-based fluids, it's a safe assumption that you should not even consider putting DOT 5 brake fluid in your vehicle. In fact, the only production vehicles sold in the U.S. that come from the factory with DOT 5 fluids today are Harley-Davidson motorcycles. Why? Because DOT 3 and DOT 4 fluids will mar the fancy paint on these machines if spilled on them.

Brake Fluid Maintenance

Regardless of how much you choose to spend on brake fluid, be forewarned that there are *no* fluids that allow you to operate indefinitely without periodic maintenance. Because chemical composition and physical properties change with temperature exposure and water content, you simply can't fill-and-forget your brake fluid. The best that a fluid can do for you is provide stable, consistent performance during use, but because all fluids will adsorb water over time, all fluids must be replaced at some point.

So how often should replacement occur? At one extreme are competition vehicles, which typically have their brake fluid changed after every lapping session. On the other extreme are show vehicles of the *Fourth of July Parade* variety, which may only need a fluid change every couple of years. For the typical enthusiast, a yearly change of fluid is usually good idea with periodic minor refreshing after significant track events.

As it sounds, there are no hard and fast rules regarding how and when brake fluid maintenance should occur, but the fluid may already be giving you signs that should not be ignored. For example, a darkening of the fluid is indicative of extreme heat exposure and/or increased water content. A spongy-feeling brake pedal around town or a partial loss of braking performance on the track can result from brake fluid boiling, or fluid fade. Both of these are sure signs that a brake fluid change is well past due.

So, what's the downside of DOT 5.1 fluids? Like most things in life, the good stuff isn't cheap. DOT 5.1 fluids typically cost three to four times as much as conventional DOT 4 fluids, but in this case you probably get what you pay for.

Brake Fluid Compatibility

As just stated, DOT 3, DOT 4, and DOT 5.1 brake fluids are all glycol ether based. Consequently, these fluids are fully compatible with one another. As a result, they can usually be interchanged or mixed with one another without concern. However, this does not mean that caution can be thrown to the wind when considering a brake fluid upgrade.

In many modern applications, the hydraulic clutch system also uses brake fluid, and in some cases, the clutch system and the brake system may even share a common fluid reservoir. The clutch reservoir above calls out DOT 3 fluid for proper operation. (Randall Shafer)

HIGH PERFORMANCE BRAKE SYSTEMS: DESIGN, SELECTION AND INSTALLATION

BRAKE FLUID

Vehicles such as hot rods and muscle cars that are driven infrequently or only at moderate speeds generally don't need to be bled as often as dedicated race vehicles. Under these benign circumstances, bleeding the brakes every other year is probably more than enough. (Randall Shafer)

These examples are not meant to indicate that you should wait for a sign from the automotive gods before changing your brake fluid. It simply means that making brake fluid inspection and maintenance a part of your regular vehicle care routine goes a long way toward ensuring optimum brake system performance.

Continued on page 68

Every caliper is equipped with at least one bleeder valve. This device allows for a controlled release of used brake fluid from the hydraulic circuit when opened. The rubber cap keeps out contamination during use. (Randall Shafer/StopTech)

ABS and Brake Fluid Selection

While it may not be obvious at first, brake fluid selection can have a considerable impact on ABS performance. Why? Because as ABS does its thing underhood, it is rapidly moving brake fluid to and from the brake caliper. If the fluid is not capable of maintaining its physical properties during this high-frequency cycling, its ability to transmit pressure may suffer. This can result in a significant reduction in brake system gain.

In general, most glycol ether-based brake fluids are suitable for use in ABS-equipped vehicles. The molecular structure of these brake fluids does not allow much air to be entrained in the fluid matrix. For this reason, most DOT 3, DOT 4, and DOT 5.1 brake fluid containers actually advertise their compatibility with ABS right on their labels.

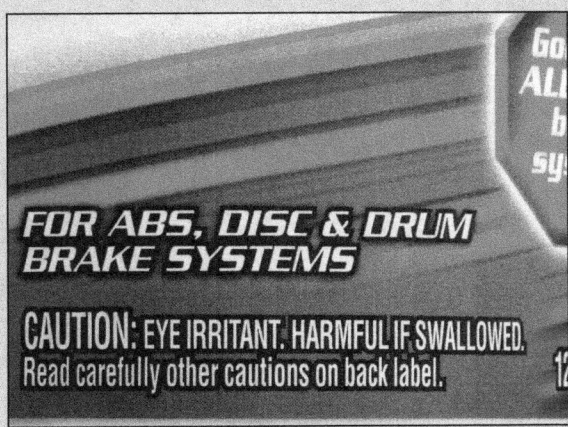

Since their glycol ether-based chemistries don't have much room for free air molecules, most DOT 3, DOT 4, and DOT 5.1 brake fluids are compatible with ABS. In many cases, this is advertised prominently on the bottle label. DOT 5 fluids, on the other hand, may end up looking like the head on a good pour of your favorite beer after ABS cycling. (Randall Shafer)

DOT 5 brake fluids are another story altogether. Because these silicone-based brake fluids do entrain a significant amount of air, they may actually foam up when cycled during a typical ABS event, resulting in extreme brake fluid compressibility. This highly undesirable side effect provides yet another reason to steer clear of DOT 5 brake fluids on most modern production vehicles.

CHAPTER 6

Brake Bleeding The Old-Fashioned Way

There are a number of high-tech tools available to bleed brake systems, but nothing beats a good old manual bleed for bonding with your vehicle. Plus, while alternative techniques may save some time in the process, the quality of a manual bleed is second to none.

Tools and Supplies Required

1. New brake fluid from a sealed container. About one pint is needed for a track bleed, three pints for a service bleed.
2. An eighteen-inch long section of clear plastic tubing. The inner diameter of the tubing should be a squeeze-fit over the exposed end of the bleeder valve.
3. A box-end wrench to open and close the bleeder valve. Choose the right size for your vehicle application, and note that the front and rear valves may be different.
4. One willing assistant to stroke the brake pedal. This tool may be the hardest to find on short notice.
5. A disposable bottle for the used brake fluid. If you choose to use an old brake fluid container, make sure it is clearly labeled to prevent its reuse!
6. One can of brake cleaner and a shop towel or two. Bleeding can get messy.

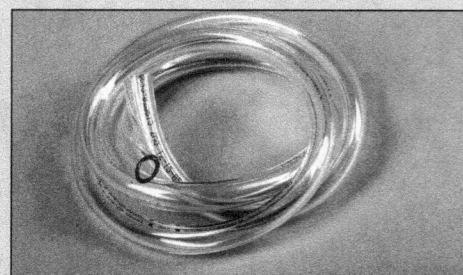

When bleeding your brakes, it's best to use a piece of clear tubing to collect and route the used brake fluid to a waste container. This allows you to see if any air bubbles are remaining in the system or not. (Randall Shafer)

A clearly marked brake fluid bottle makes for a very convenient waste fluid container, but be careful not to reuse your old fluid! Although not as glamorous, a Gatorade bottle works just as well. (Randall Shafer)

Following a brake system bleed, all of the hydraulic fittings should be cleaned with solvent and allowed to dry. This makes finding leaks and loose fittings much easier in the future. However, avoid spraying these cleaners directly on rubber or plastic parts, as this makes them hard and brittle over time. (Randall Shafer)

Vehicle Preparation

1. Loosen the lug nuts and place the entire vehicle on jack stands. Be sure that the vehicle is firmly supported before going any further!
2. Remove all four wheels. If you have open-ended lug nuts, it's helpful (but not necessary) to snugly reinstall one lug nut per corner to seat the rotor against the hub.
3. Open the hood and check the level of brake fluid in the master cylinder reservoir. Note the level of the fluid (necessary for step 17 below!) and then add fluid as needed to bring it to the MAX marking on the reservoir.

The Bleeding Process

1. Locate the outboard bleeder valve on the passenger side rear caliper (or drum brake wheel cylinder) and remove the protective rubber cap (if so equipped).
2. Place the box-end wrench over the bleeder valve.
3. Squeeze one end of the clear plastic tubing over the exposed end of the bleeder valve. Insert the other end of the clear plastic tubing into the disposable bottle.
4. While holding the disposable bottle with one hand and the wrench with the other hand, instruct your willing assistant sitting in the vehicle to apply the brakes.
5. Your assistant should pump the brake pedal three times, and then hold the pedal down firmly. It's important that you instruct your assistant not to release the brakes until instructed to do so.
6. Loosen the bleeder valve just enough to release fluid into the clear plastic tubing. Inform your assistant that the brake pedal will drop toward the floor during this step, but that they should continue to apply the brakes.
7. Once fluid has stopped flowing into the clear plastic tubing, tighten the bleeder valve gently. Note that one does not need to yank on the wrench with ridiculous force—a quick tug will suffice.
8. Instruct your assistant to release the brakes.
9. Inspect the fluid in the clear plastic tubing for the presence of air bubbles.
10. Repeat Steps 5 through 9 approximately 5 to 7 times for a track bleed or approximately 10 to 15 times for a service bleed. In either case, bleeding should continue until air bubbles are no longer present in the clear plastic tubing and the fluid appears fresh.
11. Repeat Steps 2 through 10 for the inboard bleeder valve (if so equipped).
12. Check the level of brake fluid in the master cylinder reservoir again. Add fluid to bring it back to the MAX marking on the reservoir. Don't let the reservoir run dry at any time during the bleeding process!
13. Clean any spills or drips with brake cleaner and a shop towel.
14. Repeat Steps 1 through 13 for the driver side rear, passenger side front, and driver side front hydraulic circuits. Always bleed the brakes in the same sequence to avoid skipping a caliper by accident.
15. Test the brake pedal for a firm feel. While bleeding the brakes won't necessarily cure a spongy brake pedal (there are non-brake fluid reasons that the pedal feel might be soft), the pedal should not be any worse than it was prior to the bleeding procedure.
16. Inspect all bleeder valves for signs of leakage. Re-tighten if necessary.
17. Finish the job by filling the master cylinder reservoir to the level recorded in Vehicle Preparation Step 3. Note that this means the final fluid level might not be at the MAX mark.
18. Properly dispose of the used waste fluid as you would dispose of used motor oil. Remember that used brake fluid should never be poured back into the master cylinder reservoir.

Once you're done bleeding your brake system, refill the master cylinder reservoir to the level observed prior to the start of the bleeding process. If you're also replacing the brake pads and rotors, you should fill the reservoir to the MAX mark. (Randall Shafer)

CHAPTER 6

Brake Bleeding

Brake fluid replacement is almost always performed through the process of *brake bleeding*. As the graphic name implies, this procedure allows controlled amounts of brake fluid to escape the system through a *bleeder valve* located at the wheel end of the hydraulic circuit (usually a caliper). While there are several reasons for initiating a brake system bleed, the procedure (as found in the accompanying sidebar) is typically the same.

Service Bleed

Any time a hydraulic circuit is exposed to the atmosphere, air will enter the circuit and must be purged before use. Consequently, a *service bleed* is always required after the hydraulic circuit is opened during service, repair, or upgrading. As you have already learned, when air is present in the brake fluid, input at the brake pedal merely compresses the air instead of creating system pressure. If enough air is present in the brake system, it can result in a complete loss of braking!

Because of the relatively large volume of air found in the brake system after service, a significant amount of fluid is purged during a service bleed. In fact, a service bleed usually results in a complete replacement of the brake fluid. For this reason, a service bleed procedure is also employed when upgrading fluid or performing a regular fluid replacement.

If you're driving your vehicle hard enough to put it up on two wheels, chances are you should be bleeding your brake fluid after every session on the track. (Wayne Flynn/pdxsports.com)

Track Bleed

During extreme use, brake fluid properties may degrade, making the brake fluid less robust to fade in subsequent heat cycles. In this scenario, a *track bleed* can be used to purge this small amount of brake fluid (usually confined to the brake fluid in the calipers) from the system.

This is the procedure used by race teams in the pits between track sessions. Because only the fluid at the wheel ends is exposed to high temperature, there is no need to change the entire volume of brake fluid. Mechanically, a track bleed is identical to a service bleed, but the number of bleed cycles is reduced significantly.

Summary

So what can you do to increase the performance of your brake fluid? In general, experiment with DOT 3, DOT 4, and DOT 5.1 fluids to find the right combination of boiling points, water adsorption, and cost for your application, but steer clear of DOT 5 fluids. Remember, the DOT 5 silicone-based brake fluids are not compatible with the glycol ether-based fluids. Leave the DOT 5 stuff for the two-wheel crowd!

Ultimately, your fluid choice should come down to preventing brake fluid fade. If your fluid never boils, you're done. Simply maintain the fluid at an appropriate interval and focus on the more glamorous components of your brake system. However, if brake fluid fade persists, you may have to either shorten your replacement interval or bite the bullet and pay for increased boiling point performance.

Any time the hydraulic system is opened for repair or maintenance, it needs to be bled to remove any air trapped inside at the time of reassembly. This procedure is called a service bleed and typically requires a significant amount of brake fluid on hand to completely flush and fill the system. The most time-consuming part is usually just putting the car on jack stands and removing the road wheels and tires. (Randall Shafer)

CHAPTER 7

BRAKE LINES AND HOSES

As stated back in Chapter 3, the brake lines and brake hoses have one of the easiest jobs in the brake system. They only need to transport pressurized brake fluid away from the master cylinder and to the four corners of the car. On the surface, it sounds like a simple job.

However, while the brake lines and hoses have a relatively straightforward role to play in the brake system, if they're unable to perform their task, everything goes really bad, really fast. There are few brake system failures that draw as much immediate attention as a hydraulic fluid leak. So while the job at hand may be a simple one, the importance is no less significant than for any other brake system component.

Hydraulic Circuit Design

In Chapter 5 it was briefly stated that all modern vehicles employ two completely separate hydraulic circuits to direct brake fluid pressure to the four corners of the vehicle. This step is taken in the interest of safety—if one circuit fails and is unable to generate pressure, the other remains capable of providing at least some level of brake system functionality.

Front-Rear Split

One of the simplest methods for achieving brake system redundancy is to attach the front brakes to one dedicated hydraulic circuit while placing the rear brakes on their own separate hydraulic circuit. Generally referred to as a *front-rear split*, this hydraulic architecture is found on vehicles that have relatively uniform front-to-rear static weight distributions.

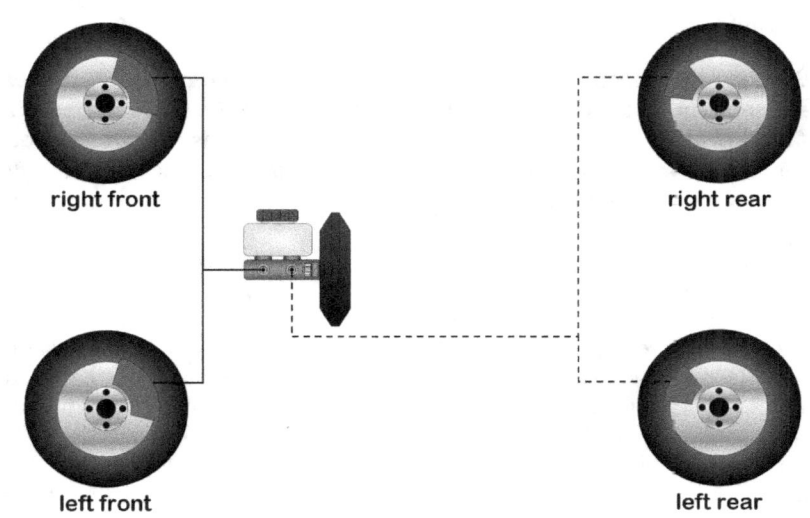

In a front-rear split design, the two front brakes (solid line) and two rear brakes (dashed line) use independent hydraulic circuits. This architecture is most common in rear-wheel drive vehicles and/or pickup trucks due to their significant rear weight distribution and large rear-brake assemblies.

The primary performance advantage of the front-rear split design is that in the event of a failed hydraulic circuit, there are still two brakes on the *same* axle that provide equal braking forces. For this reason, the vehicle won't turn or pull in either direction under failed-circuit braking.

From a manufacturing perspective, a front-rear split design only requires that a single hydraulic line be routed from the master cylinder to the rear of the vehicle. Once the hydraulic line reaches the rear axle it can be split to provide pressure to both the left rear and right rear brakes, but a single hydraulic line can be used for a majority of the distance.

One potential disadvantage of the front-rear split is that the level of deceleration available under failed-circuit braking varies with which axle experiences a hydraulic failure. In the case of a failed rear hydraulic circuit, the driver retains braking on the front axle, but a failed front circuit only leaves the driver with the rear brakes to slow the vehicle. Because the gain of the front brakes is generally much greater than the gain of the rear brakes, this can result in a significant variation in performance between the two failed conditions.

Diagonal Split

In some applications, the gain of the rear brakes may be low enough that a completely failed front hydraulic circuit would not allow the vehicle to decelerate at an

HIGH PERFORMANCE BRAKE SYSTEMS: DESIGN, SELECTION AND INSTALLATION

CHAPTER 7

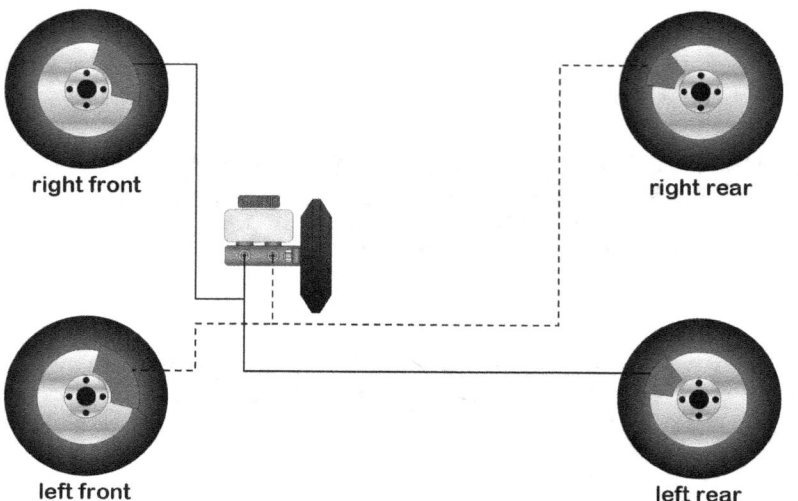

If a vehicle has a significant percentage of its weight carried on its front axle, the rear brake gain may be too low to achieve an appropriate level of deceleration during failed-circuit braking. For this reason, smaller vehicles with front-wheel drive typically employ a diagonally split hydraulic arrangement where the right front is paired with the left rear, and the left front is paired with the right rear.

acceptable level. Therefore, an alternate hydraulic design known as the *diagonal split*, or *X-split*, connects one front and one diagonally opposed rear brake assembly (the left front brake and right rear brake, for example) to each hydraulic circuit. In this fashion, regardless of which hydraulic circuit fails the remaining braking capacity is the same.

Although this symmetry in design may appear highly desirable at first, it creates its own unique performance compromise. Because the front brake gain and the rear brake gain are quite different from one another, a failed diagonal circuit will create a brake force distribution that causes the vehicle to pivot around the functioning front brake, resulting in a pull. This tendency can be amplified by vehicle suspension parameters, but fundamentally all vehicles equipped with diagonally split hydraulic circuits will try to change lanes under failed-circuit braking conditions.

In addition, the diagonal split implementation requires that two hydraulic lines be routed from the master cylinder to the rear of the vehicle. For this reason, the more complex diagonal split is also less preferred from a manufacturing and servicing perspective, but if the rear brakes are relatively small, there may not be another option.

Brake Lines

A typically hydraulic circuit consists of both *brake lines* and *brake hoses*. The difference between them is that brake lines are fabricated from mild steel, while brake hoses are made from flexible, polymeric materials.

Brake lines are typically attached to the master cylinder at one end, snaked around the vehicle like spaghetti, and terminate at the brake hose somewhere near

Smaller vehicles with smaller compliances require 3/16-inch brake lines as shown on the left, while large vehicles with excessive compliance require 3/8-inch diameter sewer pipes as shown on the right. If the brake line selected is too small in diameter, it will increase the brake system response time. (Randall Shafer)

the moving parts of a vehicle's chassis. In order to protect them from damage, brake lines are typically made from mild steel and are permanently bent to route their way around and along the vehicle's underside. For additional protection, they are usually held in place along the body with plastic clips or retainers—a brake line hanging out in midair is just asking to get caught, snagged, or otherwise damaged by a passing piece of road debris.

Because a brake line failure can be quite catastrophic, it makes sense to route them up and out of the way of any potential hazards. Clips and brackets should be used to attach individual lines to the vehicle body structure adding yet another layer of protection. (Randall Shafer/StopTech)

Another benefit of mild steel construction is that it decreases the brake line's compliance. Remember back from Chapter 3 that when a hydraulic system is pressurized it wants to expand in volume like a balloon. Mild steel helps add mechanical strength to the line, reducing its expansion when subjected to brake fluid pressure.

Flare Fittings

In order to form a leak-proof seal with the master cylinder and brake hose, a *flare*

BRAKE LINES AND HOSES

Tips for Brake Line Installation

When installing new brake lines, you should make every attempt to match the stock vehicle routing. However, if you're forced to create a new routing, there are several factors that should be considered before you start bending pipe.

1. Always use brake line the same diameter as stock. Most auto supply stores have several sizes to choose from, so measure before you go or bring a sample of the old line with you.
2. Only use mild steel tubing for your brake line. You should never use copper or aluminum lines as they are not strong enough for the high pressures found in a typical brake system!
3. Attempt to minimize the amount of brake line hanging out in midair. Wherever possible, keep the line tight against the frame or body structure to reduce the opportunity for damage. Attaching the line to the body using plastic clips or retainers is always a sound idea.
4. Route the brake line as far as possible from sources of extreme temperature, such as exhaust manifolds and catalytic converters. The heat from these devices can boil the brake fluid in the line if you get too close. If close quarters are unavoidable, be sure to install a thermal barrier or place an insulating sleeve over the lines before final assembly.
5. If you're routing brake lines in areas exposed to flying debris (along the vehicle underbody, for example), you should consider installing spiral-wrapped brake line armor. This is cheap insurance!
6. Terminate the ends of the brake line with the appropriate flare fitting for your vehicle. Many auto supply stores sell unbent lines with fittings already installed if you wish to pay a little bit extra for this convenience.

In this application, the brake lines are forced to run close to the vehicle's exhaust manifold. To prevent fluid boiling in the lines, they're wrapped with a heat-reflective shield that looks much like tin foil. (Randall Shafer)

Tube nuts are used to clamp the two mating halves of the flare fitting together. Because this is a crush-to-seal interface, these nuts should not be over tightened. Using excessive force on the wrench may seal the fitting at assembly, but probably makes the flare unusable if future servicing is required. (Randall Shafer)

fitting is used. A flare is essentially an upturned section of brake line material, which fits tightly against a seat machined into a mating component, such as a master cylinder. When the integral *tube nut* is then tightened, the force mechanically crushes the flare against the seat, forming a robust hydraulic seal.

While flare fittings are an elegant way of joining the hydraulic components together, there is a limiting factor in their design and use. Because they require mechanical deformation to seal the joint, the interface loses strength after repeated loosening and tightening cycles. In simpler terms, if you take it apart it might not seal when you put it back together.

For this reason, flare fittings have a limited useful life before they must be cut off and reformed. How many times is a function of vehicle-specific factors, but in general flares can begin to lose their sealing capability after a few installation cycles. The helpful advice here is that you should not disassemble a flared joint any more often than you must!

Brake Hoses

From the factory, nearly every production passenger vehicle has short, flexible brake hoses that run from the rigid metal brake lines to the calipers (or to the wheel cylinders in the case of drum brakes). These flexible brake hoses are necessary because the wheel ends are free to move relative to the body of the vehicle. Rigid brake lines attached to the calipers would

Because the brake calipers are typically attached to moving parts of a vehicle's suspension, it isn't possible to fabricate the entire hydraulic circuit from steel tubes. Consequently, a short piece of flexible polymeric hose is used to allow relative motion between the moving components. (Randall Shafer)

Brake Line Flares

Fortunately for the automotive enthusiast, there are essentially only two different styles of brake line flares that one can expect to encounter. The first is the SAE double flare. This flare is most commonly found on vehicles designed and manufactured in North America and consists of a 90-degree inverted cone on the brake line that seats against a protruding feature on the mating component. In these high-pressure, safety-critical applications, a simpler single flare is not used because of its more pronounced tendency to crack and leak at the brake line seam when assembled.

The second style of brake line flare is the ISO bubble flare, and is the interface of choice on many imported vehicles. Unlike the inverted SAE double flare, the ISO bubble flare actually protrudes outward from the end of the brake line, seating against an inverted feature machined into the mating component. The term metric flare is also used to describe this design, as the tube nuts are typically formed with metric threads.

So is one style of flare better than the other? Not necessarily. Properly formed, appropriately fastened, and adequately maintained, either design should provide years of leak-free operation. The most important thing to remember is that the two styles are not compatible with one another, so caution must be taken when buying bulk brake line at the parts counter to avoid mixing and matching.

A banjo bolt is frequently used to attach the flexible brake hose to the caliper body. The bolt contains a central flow-through channel, which allows for the transmission of hydraulic fluid pressure. A pair of copper crush washers is typically used to form a leak-free seal. (Randall Shafer/StopTech)

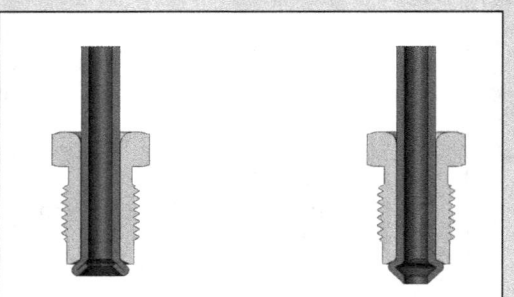

The two most common types of brake line flares are the SAE double flare (left) and the ISO bubble flare (right). When installing or repairing brake lines, the appropriate flare geometry must be used or the interface won't seal correctly. (StopTech)

not allow for the articulation of the wheel ends without subsequent failure.

Typically, these brake hoses contain a compliant polymeric inner tube to transmit brake fluid pressure from the brake lines to the caliper. While the polymeric tube does a good job of withstanding attack from the inside, it must be protected from the outside world as well. Consequently, the inner polymeric tube is wrapped, or more commonly overmolded, with a thick, rubber coating to prevent external damage.

While flexibility is good, compliance is the inevitable compromise for brake hoses. When pressurized, polymeric tubes generally have much, much higher expansion rates than mild steel lines, and for this reason, brake hoses are one of the leading contributors to unwanted brake pedal travel. More pressure results in more expansion, which results in more pedal travel. Therefore, when designing a brake system, it's highly desirable to use as much brake line as possible while minimizing the length of brake hose.

Banjo Fittings

As discussed a few paragraphs back, flexible brake hoses are commonly attached to rigid brake lines through the use of flare fittings; however, this same attachment technique is rarely used at the brake hose-to-caliper interface. Instead, brake hoses typically attach to calipers using *banjo fittings*, which consist of a single *banjo bolt* and a pair of *crush washers*. (Note that in some European applications a threaded, tapered fitting is used, but banjo fittings are far more common.)

The banjo bolt externally resembles an ordinary machine screw, but closer inspection reveals hydraulic passages cast and/or machined through the center of the bolt. These passages allow for the transmission of pressurized brake fluid from the brake hose through a radial opening in the bolt to the caliper through the bolt's center channel. Alternate designs employ fluid flow paths along channels formed in the bolt's outer diameter, but functionally the parts perform in the same fashion.

The crush washers are the sealing elements in the banjo fitting. As the banjo bolt is tightened into the caliper body, the crush washers (typically made from copper or another soft metal) are mechanically deformed against the bolt and caliper,

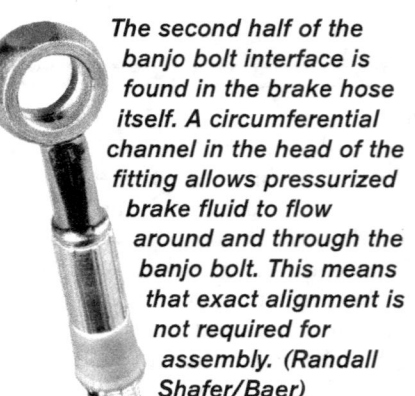

The second half of the banjo bolt interface is found in the brake hose itself. A circumferential channel in the head of the fitting allows pressurized brake fluid to flow around and through the banjo bolt. This means that exact alignment is not required for assembly. (Randall Shafer/Baer)

effectively creating a hydraulic seal. Like the flare though, once a crush washer has been used several times its ability to seal may be compromised. Therefore, their life span is finite and frequent replacement should be expected if the joint is serviced often.

While most banjo bolts feature a central flow-through channel, alternate designs exist. The bolts shown here employ multiple flow paths along their outer diameters. (Randall Shafer/Ankara Industries)

Stainless Steel Brake Hoses

Most high-performance brake hoses are identical to rubber over-molded hoses in function, but differ greatly in construction. Although their name would have you think otherwise, *stainless steel brake hoses* are not constructed from solid stainless steel; rather, they are fabricated using low-compliance Teflon inner tubing covered by protective braiding. Because the protective braiding is woven from strands of stainless steel, they are commonly referred to as *braided brake hoses, stainless steel lines*, or even simply *stainless lines* in aftermarket talk.

Under certain conditions, dirt and other abrasive contaminants can find their way between the stainless steel strands and the Teflon inner tubing. Over time these contaminants can be ground into the Teflon tubing to the point that a leak can develop. Naturally, a leak in the brake system is never a good thing. For this reason, some manufacturers also apply a clear polymeric layer over the braiding to keep abrasive debris from being trapped between the stainless steel strands and the Teflon inner tubing. Therefore, in those applications where this final design feature is not present, the hoses should be inspected and replaced on a more frequent basis.

The ends of stainless steel brake hoses are terminated with flare fittings and banjo fittings to allow for the leak-free passage of brake fluid, just like their rubber over molded counterparts. This results in most stainless steel hoses being mechanically interchangeable with over-molded rubber hoses with no additional modifications necessary.

Finally, some manufacturers have adopted the practice of placing a semi-rigid polymer strain relief over the fittings at both ends of the hose. These strain relief features reduce the abrasion that can occur where the stainless steel braiding is attached to the fittings. In some cases, stainless steel brake hoses without these strain-relief features can actually wear through the Teflon inner tubing at this critical interface.

Benefits of Stainless Steel Brake Hoses

As stated back in Chapter 3, neither brake lines nor brake hoses affect the overall brake system gain—pressure in equals pressure out. So why go about modifying them in the first place? Well, in addition to providing the high-performance racecar look, stainless steel brake hoses can provide other significant benefits in brake hose protection, driver pedal feel, and system response time.

A strain relief is an optional design add-on that can increase the useful life of a typical stainless steel brake hose. Found on one or both ends of the hose, this feature reduces the flexing at the brake hose-to-fitting interface. This hose uses plastic elements to reduce fatigue. (Randall Shafer/StopTech)

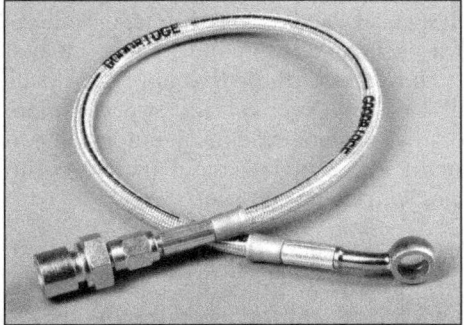

Stainless steel brake hoses provide several benefits, not the least of which is providing the racecar look. The functional improvements in protection, reduction in compliance, and enhanced system response time should not be forgotten, though. (Randall Shafer/Baer)

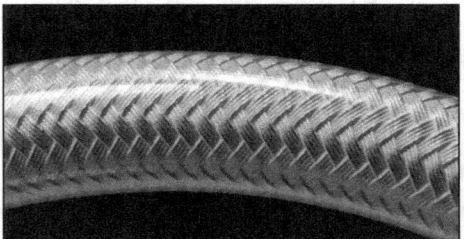

Because dirt and other abrasive contaminants can find their way between the stainless steel strands and the Teflon inner tubing, many manufacturers add a thick polymeric covering to the finished brake hose assembly. This adds cost and weight to the parts, but provides a significant increase in brake hose life. (Randall Shafer/StopTech)

One of the greatest benefits of stainless steel brake hoses is the protection they afford from stones, errant mufflers, and other flying debris. When trying to dig yourself out of a gravel trap, the last thing on your mind should be the integrity of your brake hoses. (Wayne Flynn/pdxsports.com)

While stainless steel brake hoses don't impact overall system gain, their reduced compliance can reduce brake system response time. This can result in shorter stopping distances under certain circumstances. In a racing environment, this directly correlates to faster lap times. (Wayne Flynn/pdxsports.com)

Stainless Steel Brake Hose Rumor Control

In searching the Internet for stainless steel brake hoses, it took only seconds to find the following retailer claim:

"Designed to increase braking power and shorten stopping distance giving you a firmer feel when braking and help eliminate brake fade due to hose expansion."

Let's run this statement through a filter to separate the fact from the fiction.

1. "Increased braking power" suggests that there is a benefit in overall brake system gain. However, as you have learned neither the brake lines nor brake hoses contribute toward overall brake system gain. Fiction 1, fact 0.
2. "Shorten stopping distance" does not need much explanation. Since stainless steel brake hoses can decrease the brake system response time, it's possible that slightly shorter stopping distances could result. Fiction 1, fact 1.
3. "Firmer feel" emphasizes the decreased compliance, or P-V relationship, that stainless steel brake hoses possess. For this reason, firmer feel could certainly be a benefit of installing these components. Fiction 1, fact 2.
4. "Help eliminate brake fade due to hose expansion" implies that changing brake lines can have an impact on brake fade. Sadly this is not the case, as fade is a function of either brake fluid boiling point (discussed in Chapter 6) or brake pad selection (coming up in Chapter 9). Fiction 2, fact 2.

Therefore; this episode of fact versus fiction ends up without a clear winner. If shorter stopping distances and a firmer pedal feel are your objectives, then hand over your credit card. But, if increased braking power and the elimination of brake fade are your top priorities, you should probably consider shopping for other components first.

Brake Hose Protection: Of paramount importance to racers and street drivers alike, stainless steel brake hoses provide much better impact resistance than over molded rubber hoses. This is especially true on open-wheeled formula cars where the brake hoses are literally hanging in mid-air waiting to be struck by a loose muffler, diffuser, or winglet dropped from the car just in front. Since a brake hose failure results in a complete loss of braking on the accompanying hydraulic circuit, the importance of protection cannot be understated.

Driver Pedal Feel: Once again, brake system compliance needs to be discussed. Because both types of brake hose inner tubing materials are relatively flexible (which makes them ideal for the job in one regard), they expand significantly when pressurized. Remember the P-V relationship? This expansion creates additional fluid volume in the hydraulic circuit, which is perceived by the driver as a soft or mushy pedal.

Rubber over-molding does little to limit this expansion, as rubber is also a relatively compliant material (especially in the presence of elevated brake system temperatures). A woven braid of stainless steel, however, can greatly increase the radial stiffness of the brake hose while still allowing adequate flexibility for wheel movement. In many cases, the driver feels this reduced expansion as a firmer or more responsive brake pedal.

The amount of difference in pedal feel varies by each vehicle's individual design, age, and usage. In general, vehicles with a significant amount of over-molded rubber hose or those that have seen years of use and aging typically display a more dramatic improvement when upgrading to stainless steel brake hoses than newer vehicles with shorter hoses.

System Response Time: Reduced compliance in the hydraulic circuit also has a secondary benefit to the enthusiast—it reduces the transient response time of the brake system. Because it takes time to move brake fluid into an expanding brake hose, there is an inherent delay in caliper pressure rise rate with over-molded rubber brake hoses. By switching to stainless steel brake hoses, this delay can be reduced.

In other words, stainless steel brake hoses allow the brake system to generate clamp force at the calipers more quickly. This can result in slightly shorter stopping distances in some applications, but every vehicle will display a different amount of improvement over the stock over-molded rubber brake hoses. In some cases though, the decrease in response time can be dramatic.

DOT Compliance

In addition to regulating brake fluid performance with FMVSS116, the government has established standards for automotive brake hoses under FMVSS106. If a manufacturer claims its brake hoses are *DOT-compliant*, it simply means that its brake hoses have passed all FMVSS106 requirements and the test data has been submitted to the government for official review.

Does this mean that DOT-compliant hoses are the best for your car? Not necessarily, but DOT compliance usually indicates that the manufacturer understands their product and that they're trying to hold themselves to a certain standard.

Remember that the DOT requirements must be met in full, so even if a stainless steel brake hose passes every performance test but is labeled with the wrong type of tag (or something equally trivial) it would fail certification. While this might mean something to an auto manufacturer or assembly plant, it's relatively meaningless to the high-performance enthusiast.

Another term you may hear in this context is *DOT-approved*. However, the government is not in the business of actually approving or disproving regulatory compliance—they don't typically run tests on aftermarket components themselves. Under these circumstances, one can only surmise that these manufacturers are trying to claim that their brake hoses are actually DOT-compliant, but it never hurts to ask before you buy.

Stainless Steel Brake Hose Routing

The most important factor to consider when installing your stainless steel brake hoses is that the routing of the hoses should *exactly* match the stock routing, and in those few cases where a new routing is required, be sure to follow the instruc-

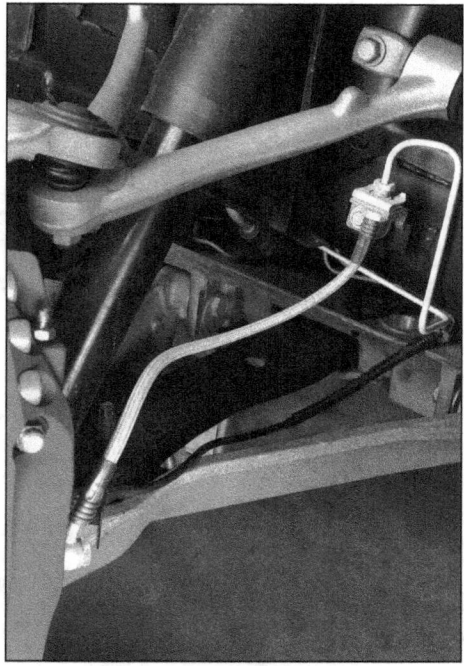

When replacing your stock rubber hoses with stainless steel brake hoses, it's imperative that you route them where the factory hoses went. Why? Because the vehicle manufacturer goes to great lengths to ensure that the original brake hose routing accommodates full vertical wheel travel, full steering travel, and other factors such as tire width variation. (Randall Shafer)

tions. Because the stainless steel braiding eventually wears through just about anything it comes in contact with, be sure that there is adequate clearance to all other moving parts under conditions of full wheel travel (up and down) and full steering (left and right).

After installation take care to examine your stainless steel brake hose routing to ensure that the fittings are not stressed under the same conditions of extreme travel and extreme steering. Of course, the hose should never come in direct contact with any part of the tire, but the hose should also not be pulled radially with respect to the end fittings either. Extra stress at the fittings can only lead to problems down the road.

Summary

So what can you do to increase the performance of your brake lines and brake hoses? After installing quality stainless steel hoses, there's not much left. If you pay attention to routing and installation details up front, all that remains is consistent follow-up with a regular inspection routine. Follow these simple, yet critical guidelines, and your lines and hoses should provide you with worry-free operation for years to come.

ABS and Stainless Steel Brake Hoses

The impact of stainless steel brake hoses on ABS performance is widely debated, but almost always comes down to a discussion about compliance. Because ABS performs its pressure-regulating activities based on the vehicle's original P-V relationship, any changes made that alter the P-V relationship could, in theory, influence ABS effectiveness.

That's the theory, anyway. From a practical perspective, the installation of stainless steel brake hoses will generally not adversely affect ABS performance. In general, ABS tends to have an easier time adapting to reduced compliance than it does reacting to increased compliance. Plus, while stainless steel brake hoses influence the P-V relationship, they don't change the overall brake system gain at all.

Every vehicle does, however, have a different level of sensitivity, so you should not interpret these generalities as absolute truths. There are certainly exceptions to the rule, and new technologies (such as PBA mentioned in Chapter 3) continue to decrease the vehicle's robustness to modification.

CHAPTER 8

BRAKE CALIPERS

While calipers need to convert hydraulic fluid pressure into clamp force, they also must look good doing it. A little advertising never hurts either. Can you guess the manufacturer of this caliper? (Randall Shafer/Baer)

In recent years, brake calipers have transformed into a prominent automotive accessory for the image-conscious consumer. Yellow, red, silver, black, and even bright gold examples can be found on the front and/or rear axles of many performance vehicles. Caliper bodies have even been converted into miniature billboards for the caliper manufacturers themselves.

While these new caliper trends are pleasing to the eye, the basic role of the caliper has remained unchanged since its inception. The caliper must simply convert the hydraulic fluid pressure generated in the master cylinder into a linear mechanical clamping force against the brake pads. At the same time, the caliper will usually locate the brake pads and supports the torque generated by the brake rotor, but these are secondary functions.

Hydraulic Gain

As you have already learned, the caliper clamp force can be calculated based upon the brake fluid pressure generated by the master cylinder and the inboard caliper piston area as follows:

Caliper clamp force (lb) = master cylinder pressure (psi) x effective caliper piston area (in²)

Note that although it wasn't mentioned explicitly back in Chapter 3, the *effective caliper piston area* is equal to the inboard caliper piston area multiplied by two.

Based on this relationship, it's common to select calipers and master cylinders in such a way as to amplify the force being applied to the master cylinder piston. Calculated much like the brake pedal ratio, the hydraulic gain of the system is equal to the effective caliper piston area divided by the master cylinder piston area. A more detailed description of hydraulic gain can be found in the sidebar, but in summary, the hydraulic gain can be increased by reducing the master cylinder area or by increasing the effective caliper piston area.

Caliper Components

It has already been stated that the caliper functionally resembles a common master cylinder, but in order to fit around the spinning rotor it must be shaped like a C-clamp. This isn't necessarily a good thing, as the clamping force generated at the open end of the caliper will always attempt to spread the caliper body apart. This distorts the caliper body, which exaggerates the P-V relationship. In short, more caliper deflection results in more brake pedal travel.

Two significant mechanical attributes of a caliper are its *stiffness* and its *strength*. Not to be used interchangeably, stiffness indicates how much deflection a caliper exhibits for a given amount of clamp force, while strength is a measure of the absolute force that can be sustained before failure of the caliper. Consequently, high stiffness is desired for good pedal feel while high strength is required for mechanical integrity.

Body

The *caliper body* is typically made of cast iron in production vehicles. It locates the piston and supports the clamp force exerted on the brake pads. While cast iron is acceptable from stiffness and strength perspectives (especially at elevated temperatures), its weight makes it undesirable

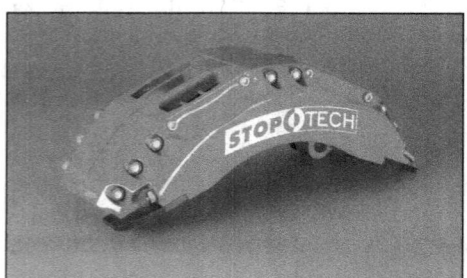

Caliper sizing and selection is generally a function of the required hydraulic gain, with larger calipers providing more output than smaller calipers. For this reason, calipers like this eight-piston monster designed for the Hummer H2 would be complete overkill on a smaller, lighter vehicle. (Randall Shafer/StopTech)

BRAKE CALIPERS

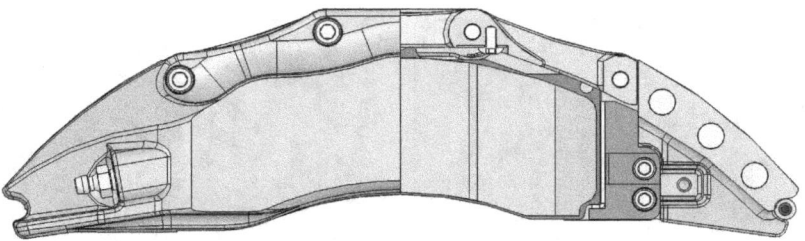

Caliper strength and stiffness are two key characteristics for optimum performance. Recent advances in computer modeling and simulation have allowed for significant improvements in both of these areas without the penalty of increased weight. (StopTech)

The basic caliper structure consists of body sections and bridge sections. In some applications, these may be discrete components assembled together. In the case of this early Porsche 911 Turbo caliper, two piston housings are bolted to two bridge sections to finalize the caliper assembly. (Randall Shafer)

Hydraulic Gain Example

If a vehicle was designed with a 0.75-inch-diameter master cylinder piston and a 2.00-inch-diameter caliper piston, one could calculate their effective areas as follows:

	Diameter (in)	Inboard Area (in²)	Effective Area (in²)
Master cylinder	0.75	n/a	0.44
Caliper	2.00	3.14	6.28

Recalling from the body text, the hydraulic gain of the brake system is simply the effective area of the caliper divided by the effective area of the master cylinder, or in equation form:

$$\text{Hydraulic gain (unitless)} = \text{effective caliper piston area (in}^2\text{)} \div \text{master cylinder piston area (in}^2\text{)}$$

Consequently, the hydraulic gain of this system would be 14.2:1 (6.28 square inches divided by 0.44 square inches). In other words, for every pound of force applied to the master cylinder piston, 14.2 pounds of clamp force is generated by the caliper.

The hydraulic relationship also dictates that the linear travel experienced by the master cylinder piston will be 14.2 times greater than the linear travel experienced by the caliper piston relative to the caliper body. For example, if the caliper piston required 0.010 inches of travel to overcome compliance, the master cylinder piston would need to travel approximately 0.142 inches (14.2 times as far) to accommodate the P-V need.

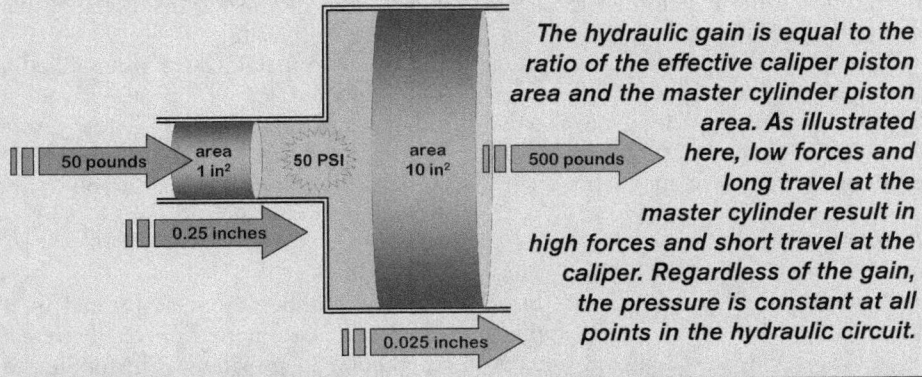

The hydraulic gain is equal to the ratio of the effective caliper piston area and the master cylinder piston area. As illustrated here, low forces and long travel at the master cylinder result in high forces and short travel at the caliper. Regardless of the gain, the pressure is constant at all points in the hydraulic circuit.

in performance applications. Consequently, aluminum alloys are employed when circumstances dictate the lowest weight possible (in fact, aluminum caliper bodies are nearly universal on modern high-performance vehicles), but their reduced stiffness can lead to excessive caliper deflection without appropriate design countermeasures.

The body consists of three main parts: an inboard body section (which almost always contains at least one piston bore), an outboard body section (which may or may not contain additional piston bores), and a bridge, which connects the two. In some applications, calipers can be fabricated from three separate components, but most often times are combined in a number of creative ways.

Bridge Reinforcement

In order to facilitate caliper inspection and brake pad replacement without caliper removal, it's common to have large openings in the caliper bridge. Unfortunately, these openings can greatly reduce the stiffness of the caliper, resulting in poor brake pedal feel. The term *open caliper* is often used to describe this type of arrangement.

Consequently, select manufacturers implement an auxiliary *bridge reinforcement* to regain the stiffness lost by open caliper design. This component is not required with *closed calipers* where pad

CHAPTER 8

In a closed caliper design, a structural reinforcement connects the inboard and outboard caliper body sections. Based on the manufacturer, it may be a removable piece bolted in place as shown above, or it may be integral to the body assembly. (Randall Shafer/StopTech)

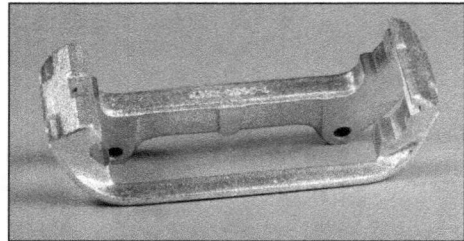

In many applications, the caliper mounting bracket must do much more than simply position the caliper relative to the rotor. For example, the C-shaped channels machined into either end of the bracket shown above serve to locate the brake pads as well as to provide axial (sliding) movement of the entire caliper assembly. (Randall Shafer/Baer)

The piston is the caliper's working element. Depending on the hydraulic fluid pressure generated at the master cylinder, thousands of pounds of force may be transmitted through these relatively small components to the brake pads. (Randall Shafer/StopTech)

replacement is performed by removing the entire caliper body from the vehicle.

Bracket

Based on the individual design, the caliper body may require a *bracket* to attach it to the suspension upright, or knuckle. Made from either aluminum or cast iron, the bracket may also serve to locate the brake pads in some applications. In the case of the floating caliper, the bracket also contains parallel channels for the caliper *slider pins* (more to come in just a few paragraphs) and is most likely designed to support the brake pad friction force as well.

Abutment Plates

In aluminum caliper applications that need to support brake pad friction force, a

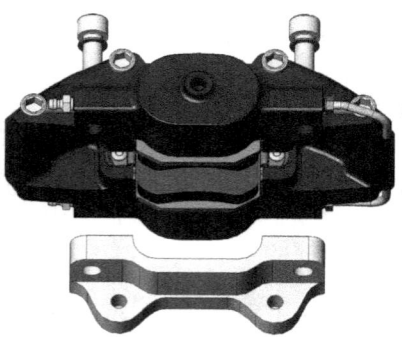

Most calipers require a bracket to attach them to the vehicle suspension. Simple brackets, like the one shown above in yellow, locate the caliper relative to the rotor without performing auxiliary functions. (StopTech)

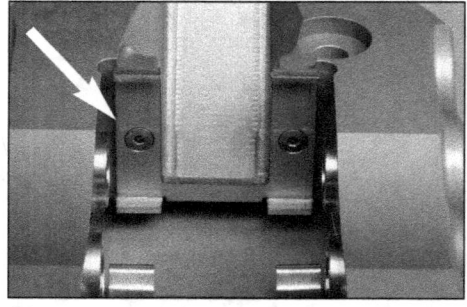

Since most high-performance calipers are fabricated from aluminum, abutment plates should be added to the caliper body to prevent wear at the brake pad interface. Calipers made from cast iron, however, don't require this additional design feature. (Randall Shafer/Baer)

pair of brake pad *abutment plates* are used to provide a durable surface at the sliding interface. These plates are usually fabricated from a thin piece of hard steel and allow for free motion of the steel brake pad backing plates relative to the aluminum caliper body without deformation of the softer body material.

Cast iron caliper bodies, due to their unique mechanical properties, typically do not require abutment plates. Note also that the abutment plates may be located in the caliper bracket in some applications.

Piston(s)

The *caliper piston* (or pistons) transmits hydraulic fluid pressure to the brake pad backing plates. Based on the application, a caliper may have between one and eight pistons, but all function in the same manner. Larger-diameter pistons generate higher forces and smaller diameter pistons generate lower forces.

In most production applications, pistons are fabricated from steel or aluminum. Titanium is used in select racing applications for its low thermal conductivity and decreased weight, but the cost of this material makes it prohibitive on typical production vehicles. Phenolic materials are found in some OEM applications, but their poor resistance to high temperatures makes them generally inappropriate for high-performance use.

Thermal Insulators

In addition to titanium pistons, *thermal insulators* may be sleeved inside of steel or aluminum pistons to reduce heat transfer from the brake pad backing plate to the piston (and ultimately to the brake fluid). Titanium and ceramic button inserts can be quite effective at keeping heat out of the hydraulic system, and they're less expensive to manufacture than billet titanium pistons.

Ceramic materials are also applied to the interior surfaces of the caliper body in some racing applications. These exotic coatings are designed to reduce heat transfer from the rotor to the caliper body, and ultimately the brake fluid.

Seal(s)

Each caliper piston is located in its bore by an elastomeric ring, or *piston seal*. In addition to providing a hydraulic seal for the pressurized brake fluid, the seal is also responsible for retracting the piston when the brakes are released. For this reason, properly designed caliper pistons seals are square in cross-section and not round like a traditional O-ring.

As shown above, piston seals are square in cross-section. This design enables the seal to pull the piston away from the brake pad when the brakes are released, greatly reducing parasitic drag. (Randall Shafer/StopTech)

In most applications, the seal is located in a trapezoidal groove found in the caliper body. The geometry of the *seal groove* is paramount to ensuring the optimum level of piston retraction. Too much retraction can result in excessive pedal travel while too little retraction can produce significant brake drag.

Dust Boot(s)

Any foreign debris that finds its way between the caliper body and caliper piston can score the sealing interface, resulting in a hydraulic leak over time. As a result, most street-oriented calipers use a *dust boot* to protect the caliper piston seal from environmental contamination.

In street applications, a dust boot is used to keep abrasive material from damaging the piston seal. Shown on top of the piston seal in the image above, the dust boot has its own locating feature machined into the piston body. (Randall Shafer/StopTech)

In most racing applications, dust boots are rarely used. Why? Because they add weight, require additional packaging space, and frequently melt when exposed to the high temperatures seen on the track. However, this ultimately results in more frequent servicing of the caliper—yet another brake system design compromise.

Crossover Tube

If a caliper has pistons located in both the inboard and outboard caliper body sections, an external *crossover tube* is used to distribute brake fluid pressure to both sides of the caliper. Typically found on the lower part of the caliper bridge, the tube should be protected as much as possible from debris, heat, and vibration.

In some applications, the crossover function can be performed by a passageway machined through caliper body itself (an interior crossover tube design). While this provides better protection from external damage, it exposes the brake fluid to much higher temperatures without the opportunity to cool as effectively.

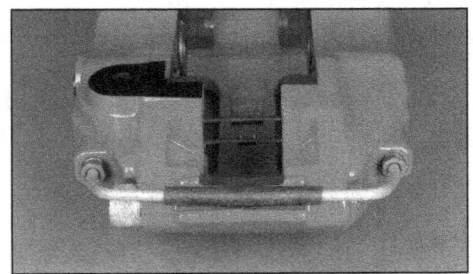

Crossover tubes are nothing more than short brake lines that transmit hydraulic fluid pressure from one side of the caliper to the other. In order to shield them from the hot air exiting the rotor, it's common to install a thermal barrier as shown above. (Randall Shafer/StopTech)

Bleeder Valve(s)

All calipers contain at least one *bleeder valve*, or *bleeder screw*, to assist in purging unwanted air from the brake fluid following hydraulic circuit maintenance. Calipers with pistons located in both the inboard and outboard caliper body sections typically implement one bleeder valve per bank of pistons.

Note that when examining a bleeder valve, the hydraulic sealing interface is not found on the threaded body, but rather at the tapered end of the valve that mates with a similar feature machined into the caliper body. For this reason, it is not uncommon for fluid remaining in the bleeder valve after service to wick out through the threads through capillary action. Although this may appear at first to be a hydraulic leak, it is in fact residual fluid making a mess and not much more.

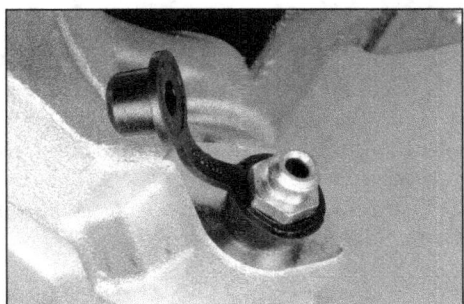

Although it was mentioned back in Chapter 7, bleeder valves are used to purge used brake fluid from the hydraulic circuit. What wasn't mentioned is that when closing the valve, excessive force can actually damage the caliper body. In most cases, only a light tug on the wrench is required for adequate sealing. (Randall Shafer/Baer)

Taper Wear

Although brake pad wear is discussed in Chapter 9, there's a secondary mode of brake pad deterioration known as *brake pad taper*, which really isn't any fault of the brake pad whatsoever. Rather, this wear-out mode is a function of geometry and caliper dynamic performance.

Radial Pad Taper

Radial pad taper is characterized by the top edge of the brake pad friction material wearing away more rapidly than the bottom edge. There are two physical factors that explain this phenomenon. First, the linear speed of the rotor is higher at the top of the brake pad than at the bottom, resulting in more heat generation. More heat always leads to increased wear.

Second, as the caliper deflects under load it tends to distort and partially relieve clamping force along the bottom edge of the brake pad. The result is increased

Around town, brake pads tend to wear in a uniform and predictable fashion, but when subjected to the stress that motorsports can bring, wear patterns and rates can vary dramatically. Fortunately, several caliper design tricks can be employed to both improve pedal feel as well as increase brake pad life. (Wayne Flynn/pdxsports.com)

Radial taper occurs for a variety of reasons, but is easily recognizable by staring at the brake pad from either end. After just one 20-minute session on the track, the brake pad shown above developed approximately 0.050 inches of additional wear along the top of the pad (left side) as along the bottom of the pad (right side). It may not look like much to the naked eye, but significantly degraded brake pedal feel is the end result. (Randall Shafer)

force at the top edge of the pad, accelerating the wear once again in this location.

In order to mitigate radial pad taper, some caliper manufacturers implement a bridge reinforcement in their designs—a stiffer caliper always produces significantly less radial taper wear. However, caliper design cannot normalize the surface speed of the rotor at different radii, and for this reason many pads employ a trapezoidal geometry to equalize the wear across the height of the pad over time.

Longitudinal Pad Taper

Longitudinal pad taper occurs when the leading edge of the brake pad friction material (where the rotor enters the caliper) wears away more quickly than the trailing edge (where the rotor exits the caliper). Again, there are two primary explanations for this observed condition. First, as the rotor first enters the brake pad, it naturally attempts to draw the brake pad friction material closer together, increasing the effective clamp force. Machine design students would call this a *self-energizing* effect, but regardless of the nomenclature the result is higher temperatures at the leading edge of the brake pad.

A secondary factor that contributes to longitudinal pad taper is a result of the erosion of the brake pad friction material during use. As the leading edge of the brake pad wears away, little bits of loose friction material and, to a lesser extent, gasses from pad resins and binders end up between the pad and rotor. The end result is that the trailing edge of the brake pad is buffered from the rotor surface by this continuous stream of debris. Consequently, the trailing edge of the pad runs cooler and wears less. Longer pads make this phenomenon even more pronounced.

Effects of Taper Wear

Regardless of the cause, brake pad taper wear can produce undesirable side effects. First, as pads are taper worn, the brake system's P-V relationship deteriorates (more brake fluid volume is required to build pressure). This is a direct result of caliper piston travel being used to seat the tapered pads and not to generate brake pad friction force. As the taper wear gets worse, the driver will notice more travel in the brake pedal before the onset of deceleration.

Second, tapered brake pads can promote pistons cocking in their bores during use, potentially leading to scoring and accelerated piston seal wear. Given enough time, this could result in a hydraulic leak.

Finally, because a brake pad requires replacement when the thinnest portion of the friction material reaches its minimum level, a tapered pad will always need to be scrapped before a non-tapered pad. While not necessarily a performance concern, this costs money.

For all of these reasons, a large percentage of caliper design revolves around simply reducing the amount of radial and longitudinal brake pad taper wear during use. Caliper clamp force may be the most critical performance parameter, but without adequate taper wear countermea-

As with radial taper, longitudinal taper can develop for a variety of reasons and invariably leads to reduced brake pad life. The longer the brake pad, the more susceptible it is to developing longitudinal taper. The brake pad above displays approximately 0.060 inches of taper wear from left (thinner leading edge) to right (thicker trailing edge). (Randall Shafer)

BRAKE CALIPERS

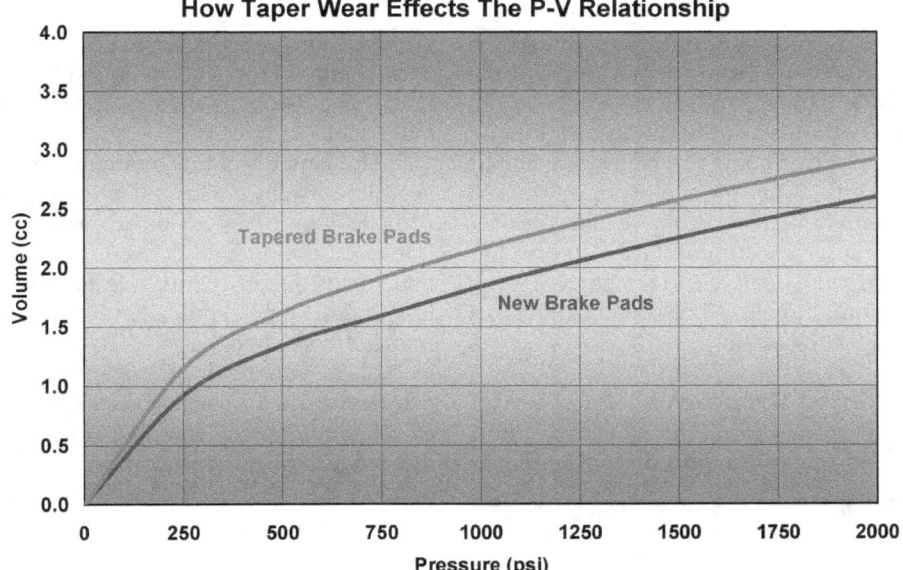

As brake pads develop taper—radial, longitudinal, or both—the P-V relationship increases. In other words, the brake pedal begins to feel spongy or soft to the driver. The blue line above is representative of a brake system with new brake pads while the red line shows the effect of taper wear.

sures the caliper's overall functionality may be compromised.

Piston Count

As already stated, a caliper may contain any number of pistons. Many modern passenger vehicle applications employ only one, while performance-oriented racing calipers may contain four or more. While a magic formula does not exist to select the proper quantity for your own application, knowing the benefits and compromises of single and multi-piston designs is critical to optimizing overall system performance.

Single-Piston Calipers

Simple, small, and cheap. These three defining characteristics make *single-piston calipers* the most common design on the road today. Employing only a single piston in the caliper body, these calipers are consequently all of the floating variety (more on this topic in a few paragraphs), and therefore aren't the most efficient. Unfortunately, while their floating characteristics make these calipers unacceptable in high-performance applications, it's the single-piston design that gets the blame.

The largest drawback of the single-piston design is the increased susceptibility to longitudinal brake pad taper when using rectangular brake pads. Because the piston loads the brake pad effectively at its center of pressure (the middle of the piston), a square-shaped pad that approximates the piston diameter provides the most desirable results (the least taper wear). Brake pad designs that increase their length in the hopes of extending the usable life of the pad only become more prone to uneven wear and poor brake pedal feel over time.

In summary, if a caliper accepts relatively square brake pads, a single-piston design makes for a compact solution. If the pads are longer than they are tall, a multi-piston caliper can be of great benefit.

Multi-Piston Calipers

There are several benefits to implementing a *multi-piston caliper* design, but by far the most significant is the ability to stagger piston bore sizes to counteract longitudinal brake pad taper. Since the amount of clamp force a piston generates is proportional to its area, many multi-piston calipers use smaller pistons at the brake pad leading edge and larger pistons at the brake pad trailing edge. Using *differential bores* provides more clamp force at the trailing edge of the brake pad, all but eliminating longitudinal brake pad taper in most applications.

The second benefit of a multi-piston caliper design is that it's possible to generate the same clamp force as a large single piston with multiple smaller pistons (think of a two-valve cylinder head compared to a four-valve cylinder head). This in turn allows for a shorter caliper body, which can, in some applications, provide more packaging flexibility. As a side note, a multi-piston caliper body can also in some cases be nominally narrower than a single-piston caliper body, but the amount of benefit varies by caliper body material selection.

Single-piston calipers are one of the most common designs on the road today. Their efficient packaging, low cost, and acceptable gain capability make them nearly the universal choice for smaller passenger vehicles. (Randall Shafer)

As the name implies, multi-piston calipers employ more than one piston. The simplest multi-piston calipers contain two pistons of equal diameter. Not only does this facilitate machining, it also reduces the number of unique parts in the caliper assembly. Consequently, equal diameters equates to lower cost. (Randall Shafer/Baer)

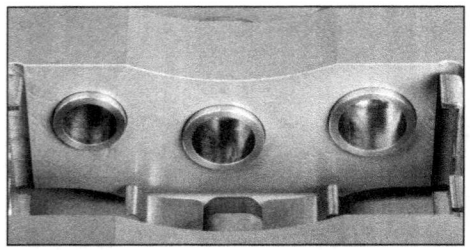

One of the biggest advantages of a multi-piston caliper is the ability to implement differential bores. By using smaller pistons on the leading edge of the brake pad (left hand side) and larger pistons on the trailing edge of the brake pad (right hand side), longitudinal taper wear can be practically eliminated. (Randall Shafer/Baer)

A third benefit of the multi-piston arrangement is that for a given packaging space, a multi-piston caliper provides a larger effective radius than a single-piston caliper. This is because the effective piston centerlines (the location of the bores in the caliper body) can be moved radially outward from the rotor center. The amount of increase is application-specific, but it's not uncommon to see an effective radius increase of five to ten percent when switching from a single-piston caliper to a twin-piston caliper.

Multi-Pad Calipers

If a caliper is designed with multiple pistons, it is also possible to employ a *multi-pad* arrangement. In these calipers, separate brake pads and abutment plates are used for each pair of caliper pistons. This results in an array of multiple short brake pads as opposed to a single, longer brake pad.

The benefits of this configuration are twofold. First, by creating additional brake pad leading edges, brake pad bite improves considerably. Second, shorter brake pads directly contribute to reduced longitudinal taper, which can significantly improve brake pedal feel.

These benefits have made multi-pad calipers nearly universal at the highest levels of motorsports. However, due to the increased cost and complexity of these designs, they are rarely found in production vehicles.

Caliper Mounting

Regardless of the number of pistons or the dimensions of their diameters, the caliper body must be attached to the suspension upright, knuckle, or axle housing in some way, shape, or form. The two most common methods are to either bolt the caliper body directly to the vehicle or to allow the caliper body to move axially relative to a fixed mounting bracket.

Fixed Calipers

The most elegant caliper mounting strategy is to attach the caliper body directly to the suspension upright, knuckle, or axle housing. Because the caliper body is not free to move relative to the vehicle, this is commonly called a *fixed caliper* design.

Since the body of a fixed caliper is mechanically locked in place, it must possess pistons in both the inboard body section as well as the outboard body section, effectively straddling the rotor. By using pairs of *opposed pistons* in this fashion, the caliper is capable of providing a clamp force through the brake pad interface.

As the only moving parts in a fixed caliper are the pistons themselves, the caliper body and mounting structure can be optimized for strength and efficiency in a relatively straightforward fashion. For this reason alone, fixed caliper mounting is the preferred strategy in any racing series or competition forum where it's allowed. Unfortunately, its increased weight, cost, and packaging space require-

---

Equivalent Piston Sizing

In order to generate a desired level of caliper clamp force, it is possible to use either one large piston or multiple smaller pistons. The following table illustrates two- and three-piston alternatives for four common single-piston calipers.

Piston Sizing For Equivalent Clamp Force

	Two-Piston Design	Three-Piston Design
Single 1.75-inch piston	2 x 1.25 inch	3 x 1.00 inch
Single 2.00-inch piston	2 x 1.40 inch	3 x 1.15 inch
Single 2.25-inch piston	2 x 1.60 inch	3 x 1.30 inch
Single 2.50-inch piston	2 x 1.75 inch	3 x 1.45 inch

As stated in the text, in order to take full advantage of the multi-piston caliper design, the piston diameters should be staggered as well. For example, instead of replacing a 1.75-inch diameter piston with two 1.25-inch diameter pistons, it would be more appropriate to install a 1.20-inch diameter piston on the leading edge and a 1.30-inch diameter piston on the trailing edge. In all cases, the total clamp force remains the same, but differential bore design can significantly increase the caliper's resistance to longitudinal brake pad taper wear.

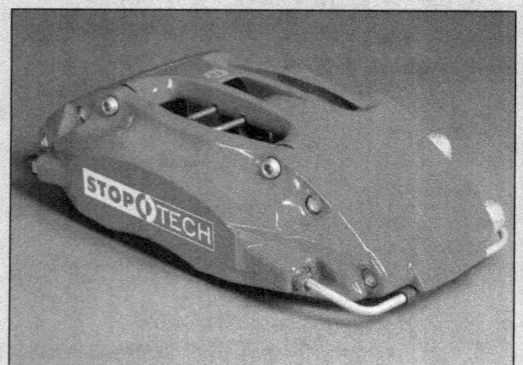

When selecting the right number of pistons for your application, there may be more than one choice. For example, the four-piston caliper shown here with differential bores of 1.50 inches and 1.65 inches has the same effective performance potential as a single-piston caliper with a piston diameter of approximately 2.25 inches. (Randall Shafer/StopTech)

Fixed calipers don't move relative to the rotor during operation—only the pistons are free to slide in and out of their bores. This 1927 Ford hot rod uses fixed-front calipers from a Jaguar that are rigidly mounted to Jaguar suspension uprights. Note that mounting the brakes out in the open like this greatly enhances convective cooling, but does not protect them from road debris or other contamination. (Randall Shafer)

While elegant in design, floating calipers can be much less efficient than their fixed counterparts. For example, friction in the slider pin assemblies, tolerances in the bracket dimensions, and the inevitable build-up of corrosion at the sliding interface can all reduce the overall brake system gain. (Randall Shafer)

ments prevent widespread implementation on typical production vehicles.

Floating Calipers

In contrast to fixed calipers, *floating calipers*, or *sliding calipers*, allow for axial translation, or float, of the caliper body relative to the rotor. A fixed mounting bracket typically locates the caliper body with a pair of lubricated slider pins that provide freedom of motion parallel to the axis of rotor rotation.

The simplest floating calipers contain a single piston, although twin-piston variants are common on many larger vehicles. In either case, all pistons are located in the inboard caliper body section and are forced against the inboard brake pad by hydraulic brake fluid pressure. However, because the caliper body is free to move axially relative to the rotor, there's an equal but opposite force on the caliper body that draws the outboard body section against the outboard brake pad. The force acting on the outboard brake pad will be equal to the force acting on the inboard brake pad, thereby generating the same clamp force as a fixed caliper, but with half the number of pistons.

In other words, a fixed caliper with two opposed 1.5-inch-diameter pistons generates the same clamp force as a floating caliper with a single 1.5-inch-diameter piston. In theory, this is a very desirable design alternative to the bulky fixed caliper.

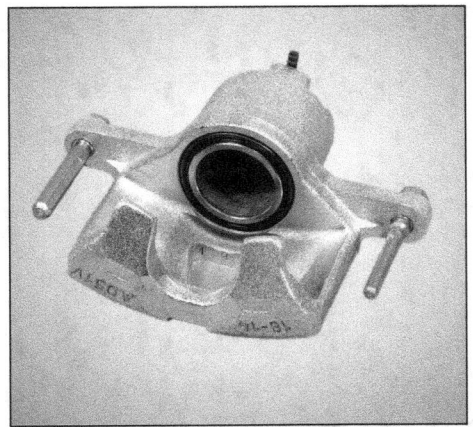

Floating calipers are designed to move axially relative to the rotor during use. A pair of lubricated slider pins as shown above can be used to locate the caliper radially relative to the rotor without constraining axial motions. Simpler caliper designs rely on brake pad alignment features for radial positioning. (Randall Shafer)

The theory breaks down once it becomes apparent that the sliding action of the caliper is subject to a variety of frictional losses. Rubbing between the slider pins and the mounting bracket, misalignment of the caliper body to the mounting bracket, and the numerous tolerances necessary for mass production all combine to make a typical floating caliper much less efficient than a fixed caliper. This results in a lower overall brake system gain when using floating calipers.

While this attribute alone may be enough to turn off the high-performance crowd, floating calipers do have some distinct advantages that make them the caliper of choice for most automotive manufacturers. As already stated, one of the primary benefits of the floating caliper is its relatively small size, which reduces both cost and weight. And because there are no pistons in the outboard body section, the clearance for wheel spokes improves, providing more flexibility in the styling department.

One-Piece (Monoblock) Calipers

One-piece calipers, or *monoblock calipers*, derive their name from the fact that they're carved from a single piece of material. Originally fabricated from garden-variety aluminum, early one-piece

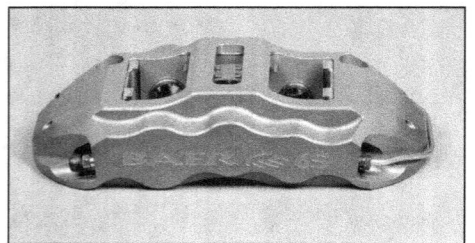

Monoblock calipers are arguably one of the sexiest components in a high-performance brake system. While their performance can be matched by two-piece calipers, their low weight makes them highly desirable in many racing applications. (Randall Shafer/Baer)

calipers were very expensive to produce because the piston bores needed to be machined at right angles from the narrow opening in the center of the caliper body. This usually dictated elaborate tooling and/or additional finishing operations, which drove up complexity and cost in the name of weight savings.

However, their biggest advantage was their relatively low weight. For this reason alone, top race teams would absorb the cost of one-piece calipers in order to gain a small weight advantage over their competitors, but street applications were few and far between.

One-piece caliper development was doing just fine until the evolution of motorsports began to catch up. As lap times dropped, higher and higher brake temperatures began to exaggerate aluminum's inherent loss in stiffness at elevated temperatures. In other words, higher speeds brought along higher temperatures, which resulted in increased caliper deflection, distortion, and poor brake pedal feel. As a result, unique alloys were formulated in order to retain stiffness at elevated temperatures.

Cost and complexity both skyrocketed to the point that certain alloys were specifically banned by race sanctioning organizations. Yet in spite of this attempt to curb costs and development, for a short while exotic aluminum alloy one-piece calipers were the only game in town.

Advances in manufacturing have slowly lowered the cost of one-piece calipers to the point that in some cases they may be considered by budget-minded enthusiasts. However, regardless of the manufacturing techniques used, one-piece aluminum calipers continue to be limited in performance by their decreased stiffness at elevated temperatures.

Two-Piece Calipers

As the name suggests, *two-piece calipers* are generally constructed from two opposing caliper body sections bolted rigidly together. While not quite as glamorous as their one-piece counterparts, the distinct advantages of early two-piece calipers were their ease of machining and corresponding lower cost. Over time, this resulted in increased proliferation of fixed calipers from auto manufacturers and simultaneously made them more accessible to budget-conscious race teams.

Although originally developed as a cost-competitive alternative to more exotic one-piece calipers, modern two-piece calipers have evolved to the point that in many applications there is little difference in performance or weight

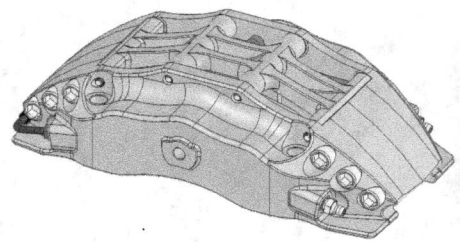

Properly designed, a two-piece caliper can actually attain higher stiffness than the more glamorous monoblock design. This is achieved through the use of steel bolts (shown in yellow above) holding the two halves together. Unfortunately, the penalty is slightly increased weight. (StopTech)

between the two designs. Through the use of computer modeling and simulation, the strategic use of steel bolts has greatly increased the stiffness of two-piece calipers without resorting to cost-prohibitive aluminum alloys. In fact, a properly designed two-piece caliper displays better mechanical properties at elevated temperatures than the most exotic one-piece caliper at the same weight.

Knockback

Whether you are driving to work on city streets or blasting around Le Mans,

When a vehicle is thrown into a corner, several parts of the chassis and suspension bend and deflect. Unfortunately, the rotor is taken along for the ride and knockback may be generated in the caliper. Note that hitting the rumble strip at the apex only makes the condition worse. (Wayne Flynn/pdxsports.com)

BRAKE CALIPERS

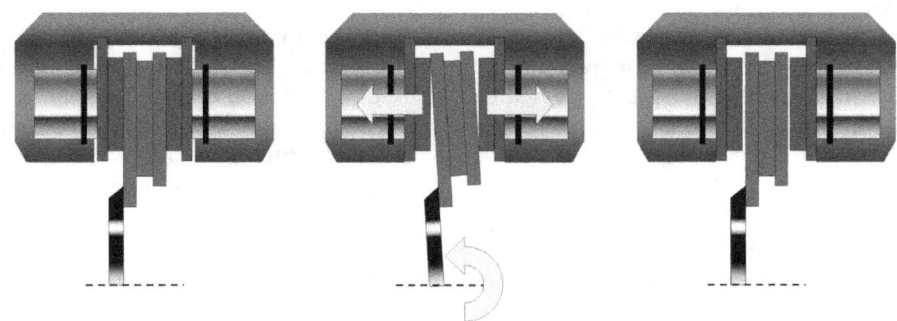

Driving straight down the road (left image), the rotor (gray) and brake pads (blue) are seated and parallel to one another. As cornering begins (center image), the rotor is deflected by the wheel hub, pushing the brake pads and pistons (silver) away from each other. After the cornering event is complete (right image), the brake pads are no longer adjacent to the rotor face (the gap shown in white). This results in additional brake pedal travel and a momentary delay in deceleration after brake pedal force is applied.

public roads and racetracks are rarely composed of just straight-aways. As such, vehicles will encounter a variety of bends, turns, and other dynamic events that impart cornering forces on the vehicle chassis and suspension. For the enthusiast, this is one of the things that make driving so enjoyable, but these cornering forces can negatively impact brake system performance behind the scenes.

Where Knockback Comes From

Because mechanical systems cannot be completely rigid, dynamic cornering forces will cause localized deflections in the loaded components. In other words, when vehicles are in the middle of a corner, stuff bends. It's not desirable, and you can pay more money to make stuff bend less, but it'll always bend to some degree. This is where *knockback* originates.

As the tire, wheel, hub, and wheel bearing deflect during cornering, the brake rotor is forced to go along for the ride. Because the caliper is attached to a more rigid suspension component (the upright or knuckle), the parallelism between the rotor and the brake pads is altered. The deflection of the rotor relative to the brake pads actually forces the brake pads away from one another, pushing the caliper pistons back into their bores a small amount. At the end of the cornering event the brake pads are physically displaced from the rotor.

The next time the brakes are applied, the brake pedal travel is used to push the pistons out of their bores and against the brake pads and rotor (back to where they were before the knockback occurred). This requires moving brake fluid into the hydraulic system from the master cylinder, and as a result the brake pedal drops away toward the floor with little resistance. Because this action does not build any brake line pressure, no brake torque is generated and for a brief moment it feels as if the vehicle is not slowing down. Only a few thousandths of an inch at the caliper piston can be perceived by a sensitive driver!

Impact of Brake System Upgrades

Unfortunately for the high-performance enthusiast, most brake system upgrades can make knockback even worse. Ironically, the very performance attributes that make the three most common brake system upgrades so desirable can all amplify and/or exaggerate the knockback phenomenon.

First, increasing rotor diameter can result in lower brake system operating temperatures, and is therefore highly desirable. However, for a given amount of deflection at the wheel hub, the larger rotor diameter increases the separating effect at the brake pad to rotor interface, pushing the pistons back even farther into their bores. On a percentage basis, the relationship is relatively linear, meaning that a 10-percent increase in rotor diameter will result in approximately 10 percent more knockback.

Second, fixed calipers are typically more efficient than floating calipers, improving pedal feel and, to a lesser extent, overall brake system gain. Unfortunately, the inefficient slider pin design actually makes floating calipers more tolerant of deflections at the wheel hub. Consequently, when upgrading to fixed calipers the brake system may actually display

Larger rotors may be just the ticket for increased thermal capacity, but be forewarned that increasing rotor diameter nearly always exaggerates knockback. For this reason, a wider rotor of the same diameter may be a more appropriate solution for increasing thermal mass. (Randall Shafer/StopTech)

Can tire selection impact knockback? Absolutely. More cornering capability invariably increases the amount of deflection in the chassis components. Consequently, knockback may become more pronounced. (Hoosier Racing Tire)

HIGH PERFORMANCE BRAKE SYSTEMS: DESIGN, SELECTION AND INSTALLATION

increased levels of knockback simply because there is less mechanical compliance to mask it.

Third, because stopping distance is limited by the tire-to-road interface, most brake system upgrades begin with tire upgrades. Since tires that stop better generally turn better, cornering performance increases as well. While this certainly is a benefit in terms of overall vehicle dynamic capability, along with increased cornering performance comes increased deflection, the key ingredient for knockback.

Knockback Countermeasures

Since knockback is a mechanical deflection condition that is only exaggerated by brake system hardware, we shouldn't blame upgraded brake system components for increased knockback. That being said, several countermeasures can be taken to prevent knockback before it becomes a performance concern and/or to alleviate the symptoms of knockback if they're already present.

Any steps taken to reduce mechanical deflections during cornering greatly reduce the possibility of knockback. While it may sound obvious, making sure that your wheel bearings are fresh and tight is the first step, but upgrading hubs and other suspension components to achieve less deflection during cornering further serves to minimize knockback. In fact, most professional race teams actually take the time to disassemble, blueprint, shim, reassemble, and upgrade the grease in their wheel bearings prior to use in order to generate as little deflection as possible.

During initial brake system design, it may be possible to increase the master cylinder area and/or reduce the caliper effective area in order to reduce the knockback effect. One or both of these parameters can alter the hydraulic characteristics of the brake system in such a way that reduces the undesirable brake pedal travel associated with deflection at the rotor. Of course, attention must still be given to overall brake system gain and brake balance, but in general, minimizing hydraulic gain can help to reduce knockback.

If knockback is already present in the brake system, it may be possible to install *anti-knockback springs* behind the caliper pistons to actively force the brake pads against the rotor, even when the brakes are not engaged. While this creates constant drag in the brake system, it can be of great help in solving otherwise terminal knockback issues. It should be noted that this is not typically a solution for street vehicles—anti-knockback springs are usually track-only components.

Finally, lightly tapping the brake pedal once or twice before each braking zone can help mitigate the effect of knockback, but only as a last resort. While this practice may not sound glamorous, many professional road racers use this technique on a regular basis. All that is usually necessary is a tap or two of the brake pedal just moments before the braking zone arrives to seat the brake pads against the rotor. Yes, it takes some getting used to, but just like heel-toe downshifting eventually it becomes second nature.

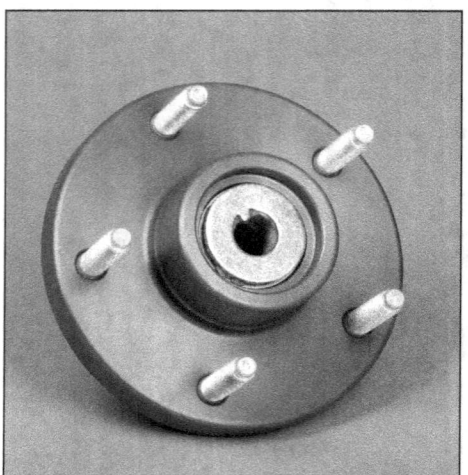

The best way to eliminate knockback is to increase stiffness at the hub. Upgraded bearings, carriers, greases, and spindles can all help to reduce deflections (and consequently knockback) during cornering. (Randall Shafer/Baer)

If either your rulebook or your wallet prohibits brake system modifications, you may be forced to deal with the knockback you have. The most reliable method is to give the brake pedal a light tap or two just prior to your braking zone to seat the brake pads against the rotor. (Wayne Flynn/pdxsports.com)

ABS and Caliper Selection

Upgrading from a single-piston floating caliper to a multi-piston fixed caliper can have a significant negative impact on ABS performance. However, you can avoid some potential performance pitfalls through careful system design and by selecting the appropriate components.

First, if caliper pistons sizes are incorrectly matched to the intended application, a caliper upgrade may also cause an unintended change in the overall brake system gain. For this reason, it's desirable that the caliper piston effective area remains unchanged when performing a caliper upgrade. The larger the change, the more difficult it is for ABS to maintain acceptable performance.

Second, changing from a floating caliper to a fixed caliper tends to increase brake system efficiency. In other words, the more efficient fixed caliper has a flatter P-V relationship than the less efficient floating caliper it's replacing. Note that this condition will exist even if the overall gain remains unchanged (remember that the P-V relationship can change independently of gain). Fortunately, ABS generally has an easier time accommodating more efficient components than less efficient components, so the potential for performance compromise is reduced.

Because every system has its own unique sensitivities, it's always best to install and test the system out prior to needing ABS on the track or on the street. Educated caliper selection is critical, but should not be considered a substitute for a solid real-world evaluation after your upgrade is complete.

Summary

So what goes into selecting the best caliper for your application? Essentially, it comes down to juggling hydraulic gain, system efficiency, weight, and packaging space. In most cases, a simple single-piston floating caliper provides more than adequate gain for most applications at a relatively modest weight. The additional benefits of low cost and flexible packaging shape explain why this design is found on an overwhelming majority of vehicles on the road today.

For the enthusiast and racer alike though, multi-piston fixed calipers are the gold standard. Their higher efficiency results in improved pedal feel under the most demanding conditions, while design features such as differential bores can greatly reduce brake pad taper. Yes, they are more bulky than their floating caliper counterparts, but that's usually a small price to pay for their enhanced performance when the green flag flies.

When the time comes to ante up for a new set of calipers, be sure to look for more than just color and piston count. While both of these attributes make for significant curb appeal, they do little toward improving ultimate performance. Focus on gain, efficiency, and weight in order to make the best selection for your application. (Randall Shafer)

CHAPTER 9

BRAKE PADS

Due to operating wear and tear, brake pads are one of the most commonly replaced components in the brake system. They also happen to have a significant impact on overall brake system gain as stated back in Chapter 3. Consequently, upgraded pads are one of the most common brake system modifications.

However, in this context the word upgrade must be used with great care. While your local auto supply store likely offers a combination of premium, high-performance, heavy-duty, and severe-use brake pads, there are no industry standards for what constitutes a premium, high-performance, heavy-duty, or severe-use brake pad.

The same lack of formal definition applies to semi-metallic, non-asbestos organic, ceramic, and other exotic brake pad chemistries. In all of these cases, the manufacturer is free to call the pads by whatever name they see fit. Consequently, brake pad selection is a bit of a black art.

Okay, so there's a lot of black art involved, but that should not discourage you from trying to find the best brake pads for your vehicle. Good materials are out there, but be forewarned that finding the best pads for your application can sometimes involve some trial and error. Therefore, you need to do some homework to determine if the four pieces of friction material inside the cardboard box are suitable for your application, because the descriptions printed on the outside of the box are not very helpful at all.

Brake Pad Terminology

Before going any farther, it's time to define the nine critical features of a typical brake pad. That's right—in some applications, there are no less than nine brake pad design features that can impact its overall performance.

Friction Materials

The brake pad *friction material* is the primary wear element for the brake system. Sometimes called the *friction puck*, this sacrificial component is the only part of the brake pad that's designed to make contact with the rotor, converting kinetic energy into heat. As a result, over time it's slowly worn away until it needs replacing.

Of all the brake pad components discussed, the friction material is arguably the most critical from a high-performance perspective. There are countless varieties of

What differentiates one brake pad from another is the physical composition of its friction material. Like a fine suit, high-performance friction materials are custom-tailored to each application with a unique blend of ingredients. (Randall Shafer)

friction materials available in the marketplace, and the paragraphs that follow provide you with the information you need to navigate through the overwhelming number of choices.

Wear Sensors

Because all friction materials eventually wear out, a *wear sensor* is typically fitted to each pair of brake pads to inform the driver that replacement is required. Although electronic sensors are found on a few high-end European applications, in most cases a simple steel spring is riveted to the brake pad backing plate to serve this purpose.

When the friction material wears to the point that replacement is necessary, the spring will contact the rotor, emitting a high-pitched squeal. This audible signal should not be ignored, for if the friction material wears completely away, the rotor, caliper, or both may be susceptible to permanent damage.

Brake pad advertising is not bound by NHTSA regulations, and unfortunately there's only so much you can find out by looking at the parts in the box. They essentially all look the same to the untrained eye. Consequently, when picking out a brake pad for your application, it pays to do a little research first. (Randall Shafer)

BRAKE PADS

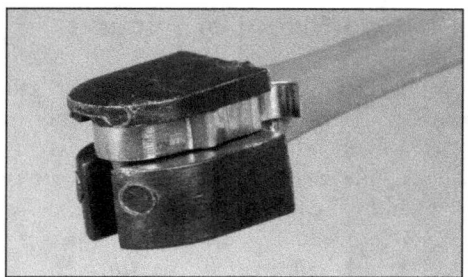

In some applications, a sensor is placed on the brake pad to alert the driver if the friction material is worn to its minimum thickness. While a spring on the backing plate can be used to emit an audible squeal under these conditions, the electronic sensor shown here informs the driver with a lamp on the instrument panel. (Randall Shafer/StopTech)

Backing Plates

Usually fabricated from simple low-carbon steel, the brake pad *backing plate* distributes forces from the caliper pistons to the friction material. Serrated features or through-holes in the backing plate can also serve to anchor and locate the friction material against the rotor and to transfer the brake pad friction force from the friction material to the caliper body.

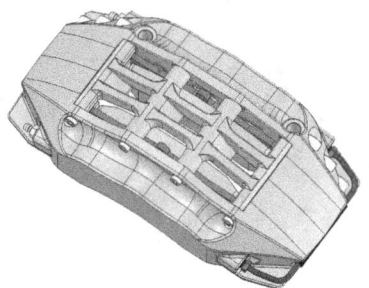

The responsibility of the backing plates (red) is to transmit the force from the caliper pistons to the friction material. They may also contain retention features such as holes or serrated edges to provide a better anchor point for the friction material. (StopTech)

Thermal Barriers

Because of their steel construction, the backing plates generally do not insulate the caliper pistons from heat very effectively. Therefore, in many racing or high-performance applications a *thermal barrier* is found sandwiched between the friction material and the backing plate.

The two most common forms of insulator are the ceramic puck and the woven mat. In either case, the insulating material is bonded or riveted in place during the manufacturing process and cannot be added on later.

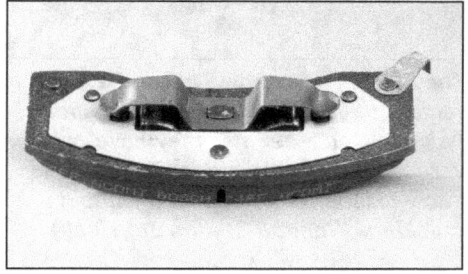

In order to reduce heat flow from the rotor to the brake fluid, a piece of insulating material can be placed between the backing plate and the caliper pistons. Stainless steel shims are the most common thermal barriers used in OEM applications and can also help to reduce certain noise frequencies. (Randall Shafer)

Adhesives

As the name implies, the brake pad *adhesive* bonds the friction material to the backing plate. While historically friction material has been held to backing plates with mechanical rivets, these high-temperature, high-strength glues are now the norm.

As you can image, selecting the proper adhesive is critical, considering a failure of the adhesive results in the friction material falling off of the backing plate. In this regard not all adhesives are created equal, and low-grade adhesives have been known to break down and de-bond in severe-duty applications.

Shims

Shims are usually thin stainless steel plates attached to the back side of the brake pad backing plate. They may also contain a thin layer of damping material (rubber in some cases) sandwiched between multiple stainless steel plates, but in any case these devices are used to damp out noises (squealing) that may be generated by the brake pad during use.

Note that the presence of shims does not necessarily guarantee noise-free performance, but in many applications they certainly help a great deal. A beneficial side

In racing applications, extreme measures are taken to keep heat out of the brake fluid. The shims shown above are fabricated from titanium, an excellent thermal insulator. Unfortunately, the cost of this material makes it impractical for production vehicles. (Randall Shafer/StopTech)

effect is that stainless steel shims can serve as an effective thermal barrier as well. For even better thermal insulation shims can be fabricated from titanium, but the cost of this material can be prohibitive.

Lubricants

Lubricants can serve two purposes. The first is to allow free motion between the brake pad and its mounts, or caliper abutment plates. This prevents binding and/or residual drag during use. This is generally a good thing.

In other applications, lubricant can be applied to the backing plate directly in an attempt to provide some measure of noise suppression. Frankly speaking, this is semi-effective at best. If this technique worked as well as some people claim, you would find it in widespread use among the vehicle manufacturers. It probably doesn't make matters worse, but don't expect a tube of goo to prevent long-term brake noise.

While advertised as a cure-all for brake noise, lubricants are really used to provide free motion between the backing plate and the caliper locating features. Too much lubricant can be detrimental though, as it collects dust, dirt, and debris over time. (Randall Shafer)

CHAPTER 9

In some applications, the leading and trailing edges of the brake pad friction material are chamfered. This is typically a countermeasure for noise, and does not have an impact on the brake pad's performance, although in theory it contributes to shorter brake pad life. (Randall Shafer)

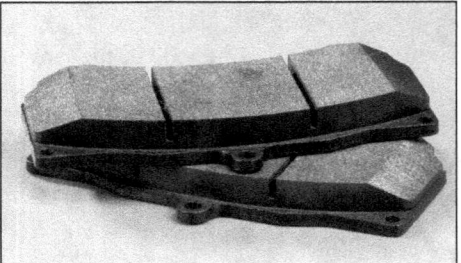

The brake pads shown above have a rectangular profile (long length, short height). Consequently, they have two vertical slots cut in the friction puck to allow for thermal expansion without cracking. (Randall Shafer/StopTech)

Chamfers

Chamfers are sometimes found ground or molded into the leading and trailing edges of the brake pad friction material itself. By angling the leading edge of the pad, there's belief that the pad and rotor are less susceptible to certain noise frequencies. Is there an element of brake voodoo involved? Certainly, but many, many vehicles come from the factory with chamfers cut into their pads for just this reason.

The downside is that the chamfers wear down with use and may lose their effectiveness over time. In the end, every application is once again different and simply having chamfers does not guarantee noise-free operation across the board.

Noise concerns aside, some high-performance brake pad manufacturers add chamfers to reduce the initial surface area of the brake pad friction material. This step is taken to increase the rate of temperature rise when the brakes are first applied, providing a more stable coefficient of friction. Although the chamfers still wear away as the pads are used, the reduced thermal mass of the friction material can offset the reduction in chamfer area, enabling rapid temperature rise rates and consistent performance over the life of the pad.

Slots

Slots are nothing more than vertical grooves cut into the face of the friction material. They're typically found evenly spaced along the pad, with one or two slots being the most common. While simple in concept, they serve a variety of purposes.

First and foremost, slots allow an escape route for brake pad dust, preventing it from building up between the pad and rotor face. Second, slots allow for thermal expansion of the friction puck at elevated temperatures, which prevents stress cracks in the puck. And finally, slots can act as redundant leading edges for the puck, which can, in some cases, increase the effective coefficient of friction of the pad.

Coefficient of Friction

Back in Chapter 3 you learned that the brake pad's primary role is to convert caliper clamp force into a frictional force, which opposes the rotation of the spinning rotor as defined by the following relationship:

Brake pad friction force (lb) = caliper clamp force (lb) x coefficient of friction (unitless)

Because most brake pads have a coefficient of friction much less than 1.0, the gain will always be less than 1:1. More precisely, the coefficient of friction value is always equal to the gain. Consequently, the friction force is always much less than the caliper clamp force.

So what is the coefficient of friction of your brake pads? Good question! While most brake pad manufacturers provide you with an approximate value over a typical temperature range, be forewarned that like a tire's mu-slip curve, anything and everything can affect the coefficient, and defining it as a single value is impossible to do.

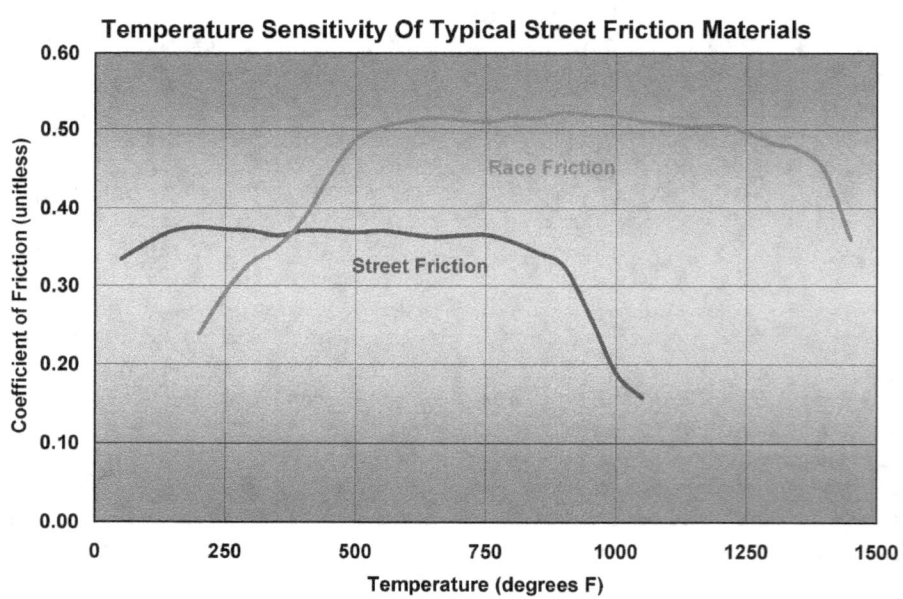

A brake pad's performance varies with temperature. For example, a typical street brake pad (blue line) might maintain consistent output until approximately 900 degrees F, but beyond this point the coefficient of friction may drop dramatically, resulting in a classic case of brake pad fade. In contrast, race friction materials (red line) may need to reach temperatures of 500 degrees F or more to achieve their steady-state output, but remain relatively stable until well past 1,200 degrees F. The objective in selecting the best pad is to find one that remains stable over the operating range your vehicle will be experiencing most often.

Brake Pad Size and Shape

If you glance back at the equation for brake pad gain again, you'll notice that consideration is not given to brake pad size or shape. That is because contrary to popular belief, the size and shape of the brake pad do not contribute toward the gain.

This point is so misunderstood that it bears repeating: The brake pad geometry (height, width, surface area, etc.) does not influence the gain! The coefficient of friction, and subsequently the gain, is independent of how big the brake pad is. As a result, bigger pads do not stop any better than smaller pads.

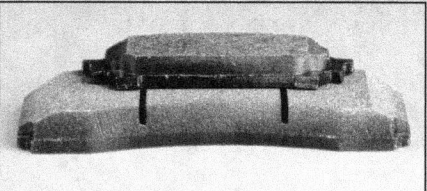

A brake pad material's coefficient of friction is independent of the size of the brake pad itself. Installing larger brake pads may increase the life of the friction material, but there will be no difference in brake system gain. (Randall Shafer/StopTech)

So why have thick pads and thin pads, tall pads and short pads? Well, there are several other very good reasons for selecting the largest pad possible. In no particular order they are:

1. A larger brake pad contains more friction material. Since friction material is a sacrificial component, if the pad contains more material to start with, it can go longer before it needs replacing. Bigger pads simply last longer.
2. A second benefit to more friction material is more thermal mass. In other words, there is more stuff present to absorb the heat. Therefore, a larger brake pad can also lead to reduced friction material temperatures.
3. A brake pad with increased surface area draws more heat away from the rotor during braking, since there is more material in direct contact with the rotor face. This can lead to decreased rotor temperatures during use. However, the heat has to go somewhere, and increased friction material temperatures may result.

Now, if a brake pad is absolutely tiny, its thermal mass may be so small that the resulting temperature rise leads to brake pad fade or, at the very least, increased wear. On the other hand, if a brake pad completely covered the face of the rotor to maximize surface area, the rotor would not be able to cool effectively. Consequently, it is theoretically possible to select a brake pad that is either too large or too small for the application.

Coefficient of Friction Stability

You have probably already concluded that a brake pad's coefficient of friction is an important parameter, but there's a characteristic even more near and dear to the high-performance enthusiast. What differentiates the good pads from the great pads is their ability to *maintain* a stable coefficient of friction (whatever that value may be) under demanding conditions.

Unfortunately, the coefficient of friction is a moving target, varying with changes in temperature, wear, humidity, age, and countless other factors not listed here. What does this mean in plain English? Only that every time the driver applies the brakes the vehicle provides a different response. Sometimes there's higher deceleration than intended and sometimes there's lower deceleration than intended. Naturally, this is neither comforting nor desirable.

Of all the factors that can influence the coefficient of friction, temperature reigns supreme. While wear and humidity may account for small fluctuations in gain, the effect of temperature, and particularly high temperature, cannot be overstated.

Brake Pad Fade

High-performance driving, towing a trailer, or blatant abuse can drive the brake pad temperature high enough that the coefficient of friction can decrease dramatically, resulting in decreased overall brake system gain. In other words, once a brake pad reaches its maximum operating temperature, *brake pad fade* may greatly reduce its ability to generate friction forces.

Brake pad fade is the result of the friction material breaking down both physically (a phenomenon known as *gassing out*) and chemically (commonly called *glazing*) while simultaneously producing a thin layer of burned brake pad material between the pad face and the rotor friction disc. Not only does this reduce the level of friction between the pad and the rotor, but the resulting gasses can also form a lubricating layer that can reduce the coefficient of friction to practically zero.

As a result, unlike brake fluid fade, where the brake pedal falls toward the floor, the primary symptom of brake pad fade is a high, hard brake pedal that doesn't produce significant deceleration, regardless of the amount of driver input force (if the gain is equal to zero, the input force doesn't matter). There may also be the unmistakable odor of fried brake pad friction material, as the gasses eventually find their way into the vehicle interior.

There are only two methods of avoiding brake pad fade. First, the temperature of the pads should be reduced to the lowest level possible through the selection of large rotors and the installation of brake cooling ducts (more to come on both of these topics in Chapter 10). The second measure is to install brake pads suited to

CHAPTER 9

While rarely experienced around town, brake pad fade is a common phenomenon on the track. Large, powerful vehicles such as this Camaro are capable of generating much more kinetic energy than smaller, less powerful vehicles, making proper brake pad selection critical to overall system performance. (Wayne Flynn/pdxsports.com)

the temperature operating range expected during use. Friction materials designed for use around town seldom provide adequate brake pad fade resistance under demanding conditions.

Friction Material Categories

Although these categories are not formally defined nor regulated by the government, it's appropriate to discuss coefficient of friction ranges based on the intended use and the expected performance of the friction material. These are rough approximations at best, but should get you well on your way toward understanding the trade-offs that must be made in friction material selection.

Street Friction Materials

Typical coefficient of friction values for *street friction materials* are in the range of 0.30 to 0.40. This means that the brake pad friction force is in the range of only 30 to 40 percent of the caliper clamp force (0.30 to 0.40 in the brake pad friction force formula). While this may seem like a severe loss in efficiency, these materials are usually easy on the rotor and don't make a lot of noise.

And therein lies the fundamental trade-off in friction material selection: Lower coefficients are typically more noise-free, vibration-free, and rotor-friendly than higher coefficients of friction. Their output suffers as a result, so the loss in overall gain must be made up by other components in the brake system.

Therefore, while street friction materials may work well under normal driving conditions (temperatures of 200 to 400 degrees F), their coefficient of friction may change dramatically as temperature increases. In other words, these materials are generally more susceptible to brake pad fade than their high-performance counterparts. Although relatively stable around town, most street friction materials begin to fade somewhere around 700 to 800 degrees F (temperatures generally experienced only when towing a trailer down a mountain or when lapping a racetrack).

High-Performance Friction Materials

High-performance friction materials usually stretch the coefficient of friction range from 0.35 to 0.45. The result is a higher overall system gain than when using street friction materials, which in

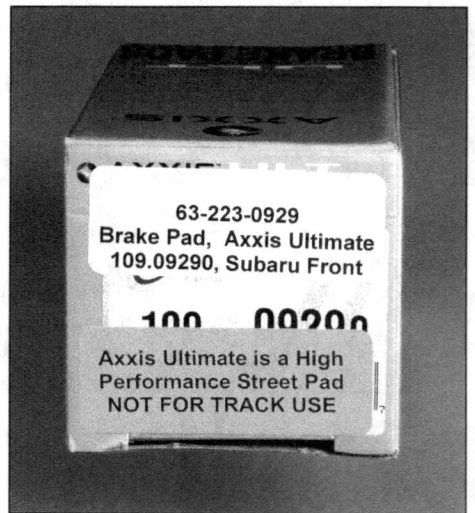

A typical street friction material is formulated for reduced noise, increased life, and minimal brake dust. However, in achieving these characteristics, the resulting temperature sensitivity may make them completely inappropriate for track use. Heed the warnings on the box! (Randall Shafer/StopTech)

Brake Pad Compressibility

Believe it or not, brake pad friction materials are pretty soft and spongy. As a result, every time you step on the brake pedal part of the force is being used to squish the molecules of the friction material closer together instead of generating brake pad friction force. While this is certainly undesirable, brake pad compressibility simply cannot be avoided.

In general, brake pads with higher compressibility exhibit a softer, spongier pedal while those with lower compressibility provide the driver with a more firm brake pedal. Unfortunately, brake pads with the highest coefficient of friction usually have the highest compressibility, so the pedal-feel benefits due to increased gain can be overshadowed.

If you're wondering why your pedal feel is still soft and mushy after installing new brake pads, compressibility could be the answer.

turn means less pedal force is required to achieve a given amount of vehicle deceleration. The vehicle brakes may feel more responsive or more powerful as a result. Of course the maximum deceleration will still be limited by the tire-to-road interface, but it will require less driver input (pedal force) to get there.

High-performance friction materials also display a higher resistance to brake pad fade. Their chemistry is designed to be more stable over a wider range of temperatures, resulting in consistent braking when the pace begins to pick up. Every compound is different, but some of these

Many friction materials are marketed to the high-performance crowd as a street-and-track solution. These street friction materials are still appropriate for daily driving, but their increased thermal performance typically comes at the expense of more noise, shorter life, and increased brake dust. (Hawk Performance)

materials are advertised to operate at temperatures up to 900 to 1,000 degrees F without a significant change in performance. This makes them good candidates for aggressive street driving, mild racetrack use, or trailer-towing applications where these temperatures are commonplace.

There is a price to pay, however. Higher coefficients usually dictate the use of more abrasive friction materials. While not true in every case, these materials generally produce more noise, dust, and vibration than their street friction material counterparts.

Racing Friction Materials

The high end of the friction spectrum is where *racing friction materials* hang out, with coefficients in the 0.50 to 0.60 range. Although still lower than 1.0, some of these

Brake Dust

One of the biggest complaints enthusiasts have regarding brake pads is the inevitable generation of brake dust. Unfortunately, brake dust is largely unavoidable, and the best one can hope for is to find a brake pad that wears at a relatively slow rate to reduce the buildup over time. Naturally, brake pads selected for high-performance attributes usually make the most dust, so a compromise must once again be endured.

Following typical street use, brake dust is relatively simple to clean—just grab the hose and go. However, in extreme situations such as track days or competitive driving, the brake dust leaving the brake pad can be so hot that it can melt and/or oxidize a wheel's protective finish. It doesn't matter whether your wheels are painted, anodized, or polished—in all cases the wheels can be permanently discolored by the glowing debris leaving the brake pad, and no amount of scrubbing will be able to make the wheel clean again.

materials can double the gain provided by street friction materials! Consequently, there can be a significant reduction in driver pedal force required to slow the vehicle down. This can be quite advantageous in cases where the brake system is downsized for weight (when removing a brake booster for example), but an appropriate level of gain is still required.

While increased gain is welcome in these applications, the real benefit of racing friction materials is their elevated resistance to brake pad fade. On-track temperatures of 1,100 degrees F and beyond require unique chemistries that remain stable and consistent in the heat of battle (no pun intended). Unfortunately, these very same chemistries make them *unstable* at cold temperatures. This is why racing friction materials require several heat-building braking events before they operate at their expected level of performance.

Unfortunately, these extreme coefficients of friction almost always come at the expense of intense squealing, increased dusting, and accelerated rotor wear. While certainly inappropriate for the street, these are the trade-offs that race teams are willing to accept for fade-free performance on the track.

Friction Material Chemistries

As if picking a brake pad from the correct friction material category wasn't difficult enough, there are also a number of *friction material chemistries* to choose between. These categories are regulated only by the pad companies' marketing department. Consequently, do not take any of these comments or observations as absolute truths—they are merely guidelines.

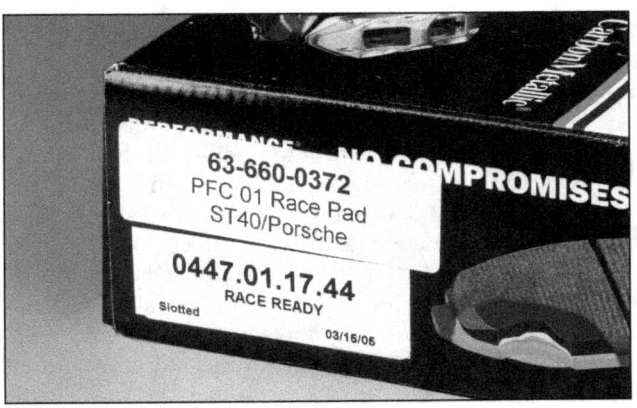

Dedicated friction materials for racing are characterized by stable performance at elevated temperatures. At low temperatures, though, their output is quite inconsistent, making them inappropriate for street use. (Randall Shafer)

Bite and Release Characteristics

Two heavily promoted brake pad characteristics are bite and release. Brake pad bite indicates how quickly the brake pad friction forces build after the brakes are applied. In other words, pads with good bite should provide more immediate brake system responses to driver inputs (a grabby response) while pads with poor bite may create a momentary delay (a lazy response).

A brake pad's release characteristic suggests how quickly the brake pad will reduce friction forces after brake pedal force is removed. A pad with good release characteristics will decrease the force immediately, while a pad with poor release characteristics may give the impression that the brakes are dragging a small amount after the pedal force is removed.

While these terms have gained widespread acceptance in the marketplace, they're only defined anecdotally. Unlike a coefficient of friction value (0.32, for example) or a maximum operating temperature (perhaps 950 degrees F), a unit of measurement does not exist to tell the consumer just exactly how much bite or release one brake pad has compared to another.

When diving into a braking zone from top speed, brake pad bite can make the difference between coming out of the corner in front or behind. The driver with better bite will be the last one to lift off the throttle and transition back on to the brake pedal. (Wayne Flynn/pdxsports.com)

In other words, good and poor are merely subjective terms, which give bite and release a purely relative meaning. When choosing brake pads from a single supplier, you may be able to differentiate between material A and material B, but it's nearly impossible to compare the bite and release characteristic claims of different manufacturers.

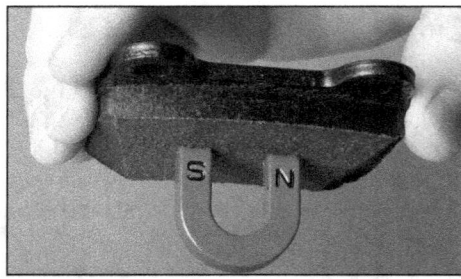

Semi-metallic brake pads get their name from the fact that up to 50 percent of the friction material is made from ferrous metals. If you're unsure if your brake pads are semi-metallic or not, just pull out a magnet and see if it sticks to the friction puck. If it does, you're holding a semi-metallic brake pad. (Randall Shafer/StopTech)

Well, some companies proclaim that their semi-metallic brake pads are 50 percent ferrous materials by weight, but this is not an industry standard by any means. It's up to the manufacturer (and usually their marketing department) to decide what constitutes a semi-metallic brake pad.

Non-Asbestos Organic Brake Pads

In the early days of the modern automobile, organic brake pads were all the rage. These materials had good wear, performance, and noise attributes even by today's standards. However, the key to their performance came from a material called asbestos, and as society now knows, asbestos isn't healthy for humans.

While asbestos-based organic brake pads were largely replaced by semi-metallic

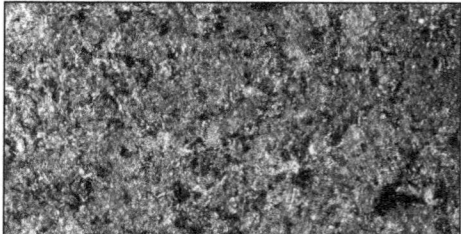

Copper is commonly added to brake pad friction materials for its lubricating properties. When exposed to the high temperatures at the rotor interface, the copper softens and melts, which can alleviate certain noise and brake roughness concerns. The characteristic copper color is usually visible upon close inspection of the brake pad. (Randall Shafer/StopTech)

Semi-Metallic Brake Pads

In general, semi-metallic brake pads are made with significant amounts of ferrous metals, or iron (think shredded steel wool). This is done primarily to increase the operating temperature range of the friction puck, as iron has relatively stable output characteristics at elevated temperatures.

A side benefit of adding ferrous metals to the compound is that the effective coefficient of friction usually increases. Not always, but usually. This results in semi-metallic brake pads usually providing a higher overall brake system gain.

Because of their desirable temperature and friction properties, semi-metallic brake pads are typically specified for high-performance and/or severe-use applications. The big downside, however, is that steel wool is generally less friendly to the rotor surface (it's quite abrasive) and as a result these pads may wear the rotors and/or squeal during use more so than the other pads described later.

So how much iron content is required to be called a semi-metallic brake pad?

pads in the 1970s and 1980s, there has been a relatively recent resurgence of organic pads. However, these new formulations do not contain asbestos, hence the name non-asbestos organic, or NAO.

In general, NAO brake pads do not contain any ferrous compounds in the friction material itself. There may be non-ferrous particulates added for lubrication (copper is a common additive), but you won't be able to stick a magnet to a NAO pad (except to the steel backing plate, of course).

Because of their chemistry, NAO brake pads provide lower coefficient of friction levels than semi-metallic pads (usually, anyway). They're also more sensitive to heat than semi-metallic pads, as their base materials change more rapidly with extreme temperatures.

So why then are NAO pads found on most new production vehicles today? Almost without exception, these compounds are used because of their elevated resistance to noise and vibration. They're typically rotor-friendly, relatively squeal-free, and go a long way toward preventing rotor thickness variation (more on this topic in Chapter 10).

So to wrap it up, NAO brake pads are great if you want quiet, smooth operation. If you're a demanding user, though, they might not be the hot ticket for your application.

Ceramic Brake Pads

Here's a tough one to nail down. Ceramic brake pads are really just the next evolution in the NAO brake pad family tree. The differentiating factor is that there's some ceramic dust thrown in the mixer when the pads are formulated. The amount of ceramic content varies by manufacturer (and is not regulated), so it's difficult to define just what a ceramic pad really is. Some manufacturers claim one- to five-percent ceramic content by volume, but every pad is different.

Just to confuse matters even more, ceramic brake pads may also contain ferrous elements. Does this mean that ceramic brake pads are also semi-metallic brake pads? That's a good question, and one without a definitive answer. Vehicle manufacturers sometimes refer to these pads as low-metallic materials, but it's just another vague marketing term.

If you believe the side of the box, ceramic brake pads claim less dust, longer

No, ceramic brake pads are not made from recycled bathroom fixtures. These pads simply contain a small percentage of marketing-chic ceramic powder by volume, but their relatively poor thermal performance usually makes them unacceptable in a high-performance application. (Hawk Performance)

life, and increased temperature performance. These pads are essentially trying to bridge the gap between NAO pads and semi-metallic pads. The end result, though, is that you end up with the brake pad equivalent of the all-season tire: middle-of-the-road performance without being particularly good at anything.

Is this bad? Maybe not, but for whatever reason ceramic pads have really caught on in the aftermarket, yet are not widely popular with vehicle manufacturers.

Exotic Brake Pads

In order to differentiate one brake pad from another, some manufacturers go to great lengths to add exotic-sounding materials to their chemistries. While certainly impressive to read in a product brochure, the benefits may or may not live up to the marketing hype.

Carbon brake pads probably have the largest amount of name recognition in the brake pad performance aftermarket, with two of the most popular being *Carbon Metallic* pads (as trademarked by Performance Friction Corporation) and *Ferro Carbon* pads (as trademarked by Hawk Performance). Properly formulated, adding carbon to a semi-metallic brake pad can greatly increase the mechanical strength of the friction material as well as increase its resistance to fade. This can, especially in high-performance applications, lead to increased brake pad life and an extended thermal operating range.

As found in bulletproof vests, *Kevlar* can also be added to brake pad chemistry to provide mechanical strength to the friction material. Unfortunately, its relatively low melting point does not lend itself to high-temperature applications. This essentially writes off Kevlar for racing or other high-performance applications.

Titanium completes the trio of brake pad additives making their way around the

Real Ceramic Brakes

Although nearly every ceramic brake pad in the automotive aftermarket is really just an enhanced semi-metallic, there are a few select applications where the rotors are manufactured from true ceramic composites. Whether it is Porsche's PCCB system on the $440,000 Carrera GT or the carbon-fiber reinforced rotors found on the $450,000 Mercedes-Benz SLR McLaren, these engineered materials can greatly increase heat capacity, significantly reduce weight, and virtually eliminate corrosion.

In other words, real ceramic brakes can reduce fade, enhance vehicle handling, improve fuel economy, and increase the service life of the brake system components. With all of these advantages, why haven't these materials found their way to more mainstream vehicles?

Quite simply, today's cost of these brake system components is approximately $10,000, or the price of a decent used car. Perhaps as economies of scale come into play affordability will increase, but until that time, enthusiasts are forced to rely on cast iron rotors and semi-metallic ceramic brake pads.

ABS and Brake Pad Selection

If you're installing non-OEM brake pads on your ABS-equipped vehicle, be advised that there are a number of factors that could lead to the degradation of ABS performance. Why? Because changing brake pads can alter not only the P-V relationship, but overall brake system gain as well.

Changes in the P-V relationship stem from brake pads with different levels of compressibility. Pads that are soft and squishy require more brake fluid volume for a given pressure than pads that are hard as a rock. In either case, the ABS algorithm is calibrated to a fixed P-V relationship by the auto manufacturer and any subsequent changes can impact ABS performance. However, as stated back in Chapter 7 relative to stainless steel brake hoses, ABS is generally robust to small changes in the P-V relationship as long as the changes reduce the overall level of compliance.

The confounding factor with non-OEM brake pads is that changes in compressibility are typically accompanied with corresponding changes in gain. Because ABS cannot differentiate between the change in the P-V relationship and the modified output characteristics, it takes an educated guess and hopes for the best. Unfortunately, the results may be far from optimized.

In the real world, most street brake pads are usually similar enough to each other that the small differences between them are readily accommodated by the ABS, at least to the extent that the average enthusiast is concerned. The switch to racing brake pads, however, may not be quite as seamless, although non-optimized ABS performance may still be better than no ABS at all. Trial and error is the only way to know for sure.

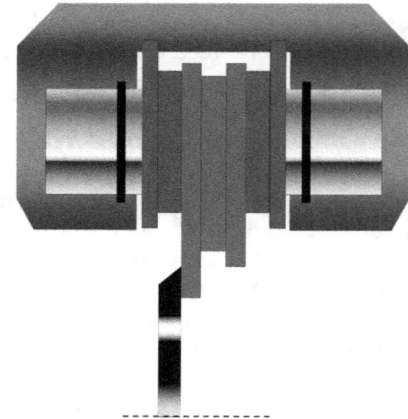

The abrasive friction mechanism generates brake pad force as the brake pads (blue), clamped by the caliper (red), directly grind away the high and low spots on the spinning rotor (gray). Over time, the rotor becomes worn thin along with the brake pads themselves. This is the primary friction mechanism for many brake pad materials when cold.

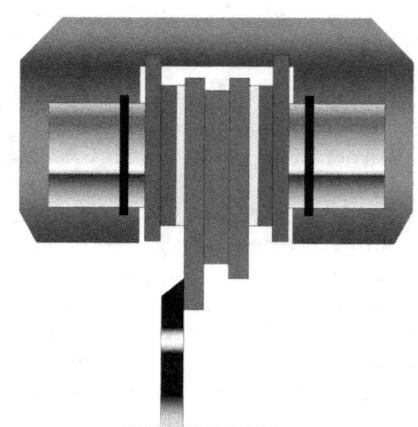

Adherent friction generates brake pad force without significantly wearing away the rotor. A sacrificial transfer layer of brake pad material on the rotor face (yellow) provides the frictional interface for the brake pads. Consequently, the rotor is spared from direct physical contact with the brake pads.

industry. Although titanium does have a marginally higher melting point than iron, its poor thermal conductivity and wear characteristics lend no real advantage over that of a high-quality semi-metallic brake pad. And while titanium is used in other vehicle components for its light weight, the percentage found in brake pads hardly even registers at the scale.

Friction Mechanisms

As the caliper squeezes the brake pads against the spinning rotor, brake pad friction forces are developed through two unique mechanisms: *abrasive friction* and *adherent friction*. In general, all pads display a bit of each with abrasive mechanisms operating in the lower temperature ranges, while adherent mechanisms become dominant as pad temperature increases. Ultimately, both mechanisms generate brake pad friction forces, but in vastly different ways.

Abrasive Friction

The abrasive mechanism generates brake pad friction forces by mechanically forcing the brake pads against the spinning rotor. This physically wears both the pads and the rotor since the high and low spots of the two mating surfaces are constantly being sheared off. Consequently, both the pads and rotor will eventually need to be replaced as they both have material removed until they are too thin to endure further service.

Adherent Friction

The adherent mechanism is altogether different. With adherent friction, a thin layer of brake pad material actually transfers to the rotor face as operating temperatures rise. When the caliper squeezes the brake pads it now forces them against this layer of brake pad material (aptly called the *transfer layer*) and *not* against the spinning rotor itself. Similar in nature to the adhesive tire forces back in Chapter 2, this brake-pad-to-brake-pad attraction and interaction produces a majority of the brake pad friction force.

With adherent friction there is much less rotor wear, but the compromise is that the brake pads wear that much quicker.

And even though rotors are not mechanically worn with adherent friction, they still need to be replaced on a regular basis to avoid other forms of mechanical failure. This is why racing rotors are typically thicker after use than when brand new. It's due to the adherent brake pad transfer layer buildup.

Brake System Break-In

When installing new brake pads and/or rotors on a vehicle, there's a certain amount of care and attention that must be given to ensure their long-term performance. In general, there are two types of brake system break-in procedures. Not coincidentally, this is a direct result of the two unique friction mechanisms just discussed.

Brake System Burnishing

Burnishing is typically performed whenever new brake pads are used with old rotors or when new rotors are used with old brake pads. Because the abrasive mechanism relies on direct contact between the brake pad friction material and the rotor, mixing and matching new and old hardware dictates that the interface must be burnished before optimum performance can be realized.

The actual process of burnishing can actually take place during everyday driving, as it simply involves wearing the two mating surfaces against each other until they are mirror images of one another. This allows for more uniform distribution of wear across the entire pad-to-rotor interface.

To avoid establishing a transfer layer, burnishing is typically performed at lower speeds and at lower temperatures. Most formal burnish procedures involve up to a few hundred stops from medium speed at large intervals to avoid significant heating of the brake system components, thereby emphasizing abrasive friction (instead of adherent friction). In the real world, though, simply driving the vehicle around town for a while is usually enough to perform an adequate, if not an ideal, brake burnish.

Brake System Bedding

Brake system bedding is typically performed when both new rotors and new pads are installed at the same time, or immediately after a brake burnish has been performed on used hardware. Also known as *bed-in*, this procedure consists of heating the brake pad friction material to its adherent temperature to initiate the formation of a transfer layer on the rotor. The material is then allowed to cool without

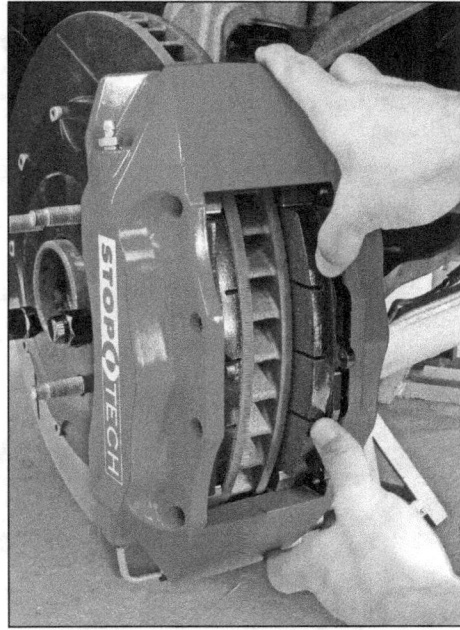

There's more to changing brake pads than just swapping in new parts and driving off. Proper brake pad break-in can be critical to the long-term performance of your vehicle's brake system.

coming to rest, resulting in an evenly distributed transfer layer around the entire rotor face. This procedure is then typically repeated one or two more times for good measure.

Different brake system designs, friction material properties, and driving conditions may require different bedding proce-

Adherent friction materials require a uniform transfer layer on the rotor face before optimum braking can occur. The shiny, freshly machined surface of this rotor indicates that it must be completely bedded-in before it is subjected to high-performance use. (Randall Shafer/StopTech)

Brake Pad Bite: How Much is Enough?

The following marketing snippets were pulled directly from a brake pad manufacturer's online catalog. All of the statements below describe the bite characteristics of five different racing brake pad compounds from the same brake pad manufacturer. The names have been changed, but can you tell the difference in bite between them?

Brake Pad A: Advanced compound matrix provides an excellent initial bite…

Brake Pad B: Outstanding initial bite at race temperatures…

Brake Pad C: Offers even higher initial bite than Brake Pad B…

Brake Pad D: This is a very high initial bite friction material…

Brake Pad E: Even higher initial bite than Brake Pad D…

No wonder it can be so difficult to pick the right brake pad—the marketing department has taken over!

Street Pad Bedding Procedure

For a stock brake system with street-oriented brake pads, a series of six to eight braking events from about 60 mph down to about 10 mph typically gets the brake components warm enough to be considered one bed-in cycle. Each of the six to eight braking events should be made at moderate to high deceleration (about 75 percent of the deceleration required to lock up the brakes and/or engage ABS) and should be made one after the other without allowing the brakes to cool in-between.

These are not extreme panic stops. Don't go overboard here.

Bedding-in brake pads requires making multiple stops from moderate speeds. The key to success is to keep the vehicle moving for the entire sequence, as coming to rest while the pads are still hot can result in uneven transfer layer deposits. For jobs like this, a racetrack comes in handy. (Daniel Mainzer)

Once the brakes have faded a bit and/or you smell friction material in the passenger compartment, the cycle is complete and you should allow the system to cool by driving at steady speeds without bringing the vehicle to a complete stop. After cooling, repeat the bed-in cycle one more time, cool down again, and you're typically good to go. In some situations a third cycle is beneficial, but two are usually sufficient.

And now a word from the lawyers: Note that these speeds and maneuvers are neither recommended nor acceptable on all public roads. While you need to get heat into the system to achieve a proper bed-in, you also need to exercise common sense and take full responsibility for your actions. Drive smart, please.

dures since too little heat during bedding prevents the material from transferring to the rotor face while overheating the friction material can generate uneven deposits. To help you through it, the sidebars provide you with the information you need to select the bedding procedure appropriate for your situation.

Summary

So what can you do to select the proper brake pad for your application? As you just read, it depends on what you're looking for. For increased gain, choose a pad with a higher coefficient of friction. For better response, chose a pad with increased bite. For improved resistance to brake pad fade, choose a pad with a higher maximum operating temperature. For reduced noise, choose a pad with chamfers, shims, and preferably one with NAO chemistry.

In all cases though, there is usually a price to pay for these increased levels of performance, and you absolutely get what you pay for. Friction material design, formulation, and manufacturing are not rocket science, but there is only so much performance that can be baked into a $9.99 set of lifetime warranty brake pads. There is a very good reason that most racing

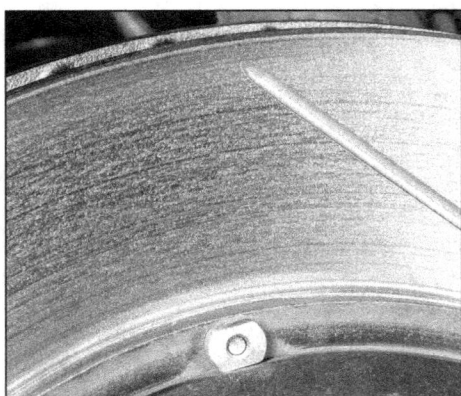

After successfully bedding-in new brake pads and rotors, a thin, uniform film of friction material will be visible on the surface of the friction disc. This transfer layer gives the friction disc a dark gray appearance and may hide the machining marks found on the rotor when it was brand-new. (StopTech)

brake pads cost hundreds of dollars—the materials that provide a consistent coefficient of friction at high temperatures cost more than those that fall apart on the third lap.

To this end, it usually pays to stick with a name-brand brake pad. Nobody can tell how well a brake pad will perform by looking at the box, so rely on the company whose name is printed on the side. In a pinch anything that fits may be able to get you through, but sticking with a name you trust will most likely be a more consistent performer than a set of *Super Stoppers* from the local discount auto parts counter.

For the ultimate in performance, be advised that one brake pad does not suit all applications. Beware of the pad that

Race Pad Bedding Procedure

For a stock brake system with race-oriented brake pads, the bed-in procedure needs to be run a bit more aggressively. Approximately 10 partial braking events are recommended from 60 mph down to 10 mph followed immediately by three or four partial braking events from 80 mph down to 10 mph. As stated in the street pad bed-in procedure, each of the partial braking events should be made at moderate to high deceleration (about 75 percent of the deceleration required to lock up the brakes and/or engage ABS) and should be made one after the other without allowing the brakes to cool in-between.

Once the brakes have faded a bit and/or you get a whiff of friction smell in the passenger compartment, the cycle is complete and you should allow the system to cool by driving at steady speeds without bringing the vehicle to a complete stop. After cooling, repeat the partial braking event procedure listed above one more time, adding two or three additional partial braking events from 100 mph down to 10 mph. In some situations, a third cycle is beneficial, but two are usually sufficient.

As before, these speeds are neither recommend nor condoned on public roads. This procedure is designed to be run in a controlled environment such as a racetrack. While you need to get heat into the system to achieve a proper bed-in, you also need to exercise common sense and take full responsibility for your actions.

Bedding-in racing brake pads is similar to bedding-in street brake pads, but the speeds are typically higher. Because the vehicle will be slowing several extra times per lap, this procedure should be performed during a practice session and not under race conditions. Brake pad fade on lap three can produce undesirable results. (Wayne Flynn/pdxsports.com)

claims to be all things to all people! In other words, the *All-Purpose Street & Track Pad* simply does not exist. Certainly there are some brake pads that blend the lines of street and track characteristics, but for optimum street and track performance, two unique brake pads need to be used. Any other selection will simply be a compromise.

Finally, don't be afraid to call the brake pad manufacturer, dealer, or distributor directly to get a recommendation. Typically a manufacturer has several pad compounds to choose from, and the best choice for your application may not be obvious. Share all of your expectations and see what they have to offer. Naturally you have to temper their recommendation with the knowledge that they're also trying to sell you their product, but it never hurts to ask.

Like the tires on your vehicle, the brake pads need to be optimized based on their intended usage. When selecting brake pads for the street, many viable options exist. However, when heading to the track, it only makes sense to swap in a set of pads more suited to the task. (Dan Gabriel Photography)

CHAPTER 10

BRAKE ROTORS

There's nothing that screams high-performance more than an oversized brake rotor sitting behind an open-spoke wheel wrapped in the widest rubber possible. No self-respecting automotive enthusiast would be satisfied with a 10-inch rotor tucked inside an 18-inch wheel. Bigger is always better, right?

Well, yes and no. There's much more to selecting the proper brake rotor than finding one that fits. Certainly the big-brake touring-car look is desirable, but selecting the wrong rotor can actually compromise overall brake system performance. It's time to find out what it takes to get the best of both worlds.

A Rotor Refresher

Although discussed separately to this point, the rotor actually performs two functions in the brake system. First, the rotor acts as the primary heat sink during the conversion of kinetic energy to thermal energy. This is where a majority of the vehicle's kinetic energy ends up during a typical braking event, and back in Chapter 1 you learned to estimate the temperature rise of the rotors by using the following equation:

Rise in temperature (degrees F)
= kinetic energy (ft-lb) ÷
weight of the brakes (lb) ÷
77.8 (assuming cast iron)

The rotor's second function was covered in Chapter 3—it is also responsible for converting the brake pad friction force into wheel torque. Because the brake pad friction force occurs at a fixed distance from the center of the spinning

Although rotors are available in a variety of different shapes, sizes, and materials, they all share a common purpose—they must first absorb then dissipate a vehicle's kinetic energy during braking. While this rotor may be horribly undersized for a road racing application, it may fit the bill perfectly for a boulevard cruiser. (Randall Shafer)

During track use, rotors are squeezed with thousands of pounds of clamp force, twisted by thousands of foot-pounds of torque, and heated to over 1,200 degrees F. Heavy cars with large engines such as these only make the demands that much more intense. (Wayne Flynn/pdxsports.com)

BRAKE ROTORS

rotor, the resulting wheel torque was calculated as follows:

Wheel torque (ft-lb) =
brake pad friction force (lb) x
[rotor effective radius (in)
÷ 12 (a conversion factor)]

Although these tasks are quite different in nature, heat absorption and torque generation occur simultaneously. In a competitive environment, the rotor is continuously compressed with thousands of pounds of caliper clamp force, generating thousands of foot-pounds of wheel torque, all while sustaining operating temperatures well over 1,000 degrees F, lap after lap after lap. It's not easy being a rotor!

Rotor Terminology

Like other parts of the brake system already discussed, a typical rotor can be broken down into several discrete components. Therefore, before going any further, it's once again necessary define the terminology.

Friction Disc

The *friction disc* is essentially the working component of the brake rotor. It's responsible for providing a mating friction surface for the brake pads, as well as supplying the thermal mass necessary for thermal energy absorption. Consequently, the friction disc experiences the highest operating temperatures of any brake system component.

Friction discs are usually made from cast iron due to its inherent strength, energy absorption characteristics, and temperature robustness. Other materials can be used in select racing applications (more to come on this topic later in this chapter), but when comparing cost to performance, cast iron simply can't be beat.

Rotor Hat

The rotor *hat*, also known as the *mounting bell*, serves to locate and attach the friction disc to the vehicle's wheel hub or spindle. In doing so, the torque generated in the friction disc is transferred by the hat to the hub, through the wheel, and ultimately to the tire contact patch.

The rotor hat can either be integral to the friction disc, or it can be a separate component assembled to the friction disc. In either case, the hat also provides the primary mechanical heat transfer path from the friction disc to other vehicle components at the wheel end.

The rotor hat couples the friction disc to the wheel hub. In many production vehicle applications, it's integral to the friction disc, but in high-performance applications, it may be a separate component. The hats shown here are machined from billet aluminum in order to reduce rotating inertia. (Randall Shafer/StopTech)

Integral rotor hats are made from the same material as the friction disc—cast iron in most cases. Discrete rotor hats can be made from a variety of materials, with aluminum alloys being the most common due to their low weight and relatively modest cost. In more exotic applications magnesium alloys can be employed, but these are beyond the budget of most automotive enthusiasts.

Two-piece rotors allow for relative movement between the friction disc and hat at temperature. Specialized fasteners are used to provide this freedom while simultaneously transmitting thousands of foot-pounds of brake torque. (Randall Shafer/StopTech)

Since most rotor hat mounting methods allow for some unrestricted axial motion, they may rattle around when cold. Although not present on the racing rotor shown, anti-rattle springs are typically employed on street applications. (Randall Shafer)

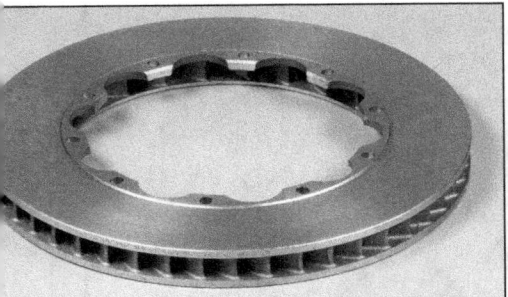

The friction disc is where all the action takes place. Because of its ideal mechanical properties and reasonable cost, gray cast iron is the predominant material of choice for nearly every friction disc today. The hazy film shown covering this friction disc is a coating to prevent corrosion before installation. (Randall Shafer/StopTech)

In the quest to further reduce rotating inertia, it's possible to use rotor hats made from exotic alloys. The hat shown above (already attached to a friction disc) was machined from a magnesium alloy. While cost prohibitive, it provides the lightest rotor assembly possible. (Randall Shafer)

Mounting Hardware

Most two-piece rotors are designed to allow the friction disc to thermally expand and contract radially without binding or distortion during use. For this reason, specialized *mounting hardware* must be used to constrain the rotor axially without preventing radial movement at high temperatures.

Unfortunately, most designs of this nature also permit some axial movement of the friction disc when cold. While not an issue for a dedicated racecar, this can lead to unwanted noises and vibrations on a daily-driven vehicle. Consequently, some rotor manufacturers take the extra step of installing an anti-rattle feature to alleviate this annoyance condition.

Thermal Break

When using a two-piece rotor, it's possible to install a *thermal break*, or insulator, between the friction disc and the rotor hat to reduce the flow of heat into vehicle components at the wheel end. Similar to the thermal barriers used in brake pad design, these devices are most typically used when there is a concern with wheel bearing longevity. However, the heat must go somewhere, and higher friction disc temperatures are normally the accepted tradeoff.

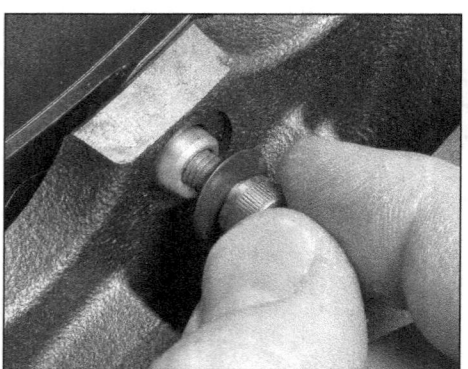

Some two-piece rotors may contain a thermal break to reduce the flow of heat from the friction disc to the mounting hat. This particular design uses a conical washer made from an insulating material to act both as an anti-rattle spring as well as a thermal break. (Randall Shafer/StopTech)

Rotor Mounting Tips

When installing brake rotors, it pays to take a few extra moments to properly prepare the mating surfaces and components. A little care upfront can prevent brake-induced headaches down the road.

1. Be sure that the hub mounting face is free of deposits, corrosion, or other junk that may have accumulated over the last 50,000 miles. A piece of Scotch-Brite and a bit of elbow grease should be all you need to ensure a clean mounting face. Be extra sure to inspect and clean the areas around the wheel studs.
2. If you are reinstalling used rotors, the same preparation comments go for the front and back surfaces of the rotor mounting hat. No crud allowed!
3. Inspect the mating wheel mounting face to ensure that it is flat and free from debris. A quick hit of Scotch-Brite should take care of any light corrosion you may need to address.
4. Finally, when mounting your wheels, tighten the lug nuts in the manufacturer's recommended sequence (usually a star-shaped pattern) and tighten them progressively to their appropriate torque. Over-tightening is a guaranteed way to distort the rotor, which can ultimately result in unwanted brake vibration.

Taking your time during rotor installation can prevent several brake-related problems in the miles that follow. At the very least, be sure that all rotor hat mounting surfaces are clean and free of corrosion. A few minutes with Scotch-Brite is usually all that's required. (Randall Shafer)

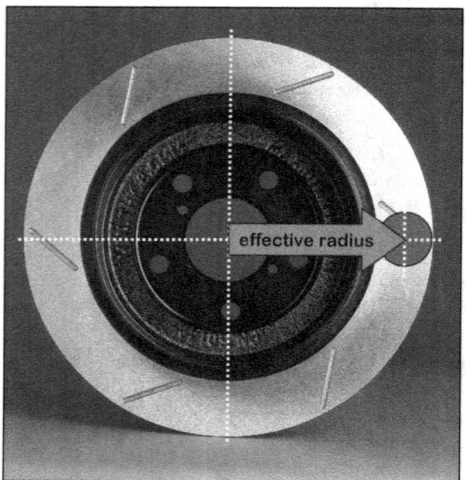

The effective radius is the lever arm that converts the brake pad friction force into torque. As shown above, it's not the same as the rotor radius, but rather the distance from the center of the rotor to the center of the caliper piston (blue). (Randall Shafer/StopTech)

BRAKE ROTORS

Effective Radius

The rotor generates torque because it's able to support the brake pad friction force at a fixed distance from its center of rotation. A rotor's *effective radius* is the virtual lever through which the brake pad friction force acts to create this torque. While there is debate among the engineers over where the force really acts, in this situation it works well enough to assume the brake pad friction force acts through the centerline of the caliper piston, or pistons. Based on this assumption, the rotor effective radius can then be estimated as follows:

Rotor effective radius (in) =
[rotor diameter (in) ÷ 2] –
[caliper piston diameter (in) ÷ 2]

(If you are into the nitty-gritty details, you should note that this equation assumes the caliper pistons to be tangent to the outer diameter of the brake rotor, which may not be true in all cases. However, it's a small detail that should not keep you up at night.)

Rotor Sizing

At this point you're well aware that heat is the primary enemy of the brake system. The hotter the brakes, the higher the likelihood of accelerated brake pad wear, brake fluid fade, and other assorted brake system maladies. Therefore, larger rotors are installed wherever possible to increase thermal mass. This results in lower brake temperatures, and lower brake temperatures result in happier brake system components.

In theory, a given percentage increase in thermal mass generates an equal percentage decrease in rotor temperature. According to the math, adding 25 percent to the brake system thermal mass should reduce brake temperatures by 25 percent. In the real world, it ends up not quite working out that perfectly, but the trend certainly holds true. This is one case where bigger is *definitely* better—up to a point.

Static Weight and Rotational Inertia

Although super-sizing looks appealing at first, rotor *static weight* and *rotational inertia* can be just as important to overall vehicle performance. While increased thermal mass can do wonders for brake temperatures, the corresponding increased static weight and rotational inertia can create significant negative side effects.

Static weight simply refers to the physical heft of the rotor. Because the rotor is hanging out at the end of the suspension arms, it's considered part of the

Rotor size impacts more than just the effective radius and thermal mass. The rotational inertia of the rotor can also play a factor in vehicle handling. If the front rotor shown on this sport bike were to grown significantly in diameter or width, the bike would be much more reluctant to lean over for a corner. (Randall Shafer)

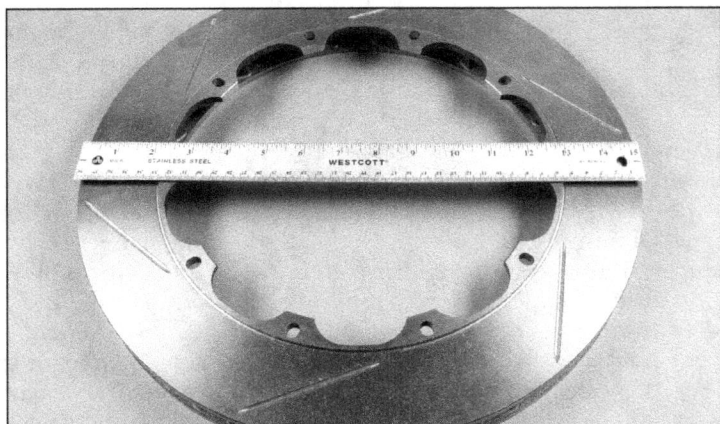
Super-sizing may sound appealing at first, but in the game of thermal management, bigger is not necessarily better. While this 15-inch friction disc has an incredible amount of thermal mass, it would be complete overkill on a 1,900-pound formula car. (Randall Shafer/StopTech)

Brake sizing, and more specifically rotor sizing, comes down to the compromise between temperature and weight. Larger brakes run at cooler temperatures, but at the expense of more vehicle weight to accelerate. Smaller brakes may enhance straight-line speed, but experience much higher temperatures. The right answer depends on the application. (Randall Shafer/StopTech)

Carbon/Carbon Brakes

In a carbon/carbon braking system, both the rotor friction disc and the brake pad friction material are manufactured from carbon composites. Although they're incredibly expensive and inappropriate for street use, they're used in every category of racing where they're allowed. Why? Because of their significant reduction in rotating inertia (they're lighter!). While this can be an advantage in all forms of motorsports, it can be especially useful on high-speed super speedways to reduce gyroscopic precession (the resistance to turning a rotating object) at corner entry.

If your wallet can sustain the price (and if your sanctioning body doesn't forbid them), then carbon/carbon brakes are the way to go. While they don't offer an improvement in gain over conventional racing brakes, the reduction in rotational inertia can be a huge advantage. (Wayne Flynn/pdxsports.com)

The disadvantages of a carbon/carbon brake system include the exorbitant cost, delayed response to driver inputs (the materials must be warm before they become effective), and some difficulty in modulation (their characteristics are not particularly linear). And, contrary to what you may hear in the paddock, the effective coefficient of friction of a carbon/carbon brake system is no different than that of modern racing brake pads used with gray cast iron friction discs (in other words, there are no significant gain impacts).

vehicle's *unsprung weight*. A separate book is needed to dive into why unsprung weight matters, but in summary the weight of the rotor must be vertically controlled along with the rest of the moving parts of the vehicle's suspension. As a result, adding unsprung weight may require changes in the vehicle's spring rates or damping characteristics to optimize suspension motions. From a vehicle ride and handling standpoint, less static weight is always best.

Increased rotational inertia brings another measure of concern. A spinning rotor is nothing more than a flywheel, storing rotational energy. Therefore, every time the driver desires to decelerate the vehicle, not only must enough force be generated to slow the vehicle down, but additional force must be added to stop the rotating parts from spinning. The same is true for a vehicle pulling away from rest—some portion of the engine's energy must be used to overcome the inertia of the rotating components as the vehicle accelerates. For these reasons, it's desirable to reduce the parasitic losses due to rotational inertia as much as possible.

What you are left with is the classic trade-off in rotor selection: Larger rotors are better for temperature control while smaller rotors are better for vehicle dynamics. The best compromise lies somewhere in-between. The moral of this story is that the right-sized rotor is just large enough to keep temperatures in check, and not one ounce heavier.

Rotor Cooling

So far, this chapter has been emphasizing the rotor's role in absorbing large amounts of thermal energy during braking. However, the rotor's ability to cool itself after braking is equally important. After all, if a rotor continuously absorbed energy and never was given a chance to cool, the temperature would continue to rise until the rotor melted!

If a rotor is heated to a temperature higher than its surroundings, it attempts to equalize its temperature by dissipating some of its energy to other stuff nearby. This process is called *heat transfer* and can only occur through one of three distinct mechanisms.

Conduction

The first heat transfer mechanism is known as *conduction*. This is the transfer of heat from a warmer object to a cooler object through physical contact. Whether it's a metal spoon in a bowl of hot soup or the sensation you feel walking barefoot across a cold tile floor, heat always flows from the warmer object to the cooler object if there is direct contact between them.

In the brake system, the rotor friction disc cools itself by conduction in many ways. One conductive path starts at the rotor friction disc, flows through the brake pad friction material and backing plate, transfers into the caliper pistons, and ends up warming the brake fluid. Along the way the heat may also take a detour to warm the caliper body. Another path from the rotor friction disc flows to the rotor hat, through the hub, and into the wheel bearing elements, ultimately heating up the wheel bearing grease. Simultaneously, some heat may flow into the wheel, lug nuts, and wheel studs. Given enough heat, there may also be measurable temperature rise in the suspension knuckles.

Conduction is also the mechanism the rotor friction disc employs to transfer heat away from the brake pad interface (where the heat is first developed) to the material at its core. While different rotor designs are used to exploit this phenomenon, for now it's enough to state that all heat flow through the rotor is through conductive means.

The amount of conductive heat transfer is proportional to the difference in temperature between the warmer object and the cooler object. Therefore, if the temperature difference between the warmer object and the cooler object is doubled, the rate of conductive heat transfer will double as well (at least in theory).

While driving around town, approximately half of the total thermal energy stored in the rotor friction disc is dissipated through conduction. On track though, when the mechanism of radiation becomes more significant, conductive cooling accounts for a much smaller percentage of the total heat transferred.

Convection

Unlike conduction, which relies on physical contact between solid objects for heat transfer, *convection* is the transfer of heat through fluid flow. From cooking the Thanksgiving turkey in a convective oven to quenching a red-hot piece of wrought iron in a bucket of water, examples of convective heat transfer can be found in nearly every aspect of daily life.

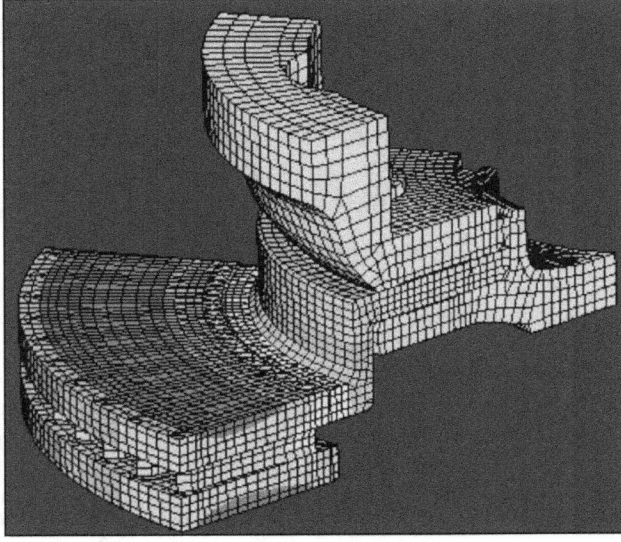

Given enough time, thermal energy flows from areas of higher temperature to areas of lower temperature. This computer simulation shows the friction disc at the highest temperatures during use (red and yellow), which results in heat flowing to cooler components such as the wheel and hub (both in blue). This analysis also shows the heat flow through the friction disc itself, with the vanes running at a cooler temperature (yellow) than the rubbing surface (red). (Delphi Corporation)

Since air is a fluid, it's the primary medium through which a rotor friction disc performs convective cooling; however, any component of the brake system that is warmer than the surrounding air will also cool through convection. In other words, any part of the rotor friction disc, brake calipers, hubs, and/or wheels exposed to air will cool through convective means.

As with conduction, the amount of convective heat transfer is proportional to the difference in temperature between the warmer object and cooler fluid. Therefore, if the temperature difference between the warmer object and the cooler object is doubled, the rate of convective heat transfer will double. For this reason, it's highly desirable to provide a constant supply of cool air to as many exposed brake system components as possible to increase the rate of convective heat transfer.

At low temperatures, approximately half of the total thermal energy stored in the rotor friction disc is dissipated through convection, but this amount may vary significantly with changes in speed. On track when the mechanism of

Heat transfer through convection becomes more effective if cool air can be provided to the rotor. This Z06 Corvette comes equipped with front and rear brake cooling ducts from the factory to enhance convective cooling. The mesh screening prevents road debris from contaminating the rotors. (Randall Shafer)

Around town, brake cooling through radiation is nearly negligible. However, on the track, it can become quite significant. This vehicle has heat-reflective sleeves placed over its rubber ball joint boots to prevent them from melting due to extreme heating through radiation. (Randall Shafer)

CHAPTER 10

Brake Cooling Ducts

One of the least expensive, yet highly effective, brake system modifications is to install a set of brake cooling ducts. As you've probably already guessed, brake cooling ducts direct cooler air from the leading edge of the vehicle to the warmer brake system components in order to increase the amount convective heat transfer.

A properly designed brake cooling duct collects air from a high-pressure area on the leading edge of the vehicle. At the inlet, every attempt should be made to funnel as much air from this high-pressure source as possible. Several commercially available designs and patterns exist, so there's usually no need to fabricate an inlet from scratch.

The hose itself should be no less than three inches in diameter. While many race catalogs feature high-temperature products for this purpose, it's not uncommon to see hoses fabricated from flexible dryer ducting supplied by the local home improvement store in the race paddock area. It's not glamorous, but it works.

The hose should be routed in the most direct manner possible as to not disturb the flow of air to the rotor. Care should be taken to ensure that the wheel and tire do not contact or otherwise mutilate the hose when the steering wheel is turned (yes, this is the voice of experience talking).

Finally, the hose should be terminated at a backing plate to direct the cool air to the center of the vented rotor. Without a backing plate, the cool air may not find its way to the rotor at all, in which case the benefit of the ducts may be compromised.

Properly designed brake cooling ducts can greatly increase the effectiveness of convective cooling on track. The path from the duct inlet to the rotor should be as direct as possible to minimize flow restrictions. After installation, be sure that the tire won't make contact with the duct under full steering conditions! (StopTech/Davis Motorsports)

The most important step in adding brake cooling ducts is to direct the incoming stream of air to the center of the rotor. A good set of backing plates force the air to the vane inlets without letting it escape to the free air in the fender well. (StopTech)

radiation becomes more pronounced, convective cooling remains significant but accounts for a lower percentage of the total heat transferred.

Radiation

Whereas conduction and convection both rely on a physical interface to transfer heat from a warmer object to a cooler object, *radiation* is the transmission of energy through the emission of electromagnetic waves. Photons, traveling at the speed of light, transfer energy from the sun to the earth in this fashion.

Unlike conduction and convection, the rate of irradiative heat transfer is proportional to the difference in temperature between the warmer object and its surroundings *raised to the fourth power*. Therefore, if the temperature difference between the warmer object and its surroundings is doubled, the rate of irradiative heat transfer will increase by *sixteen times*.

For this reason, the cooling contribution of radiation is negligible at low temperatures, but grows significantly as temperatures increase. While practically

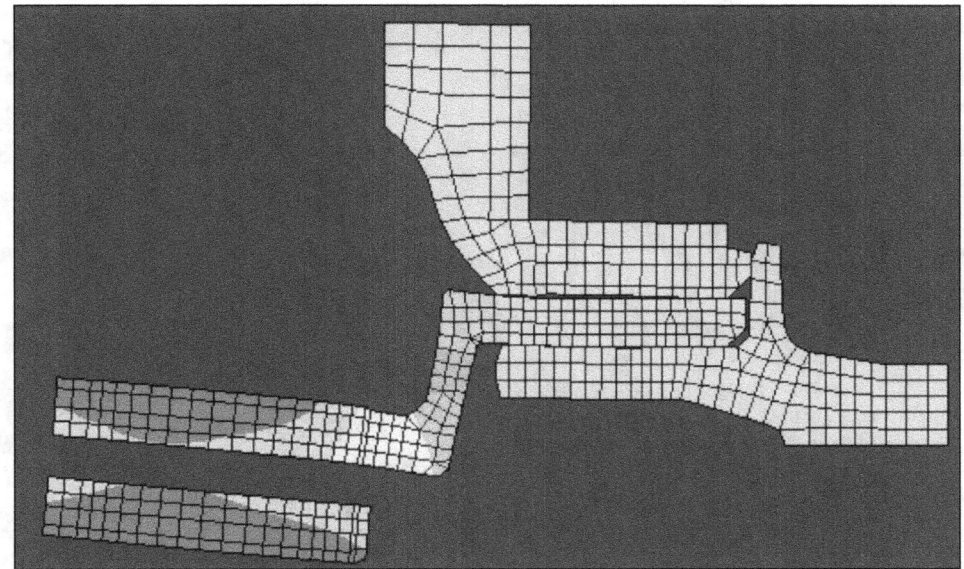

One compromise of the one-piece rotor design is its tendency to distort at high temperatures. As this simulated cross-section shows, the outboard friction disc runs at a cooler temperature (less red) than the inboard friction disc (more red). This is because it's attached to the rotor hat, allowing for better conductive cooling. As a result, the friction disc warms unevenly and distorts upward. This phenomenon is known as rotor coning and leads to radial taper wear of the brake pads. (Delphi Corporation)

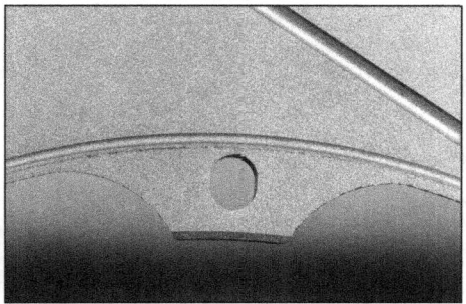

In order to provide unrestricted growth at elevated temperatures, the rotor friction disc and hat cannot be rigidly bolted together. In the application shown above, they're assembled using slotted attachment features, allowing for free radial movement. This can greatly reduce rotor coning. (Randall Shafer/StopTech)

non-existent around town, irradiative heat transfer may account for up to half of the total rotor friction disc cooling when on track, albeit for very short durations.

In order to deflect this large amount of radiant energy away from neighboring brake system components, *radiant barriers* can be selectively applied. These ceramic coatings are commonly found on the inner surfaces of brake calipers, and can significantly reduce irradiative heat transfer to the caliper body.

One-Piece (Fixed) Rotors

As their name implies, *one-piece rotors* are formed from one continuous piece of cast iron. This means that the rotor friction disc and hat are bound to one another rigidly, which under most circumstances, is a good thing. Due to their low cost, simple design, and adequate thermal performance, one-piece rotors are the norm for nearly every road-going production vehicle today.

Because one-piece rotors are asymmetric by design (the hat is only attached to one of the two friction discs), the inboard and outboard rotor friction discs thermally expand at different rates. This results in radial distortion of the friction disc, or *rotor coning*, when subjected to high temperatures. In even moderate cases, rotor coning can lead to radial brake pad taper and/or poor brake pedal feel. Consequently, much of the art of one-piece rotor design revolves around gooseneck-shaped hat sections to minimize the coning effect.

Just because a rotor is made from one piece of gray cast iron doesn't mean that it can't have performance aspirations. This one-piece rotor measures 14.0 inches in diameter and 1.3 inches in width—enough thermal mass for nearly any application. (Randall Shafer/StopTech)

Unfortunately, not even geometric design tricks can prevent the unwanted conductive heat transfer that occurs from the friction discs to the rotor hat section (and ultimately to the wheel bearings) with one-piece rotors. When combined with their tendency to distort at high temperatures, it becomes apparent that one-piece rotors are ultimately unacceptable in a high-performance application.

Two-Piece (Floating) Rotors

In order to overcome the inherent shortcomings associated with garden-variety one-piece rotors, *two-piece rotors* are standard equipment in any serious

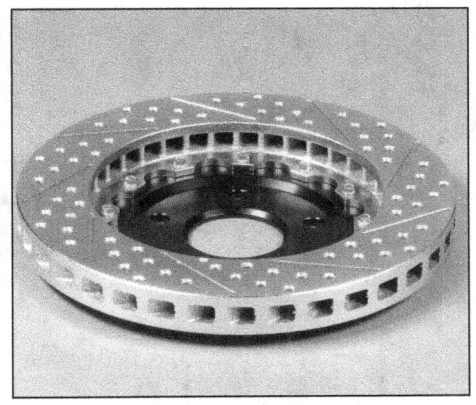

As their name suggests, two-piece rotors consist of a separate friction disc and rotor hat assembled together. While there are many advantages to this design, a primary benefit is reduced rotational inertia. (Randall Shafer/Baer)

CHAPTER 10

If two-piece rotors are used in environments where road salt is present, corrosion can form more readily between the friction disc and rotor hat. Over time, this can reduce float and increase stress at the attachment points. Consequently, rotors used in this environment should be plated with a material such as zinc. (Randall Shafer/StopTech)

high-performance application. Although more expensive to produce and more temperamental to maintain than their one-piece cousins, the performance of a properly designed two-piece rotor is second to none.

As stated earlier, two-piece rotors are designed to allow the rotor friction disc to expand and contract radially during use. This is accomplished by fastening the cast iron friction disc to the rotor mounting hat with specialized hardware that allows for radial movement, or *float*, between the two. This in turn prevents rotor coning at high temperatures. Consequently, radial brake pad taper due to rotor distortion is all but eliminated.

Note that based on the mounting design, axial float can also be provided.

Solid rotors are typically found on the rear axle of many modern, front-wheel-drive vehicles. Why? Because the thermal needs in these applications are quite low. However, it's not uncommon to also find them on the front axle of many lightweight home-built hot rods. (Randall Shafer)

When coupled with radial float, both running drag losses and knockback sensitivity can be greatly reduced.

A second advantage is that two-piece rotor hats are typically fabricated from lightweight materials, thereby reducing the overall rotational inertia. In most applications, aluminum is the material of choice due to its low weight, reasonable cost, and ease of machining. More exotic metals like magnesium can also be used, but as already stated their cost makes them scarce in all but the highest levels of racing.

Benefit number three is reduced conductive heat transfer through the rotor hat. Because the rotor friction disc and rotor hat are typically fabricated from dissimilar materials, the rate of conductive heat transfer is slower through a two-piece rotor than it is through a one-piece rotor. In applications where wheel bearing longevity is a concern, this can be quite an advantage. Of course the heat must go somewhere else instead, so this should not be confused with a free

Wheel Design and Rotor Cooling

Convective cooling relies on cool air absorbing heat from the rotor's warm surface. However, once the air has increased in temperature, it needs somewhere to go so that fresh, cool air can take its place in the convective cooling cycle. In short, an appropriate escape route is needed for the used, warm air to be drawn away from the vehicle. For this reason, most racing wheels have large, open-spoke designs to maximize the amount of airflow around the rotor itself, thereby enhancing the overall convective cooling.

In addition to holding the tires in place, wheels can also play a part in brake cooling. Choosing a wheel with a large amount of open area can provide an efficient outlet for warm air exiting the rotor vanes. (The Tire Rack)

In racing applications, a fan-type device can be fitted to the wheel face to draw warm air from the fender area out into the fast-moving air stream. In most street applications there is little need to go to these extreme measures, but be sure to avoid wheel designs or wheel covers that smother the airflow through the wheel face, attractive as they may be. For the best brake system performance, select a wheel with the most rotor showing.

In order to enhance convective cooling, two solid rotors can be connected together with a series of webs or vanes. Due to their superior thermal capabilities, vented rotors are found on the front axle of most vehicles on the road today. In this photo you can also observe material removed from the outer diameter of the friction disc for balancing purposes. (Randall Shafer/StopTech)

Curved-vane vented rotors use discrete left-handed and right-handed rotor friction discs. The curved internal profile of the vanes incrementally increases the pumping efficiency, drawing more cool air through the center of the rotor. The rotor above uses vanes of varying lengths to further maximize convective cooling. (Randall Shafer/StopTech)

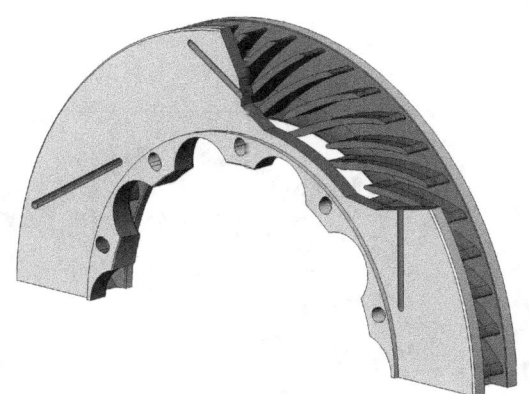
Both curved vane rotors and differential vane rotors are directionally sensitive. In other words, they're designed to operate best when installed on one side of the vehicle or the other. The cut-away image shown above illustrates the vane orientation for a rotor on the left-hand side of a vehicle (normally spinning counter-clockwise). The right-hand side part would have the vanes swept in the opposite orientation. (StopTech)

lunch. Increased rotor temperatures will most likely be observed, but at least the wheel bearings will be happier.

The final advantage of the two-piece design is that when the rotor friction disc needs replacing, the rotor hat can typically be reused. The mounting hardware probably should be tossed out with the used friction disc, but reusing the hat can be a significant cost savings.

So what are the compromises that must be made with two-piece rotors? Besides the aforementioned rattling around under certain conditions, two-piece rotors certainly carry a premium price tag due to their intricate design and manufacturing complexity. In addition, corrosion between the rotor friction disc and rotor mounting hat in daily-driven street applications can reduce the float over time, but regular inspections should detect any signs trouble before it becomes a performance concern.

Solid Rotors

Not to be confused with one-piece rotors, *solid rotors* use a friction disc machined from a solid piece of gray cast iron without internal cooling passages. In other words, solid rotor friction discs are nothing more than a giant metallic Life Saver.

Because the convective heat transfer mechanism is only able to act against the outer surface of the solid rotor friction disc, the material at the core of the friction disc does not have an efficient method of dissipating its thermal energy. And while some degree of convective cooling still occurs at the outer surface, the airflow patterns are quite random and turbulent.

The simplest vented rotors use multiple radial vanes. As the rotor spins at increasing speed, these vanes create a pumping effect, drawing cool air through the center of the rotor. This in turn increases heat transfer due to convective cooling. (Randall Shafer)

In carbon/carbon brake applications, it would be extremely difficult to construct internal cooling vanes, straight, curved, or otherwise. Consequently, a series of straight radial holes are used to allow airflow through the rotor friction disc. (Randall Shafer)

Cross-drilling rotors may do more harm than good, but the holes certainly do give you the high-performance look. When cross-drilling the holes, it's imperative that they never intersect the internal rotor vanes, as this could lead to rapid failure of the friction disc. (Randall Shafer/StopTech)

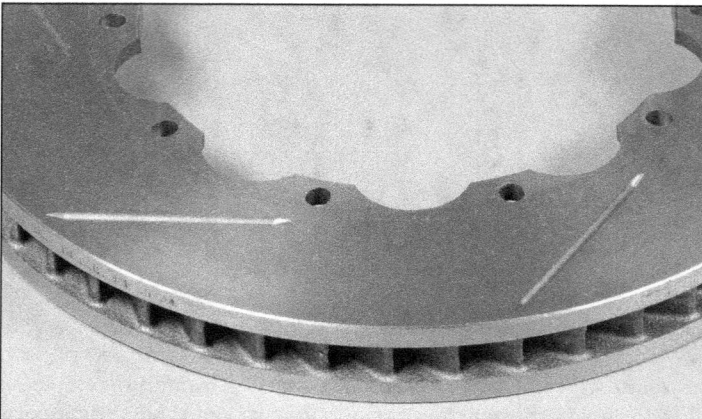
Slotted rotors are the performance standard found in all classes of racing where they're allowed. These shallow grooves machined in the face of the friction disc continuously wipe away the glazed friction interface, exposing fresh material for the next brake application. Brake pad life certainly can suffer, but the end result is much more consistent brake system gain. (Randall Shafer/StopTech)

In summary, while solid rotors may provide acceptable performance on small, lightweight vehicles, they're typically avoided in high-performance applications due to their poor convective heat transfer characteristics.

Vented Rotors

In applications where significant heat is expected, *vented rotors* are the norm. Vented rotors consist of two solid friction discs joined together with a series of central support webs, or *vanes*, which act as internal cooling passages. When spun at high speed, these vanes force air through the center of the rotor, increasing rotor convective cooling. This mechanism alone can greatly reduce rotor operating temperatures.

Straight Vanes

Due to their ease of manufacturability, *straight vanes* are the most common type of vane design. These vanes extend radially from the inner diameter of the friction disc outward. This design is often used in high-volume production vehicles because the same part can be used on both sides of the vehicle.

Curved (Directional) Vanes

Curved vanes are shaped like arcs to increase the volume of air pumped through the rotor's internal cooling passages. This can greatly enhance the convective cooling capability of the rotor. While this dictates unique (and more expensive) left-handed and right-handed, or *directional*, rotors, they are universally used in racing applications where cast iron rotors are mandated. As a side benefit, due to their sweeping design, curved vanes can also help to reduce the spread of radial cracking in the friction disc.

Differential Vanes

The need for increased rotor cooling in severe applications has recently led to the development of *differential*

The slotting pattern doesn't matter as much as the number of leading edges created. More slots yield more cleaning action at the expense of decreased brake pad life. Like everything else in brake system design, it's an exercise in balancing compromises. (Wayne Flynn/pdxsports.com)

BRAKE ROTORS

vanes. These rotors use curved vanes of alternating lengths. Airflow studies have indicated that alternating the vane inlet geometry can increase the volume of air pumped through the rotor without a significant sacrifice in cooling passage surface area. As a result, even more convective cooling is realized than with conventional curved vanes.

Pillars

In some vented rotor applications, vanes can be replaced with *pillars* or *islands* to separate the two solid friction discs from one another. When properly implemented, these alternative designs can provide a measure of dimensional stability to the rotor, but will be more inefficient from an airflow perspective. They are non-directional, however, so their low cost and ease of manufacture make them an attractive design compromise.

Cross-Drilled Rotors

Cross-drilled rotors display a pattern of non-intersecting radial holes along the friction disc face. While these design features certainly convey the high-performance image, unless your vehicle is using brake pads from the 1950s, they're probably not doing very much for your overall brake system performance.

Rotors were first cross-drilled because early brake pad materials produced a significant amount of volatile gasses when heated to racing temperatures (see *gassing out* in Chapter 9). These gasses (along with brake pad material worn away at the frictional interface) would form a thin boundary layer between the brake pad face and the rotor, acting as a lubricant. The end result was an effective reduction in the coefficient of friction between the brake pad and the rotor, a condition not too much unlike conventional brake pad fade.

Because friction materials at the time could not be formulated to avoid this condition, rotors were cross-drilled to give the inevitable gasses an escape path away from the frictional interface. It was an effective solution at the time, but today's friction materials do not exhibit the same level of gassing out as older friction materials.

A secondary benefit was that the very same brake pads that were subject to gassing out also displayed very low levels of bite. By drilling dozens of holes in the friction disc, the effective bite increased significantly, albeit at the sacrifice of brake pad longevity. However, modern friction materials have increased their bite to such a level that cross drilling is no longer required to make up for low brake pad output.

For these reasons, cross-drilled holes have carried over in modern brake systems more as a cosmetic feature than as a

Why just cross-drill or slot when you can cross-drill and slot? That would make this a one-piece, vented, cross-drilled, and slotted rotor. In this particular application, the rotor hat also integrates the wheel bearing inner races and wheel studs, making it even more complex to describe. (Randall Shafer/Baer)

Regardless of the slotting pattern used, individual slots should never extend to the edge of the rotor. In the case of the rotor shown, cracks are quite likely to develop at the point where the slot continues out past the outer diameter of the friction disc (a thermal stress riser). (Randall Shafer)

Cryogenic Treatment

The cryogenic treatment of brake rotors has recently been advertised as the miracle cure for rotor wear, rotor cracking, and brake pad life. Although every manufacturer has their own proprietary process, in general these treatments slowly cool the rotors to extremely low temperatures (around -300 degrees F) and then just as slowly warm them back up to room temperature. If you read the testimonials, it doesn't matter if you treat machine tools, aluminum baseball bats, valve springs, gun barrels, or brass trombones—they all can benefit from the chilling process in some way.

Proponents of cryogenic treatment claim that the rotor's gray cast iron grain structure is changed or refined by the process. However, there is considerable debate about its effectiveness since the claims are backed entirely by anecdotal evidence. To date, no scientific and/or quantitative engineering studies have been published that can prove or disprove the benefits. In fact, when researching for this book, I found absolutely no published data, only statements of, "the life of the brake rotor has increased by over three times," "treated rotors easily last all weekend," and that treated rotors "reduce or eliminate warping."

Conversely, there does not appear to be any harm to the process either...unless one considers the negative impact to the checkbook.

Every rotor has its minimum recommended thickness cast, stamped, or machined on its periphery. While easily discernable when new, with time and corrosion the marking may become difficult to read. If you can't make out the numbers, chances are the disc should be replaced anyway. (Randall Shafer)

Heat checking is the first phase of rotor cracking. Unfortunately, this is simply the result of using friction discs made from gray cast iron and is largely unavoidable. The heat check marks shown on this particular rotor are not quite large enough to merit replacement, but will be once they reach the edge of the friction disc. (StopTech/Davis Motorsports)

performance feature. While occasional benefits may be seen in rotor cooling (the holes can act as additional inlets for air entering the vanes), these gains can be offset by an overall reduction in thermal mass. More holes equal less gray cast iron to absorb thermal energy.

In addition, cross-drilled holes invariably create thermal stress risers in the friction disc, which can accelerate rotor cracking. While some manufacturers cast these holes at the foundry, they still self-destruct more quickly than a solid-faced rotor. Yes, chamfering, radiusing, and/or peening the hole inlet can help to slow down the propagation of cracks, but without exception a rotor with discontinuities in the friction disc cannot be expected to last as long as a rotor that is left unmolested.

So are cross-drilled rotors to be avoided at all costs? Not necessarily. In applications where there is too much thermal mass, drilling the rotors like Swiss cheese can help to reduce rotational inertia. Look at any performance motorcycle, lightweight formula car, or race kart for an example. These rotors will certainly crack sooner and wear out their brake pads at a higher rate than their non-cross-drilled counterparts, but that's the tradeoff made in exchange for enhanced performance in other areas.

Slotted Rotors

In contrast to cross-drilling dozens of holes through the rotor, slotting consists of machining a few shallow grooves across the face of the friction disc. Typically one to two millimeters deep and two to four millimeters wide, these slots can take on a variety of designs and pat-

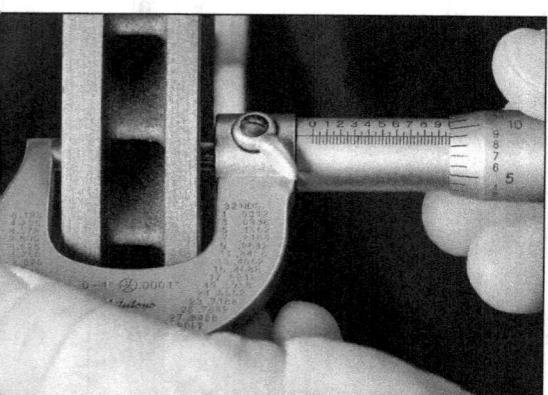

Before a rotor can be resurfaced, you must check its thickness. The dimension measured needs to be greater than the rotor's minimum thickness, since material is removed during the turning process. (Randall Shafer)

Circumferential grooves on the face of the rotor friction disc can occur for a variety of different reasons; however, if they aren't significantly deep or wide, they're not reason for immediate concern. The grooves above were generated due to the cross-drilling pattern of the rotor itself. (Randall Shafer)

Friction disc cracking is one of the most catastrophic failure modes of the rotor assembly. Felt at first as a severe vibration under braking, if ignored long enough it can lead to fragmentation of the entire brake assembly. A cracked rotor needs to be replaced immediately, if not sooner.

BRAKE ROTORS

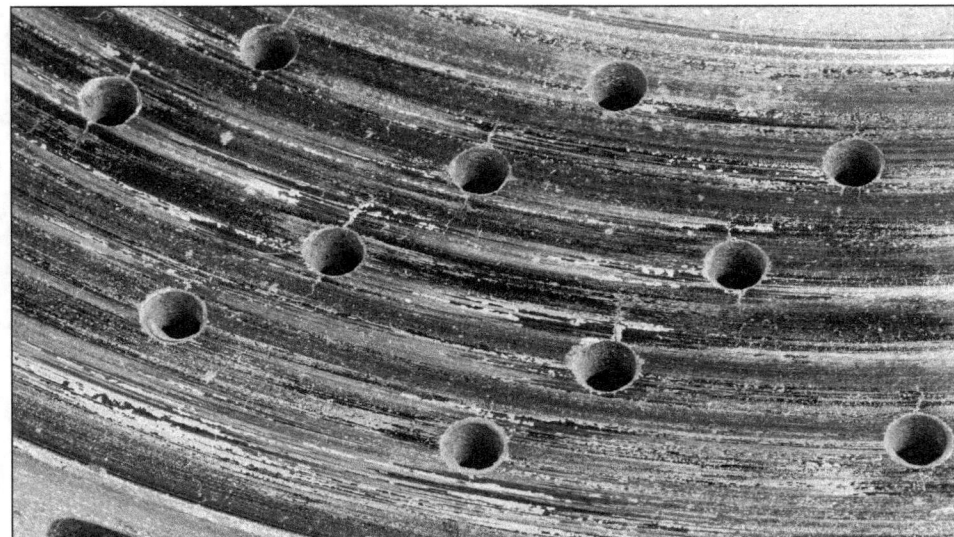

The cross-drilled rotor shown here is in the early stages of crack propagation. What starts as short radial heat check marks eventually migrate all the way to the edge of the friction disc, resulting in catastrophic failure. While this rotor doesn't need to be replaced quite yet, inspection frequency should increase at this point. (Randall Shafer)

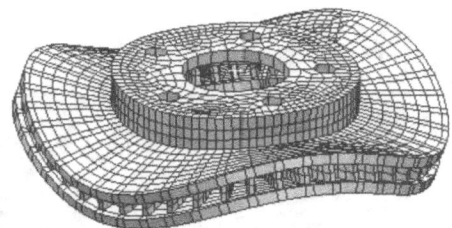

Contrary to popular belief, rotors don't warp like the image above would have you believe. Brake vibration is actually the result of friction disc thickness variation, not mechanical deformation of the rotor itself. (Delphi Corporation)

Rotor Inspection

Due to the intense thermal cycling and mechanical stresses experienced by the rotor friction disc during use, over time it may be subjected to a variety of different wear-out modes. Every rotor and every application is slightly different, but the short list that follows describes the most common means of rotor fatigue and failure. A regular inspection and maintenance schedule goes a long way toward identifying and correcting these conditions before they lead to a more catastrophic conclusion.

terns. Whether the design is simple straight lines, an array of semi-circles, or an elliptical pattern reminiscent of a child's Spirograph creation, slotted rotors can offer many of the benefits of cross-drilled rotors without many of the negative side effects.

First, although modern brake pad friction materials are vastly superior to materials formulated in the recent past, in extreme cases there still may be a small amount of gassing out and/or brake pad dust lubricating the pad-to-rotor interface. This can result in varying gain from stop to stop. Under these conditions, slots give the gasses and incandescent particles somewhere to go, thereby stabilizing the output of the frictional interface during a single stop without significantly impacting the rotor's thermal mass.

A second benefit is that slots can actually help to maintain a stable coefficient of friction over time. During high-speed use, the brake pad friction material found at the friction disc interface can actually get so hot that its chemistry can change. This effect is commonly known as *glazing* and results in a lower coefficient of friction between the pad and the rotor. Slots prevent this condition by slowly shaving away the glazed face of the brake pad friction material, uncovering fresh material each time the brakes are applied. (Of course, cross-drilled holes perform this same function, but at a much higher rate.)

Finally, the advent of modern friction materials has all but eliminated the need for rotor features that enhance brake pad bite; however, in some cases more bite can still be desirable. In these applications, slots can function as leading edges to moderately increase the effective coefficient of friction between the brake pad and the rotor friction disc. It seems that there are as many slotting patterns available as there are brake manufacturers, but the design does not significantly increase bite, if at all. It's a simple matter of more slots equaling more leading edges, which results in increased bite.

The tradeoffs of slotted rotors are similar to those for cross-drilled rotors, but generally less severe. Without a doubt, increased dusting and shorter brake pad life should be expected if slotted rotors are used on the street. For the racer, though, these compromises are readily accepted for brake pad output stability and moderately increased bite. And, while there may still be a small concern over creating stress risers in the face of the rotor, if the slots are shallow and cut properly they won't accelerate rotor cracking to a significant degree (unless they are incorrectly machined past the outer diameter of the friction disc).

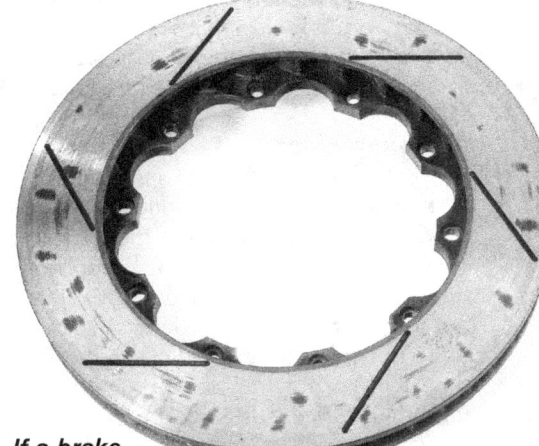

If a brake pad is overheated, it may break down and smear random deposits of friction material on the surface of the friction disc. This can result in localized areas of increased and/or decreased wear. Consequently, these deposits are typically the number one cause of brake vibration during high-performance use. (StopTech)

Abusing the friction disc can also lead to brake vibration. While the entire rotor shown here appears red hot to the naked eye, it may also develop localized areas of extreme temperature, or hot spots. These regions wear more quickly, resulting in accelerated disc thickness variation. (Hawk Performance)

Minimum Thickness

If the brake pads are operating in a predominantly abrasive mode, they will slowly wear away the rotor friction disc. Mechanically, this is no different from turning the rotors continuously on a lathe, but the wear pattern experienced is rarely uniform across the entire face of the friction disc. For this reason, it's common to *turn* or *resurface* the rotor friction disc when new brake pads are installed to re-establish the interface.

When determining whether a rotor should be turned or replaced, the important factor is not how many times it has been turned in the past, but rather how thick the rotor is. Nearly every rotor available has a *minimum thickness* number cast into the back side of the hat section or stamped into the outer diameter of the friction disc. This number is the minimum thickness recommended by the manufacturer after the rotor has been turned, not before.

As a rule of thumb, turning a well-used rotor usually results in taking off at least 0.025 inches of material per side, so be sure to measure beforehand to see if the rotor is a candidate for turning. If you don't have the tools necessary to measure and make the determination yourself, most auto parts stores will be happy to check them for you.

Finally, in racing applications rotors are rarely turned, if ever. This is because turning removes gray cast iron from the rotor friction disc, thereby reducing its thermal mass. Therefore, if a race team has used a rotor to the end of its useful life, it will most likely be replaced outright with a brand new part and not resurfaced. (In fact, most used race rotors are actually *thicker* than new rotors due to the heavy transfer layer build-up on the friction disc.)

Bluing

During severe use, the rotor friction disc may become discolored. In most cases, it acquires a light blue tint after intense thermal cycling (not to be confused with the friction disc discoloration due to the brake pad transfer layer). Although this *bluing* phenomenon is physical evidence of thermal stress, it's quite normal under repeated hard braking and is typically not a cause for concern. However, bluing does indicate that reduced rotor life may be expected, so be sure to monitor the friction disc for other signs of failure and fatigue on a more regular basis.

Grooving

In many applications, it's common to observe concentric, shallow *grooves* on the face of the rotor friction disc. These features can be caused by road

Localized corrosion can also contribute to disc thickness variation. In the image, one can plainly see the outline of the brake pad left in the friction disc. Over time, this results in asymmetric wear rates along the rotor circumference. (Randall Shafer)

debris temporarily caught between the pad and the rotor, a brief overheating of the rotor friction disc, voids in the brake pad material surface, or improper brake pad bedding. (Note that grooving can be initiated by cross-drilling the friction disc as well!) While generally not a major cause for concern, be on the lookout for deep scoring or pitting of the friction disc face—both are valid reasons for rotor replacement.

Heat Checking

Rotor friction disc *heat checking* is the first step down the path of rotor cracking. In fact, heat check marks are actually just very small surface cracks caused by excessive thermal cycling. While heat check marks are not necessarily a concern on their own, they are a warning sign that the disc is not receiving adequate cooling air and/or is experiencing intense thermal stress.

Cracking

Cracking is a catastrophic mechanical failure of the rotor friction disc. In its most benign manifestation, cracking is felt as a severe brake vibration to the driver, while in more extreme cases it can lead to separation of the rotor from the vehicle in the form of shrapnel. In either case, rotor cracking is to be avoided at all costs.

Cracking is typically attributed to the heat cycling of gray cast iron, but the details are sketchy at best. Even material scientists have a hard time explaining the exact reasoning for this failure! However, most agree that rapid heating and subsequent cooling of the rotor around 900 degrees F creates internal stresses in the gray cast iron matrix, which are then relieved by the cracking of the material. Precise control of friction disc chemistry can be used to resist cracking in some applications, but cracking will still occur, albeit at a reduced rate.

When inspecting the rotor friction disc for signs of distress, it's sometimes difficult to differentiate between acceptable heat checking and unacceptable cracking. While no hard and fast rules apply, any time any crack reaches the edge of the rotor friction disc, it's past time for immediate replacement.

Warping

Rotor *warping* is probably the most talked-about variety of rotor failure, both on the street and at the track. It seems that every driver has a story about a vehicle with rotors that were warped so badly that the vibrating brake pedal would give them a therapeutic foot massage.

Unfortunately, this condition is grossly misunderstood, improperly diagnosed, and is typically not a result of any sort of rotor deformation at all. In fact, rotors do not warp, period. The real culprit behind these brake vibrations is rotor friction disc *thickness variation*, or TV.

Thickness Variation

TV is the difference in rotor friction disc thickness between its thickest and thinnest locations. The vibration felt in the steering wheel, floorboard, and brake pedal is caused by the brake caliper piston extending and retracting (and consequently increasing and decreasing brake torque) as it tries to follow the rotor's varying surface thickness. Anecdotally, it only takes a tiny amount of TV in the rotor friction disc (a few ten thousandths of an inch) to generate significant brake vibrations.

While the impact of TV can be almost imperceptible at first, as the brake pads start riding up and down the high and low spots on the rotor friction disc surface, more and more TV is generated until the vibration is much more evident. This downward spiral ends only when the vibration is so severe that the driver refuses to continue until the situation is resolved.

One of the most effective ways to avoid thickness variation is to observe the vehicle manufacturer's recommended specification when tightening lug nuts. Over-tightening can lead to physical distortion of the rotor assembly, which could ultimately result in long-term disc thickness variation. (Randall Shafer)

CHAPTER 10

The only sure-fire way to alleviate brake vibration is to replace the offending rotors. Rotor turning may mask the effects short-term, but in many cases the problem is bound to reappear. If you do end up replacing rotors, be sure to follow the guidelines in this chapter to prevent its reoccurrence in the future. (Randall Shafer)

Uneven Transfer Layer Deposits

So, how does TV occur in the first place? In general, there are three mechanisms through which TV is initiated and propagated, but for the racer and track enthusiast alike the most common mode of TV is created by an uneven transfer layer of brake pad material to the rotor friction disc.

That last point should be restated again, just so there are no misunderstandings: *Uneven brake pad deposits on the rotor friction disc are the number one, and almost exclusive, cause of brake vibrations.*

Improper bed-in of new brake pads is usually to blame here, but bringing a vehicle in from the racetrack without cooling the brakes can also create this condition. Given enough heat and time, most brake pads are more than willing to continue their adherent bonding while at rest, and transfer to the rotor in small, seemingly random spots. Overheating the brake pad material can also generate an uneven transfer layer as it breaks down and splotches (a highly technical term!) on the rotor face.

Regardless of the cause, the uneven transfer layer deposits wear at a different rate than the surrounding rotor friction disc material. On and on it goes until the high spots and low spots on the rotor face are severe enough to be felt in the brake pedal by the driver.

Hot Spotting

The second most common source of TV begins with overheating the rotor friction disc. When operating at extreme temperatures, the friction disc can develop evenly spaced, localized areas along its circumference that are much hotter than the surrounding material. These *hot spots* wear more quickly than the adjacent cooler material, creating a thick-and-thin wear pattern. As the friction disc cools, these thick and thin spots remain and will propagate with use until the driver senses the TV.

Corrosion

Although less glamorous than transfer layer uniformity and hot spotting, TV can also be initiated when a vehicle is parked for an extended period of time. While sitting motionless, a thin layer of *corrosion* can form between the brake pad and the rotor friction disc. Sitting in humid or damp environments combined with use of the parking brake can greatly accelerate this condition.

When the vehicle is eventually moved, there will be a localized thick spot (an unintended transfer layer of corrosion) on the rotor friction disc that wears at a different rate than the surrounding material. At first, the condition is undetectable, but it will continue to get worse over time as the friction disc wears unevenly.

Preventing Thickness Variation

In order to avoid TV in the first place, there are several steps that can and should be taken. First, be sure to follow the manufacturer's recommended procedure for bed-in when installing new brake pads and/or rotor friction discs. These procedures have been developed to reduce the opportunity for uneven brake pad material deposition on the rotor face. In the absence of instructions from the manufacturer, the procedures found back in the Chapter 9 sidebars can be used as a good starting point.

Second, during track days, make absolutely sure to run a cool-off lap or two before coming into the pits and *never* use the parking brake. It also helps to avoid keeping your foot on the brake pedal after coming to rest in the paddock. Any time hot brakes are allowed to

ABS and Rotor Selection

If you choose to replace your stock rotors with aftermarket rotors of the same size, the overall brake system gain will remain unchanged. It doesn't matter if the rotors are one-piece, two-piece, solid, or vented; the gain is only a function of the effective radius. As a result, a stock-sized upgrade is almost always transparent to the ABS.

However, if you're upsizing your rotors in an attempt to increase thermal mass, it's imperative that the effect of the larger effective radius be offset with the selection of smaller caliper pistons. While this is also necessary to maintain appropriate brake balance, returning the overall brake system gain to stock levels also reduces the opportunity for an ABS calibration mismatch. Some big brake kit suppliers do this homework for you, but be sure to ask since your ABS performance could be compromised if this critical step is skipped.

As a final note, it has already been mentioned elsewhere in this chapter that slotting and/or cross-drilling can be used to increase the initial bite of the brake pads. In most applications, this change in gain is small enough and transient enough that the ABS is not adversely affected. However, one last disclaimer must be made that every application has a different sensitivity. As always, your results may vary.

---

sit motionless, adherent molecular bonds may continue to form between the brake pad material and the existing transfer layer. The result is nearly instantaneous TV generation.

Third, keep your brakes as cool as possible during aggressive driving to reduce the opportunity for hot spots. A set of brake cooling ducts goes a long, long way in this regard. Remember, cool brakes are happy brakes.

Fourth, if your vehicle is typically left outside for extended periods of time, it might be best to select a non-semi-metallic brake pad. NAO and/or some ceramic brake pads can reduce the tendency to generate corrosion between the brake pad and the rotor friction disc. While they are not usually recommended for high-performance applications, they don't rust as fast, and over time this may reduce the generation of TV on your garage queen.

Fifth, when installing your wheels and tires, make sure to tighten your lug nuts in the manufacturer's recommended pattern and take several passes to reach maximum torque. In some applications, uneven tightening of the lug nuts can physically distort the rotor hat enough that during normal driving thick and thin spots may develop on their own. (Arguably, two-piece rotors may be more robust to an uneven torque sequence than one-piece rotors, but your wheels will appreciate it in either case.)

Curing Thickness Variation

In some applications where brake vibration has *just* begun, it may be possible to remove any uneven transfer layer deposits from the rotor face by using a super-abrasive brake pad for a brief period. Unfortunately, this is a hit-and-miss strategy, and if uneven rotor wear has already started then it's too late anyway.

Abrasive brake pads cannot make a rotor flat again; they can only smooth off uneven brake pad deposits.

Turning rotors can sometimes alleviate brake vibrations in the short-term, but typically is not an appropriate solution in high-performance applications (removing cast iron reduces thermal mass after all). If the rotor has been heated to the point that its chemistry has changed (for you metallurgists, if localized areas of cementite have formed), then the vibration very quickly comes back. This is because the softer areas of the rotor friction disc face wear away at an increased rate. Note that in some cases, turning rotors may not cure vibration even for a short time, as the harder spots in the friction disc can actually deflect the brake lathe cutting tool, creating an uneven surface on the rotor face.

Finally, the only absolute long-term solution to purging brake vibration is to replace the rotors and properly bed-in the new parts to ensure an even transfer layer. It may sound like a brute-force approach, but a rotor friction disc that has been hot spotted or worn into a state of extreme TV might not be salvageable.

Summary

So, what's the secret rotor recipe? Again, there's no absolute right or wrong answer, but like most modifications there are rotors that have significant performance benefits and those that simply look the part.

If ultimate performance on track is your goal, you are probably in the market for relatively large (for increased thermal mass), slotted (for decreased glazing), two-piece (for reduced radial taper) rotors with differential vanes (for enhanced convective cooling) and aluminum hats (for reduced rotational inertia). However, if the racer image is the most important factor to you, feel free to break out the drill press and be prepared to replace your brake pads on a regular basis. Like every other component discussed, rotor selection is all about managing compromises.

CHAPTER 11

SPORTS CAR BRAKE UPGRADE

Now that you've read and understand everything about brakes (right?), it's time to explore four different brake improvement projects. In other words, it's time to grab the wrenches and head out to the garage to bolt on some high-performance brake hardware. Each upgrade scenario has its own set of unique conditions and constraints, but by referencing these four chapters, you'll be better prepared to address any challenges your own vehicle may throw at you.

To kick things off, we're going to get our hands dirty (literally) walking through the installation of two-piece rotors, high-performance brake pads, four-piston fixed calipers, and stainless steel brake hoses behind the front wheels of a modern sports sedan—the quintessential *big brake upgrade*. It's important to note that these same steps and considerations apply to practically any vehicle going through a front disc brake upgrade. Whether you are working on a late-model Camaro, an Acura Integra, an Audi A6, or a Ford GT,

While most brake upgrades can be performed by the average enthusiast, remember that you're tinkering with one of your vehicle's most important safety systems. For this reason, you need not only your tools, jack, and jack stands, but also a healthy dose of experience and common sense. If you question your abilities in the least, enlist the services of a professional. (Randall Shafer)

118   HIGH-PERFORMANCE BRAKE SYSTEMS: DESIGN, SELECTION AND INSTALLATION

the fundamental sequence of events remains the same.

However, in parallel with selecting and installing the upgraded components, we also take the time to address system-level characteristics such as gain, balance, and pedal feel. For this reason, we frequently reference equations from Chapters 1 through 4 in order to juggle these sometimes conflicting requirements while optimizing overall brake system performance.

The Vehicle

Representative of many compact sports cars on the market today, the BMW 330i is a competent performance machine. Like several other vehicles of this nature, this particular example is used primarily for commuting and driving around town, but on weekends it is driven to the limit at high-speed driving schools and racetrack lapping events. Consequently, a high-performance brake system upgrade was desired that would balance the needs of street and track use.

The Objective

Although its six-cylinder engine produces only a modest 235 hp, this car's 3,300-pound curb weight contributes to significant brake system temperatures when driven aggressively. Being a BMW, there is certainly autobahn DNA in the brake system design, but like any production passenger vehicle, its stock brake system hardware is biased toward high-speed cruising more than toward generating fast lap times around a road course.

In fact, that last statement is true for practically *any* street-driven vehicle. Whether you drive a turbocharged sport compact, a high-performance V-12 exotic, a or a modern muscle machine, brake systems designed for street use simply don't cut it when driven hard on track.

Although increasing the BMW's brake system thermal capacity quickly became the primary objective, we wanted to make this improvement without making any sacrifices when driving around town. In other words, a dedicated, race-only solution with dual master cylinders and aggressive brake pads was not a viable option.

Therefore, the plan was to replace the brake rotors and calipers with pieces more suited toward high-performance driving while retaining the stock apply system hardware. An equally important objective was to accomplish this task while maintaining stock brake system gain and brake balance. Without the constraints of sanctioning body rules and regulations, our only limiting factor was our checkbook.

Removing the wheels and supporting the vehicle on suitable jack stands is usually the most safety-critical step in any brake system installation. Once you have the vehicle safely in the air, you have easy access to its stock brake system components. Regardless of which make and model you're working on, the stock front brakes probably look a lot like this. (Randall Shafer)

Picking the Right Parts

Even though the vehicle's front-to-rear weight distribution is a respectable 50/50 at rest, under 1.05g of deceleration, the weight distribution shifts to approximately 80/20. Typical of most production-based vehicles, this suggests that the rear brakes are probably not the primary area of concern. As a result, we elected to focus on the thermal mass and performance of the front brakes while leaving the rear brakes alone.

Fortunately, a complete front big brake upgrade kit is available for this vehicle from StopTech. While the kit consists of upgraded front rotors, calipers, brake hoses, and brake pads (smart parts), the icing on top is that the individual components are designed to be compatible from a gain and balance perspective as well (smart system).

Front Rotors

As with any thermal mass upgrade, the most important step is to select and install new front rotors. The stock 330i rotors measure 12.8 inches in diameter and 1.0 inch

The objective of this project was to select and install a brake system that's capable of great around-town driving while being able to sustain the abuse of weekend track events. For this reason, we decided to focus on the front brake system components, as they were the limiting factor for the brake system's thermal performance. (Randall Shafer)

Begin by removing your rotor's retaining fastener. Measuring 12.8 inches in diameter and 1.0 inch in thickness, the stock 330i's front rotors certainly aren't undersized for daily driving. However, when exposed to the rigors of track use, the system is barely capable of maintaining adequate performance for even three laps. (Randall Shafer)

Our project 330i came with floating, cast-iron front calipers containing single 2.2-inch diameter pistons. They unbolt from the brackets as shown. We swapped them for four-piston aluminum fixed calipers to increase efficiency and to reduce weight. (Randall Shafer)

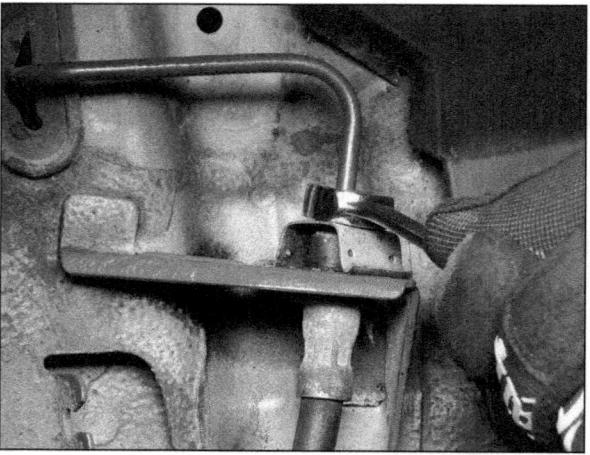

At some point, performing a brake upgrade requires opening the hydraulic circuit. Brake line fasteners are notorious for corroding in place, and as a result, it's a good idea to only service them with flare nut wrenches available from most tool suppliers. In any case, be prepared to clean up spilled brake fluid before it gets a chance to mar your vehicle's paint. (Randall Shafer)

in thickness and are tucked underneath stock 18-inch diameter wheels. In theory, a pair of 14.0-inch diameter rotors would have fit inside the stock 18-inch diameter wheels, but since we wanted to run 17-inch diameter wheels at track days, we selected 13.1-inch rotors that are 1.3 inches thick.

To further improve rotor cooling, we chose friction discs with differential vanes to replace the straight-vaned stock parts. We also went with a two-piece design to reduce radial brake pad taper at elevated temperatures, with the added benefit of reduced rotational inertia. Finally, we chose to have the friction discs slotted. (Although the additional leading edges reduce brake pad life on the street, in this application their on-track performance benefits justify the compromise. Plus, the slots provide the desirable high-performance look, too!)

Front Calipers

The stock 330i floating calipers are made from cast iron and incorporate a single 2.2-inch diameter piston. It didn't take very long to decide to upgrade to a pair of aluminum, two-piece, multi-piston fixed calipers. After all, decreased weight, increased efficiency (better pedal feel), and optimized pressure distribution across the brake pad backing plate (reduced taper wear) are desirable both on the street as well as on the track.

To take full advantage of the multi-piston geometry, StopTech implements differential piston bores of 1.3 inches and 1.5 inches in this application to reduce longitudinal brake pad taper. While this design increases brake pad life on its own, the calipers also use larger brake pads than stock, providing an increased amount of friction material for longer brake pad life.

Note that because the StopTech calipers are a universal design, 330i-specific mounting brackets are required to attach them to the stock suspension uprights. Fortunately, they were included in the kit, alleviating the need to fabricate custom brackets.

Hoses, Fluids, and Pads

While filling up our shopping cart, we also decided to upgrade the stock rubber overmolded brake hoses with high-performance stainless steel brake hoses. Although there was no reason to upgrade based on thermal needs alone, the reduced compliance would provide improved brake pedal feel.

For brake fluid, we chose Motul RBF600, a high-performance DOT 4 blend. A dry boiling point of 594 degrees F indicates that brake fluid fade shouldn't be an issue when new, and a wet boiling point of 421 degrees F suggests performance should be maintained even with a significant amount of moisture adsorbed into the fluid. (In spite of these quality numbers though, brake bleeding on track days is still a good idea to keep the brake pedal as firm as possible.)

Like many performance street cars, this one will be primarily driven on public roads, so we wanted to select brake pads that would perform well at low temperatures. However, well-rounded cars like this also see the track, so high-temperature robustness was just as necessary to prevent brake pad fade. To satisfy these conflicting needs, we ended up going with two sets of brake pads—one material for around-town driving and another material for hot laps on the weekend.

For street use, we chose a semi-metallic brake pad friction material to replace the stock non-asbestos organic material. Why? To allow for moderately increased thermal performance during spirited driving while maintaining acceptable levels of wear and noise. On the track though, the street brake pads will be replaced with a dedicated racing compound specifically designed to deal with the heat generated under green flag conditions. (Unfortunately, the elevated levels of rotor wear, brake dust, and noise from the race pads would make them unacceptable on a daily basis.)

Bolting Them On

Once the new brake hardware arrived, it was time to unpack the boxes, roll out the tool box, and get dirty. The following paragraphs walk you through some of the more unusual and complex steps we encountered on the BMW, but don't forget that these same basic steps and sequences apply to nearly any front big brake kit installation.

Stock Caliper Removal

When performing a front brake upgrade, the first step is typically to loosen the two bolts securing the stock caliper to the suspension upright. Note that a significant amount of torque is used to secure these fasteners in most applications, and therefore it's not uncommon to need the longest breaker bar in the tool box to start working them free. Since our bolts would be reused later in the installation, we cleaned them with a wire wheel and set them aside.

After loosening the brake-hose-to-brake-line fitting, we removed the caliper from the vehicle. During this step is it critical to

System Performance: Gain and Balance

While sizing up this project, we performed a few quick calculations to ensure that brake balance and gain were not significantly altered from the stock configuration. Before going any further, however, please note that if the thought of performing all of these calculations on your own has your head spinning, never fear. The point of this exercise is to show you what is involved in selecting the right parts for your own application. By knowing the steps (even without being able to perform them all yourself), you know the right questions to ask the person who is trying to sell you their product. A quality brake system supplier is able to do the math for you.

Using actual values for our front calipers and rotors and recalling select equations from Chapters 3 and 8, the following numbers were generated:

	Effective Piston Area (in^2)	Rotor Effective Radius (in)
Stock 330i:	3.95	5.52 (measured)
StopTech:	3.15	5.62 (measured)

Next, assuming rear brake gain and master cylinder pressure to be constant between the two designs (both were left untouched during this upgrade), the relative gain and balance impacts due only to the front rotor and caliper changes were found to be:

	Gain (compared to stock)	Balance (% front)
Stock 330i:	100%	80% (estimated)
StopTech:	81% (19% reduction)	76% (4% reduction)

In other words, without taking brake pad coefficient of friction into account, the upgraded components decreased front brake gain by 19 percent and increased rear bias by 4 percent. Since this is an unfavorable situation, the front brake pad material coefficient of friction was increased from approximately 0.32 (an estimated value for the stock brake pads) to 0.38 (a value provided by the upgraded brake pad manufacturer) to increase the gain of the front brakes with the following results:

	Gain (compared to stock)	Balance (% front)
Stock 330i (w/ 0.32):	100%	80% (estimated)
StopTech (w/ 0.38):	96% (4% reduction)	79% (1% reduction)

In summary, by using a bit of math it was possible to verify that the vehicle's stock gain and balance characteristics would be unchanged by the high-performance components. And, while it's possible for you to perform these same calculations in the garage, don't be afraid to ask your brake system supplier if they have done the number crunching too!

Since this car would be driven both on the street and at the track, we selected two different friction materials (one street, one track). While it requires swapping the brake pads for track days, performance is optimized under both conditions without compromise. (Randall Shafer/Hawk Performance)

In this particular application, tight clearances between the caliper mounting bracket and the suspension upright prevented the bracket from simply bolting in place. We spent a few minutes with a die grinder removing excess material from the upright mounting ears. Depending on your vehicle, it may also be necessary to remove a small amount of material from the lower control arm, too. (Randall Shafer)

With the flexible brake hose loose from the brake line, the caliper and brake hose were removed from the vehicle as an assembly. In most applications, the brake pads come out too, but you may need to wiggle them around a bit first if they've worn themselves into the rotor friction disc. (Randall Shafer)

remember that the caliper and brake hose are still filled with brake fluid! For this reason, be sure to have a brake fluid-friendly location set aside to place the caliper (like a drain pan), as brake fluid will probably trickle out of the brake hose once you set it down.

Stock Rotor Removal

We had a little trouble getting the stock rotor off. Over time, a layer of corrosion had bonded the hat section to the wheel bearing hub. Armed with a non-marring rubber mallet, it took several blows to dislodge both front rotors from the vehicle. If you experience the same condition, it helps to leave two wheel bolts (or lug nuts) loosely screwed into each hub to keep the rotors from flying onto the ground once they break free.

With the front rotor removed, we cleaned the wheel bearing hub face with a Scotch-Brite pad to allow the upgraded rotor to sit flat on the mounting surface. Regardless of your vehicle, this is an important step that can help prevent brake vibrations down the road and should *not* be skipped.

Caliper Bracket Installation

Before attaching the new rotor and caliper to the suspension upright, we installed our BMW-specific mounting bracket. (Note that this step may not be necessary if your new calipers are manufactured specifically for your vehicle.) Although we could have purchased new fasteners, our kit was designed to reuse the bolts from the stock caliper. Taking a hint from the factory, it's useful to apply a small amount of thread-locking adhesive to these fasteners to prevent the joint from loosening while in service.

Rotor Installation

Test-fitting the caliper to its mounting brackets at this point indicated that the rotor dust shield needed to be modified slightly before the rotor could be installed. We used a manual nibbler tool for the trimming, but in a more extreme racing application we probably would have removed the shield from the vehicle.

Like the stock rotor we had just removed from the vehicle, the new rotor was designed with a retention fastener located in the hat section. Consequently, we slid the rotor on the wheel bearing hub pilot and gently tightened the fastener to secure the rotor in place. If your vehicle uses this same hardware, be sure to apply a dab of anti-seize compound to the fastener to make sure you can get it off in the future.

Caliper Installation

With the rotor in place, we could bolt the caliper to its bracket with a pair of radial studs (part of the BMW bracket assembly) and self-locking nuts. The attaching geometry may be different in your application, but regardless of the design don't forget to

If your rotor has been on the vehicle for a while, it may be necessary to resort to brute force to break it free. Use a rubber mallet to protect the rotor. Note the wheel bolts loosely installed to catch the rotor once it breaks free, preventing damaged parts and broken toes. (Randall Shafer)

SPORTS CAR BRAKE UPGRADE

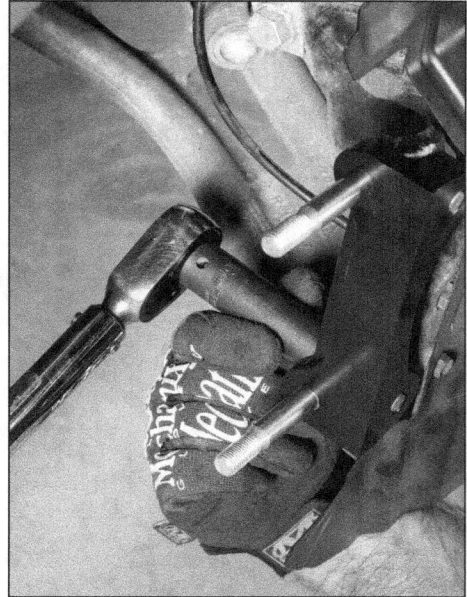

Once we had "modified" our suspension upright, the bracket bolted right in place. Due to the high loads and temperatures experienced by these fasteners, we applied a high-temperature thread-locking adhesive and then tightened them to specification with a torque wrench. Attention to detail like this is highly recommended regardless of the vehicle you are modifying. (Randall Shafer)

use a torque wrench to ensure a sufficient clamp load.

The next step was to load the brake pads into the calipers. Being an open-caliper design, our pads slid into place through an opening in the top of the caliper body. The caliper bridge reinforcement was then bolted in place, serving both to increase the strength of the caliper as well as to hold the brake pads in place. This is

Installing larger calipers may require you to remove a little material from the rotor dust shields. In this particular application, only a small amount needed to be trimmed from the lower edges, but you may need to remove the shields completely in some applications. (Randall Shafer)

another area where your particular brand of caliper may require a different technique, so be sure to read the instructions.

Hoses And Fluids

After installing the new brake hardware, it's usually time to reconnect the hydraulic system. We used a flare nut wrench to prevent damage to the tube nut while attaching the new stainless steel brake hose to the stock brake line, and you should do the same.

When taking this step at home, pay careful attention to route all new hoses following the same path as the stock hoses. Then, with everything tightened down, turn the steering from full left lock to full right lock to ensure that the new hoses are able to move freely without contacting the wheels, tires, or any suspension components. It's important to identify and correct interference issues now instead of five miles down the road!

Once our new brakes were bolted in place, we followed the brake-bleeding procedure found in Chapter 6 to remove the air trapped in the new components. To guarantee that all of our old brake fluid had been replaced by our new DOT 4 fluid, we bled both the front and rear brakes twice, eliminating the possibility that old fluid was still present in the system.

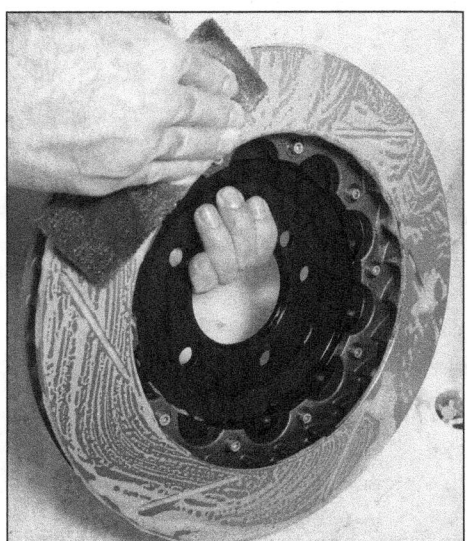

Some rotors are shipped with an anti-corrosion coating, so be sure to scrub them down completely with soap and water before installation. After a few minutes in the washtub, they'll ready to install. (Randall Shafer)

Some vehicles have a fastener that secures the rotor to the wheel bearing hub. Not only does this keep the rotor from falling on the floor, it holds the components parallel to one another during brake fluid bleeding and brake pad replacement. (Randall Shafer)

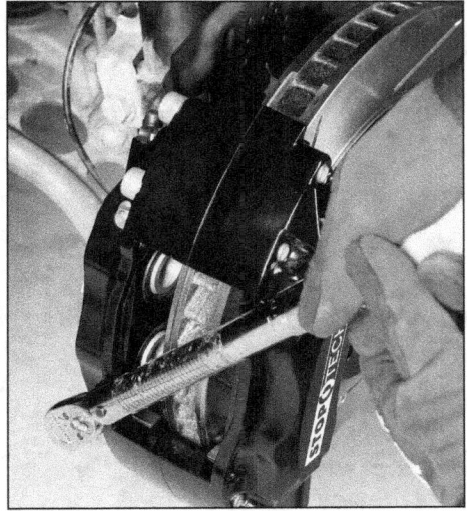

With the caliper seated firmly against the mounting bracket, we torqued down the nuts to specification. Note that after caliper installation, it's a good idea to spin the rotor gently to ensure that the friction disc is centered in the caliper body opening. (Randall Shafer)

Although this vehicle is destined for future track use, we installed a brake pad friction material more suited to day-to-day operation. Once at the track, the removable caliper bridge will facilitate rapid brake pad changes. (Randall Shafer)

Reattaching the brake line can be one of the messiest jobs in a typical brake upgrade project. Most vehicles incorporate a spring element to locate the brake line in the body bracket during assembly, so be prepared to use both hands (and sometimes a third) to make the connection. Put a rag under the joint to keep the mess to a minimum. (Randall Shafer)

While we could have chosen a bunch of different parts, we wanted a system that would work great without compromises. Our upfront attention to detail and a solid understanding of brake system fundamentals allowed us to make the proper selections. (Randall Shafer)

(This is a good time to restate that used brake fluid should be disposed of properly. In most cases this means recycling it like motor oil, but check with your local shop to determine what your options are.)

Wheels and Tires

With the brake upgrade complete, the final step was to install the wheels and tires. Unfortunately, the larger dimensions of the upgraded calipers would not fit under the stock wheels—the wheel spokes would contact the caliper body. We knew this ahead of time, so we found a set of wheels that were the same size as stock, yet allowed sufficient clearance to the brake calipers. As an added benefit, the new wheels weighed approximately 10 pounds less per wheel than the stock parts *and* provided larger openings for enhanced brake cooling.

In order to minimize the impact to ABS, stock replacement tires in stock sizes were selected and mounted on the upgraded wheels. Normally this would have been an opportunity for an upgrade, but because the stock tires were already designed for maximum performance in both dry and wet conditions, there wasn't much room for improvement.

The Results

Upfront attention to system-level details (specifically, the gain and balance relationships) allowed for an increase in thermal mass (larger rotors), decreased brake pad taper wear (differential caliper bores and

Using the 330i's stock wheels would have required a set of 0.6-inch hubcentric wheel spacers to provide the necessary axial caliper clearance. We chose to upgrade the wheels instead. (Randall Shafer)

two-piece rotor design), and reduced compliance (stainless steel brakes hoses and fixed caliper mounting) without creating other brake system performance compromises. As this upgrade proved, smart parts *can* contribute to a smart system.

In addition to these brake system performance enhancements, attention to material selection also proved to be beneficial. By converting from stock cast iron calipers and rotor hats to aluminum components, the overall weight of this brake system decreased by a total of 12 pounds in spite of the fact that the thermal mass of the friction discs increased. When coupled with the 10-pound savings realized at each wheel, a total of approximately 52 pounds was removed from the vehicle during the upgrade. Although it usually comes at a price, reduced weight always provides enhanced vehicle performance, no matter what you drive.

Finally, the extra care taken to maintain stock tire performance, stock gain levels, and stock balance characteristics minimized the impact to ABS. While this may not have been the glamorous part of the upgrade, well-planned brake system upgrades become that much more important as vehicles become more and more reliant upon these electronic technologies.

Wheel Clearance Made Easy

When budgeting for your own brake upgrade, you should determine up front if your new rotors and calipers will fit inside your existing wheels. In many cases, adding the cost of a new set of wheels (not to mention tires!) with the proper clearance can double the cost of your brake upgrade project!

The first wheel fitment parameter is the *radial clearance* to the caliper body. As rotors get larger in diameter, the calipers are moved outward from the wheel center, reducing the clearance with the inner wheel rim. Each application has its own tolerances, but in general, the following guidelines apply:

Rotor Diameter (in)	Minimum Wheel Diameter (in)
12	16
13	17
14	18
15	19

However, even if the new calipers have adequate radial clearance to the rim of your existing wheels, there may still be a concern with *axial clearance*—in other words, they might hit the back side of the wheel spokes. In many cases, the shape and pattern of the wheel spokes are the limiting factor in establishing adequate clearance to the upgraded brake system components. Most systems only require a gap two to three millimeters wide between the caliper body and the back of the wheel spokes, but quite often the stock wheel design just won't cut it.

So how can the average enthusiast determine in advance what packaging pitfalls lay before them? One alternative is to use manufacturer-provided templates to measure your wheels before making your decision. Another option is to follow a manufacturer's recommended procedure for measuring critical dimensions in advance of bolting the parts together. However, both of these methods require information from your brake system supplier, which may not always be available for your application.

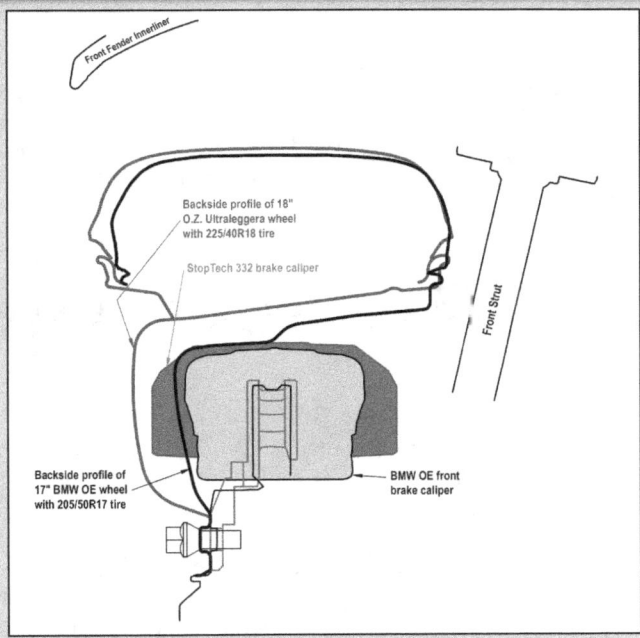

As illustrated above, the upgraded calipers (red) were significantly wider than the stock 330i calipers (pink). Although there was plenty of radial clearance (distance to the rim), we needed a set of wheels with more axial clearance (distance to the spokes). Using proprietary design tools, the team at The Tire Rack was able to take the guesswork out of determining which wheels would fit over the upgraded brake components.
(The Tire Rack)

The high-tech alternative to determine wheel clearance is to use computer-assisted design tools. For example, the engineers at The Tire Rack have developed a process that enables them to overlay most typical brake upgrade profiles with wheels from their extensive catalog. Now, instead of fitment through trial and error, checking for proper clearance is just a mouse click away.

Although increasing thermal mass and improving pedal feel were high on our list of original objectives, the enhanced curb appeal is nice, too. While the new brake system works great both on the street and at the track, the car even looks better standing still.
(Randall Shafer)

CHAPTER 12

RACECAR BRAKE UPGRADE

The brake system components found on competition vehicles have complex and demanding requirements placed on them. Combining high speeds, repetitive braking, and little time for cooling in-between, racetracks have the capability of exposing weaknesses in even the very best stock braking systems in only a few laps. Naturally, the consequences of brake system failure under these conditions is to be avoided at all costs, so when preparing a vehicle for competition, the brake system is usually given priority over more discretionary items.

At the same time, purchasing and installing a big brake kit may not be a viable solution for improving your brake system performance. Constraints such as sanctioning body rules, regulations, or simple budgetary limitations often dictate that the only way to address brake system performance on track is to stick with the factory hardware and improvise. In other words, not everyone has the luxury of bolting on a set of 14-inch floating rotors and 6-piston calipers to address their brake system performance concerns.

No matter what you race, always check your sanctioning body's rulebook before buying any new brake parts, as certain modifications may be prohibited. Consequently, it may require more creativity than cash to make significant brake system performance improvements. In cases like this, a solid understanding of brake system fundamentals ensures that your elbow grease is applied in the correct areas. (Randall Shafer)

Racing in vintage classes may require participants to adhere to arcane rules and regulations from the past. While this is certainly part of the allure of vintage competition, it may prevent you from using modern brake system technology. The 1972 Porsche 911 modified in the pages that follow falls exactly into this category. (Daniel Mainzer)

To provide you with ideas to help you choose your own upgrades, this chapter illustrates some of the most common brake system modifications when racing a production-based vehicle. Note that any time you embark on a project such as this, you should not be second-guessing your design, fabrication, or installation abilities. If in doubt, enlist the services of a professional to ensure that the integrity of the modified components is not compromised in any way!

The Vehicle

In contrast to the daily-driver BMW modified in Chapter 11, the focus of attention in Chapter 12 is a 1972 Porsche 911 prepared exclusively for road racing. Competing primarily in the PCA GT-4s category, this vehicle is occasionally run in SCCA Club Racing events in the GT2 category as well as SVRA group 10c competition. It is truly a jack of all trades, and, as a result, must comply with sanctioning body requirements in multiple classes simultaneously.

The Objective

With approximately 280 hp at the crankshaft and weighing in at just 2,000 pounds, this vehicle is capable of generating a significant amount of kinetic energy in a very short amount of time. Consequently, the stock brake system, designed for much less power and significantly more weight, was not able to keep up with the rest of the vehicle's performance capability.

While brake fade was being managed through friction material selection and a brake fluid upgrade, brake pad taper, brake pad life, and rotor cracking were all causing headaches on track. In addition, there was no adjustability in the stock brake system to adjust the brake balance for the vehicle in full race trim, resulting in extended stopping distances.

Therefore, the objective of this upgrade was to increase the thermal capacity of the brake system in order to reduce brake temperatures to more manageable levels without causing unwanted changes in brake system gain or brake balance. At the same time, a caliper upgrade was deemed necessary to reduce taper wear and consequently improve brake pedal feel. However, between a typical club racer's budget and a vintage racing requirement to maintain a 15-inch wheel diameter, a typical big brake upgrade was not on the agenda.

Front Brake Upgrade

The first step in the upgrade was to do some research to find out if any other models were offered by the same manufacturer that came with more robust brake-system hardware. Fortunately, Porsche offered an upgraded brake system on the 911 Turbo models, which fits under 15-inch wheels while still being reasonably affordable (in relative terms) when purchased used.

As a result, this was the chosen upgrade path: bolt on the Turbo parts. The only problem was that they didn't just bolt on.

Rotor Selection and Modification

To address brake system temperatures, the first order of business was to select new front rotors. The stock 911 front rotors measured 11.1 inches in diameter and 0.8 inches in thickness—not too bad for 1972, but relatively small by contemporary standards. The Turbo rotors were a more significant 12.0 inches in diameter and 1.3 inches in thickness,

Although it was world-class at the time, the stock 911 brake system from 1972 is only considered average by modern standards. Between the additional horsepower and modern race tires installed for competition, it didn't take many laps to realize the need for increased thermal capacity. The vintage brake systems found on Camaros, Corvettes, and Mustangs from the same era typically don't fare too well, either. (Randall Shafer)

The custom, two-piece front rotor shown on the left is 0.9 inches larger in diameter than the stock 911 rotor shown on the right, but even more impressive was the 0.5-inch growth in thickness. While thermal mass increased significantly (approximately five pounds per rotor), fabricating the hats from aluminum offset some of the rotational inertia impacts of the new rotors. (Randall Shafer)

After a significant amount of trial and error, the owner bolted the custom front rotors and hats onto the front suspension. The friction discs selected are neither slotted nor cross-drilled to reduce cost, but their curved vane geometry is clearly visible. (Randall Shafer)

The front Turbo calipers were a four-piece design (one inboard piston housing, one outboard piston housing, and two bridge pieces) in contrast to the stock 911 aluminum monoblock calipers. The cross-shaped piece of wire on the top of the caliper acts as the brake pad retaining device. (Randall Shafer)

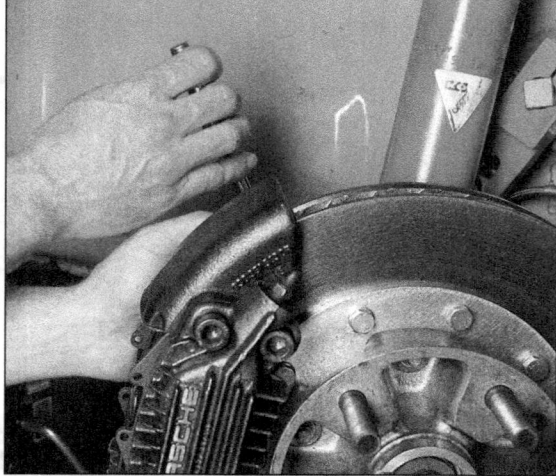

The front Turbo calipers bolted on to the stock 911 front suspension with little modification at all. The 3.5-inch center-to-center caliper fastener placement was common to both caliper bodies, requiring only a few small spacers to align the caliper body with the rotor friction disc. Owners of many American vehicles of this vintage will have similar luck finding parts that practically bolt on without significant modification. (Randall Shafer)

but the hat geometry would not allow for a bolt-on installation. Consequently, aftermarket two-piece friction discs (using Turbo rotor dimensions) with custom hats were the first modification.

While custom hats are readily available in the aftermarket, the owner fabricated a pair in the shop from a piece of 6061 aluminum. The only downside to the home-built hats was that it was not possible to implement a floating interface between the friction disc and the hat. Instead, the two were bolted rigidly together using aircraft-grade hardware. Although the weight savings of a two-piece rotor would be realized, the larger rotor would be no more robust to coning than the stock 911 rotor.

In a cost-savings move the front rotors were not slotted, nor were they cross-drilled for fear of reduced durability. However, the curved-vane design of the larger rotors was expected to move more cool air through the friction disc than the straight-vaned stock rotors, so the benefit was more than size alone.

Caliper Selection and Modification

To accompany the front rotor upgrade, the owner purchased a pair of Turbo calipers at a local swap meet. Compared to the stock 911 two-piston calipers, the Turbo four-piston calipers certainly looked much more like racecar parts. The fact that they fit under the stock 911 15-inch wheels using only a pair of custom bracket spacers sealed the deal.

Functionally, the Turbo calipers used a larger brake pad than the stock 911 calipers, providing increased friction material volume for better brake pad life and lower brake pad temperatures. The

In order to cool the front rotors more effectively, the owner installed brake duct openings in the front air dam. Three-inch flexible hosing was selected to route the air around the tire, with custom-built backing plates used to direct the incoming air to the rotor center. If your rulebook allows, you should consider this a mandatory upgrade on the racecar sitting in your garage. (Randall Shafer)

If you are unsure about cutting holes in the front fascia of your vintage racecar for brake cooling ducts, it may also be possible to mount them in an air dam. The yellow Corvette on the left has a pair of ducts mounted in exactly this fashion, eliminating the need to modify the stock bodywork. (Wayne Flynn/pdxsports.com)

four-piece construction of the Turbo calipers also provided increased stiffness compared to the stock 911 monoblock calipers, but with the penalty of a slight weight increase.

Although the Turbo calipers used four pistons, they did not contain differential bores. Instead, all four bores measured 1.5 inches in diameter. However, compared to the stock two-piston 911 caliper, the pressure distribution across the brake pad backing plate was improved and consequently *was* expected to decrease the occurrence of longitudinal brake pad taper by some amount.

Brake Cooling Duct Installation

The final step to reduce the operating temperature of the new front rotors was to install brake cooling ducts in the front fascia. If the rulebook allows, this is one modification that should never be passed over—increased convective heat transfer is always of benefit.

Rear Brake Upgrade

Step two of the project involved upgrading the rear brakes to match the increased thermal capacity of the front brakes. In many applications, the rear brakes perform so little work that an upgrade is not necessary, but the significant rearward weight bias of the 911 dictates that the rear brakes will see their fair share of thermal stress on the track.

Rotor Selection and Modification

Unlike the front rotor upgrade, which required unique hats for installation, the rear rotor upgrade was a straightforward

System Performance: Gain and Balance

Before the new rotors and calipers were bolted in place, a quick check was performed to determine the possible effects on brake balance and gain. Using several of the relationships from Chapters 3 and 8, the following parameters were calculated:

	Effective Piston Area (in^2)	Rotor Effective Radius (in)
Stock 911 front brakes:	2.80	4.62 (estimated)
Turbo front brakes:	3.51	5.24 (estimated)
Stock 911 rear brakes:	1.76	4.96 (estimated)
Turbo rear brakes:	2.19	5.47 (estimated)

While the stock 911 (right) and Turbo (left) rear rotors may look similar, there's a significant four-pound difference in thermal mass. This is due to a 0.7-inch growth in diameter and 0.3-inch increase in friction disc thickness. (Randall Shafer)

Next, assuming brake pad coefficient of friction and master cylinder pressure to be constant between the two designs, the relative gain and balance changes due only to the rotor and caliper upgrades were found to be:

	Gain (compared to stock)	Balance (percent front)
Stock 911 brakes:	Baseline	60%
Turbo brakes:	140%	60%

In other words, the Porsche engineers did a pretty good job of designing this brake system in the first place—the balance with the Turbo components remained essentially unchanged from the stock 911 configuration. Unfortunately the gain increased by approximately 40 percent, but that is addressed later in the upgrade.

While the stock 911 rear brakes look trick with their cast-in-place holes, this is not the best solution for the demands of track use—notice the cracks propagating from several of the openings. It doesn't help that the extreme rearward weight bias (and corresponding rearward brake balance) of the Porsche 911 platform leads to increased rear brake temperatures. (Randall Shafer)

It took some significant machining to bolt the Turbo rear caliper on to the stock 911 rear suspension. In addition to relocating the mounting bosses, material also needed to be removed by hand around the crossover tube. For work like this, it's best to consult with a professional. (Randall Shafer)

affair. Upsizing to 12.1-inch diameter Turbo rear rotors from the stock 911 11.4-inch rotors was the easy part, since the Turbo rotors' one-piece integral hats fit the stock 911 rear upright. Increasing the thickness from 0.8 inches to 1.1 inches also helped to increase thermal mass, and all without the need for a return trip to the machine shop.

Unfortunately, the Turbo factory rotors were equipped with holes *cast* into the rotor friction disc. While arguably more robust than typical cross-drilled holes, this would still result in premature cracking over time. However, in this case the shortened rotor lifespan would be more than offset by their fire-sale pricing.

Caliper Selection and Modification

The rear Turbo calipers, also procured through creative wheeling and dealing, were visually identical to the front Turbo calipers. Their difference was only in piston sizing—four 1.2-inch diameter pistons in the rear versus four 1.5-inch pistons in the front. Naturally, the reduction in rear piston area was necessary to enable proper brake balance from the factory.

Unlike the front Turbo calipers, which bolted on without modification, the rear Turbo caliper mounting bosses

The owner swapped in stainless steel brake hoses to replace the stock 911 rubber brake hoses, but also used stainless steel brake hoses to replace short but complex sections of stock brake lines (shown to the right of the body bracket fitting). While not ideal, this was cheaper than finding expensive pre-bent brake lines. Note the safety wire holding the black brake tube retaining clip to the body bracket—a subtle modification that indicates the owner was not afraid to sweat the details. (Randall Shafer)

Once the caliper machining was complete, the owner bolted it over an unmodified Turbo rotor. Although these upgraded components significantly improved brake system performance, the brake balance of the stock 911 was maintained. (Randall Shafer)

Depending on your setup, you may be forced to modify the factory brake pedal arm to accept a balance bar. This is not a job for the inexperienced fabricator! The round tube welded in place to position the balance bar fulcrum is offset to the right since the vehicle generally requires more front brake force than rear brake force. And yes, that's authentic racecar dirt in the pedal box. (Randall Shafer)

needed to be removed and relocated in order to attach to the rear suspension. The center-to-center mounting dimension needed to be reduced by one-half inch and was moved outward on the caliper body by approximately the same amount. Because templates were not available for this modification, a significant amount of trial-and-error and test fitting was involved to ensure dimensional accuracy and mechanical integrity.

(Note that a brake system modification of this nature is not for the novice, and is only discussed here to demonstrate just how far one can go in making non-standard brake parts fit. A similar swap for your vehicle may be easier or more difficult, depending on any number of factors.)

Apply System Upgrade

In order to match the Turbo caliper's compliance characteristics as well as to allow brake balance adjustment while on the track, several additional changes were made to the vehicle's apply system. While not as glamorous as the big rotor and caliper upgrades, these final modifications were just as necessary to ensure optimum performance of the entire brake system.

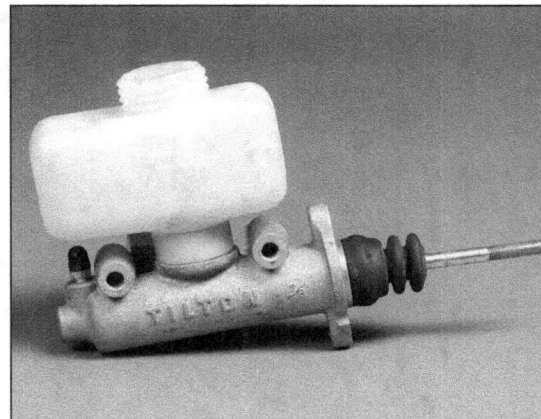

In order to provide enough brake fluid to fill the upgraded calipers, both master cylinders were upsized to 7/8-inch pistons. The Tilton part shown here was originally procured at a swap meet, but its overall length proved to be too long to fit under the floorpan. The owner ended up using a more compact version of the same part to fit the tight packaging requirements. (Randall Shafer)

System Performance: Compliance and Gain

When comparing the stock 911 calipers to the upgraded Turbo calipers, a significant increase in effective caliper piston area was observed:

Effective Piston Areas (in^2)

	Front (each)	Rear (each)	Total (full vehicle)
Stock 911 front brakes	2.80	1.76	9.12
Turbo front brakes	3.51	2.19	11.41

Therefore, without taking caliper stiffness into account, a compliance increase of approximately 25 percent was expected when upgrading from the stock 911 calipers to the Turbo calipers. For this reason, the master cylinders were upgraded from 3/4-inch pistons to 7/8-inch pistons, providing 31 percent more volume for a given master cylinder piston displacement.

Because the stock 911 used a tandem master cylinder, the brake pedal box needed to be modified to accept dual master cylinders. The lower portion containing the brake pedal fulcrum and clutch pedal assembly was essentially left unchanged, while the firewall-mounted portion was redesigned and reinforced to accept the new hardware. (Randall Shafer)

Normally, the corresponding 31-percent *decrease* in gain would have a negative impact on driver required leg forces. However, because the calipers and rotors contributed to a 40-percent *increase* in brake system gain, these two effects nearly cancel one another out, resulting in an overall brake system gain within a few percent of the stock 911 brake system.

Since this vehicle would not be driven on public roads, a dedicated racing brake pad was selected. While the noise, dust, and wear of the Hawk 9012 compound would make this racecar unlivable on the street, its thermal robustness and stable coefficient of friction on the track make it a sensible choice. (Randall Shafer/Hawk Performance)

The new brake hardware not only promised increased performance on the track, but looked the part as well. While many hours were spent in the shop making all the pieces work together, it was the management of brake system attributes such as balance and gain that paid the greatest dividends. Your racecar deserves the same level of attention, doesn't it? (Randall Shafer)

Brake Pedal Modification

The first apply-system upgrade actually occurred prior to the rotor and caliper upgrades. When first prepared for racing, the stock 911 brake pedal arm was modified to accept a balance bar, allowing for driver adjustment of brake balance with the stock 911 brake system. Because the strength of the brake pedal arm is so critical to overall brake system performance (and vehicle safety!), this work was performed by a shop with a significant amount of experience in this area. Like the caliper modification described earlier, this was not a job for the first-time fabricator.

Concurrent with the pedal arm modification, the remaining pedal support box was also reworked to accept dual master cylinders. Due to the floor-mounted pedal assembly in this particular vehicle, the master cylinders were mounted underneath the body structure and not under the hood. A remote adjustment knob for the balance bar mechanism completed the hardware upgrades inside the passenger compartment.

Master Cylinder Upgrade

The final upgrade was to increase the size of the master cylinders to account for the increased compliance due to the larger Turbo calipers (larger caliper pistons almost always lead to more compliance). Since the vehicle had previously been outfitted with a pair of 3/4-inch master cylinders to work with the stock 911 brakes, a pair with 7/8-inch pistons (the next largest commonly available size) were selected and installed. Based on the ratio of the old and new master cylinder piston areas, a displacement increase of 31 percent was expected with a corresponding 31-percent decrease in gain.

Hoses, Fluids, and Pads

In classic racecar fashion, the stock 911 flexible rubber brake hoses were replaced at all four corners with stainless steel brake hoses. While this modification was not expected to improve brake system thermal capacity, protection from debris on the track and improvement in brake pedal feel was worth the modest investment, even on a budget.

For brake fluid, a conventional DOT 4 formulation from Castrol was used. Although its dry and wet boiling points are not the highest advertised, the budget-friendly price and general availability at most auto parts stores make it a sensible choice in this application.

Finally, the owner chose dedicated racing brake pads from Hawk Performance. While several materials were available, the 9012, or Blue, compound was selected for its high durability and relatively low cost. Compared to other materials in the Hawk catalog, this compound was expected to be a slight compromise in ultimate output and initial bite, but previous experience with the same material in the stock 911 calipers made the decision relatively straightforward.

The Results

When the wrenches were finally put away, all of the brake system upgrade objectives were met without investing in a high-dollar big brake kit. By converting to parts-bin Porsche 911 Turbo brakes, overall thermal mass increased by 18 pounds, brake pad volume increased significantly, caliper stiffness was improved, and on-the-fly adjustability was provided, all while maintaining appropriate levels of brake system gain and brake balance. There certainly was a good amount of skilled fabrication and elbow grease involved, but more often than not this level of modification and creativity is required when you're racing on a budget within the constraints of a rulebook.

CHAPTER 13

MUSCLE CAR BRAKE UPGRADE

In addition to swapping big disc brakes for small disc brakes, another common brake system upgrade involves converting a vehicle originally equipped with *drum brakes* to disc brakes. Up to this point in the book, drum brakes have been ignored, as their poor thermal characteristics and non-linear torque output make them undesirable in high-performance applications. However, for this very reason, older vehicles originally equipped with drum brakes make ideal candidates for disc brake conversions.

Chapter 13 exposes you to some of the unique steps involved in the process of converting a vehicle with rear drum brakes to rear disc brakes. Because many of the brake system design factors are similar to those already covered in Chapters 11 and 12, they are not recounted here. Yet gain, balance, and thermal capacity still need to be primary considerations when upgrading your vehicle, regardless of its age or intended use.

The Vehicle

Compared to the race-prepared Porsche 911 examined in Chapter 12, a relatively stock 1972 Chevrolet Nova may seem a bit understated. Although both vehicles were built in the same year, the

When this Chevy Nova was built in 1972, drum brakes had been replaced on most vehicles' front axles by disc brakes, but drums were still commonly found out back. Primarily because of their low cost, low weight, and superior parking brake performance, drums can still be found in modern rear brake applications where thermal requirements are low. (Baer)

Solid axles, leaf springs, and drum brakes—all standard fare for the times. Like many cars of the era, this Nova's drums were cast with fins on the outer diameter for enhanced convective cooling, but were still thermally inefficient even by contemporary standards. (Baer)

HIGH-PERFORMANCE BRAKE SYSTEMS: DESIGN, SELECTION AND INSTALLATION 133

Nova was much more likely to see time at the drag strip than at the racetrack. Its front disc and rear drum brakes were common for vehicles of the era, and were relatively well-suited for boulevard cruising and sprinting from stop sign to stop sign. However, improved braking performance shouldn't be limited to vehicles with road course aspirations, and the owner of this particular vehicle had three distinct objectives in mind.

The Objective

The Nova's original rear drum assembly measured a diminutive 9.5 inches in diameter and used a ⁷/₈-inch wheel cylinder, common hardware to be found hanging off the ends of a GM 10-bolt rear end in 1972. While properly sized from a gain and balance perspective, the non-linear pedal feel of the drum brake design made modulation difficult at best when braking near the vehicle's limit of adhesion. Thermally, though, the drum brake proved to be woefully inadequate, as no more than a couple stops from moderate speeds were enough to produce rear brake pad fade and a dramatic drop-off in brake system performance.

Therefore, in order to improve pedal feel and enhance the resistance to fade, the objective was to replace the old-school drum brakes with a pair of modern disc brake assemblies. Of course, the improved visual appearance of the disc brakes would score big points at the Saturday night cruise-in as well.

Picking The Right Parts

Rear Rotors

Since the owner desired to maintain the original 15-inch steel wheels, 12.0-inch diameter rear rotors were the largest that could be installed. Measuring 0.8 inches in thickness, the vented friction discs provided by Baer had substantially more thermal mass than the stock drum assemblies.

For primarily aesthetic reasons, the rotors were both slotted *and* cross-drilled. Although out of place on a competition vehicle, this rotor treatment provided a unique look that was desired in this particular application. It also helped that they matched the front rotor upgrade, which had been performed earlier.

Drum Brakes 101

Although drum brakes and disc brakes may appear quite different at first glance, they both use similar principles to convert hydraulic fluid pressure into torque, while at the same time converting kinetic energy into heat. In both systems, pressure is converted into force, force is converted into torque, and energy is converted at a friction interface.

Drum brake wheel cylinders perform the same function as disc brake calipers. Located inboard of a rotating drum, two opposed pistons in each wheel cylinder are subjected to fluid pressure from the hydraulic circuit. Based on the piston diameters, this pressure is converted into a pair of linear forces acting against brake shoes, which function in the same capacity as the brake pads in a disc brake system.

A variety of designs exist to transmit and amplify the wheel cylinder linear forces, but all serve to expand the brake shoes out against the rotating drum. Based on the drum geometry, the sum of these forces is then converted into torque. While there are many ways to arrange the internal components to enhance gain, the end result is a pressure-to-torque relationship that is not typically as linear as that provided by a disc brake assembly.

Drum brake wheel cylinders convert hydraulic fluid pressure into linear force (yellow arrows) as a function of their piston diameters. Through various design techniques, this force is amplified (red arrows) as it forces the brake shoes out against the rotating drum. It's important to note that the force distribution along the length of the pad (as well as between the leading and trailing pads) is never uniform, resulting in uneven friction material wear. (Delphi Corporation)

Acting much like a disc brake rotor, the drum's temperature rises as kinetic energy is converted into heat at the friction interface. Unfortunately, the rubbing surface of the drum is located inside of the brake assembly, resulting in inefficient convective cooling. For this reason, drums typically contain fins on their outer diameter to enhance what little convective cooling is available externally.

There are many, many more design differences that differentiate drum brakes from disc brakes, but in summary they are both engineered to accomplish the same task. For the enthusiast, though, the poor thermal performance of drum brakes is reason enough to make them an inappropriate choice for any high-performance application.

In order to examine the inner workings of a drum brake, it's necessary to remove the drum as shown above. The design of the drum also dictates that cooling air is not able to reach the working elements of the drum brake during operation, resulting in thermal performance that is always inferior to conventional disc brakes. (Baer)

Converting a typical muscle car from rear drum brakes to disc brakes usually means taking apart the vehicle's rear end. While not very complex from a mechanical perspective, it does result in a significant mess if you're not using a large enough drain pan. Here, the differential cover has already been removed and one C-clip extracted. (Baer)

Although two-piece rotors were initially considered for their lower weight and enhanced visual appeal, in the end, it was decided to use one-piece rotors to keep the budget reasonable. Curved vanes were within financial reach though, and were expected to further aid convective cooling, even during around-town use.

Rear Calipers

Replacing the drum brake wheel cylinders were a pair of floating calipers with single 1.6-inch diameter pistons, also provided by Baer. While not as visually exciting as fixed multi-piston calipers, the tight packaging constraints of the steel wheels dictated the more compact floating design.

In contrast to the cast iron attachment brackets, the caliper bodies were fabricated from lightweight aluminum. A pair of slider pins served to locate the two relative to one another while simultaneously providing the required axial float.

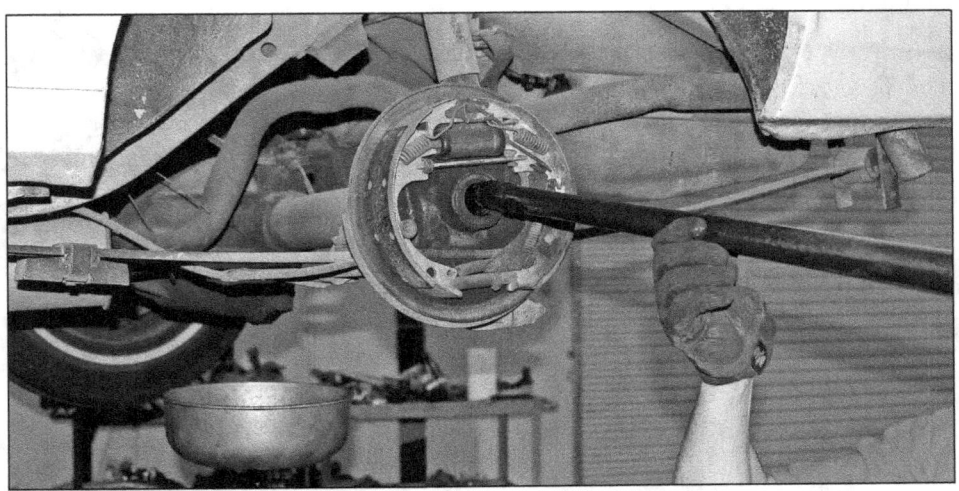

When removing the axle shafts from the rear end, take your time to avoid damaging the seals found at the ends of the axle housing. The splines machined in the ends of the axle shafts can tear or rip the seals if you aren't careful. Of course, with the axles removed, it might not be a bad idea to replace the seals anyway. (Baer)

Bolting Them On

The very first step in any drum brake service procedure is to remove the cast iron drums from the vehicle. Unfortunately, this can prove to be quite a challenge, since drums tend to firmly corrode themselves in place over time. However, this is not altogether different from servicing a vehicle with disc brakes, as you can usually break the drums free with some brute force and a mallet.

In this particular application, the corrosion was not significant, but because the brake shoes had machined their way into the drum diameter, there was a ridge on the inside of the drum that prevented its removal. For this reason, it was necessary to not only get out the mallet, but also to externally adjust the drum internal components to completely retract the brake shoes.

Axle Disassembly

When performing your own rear drum-to-disc conversion, one of the most unique steps is the partial disassembly of the rear axle. As with many rear-wheel drive vehicles built in North America in this timeframe, the axle shafts were retained by a pair of C-clips found in the differential. Because the drum brake backing plates were sandwiched between the solid axle housing and the axle shafts, the first step was to drain and tear down the rear end.

In order to gain access to the C-clips in the differential, it was first necessary to loosen the differential cover and drain the fluid out of the rear end. Once this messy step was complete, the cover was removed completely and set aside, exposing the inner components of the differential assembly.

Following the removal of the differential pin and C-clips, the axle shafts could then be removed from the axle housing. Each application has a slightly different mechanical arrangement, but when removing the axle shafts from the housing, it's important to prevent damage to the outboard housing seals and the axle shaft splines. Once free from the vehicle, the axle shafts were carefully set aside and the brake upgrade could begin.

Stock Backing Plate Removal

With the axle shafts out of the way, removing the drum brake backing plates was a relatively straightforward affair. As with most drum brakes, four fasteners secured each backing plate to a smaller mounting flange welded to the axle housing. After uncoupling the mechanical parking brake cables and disconnecting the brake lines, both assemblies could be easily removed from the axle housing.

In preparation for the adapter bracket installation, the mounting flanges were inspected for damage, checked for flatness, and cleaned up with a Scotch-Brite pad. Since the axle housing seals were not to be replaced during this installation, they too were inspected for any damage that may have occurred during the axle shaft removal process.

Adapter Bracket Installation

Because the axle housing mounting flanges were too small to allow the new calipers to bolt directly to them, an adapter bracket was needed. Fabricated by Baer from heavy-gage steel, the plated brackets were designed to not only locate the calipers relative to the rotors, but also to provide adequate clearance to all moving underbody components.

With the adapter bracket fasteners torqued to specification, the axle shafts could be reinstalled. Before sliding them into the housing, however, one last check was made to ensure that the adapter brackets were installed in the correct orientation. While it was necessary at this point to reinstall the axle shaft C-clips and

Because this was a southern vehicle, there was no problem removing the fasteners that held the drum brake backing plates to the axle housing. You can use air tools extensively during disassembly, but be sure to use hand tools and torque wrenches when you're putting things back together. (Baer)

Once the drum brake backing plates were removed from the axle housing, small vinyl caps were placed over the ends of the disconnected hydraulic lines. While some brake fluid leakage is inevitable when performing an upgrade like this, keeping the mess to a minimum is always a good idea. (Baer)

The new caliper brackets were attached to the same mounting flanges used to locate the drum brake backing plates. The 16 mounting holes drilled around the circumference of this bracket indicate that it's a universal design. Consequently, it's critical to identify the correct bracket orientation for your individual application. (Baer)

differential pin, the differential cover was intentionally left off the vehicle, just in case the axles needed to come back out again later. Taking apart the rear end a second time should be avoided at all costs!

Rotor Installation

At this point, the steps began to mirror those found in Chapter 11. Installing the rotors consisted of simply sliding them over the ends of the axle shafts. However, because the axle shafts did not have provisions for retention fasteners like the BMW did, the rotors were instead loosely retained with a pair of lug nuts.

Note that when installing your own rotors on vehicles of this vintage, it's quite common to encounter a significant amount of resistance due to corrosion on the end of axle shaft. Under no circumstances should you *ever* force the rotors on to their mounting surfaces. Spend the time necessary to clean the axles until the rotors slide on freely without needing additional persuasion.

Based on prior experience with vehicles of this vintage, a light film of anti-seize was applied to the pilot feature on the end of the axle shaft. In the future, this would hopefully allow for removal of the rear rotors without a mallet.

Because the rotors used curved vanes, one last check was made to ensure that the proper rotor had been installed on each side of the vehicle. Even though the vehicle was not expected to see intense thermal cycling, it was just as important that the slot geometry and cross-drilled hole patterns mirrored those found on the front rotors.

Caliper Installation

The next step was to mechanically bolt the new calipers to the adapter brackets. To simplify the process, the brake pads were removed from the calipers first, allowing the rotor to spin freely relative to the caliper body. After making sure that the friction discs were centered in the caliper mounting brackets, the fasteners were tightened to specification.

Because the brake pads came loaded in the caliper bodies from the manufacturer, there was no need to remove any

With the new rotor held in place, a couple lug nuts were used to secure it to the axle shaft. This holds the rotor parallel to the caliper bracket during installation, making caliper installation much easier. (Baer)

At this point, the project mirrored the caliper installations covered in Chapters 11 and 12—just reconnect the brake lines, perform a service bleed, and button up the rear axle. Because this vehicle was not expected to experience extreme brake temperatures during everyday use, fresh DOT 3 brake fluid (from a sealed container, of course) was deemed more than adequate. (Baer)

Parking Brake Considerations

One of the last issues to address when converting from rear drum brakes to disc brakes is parking brake functionality. Based on the hardware you have selected, there may not be a mechanical provision to maintain the parking brake feature. As a result, this important safety component is left disconnected (and consequently non-functional) all too often.

The steel bracket shown hanging from the lower left side of the caliper body served to locate and attach the stock parking brake cable to the caliper's built-in mechanical parking brake components. If you're swapping from drums to discs and you want to keep your parking brake, make sure your new hardware allows you to do so. On a street-driven vehicle, this is highly recommended. (Baer)

Based on the design of your upgraded brake system, a mechanical parking brake may be actuated through the caliper, or it may function through a dedicated mini-drum brake located in the hat section of the rotor. In either case, it's always best to select components that allow you to retain the convenience and safety provided by this critical feature. It may not be the most glamorous part of your brake system upgrade, but it certainly could prove to be the most important.

caliper or bracket fasteners for brake pad installation. For future pad replacement, though, it would be necessary to remove one caliper slider pin from each assembly to pivot the caliper bodies out of the way.

As with many drum-to-disc conversions, the stock brake lines did not have enough flexibility in their routing to connect directly to the new calipers. Thankfully, two pre-bent pieces of brake line were included with the rest of the upgraded brake system hardware just for this reason, saving an unexpected trip to the auto parts store.

Proportioning Valve Installation

Due to the increased gain provided by the new rear disc brake assemblies, it was necessary to install a new proportioning valve to modify the rear brake line pressure. After disabling the stock proportioning valve by removing its internal components, an adjustable valve was installed underhood adjacent to the master cylinder. The new proportioning valve was initially adjusted to its lowest, or most front-biased, setting by turning the knob completely counter-clockwise. Later testing would be used to adjust the valve by trial and error for optimum brake balance.

Buttoning it Up

With the brake hardware installation complete, it was time to fill the hydraulic system with fresh brake fluid. Because this was not an extreme-use application, there was no need to pay extra for DOT 4 levels of performance. Consequently, an off-the-shelf DOT 3 brake fluid was used to fill the entire brake system using the service bleed procedure found in Chapter 6. Since the front brakes had not been serviced recently, they were bled as well for good measure.

The final step was to reinstall the differential cover (note that this was also an appropriate time to verify that the differential pin and C-clips had been reinstalled). Because the differential fluid had been drained into a waste drum earlier in the process, it was necessary to refill with new fluid to the manufacturer's recommended level (in this case, even with the inspection hole).

The Results

Although fixed multi-piston calipers and two-piece floating rotors would have certainly been the highest-performance route to take in this project, the relatively straightforward single-piston sliding calipers and one-piece vented rotors proved to be the biggest bang for the buck. Even without the high-dollar hardware, significant improvements were still made in thermal mass, brake system cooling, brake pedal feel, and visual appeal.

In closing, when selecting the components for your own rear brake upgrade, be sure to manage your wants against your needs. Don't forget that while the rear brakes are important to overall brake system performance, the front brakes are where most of the action occurs. Resist the temptation to overspend at the rear and direct your budget to the components that matter most—the front rotors and calipers.

You can typically use a bead of RTV sealant on the differential housing to seal the cover in place instead of using a traditional paper gasket. Don't forget to refill the rear end with the appropriate fluid! (Baer)

Of course, not only rear drum brakes are candidates for an upgrade. If your vehicle is equipped with front drum brakes like this 1966 Pontiac GTO, they also can be swapped for more modern disc brakes, and it won't even require tearing down your rear end. (Randall Shafer)

CHAPTER 14

Hot Rod Brake Upgrade

In many ways, hot rod builders are on their own when it comes to brake system component selection and system design. Unlike any of the production-based brake upgrades discussed this far, building a hot rod from scratch (or even from a kit) entails a unique collection of brake system considerations and constraints. With custom frames, powerful drivelines, modified bodies, and cut-and-paste suspension systems, there is little opportunity to learn from the original vehicle when the time comes to create your own hot rod brake system.

Yet the laws of physics still apply in these applications, making basic brake system design criteria just as important here as they were in Chapters 11, 12, and 13. The pages that follow will expose you to some of the most common design compromises, hardware considerations, and installation pitfalls that are either unique to, or exaggerated by, hot rod brake systems.

The Vehicle

The subject of this hot rod brake upgrade project began life as a 1940 Ford pickup truck. Although it still possesses some token bits of the original body and frame, little else resembles what rolled off of the assembly line over 60 years ago. Custom roadster coachwork, independent front suspension, Chevy power under the hood, and a host of complex chassis changes only begin to describe the level of change this truck has experienced.

Although originally equipped with hydraulic brakes (mechanical brakes were only dropped the year before in 1939), the single-circuit master cylinder and four-wheel drum brake layout was dated at

We were fortunate to catch this 1940 Ford hot rod pickup in the middle of its own brake upgrade project. When embarking on your own hot rod brake system upgrade, it sure helps to have the vehicle up off the ground in a clean and well-lit garage. If possible, having most of the body and powertrain out of the way makes the job that much easier. (Randall Shafer)

best. Therefore, as long as the rest of the truck was being significantly modified and updated, the brake system was upgraded as well.

The Objective

Like most vehicles of this type, this hot rod was primarily designed for cruising along on a Sunday afternoon drive. Therefore, increased thermal capacity was not high on the list of needs or wants. At the same time, optimizing brake pedal feel was not critical for the truck's intended use. In short, the most important brake system performance requirement was to slow the truck in a stable fashion during emergency-type events. Naturally, the parts had to look good (since that's a big part of what hot rodding is all about), but performing a single stop quickly and reliably from a moderate speed was the most stringent brake system performance design target.

Front Brake Upgrade

The forward frame rails of the truck had already been modified to accept one of the most common independent front

HIGH-PERFORMANCE BRAKE SYSTEMS: DESIGN, SELECTION AND INSTALLATION

CHAPTER 14

It took a significant amount of modification to adapt a Mustang II front suspension to the stock front frame rails. However, the front brake hardware remains essentially unchanged from the Mustang II design. Note that many hot rodders upgrade their Mustang II front end with a set of 11.0-inch diameter rotors and aftermarket caliper mounting brackets. (Randall Shafer)

The Mustang II front brake calipers contain relatively large brake pads held in place by floating caliper bodies. The single piston in each caliper was designed to be offset relative to the center of the rotor friction disc, resulting in a larger effective radius. In plain English, this means higher gain is possible in a smaller package. (Randall Shafer)

suspensions used in the hot rodding community. Lifted straight from a Ford Mustang II, this setup can be found hanging off the front end of countless hot rods today. In this application, the upper and lower control arms had already been replaced with custom tubular pieces, but the front uprights, bearings, and brake hardware were straight from the Ford parts bin.

Chosen more for availability and fitment than for thermal mass and effective radius, the front rotors measured a relatively small 9.0 inches in diameter and 0.9 inches in thickness. Although the straight vanes in the vented friction discs were not expected to be as efficient as curved vanes would have been, any front rotors would be more thermally robust that the stock front drums.

Like the front rotors, the front calipers were chosen more for convenience than for performance. These remanufactured single-piston calipers were based on the original Mustang II floating design. Their compact dimensions were the final consideration, as this would lead to flexibility in wheel selection later in the project.

Although a more modern Ford rear axle had been installed, in the interest of both time and money it was decided to leave the rear drum brakes in place. Of course they would receive a fresh coat of paint and fresh internal components, but with so little weight over the rear tires there was no reason to improve their performance. Even though it was still a pickup truck, its heavy hauling days were over.

Brake Pedal Considerations

In 1940, vacuum boosters were still several decades away from becoming mainstream brake system components. Therefore, because the truck was originally built without a vacuum booster (in other words, built with manual brakes), the brake pedal ratio was exceptionally high compared to conventional standards. Employing a pedal ratio of approximately 8.0:1, the stock brake pedal was required to swing through a relatively long arc as brake pressure was generated in the master cylinder.

Since the truck's master cylinder was originally mounted beneath the floor of the vehicle, retrofitting a vacuum booster,

While the stock single-circuit master cylinder was swapped for a tandem unit, its location under the vehicle was retained. The tight confines dictated that an opening be cut in the floorpan to allow access to the brake fluid reservoir. Check out the elegant routing of the custom-bent brake lines! (Randall Shafer)

HOT ROD BRAKE UPGRADE

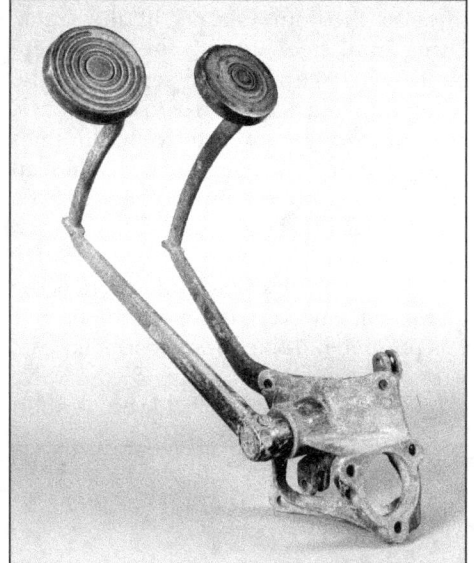

This hot rod builder chose to retain the long, spindly stock brake pedal on the right without modification. Without the benefit of a vacuum booster, the pedal ratio needs to be as high as possible to maximize overall brake system gain. The pedal on the left originally operated the clutch, but was later removed since an automatic transmission was being installed. (Randall Shafer)

For improved pedal spacing, it was necessary to cut off the brake pedal pad prior to installing the brake pedal assembly. Once the final positioning of the steering column and floorpan were determined, the pedal pad was welded back in place. Notice the aftermarket chrome throttle pedal seen hanging off of the firewall to the right. (Randall Shafer)

even one with a relatively small diameter, would have been difficult at best. While upgrading to vacuum-assisted brakes would have been desirable from both a gain and pedal feel standpoint, in the end the stock manual pedal assembly was kept intact. In fact, with the exception of a

Residual Pressure Valves

In many hot rod applications, the master cylinder is mounted below the hydraulic components at the wheel ends (disc brake calipers and drum brake wheel cylinders). Thanks to gravity, this arrangement results in brake fluid flowing from the wheel end components back to the master cylinder reservoir when it's not pressurized. When the brakes are next applied, reduced pressure is available, accompanied by excessive brake pedal travel. In order to prevent this phenomenon from occurring, a residual pressure valve can be installed in one or more of the brake lines. Acting much like a one-way flow restrictor at low pressures, these devices hold a constant amount of pressure at the wheel ends, preventing fluid from draining back to the master cylinder when the brakes are not applied.

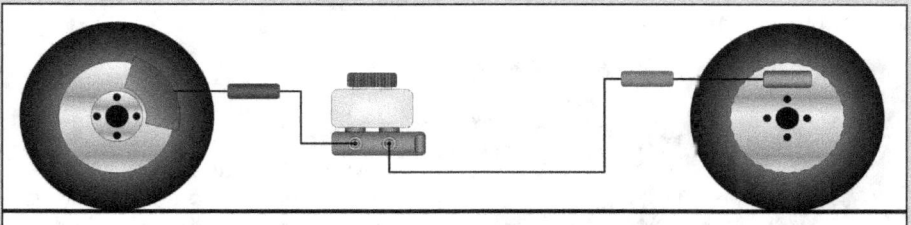

Any time you're using a low-mounted master cylinder, it'll be necessary to install one residual pressure valve for each hydraulic circuit (blue and red). As long as they're installed in the proper orientation, their physical location in the hydraulic system doesn't matter. For ease of service and inspection, though, it makes sense to mount them where they'll be readily accessible.

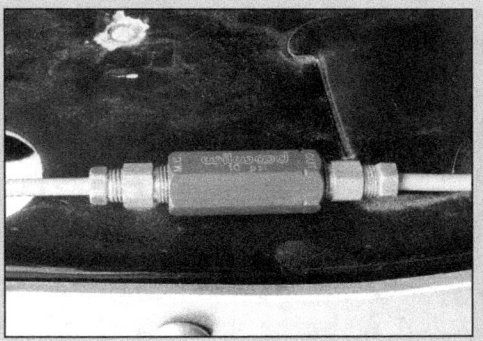

When using a residual pressure valve, it's important to install it in the correct orientation. For this reason, the inlet and outlet port assignments are usually stamped or engraved in the valve body. The 10-psi rating found etched into this valve indicates that it's suitable for use with drum brake hardware. A 2-psi valve would be used for disc brakes. (Randall Shafer)

Based on the type of brake being used at a particular corner, different levels of residual pressure are appropriate to prevent drain back. Generally speaking, disc brakes require approximately 2 to 5 psi valves, while drum brakes, due mostly to their built-in retraction springs, work best with 10-to-15 psi valves.

If you're unsure of the relationship between your master cylinder and the wheel end components, it's best to be conservative and install a pair of valves. Even if drain back is not a problem, installing these valves does not pose any other negative performance impact to your vehicle's brake system operation. When in doubt, it's better to be safe than sorry.

thorough visual inspection and a fresh coat of paint, the pedal was lifted straight from 1940 without alteration.

Master Cylinder Upgrade

Because hydraulic brake systems were still in their infancy when the truck was originally built, government regulations had not yet matured to the point of requiring parallel hydraulic circuits. As a result, the stock single-circuit manual brake system was in need of attention, if for no other reason than to bring it up to modern safety standards.

In order to provide hydraulic redundancy, a tandem master cylinder was selected from General Motors' parts bin. An aluminum adapter plate was necessary to connect the two-hole mounting flange to the three-hole brake pedal box, and a special pushrod was needed to transmit the force from the brake pedal arm to the piston.

Brake Line and Proportioning Valve Installation

With one hydraulic circuit pressurizing the front brakes and the second circuit taking care of the rear brakes, it became necessary to install new brake lines to the four corners of the truck. Using mild steel tubing, the lines were bent with large radii and secured to the body with clips every 12 to 18 inches. Special care was taken to route the lines away from exhaust system heat, and all were located up and out of the way from potential debris bouncing off of the road surface.

While the new brake lines were being fabricated, a universal proportioning valve was plumbed in-line to the rear brakes. As with the Nova in Chapter 13, the valve was initially adjusted to its lowest, or most

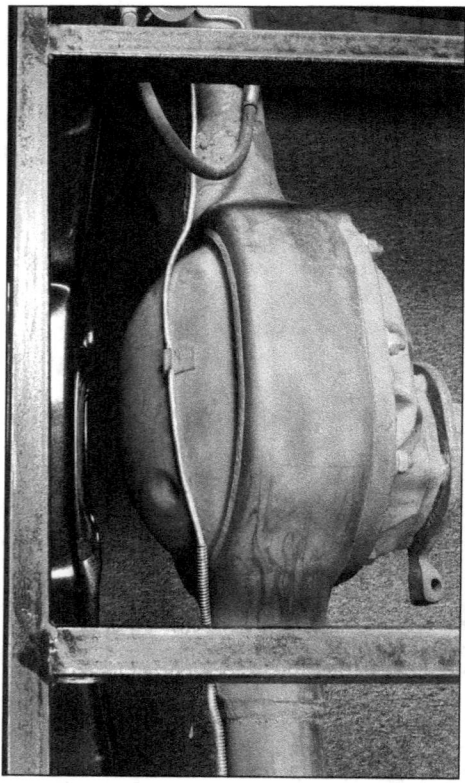

A common mistake when routing custom brake lines is to lay them directly on top of the rear axle. While this certainly protects the lines from debris from the roadway below, it can subject them to being pinched between the axle and the chassis. This becomes even more important with modified hot rod suspensions that lower the vehicle ride height. Consequently, it's best to route them along the backside of the axle housing as shown. (Randall Shafer)

Common Hot Rod Brake Pitfalls

In order to raise the overall level of safety in the scratch-built hot rod world, several clubs and organizations are making technical inspection a requirement for entry into select shows and competitions. Learning from others' mistakes, the following series of errors should be on your checklist of concerns to address prior to finishing your project.

1. Brake lines should never be unsecured for more than 18 inches at a time. Tight-fitting clips designed for use with the appropriate diameter brake lines should be used generously when plumbing your project. Loose-fitting clips can in some cases be worse than no clips at all.

2. Brake hoses should be attached to the body or frame wherever they are coupled to the rigid brake lines. It's not enough to simply clip the brake line to the body by itself, as the joint will fatigue over time.

3. Brake hoses should be routed in such a way that they do not contact any part of the body, frame, suspension, or tire under any conditions. The easiest way to check is to remove the suspension spring and move the tire through its full range of vertical travel while turning the steering wheel from lock to lock.

4. Always be sure to check brake hose routing to ensure that the hose is not stretched beyond its limits under conditions of full steering with full vertical wheel travel. A hose that is too tight may suddenly separate from the caliper, resulting in a serious brake system failure.

5. Revised suspension geometries can result in unfavorable locations for the brake system components. Take your time to verify that the calipers and rotors do not contact any other parts of the vehicle suspension while going through their full range of motion.

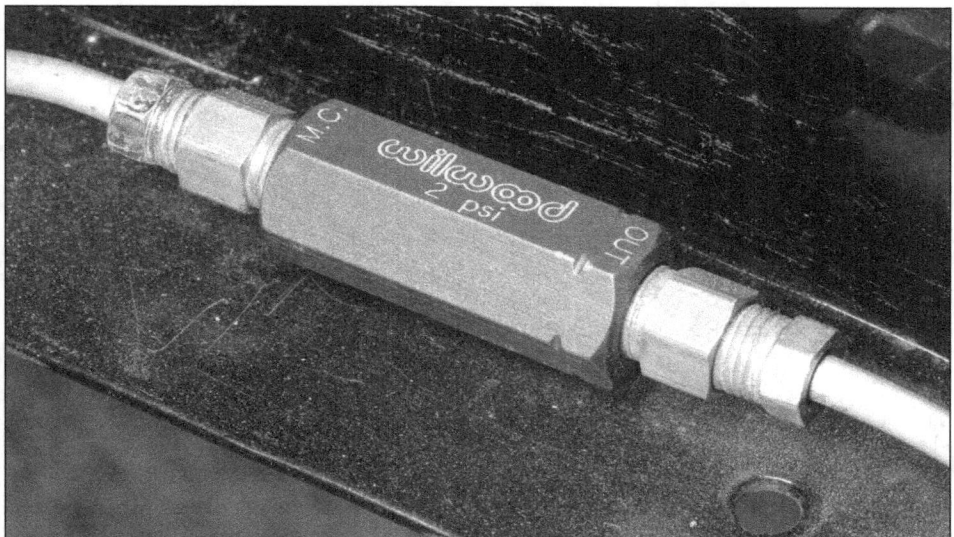

New brake lines were fabricated from scratch using SAE double flares and tube nuts at all sealing interfaces. However, the residual pressure valves were manufactured with tapered fittings at both ends. Consequently, brass adapters were needed to secure the brake lines to the valves. (Randall Shafer)

stainless steel lines for their aesthetic appeal, consider yourself forewarned.

Brake Hoses

Once the new brake lines were installed, it was necessary to connect the rigid hydraulic lines to the moving parts of the brake system. At both the front and rear ends of the truck, conventional rubber overmolded lines were selected for their availability and relatively low cost. Stainless steel brake hoses, with their attractive stainless steel braiding, would certainly have made an improvement in pedal feel, but with an 8.0:1 pedal ratio they were deemed to be overkill.

To prevent brake line fatigue at the brake hose interfaces, a bracket was used to secure both sides of each fitting to the truck's chassis. Left unsupported, long-term vibration of the joints could have led to potential damage or failure.

Brake Fluid Selection

Although Chapter 6 condemned silicone-based DOT 5 brake fluids for use in practically any vehicle application, in this situation it was the appropriate choice. Why? Because the brake fluid properties most important to the typical hot rod owner differ greatly from those held in the highest regard by the track-day enthusiast.

The number one brake fluid requirement in this application (as in most hot rod applications) was protecting the vehicle's

front-biased, setting by turning the knob completely counter-clockwise. Once the vehicle was drivable, the valve would be adjusted for increased deceleration until the limit of braking stability was reached.

In some hot rod applications, there may be a desire to fabricate the brake lines from corrosion-resistant stainless steel tubing. While this material is certainly acceptable from a strength perspective, the downside is that it is not as ductile, or as soft, as mild steel tubing. For this reason, stainless steel flares are much more prone to leakage, so if you must install

Unlike several other calipers already described in this book, the Mustang II front calipers did not incorporate banjo fittings at the brake hose interface. Rather, a straight threaded fitting was machined into each caliper body, requiring only a single copper crush washer to form a robust hydraulic seal. Note also the unusual nylon rings molded around the brake hose for protection. (Randall Shafer)

Shown here from beneath the vehicle, most hot rods employ a hand-actuated parking brake assembly. A simple lever arrangement (similar to the brake pedal) amplifies the force applied by the driver, and two cables distribute the force between the left-hand and right-hand rear drum brakes. The threaded rod allows for cable pre-tensioning and adjustment after installation. (Randall Shafer)

CHAPTER 14

While it might seem obvious, the parking brake handle should be mounted out of the way of the vehicle's primary controls, yet within easy reach of the driver. The small trap door cut in the driver's side floorpan allows access to the master cylinder reservoir. (Randall Shafer)

brake was completely removed, a stand-alone parking brake actuation system was installed in a final nod to vehicle safety. Operated by hand, the lever and cable system integrated neatly with the stock rear drum brake assemblies.

(Note that while a parking brake is certainly of benefit to those in and around the vehicle, in many states a functioning parking brake is required to license your hot rod for use on public roads. In addition, most major shows and competitions require that a functioning parking brake be installed before a vehicle is eligible for judging or awards.)

The Results

When sized up against the three brake system upgrades covered in Chapters 11, 12, and 13, several unique compromises were made in the design and installation of the hot rod brake system. From the reduced importance of thermal mass to the decision to fill the hydraulic circuits with silicone-based DOT 5 brake fluid, differences could be found at nearly every step in the process. Yet in spite of these apparent contradictions in design philosophy, all of the stated objectives were met.

By comparing and contrasting these four diverse projects, it becomes obvious that in brake system design there is never just *one right answer*. Every individual vehicle must be evaluated for its intended use and expected levels of performance. For this reason, what works well on a dedicated competition vehicle may be totally out of place and/or inappropriate for a weekend cruiser, and vise-versa. However, the fundamental characteristics of gain (component physical dimensions), balance (brake proportioning), thermal mass (rotor sizing), and stopping distance (tire output) should always make their way to the top of your list of critical design factors, regardless of your application.

paint from damage. In the hot rod world it's not uncommon to have small brake fluid leaks and spills from time to time, and in the interest of avoiding damage to the show-quality finishes, DOT 5 fluids are commonly accepted in spite of their poor pedal feel characteristics.

Because the truck's new brake system was assembled from dry components, there was no concern of mixing the DOT 5 fluid with non-silicone-based fluids already in the hydraulic circuit. If this had not been the case, the entire system would have been first removed from the vehicle, disassembled, and cleaned until all traces of glycol-based fluids were removed.

Parking Brake Installation

In contrast to the Porsche 911 racecar in Chapter 12 where the parking

Although tiny by modern performance car standards, most hot rod brakes only need to be up to the thermal stresses imposed by cruising on Saturday night. While these brakes would not fare too well on a road course, neither would the rest of the vehicle. An upgrade of this nature clearly demonstrates that brake system design is all about making the appropriate compromises to meet your brake system goals. (Randall Shafer)

More great titles available from CarTech®...

S-A DESIGN

Super Tuning & Modifying Holley Carburetors — Perf, street and off-road applications. (SA08)
Custom Painting — Gives you an overview of the broad spectrum of custom painting types and techniques. (SA10)
Street Supercharging, A Complete Guide to — Bolt-on buying, installing and tuning blowers. (SA17)
Engine Blueprinting — Using tools, block selection & prep, crank mods, pistons, heads, cams & more! (SA21)
David Vizard's How to Build Horsepower — Building horsepower in any engine. (SA24)
Chevrolet Small-Block Parts Interchange Manual — Selecting & swapping high-perf. small-block parts. (SA55)
High-Performance Ford Engine Parts Interchange — Selecting & swapping big- and small-block Ford parts. (SA56)
How To Build Max Perf Chevy Small-Blocks on a Budget — Would you believe 600 hp for $3000? (SA57)
How To Build Max Performance Ford V-8s on a Budget — Dyno-tested engine builds for big- & small-blocks. (SA69)
How To Build Max-Perf Pontiac V8s — Mild perf apps to all-out performance build-ups. (SA78)
How to Build High-Performance Ignition Systems — Guide to understanding auto ignition systems. (SA79)
How To Build Max Perf 4.6 Liter Ford Engines — Building & modifying Ford's 2- & 4-valve 4.6/5.4 liter engines. (SA82)
How to Build Big-Inch Ford Small-Blocks — Add cubic inches without the hassle of switching to a big-block. (SA85)
How To Build High-Perf Chevy LS1/LS6 Engines — Modifying and tuning Gen-III engines for GM cars and trucks. (SA86)
How To Build Big-Inch Chevy Small-Blocks — Get the additional torque & horsepower of a big-block. (SA87)
Honda Engine Swaps — Step-by-step instructions for all major tasks involved in engine swapping. (SA93)
How to Build High-Performance Chevy Small-Block Cams/Valvetrains — Camshaft & valvetrain function, selection, performance, and design. (SA105)
High-Performance Jeep Cherokee XJ Builder's Guide 1984–2001 — Build a useful Cherokee for mountains, the mud, the desert, the street, and more. (SA109)
How to Build and Modify Rochester Quadrajet Carburetors — Selecting, rebuilding, and modifying the Quadrajet Carburetors. (SA113)
Rebuilding the Small-Block Chevy: Step-by-Step Videobook — 160-pg book plus 2-hour DVD show you how to build a street or racing small-block Chevy. (SA116)
How to Paint Your Car on a Budget — Everything you need to know to get a great-looking coat of paint and save money. (SA117)
How to Drift: The Art of Oversteer — This comprehensive guide to drifting covers both driving techniques and car setup. (SA118)
Turbo: Real World High-Performance Turbocharger Systems — Turbo is the most practical book for enthusiasts who want to make more horsepower. Foreword by Gale Banks. (SA123)
High-Performance Chevy Small-Block Cylinder Heads — Learn how to make the most power with this popular modification on your small-block Chevy. (SA125)
High Performance Brake Systems — Design, selection, and installation of brake systems for Musclecars, Hot Rods, Imports, Modern Era cars and more. (SA126)
High Performance C5 Corvette Builder's Guide — Improve the looks, handling and performance of your Corvette C5. (SA127)
High Performance Diesel Builder's Guide — The definitive guide to getting maximum performance out of your diesel engine. (SA129)
How to Rebuild & Modify Carter/Edelbrock Carbs — The only source for information on rebuilding and tuning these popular carburetors. (SA130)
Building Honda K-Series Engine Performance — The first book on the market dedicated exclusively to the Honda K series engine. (SA134)

Engine Management-Advanced Tuning — Take your fuel injection and tuning knowledge to the next level. (SA135)
How to Drag Race — Car setup, beginning and advanced techniques for bracket racing and pro classes, and racing science and math, and more. (SA136)
4x4 Suspension Handbook — Includes suspension basics & theory, advanced/high-performance suspension and lift systems, axles, how-to installations, and more. (SA137)
GM Automatic Overdrive Transmission Builder's and Swapper's Guide — Learn to build a bulletproof tranny and how to swap it into an older chassis as well. (SA140)
High-Performance Subaru Builder's Guide — Subarus are the hottest compacts on the street. Make yours even hotter. (SA141)
How to Build Max-Performance Mitsubishi 4G63t Engines — Covers every system and component of the engine, including a complete history. (SA148)
How to Swap GM LS-Series Engines Into Almost Anything — Includes a historical review and detailed information so you can select and fit the best LS engine. (SA156)
How to Autocross — Covers basic to more advanced modifications that go beyond the stock classes. (SA158)
Designing & Tuning High-Performance Fuel Injection Systems — Complete guide to tuning aftermarket standalone systems. (SA161)
Design & Install In Car Entertainment Systems — The latest and greatest electronic systems, both audio and video. (SA163)
How to Build Max-Performance Hemi Engines — Build the biggest baddest vintage Hemi. (SA164)
How to Digitally Photograph Cars — Learn all the modern techniques and post processing too. (SA168)
High-Performance Differentials, Axles, & Drivelines — Must have book for anyone thinking about setting up a performance differential. (SA170)
How To Build Max-Performance Mopar Big Blocks — Build the baddest wedge Mopar on the block. (SA171)
How to Build Max-Performance Oldsmobile V-8s — Make your Oldsmobile keep up with the pack. (SA172)
Automotive Diagnostic Systems: Understanding OBD-I & OBD II — Learn how modern diagnostic systems work. (SA174)
How to Make Your Muscle Car Handle — Upgrade your muscle car suspension to modern standards. (SA175)
Full-Size Fords 1955–1970 — A complete color history of full-sized fords. (SA176)
Rebuilding Any Automotive Engine: Step-by-Step Videobook — Rebuild any engine with this book DVD combo. DVD is over 3 hours long! (SA179)
How to Supercharge & Turbocharge GM LS-Series Engines — Boost the power of today's most popular engine. (SA180)
The New Mini Performance Handbook — All the performance tricks for your new Mini. (SA182)
How to Build Max-Performance Ford FE Engines — Finally, performance tricks for the FE junkie. (SA183)
Builder's Guide to Hot Rod Chassis & Suspension — Ultimate guide to Hot Rod Suspensions. (SA185)
How to Build Altered Wheelbase Cars — Build a wild altered car. Complete history too! (SA189)
How to Build Period Correct Hot Rods — Build a hot rod true to your favorite period. (SA192)
Automotive Sheet Metal Forming & Fabrication — Create and fabricate your own metalwork. (SA196)
How to Build Max-Performance Chevy Big Block on a Budget — New big-block book from the master, David Vizard. (SA198)
How to Build Big-Inch GM LS-Series Engines — Get more power through displacement from your LS. (SA203)
Performance Automotive Engine Math — All the formulas and facts you will ever need. (SA204)
How to Design, Build & Equip Your Automotive Workshop on a Budget — Working man's guide to building a great work space. (SA207)
Automotive Electrical Performance Projects — Featuring the most popular electrical mods today. (SA209)
How to Port Cylinder Heads — Vizard shares his cylinder head secrets. (SA215)

S-A DESIGN RESTORATION SERIES

How to Restore Your Mustang 1964 1/2–1973 — Step-by-step restoration for your classic Mustang. (SA165)
Muscle Car Interior Restoration Guide — Make your interior look and smell new again. Includes dash restoration. (SA167)
How to Restore Your Camaro 1967–1969 — Step-by-step restoration of your 1st gen Camaro. (SA178)

S-A DESIGN WORKBENCH® SERIES

Workbench® Series books feature step by step instruction with hundreds of color photos for stock rebuilds and automotive repair.

How To Rebuild the Small-Block Chevrolet — (SA26)
How to Rebuild the Small-Block Ford — (SA102)
How to Rebuild & Modify High-Performance Manual Transmissions — (SA103)
How to Rebuild the Big-Block Chevrolet — (SA142)
How to Rebuild the Small-Block Mopar — (SA143)
How to Rebuild GM LS-Series Engines — (SA147)
How to Rebuild Any Automotive Engine — (SA151)
How to Rebuild Honda B-Series Engines — (SA154)
How to Rebuild the 4.6/5.4 Liter Ford — (SA155)
Automotive Welding: A Practical Guide — (SA159)
Automotive Wiring and Electrical Systems — (SA160)
How to Rebuild Big-Block Ford Engines — (SA162)
Automotive Bodywork & Rust Repair — (SA166)
How To Rebuild & Modify GM Turbo 400 Transmissions — (SA186)
How to Rebuild Pontiac V-8s — (SA200)

HISTORIES AND PERSONALITIES

Quarter-Mile Chaos — Rare & stunning photos of terrifying fires, explosions, and crashes in drag racing's golden age. (CT425)
Fuelies: Fuel Injected Corvettes 1957–1965 — The first Corvette book to focus specifically on the fuel injected cars, which are among the most collectible. (CT452)
Slingshot Spectacular: Front-Engine Dragster Era — Relive the golden age of front engine dragsters in this photo packed trip down memory lane. (CT464)
Chrysler Concept Cars 1940–1970 — Fascinating look at the concept cars created by Chrysler during this golden age of the automotive industry. (CT470)
Fuel Altereds Forever — Includes more than 250 photos of the most popular drivers and racecars from the Fuel Altered class. (CT475)
Yenko — Complete and thorough story of the man, his business and his legendary cars. (CT485)
Lost Hot Rods — Great Hot Rods from the past rediscovered. (CT487)
Grumpy's Toys — A collection of Grumpy's greats. (CT489)
Woodward Avenue: Cruising the Legendary — Revisit the glory days of Woodward! (CT491)
Rusted Muscle — A collection of junkyard muscle cars. (CT492)
America's Coolest Station Wagons — Wagons are cooler than they ever have been. (CT493)
Super Stock — A paperback version of a classic best seller. (CT495)
Rusty Pickups: American Workhorses Put to Pasture — Cool collection of old trucks and ads too! (CT496)
Jerry Heasley's Rare Finds — Great collection of Heasley's best finds. (CT497)
Street Sleepers: The Art of the Deceptively Fast Car — Stealth, horsepower what's not to love? (CT498)
Ed 'Big Daddy' Roth — Paperback reprint of a classic best seller. (CT500)
Car Spy: Secret Cars Exposed by the Industry's Most Notorious Photographer — Cool behind-the-scenes stories spanning 40 years. (CT502)

CarTech®, Inc. 39966 Grand Ave., North Branch, MN 55056. Ph: 800-551-4754 or 651-277-1200 • Fax: 651-277-1203
Brooklands Books Ltd., PO Box 146 Cobham, Surrey KT11 1LG, England. Ph: 01932 865051 • Fax 01932 868803
Brooklands Books Aus., 3/37-39 Green Street, Banksmeadow, NSW 2019, Australia. Ph: 2 9695 7055 • Fax 2 9695 7355

Visit us online at www.cartechbooks.com for more info!

More Information for Your Project ...

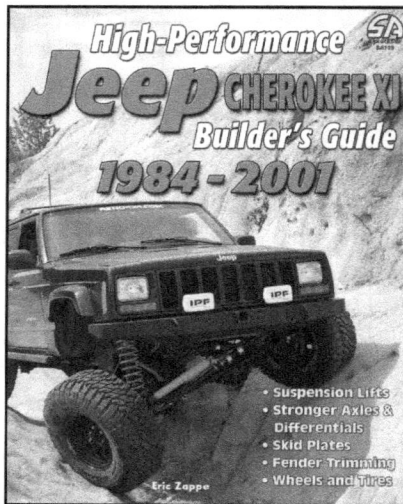

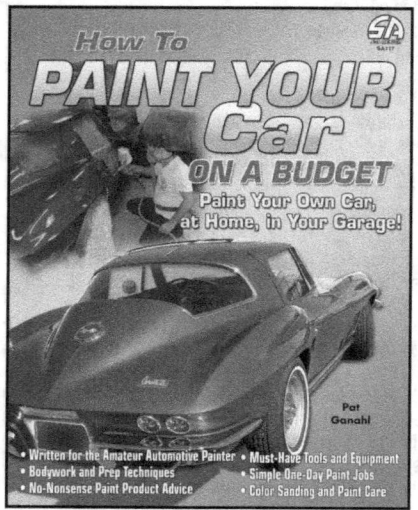

HIGH-PERFORMANCE JEEP CHEROKEE XJ BUILDER'S GUIDE: 1984 – 2001 by Eric Zappe, Ready to turn your Jeep Cherokee XJ into a trail-worthy machine? This book shows you how to build a useful, capable Cherokee for mountains, the mud, the desert, the street, and everywhere in between. Author Eric Zappe explains how to upgrade your Cherokee's suspension, axles, differentials, engine, transfer case, wheels and tires, skid plates, and more, using aftermarket and salvage yard upgrades. Zappe even has special sections covering basic driving and recovery techniques, and a number of built-up Jeeps to give you ideas for your own Cherokee. Also includes a detailed account of a group of XJs making a run through the famous Rubicon trail. Softbound, 8-1/2 x 11 inches, 144 pages, approx. 300 color photos. **Item # SA109**

HOW TO BUILD HIGH-PERFORMANCE IGNITION SYSTEMS by Todd Ryden, The complete guide to understanding automotive ignition systems, from old-school points & condensers to modern computer-controlled distributorless systems, from bone-stock to totally aftermarket. Covers the various components, systems, & subsystems, explaining the theory behind the operation & how the parts work together to achieve the ultimate goal of efficient combustion. Coils, wires, spark plugs, distributors, magnetos, inductive systems, CD ignitions, multiple-spark systems, computer ignition controls, rev limiters — all are covered for both street & race applications. This book helps you understand your car's ignition and choose the right components for your performance needs. Softbound, 8-1/2 x 11 inches, 128 pages, 250 b/w photos. **Item # SA79**

HOW TO PAINT YOUR CAR ON A BUDGET by Pat Ganahl Author Pat Ganahl unveils dozens of secrets that will help anyone paint their own car. From simple scuff-and-squirt jobs to full-on, door-jambs-and-everything paint jobs, this book covers everything you need to know to get a great-looking coat of paint on your car and save lots of money in the process. Covers painting equipment, prep, masking, painting and sanding products & techniques, plus real-world advice on budgeting wisely. Softbound, 8-1/2 x 11 inches, 128 pages, 400 color photos. **Item # SA117**

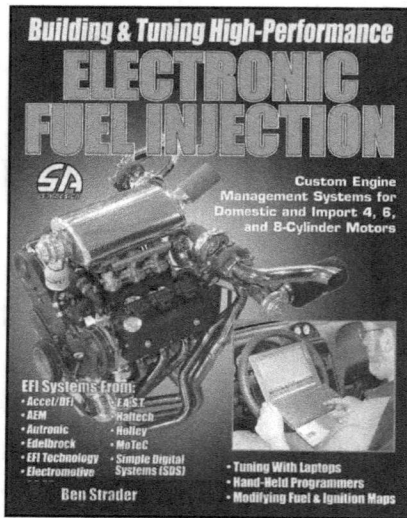

HIGH-PERFORMANCE BRAKE SYSTEMS: DESIGN, SELECTION, AND INSTALLATION by James Walker, Jr. This book uses over 330 photos and plain English to help you understand how and why your brake system works, what each of the components does, and how to intelligently upgrade your brakes for better performance. There are chapters showing you how to choose and install the most effective rotors, calipers, pads, and tires for your sports car, muscle car, race car, and street rod. You will even find special sidebars detailing how each upgrade will affect your ABS. Whether you are a casual enthusiast, a weekend warrior, or a professional racer, this book will tell you everything you need to know about brakes. Softbound, 8-1/2 X 11 inches, 144 pages, 330+ color photos. **Item # SA126**

ENGINE BLUEPRINTING is simply the best book available on basic engine preparation for street or racing. Rick Voegelin's writing and wrenching skills put this book in a class by itself. Includes pros' secrets of using tools, selecting and preparing blocks, cranks, rods, pistons, cylinder heads, selecting cams and valve train components, balancing and assembly tips, plus worksheets for your engine projects, and much more! Softbound, 8-1/2 x 11 inches, 128 pages, over 400 photos. **Item # SA21**

BUILDING & TUNING HIGH-PERFORMANCE ELECTRONIC FUEL INJECTION by Ben Strader, Author Ben Strader (founder & senior instructor of EFI University) gives a detailed account of what you want to accomplish with your EFI system, then shows you how to get there. You'll learn to: define air & fuel requirements based on horsepower & RPM; set up your base fuel & ignition maps to get things up and running fast; tweak your fuel & timing maps for light- and heavy-load situations; & adjust timing for cold-starting or high-boost conditions. Strader also describes the systems from 11 respected EFI manufacturers, helping you weigh the info on cost, features, tunability, and ease of installation. Softbound, 8-1/2 x 11 inches, 128 pages, 300 b/w photos. **Item # SA83**

www.cartechbooks.com or 1-800-551-4754

www.ingramcontent.com/pod-product-compliance
Lightning Source LLC
Chambersburg PA
CBHW051412070526
44584CB00023B/3393